AF587807

# Practical Software Test Analysis

Adam Roman · Matthias Hamburg

# Practical Software Test Analysis

## A Self-Study Companion for the ISTQB® Test Analyst Exam

Adam Roman
Faculty of Mathematics and Computer Science
Jagiellonian University
Krakow, Poland

Matthias Hamburg
German Testing Board e.V.
Erlangen, Germany

ISBN 978-3-032-27985-9 ISBN 978-3-032-27986-6 (eBook)
https://doi.org/10.1007/978-3-032-27986-6



This Springer imprint is published by the registered company Springer Nature Switzerland AG
The registered company address is: Gewerbestrasse 11, 6330 Cham, Switzerland

**Competing Interests** The authors have no competing interests to declare that are relevant to the content of this manuscript.

# Conventions Used in This Book

The following conventions are used in this book.

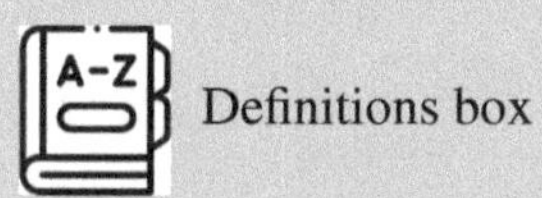


The boxes labeled "Definitions" provide definitions of terms used in individual sections of the syllabus as keywords that must be known for the ISTQB® Certified Tester—Test Analyst exam. The definitions are taken from the official ISTQB® glossary of testing terms (www.glossary.istqb.org).

The boxes marked "Example" provide examples illustrating the concepts, techniques, or methods introduced.

The material marked as "Optional" goes beyond the scope of the Test Analyst syllabus. It usually consists of more advanced content related to the syllabus, but illustrating more complex issues or methods. Those who use the book to prepare for the certification exam can safely skip this content.

Case study box

The boxes marked "Case study" refer to the case studies, mainly to a food ordering application called FoodApp, described on pages 22–23. The content provided there shows how the tools introduced in a given chapter can be used in practical applications. By using the same case study throughout the book (with only a few exceptions), the reader can see how the entire set of methods, approaches, and techniques in the field of test analysis can be used in a single IT project.

# Contents

**Part I ISTQB® Test Analyst Certificate, Syllabus, and Exam**

**Introduction** ... 3

**Tasks and Competencies of a Test Analyst** ... 5
Dimensions of Competence ... 6
What a Test Analyst Should Know ... 6
Using the Standard Terminology ... 7
Using International Standards ... 8
The ISTQB® Test Analyst Syllabus and Certificate ... 10
Introduction to ISTQB® ... 10
Test Analyst Certificate in Relation to ISTQB® Portfolio ... 10
History of the Test Analyst Certificate ... 12
How the Syllabus is Structured ... 12
The ISTQB® Test Analyst Exam ... 15
Requirements for Candidates ... 15
Training ... 15
Exam Rules ... 16
Exam Structure ... 17
Question Types ... 19
Tips: Before and During the Exam ... 21
Case Study ... 22

**Part II The Syllabus Content**

**Chapter 1 The Test Analyst's Tasks in the Test Process** ... 27
Introduction to the Test Analyst's Tasks in the Test Process ... 27
1.1 Testing in the Software Development Lifecycle ... 29
Sample Questions ... 35
1.2 Involvement in the Test Activities ... 36
1.2.1 Test Analysis ... 36
Sample Questions ... 41

1.2.2 Test Design ... 41
Sample Questions ... 45
1.2.3 Test Implementation ... 46
Sample Questions ... 49
1.2.4 Test Execution ... 50
Sample Questions ... 58
1.3 Tasks Related to Testware ... 58
1.3.1 High-Level and Low-Level Test Cases ... 59
Sample Questions ... 62
1.3.2 Quality Criteria for Test Cases ... 63
Sample Questions ... 67
1.3.3 Test Environment Requirements ... 68
Sample Questions ... 71
1.3.4 Determining Test Oracles ... 72
Sample Questions ... 77
1.3.5 Test Data Requirements ... 78
Sample Questions ... 82
1.3.6 Developing Test Scripts Using Keyword-Driven Testing ... 83
Sample Questions ... 87
Exercise 1—Keyword-Driven Testing ... 88
1.3.7 Tools Applied in Managing the Testware ... 89
Sample Questions ... 91

**Chapter 2 The Test Analyst's Tasks in Risk-Based Testing** ... 93
Introduction to the Test Analyst's Tasks in Risk-Based Testing ... 93
2.1 Risk Analysis ... 94
Sample Question ... 104
2.2 Risk Control ... 105
Sample Questions ... 121
Exercise 2—Determining the Scope of Regression Testing ... 123

**Chapter 3 Test Analysis and Design** ... 125
Introduction to Test Analysis and Design ... 125
3.1 Data-Based Test Techniques ... 127
3.1.1 Domain Testing ... 127
Sample Questions ... 138
Exercise 3—Domain Analysis ... 139
3.1.2 Combinatorial Testing ... 140
Sample Questions ... 156
Exercise 4—Combinatorial Testing ... 157
3.1.3 Random Testing ... 158
Sample Questions ... 165
3.2 Behavior-Based Test Techniques ... 166
3.2.1 CRUD Testing ... 166
Sample Questions ... 171
3.2.2 State Transition Testing ... 171

Sample Questions ..... 185
Exercise 5—State Transition Testing ..... 186
3.2.3 Scenario-Based Testing ..... 186
Sample Questions ..... 201
Exercise 6—Scenario-Based Testing ..... 204
3.3 Rule-Based Test Techniques ..... 205
3.3.1 Decision Table Testing ..... 205
Sample Questions ..... 220
Exercise 7—Decision Table Testing ..... 221
3.3.2 Metamorphic Testing ..... 222
Sample Questions ..... 233
Exercise 8—Metamorphic Testing ..... 234
3.4 Experience-Based Test Techniques ..... 234
3.4.1 Test Charters Supporting Session-Based Testing ..... 234
Sample Questions ..... 241
Exercise 9—Preparing Test Charters for Session-Based Testing ..... 243
3.4.2 Checklists Supporting Experience-Based Test Techniques ..... 243
Sample Questions ..... 251
Exercise 10—Preparing Checklists for Experience-Based Testing ..... 252
3.4.3 Crowd Testing ..... 252
Sample Questions ..... 259
3.5 Applying the Most Appropriate Test Techniques ..... 260
3.5.1 Selecting Test Techniques to Mitigate Product Risks ..... 260
Sample Questions ..... 269
Exercise 11—Test Technique Selection ..... 270
3.5.2 Benefits of Automating the Test Design ..... 271
Sample Questions ..... 277

**Chapter 4 Testing Software Quality Characteristics** ..... 279
Note on the Relation Between the Syllabus and the ISO 25010 Standard ..... 279
4.1 Functional Testing ..... 281
Sample Questions ..... 289
4.2 Usability Testing ..... 290
Sample Questions ..... 301
4.3 Flexibility Testing ..... 302
Sample Questions ..... 315
4.4 Compatibility Testing ..... 316
Sample Questions ..... 321

**Chapter 5 Software Defect Prevention** ..... 323
Introduction to the Software Defect Prevention ..... 323
5.1 Defect Prevention Practices ..... 324
Sample Questions ..... 334
5.2 Supporting Phase Containment ..... 334
5.2.1 Using Models to Detect Anomalies in Specifications ..... 335
Sample Questions ..... 343

Exercise 12—Using Test Models to Detect Defects in a Specification .... 344
5.2.2 Applying Review Techniques .... 344
Sample Questions .... 360
Exercise 13—Review Techniques .... 361
5.3 Mitigating the Recurrence of Defects .... 362
5.3.1 Analyzing Test Results to Improve Defect Detection .... 362
Sample Questions .... 381
Exercise 14—Improving Defect Detection .... 382
5.3.2 Supporting Root Cause Analysis with Defect Classification .... 383
Sample Questions .... 392

**Part III Answers to Questions and Exercises**

**Answers to Sample Questions** .... 395
Chapter 1 .... 395
Chapter 2 .... 403
Chapter 3 .... 405
Chapter 4 .... 417
Chapter 5 .... 420

**Solutions to Exercises** .... 425
Solution to Exercise 1 .... 425
Solution to Exercise 2 .... 427
Solution to Exercise 3 .... 428
Solution to Exercise 4 .... 432
Solution to Exercise 5 .... 436
Solution to Exercise 6 .... 438
Solution to Exercise 7 .... 439
Solution to Exercise 8 .... 440
Solution to Exercise 9 .... 441
Solution to Exercise 10 .... 443
Solution to Exercise 11 .... 444
Solution to Exercise 12 .... 445
Solution to Exercise 13 .... 447
Solution to Exercise 14 .... 448

**References** .... 451

**Index** .... 455

# About the Authors

**Prof. Adam Roman** Ph.D., D.Sc., is a professor of computer science and a research and teaching fellow at the Institute of Computer Science and Computer Mathematics at Jagiellonian University in Krakow, Poland, where he has been giving lectures and seminars on software testing and quality assurance for more than 15 years. He is the head of the Software Engineering Department and the co-founder of the "Software Testing" postgraduate studies at Jagiellonian University. His research interests include software measurement, defect prediction models, and effective test design techniques.

Adam Roman is a member of many ISTQB® working groups, including Foundation Level WG, Advanced Level WG, Expert Level WG, and Glossary WG. He is the co-author of several ISTQB® syllabi, including the Advanced Level—Test Analyst v4.0 syllabus. He is an ISTQB® accredited trainer and vice-president of the Polish Quality Board (www.pqb.org.pl).

Within ISO, he is a member of the team working on the international standard "ISO/IEEE 29119 Software Testing Standard." Adam Roman is the author of several monographs on software testing: "Testing and Software Quality. Models, Techniques, Tools" (in Polish), "Thinking-Driven Testing," "ISTQB® Certified Tester Foundation Level. A Self-Study Guide Syllabus v4.0," and many scientific and popular publications in the field of software testing. Adam Roman is the speaker at many Polish and international testing conferences (including EuroSTAR, TestWell, TestingCup, and TestWarez). He holds several certifications, including ASQ Certified Software quality engineer, ISTQB® Full Advanced Level, and ISTQB® Expert Level—Improving the Test Process.

**Dr. Matthias Hamburg** Ph.D. graduated from the University of Bonn in mathematics and computer science, where he received his doctorate in differential geometry in 1986. Since then, he has worked in the software development industry. Since 1997, he has specialized in software testing. In his last industrial position, he was a managing consultant for software testing at Sogeti Germany. His professional focus is on test analysis, test management and test process improvement. As a long-standing active member of the German Informatics Society and a member of the IEEE Computer

Society, he is particularly committed to the application of scientific innovation in IT practice. After retiring at the end of 2019, he continues his involvement in the German Testing Board (GTB) and in the International Software Testing Qualifications Board (ISTQB®) on a voluntary basis. Having served for ten years as chair of the ISTQB® Glossary Working Group, he is the product owner of the Glossary app. In addition, he leads the task force for the ISTQB® Advanced Level Test Analyst syllabus. In these roles, he continues to be an active practitioner of testing and enjoys piloting innovative methods.

# Abbreviations

| | |
|---|---|
| API | Application Programming Interface |
| BPMN | Business Process Model and Notation |
| CI/CD | Continuous Integration/Continuous Delivery |
| CoQ | Cost of Quality |
| COTS | Commercial Off-the-Shelf |
| DDP | Defect Detection Percentage |
| DRE | Defect Removal Efficiency |
| EFSM | Extended Finite State Machine |
| FSM | Finite State Machine |
| ISTQB® | International Software Testing Qualifications Board |
| KLOC | Kilo Lines of Code |
| LO | Learning Objective |
| LOC | Lines of Code |
| MBT | Model-Based Testing |
| MR | Metamorphic Relation |
| MT | Metamorphic Testing |
| OS | Operating System |
| PCE | Phase Containment Effectiveness |
| RCA | Root Cause Analysis |
| SDLC | Software Development Lifecycle |
| TC | Test Case |
| UML | Unified Modeling Language |
| WCAG | Web Content Accessibility Guidelines |

# Part I
# ISTQB® Test Analyst Certificate, Syllabus, and Exam

# Introduction

In today's rapidly changing world of software development, test analysis has become not just a supporting activity but the foundation for successful project delivery. The quality of testing, and in particular the precision of test analysis, can mean the difference between success and failure. Today's software systems are increasingly complex, connected, and intelligent. The implementation of artificial intelligence, in particular, large language models, introduces undefined behaviors that challenge traditional testing paradigms. At the same time, the shift to DevOps, containerization, microservices, and cloud-native architectures requires more flexible, automated, and adaptive test strategies. In this dynamic context, test analysis—the process of reviewing, interpreting, and decomposing requirements to define "what to test" and "how to test"—is a critical bridge between ambiguous specifications and executable, precise test cases.

Test analysis enables early defect detection, promotes effective test design, and aligns testing with business and technical objectives. It structures often chaotic software requirements and clarifies ambiguities before they become costly production defects. In modern IT environments, where continuous integration and deployment processes are the norm, high-quality test analysis ensures that automated tests are both meaningful and easy to maintain. Without this discipline, automation can become a costly illusion of quality. Today's software is not just code—it is a composition of services, containers, APIs, third-party integrations, and now increasingly machine learning components. Because these components are often deployed on distributed cloud platforms, testing is less about verifying isolated functions and more about validating behavior under variability, with a business perspective in mind.

While tools and platforms may change, the core competency of a test analyst remains the same: mastery of analytical skills and test techniques. These competencies are the lens through which test analysts view software systems, revealing risks, assumptions, and gaps. But testing in real-world conditions is more than just designing test cases. Effective test analysis must address and resolve several practical challenges, such as the test oracle problem (especially in AI-based systems

 
A. Roman and M. Hamburg, *Practical Software Test Analysis*,
https://doi.org/10.1007/978-3-032-27986-6_1

with subjective or probabilistic outcomes), test case quality (to ensure test cases are correct, easy to maintain, and aligned with business value), risk-based testing, test design automation, defect prevention, phase containment, or reducing the defect recurrence. All these issues fall within the scope of a test analyst's responsibilities.

This publication has been written with two main objectives in mind. The first is to present issues related to test analysis—a key intellectual phase in the testing process, which determines the quality, effectiveness, and efficiency of the designed tests. The second objective is to provide self-study material for those wishing to obtain the ISTQB® Advanced Level—Test Analyst certificate.

Therefore, the main target groups of readers are:

- software testers who deal with test analysis and design issues in IT projects on a daily basis,
- people who want to prepare for the ISTQB® Certified Tester—Advanced Level Test Analyst exam based on the version 4.0 syllabus published in 2025,
- anyone who wants to further their education and expand their knowledge of analytical activities related to the testing process in organizations.

The structure of the book is consistent with the Test Analyst syllabus v4.0. However, in addition to presenting the content described in the syllabus, the book contains many practical examples showing how the presented knowledge can be applied in real IT projects. Many examples are based on a case study, which is a practical example of an actual IT project. We have also included a number of sample codes in Python that illustrate how to automate not only the execution but also the design of test cases and the generation of test data. In some places, there is additional, optional (i.e., not obligatory for the exam), more advanced material that expands on the content presented in the syllabus.

The book also contains **72 sample exam questions** that could appear on the exam, two for each of the 36 learning objectives described in the syllabus. These are original questions, not duplicates of those contained in the official ISTQB® document containing a sample exam. In addition to sample questions, the book also includes **14 exercises**, one for each learning objective at level K3 or K4 (see Section "Learning Objectives and K-Levels" on page 13). The exercises are helpful in the practical application of the methods discussed in these learning objectives.

The book consists of three main parts:

- Part I describes the certificate, syllabus, and exam rules for ISTQB® Certified Tester—Advanced Level Test Analyst v4.0.
- Part II, the main part of the book, discusses the content in accordance with the syllabus.
- Part III contains answers to sample questions and exercises.

# Tasks and Competencies of a Test Analyst

A **test analyst** is a testing role primarily focusing on functional, black-box, and experience-based testing to verify that the software behaves as expected from an end-user perspective. Test analysts are also responsible for testing the "user-related" software quality characteristics, such as usability or flexibility. Moreover, they are involved in some elements of test process improvement, specifically, defect prevention. Test analysts do most of their work in test analysis, test design, test implementation, and test execution.

The core test analyst responsibilities include:

- implementing test strategy with focus on business requirements,
- analyzing requirements and specifications to understand the software's functionality, the scope of testing, and to determine whether the business objectives can be met by the system being developed,
- performing risk analysis,
- performing reviews of requirements and testware (e.g., test plans, test cases),
- designing test cases by using appropriate test techniques and test approaches,
- executing tests manually,
- reporting on test progress,
- analyzing test execution results to improve test process (e.g., defect prevention).

This role requires a combination of analytical skills, business domain knowledge, attention to detail, communication skills, and a strong understanding of the Software Development Lifecycle. The test analyst complements the roles of a technical test analyst (focused on non-functional, white-box, low-level, "technical" testing) and a test manager (responsible for managing the test project, test process, and test team). Test analysts collaborate with many different stakeholders, especially with those who play business-related roles. Examples include project managers, product owners, clients, or business analysts.



A. Roman and M. Hamburg, *Practical Software Test Analysis*,
https://doi.org/10.1007/978-3-032-27986-6_2

## Dimensions of Competence

The competence of a test analyst can be understood across three key dimensions: cognitive competence, social competence, and subject matter competence. This book focuses specifically on the cognitive dimension—knowledge and reasoning related to testing tasks such as analyzing requirements, designing test cases, evaluating risks, and interpreting results. While social competence (e.g., collaboration, communication, and negotiation skills) and subject matter competence (e.g., specific business or technical domain expertise) are essential for a well-rounded test analyst, they fall outside the scope of this book. The cognitive competencies discussed here represent generic and transferable knowledge applicable across all branches of the software industry, including business IT systems, digital entertainment, embedded technologies, and safety–critical applications.

Analytical skills, critical thinking, and logical thinking are essential for a test analyst because they form the foundation for making informed, objective decisions throughout the testing process. Good analytical skills enable a test analyst to break down complex requirements, identify gaps or ambiguities, and understand how different components of the system interact. Critical thinking is crucial for evaluating the quality and testability of requirements, performing risk analysis, and determining the most effective test approach. Logical thinking supports the creation of consistent, traceable, and well-structured test cases that align with business goals and ensure required coverage. Together, these skills allow the test analyst to uncover hidden defects, spot inconsistencies early, and contribute meaningfully to product quality and risk reduction—all while maintaining a user-focused perspective.

## What a Test Analyst Should Know

A test analyst should possess a solid understanding of the fundamental principles of software testing, such as those outlined in the ISTQB® Foundation Level syllabus. This foundational knowledge serves as a prerequisite for effectively performing the responsibilities of the role, including test analysis, design, implementation, and execution. The following areas from the ISTQB® Foundation Level syllabus are particularly important:

**Fundamentals of Testing**. A test analyst must understand why testing is necessary, know the most important testing principles, and the test process, including test planning, test monitoring and control, test analysis, test design, test implementation, test execution, and test completion. This foundation helps ensure that testing is not ad hoc but instead follows a structured, purposeful approach aligned with project goals.

**Testing Throughout the Software Development Lifecycle**. Test analysts should know how testing fits into various software development models (e.g., sequential, iterative, incremental) and how the timing and objectives of test activities vary accordingly. This enables the test analyst to adapt their test activities to the development context, ensuring relevance and efficiency.

**Static Testing**. The ability to participate in and conduct reviews is crucial. Test analysts must understand how to analyze work products like requirements and user stories before code is written, which helps in defect prevention and early validation of business needs.

**Test Analysis and Design**. One of the most critical areas of knowledge is the application of black-box test techniques such as equivalence partitioning, boundary value analysis, decision table testing, or state transition testing. These techniques help the test analyst design effective and efficient test cases to verify that the system behaves as expected from a user's perspective. Additionally, understanding experience-based techniques (e.g., error guessing, exploratory testing, checklist-based testing) equips test analysts to uncover issues that structured techniques might miss.

**Managing the Test Activities**. While test management is a separate role, a test analyst must understand the basics of test planning, test estimation, test monitoring and control. This includes knowing how to report test progress, manage defects, and understand different test levels and types.

**Test Tools**. Test analysts should be aware of the types of tools that can support test activities, such as test management tools, defect tracking tools, and tools for test design or data generation. While deep technical expertise is not required, knowing what tools are available and how they support the process is useful for increasing test efficiency and traceability.

While practical experience in testing is not strictly required, it can greatly enhance a test analyst's ability to apply theoretical concepts to real-world projects. Additionally, having some familiarity with the other Advanced Level core syllabi, such as those for the test manager, technical test analyst, or test automation engineer, can provide valuable context and improve collaboration across testing roles. However, such knowledge is considered helpful but not essential for mastering the competencies specific to the test analyst.

## Using the Standard Terminology

In the field of software testing, clear and consistent communication is essential, especially when working in cross-functional or international teams. This is where keywords and the use of standardized terminology become invaluable. The ISTQB® has established a common language of testing through its syllabi and the ISTQB® Glossary of Terms, which ensures that all testing professionals share a mutual understanding of key concepts and terms, regardless of their location, organization, or industry domain.

Using standard terminology offers several important advantages:

- clarity and precision—by reducing ambiguity and misinterpretation of testing terms during communication among team members, stakeholders, and clients,
- efficiency—by streamlining documentation, reporting, and training by using widely understood and accepted language,
- consistency across projects—by supporting and maintaining uniform test processes, especially when individuals move between projects or organizations,
- global recognition—as ISTQB® is internationally recognized, its terminology supports collaboration on global software initiatives and outsourcing,
- improved learning and certification preparation—because standard terms make it easier to study for certifications, follow industry literature, and understand specifications and best practices.

The ISTQB® Glossary (available at www.glossary.istqb.org) is a searchable online database of testing terms defined by the ISTQB®. It is maintained and regularly updated to reflect the evolution of the software testing field and to align with changes in the syllabi. The glossary is available in multiple languages and can also be downloaded in a customizable form in a PDF file.

Each ISTQB® syllabus explicitly identifies keywords in the learning objectives. These keywords are included in the glossary to reinforce their standard meanings and ensure candidates and professionals are using the correct definitions. The keywords listed in the ISTQB® syllabi represent core terms that candidates are expected to understand and use precisely.

## Using International Standards

There are several important international standards for software testing and quality that a test analyst should be familiar with. These standards provide structured processes and terminology that ensure consistency across testing projects, teams, and organizations. For a test analyst, this means fewer ambiguities in how quality is assessed, and tests are designed, executed, and reported. In global or multi-vendor environments, using international standards facilitates collaboration and aligns with best practices.

Below, we describe the most important standards from the test analyst's point of view. Part of the Test Analyst syllabus is based on them.

**ISO/IEC/IEEE 29119—Software testing standard** is an international standard for software testing that provides a globally agreed-upon framework for testing processes, documentation, techniques, and more. It aims to ensure consistent, quality-focused software testing practices across different organizations and industries. The four most important parts of this standard are:

- ISO/IEC/IEEE 29119-1: General concepts [1] defines the fundamental concepts, terminology, and principles used throughout the other parts of the standard. It establishes a shared vocabulary for clear communication with stakeholders.
- ISO/IEC/IEEE 29119-2: Test processes [2] outlines the test processes that can be used at any stage of the Software Development Lifecycle. It provides a structured approach to planning, designing, and executing tests, ensuring consistent application of processes, and improving traceability and repeatability.
- ISO/IEC/IEEE 29119-3: Test documentation [3] defines templates and guidelines for standard test documentation. These documents can be adapted to specific projects and organizations.
- ISO/IEC/IEEE 29119-4: Test techniques [4] describes a range of test design techniques, divided into three main categories: specification-based (black-box), structure-based (white-box), and experience-based. It provides a toolkit of proven techniques for effective test case design. Test techniques are discussed in Chap. 3 of this book.

The fifth part, ISO/IEC/IEEE 29119-5—Keyword-Driven Testing [5], focuses specifically on keyword-driven testing discussed in Sect. 1.3.6 of this book.

**ISO/IEC 25010—Product quality model** [6] defines a quality model for software products. It identifies nine key quality characteristics and their subcharacteristics (see Chap. 4) that describe what makes software "good" from a user and business perspective. It helps the test analyst identify non-functional requirements, not just functional ones, and provides a common language for discussing quality with developers, stakeholders, and clients.

**ISO/IEC 25019—Quality-in-use model** [7] defines a quality-in-use model composed of three characteristics and their subcharacteristics that can influence stakeholders when products or systems are used in a specified context of use.

**IEEE 1044—Standard classification for software anomalies** [8] defines a standardized way to identify, classify, and manage software anomalies. Standard classification helps identify patterns in anomalies, aiding in analyzing root causes, which allows test analysts to contribute to preventing similar defects in the future, enabling tracking of defect trends over time, and focusing on high-risk areas, improving test design and coverage.

**ISO/IEC 20246—Work product reviews** [9] provides guidance for conducting work product reviews, a key part of static testing. It gives test analysts a structured approach to reviewing work products, allowing early defect detection and stronger static testing practices, which improve quality and reduce testing effort later in the lifecycle.

## The ISTQB® Test Analyst Syllabus and Certificate

### *Introduction to ISTQB®*

ISTQB® (International Software Testing Qualifications Board, www.istqb.org) is an organization promoting software testing, active since November 2002. It brings together ca. 70 organizations (known as national boards), representing more than 130 countries worldwide. ISTQB® maintains its products—syllabi related to different areas of software testing—and certifies testers through exams based on these syllabi. The ISTQB® scheme is a de facto standard in software testing. As of May 2026, ISTQB® has administered 1.5 million exams and issued more than 1.1 million certificates in over 130 countries.

### *Test Analyst Certificate in Relation to ISTQB® Portfolio*

Figure 1 presents the portfolio of ISTQB® products.

The core of the portfolio is the "**Certified Tester—Foundation Level**" syllabus, which is a prerequisite for obtaining further certifications. After obtaining the Foundation Level certificate, there are a number of options for further development. The "core advanced" path contains syllabi describing standard software testing practices at an advanced level. This path consists of four syllabi:

- **Test Analyst**—focused on the "business" side of testing, functional testing, black-box and experience-based techniques, and defect prevention; this book is based on this syllabus.
- **Technical Test Analyst**—focused on the technical rather than the business side of testing, in particular non-functional testing, white-box techniques, static and dynamic analysis.
- **Test Management**—focused on the managerial role in testing (such as test manager, test lead, or similar).
- **Test Automation Engineer**—focused on classic issues related to test automation.

Those who hold the Test Management certificate may apply for an expert level certificate, for which ISTQB® offers two programs:

- **Test Management**—covering topics beyond the content presented in the Advanced Level—Test Management syllabus.
- **Improving the Test Process**—covering topics related to improving the test process within an organization.

In addition to the "core" path, ISTQB® also offers a "specialist" path, which includes many syllabi covering more specific areas of testing. This path is divided into three main groups of syllabi:

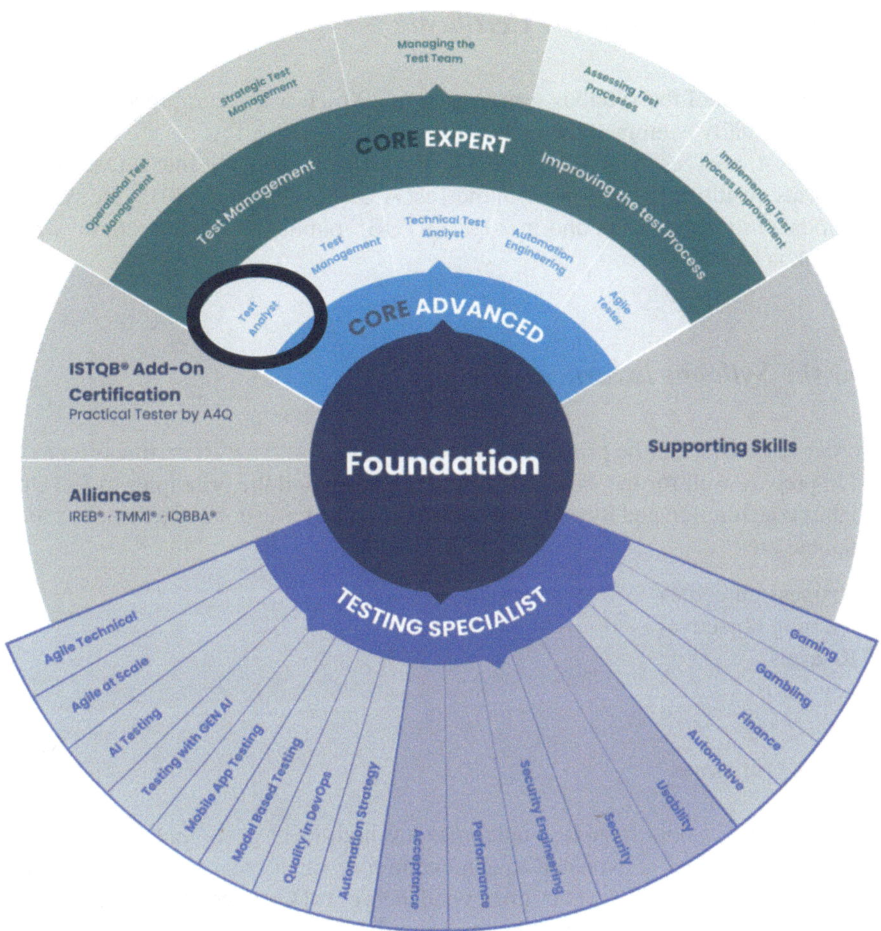


**Fig. 1** ISTQB® portfolio with the test analyst syllabus marked

- Technologies and approaches—grouping syllabi related to specific technologies or approaches in testing, e.g., testing in Agile projects, AI testing, mobile application testing, model-based testing, test automation strategy.
- Quality characteristics and test levels—grouping syllabi devoted to testing specific quality characteristics (e.g., performance, security, usability) or testing at specific test levels (e.g., acceptance testing).
- Testing in particular domains—grouping syllabi devoted to testing applications in specific business areas, e.g., testing in the automotive industry, game testing, or testing of gambling devices.

## *History of the Test Analyst Certificate*

The first version of the syllabus was created in 2007. It was a comprehensive document that actually combined the material from three syllabi: Test Analyst, Technical Test Analyst, and Test Manager. In 2012, this syllabus was split into three separate documents, resulting in version 2.0 of the Test Analyst syllabus. In 2019, the syllabus was updated to version 3.0, and in 2025, ISTQB® published version 4.0, on which this book is based.

## *How the Syllabus is Structured*

In order to understand the principles of the ISTQB® Test Analyst certification exam and to prepare well for the exam, it is good to understand the principles of ISTQB® syllabus construction and its relation to the exam. The basic concepts that need to be explained are:

- business outcomes,
- learning objectives,
- K-levels,
- keywords.

### Business Outcomes

In the ISTQB® syllabi, business outcomes are high-level goals that describe what a certified individual is expected to achieve in a practical, real-world context after completing the certification. They go beyond theoretical knowledge, focusing on how the acquired skills and understanding will benefit the organization and contribute to project and business success.

Business outcomes connect what is learned in the syllabus to the practical tasks a testing professional performs on the job. They ensure that the training and certification process is not just academic but also has direct relevance to workplace performance. Each business outcome articulates how the certified tester adds tangible value to the organization, for example, through better test design, improved risk identification, or more efficient test execution.

Business outcomes serve as an organizing principle for the syllabus. All learning objectives, knowledge areas, and keywords are ultimately designed to support the achievement of these outcomes. They help shape the exam by focusing on practical application, not just memorization.

For employers, business outcomes clarify what to expect from a certified professional. For training providers, they help design courses that focus on real-world competence, not just theoretical knowledge.

In Table 1, nine business outcomes for the Test Analyst v4.0 syllabus are presented.

**Table 1** Business outcomes for the test analyst v4.0 syllabus

| Code | Business outcome description |
|---|---|
| TA-BO1 | Support and perform appropriate testing based on the Software Development Lifecycle followed |
| TA-BO2 | Apply the principles of risk-based testing |
| TA-BO3 | Select and apply appropriate test techniques to support the achievement of test objectives |
| TA-BO4 | Provide documentation at appropriate levels of detail and quality |
| TA-BO5 | Determine the appropriate types of functional testing to be performed |
| TA-BO6 | Contribute to non-functional testing |
| TA-BO7 | Contribute to defect prevention |
| TA-BO8 | Improve the efficiency of the test process with the use of tools |
| TA-BO9 | Specify the requirements for test environments and test data |

## Learning Objectives and K-Levels

The Test Analyst syllabus is built around a set of so-called learning objectives (LOs). The LOs are listed at the beginning of each chapter and are associated with a specific business outcome. An LO describes the gain in cognitive competence to be achieved for a given content. Less formally, an LO describes what a candidate can (and should) learn about a given section of the syllabus. LOs relate to individual subsections of the syllabus and are listed before each section.

Each LO has a unique code, consisting of a prefix encoding syllabus symbol (e.g., "TA" for the Test Analyst syllabus) and a three-part number. The individual numbers indicate the chapter number, the section number, and the sequence number of the LO within that section. The Test Analyst syllabus is structured so that each section of the document corresponds to exactly one LO (e.g., Sect. 1.3.2 refers to the LO TA-1.3.2).

The K-level is a value that signifies at what level a given LO will be verified in an exam question. Since the Test Analyst syllabus is at the advanced level, LOs appear in three possible K-levels, K2, K3, and K4:

**K2—Understand**. With LOs at the K2 level, the candidate is expected not only to remember the definitions of certain concepts but also to understand them so that, for example, they can compare two concepts, identify the advantages and disadvantages of certain approaches in testing, etc.

**K3—Apply**. With LOs at the K3 level, the candidate is expected to know and understand a specific method or technique of operation and be able to apply it in practice. Questions based on K3 LOs often take the form of "exercises" in which, for example, a specific test technique should be used to achieve the required coverage or identify defects in a work product.

**K4—Analyze**. With LOs at the K4 level, the candidate can separate information related to a procedure or technique into its constituent parts for better understanding and can distinguish between facts and inferences. A typical application is to analyze a document, software, or project situation and propose appropriate actions to solve a problem or task.

The Test Analyst syllabus does not include learning objectives at level K1 (remember), but knowledge of the keywords from the syllabus is required at this level (see below).

K-levels are a concept derived from Bloom's revised taxonomy [10].

## Glossary and Keywords

Keywords are important test-related terms that appear in the syllabus. These terms may appear on the exam without explanation. The examinee is expected to know their definitions (K1) and understand them (K2). The set of keywords applicable to a chapter of the syllabus is given at the beginning of that chapter.

The syllabi enumerate keywords but do not define them. Their official definitions are given in the ISTQB® Glossary of testing terms. It is a general rule that the candidate must understand the keywords' definitions in addition to the LOs described in the syllabus.

The ISTQB® Glossary is available as a web application http://glossary.istqb.org (the subsequent hyperlinks for IREB and IEEE). Its purpose is to standardize testing terminology by providing unambiguous definitions for the terms that have a specific meaning in software quality assurance and testing. The glossary is multilingual, with more than 20 languages available. It also provides a quiz for practicing the keywords of a syllabus, like the Advanced Level Test Analyst. For the requirements engineering terminology, we refer to the IREB® CPRE glossary (https://cpre.ireb.org/en/downloads-and-resources/glossary). An online glossary of software engineering terms can be found on the IEEE/ISO Software Engineering Vocabulary website (https://pascal.computer.org/sev_display/index.action).

## Syllabus Content

The Test Analyst syllabus consists of five main chapters with examinable content.

**Chapter 1—The Tasks of the Test Analyst in the Test Process** describes the test analyst's involvement in various Software Development Lifecycles and test activities. It also discusses tasks performed by the test analyst related to work products such as test cases, test environment requirements, test oracles, test data requirements, and test scripts.

**Chapter 2—The Tasks of the Test Analyst in Risk-Based Testing** discusses how the test analyst contributes to product risk analysis and how to analyze the impact of changes to determine the scope of regression testing.

**Chapter 3—Test Analysis and Test Design** describes several black-box test techniques (categorized into data-based, behavior-based, and rule-based techniques) and experience-based test techniques (session-based testing, crowd testing). It also discusses how to select appropriate test techniques to mitigate product risks.

**Chapter 4—Testing Quality Characteristics** explains how to perform several types of functional testing and how to use the specific knowledge of functionality to contribute to non-functional test types being in scope of the test analyst responsibilities, such as usability testing, flexibility testing, and compatibility testing.

**Chapter 5—Software Defect Prevention** discusses various defect prevention practices related to phase containment (using models to detect defects, applying review techniques) and how to mitigate the recurrence of defects by analysis of test results and using defect classification to support root cause analysis.

## The ISTQB® Test Analyst Exam

### *Requirements for Candidates*

The entry criterion for taking the ISTQB® Certified Tester Advanced Level Test Analyst exam is that candidates have an interest in test analysis and test design. The ISTQB® Foundation Level certificate shall be obtained before taking the Advanced Level Test Analyst certification exam.

### *Training*

Preparing for an ISTQB® certification exam requires a structured understanding of the syllabus content, terminology, and intended business outcomes. While self-study using official syllabi, sample exams, and the ISTQB® Glossary is possible and often effective, many candidates choose to enroll in accredited training courses to deepen their understanding and improve their chances of passing the exam. Accredited training refers to training courses that have been officially reviewed and approved by an ISTQB®-recognized member board. These courses are delivered by accredited training providers and are designed to fully cover the syllabus content in alignment with ISTQB® standards. Choosing an accredited training offers several key benefits:

- Structured learning experience—accredited courses follow the official syllabi closely and are organized to support both theoretical learning and practical application.
- Qualified trainers—instructors are typically certified experts with practical experience, capable of clarifying complex concepts and answering candidate questions effectively.

- Up-to-date material—course content is kept current with the latest versions of the ISTQB® syllabi and terminology.
- Sample questions, real-life examples, practical exercises, and exam preparation—accredited trainings often include mock exams and are required to present syllabus content with real-life examples; moreover, each K3 and K4 learning objective must be accompanied by a practical exercise which bridges the gap between theoretical knowledge and real-world application, ensuring that candidates can not only recall concepts but also use them effectively in practical scenarios.

Many training providers also offer flexible formats, including classroom-based, online live sessions, and self-paced e-learning, making it easier for candidates to fit training into their schedules. Candidates can find information about accredited training providers and available courses through the following official sources:

- ISTQB® website (https://istqb.org)—provides general information and links to national boards.
- National or regional ISTQB® member boards—each country or region typically has a local ISTQB® board (e.g., UK and Ireland Testing Board in the UK, American Software Testing Qualifications Board in the USA, German Testing Board in Germany, etc.), which maintains a list of accredited providers and approved courses in a given country or region.
- Training provider websites—accredited providers often publish detailed course information, schedules, and pricing on their own websites.

To be accredited, a training provider must meet strict quality criteria, including:

- Syllabus alignment—course content must fully cover the learning objectives, business outcomes, and terminology defined in the relevant ISTQB® syllabus.
- Qualified trainers—instructors must hold relevant ISTQB® certifications and demonstrate expertise in the subject area.
- Training materials review—all courseware (slides, handouts, exercises, etc.) must be reviewed and approved by an official accreditation body to ensure accuracy and quality.
- Feedback and continuous improvement—accredited providers must gather participant feedback and continuously improve their offerings based on evaluations and updates to ISTQB® standards.

The accreditation process is rigorous and ensures that the training meets the global quality standards expected by ISTQB® and its stakeholders.

## *Exam Rules*

In general, the rules are similar to the ones for the Foundation Level exam, but there are also some differences.

- The ISTQB® Certified Tester Advanced Level—Test Analyst exams are based on the Test Analyst syllabus. As of 2024, version 4.0 of the syllabus is in effect.
- All LOs included in the syllabus are subject to examination.
- The order of questions is random.
- No information about the LO is given in the question's content.
- The examinee is expected to know the definitions of the keywords specified in the syllabus.
- The exam consists of a set of **45 multiple-choice questions** based on the LOs.
- The distribution of questions is precisely defined (see Section "Exam Structure").
- Each question strictly covers a certain learning objective and cannot go beyond it—knowing that is helpful when learning for the exam and also during the exam (it is easier to justify why a given answer is correct or incorrect, when you know the corresponding learning objective).
- K2 question is worth 1 point, K3—2 points, and K4—3 points. Providing the correct answer (i.e., marking all and only correct answers) will result in the award of full points for the question. In any other case, the candidate gets 0 points.
- The maximum possible score for the exam is **78 points**. To pass, you must score at least **65%** (**51 points**).
- The time allotted for the exam is exactly **120 min**. If the language of the exam is not the candidate's native language, the candidate is allowed an additional 25% of the time (i.e., 150 min in total).
- If you fail the exam, you can retake it as many times as you like.

Examinations can be taken as part of an accredited training course or on your own (for example, at an examination center or as part of a public examination). Completion of an accredited course is not a prerequisite for taking the exam, but attending such a course is recommended, as it allows you to better understand the material and significantly increases your chances of passing the exam.

The certificate is issued for life; it does not need to be renewed (in particular, when a new version of the syllabus is published, the certificate earned remains valid, regardless of which version of the syllabus it applies to).

## *Exam Structure*

In Table 2, the structure of the Test Analyst exam is shown. The LOs are gathered into groups, and for each group, there is a required number of questions in the exam. For example, there must be exactly one question that covers LO TA-1.1.1 (so you may be sure that this LO is covered). There will be two questions from LOs TA-1.2.1, TA-1.2.2, TA-1.2.3, and TA-1.2.4. You do not know *which* LOs exactly will be covered. The LO TA-2.2.1 will be covered by two questions, etc.

Table 2 gives you an idea of which parts of the syllabus will be covered more and which not so much. This allows you to properly allocate your time and effort when preparing for an exam. For example, notice that only Chap. 3 will be covered by

**Table 2** Structure of the test analyst exam

| LO | K-level | Number of questions per LO (group)[a] | Points per question | Summary |
|---|---|---|---|---|
| **Chapter 1** | | | | |
| TA-1.1.1 | K2 | 1 | 1 | There are a total of 8 questions required for Chap. 1<br>K2 = 7<br>K3 = 1<br>K4 = 0<br>Number of points for this chapter = 9 |
| TA-1.2.1 | K2 | 2 | 1 | |
| TA-1.2.2 | | | | |
| TA-1.2.3 | | | | |
| TA-1.2.4 | | | | |
| TA-1.3.1 | K2 | 4 | 1 | |
| TA-1.3.2 | | | | |
| TA-1.3.3 | | | | |
| TA-1.3.4 | | | | |
| TA-1.3.5 | | | | |
| TA-1.3.7 | | | | |
| TA-1.3.6 | K3 | 1 | 2 | |
| **Chapter 2** | | | | |
| TA-2.1.1 | K2 | 1 | 1 | There are a total of 3 questions required for Chap. 2<br>K2 = 1<br>K3 = 0<br>K4 = 2<br>Number of points for this chapter = 7 |
| TA-2.2.1 | K4 | 2 | 3 | |
| **Chapter 3** | | | | |
| TA-3.1.3 | K2 | 1 | 1 | There are a total of 22 questions required for Chap. 3<br>K2 = 4<br>K3 = 16<br>K4 = 2<br>Number of points for this chapter = 42 |
| TA-3.2.1 | K2 | 1 | 1 | |
| TA-3.4.3 | K2 | 1 | 1 | |
| TA-3.5.2 | K2 | 1 | 1 | |
| TA-3.1.1 | K3 | 2 | 2 | |
| TA-3.1.2 | K3 | 2 | 2 | |
| TA-3.2.2 | K3 | 2 | 2 | |
| TA-3.2.3 | K3 | 2 | 2 | |
| TA-3.3.1 | K3 | 2 | 2 | |
| TA-3.3.2 | K3 | 2 | 2 | |
| TA-3.4.1 | K3 | 2 | 2 | |
| TA-3.4.2 | K3 | 2 | 2 | |
| TA-3.5.1 | K4 | 2 | 3 | |

(continued)

**Table 2** (continued)

<table>
<tr><th>LO</th><th>K-level</th><th>Number of questions per LO (group)[a]</th><th>Points per question</th><th>Summary</th></tr>
<tr><td colspan="5">Chapter 4</td></tr>
<tr><td>TA-4.1.1</td><td>K2</td><td>1</td><td>1</td><td rowspan="4">There are a total of 4 questions required for Chap. 4<br>K2 = 4<br>K3 = 0<br>K4 = 0<br>Number of points for this chapter = 4</td></tr>
<tr><td>TA-4.2.1</td><td>K2</td><td>1</td><td>1</td></tr>
<tr><td>TA-4.3.1</td><td>K2</td><td>1</td><td>1</td></tr>
<tr><td>TA-4.4.1</td><td>K2</td><td>1</td><td>1</td></tr>
<tr><td colspan="5">Chapter 5</td></tr>
<tr><td>TA-5.1.1</td><td>K2</td><td>1</td><td>1</td><td rowspan="5">There are a total of 8 questions required for Chap. 5<br>K2 = 2<br>K3 = 4<br>K4 = 2<br>Number of points for this chapter = 16</td></tr>
<tr><td>TA-5.3.2</td><td>K2</td><td>1</td><td>1</td></tr>
<tr><td>TA-5.2.1</td><td>K3</td><td>2</td><td>2</td></tr>
<tr><td>TA-5.2.2</td><td>K3</td><td>2</td><td>2</td></tr>
<tr><td>TA-5.3.1</td><td>K4</td><td>2</td><td>3</td></tr>
<tr><td colspan="4">Total: 120 min for 45 questions, 78 points</td><td></td></tr>
</table>

[a] if there are fewer questions to distribute between LOs in a group of LOs, then each question must cover a different LO

almost half of the questions, and you can get 54% points (42 out of 78) for answering these questions. This means that Chap. 3—"Test Analysis and Test Design"—is a very important chapter. This is because the test analyst's main tasks are test analysis and test design using test techniques. On the other hand, there will be only four questions for Chap. 4, and you can get only 4 out of 78 points for them. This does not mean that Chap. 4 is not important. It only means that you should spend less time learning it, compared to Chap. 3.

## *Question Types*

The ISTQB® allows seven different types of multiple-choice questions—Type-A, Roman, Ordering, Matching Select, Matching Drag, Grouping, and Pick-Two. Each is discussed in detail below.

A multiple-choice question consists of two parts—a stem and response options (or response area). Stem contains a question phrase and sufficient information to select the correct response option(s). A problem statement or a scenario may enhance the stem. Response options contain possible answers and appear for Type-A, Roman, Matching Select, and Pick-Two types of questions. Response areas appear for

Ordering, Matching Drag, and Grouping types of questions. They contain a number of options which need to be arranged in a certain way.

**Type-A-type** questions include a stem and four response options, including a single correct option. Each of the four response options consists of an answer to the question in the stem. In order to receive credit for correctly answering a Type-A-type question, the candidate must select the correct response option.

**Roman-type** questions include a stem and four response options, including a single correct option. The stem consists of a limited amount of information and five statements, each preceded by a roman numeral. Each of the four response options consists of two or three roman numerals, representing the TRUE statements. In order to receive credit for correctly answering a Roman-type question, the candidate must select the correct response option containing the correct combination of TRUE statements from the choices provided in the set of five statements.

**Matching Select-type** questions include a stem and four response options, including a single correct option. The stem consists of two lists. Each list contains four items, the first four represented by a number and the second four with a capital letter. Each of the four response option consists of 4 pairs. Each pair consists of an item from the first list paired with an item from the second list. In order to receive credit for correctly answering a Matching Select-type question, the candidate must select the correct response option containing the correct pairing of the two lists.

**Pick-Two-type** questions include a stem and five response options, including two correct options. Each of the five response option consists of an answer to the question in the stem. In order to receive credit for correctly answering a Pick-Two-type question, the candidate must select the two correct response options. If both of the selected options are correct, then the candidate is awarded all the points assigned to the question; otherwise, they are awarded none.

These four types of questions are the most popular, and almost all exam questions are of one of these types. Recently, ISTQB® introduced three new types of questions described below.

**Ordering-type** questions are used to measure the candidate's ability to correctly order items in a sequence. Ordering-type questions include a stem and framing to order items correctly. The stem contains a list of four or five items to order. The candidate must then order the items. In order to receive credit for correctly answering an ordering-type question, the candidate must order all items correctly with regard to the other items. If all items are ordered correctly, then the candidate is awarded all the points assigned to the question; otherwise, they are awarded none.

**Matching Drag-type** questions include a stem and framing to match items correctly. The stem contains two lists of four items each. In order to receive credit for a Matching Drag-type question, the candidate must match all items in the first list to the correct item in the second list, leaving no item unmatched on any one of the lists. If all items are matched correctly, then the candidate is awarded all the points assigned to the question; otherwise, they are awarded none. For use in paper exams, "drag" can be replaced with "draw" for easier understanding by the candidate.

**Grouping-type** questions are used to measure the candidate's ability to identify items with shared characteristics. Grouping-type questions include a stem and framing to group items correctly. The stem contains a list of between four and seven items and a second list of between two and four groups. There is no indication from the size of the groups as to how many items go into each group. Note that questions with four items and four groups are equivalent to the Matching Drag-type question. In order to receive credit for correctly answering a grouping-type question, the candidate must group all items in the first list into a group from the second list. Correct answers cannot result in any empty groups, nor can an item be in more than one group, but there can be a different number of items in different groups. If all items are grouped correctly, then the candidate is awarded all the points assigned to the question; otherwise, they are awarded none.

## *Tips: Before and During the Exam*

In addition to the syllabus, ISTQB® also publishes one or more sample exams. These exams are a handy preparation tool because they train both your knowledge and your exam performance skills. Sample exams let you get used to the specific question format. Every wrong answer points directly to a concept you need to review, which is much more efficient than rereading the whole syllabus blindly. The real ISTQB® exam has a fixed time limit, so practicing with timed sample exams helps you pace yourself so you can finish without rushing. Reading the syllabus is passive learning; answering exam-like questions forces you to recall and apply knowledge, which strengthens memory retention. If you take sample exams under realistic conditions—quiet environment, timer running—you train your brain and body to perform under pressure.

During the real exam:

- Read the questions carefully—sometimes one word changes the whole meaning of the question or is a clue to give the correct answer.
- Pay attention to keywords (e.g., in what Software Development Lifecycle model the project is run).
- Try to match the question with the learning objective—then it will be easier to understand the question's idea and justify the correctness and incorrectness of individual answers.
- Be careful with questions containing negation (e.g., "Which of the following is NOT…")—in such questions, three answers will be true statements, and one will be a false statement. You need to indicate the answer containing *the false statement*.

- Choose the option that directly answers the question. Some answers may be completely correct sentences, but they do not answer the question asked—for example, the question is about the risks of automation, and one of the answers mentions some benefit of automation.
- Guess if you do not know which option to choose—there are no negative points, so it doesn't pay to leave questions unanswered.
- Remember that answers with strong, categorical phrases are usually incorrect (e.g., "always," "must be," "never," "in any case")—although this rule may not apply in all cases.

## Case Study

Below we present a case study that will serve as a guiding example throughout this book. This example will be used to illustrate the content discussed in subsequent chapters.

FoodApp is a mobile application for ordering food. The application consists of three main subsystems:

- Client Component,
- Delivery Management Component,
- Courier Component.

The Client Component is used by customers who order food. Once a client's app user registers, they are able to browse restaurants or find them by filtering with several criteria such as restaurant type, food type (e.g., vegan/vegetarian), and distance. They can view menus, place orders (basket functionality), make payments, track deliveries, and view order history. The app will offer different payment methods.

The Delivery Management Component allows the restaurant owners to monitor orders and their status, monitor couriers in real time, request couriers to take an order, manage delivery rates, and compensation fees. It also allows the portfolio management, i.e., to manage associated restaurants and the pools of couriers (their master data and availabilities). Restaurant owners will also be able to define different discount types and promotions.

The Courier Component is used by people who deliver the food. It allows taking an open order, seeing orders to realize, calculating an optimal route, browsing the routes, and checking the delivered orders.

The high-level, logical view of the FoodApp is presented in Fig. 2.

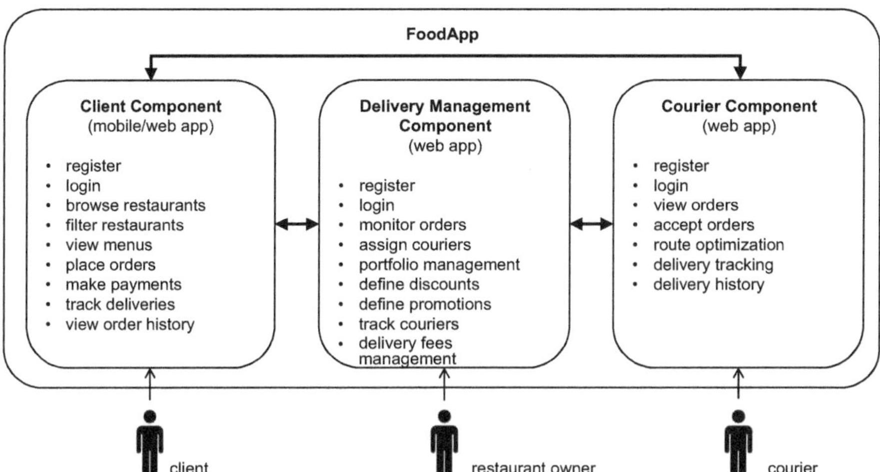


**Fig. 2** High-level, logical view of the FoodApp

The application is a commercial off-the-shelf (COTS) application, which means that there may be a large number of potential users with different environment configurations (e.g., phone type, screen size, memory, etc.). Users will come from different countries, have different cultural backgrounds, and speak different languages.

The application is primarily designed for mobile devices, but a web version is also available for desktop computers. A survey conducted among potential users of the application revealed that ease of installation and an intuitive and aesthetic user interface are very important to customers. In turn, interoperability is a very important feature for the development team due to the modular nature of the application, which is developed in a microservice architecture.

# Part II
# The Syllabus Content

# Chapter 1 The Test Analyst's Tasks in the Test Process

**Keywords** High-level test case · Keyword · Keyword-driven testing · Low-level test case · Software Development Lifecycle · Test analysis · Test analyst · Test case · Test condition · Test data · Test design · Test environment · Test execution · Test implementation · Test oracle · Test script · Testware

## Introduction to the Test Analyst's Tasks in the Test Process

**Definitions**

**Test analyst**: A person responsible for test analysis, test design, test implementation, and test execution, focusing on non-technical aspects of software.

Testing is a process within the Software Development Lifecycle that evaluates the quality of a component or system and related work products.

As with any process, testing is a structured set of activities, work products, roles, and responsibilities. Figure 1.1 illustrates the main activities of testing and the main roles that are used in the ISTQB® test process with a simple BPMN diagram.

The BPMN diagram has two swim lanes for the two main roles: test management and dynamic testing. The swim lanes contain the main activities for which the roles are responsible.

The test management role bears the main responsibility for test planning, test monitoring, test control, and test completion. Their skills are covered in the ISTQB® Advanced Level—Test Management syllabus.

 
A. Roman and M. Hamburg, *Practical Software Test Analysis*,
https://doi.org/10.1007/978-3-032-27986-6_3

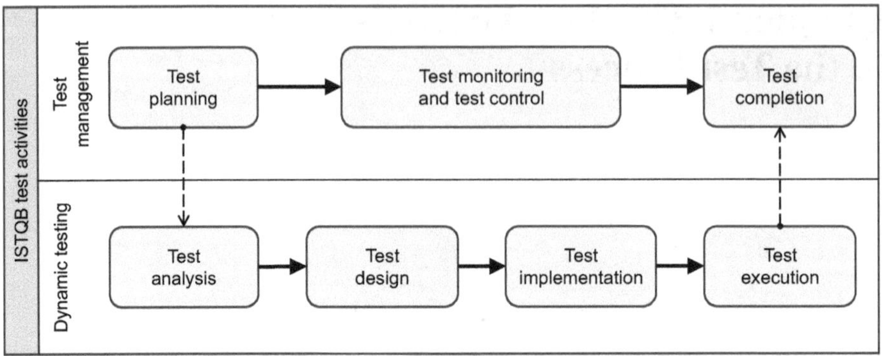


**Fig. 1.1** Test roles and test activities in ISTQB®

The dynamic testing role bears the main responsibility for test analysis, test design, test implementation, and test execution. Their skills needed in the software development industry depend on various factors, including:

- independence from development,
- the test levels they are involved in,
- the quality characteristics in focus.

Among the various specializations of this role, test analysts are responsible for testing the software's business aspects. In the ISTQB® Advanced Level Test Analyst certification, the test analyst is understood as a role that:

- is independent from development and tests based on the specification rather than on the technical design of the software,
- is mostly involved in higher test levels like system testing, system integration testing, and acceptance testing,
- performs mainly functional testing but also contributes to user-focused, non-functional testing, such as usability, adaptability, installability, or interoperability testing.

The software industry spends a major effort on independent quality control. Therefore, it needs test analysts who are testing on higher test levels from a user or business perspective. Empirical studies confirm that professional, systematic independent testing leads to a higher product quality,,. If software providers and clients are organized in separate organizations, both sides will need test analysts: for system testing on the provider's side, and for acceptance testing on the client's side.

Other testing roles focusing on structure-based and less independent testing, on early test levels, or on specific non-functional quality characteristics like security or performance efficiency are covered in other ISTQB® certification products, see Fig. 1 in Chapter "Tasks and Competencies of a Test Analyst".

## 1.1 Testing in the Software Development Lifecycle

TA-1.1.1 (K2) Summarize the involvement of the test analyst in different Software Development Lifecycles

**Definitions**

**Software Development Lifecycle (SDLC)**: The activities performed at each stage in software development, and how they relate to one another logically and chronologically.

The organization of test activities can vary based on the Software Development Lifecycle (SDLC, also called lifecycle model) being utilized. As a result, the involvement of test analysts in these activities may differ depending on the chosen SDLC model. There are three primary SDLC model types in software development: sequential, incremental, and iterative. In practice, models are rarely implemented in these pure forms. However, understanding these model types helps test analysts anticipate specific tasks and determine the best ways to engage in the test process.

### Sequential Development Models

In sequential development models, activities are carried out in distinct phases, as shown in Fig. 1.2. Each phase encompasses a specific set of activities, with minimal overlap between them. A new phase starts only after the previous one has been completed, relying on the deliverables from earlier phases. At the end of each phase, reviews are typically conducted to assess the quality of the deliverables and determine if they are suitable for the next phases. A phase concludes when all of its deliverables have been completed.

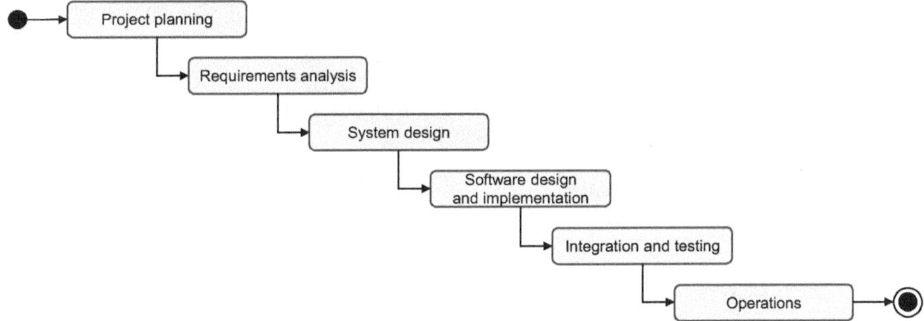


**Fig. 1.2** Example of a sequential SDLC

**Table 1.1** Examples of the test analyst's tasks in a sequential SDLC

| Phase | Tasks of the test analyst |
|---|---|
| Project planning | • Evaluate the impact of failure risks for the combinations of the main features (from client registration to restaurant promotions to courier route planning) and quality characteristics (functional completeness, functional correctness, functional appropriateness, usability, adaptability, installability, interoperability) and suggest to the test manager the test levels to mitigate them best. For example, failures in the functional completeness of restaurant filtering may have a medium impact, while failures in the functional correctness of making payments will certainly have a critical impact<br>• Consult the test manager on the appropriate test techniques to use, e.g., metamorphic testing for the geographic features due to the oracle problem in geographic orientation<br>• Consult the test manager in estimating the cost and lead time for test activities, including reviews, dynamic test activities, and providing the test infrastructure (e.g., by indicating the test doubles and test data needed)<br>• Consult the test manager in deciding on test design automation, indicating its benefits and the resources needed |
| Requirements analysis | • Review the requirements for testability<br>• Define test conditions for the respective test levels (system testing, system integration testing, acceptance testing) based on the test techniques foreseen in the test plan |
| System design | • Create test models of system behavior, e.g., classification trees for restaurant filtering, state diagrams for order processing, decision tables for pricing and discounting, or metamorphic relations for distance calculations. Provide feedback on anomalies detected in the models<br>• Review the design specifications for testability<br>• Define test conditions to cover the system design specification items |
| Software design and implementation | • If model-based testing is used, generate test cases from the models (e.g., combinatorial tests from the classification trees, state transition tests, or decision table tests)<br>• Design test cases manually otherwise<br>• Design test procedures and (if foreseen) keyword-driven test scripts for automation<br>• Define test suites, e.g., one per associated risk level for each subsystem<br>• Specify the test data requirements for restaurants, menus, couriers, user personas, etc.<br>• Specify the test environment requirements, including the mobile devices and platforms, restaurant applications, banking systems, and navigation systems |
| Integration and testing | • Execute the test suites by descending risk level<br>• Report defects |
| Operations | • Design tests for reproducing failures in production in the test environment<br>• Run confirmation tests after defect fixing<br>• Conduct impact analysis of maintenance changes and define appropriate regression test suites |

The tasks of the test analyst often evolve over time, depending on the activities associated with each phase of the SDLC. In the early phases, the test analyst primarily focuses on supporting test planning, which may involve contributing to the test strategy, conducting product risk analysis, or estimating test efforts. Table 1.1 shows some examples of the test analyst's tasks in a sequential SDLC.

As the test basis is developed, test analysis can begin. For instance, if the requirements are part of the test basis, the test analyst can engage in collaborative requirements analysis or participate in requirements reviews, as well as create test conditions or define acceptance criteria for user stories. If the test basis includes aspects of system design, the test analyst can take part in the system design phase by creating test models, reviewing design specifications, and developing test conditions that address the design elements.

Test design and implementation run parallel to software design and implementation. Typical deliverables that fall under the test analyst's responsibilities include test cases, test procedures, test data requirements, and test environment specifications.

In the later phases of the SDLC, the test analyst executes the tests and assists with test completion activities.

Popular sequential SDLCs include the waterfall model and the V-model, .

**Case Study**

Let us assume that, in our FoodApp case study, development follows the sequential SDLC in Fig. 1.2. Table 1.1 gives some specific examples of the test analyst's involvement in the phases if they are responsible for dynamic system testing:

### Incremental Development Models

Incremental development models divide software into smaller, manageable increments. An increment refers to the software product delivered, and each increment provides a usable solution for specific requirements that can be deployed and utilized in an operational environment. Each new increment extends the previous one by adding additional features, as shown in Fig. 1.3. In contrast to sequential development, which can take a long time (even several years for complex projects), an increment is typically developed from a few days to a few months at most.

Each increment is developed and tested independently. Consequently, the test analyst performs the same activities for each increment, including test analysis, test design, test implementation, test execution, and test management support. However, in incremental development, the test analyst must carefully distinguish between testing new features and conducting regression testing.

As with any SDLC, one part of testing focuses on new or modified features. In the early increments, the emphasis is primarily on testing the new features.

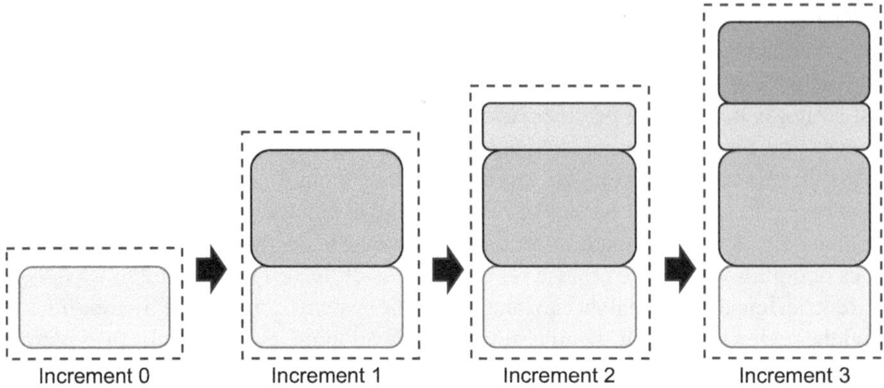


**Fig. 1.3** Symbolic example of incremental product delivery

In incremental SDLCs, regression testing requires special attention compared to sequential development. Due to frequent changes, the risk of regression increases with each increment. To effectively mitigate this growing risk with an affordable effort, it is crucial to use automated test execution for the regression test suites. Therefore, the test analyst should design regression test suites from the early increments onward and support their automation. To prevent the test suites from wearing out and becoming ineffective, as outlined in Sect. 1.3 on testing principles, the test analyst must also pay particular attention to refactoring and organizing these regression test suites carefully.

In some incremental SDLCs, developers introduce new features in each increment while leaving the implementation of existing features unchanged. For such increments, the test analyst should typically build regression test suites based on a risk analysis. The risk impact of unchanged features typically remains the same, while their risk likelihood depends on the likelihood of side effects from the changes made.

Moreover, the test analyst should be aware that this development approach can often lead to increased software complexity and decreased maintainability. The test analyst may observe higher defect rates, increased defect clustering, and slower defect resolution as indicators of these issues. In such cases, it is essential for the test analyst to provide feedback to the development team regarding the need for code refactoring. Addressing this technical debt often requires dedicated increments focused specifically on refactoring. However, code refactoring can significantly impact the system and carries a high risk of regression, which the test analyst must manage by assembling and executing comprehensive regression test suites.

Other incremental development lifecycles maintain clean code design by refactoring code sections as necessary during each increment. In these situations, regression testing should focus on the areas of highest risk due to refactoring. Additionally, regression test suites will be needed for the critical unchanged features that may be impacted by the changes made.

## Case Study

Let us assume that, in our FoodApp case study, development follows an incremental SDLC like in Fig. 1.3. Increment 0 develops an initial skeleton application. This increment is not yet useful for the stakeholders but is rather intended as a proof of concept. Increment 1 is the minimal viable product (MVP), while Increment 2 is the minimal marketable product (MMP), which will be launched into operation. Increment 3 is planned to focus on refactoring. (Note that, in practice, incremental development usually means much more and smaller increments, but this example should be good enough to illustrate the test analyst's involvement in various increment types.)

Table 1.2 gives some specific examples of the test analyst's involvement in dynamic system testing through the various increments.

**Table 1.2** Examples of the test analyst's involvement in incremental SDLCs

| Increment | Features | Specific focus of the test analyst's activities |
|---|---|---|
| Increment 0 | Clients<br>• Client registration<br>• View menu<br>• Place orders<br>Delivery management<br>• Request couriers to take an order.<br>Couriers<br>• Take order<br>• Deliver order | • Perform all dynamic test activities: Test analysis, design, implementation, and execution, as foreseen in the test plan<br>• Support the specific objective of this MVP (proof of concept) with focused testing of functional appropriateness, usability, and interoperability<br>• Design regression test suites for future increments covering the implemented features<br>• Support the automation of the regression test suites |
| Increment 1 | Clients<br>• Select restaurant<br>• Pay order with credit card<br>Delivery management<br>• Monitor order status<br>Couriers<br>• See orders to realize<br>• Check delivered orders<br>Non-functional<br>• Integration on the latest Android and iOS platforms<br>• Availability on app stores | • Testing the new features with focus on functional correctness and completeness<br>• Regression testing of the increment 0 features<br>• Support usability testing<br>• Extend the regression test suite to include the new features<br>• Perform adaptability testing on the Android and iOS platforms, popular browsers, and devices<br>• System integration testing, including bank payment systems and restaurant systems<br>• Perform installability testing |

(continued)

**Table 1.2** (continued)

| Increment | Features | Specific focus of the test analyst's activities |
|---|---|---|
| Increment 2 | Clients<br>• Filter restaurants<br>• Track order delivery<br>• View order history<br>• Pay order with bank transfer or mobile wallet<br>Delivery management<br>• Manage delivery rates and compensation fees<br>• Manage discounts and promotions<br>Couriers<br>• Calculate an optimal route<br>• Browse routes | • Testing the new features dedicated to functional correctness and appropriateness<br>• Regression testing based on impact analysis and defect cluster history of the increment 0 and 1 features<br>• Maintain and extend the regression test suite<br>• System integration testing of new payment types and navigation systems |
| Increment 3 | • Refactoring<br>• Extension to desktop computers<br>• Integration of additional popular mobile platforms and stores | • Comprehensive regression testing<br>• Adaptability testing to desktop computers and mobile platforms |

## Iterative Development Models

In **iterative development models**, the development process is cyclical, involving repeated cycles of prototyping, testing, refining, and deployment (see Fig. 1.4). The term "iterative" refers to the SDLC activities performed and the work products produced. Each iteration follows the same pattern of activities, deliverables, and roles. A well-known example of an iterative development model is the spiral model by Boehm.

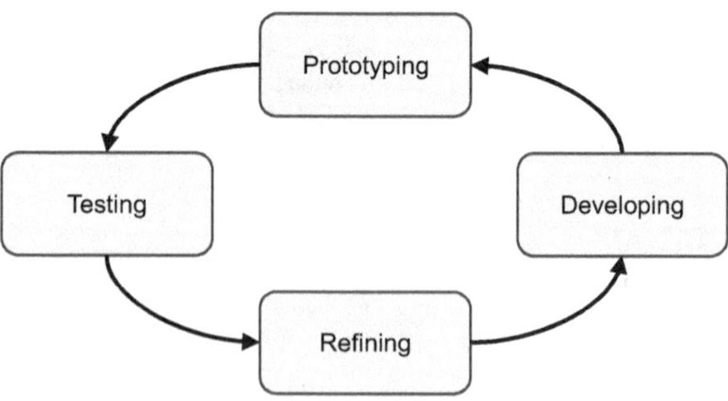


**Fig. 1.4** Sample activities in an iterative development lifecycle model

In an iterative Software Development Lifecycle, the role of the test analyst is dynamic and adaptive. The test analyst works closely with developers and business representatives, adjusting to the evolving product. As the software evolves, the test analyst modifies test conditions and test cases accordingly, providing feedback to improve the test process in each iteration. The more frequently iterations occur, the more essential it becomes for the test analyst to maintain and develop regression tests.

### Hybrid Models

An SDLC may incorporate elements from various models, along with specific techniques and approaches. For example, Agile software development combines aspects of both iterative and incremental models. In these instances, the involvement of the test analyst will vary based on the specific characteristics of the SDLC and the way these elements are integrated. A best practice that applies to all SDLC models is to involve the test analyst from the initial phases of the development process.

**Test Analyst in Scrum**

Scrum is a popular software development framework embedded in the iterative and incremental Software Development Lifecycle. In Scrum development, the test analyst should be involved in activities such as defining user stories and acceptance criteria, estimating the user stories with planning poker, creating and maintaining automated regression test suites, performing experience-based testing, or designing tests for demo sessions.

## Sample Questions

### Question 1.1.1A

You are a test analyst for acceptance testing in sequential software development of a system for making appointments with city authorities. Your main test objective, as stated in the test plan, is to verify that the system fulfills its requirements.

The project plan is reviewed and approved by the stakeholders. In the current phase, business analysts collect the requirements. Which of the following test tasks should you perform during this phase?

(a) Support the test effort estimation required for testing these requirements.

(b) Review the requirements from the perspective of test conditions.
(c) Design test cases and the corresponding test data to cover the requirements.
(d) Prioritize the test procedures related to the requirements for execution.

Select ONE answer.

**Question 1.1.1B**

Your company is developing an online hiking guide. The team delivers a new version with a few new features to hikers every week. As a test analyst, how do you contribute to the team's work?

(a) You focus on regression testing and only test the happy paths of the new or modified features.
(b) You focus on testing the new or modified features and always run the same standard regression test suite.
(c) You carefully assemble the regression test suite and refactor it whenever necessary.
(d) You perform test analysis during the first weeks and focus on test execution during the remaining weeks.

Select ONE answer.

## 1.2 Involvement in the Test Activities

### *1.2.1 Test Analysis*

TA-1.2.1 (K2) Summarize the tasks performed by the test analyst as part of test analysis

**Definitions**

**Test analysis**: The activity that identifies test conditions by analyzing the test basis.

**Test condition**: A testable aspect of a component or system identified as a basis for testing.

The overall process of test analysis is shown in Fig. 1.5. The most crucial input for test analysis and design is the test basis. The test manager typically defines during test planning what information the test basis should contain. During test planning,

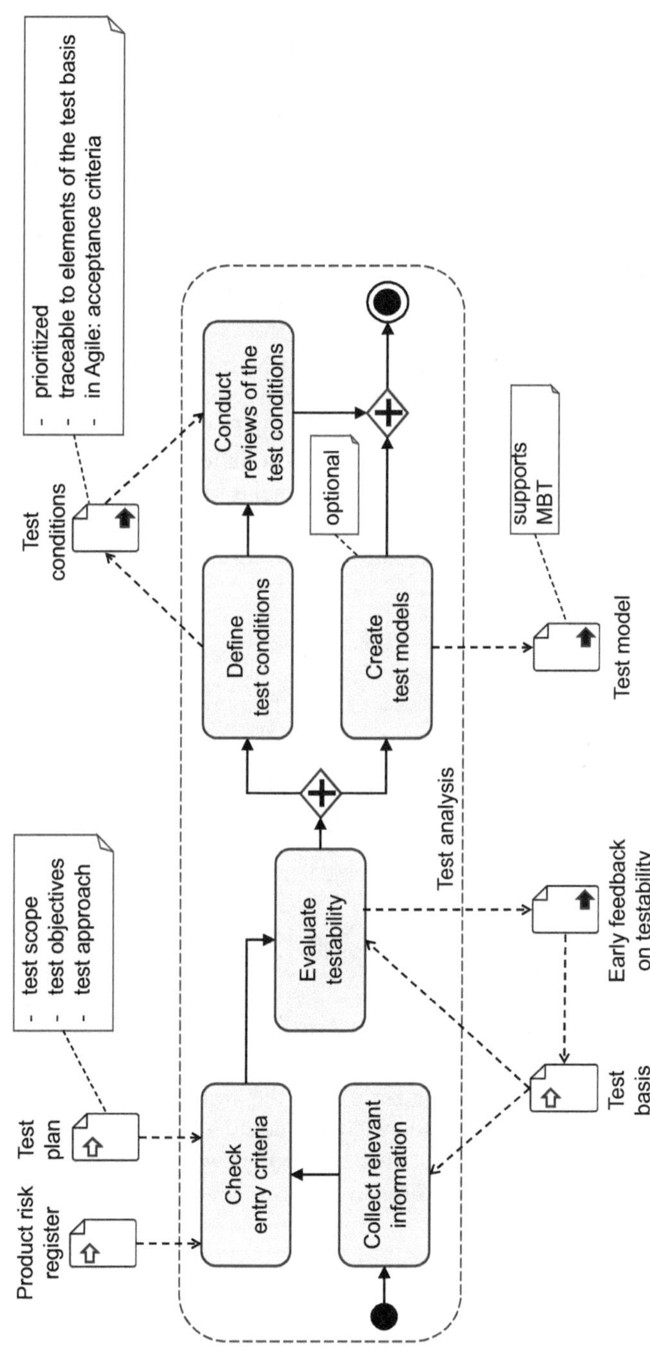


**Fig. 1.5** Test analyst's tasks in test analysis

the test basis does not have to be fully available or usable, but it should be clear where the test analyst can locate it when test analysis begins. Even if the test analyst participated as a consultant during test planning, the test analysis activity is often the first time they will engage with the test basis.

Therefore, when beginning test analysis, the test analyst should verify that the test basis is available and contains all the required information. If it does not, the test analyst must gather additional relevant information.

Test analysis and design according to the intended test approach may require further documentation. This can include relevant standards or regulatory requirements, organizational guidelines for the supported business processes, interface specifications, and system documentation for existing systems and platforms that need integration.

Furthermore, the test basis typically consists of both documentation and verbal information. For instance, insights gained from conversations during collaborative user story writing may be essential (see Sect. 4.5.1). The test analyst may need to engage with various stakeholders to collect this information.

Changes to the test basis may necessitate adjustments to the test scope. Therefore, the test analyst should carry out these activities as early as possible to prevent later rework. The test analyst must communicate the need for adjustments and coordinate these changes with test management.

**Case Study**

In our FoodApp case study, the test analyst may consult national data protection regulations, national working hours' regulations for courier drivers regarding driving and rest periods, accessibility standards for the Client Component, or the interface specifications of the geographical navigation systems that interact with the FoodApp.

Non-documented verbal information may include courier and restaurant representatives indicating which usage scenarios are frequently used, customer support indicating feedback from clients for previous versions of the FoodApp, or software architects describing how the integrated user registration system works and how an update rollout of the Client Component works.

Incorporating accessibility standards into the test basis for the Client Component may expand the test scope by including a validation of required accessibility levels. The test analyst must collaborate with test management to identify where to integrate this additional task.

To proceed effectively with test analysis, the test analyst checks the following entry criteria:

- Test planning has been performed, and the test scope, test objectives, and test approach are clear. Otherwise, there is a risk that the organization expects more from the test analyst than the budget allows or that the test analyst will not focus on the aspects that stakeholders expect from them.
- The test basis (containing information such as requirements or user stories) is available. Otherwise, there is no solid basis for the tests that ultimately justifies the test results.
- The product risks already identified have been evaluated and documented if required. Otherwise, the efforts of the test analyst will not be appropriately targeted at the product risks of the test object and will not adequately minimize them.

**Case Study**

Assume that an incremental SDLC is used to develop the FoodApp, in which a test plan is provided by the test manager. In such a case, the test analyst should especially check among others:

- Is it clear which integrated standard components and features are in the generic test scope, e.g., the customer registration and authentication, the geographic navigation of the couriers, or the bank payment authorization?
- Is it clear which features are to be implemented and tested in the current version?
- Does the current increment have specific test objectives like improving the user experience, verifying that there is no regression after refactoring, or validating the functional appropriateness for couriers?
- Is a model-based test approach foreseen for the new features, manual black-box testing, or rather exploratory testing?
- Is the risk register (if foreseen) completed by the stakeholders, aligned, and approved by the test manager?

The test analyst evaluates the test basis to identify any defects and assess its testability, providing early feedback to the product owners. This evaluation may involve modeling the system behavior according to the test techniques that will be applied (see Chap. 3 and Sect. 5.2.1). Review techniques are also utilized as part of the process (see Sect. 5.2.2). If defects in the test basis are not fixed immediately, they must be documented. Additionally, the test analyst determines the necessary test oracles (see Sect. 1.3.4).

**Case Study**

Suppose the next increment of the FoodApp will implement some types of restaurant discounts and promotions. If decision table testing should be used, the test analyst can model the corresponding business rules in a decision table. By that, they may detect anomalies like overlapping rules, inconsistencies, gaps, or high complexity. The decision table will also act as a test oracle, its actions containing the expected outcomes for each rule. Alternatively, if equivalence partitioning or domain testing is foreseen, the test analyst can model some equivalence partitions in a perspective-based reading and provide review feedback to the product owner. In this case, the test analyst should check if the business rules are clear enough to serve as a test oracle.

The test analyst defines and prioritizes test conditions for each test item in scope. The test conditions address the test objectives (see, Sect. 1.1) and must be traceable to the elements of the test basis. The scope and focus of the test conditions take the product risks into consideration. In incremental or iterative development models, this includes determining the scope of regression testing based on an impact analysis. In Agile software development, test conditions can be expressed as acceptance criteria that reflect the risks of the user stories.

**Case Study**

Test conditions for the restaurant discounts and promotions should cover the different types of discounts and promotions possible (e.g., free delivery, percentual price reduction, bonus for the next order), the customer types eligible (e.g., new customers, loyal customers according to some criteria, former regular customers who have not ordered for some time), validity periods of the offer, the types of dishes in the offer, or the minimum purchase amount. The risk levels should determine the rigor of testing. For instance, if the parameters are mainly independent, combinatorial coverage types like base choice for low risks and pairwise for higher risk levels will suit. In case of dependencies between the parameters, decision table testing may be suitable, with minimization depending on the risk level.

An unchanged feature that is likely to be impacted and needs comprehensive coverage is client billing, while the route calculation and display are unlikely to be impacted in this increment.

The test analyst can proceed in stages, starting with high-level test conditions such as "promotional free delivery provided" and "free delivery not provided." Next, the test analyst defines more detailed test conditions such as "free delivery provided to the new customer," "free delivery not provided because not a new customer," or "free delivery period expired." This approach supports sufficient coverage and enables an early start to the test design, e.g., for user stories that still need to be refined.

The test analyst involves the stakeholders in reviewing the test conditions to ensure that the test basis is clearly understood and that testing is aligned with the test objectives.

## Sample Questions

### Question 1.2.1A

Which of the following tasks is part of the test analysis activity?

(a) Collect information missing from the test basis.
(b) Consult the test manager in defining the test basis.
(c) Capture the traceability between the test basis, test conditions, and test cases.
(d) Create test conditions using keywords in keyword-driven testing.

Select ONE answer.

### Question 1.2.1B

Which of the following is **NOT** a part of the test analysis activity when performing testing for the ticket reservation system?

(a) Deciding to test the online payment process before seat selection features, because payment failures have the highest customer impact.
(b) While reviewing the system requirements document, confirm that it correctly describes the seat-locking logic during payment.
(c) Logging a defect stating that the requirement for refund timelines is missing from the specifications.
(d) Designing a test case to verify that a user can reserve three seats for a 7 pm movie and receive an email confirmation within 5 min.

Select ONE option.

## *1.2.2 Test Design*

TA-1.2.2 (K2) Summarize the tasks performed by the test analyst as part of test design

**Definitions**

**Test design**: The activity that derives and specifies test cases from test conditions.

Test design describes how to perform testing to achieve the stated test objectives. The approach taken for test design is influenced by various factors, including required coverage, the test basis, the SDLC, project constraints, and the knowledge and experience of the testers involved. The overall process of test design is shown in Fig. 1.6.

In this activity, the test analyst uses the test conditions and the test basis as the primary source of information to design tests that determine in detail how testing will be performed. Typically, tests will be documented as test cases. While the test conditions define *what* needs to be tested, the test cases outline *how* the tests will be executed. The test objectives, approach, and techniques to be employed have been defined by the test management in the test plan, used in test analysis, and are also essential for the test analyst during the test design. A systematic approach that uses

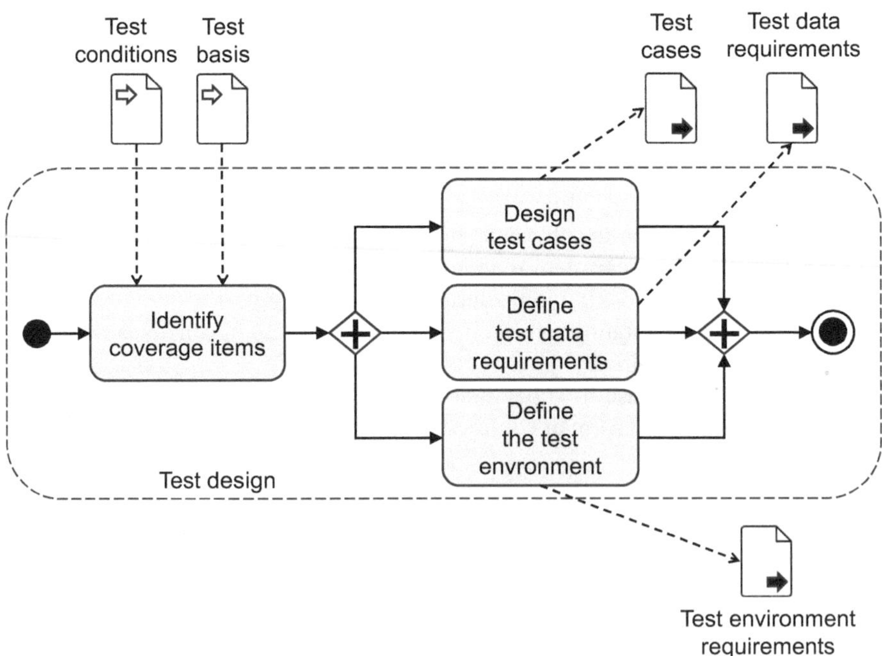


**Fig. 1.6** Test analyst's tasks in test design

established test techniques is ideal for test design. Without this approach, testing can become ad hoc and lack both effectiveness and efficiency.

Test cases can be specified at various levels of abstraction, ranging from high-level to low-level. During test design, the test analyst determines when it is appropriate to use low-level or high-level test cases (see Sect. 1.3.1). In both instances, the test analyst must establish clear pass/fail criteria for the tests.

The test analyst designs the test cases for new and changed test conditions. For regression testing, selecting existing high-level test cases or adapting existing low-level test cases based on their prioritization is typically sufficient.

Like any work product, the test cases must meet specific quality criteria in order to best fulfill their purpose (see Sect. 1.3.2). In particular, test cases play a vital role in communication and must be easily understood by all relevant stakeholders. Since test cases may not always be executed by their authors, it is essential that other testers can comprehend how to execute them, understand their objectives (i.e., the underlying test conditions), and recognize their significance. Additionally, test cases should be understandable to developers who may need to implement or re-run the tests in the event of a failure, as well as to auditors who may need to review and approve them.

During test design, the test analyst must also establish traceability among the test basis, test conditions, and test cases. The effort invested in creating and maintaining these relationships yields significant benefits. Firstly, the test results of test case execution (whether it passes or fails) can be traced back to elements of the test basis, such as specific requirements, features, and interfaces. This enables test managers to assess the quality of the software in terms familiar to the stakeholders. Secondly, changes to elements of the test basis are inevitable. When such changes occur, traceability will enable the test analyst to efficiently identify which test cases are impacted and need adjustment. This proactive approach ensures that the testing remains relevant and effective in the face of evolving requirements.

**Case Study**

In the example above of the FoodApp increment implementing restaurant discounts and promotions, suppose the business rules for discounts are defined in a textual specification. According to the test plan, they shall be tested with decision table testing. The product risk analysis assigned a high-risk level to the client-facing aspects of this feature, due to its complexity and business criticality. Decision table testing shall be applied.

Consider, for example, the test condition “free delivery promotion for any combination of customer type, validity period, and minimum purchase amount.”

Deriving high-level test cases from the decision table rules will be an appropriate option, e.g.:

- Preconditions:
  - Free delivery promotion for new customers provided for any order in the first x days of their registration.
  - Customer has registered at most x days earlier than the order date.
- Action:
  - Customer places an order with a delivery distance within the limit.
- Expected Results:
  - FoodApp accepts the order.
  - The customer bill contains no delivery fee.
  - The courier will receive the delivery fee.
  - The FoodApp organization will be charged for the delivery fee.

The test case should be traceable to the decision table for free delivery promotions, which in turn will be traceable to the respective requirements.

In experience-based testing, test cases may not always be documented. Instead, test execution can be guided by test conditions on appropriate levels of abstraction. Instead of designing traditional test cases, the test analyst can design test charters for session-based testing, which concentrate on specific test conditions. Alternatively, the test analyst can design high-level test cases based on high-level objectives.

When the tests are designed, details of the test environment and test data required for test execution also become clear. Some of these must be prepared by various responsible parties and, therefore, requested in good time. For this reason, the test analyst also has the task of defining the test environment requirements (see Sect. 1.3.3) and specifying the requirements for test data (see Sect. 1.3.5).

**Test Environment and Test Data in Test Design**

Designing tests for client registration may indicate the need for an email server and viewer in the test environment. This setup captures test emails without the risk of sending them to actual users. The requirements should specify the platform on which the email server and client will operate. Additionally, if two-factor authentication is implemented, the test environment may require extra components, such as mobile devices capable of receiving SMS notifications or authenticator apps.

Testing client profile management may need virtual banking services in the test environment to verify the validity of credit cards. Test data requirements may indicate the credit cards in the banking system needed for testing (e.g., valid, expired, blocked credit cards).

Suppose the test approach opted for synthetic test data. In this case, the test analyst may require procedures for saving and restoring the test data to enable re-running tests with the same inputs. In addition, time shifts of the test database should make the test data suitable for executing time-dependent tests on any day (e.g., testing expired promotions for new customers).

The test analyst uses the exit criteria established in test planning to determine when sufficient test cases have been designed. A common exit criterion for test design is the achieved level of coverage. Additionally, other factors such as residual risk levels or project constraints like budget or time can also indicate when the test design may conclude.

Test design can be supported by tools, but should be tool- and technology-agnostic to ensure flexibility and tool independence.

## Sample Questions

### Question 1.2.2A

During which activity should a test analyst complete the requirements for the test environment?

(a) During test planning, when the test scope and objectives become clear.
(b) During test analysis, when the test conditions become clear.
(c) During test design, when the test cases become clear.
(d) During test implementation, when the test environment is prepared.

Select ONE answer.

### Question 1.2.2B

Which of the following activities is a part of the test design?

(a) Defining test conditions.
(b) Organizing test procedures into test suites.
(c) Specifying requirements for test data.
(d) Comparing actual results to expected results.

Select ONE answer.

### 1.2.3 Test Implementation

TA-1.2.3 (K2) Summarize the tasks performed by the test analyst as part of test implementation

**Definitions**

**Test implementation**: The activity that prepares the testware needed for test execution based on test analysis and design.

**Test script**: A sequence of instructions for the execution of a test.

Test implementation aims to ensure that all necessary testware required for executing tests is ready and available when development releases the test object for testing and deploys it in the test environment. This allows the test analysts and testers to start test execution without delay and proceed quickly without unnecessary interruptions. Such good preparation is important because test execution is typically on the critical path of software development, meaning that delays in this activity would most likely have an impact on the overall timeline.

The overall process of test implementation is shown in Fig. 1.7. The main deliverables of test implementation are test suites, test data, and test environments. Consequently, the test analyst has three primary tasks in this activity:

- creating the test suites,
- acquiring or generating the test data,
- ensuring that the test environment is properly set up by the designated parties.

The main inputs for this process consist respectively of:

- test cases,
- test data requirements,
- test environment requirements.

In addition, the test plan may include other relevant input. For example, test objectives and test scope indicate which aspects to focus on. Roles and responsibilities determine who has to set up and provide the requested test doubles and service virtualization in the test environment, or a required anonymization procedure for test data.

Typically, the test cases designed need preconditions to be met for successful execution. When executed in an appropriate order, their results can establish the preconditions for subsequent test cases. To take advantage of this interaction, the

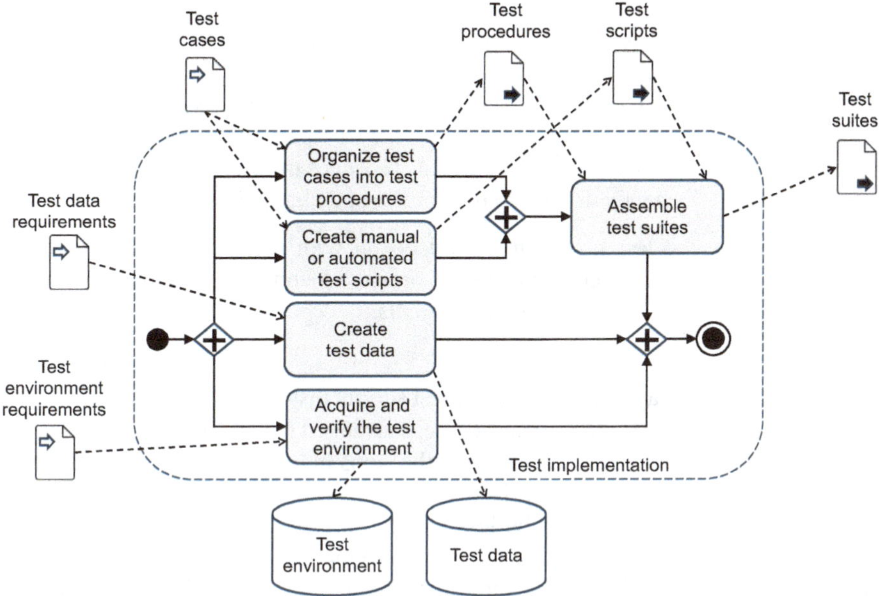


**Fig. 1.7** Test analyst's tasks in test implementation

test analyst can assemble test procedures containing steps in execution order, most of which execute test cases. In addition to the test cases, the test procedures shall include any steps needed for setting up any initial preconditions (e.g., loading test data from a data repository), verifying expected results and postconditions, and resetting the test data and environment following execution (e.g., resetting the database or resetting the state of mock objects and other test doubles).

**Case Study**

For testing the free delivery promotion in our FoodApp, the test analyst may assemble the following test procedure:

Step 0a (setup): Select a restaurant R1 from which to order and an address A1 within delivery distance.
Step 0b (setup): Verify that free delivery promotion for new customers is provided for any order in the first x days of their registration.
Step 0c (setup): Search for a courier F1 who is available.
Step 1: Run the regression test case registering a new customer C2 with address A1.

Step 2: Run the new test case for food ordering of customer C2 from restaurant R1.
Step 3: Run the regression test case for courier F1 delivering the order to customer C2.
Step 4: Verify that the booking for customer C2 does not charge the delivery fee and that the delivery fee is paid to the courier and charged to the organization.

Of course, the test procedure could go on with more test cases for this promotion type. If needed, it may also contain a technical cleanup at the end, resetting the database to its original contents.

The test analyst may choose to create test scripts instead of test procedures. Both test scripts and test procedures consist of steps arranged in execution order. However, the key difference between the two is that the steps in test scripts consist of instructions, while test procedures comprise test cases. As a result, test scripts operate at a more technical level and may be less suitable for test analysts who are focused on business aspects. However, test scripts can be more appropriate for test automation, such as in keyword-driven testing. If automated test execution is planned, the test analyst should recommend test cases that are suitable for automation—typically those that cover the higher risk levels—to the test automation engineers.

The test analyst prioritizes the test procedures and test scripts for execution based on the criteria established during risk analysis and test planning. They create test suites that contain the test procedures or scripts to be executed on the current version of the test object. This enables related tests (e.g., for new features or regression testing) to be executed together in a specific test run.

**Case Study**

The prioritized list of test suites for the new FoodApp increment could be:

1. high-priority happy cases for discounts and promotions,
2. automated regression test suite for billing,
3. medium-priority test cases for discounts and promotions,
4. automated regression test suite for delivery management,
5. automated regression test suite for courier features,
6. low-priority edge and negative test cases may be tested with exploratory testing. The test analyst can prepare test charters rather than specifying test cases, procedures, scripts, or suites.

Simultaneously with creating new testware from test cases, the test analyst should also update the traceability between the test basis and the new testware, which includes test procedures, test scripts, and test suites.

The test analyst can also assist the test management in defining a test execution schedule, including resource allocation, to enable efficient test execution by defining the test execution order (see, Sect. 5.1.5).

The level of detail and the associated complexity of work carried out during test implementation depend on the importance of fast test execution. In addition, it may be influenced by the level of detail of the test conditions and test cases. In some cases, regulatory rules apply, and testware should provide evidence of compliance with applicable standards.

**Testing in CI/CD Pipeline**

In the case of continuous integration and continuous deployment (CI/CD), the tests in the CI/CD pipeline must be fully automated. Therefore, the test suites must contain automated test scripts, and careful test implementation should ensure that automated test execution runs smoothly.

In addition to specifying the tests at the level of detail needed for swift execution, the test analyst should also care for two other prerequisites of test execution: test data provisioning and test environment readiness.

The test analyst creates input and environment data to load into databases and other repositories (see Sect. 1.3.5). The test data requirements aim to ensure that this data will be fit for purpose to support the specific test objectives.

The test analyst should also verify that the test environment is fully set up, meets the needs specified in the test environment requirements, and is ready for test execution (see Sect. 1.3.3). This is best carried out by designing and running a smoke test. The test environment should reveal defects in the test object through test execution, operate normally when failures do not occur, and adequately replicate, if required, the production or end-user environment.

## Sample Questions

### Question 1.2.3A

Match the following examples (1–4) with the corresponding tasks in the test implementation (A–D):

Example activities:

1. Create and run a small test suite that invokes all interfaces provided by service virtualization.
2. Indicate the dependencies and priority of manual test procedures, and the skills needed for executing them.
3. Use the prioritization criteria from the test plan and the risk levels from product risk analysis to group related test scripts and test procedures for execution.
4. Migrate the test database from the previous to the new structure after refactoring.

Tasks in test implementation:

A. Create test suites.
B. Create test data.
C. Verify the test environment setup.
D. Assist the test manager in defining a test execution schedule.

(a) 1-C, 2-D, 3-B, 4-A.
(b) 1-D, 2-C, 3-A, 4-B.
(c) 1-C, 2-D, 3-A, 4-B.
(d) 1-A, 2-B, 3-C, 4-D.

Select ONE answer.

**Question 1.2.3B**

Which of the following takes place during the test implementation?

(a) The test analyst manually executes tests following the exploratory testing approach.
(b) The test analyst determines in which areas low-level test cases are appropriate.
(c) The test analyst defines more detailed test conditions based on a high-level one.
(d) The test analyst assists a test manager in defining a test execution schedule.

Select ONE answer.

### 1.2.4 Test Execution

TA-1.2.4 (K2) Summarize the tasks performed by the test analyst as part of test execution

**Definitions**

**Test execution**: The activity that runs a test on a component or system producing actual results.

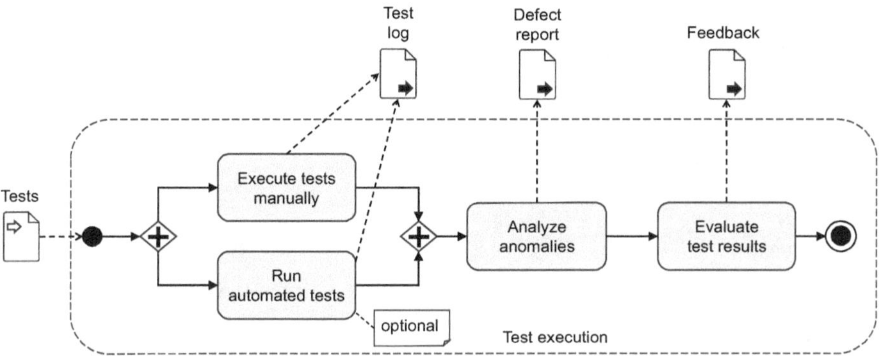


**Fig. 1.8** Test analyst's tasks in test execution

During test execution, test suites are run on a specific version of the test object. This process of executing a test suite on a particular version is referred to as a test run and is recorded in a test log. The executed test suites may consist of both test procedures and test scripts, which in turn contain individual tests. The primary tasks of the test analyst during test execution are executing tests manually and analyzing anomalies. Executing tests includes comparing actual against expected results and logging execution details and results. Analyzing anomalies includes reporting defects. In addition, the test analyst may run automated tests and evaluate test results to provide feedback.

The overall process of test execution is shown in Fig. 1.8. The input to test execution is visualized as tests, which may be organized as single test cases, test procedures, test scripts for manual or automatic execution, or even test charters for exploratory test sessions.

The test analyst performs tests manually, which involves executing designated test procedures and manual test scripts, as well as conducting exploratory testing. For exploratory testing, the test analyst may utilize session-based testing along with test charters (see Sect. 3.4.1).

The test analyst can also run automated test scripts, but that may be the task of developers, test automation engineers, or technical test analysts. Running test scripts and especially analyzing them in case of failures usually require technical skills not in the scope of a test analyst.

The combination of manual and automated tests should encompass the three key areas:

- testing the new or changed features,
- confirmation testing (i.e., re-running tests that previously failed to confirm that after defect fixing, the failures do not occur anymore in the current version of the test object),
- regression testing of unchanged features.

If test management has set a test execution schedule, the tests are carried out in the intended sequence and personnel assignment.

**Case Study**

The next increment of FoodApp delivers the following backlog items:

- five defects found in earlier increments of the Client Component have been fixed,
- two new delivery management features were implemented: manage delivery rates and compensation fees.

During test design, the test analyst has designed high-level test cases for the happy paths and the most important variants of the new features. For other special and negative cases, test charters for exploratory test sessions are defined.

They also selected the test cases for existing features that have failed due to the defects that will be fixed in this release. The test analyst ensured that these test cases were automated and included in a new regression test suite.

During test implementation, the test analyst prepared the test data needed. The test environment remains unchanged. The test analyst included the regression test suites for this increment in the CI/CD pipeline. When the new version is deployed in the test environment, the regression tests are run.

Test execution starts with the CI/CD pipeline. It executes the automated regression test suites automatically. The test analyst and the test automation engineer collaborate in analyzing the anomalies and fixing any issues not due to software defects. After fixing, they re-run the suites. If the regression test finds new defects in the test object, the test analyst comments on the defect reports generated by the CI/CD pipeline. The test management tool updates the traceability automatically.

Next, the test analyst starts the automated confirmation tests and the automated test suite for the new features. Again, the test analyst and the test automation engineer collaborate in analyzing the anomalies, fixing issues, re-running the test suites, and reporting defects. Traceability updates are automated.

Finally, the test analyst and additional testers perform the exploratory test sessions defined in the test charters. They document the results manually on session sheets. Defects of the test object found are reported in the defect management tool.

It is usually necessary to log the test execution. The log documents who performed each test case, when, and with what result, including the actual results and any anomalies. If detailed logs are required by the test plan, test management tools can automate the logging and relieve the test analyst of documentation work (see Sect. 1.3.7). Exploratory session-based testing typically involves lightweight logging on session sheets.

If anomalies occur when running a test manually or automatically, the test analyst must analyze their likely causes. Anomalies include deviations of actual from expected results, missing data objects or incorrect data required by the postconditions, or unexpected events such as system crashes, error messages, or warnings. Such an anomaly may result from a defect in a test object, but there may be other reasons as well. Being familiar with the test basis and the testware, the test analyst can check for the following:

- Can misunderstandings of the specification be excluded?
- Is the test case justified and correct based on the specifications?
- Are all preconditions regarding the test data met?
- Are all preconditions regarding the test environment met?
- Have all test cases on which this test depends been passed?
- Are the input test data for the test case correct?
- Are the expected results of the test case correct?
- Are the postconditions of the test case correct?

Test analysts usually have little insight into the structure of the test object and can therefore only analyze technically caused anomalies to a limited extent. Nevertheless, they should not immediately report such anomalies as defects to the development team. With the support of other parties, like infrastructure management or test automation engineers, they may also check:

- Is the platform for the application operating nominally?
- Are all components of the test object deployed and available?
- Are all components of the test environment available?
- Is the automated test script correct?
- Are there hidden technical dependencies between the test cases?

Analysis may reveal causes that can be fixed immediately by the test analyst or supporting technical staff, e.g., adding a missing action to the test case, correcting wrong attribute values of test data objects, or setting up the missing link to a mock object needed in the test environment.

The test analyst communicates defects based on the observed failures to the parties who can fix them. Depending on the organization's structure, they can directly contact them or communicate via a single point of contact (SPOC).

If needed, test analysts have to document anomalies in defect reports to be handled by defect management. This is typically the case in larger organizations when several people are involved in defect detection, analysis, resolution, and solution confirmation. How to create a defect report is handled in Sect. 5.1, and the defect management lifecycle in Sect. 2.2.

The test analyst must ensure that the most recent test run and its corresponding results are traceable back to the relevant testware. To achieve this, the test analyst needs to update the traceability relationships. This process helps stakeholders understand the most current execution status of each test suite, test case, test condition, product risk item, or specification element. This information allows for the transformation of test results into high-level risk or coverage information, enabling stakeholders to make informed decisions. For example, it provides clarity on how many test cases related to a test condition have passed or failed. Test management tools can assist in automating this documentation activity, making the process more efficient (see Sect. 1.3.7).

In addition to these typical tasks, the test analyst evaluates the test results, including the following tasks:

- Recognizing defect clusters, which may indicate the need for more testing of a particular part of the test object (see Sect. 5.3.1).
- Manually re-executing automated tests that have failed to make sure that the test automation did not produce a false-positive result.
- Suggesting additional tests based on what was learned during previous tests.
- Identifying new risks from information obtained when performing test execution.
- Suggesting improvements to test design or test implementation (e.g., improvements to test procedures) or even to the system under test.
- Suggesting improvements to the regression test suites, including refactoring, scope adjustments, and test automation (see Sect. 2.2).

**Benefits of Traceability**

In an iterative and incremental development process, an increment was planned to deliver features 1–4 for system testing. During test analysis and design, the test analyst designed five test cases for these features and created traceability links between them as indicated in Fig. 1.9 with solid lines. When it came to deployment in the test environment, the development team stated in the release notes that only features 1–3 had been implemented, while feature 4

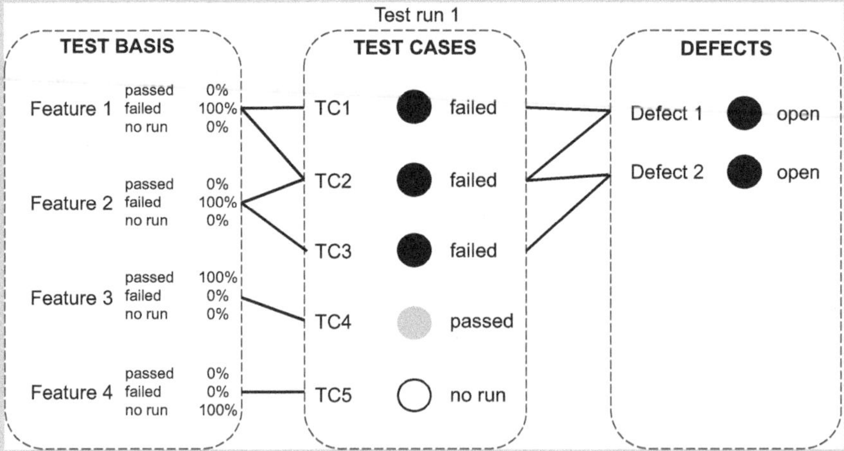


**Fig. 1.9** Traceability links and results after test run 1

As a result, the test analyst removed test case TC5 from the test suite and executed test cases TC1 to TC4 in test run 1. The test results revealed that the test cases TC1, TC2, and TC3 failed, while test case TC4 passed. Analysis showed that the failures were caused by two distinct defects: defect 1 impacted TC1 and TC2, while defect 2 impacted TC2 and TC3. The test analyst documented these relations, and updating the traceability led to revised coverage indicators for the test basis.

Consequently, stakeholders were able to see that features 1 and 2 have completely failed, feature 3 has passed, and feature 4 has not been tested. Based on this information, along with the details in the defect reports regarding the issues encountered and their associated severity, the stakeholders decided against deploying this increment in the live environment. Fixing the two defects was included in the scope of the next increment.

During the following increment, the development team addressed defects 1 and 2 and completed implementing feature 4. The test analyst assessed the risk of feature 3 being impacted as low and prepared a test suite that included test cases TC1 to TC3 and TC5.

When the new version was deployed in the test environment, the test analyst executed this test suite, and the results are shown in Fig. 1.10. Re-testing TC1 to TC3 confirmed that the failures caused by Defect 1 and Defect 2 no longer occur. However, TC3 revealed a new minor defect that had been masked in the previous increment, resulting in a failure for TC3. Additionally, TC5 failed due to another minor defect.

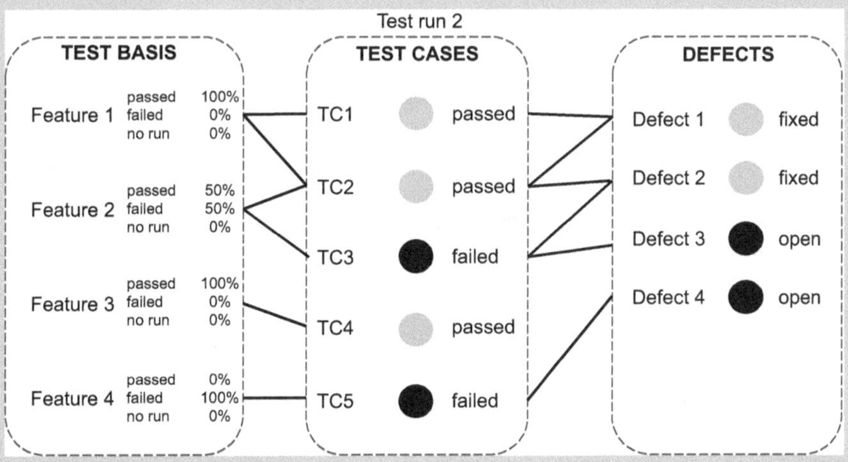


**Fig. 1.10** Traceability links and results after test run 2

The test analyst then updated the traceability, which led to the revised coverage indicators for the test basis indicated in Fig. 1.10. Consequently, stakeholders could see the test results related to each feature. With this information, along with the details from the defect reports, the stakeholders decided to deploy the new version of the software in the live environment.

### Practical Considerations on Traceability

**Tool Support**. The above example only gives a first impression of how complex traceability can become. To maintain it efficiently, using appropriate tools is highly recommended. Common test management tools can provide some level of support in this area. If tool support is unavailable, storage structures and test naming conventions may help capture a rough traceability between test cases and parts of the test basis. For example, test cases can be sorted into folders per feature, or their names can start with the test condition. But such structures do not achieve the benefit of traceability.

**Consistency**. The test analyst is responsible for ensuring the consistency of test cases and their associated defects:

- If the most recent execution of a test case fails, at least one open defect must be associated.
- If all defects related to a test case are closed, the test case must have passed.
- If all test cases associated with a defect have passed, that defect must be marked as closed.

If test cases and defects must be documented according to the test plan, then these criteria are essential. If they are not met, the documentation will be inconsistent, and stakeholders looking at it will be confused. They will ask the test analyst questions like: Why did this test case fail, and no defect was reported? Why did this test case fail after having fixed all its defects? Why is this defect still open if it causes no failure anymore? However, test management tools often fail to verify these criteria automatically, leaving inconsistencies for the test analyst to resolve.

**Timeliness**. Stakeholders expect the test analyst to evaluate the quality of the latest tested version of the test object. This expectation also applies to unchanged features, which are usually only tested incompletely in regression testing. However, traceability typically shows the status of the latest execution of each test case, even if this execution only took place with earlier software versions. Typically, such test cases are labeled as "passed," which might be misleading. While this is better than labeling them as "not executed," a more precise marking, such as "previously passed," is unusual. This is illustrated in the example above with feature 3 and TC4.

In sequential Software Development Lifecycles, the test manager might provide for comprehensive regression testing of the test object before going live. However, in incremental lifecycles, this is not a realistic option. This underlines the importance of careful risk-based selection of regression tests (see Sect. 2.2). Test analysts must be prepared to explain the reason why test cases are labeled as "passed" even though they were not executed on the latest version of the test object.

**Severity**. The criticality of an element of the test basis, the priority of the assigned test cases, and the severity of a defect in a traceability chain do not have to correspond. Criticalities and priorities will not normally increase in the forward chain of traceability, but they may decrease. As a result, a highly critical feature or test condition may fail simply because a cosmetic defect has occurred in an associated test case. In principle, this could be visualized by displaying an overall severity level of all associated defects (e.g., as a maximum). However, the usual tools do not support this. Therefore, the test analyst or test manager usually has to qualitatively assess the impact of a feature or test condition failure.

**Granularity**. In the example above, the dashboard presents the features of the test object for simplicity. More detailed and fine-grained entities, such as test conditions or coverage items, would provide a more meaningful evaluation. However, these require higher maintenance efforts, even with the assistance of tools. This creates a trade-off between the significance of the traceable entities and the maintenance effort needed for traceability. While the ISTQB® recommends using test conditions, each organization must make its own decision regarding their use.

**Dimensions**. In some software lifecycle models, such as the V-model, specifications are refined in stages, beginning with requirements and progressing through system specifications, technical specifications, and component specifications. Development employs traceability to connect requirements with elements of the system specification, which in turn link to elements of the technical specification and finally to specific components. This dimension is often referred to as vertical traceability.

Corresponding test levels, such as the acceptance test, system test, integration test, and component test, use the respective level of the specification as their test basis. The traceability of test cases and results on these test levels to elements of their test basis is typically called horizontal traceability. Combining horizontal traceability with vertical traceability informs stakeholders on the test results on lower test levels, e.g., unit testing, in terms of high-level specification items, e.g., user requirements. In our example above, horizontal traceability indicates that feature 4 has failed. Vertical traceability of Feature 4 may link to a user requirement, e.g., "As a restaurant owner, I want to offer my customers a special promotion with free delivery to attract them back to my restaurant." So, stakeholders can see that the implementation of this requirement has a defect. Advanced test management tools support such combinations of horizontal and vertical traceability.

## Sample Questions

### Question 1.2.4A

The release notes of the test object announce the fixing of defects reported earlier. The test analyst has executed the associated confirmation tests. Which of the following tasks shall the test analyst perform **NEXT**?

(a) Updating the traceability between the test basis and the latest test results.
(b) Analyzing the anomalies that have led to the defects fixed for their likely causes.
(c) Performing a root cause analysis of the defects to support defect prevention.
(d) Running the regression test suite to verify that defect fixing did not cause side effects.

Select ONE answer.

### Question 1.2.4B

Which of the following sentences about the activities of a test analyst during the test execution is **FALSE**?

(a) The test analyst updates the business requirements to match the system's actual behavior.
(b) The test analyst executes tests according to the test execution schedule.
(c) The test analyst identifies new risks from information obtained when performing test execution.
(d) The test analyst executes tests manually, but they can also run automated test scripts.

Select ONE answer.

## 1.3 Tasks Related to Testware

Test analysts are not only responsible for the execution of their tasks, but also for the quality of their deliveries. This includes test cases, test environments, test data, test oracles, and test scripts. This section discusses the tasks of test analysts related to the quality of the testware delivered, as well as the types of tools available for managing it.

### *1.3.1 High-Level and Low-Level Test Cases*

TA-1.3.1 (K2) Differentiates between high-level and low-level test cases

**Definitions**

**High-level test case**: A test case with abstract preconditions, input data, expected results, postconditions, and actions (where applicable).
**Low-level test case**: A test case with concrete values for preconditions, input data, expected results, postconditions, and a detailed description of actions (where applicable).

A high-level test case, also known as an *abstract test case* or *logical test case*, outlines the conditions under which the test object is evaluated. It indicates which test conditions are covered by the test case. However, they do not contain specific details or values for preconditions, input data, expected outputs, or postconditions. These are all expressed at an abstract level.

**A High-Level Test Case**

**Title**: Delivery fee for small orders.

**Preconditions**

The customer is authenticated and logged in.

FoodApp has a configured minimum order amount for free delivery.

A standard delivery fee is defined in FoodApp.

**Inputs**

The customer selects dishes from a restaurant menu such that the total is less than the minimum for free delivery and proceeds to checkout.

**Expected Results**

The invoice includes the selected dishes and the standard delivery fee applied.

**Postconditions**

The customer can complete the payment, continue shopping, or cancel the order.

Typically, a test analyst begins by designing high-level test cases that clearly define the test conditions they address. These test cases are well-suited for creating traceability links to the test conditions, ensuring comprehensive coverage. Consequently, test plans often require the documentation of high-level test cases, typically in a test management tool.

If the test approach allows for lighter documentation, high-level test cases can also guide the test analyst in formulating test objectives in a test charter for session-based testing. This allows the test analyst to expand on these objectives during the test execution (refer to Sect. 3.4.1).

High-level test cases provide a rough outline of the type of test data and test environment required for execution. As illustrated by the example above, some of these requirements may be explicit, such as the standard delivery fee or the minimum order amount for free delivery. Other requirements may be less obvious, like the presence of a menu featuring dishes below the minimum order amount. Experienced test analysts can identify the necessary test data and environments, prepare everything required during test implementation, and execute the high-level test case manually.

High-level test cases can serve as the basis for developing low-level test cases. Also known as *concrete* or *physical test cases*, low-level test cases provide a detailed refinement of high-level test cases. Documenting low-level test cases is particularly important when test implementation and execution are automated, when the test plan requires thorough documentation or logging of test activities, or when testers need precise and detailed instructions, such as in cases where tasks are outsourced to countries with lower labor costs.

For this purpose, low-level test cases offer an in-depth description of the necessary data to be prepared, the actions the tester must take (if applicable), and the verification of expected results. These test cases are characterized by specific preconditions, input data, expected results, and postconditions, as illustrated in our example below.

**A Low-Level Test Case Implementing the High-Level Test Case Above**

**Title**: Delivery fee for small orders.

**Preconditions**

- The Customer C1 is authenticated and logged in.
- FoodApp has a configured minimum order amount for free delivery of 30€.

- A standard delivery fee of 5€ is defined in FoodApp.
- Restaurant R1 offers on its menu dishes including:
    01. Pizza Margherita 10€.
    02. Noodles Bolognese 8€.
    03. Wiener Schnitzel 20€.

**Step 1**

- **Inputs/Actions:**

Customer C1 selects restaurant R1.

- **Expected Results:**

FoodApp displays the menu of restaurant R1.

**Step 2**

- **Inputs/Actions:**

Customer adds dishes 01 and 02 from the menu to the shopping cart.

- **Expected Results:**

FoodApp displays information that 2 dishes are selected for a total of 18€.

**Step 3**

- **Inputs/Actions:**

Customer selects "Place order."

- **Expected Results:**

FoodApp displays the invoice data, including:

- The name of the restaurant R1.
- A detailed list of the dishes ordered and their prices, i.e., Pizza Margherita for 10€ and Noodles Bolognese for 8€.
- A subtotal of 18€ for the selected dishes.
- The standard delivery fee is 5€.
- A total payable amount of 23€.
- An information message "Order for just €12 more for free delivery."

**Postconditions**

- The customer is presented with options to:
    - Complete payment.
    - Continue shopping at restaurant R1.
    - Cancel the order.

One high-level test case can be implemented in one or more low-level test cases. For instance, a test analyst might generate different minimum order amounts, delivery fees, users, restaurants, and dishes for a single high-level test case. However, it is important to note that all these low-level test cases will be associated with the same test condition (such as the delivery fee for small amounts). Additional low-level test cases related to the same high-level test case will not contribute to coverage.

**Rigorous Coverage with Low-Level Test Cases**

If the test analyst aims to enhance test depth by incorporating test conditions related to data (e.g., boundary values), behavioral aspects (e.g., state transitions), or business rules (e.g., decision tables), they need to create the relevant test conditions and ensure that the additional test cases, whether high-level or low-level, are traceable to them.

As can be seen in the example above, creating low-level test cases for a high-level test case is more than just filling in concrete values. It is also a step from conceptual to technical, specifying the detailed steps, actions, and verifications needed to evaluate the test object under the given test condition. It is often deferred from test design to test implementation, especially if specific test data is needed. The test analyst must ensure that everything necessary to execute the low-level test cases is known.

Documenting high-level test cases in test design involves less documentation effort but may delay the implementation details until a critical phase in testing. Conversely, documenting low-level test cases requires substantial documentation and maintenance efforts, but it facilitates quicker execution later on. In practice, most test cases are hybrid, being concrete in some areas while abstract in others. This hybrid nature often arises from a trade-off between the maintainability and comprehensibility of the test cases.

In the example above, the test analyst may choose to keep all specific data abstract if the test data offers sufficient variety. However, providing a detailed description of the test steps and expected results—including the specific message text anticipated in step 3—will be beneficial.

## Sample Questions

### Question 1.3.1A

In a border control system, you are testing the following test condition: "Individuals aged 12 and above are required to provide fingerprints." You design the following test case:

Test Case ID: TC01

**Title**: Fingerprint for ages 12 and above.

**Input**: The birth date of the traveler, with birth date < current date—12 years.

**Expected Output**: Prompt "Please place your right index finger in the fingerprint reader."

What kind of test case is this?

(a) A high-level test case because it contains abstract data like birthdate.
(b) A low-level test case because it contains concrete data like 12 years.
(c) Not a valid test case because it contains both abstract and concrete data.
(d) A valid hybrid test case because it contains both abstract and concrete data.

Select ONE answer.

**Question 1.3.1B**

What is the difference between high-level and low-level test cases?

(a) High-level test cases are expressed at an abstract level. Low-level test cases do not contain concrete information for input data.
(b) High-level test cases are suitable for ensuring that tests cover all relevant test conditions. Low-level test cases refine high-level test cases.
(c) High-level test cases are designed by test analysts and technical test analysts. Low-level test cases can be designed by both testers and developers.
(d) High-level test cases are designed using black-box test techniques. Low-level test cases are designed using experience-based test techniques.

Select ONE answer.

## *1.3.2 Quality Criteria for Test Cases*

TA-1.3.2 (K2) Explain the quality criteria for test cases

**Definitions**

**Test case**: A set of preconditions, inputs, actions (where applicable), expected results and postconditions, developed based on test conditions.

**False-negative result**: A test result which fails to identify a defect that is actually present in a test object.

**False-positive result**: A test result in which a defect is reported although no such defect actually exists in the test object.

Test cases are the central work product of dynamic testing. They are a result of the test design, in which the test analyst specifies how testing is to take place. As the person responsible, the test analyst must therefore ensure the quality of the test cases.

The format and level of detail for test cases depend on the specific context of the project and product. These aspects should be discussed and agreed upon within the test team. Mandatory attributes of the test cases are determined by the definition of the term given above. Despite these fixed basic conditions, the quality of test cases can vary greatly.

**Standard Attributes of a Test Case**

The syllabus also refers to the international standard as an example of a list of attributes. However, it should be noted that the contents of this standard are not examinable according to the rules outlined in Chapter "Tasks and Competencies of a Test Analyst" of the syllabus. Nonetheless, the attributes of a test case listed in Section 8.3 of this international standard are similar to those defined by ISTQB® and worth considering:

- unique identifier (needed for traceability; typically, a technical ID either generated or created manually according to a notation scheme),
- objective (typically in the form of a title),
- priority (of running the test case in test execution),
- traceability,
- preconditions,
- inputs,
- expected results (which include both expected outputs and postconditions).

As for any type of work product, the quality of a test case means "the characteristics that bear on its ability to satisfy stated or implied needs". Therefore, in order to understand the criteria of test case quality, the test analyst must be aware of the needs for its use.

In the first place, stakeholders require test cases to provide an appropriate evaluation of the quality of the test object and find the defects before they cause harm in production. These needs are addressed by test techniques and traceability, which are topics discussed in other dedicated sections of the Test Analyst certification.

But there are other stated or implied needs as well, addressing mainly the quality of test case documentation. Test cases must not only be executable as desired but must also provide relevant information about the coverage and significance of the test results and be maintainable for use over the entire software lifecycle.

Neglecting test case quality can lead to many problems, such as reduced comprehensibility, execution delays due to unclear results, or high maintenance costs. Such problems typically accumulate over time, leading to quality debt: They will increasingly obstruct the work of the test analyst, while eliminating them will require more and more effort. Defining quality criteria for test cases in an organization is the first step toward more executable, comprehensive, and maintainable test cases.

The syllabus mentions the quality criteria listed below, which can be grouped based on the specific needs they address. For each criterion, we provide an example for better clarity.

Quality criteria related to the need for successful execution of the test case include:

- **Feasibility**. It must be possible to execute a test case.
  A common scenario is when a test case becomes outdated due to changes in the test object. For example, there may be existing test cases for orders made by unregistered customers. If the customer policy is updated to require prior registration on FoodApp, those test cases will no longer be feasible following the change.
- **Precision**. There should be only one interpretation of a test case to avoid false-negative and false-positive test results. Ambiguous terms like "suitable," "as needed," or "several" should be avoided.
  For example, an expected result "The app displays a mouseover tooltip for the output GUI elements as needed" will be ambiguous. It neither states when a tooltip is expected nor the text of the tooltip. If the requirement for tool tips is specified, the test analyst should replace "as needed" with "as specified."
- **Correctness**. A test case must facilitate accurate verification of the test conditions on which it is based.
  For example, assume that the test basis specifies: "Given the detail display of an element from a list, when the user closes this detail display, the system shows the list again." The test analyst might require that the expected results include the list display positioned at the same place from which he selected the element for detailed display. However, this is an assumption that is not necessarily correct.
- **Conciseness**. The granularity of test cases (i.e., one large test case with many test actions versus several smaller test cases) should correspond to the test basis and test conditions. Smaller test cases focused on a few coverage items are preferable: they simplify root cause analysis, can be combined freely into test procedures and test suites, and do not block further test execution if one fails.
  For example, separate short test cases for creating a small order with a delivery fee, "cancel order and change restaurant," "create a large order with free delivery," and "place order and pay" are relatively concise. These four short test cases offer the above-mentioned advantages of fast failure cause analysis, flexible combination, and independent execution. On the other hand, the test analyst must incorporate them during test implementation into test procedures or scripts for execution, which contain steps establishing their preconditions and checking their postconditions. For a single large test case that combines all four, no additional steps

would be required. Nevertheless, the advantages of the four concise test cases outweigh this disadvantage.

Quality criteria related to the need for relevant information provided by the test results include:

- **Completeness**. All necessary attributes should be present, including the required test data and a clear expected result to avoid doubt when comparing with the actual result.
  For example, assume that the test basis specifies: "Customers can filter restaurants for food types (vegetarian, vegan)." The test case specifies as input a search with food type "vegetarian" and selection of a restaurant from the list. The expected result says that the restaurant selected shall offer vegetarian food on its menu. However, this test case fails to verify that the result list contains *all* restaurants satisfying the filter criteria. This might miss a critical defect of incomplete search result lists.
- **Traceability**. Test cases should be traceable to test conditions, requirements, and risks to enable the test analyst to keep them up to date as described in, Sect. 1.3.4.
  For example, a test case "search with food type 'vegetarian'" should be traceable to a test condition "restaurant search for various food types," the requirement "As a customer, I want to be able to filter restaurants which offer specific food types," and to the risk that the hit list does not contain the correct restaurants.
- **Necessity**. Every test case should cover a clear test objective, as expressed in its title or summary. Duplicates should be avoided. Things that should not be tested should not have test cases designed.
  For example, if the test plan determines that each choice coverage of the restaurant search criteria, restaurant type, cuisine, and food type is sufficient, then there is no point in adding a test case for the combination of (family restaurant, Italian cuisine, seafood) if all single values of this combination are already covered in other combinations. Another typical example of unnecessary testing is verifying a feature of a reliable built-in component, e.g., testing a non-numeric input in a numeric GUI input field.

Quality criteria related to the need for maintainable tests during the Software Development Lifecycle include:

- **Understandability**. Test cases may be reviewed, modified, and executed by people other than the author. The test analyst should write test cases in a language and format understandable to all stakeholders involved without explaining the obvious. Complex test cases should be simplified or split up.
  For example, the expected result of a successful order in FoodApp should not be worded as "Dupe printed" but rather as "Order ticket printed at the restaurant," because the testers may not be familiar with the technical jargon of restaurant management.
- **Consistency**. Consistency in language, formatting, and structure makes the test cases easier to understand and maintain. The test analyst may use a glossary for this purpose.

Examples of inconsistent wording include the use of synonyms and homonyms. For instance, if test cases refer to customers in some instances and to clients, users, or testers in others, this inconsistency could confuse testers and other stakeholders. If the term “child” is used to represent the age group of 0–17 years in one context and 3–12 years in another, it is likely to lead to confusion.

As the examples show, some quality criteria for test cases can address more than one of the needs mentioned. For example, if all test cases are executable, this not only facilitates test execution on the current software version, but also their maintenance and the transparency for stakeholders about the planned and achieved coverage.

All quality criteria are affected by the maintenance of the test object in the software lifecycle, which is why the test analyst must maintain the test cases with each version of the test object.

## Sample Questions

### Question 1.3.2A

What can go wrong if a test case is not documented precisely?

(a) Test execution may not be able to decide whether the test run passed or failed because of missing information.
(b) Stakeholders will not recognize which test conditions are impacted when the test case fails.
(c) The test analyst will need much effort to make the test case executable again for future software versions.
(d) Test execution might misinterpret the test result as failed and cause a defect report, which will be rejected.

Select ONE answer.

### Question 1.3.2B

Consider the following excerpt from a test case for a ticket reservation system confirming that the seat selection feature works for available seats:

- Navigate to the movie’s booking page.
- Choose a suitable seat from the seating chart.
- Proceed to checkout.

Expected Result: The system should reserve the seat and proceed to payment.

Which test case quality criterion is violated by the use of the word “suitable”?

(a) Precision.
(b) Feasibility.
(c) Traceability.
(d) Correctness.

### *1.3.3 Test Environment Requirements*

TA-1.3.3 (K2) Give examples of test environment requirements

**Definitions**

**Test environment**: An environment containing hardware, instrumentation, simulators, software tools, and other support elements needed to perform a test.

Dynamic testing does not usually run in the production environment so as not to disrupt live operation. Organizations set up test environments in which testing only takes place. The test environment is a critical success factor for both manual and automated test execution.

- A general expectation of the test environment is that the test results accurately reflect the behavior of the test object in live operation. A test case that passes or fails in the test environment should have the same test result when executed in production. Shortcomings in the test environment can otherwise impair the reliability of the test results delivered by the test analyst.
- A specific need of the test analyst regarding the test environment is testability. The test environment must support establishing test conditions for the test object, performing the tests, and determining whether those test conditions have been met. For example, if the test analyst needs to test various responses from banking systems when charging a bill, the test environment should support simulating these responses and verifying their contents.
- A related need is support for defect detection. This includes the ability to create the test conditions and recognize the failure caused by a defect, but also to analyze the cause of failure. For example, in interoperability testing, the test environment should support interface logging. This allows the test analyst to understand whether the sender has sent the wrong message or the receiver has misinterpreted a correct message.
- However, the test analyst must also be aware of the effort and costs involved in setting up and maintaining a test environment. Features they request from the test environment may imply high effort and cost. If necessary, they must be able to justify the cost–benefit ratio of a test environment to the stakeholders with lower overall test costs. For example, the costs of setting up and maintaining a production-like instance of the server platform in a web service with high data volume and availability might be higher than the benefit of having it always available for running tests.

Ideally, a test environment is robust, predictable, and integrated with the test automation framework, if required.

- Robustness (also known as *fault tolerance*) refers to the ability of a test environment to function as intended despite the presence of hardware or software defects (also known as *faults*). The likelihood of encountering such defects during testing is relatively high. Ensuring robustness helps reduce the impact of interruptions or obstructions during test execution.
- A test environment is considered predictable when its owners can reliably predict its availability. This involves not only setting up the environment but also maintaining it throughout test execution. For instance, if the infrastructure support team is responsible for both live operations and testing, critical operational incidents may attract all their resources and lead to delays in setting up the test environment, which in turn can affect the development timeline.
- Test automation frameworks usually access the test environment via its interfaces. Standard automation frameworks support the common interface types like HTML web GUI or REST API's. The less common an interface of the test environment is, the more difficult it is to automate the tests for inputs or outputs via that interface. For example, if the FoodApp has an interface to a biometric authentication system, it will probably be better to use a test double for the authentication system than to ask test automation to trigger the biometric interface (i.e., fingerprint reader or face recognition camera).

As the main user, the test analyst must be able to express their requirements for the test environment clearly and on time.

The test analyst may define the test environment requirements during test design based on the analysis of:

- Test conditions, test cases, and test data requirements, such that test environment requirements describe the conditions necessary to set up and maintain the test environment to ensure the preconditions of the test execution are met. For example, if sending emails to customers needs to be tested, the test analyst can request an email system in a sandbox environment.
- Test levels and test types, which influence the trade-off between test environment flexibility and similarity to the production environment. For example, for an interface to a card reader, a simulator that facilitates test automation and flexible test data generation may be required for system testing, but system integration testing may require the actual hardware with test cards.
- Availability and independence of components and systems, which may indicate the need to use test doubles (e.g., stubs or drivers). This is the case, for example, with components that will be delivered by third parties on an uncertain date.

**Test Environment in the Test Plan**

The ISTQB® Foundation Level Syllabus, Sect. 1.3.3, states that the test environment requirements are a work product of test design. At the same time, Sect. 5.1.1 mentions that a test plan typically includes test environment requirements. This is because basic, generic test environment requirements can be ideally identified early during test planning. However, more specific requirements often need detailed information regarding how the tests should be executed. This approach aids in early estimation and planning. In addition, it also relieves the test analyst from repeating the same requirements for each test cycle.

In Software Development Lifecycles that utilize CI/CD pipelines or adopt a DevOps approach, it is essential to automate the setup of the test environment as much as possible. Typically, operations teams create and maintain scripts that automate the setup of the appropriate test environment using configuration parameters. Consequently, instead of documenting the requirements, the test analyst will focus on setting these configuration parameters.

The test environment requirements describe the test environment items. Based on the ISO standard for test documentation, the syllabus indicates that such requirements should include the following information for each test environment item:

- unique identifier (typically, needed for traceability purposes),
- description (in sufficient detail to implement it as required),
- responsibility (describes who is responsible for making it available),
- period needed (identifies when and for how long the item is needed),
- fidelity (the degree to which this item represents or deviates from the production environment).

The requirements should also address the test environment's overarching needs, including setup, backup and restore, security needs, the ability to change the test environment, and roles and authorization.

**Generic and Specific Test Environment Requirements**

The generic test environment requirements in the test plan of the FoodApp could include the following:

- Dedicated Server: The server should support backup and restore, time travel, and scripts for loading and unloading test data. The development team should define the technical specifications for the hardware platform, database management system, and related components.

- FoodApp Administration Client: One PC client, with the current Windows OS version and the web browser DuckDuckGo.
- Restaurant Client Devices: Simulated on one PC client, with the current Windows OS version and the web browsers Chrome, Edge, Opera, and Firefox. Playwright client for test automation.
- Customer Client Devices: An emulator for Apple devices and a simulator for Android mobile devices, on which the most popular devices and platforms can be configured. Should include both mobile phones and tablets. Test automation with Appium.
- Courier Client Devices: At least three mobile phones with popular hardware, only Android, with GPS features and navigation system for the field test.
- Test Double of the Banking System: It should support synthetic test data like credit cards.
- GPS System: It should have an interface that shares the location and route information of the couriers with the FoodApp.

Specific test environment requirements defined by the test analyst during test design could include the following:

- For two-factor authentication with time-based one-time passwords—customer client devices: the most popular authenticator apps should be installed each on a different device.
- For test cases that need real customer client devices for some reason (e.g., to access their geographic location)—customer client devices: four mobile phones with popular hardware, two Android and two iOS.

The test analyst should document test environment requirements clearly, compactly, and coherently. These can use diagrams or tables, can reference existing test environments, and focus on the specific needs of the test level. The relevant stakeholders (e.g., developers, technical test analysts, test automation engineers, business analysts, sponsors, and product owners) should also review, approve, and update test environment requirements.

## Sample Questions

### Question 1.3.3A

Which of the following statements about test environment requirements is correct?

(a) They should be defined during test planning and recorded in the test plan so that they can be implemented in time.
(b) They should include the need for administration and maintenance of the test environment items.

(c) They should be as close as possible to the production environment so that the test results are reliable.
(d) They should be written in plain text to make them easily understandable by all relevant stakeholders.

Select ONE answer.

**Question 1.3.3B**

Match the following attributes of a test environment requirement (1–4) with their purpose (A-D).

1. Unique identifier.
2. Description.
3. Period needed.
4. Fidelity.

A. Ensure the availability during test execution.
B. Support the traceability to test conditions and test cases.
C. Enable a correct implementation.
D. Indicate whether it should be flexible or production-like.

(a) 1B, 2C, 3A, 4D.
(b) 1B, 2A, 3D, 4C.
(c) 1C, 2D, 3A, 4B.
(d) 1D, 2C, 3B, 4A.

Select ONE answer.

### *1.3.4 Determining Test Oracles*

TA-1.3.4 (K2) Explain the test oracle problem and potential solutions

**Definitions**

**Test oracle**: A source to determine an expected result.

**Pseudo-oracle**: An independently derived variant of the test item used to generate results, which are compared with the results of the original test item based on the same test inputs.

**Model-based testing**: Testing based on or involving models.

**Property-based testing**: A test approach in which test results are verified using specified relations between inputs and expected results of a test case.

**Metamorphic testing**: A test technique in which test conditions are metamorphic relations.

When test analysts conduct dynamic testing, they provide inputs to the test object, which then processes these inputs to produce actual results. To verify these actual results, test analysts need expected results for comparison. Therefore, a test oracle is necessary to determine the expected results for the inputs used (see Fig. 1.11).

When the tests are executed, comparing the actual results against the expected results reveals whether the test has passed or failed. Assertions may be built into test automation code or in the test object itself to implement the verification of the actual results, supporting an automated test oracle. They are executable statements that verify the state or behavior of the test object and throw an exception if the comparison fails. When built in the test object, they usually only verify what is necessary for the continuation of the task.

A complete and accurate test basis ideally provides the test oracle. This may have the form of a textual specification written in natural language or a formal specification.

When documentation is incomplete or absent, human experience or knowledge of the test object can complement the test oracle. For instance, test analysts might interview domain experts to determine the expected results for complex inputs.

The expected results for specific inputs are usually determined during test implementation. In such cases, test oracles can already be used during test implementation. In situations where there are only a few low-level test cases, this can be done manually, making human test oracles sufficient. However, an automated test oracle may be necessary for cost-effectiveness, particularly if inputs are generated automatically or if relying on human oracles is expensive. Formal specifications in the test basis aid in the development of an automated test oracle.

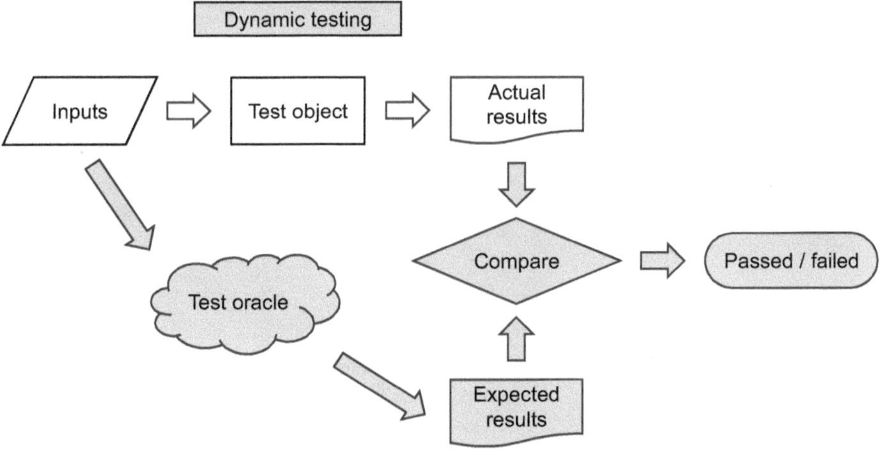


**Fig. 1.11** Test oracle

It is important to note that the need for an automated test oracle is basically independent of automated test execution. However, in practice, automated test execution often includes automated test oracles and automated verification of results. This approach is especially recommended in CI/CD environments.

The availability of a cost-effective test oracle can be influenced by the quality and completeness of the test basis or system characteristics. The challenge of finding a suitable test oracle is referred to as the "test oracle problem." Several factors contribute to this problem, including:

- data-related complexity as seen in big data, legacy systems with several generations of data structures, or route optimization,
- non-determinism, where more than one result may be considered correct, as seen in AI-based systems,
- probabilistic behavior found in applications like gambling and computer games,
- missing or ambiguous requirements.

Some known solutions to the test oracle problem are explained below.

**Human oracles** (Fig. 1.12) use the capability of humans to determine the expected results.

Humans can serve as a test oracle when the oracle problem is manageable, meaning the effort and time required to determine the expected results remain feasible. This is often true when only a few low-level test cases are designed or when those low-level test cases do not change significantly between test cycles. Additionally, human oracles are preferred in certain test approaches, such as exploratory testing. However, human resources can be expensive and scarce. This is especially true when test analysts need to consult with domain specialists who have limited availability, or when there is very limited time for test implementation and execution, as seen in continuous integration and deployment processes.

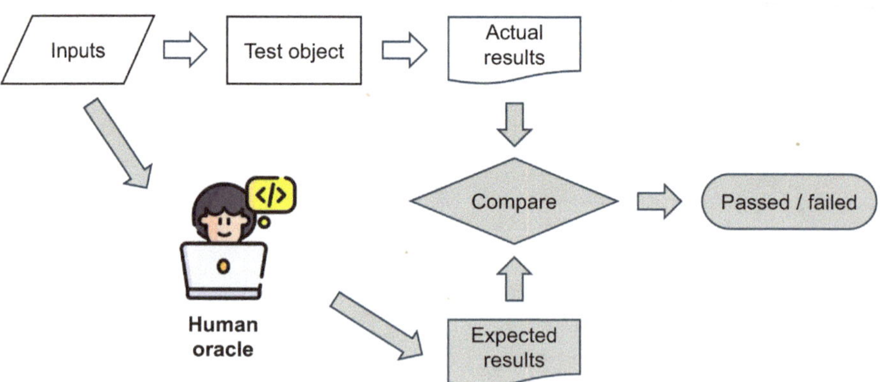


**Fig. 1.12** Human oracle

**Pseudo-oracles** (Fig. 1.13) are variants of the test item that are developed independently of it. They provide a fully automated solution to the oracle problem, capable of generating expected results for any given input. They are only pseudo-oracles and not full oracles because, just like any implementation, they might have defects. Therefore, they cannot guarantee the expected result. Their effectiveness as a test oracle largely depends on how well they implement the test basis.

Examples of pseudo-oracles include legacy systems used in software migration, backup variants in fault-tolerant systems, simplified versions of the test object, and the dual or multiple development of the same highly critical system.

Pseudo-oracles represent the most comprehensive automated solution to the oracle problem. They are often used when testing critical systems. However, creating a high-quality, dedicated pseudo-oracle for a complex test object can be costly. Lightweight pseudo-oracles may focus on the most critical quality characteristics, such as functional accuracy, and can employ straightforward tools like spreadsheets or scripts.

The practice of executing the test object alongside the pseudo-oracle and automatically comparing their results is also known as back-to-back testing.

**Model-based testing** (Fig. 1.14) may formalize the test oracle as part of the test model. This requires a formal model of inputs, outputs, and the behavior of the test object. It enables the generation of expected outputs and the derivation of tests from the model.

Typically, MBT models contain a behavior model and test selection criteria, from which a set of high-level test cases can be generated. To support the test oracle, additional model elements are needed, such as an object model of test data and a model containing the relationship between the inputs in the test data, behavior elements, and the outputs in the test data.

Behavior-based test techniques often involve the implementation of an automated test oracle. For example, in a state-based technique, test cases consist of sequences of state transitions. Hence, the outputs connected to the state transitions determine

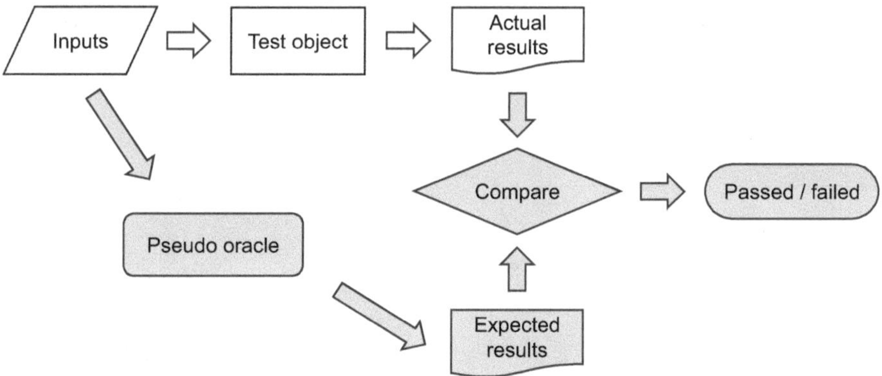


**Fig. 1.13** Pseudo-oracle

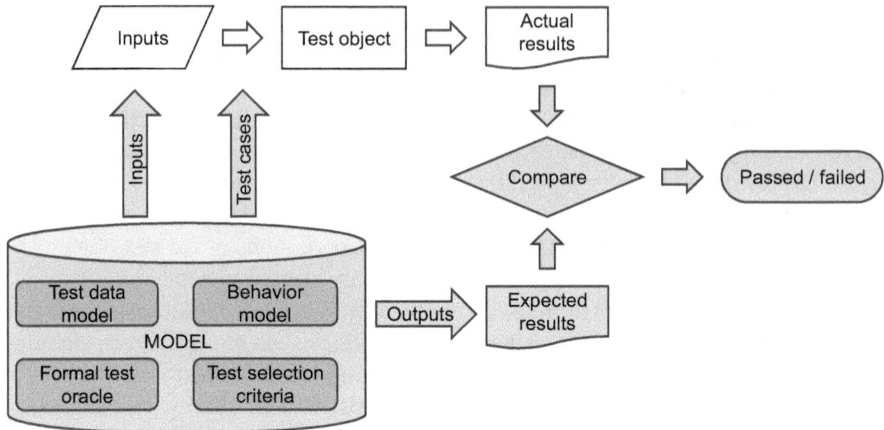


**Fig. 1.14** Model-based testing as a test oracle

the expected output, and the resulting state of the last transition provides the post-condition (see Sect. 3.2.2). Similarly, in scenario-based testing, scenarios contain the sequences of interactions between the actor and the test object, including the expected results (see Sect. 3.2.3).).

**Property-based testing** (Fig. 1.15) uses specified properties of the test object to verify relations between the input and the expected result of individual test cases.

If such a relation is not met, we can be sure that the test case fails. However, passing the test case only provides a limited degree of confidence that the specification has been fulfilled.

One example is a text search in big data. The results list should contain all entries in which the searched text appears. Verifying the completeness of the results list typically constitutes an oracle problem. A property-based test could be limited to checking the results list to see whether all hits contain the searched text.

In practice, the shortcoming of incomplete verification can be alleviated by executing the same high-level test case with numerous concrete inputs, typically generated by a random generator.

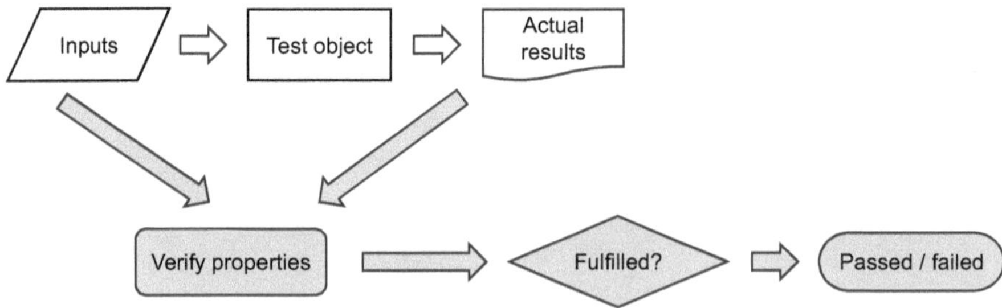


**Fig. 1.15** Property-based testing as a test oracle

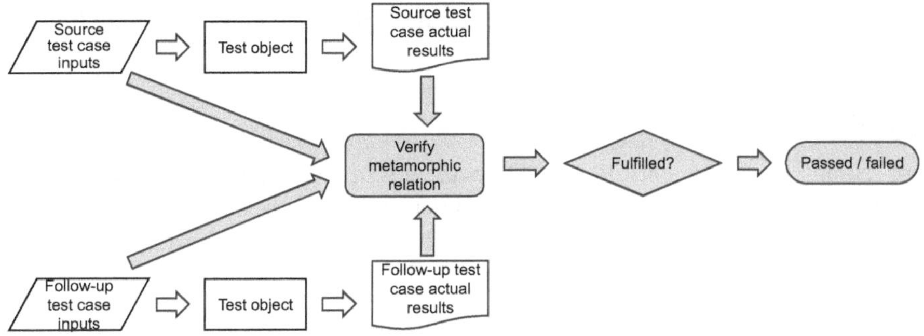


**Fig. 1.16** Metamorphic testing as a test oracle

This solution is well-suited for test automation, but its effectiveness depends on the relations, which may be difficult to determine.

**Metamorphic testing** (Fig. 1.16) verifies that the test object responds to certain changes in input with consistent changes in output, in accordance with a metamorphic relation. To do this, a test procedure consisting of a source test case and corresponding follow-up test cases is executed, and the metamorphic relation of the actual results is verified.

For example, metamorphic testing can be used in the safety testing of AI-based autonomous vehicle control systems in a simulated environment. The test analyst first defines source test cases using driving scenarios of interest under good environmental conditions. Next, the test analyst generates various follow-up test cases using the metamorphic relations identified. For example, they can rotate the route map by any angle, or change the lighting or visibility conditions (night, twilight, backlighting, fog, rain). The expected behavior should remain similar, e.g., staying in lane, avoiding obstacles, not colliding with other traffic participants, or not driving faster than in the source test case.

For more details on metamorphic testing, see Sect. 3.3.2).

## Sample Questions

### Question 1.3.4A

Which of the following factors **MOSTLY** indicates the presence of an oracle problem?

(a) The requirements are described in great detail in a very extensive specification.
(b) Critical details of system behavior are known only to selected experts who are rarely available to testers.
(c) A system behavior is required in which only one output is correct for any specific combination of system state and input.

(d) The amount of test data available for some of the test conditions is very limited.

Select ONE answer.

**Question 1.3.4B**

For complex components, a test team creates a simplified implementation of the requirements in parallel with development to correctly and efficiently predict the expected results of the software without having to comply with all software development guidelines in the delivery context.

Which solution to the oracle problem does this team use?

(a) Model-based testing.
(b) A human oracle.
(c) Metamorphic testing.
(d) A pseudo-oracle.

Select ONE answer.

### *1.3.5 Test Data Requirements*

TA-1.3.5 (K2) Give examples of test data requirements

**Definitions**

**Test data**: Data needed for test execution.

The test analyst identifies and requests the test data that may require preparation or provisioning for test execution. While generic requirements can be mentioned early in test planning, most details are typically clarified later during test design. This is why the Certified Tester Foundation Level syllabus mentions the test data requirements both in Sect. 5.1.1). as a typical content of a test plan and in Sect. 1.3.3 as a test design work product.

**Standard Attributes of a Test Data Requirement**

The syllabus refers to the international standard as an example of a list of attributes. However, it should be noted that the contents of this standard are not examinable according to the rules outlined in Chapter "Tasks and Competencies of a Test Analyst" of the syllabus. Nonetheless, the attributes of a test case listed in Section 8.5 of this international standard are worth considering:

- Unique identifier.
- Description—defines the names and values of the test data elements, and any relevant aspects as indicated above.
- Responsibility—the person or organization unit responsible for making the data available.
- Period needed—when and for how long the test data is needed.
- Resetting needs—whether the test data needs to be reset during test execution to its original values.
- Archiving or disposal—when and how the test data should be archived or disposed of after test execution.

Apart from the period needed, this book also uses these attributes in the example Table 1.3.

**Table 1.3** Some example test data requirements for the FoodApp case study

| ID | Description | Responsibility | Resetting needs | Archiving/disposal |
|---|---|---|---|---|
| TD01 | Copy the registered restaurants from the live system to the test instance of the geographic database | IT operations | No | Dispose |
| TD02 | Provide 4 synthetic test clients with valid credit cards | IT operations | Yes | Archive |
| TD03 | Provide a synthetic client who used up his credit to the limit | IT development | No | Dispose |
| TD04 | Provide a restaurant with a promotion period ending today | IT development | Yes | Dispose |
| TD05 | Provide 2 synthetic clients with the same name | Test team | No | Archive |

Table 1.3 shows some examples of test data requirements. The period needed is the same for all of them: the test execution period of the current increment.

In the example above, requirements TD01 and TD02 are generic and usually defined in the test plan. In contrast, requirements TD03 to TD05 are specific to particular test cases and are typically established during the test design phase.

When defining test data requirements, the test analyst must consider several factors, including the purpose, format, and context of use:

**Similarity with Production Data.** When testing, there are two primary approaches to handling data: using a copy of production data or generating synthetic data.

Using production data has the advantage of reflecting real-world scenarios. If a test object fails to process specific combinations of test data correctly in the test environment, it is likely to encounter the same issue in production. However, production data can lack variability. For example, restaurants may be missing where the length of a courier's route from their location is exactly at the border of their operating radius. Additionally, some test objects may not have any production data available, particularly if major features are newly developed. In our case study, this may be the case in increments when restaurant chains or courier pools are newly introduced. In such cases, synthetic data becomes essential.

Unlike production data, synthetic data allows for controlled variability. If efficient data generation procedures are in place, it optimally provisions the test cases in scope. However, synthetic data may not capture some of the uncommon data combinations present in real-world scenarios, which can lead to failures. In our case study, geographical locations, such as a restaurant on the opposite shore of Lake Zurich, which is only 1 km away by ferry but over 15 km away by road, could be missing from synthetic test data. To enhance the effectiveness of synthetic data, it should reflect realistic business and technical scenarios. It should mimic key aspects of production data, including patterns, distributions, and outliers that fall within the test scope. Developing personas can assist in this process by providing user-centered profiles that help create data representing diverse user behaviors and scenarios.

**Confidentiality**. Sensitive test data, such as personal information, requires protection. Pseudonymized data substitutes personal information with artificial identifiers, while anonymized data removes any identifiable information about individuals altogether. In our case study, for example, the attributes of the registered restaurants from production could be used unchanged. The names and email addresses of restaurant owners should be pseudonymized, but their (business) postal addresses may be used unchanged. On the other hand, if live courier data is used, the personal data of the couriers should be anonymized.

If necessary, the test analyst must comply with data protection regulations, such as the General Data Protection Regulation (EU-GDPR 2018) in the European Union or (US-HIPAA 2024) in the USA. Typically, the test analyst is not responsible for creating the pseudonymization or anonymization procedures. However, they are responsible for defining the requirements and determining which attributes need to be modified and in what way. The procedure must balance data protection with the usability required for testing.

**Purpose**. Test data is crucial for determining preconditions and expected results that impact the system state and its configuration. In addition to the business entities, it also includes establishing relations between products, departments, and categories (e.g., in our case study, which menu items have which food types and which restaurants offer them). Transactional data should also be considered. For example, if time-dependent preconditions are needed (e.g., events that happened in the past or in the future, like the expiry of a promotion period), then data aging might be needed (see below).

Another aspect to be considered is user roles. If roles and responsibilities are not relevant at the test level, users with universal permissions can facilitate testing. However, if user roles and responsibilities are to be validated, the test analyst must request users in the relevant roles and with the appropriate permissions.

**Coverage Criteria**. Test data must align with the coverage criteria for the chosen test technique. In addition to valid test data, this may also require invalid test data, such as for negative tests. Appropriate test data requirements, like TD03 to TD05 in Table 1.3, are typically defined during test design.

**Data Format**. Systematic data management (e.g., in API testing) may require structured data (e.g., CSV, JSON, XML, or database). In our case study, the interfaces to restaurants, banks, and the geographic route system provide examples of such formats.

**Traceability**. The test analyst should think long-term and maintain an overview of which test data is needed for which test cases. Traceability ensures test data maintainability when changes are made to test cases.

**Maintainability**. Hard-coded test data in low-level test cases should be avoided to facilitate defect detection and maintenance. Test cases should separate test logic from test data (see 1.3.2 above). For example, in our case study, when testing the courier's range of action, it makes more sense to formulate abstract test cases with ON and OFF points for the range of action than concrete test cases with specifications such as 5.00 or 5.01 km distance, since the standard range of action might change.

**Dependencies**. Dependencies between data entities and attributes lead to complexity in data creation or generation. For example, credit cards need an owner and a financial institution. Whether such data is created manually or generated by procedures, they need to follow a procedure that ensures referential integrity. If the test analyst creates synthetic data manually, they must make parent entities and referenced data available before creating a child entity. If, on the other hand, the test data is to be generated by procedures created by other parties, the test analyst must indicate the dependencies in the test data requirements. The test analyst must also consider dependencies when they require a subset of production data in the test environment. Subsetting is typically needed when testing with production data, where the test environment has a smaller capacity than production for cost reasons.

**Availability**. Sometimes the test data is provided by external systems or services at interfaces that are not yet available. Service virtualization can address missing data by simulating absent or inaccessible services to interact with external systems or services.

**Time Sensitivity and Data Aging**. Test conditions often contain temporal attributes and their relationships to each other or to the current time. For example, the behavior of an application may depend on the age of the user, which is calculated as the difference between the current day and the date of birth. Such test conditions are time sensitive. Test cases involving outdated or time-sensitive data may impact system behavior in unexpected or inaccurate ways. Therefore, the test analyst should indicate the need for data aging (i.e., consistently transferring the temporal test attributes to fit the time of test execution).

## Sample Questions

### Question 1.3.5A

Which of the following statements about test data requirements is correct?

(a) Linking test data requirements with the test cases that use them supports the maintenance of the test data.
(b) The test data requirements should specify the data content, not the data format.
(c) The test data only needs to be required in advance if data-based test techniques are used.
(d) The test data required must be usable for testing at any time without modification.

Select ONE answer.

### Question 1.3.5B

Match the following needs of a test analyst regarding test data (1–4) with the key aspects of a test data requirement (A–D).

1. Support every condition value and the validation of every action occurring in the rules of the decision table to be tested.
2. Store the test data in spreadsheets that can be referenced by high-level test cases.
3. For each product in the test database, all referenced categories and price plans must also be in the test system.
4. The synthetic data generated for testing the new features should support realistic business scenarios.

A. Maintainability.
B. Similarity with production data.
C. Coverage criteria.
D. Dependencies.

(a) 1B, 2C, 3D, 4A.
(b) 1D, 2A, 3B, 4C.
(c) 1C, 2D, 3B, 4A.
(d) 1C, 2A, 3D, 4B.

Select ONE answer.

### *1.3.6 Developing Test Scripts Using Keyword-Driven Testing*

TA-1.3.6 (K3) Use keyword-driven testing to develop test scripts

**Definitions**

**Keyword**: A phrase that represents specific actions to be performed during test execution.

**Keyword-driven testing**: A scripting technique in which test scripts contain high-level keywords and supporting files that contain low-level scripts that implement those keywords.

Keyword-driven testing (see the definition above) is often used to support test automation, even though in principle it can also be used in manual testing. It enables test analysts to create test scripts that can be efficiently automated without possessing technical knowledge of programming or test automation tools themselves. According to, Sect. 1.3.1, this is a test implementation activity. To start with, we illustrate the idea of this technique with an example from our case study.

Assume the test analyst has designed the following test case for the FoodApp:

TC1: Successful restaurant search with filter set

- Preconditions: A client CL1 is logged in. CL1 is at a location serviced by FoodApp. Three restaurants, RE1, RE2, and RE3, are within 5 km of CL1's location. RE1 offers only vegetarian food, RE2 offers both vegetarian and non-vegetarian dishes, and RE3 offers only non-vegetarian dishes.
- Action: CL1 sets the search filter to vegetarian food and searches for restaurants within the standard 5 km radius. CL1 views the menu of RE2.
- Expected Results: The app displays RE1 and RE2 on the map, but does not display RE3. The app displays the menu of RE2.
- Postconditions: The user can select any dishes from the menu of RE2.

Table 1.4 provides an example of a keyword-driven test script for the test case above.

If keyword-driven testing is used, the test analyst creates high-level test scripts using keywords. The implementation of the keywords, i.e., designing the low-level, machine-readable scripts that execute them, is the responsibility of the technical test analyst, test automation engineer, or developer.

The tasks of the test analyst in keyword-driven testing include:

- identifying and specifying keywords and their parameters,

**Table 1.4** Simple keyword-driven test script

| Step | Action keyword | Parameter values | Verification keyword | Parameter values |
|---|---|---|---|---|
| 1 | Login client | CL1.email, CL1.password | Verify the client name and street map are displayed | CL1.name, CL1.location, 5 km |
| 2 | | | Verify the restaurant is shown | RE1 |
| 3 | | | Verify the restaurant is shown | RE2 |
| 4 | | | Verify the restaurant is shown | RE3 |
| 5 | Set restaurant filter | Vegetarian | Verify the restaurant is shown | RE1 |
| 6 | | | Verify the restaurant is shown | RE2 |
| 7 | | | Verify the restaurant is not shown | RE3 |
| 8 | Select restaurant | RE2 | Verify the menu is displayed | RE2 |
| 9 | | | Verify that all dishes on the menu are selectable | RE2 |

- specifying the keyword test cases, i.e., test scripts using keywords,
- specifying the additional steps to the test scripts using keywords such as preconditions, verification actions, and cleaning up the test environment after the test,
- maintaining keyword test cases to reflect changes to the test object,
- executing keyword test scripts, either automated or manually,
- analyzing failed keyword test cases to determine the cause of the failure.

The test analyst identifies and specifies keywords by analyzing the test basis or collaborating with the stakeholders. The goal is to provide a basic set of reusable keywords such that the test scripts can be entirely composed of these keywords. To accomplish this, the test analyst must understand the characteristics of keywords.

**Action and Verification Keywords**. Based on their purpose, keywords can be categorized into two main types: action keywords and verification keywords (see Table 1.4).

Action keywords must interact with the test object (e.g., executing functions, submitting data, navigating within the test object), the test environment (e.g., setting up configurations and activating simulators), or other components or systems (e.g., triggering an interface of the test object). Examples for our FoodApp case study include:

- Login client (email address, password).
- Set restaurant filter (list of food types).
- Select restaurant (restaurant ID).
- Import restaurants (list of restaurants).
- Connect to the GPS navigation system (system identifier).
- Trigger credit card payment (card data, amount).

Verification keywords represent assertions to evaluate whether the actual result produced by the test object matches the expected result. Naming standards for the action verb are helpful. Typically, teams decide to use one of the verbs verify, validate, check, or assert. These can be used as synonyms. Examples for our FoodApp case study include:

- Verify client name and street map are displayed (client, location, action radius).
- Verify restaurant is shown (restaurant ID).
- Verify restaurant is not shown (restaurant ID).
- Verify menu is displayed (restaurant ID).
- Verify all dishes on the menu are selectable (restaurant ID).
- Verify successful import.
- Verify GPS connections.
- Verify payment confirmation.
- Verify payment rejection.

**Abstraction Layers of Keywords**. Keywords operate on at least two levels of abstraction: the domain layer and the test interface layer.

Domain layer keywords are tied to business-related actions and reflect the terminology specific to the application domain. They can encompass complex tasks, such as registering a client or placing an order, which may involve multiple interactions with the test object. These keywords abstract away from the technical details of the test object's interface and align well with the typical knowledge and needs of test analysts. All examples referenced in Table 1.4 are domain layer keywords.

In contrast, test interface layer keywords function at the lowest level of abstraction. They correspond to technical actions, such as selecting an item from a dropdown, clicking a button, or verifying the contents of a specific field in the user interface. These keywords interact directly with test objects, items in the test environment, or other components or systems through their test interfaces. As a result, they are heavily influenced by the software design.

Additionally, intermediate layers may be implemented to enhance the maintainability of keywords.

**Atomic and Composite Keywords**. Keywords can be classified as atomic or composite. For instance, the domain-level keyword "Verify client name and street map are displayed" is a composite keyword. It consists of two parts: "Verify client name is displayed" and "Verify the street map is displayed," which may also be used separately. The main purpose of composite keywords is to promote reusability. When a specific combination of previously defined actions or verifications appears multiple times in test scripts, it can be replaced with a composite keyword to streamline the process.

Essentially, a keyword's structure and level of abstraction are independent of each other. However, composite keywords often operate at a higher level of abstraction, while atomic keywords typically reside at the test interface layer.

**Quality Criteria for Keywords.** When specifying keywords, the test analyst must keep in mind that keywords must:

- contain a verb (+ noun),
- use the imperative form of the verb (+ noun),
- be unique in their meaning,
- be adequately documented,
- reflect the vocabulary of the application domain (only required for domain layer keywords),
- be reusable.

**Composing Keyword Test Cases.** The test analyst may create an initial library of keywords during test analysis. When analyzing the test basis, they look for interactions between the test object and its environment (e.g., users, other systems, and devices). Consider, for example, the user story "As a client, I want to set filter criteria, such that I can find my favorite type of dishes at any restaurant offered in FoodApp," with the acceptance criteria "Any combination of meat, fish, vegetarian, and vegan dishes is selectable for a filter." The test analyst may specify an (action) keyword "Set restaurant filter" with a parameter "list of food types." The test analyst checks whether the identified keywords reside on the appropriate abstraction layer.

When creating a keyword test script for a new test case, the test analyst may recognize some missing keywords and immediately specify them. Keyword test cases may be written in various formats, such as lists or tables, like in Table 1.4.

Keywords may change over a project's lifetime and are prone to becoming redundant. The recommendations mentioned in this section aim to avoid redundancy and reduce maintenance efforts.

Although keyword-driven testing is a technique created for automated test scripts, manual testing can also benefit from it. If applied for manual testing, it effectively supports a later transition from manual to automated testing.

More details on test execution automation and keyword-driven testing are available in the ISTQB® Core Advanced Technical Test Analyst and Test Automation Engineering syllabi, and in the international standard ISO 29119-5.

## Sample Questions

### Question 1.3.6A

In a vehicle insurance quote app, customers provide their vehicle and personal information through multiple screens to obtain a quote. The test plan provides for keyword-driven testing with business-level keywords. Existing keywords are available for features that were released in previous increments. The next increment introduces the following new user story:

USt1: As a customer, I want to receive a warning when I enter data and then select an action that causes the app to lose this data. I want the option to either proceed with the action or cancel it and return to the last data entry screen, so I do not have to re-enter my data by mistake.

Which of the following keywords should be added for testing this user story?

(a) Name: Enter valid data on Quote-Screen-1.
Parameters: Vehicle data.
Description: Enter valid data for all attributes of a vehicle on Quote-Screen-1.

(b) Name: Data loss warning.
Parameters: None.
Description: Check that the system displays a dialog with a data loss warning and two possible options: accepting the data loss or returning to the previous screen.

(c) Name: Accept data loss warning.
Parameters: None.
Description: In the data loss warning dialog, select the option to proceed and lose the data entered.

(d) Name: Confirm data loss action.
Parameters: None.
Description: In the data loss warning dialog, press the button "Confirm."

Select ONE answer.

### Question 1.3.6B

You are testing the fuzzy search of a vocabulary application using keyword-driven testing. The vocabulary contains a list of terms consisting of a name and a definition. The fuzzy search shall treat upper-case letters as lower-case and hyphens as spaces.

The following keywords are available:

- Empty()—empties the vocabulary.
- AddTerm(Name)—adds a term with the given name to the vocabulary.
- SearchForText(SearchString, ResultList)—fuzzy search for a text string occurring in the vocabulary that returns a result list of all terms whose name contains the search string.

- VerifyIsInList(Text, ResultList) —Verify that a given text occurs as a name in a search result list.
- VerifyIsNotInList(Text, ResultList)—Verify that a given text does not occur as a name in a search result list.

Using these keywords, you intend to execute the following sequence of keyword test scripts in a test suite:

(i) Empty(); AddTerm('ad hoc testing'); SearchForText('ad-hoc', L1); VerifyIsInList('ad hoc testing', L1).
(ii) AddTerm('A/B testing'); SearchForText('a/b', L2); VerifyIsInList('A/B testing', L2).
(iii) AddTerm('test-first development'); AddTerm('test-driven development'); SearchForText('Test F', L3); VerifyIsInList('test-first development', L3); VerifyIsNotInList('test-driven development', L3).
(iv) AddTerm('keyword-driven testing'); SearchForText(Keyword Driven, L4); VerifyIsInList('keyword-driven testing', L4).
(v) AddTerm('MC/DC'); SearchForText('mc-dc',L5); VerifyIsNotInList('MC/DC', L5).

Which of these test scripts covers the following acceptance criteria: "The fuzzy search shall treat hyphens as spaces"?

(a) (i), (iii), and (v).
(b) (i), (iv), and (v).
(c) (ii), (iii), and (iv).
(d) (i), (iii), and (iv).

Select ONE answer.

## Exercise 1—Keyword-Driven Testing

TA-1.3.6 (K3) Use keyword-driven testing to develop test scripts

You are part of a test team testing an online banking application. The application has the following features:

- login,
- check account balance,
- transfer funds from one account to another,
- logout.

Each user (identified by their login) has one bank account (a 6-digit number) associated with them.

1. Create a list of keywords that could be used to automate testing for the above functionalities. Each keyword should represent a distinct action or operation in the application. The keywords should allow the tester to:

- set up preconditions (account creation),
- use the application's features (i.e., action keywords),
- assert expected results and postconditions (i.e., verification keywords).

For each keyword, describe its purpose, parameters (if any), and expected behavior.

2. Identify test conditions for the online banking application.
3. Using the created set of keywords, design test scripts that cover the identified test conditions. Indicate which parts of the test script cover which test conditions.

### *1.3.7 Tools Applied in Managing the Testware*

TA-1.3.7 (K2) Summarize the types of tools applied in managing the testware

**Definitions**

**Testware**: Work products produced during the test process for use in planning, designing, executing, evaluating, and reporting on testing.

During dynamic testing, the test analyst creates, maintains, and uses a variety of work products that are interrelated. As described in Sect. 1.2, they include the output of various test activities:

- test analysis: test conditions and test models (see Fig. 1.5),
- test design: test cases, test data requirements, and test environment requirements (see Fig. 1.6),
- test implementation: test data, test environments, test procedures, test scripts, and test suites (see Fig. 1.7),
- test execution: test runs, test logs, defect reports, and feedback (see Fig. 1.8).

Given this complexity, proper management of the work products and their relations is essential. Appropriate tools can assist test analysts in managing testware. These tools can also provide an overview of work product status and support test monitoring and control. For example, if a test fails during test execution, they enable the test analyst to review results from previous test runs and analyze when defects occurred.

The Syllabus classifies tools that assist in testware management into the following categories:

- **Test management tools** provide a repository of all relevant testware, including test conditions, test cases, test scripts, test suites, and test runs. They also support the test analyst in recording the traceability between these work product items.

For example, see Figs. 1.9 and 1.10 in Sect. 1.2.4. Since traceability is a many-to-many relation, test management tools typically visualize it in a traceability matrix. Test management tools also facilitate the retrieval of test cases, scheduling test runs, recording test results, and overall reporting of test progress and quality. For instance, these tools can generate graphs that visualize the number of test cases based on their execution status (such as not run, passed, or failed) within a test suite.

- **Defect management tools** facilitate both the structured recording of defect reports with all necessary information and the defect workflow (for details, see, Sect. 3.2). This also includes prioritization and monitoring of workflow steps, including clarifications, resolution, deployment of fixes, and confirmation testing.
- **Test data management tools** assist in manually editing, automatically generating, and maintaining test data while also ensuring the protection of sensitive information (see Sect. 1.3.5). For example, they can provide features for random but valid input data generation, client name obfuscation, time travel, or test data backup and restore.
- **Configuration management tools** are not specific to testing but are generally used in software development. When correctly applied to test work products, they facilitate test-related activities within the development, release, and operation processes. Their benefits include managing the configuration and availability of test environments. Another example is the information on which versions of the test cases have been executed in a particular test run, on which versions of the test object, test environment items, and test data.
- **Requirement management tools** are primarily used in requirements engineering, but they are also important for test analysts since requirements are a crucial part of the test basis. These tools help document and track high-level requirements, ensuring that they are clearly defined, versioned, and traced throughout the SDLC. It is essential that requirements are traceable to test conditions and test cases. Therefore, the requirement management tool used by an organization must have a suitable interface to enable the identification of test cases affected by any changes to the requirements. Additionally, these tools facilitate reporting to stakeholders on test progress in relation to requirements, allowing for easy visualization of how many test cases linked to a requirement have passed, failed, or remain unexecuted.

The role of the test analyst involves supporting the management of testware. This includes the following responsibilities:

- **Selecting Work Products**: Choose the appropriate subset of work products for the current test level. For instance, for each increment in our case study, the whole team (including product owner, development, and quality assurance) may determine the scope. Based on this scope, the test analyst should select the version and subset of requirements and specification items that will serve as the test basis for system testing. The selected subset should align with the scope of the current increment of the FoodApp.

- **Organizing Test Cases**: Define a suitable structure for organizing test cases within the test management tool. Most tools support custom attributes and folder structures. It is advisable to use functional structuring (e.g., by features or modules), technical structuring (e.g., by test type or environment), or a combination of both. In contrast, organizing folders by increments may hinder change impact analysis and the creation of regression test suites.
- **Adding Metadata**: Include metadata in test cases, such as estimated test execution effort, required test environment, or test data, and dependencies on other test cases.
- **Ensuring Traceability**: Create and maintain traceability relationships to ensure a clear connection between requirements, test conditions, tests, test runs, and defects.
- **Creating Regression Test Suites**: Combine relevant test cases into regression test suites for both manual and automated test execution. This should be based on impact analysis, dependencies, priorities, and other relevant factors (see Sect. 2.2).
- **Managing Configuration**: oversee the configuration of test cases to ensure consistency in versions for test cases, test items, test data, and test environments during a test run. This task also includes identifying outdated test cases.

Tools assist test analysts in organizing, tracking, and ensuring the quality of testing more effectively than relying on simple manual methods. However, it is essential for test analysts to know how to structure their work and to understand which tools to use and how to apply them effectively. Tools do not replace human capabilities. The popular statement by software engineer Grady Booch also holds true for test analysts: “A fool with a tool is still a fool.”

## Sample Questions

### Question 1.3.7A

As a test analyst in system testing, you establish the traceability of your test results to the requirements, to show how many test cases have passed, failed, or were not executed for each requirement. To this end, you are using the following traceability links:

- Every test case is linked to the test result (passed/failed) of its latest execution.
- Every test case is linked to the system specification items addressed (horizontal traceability).
- Every system specification item is linked to the requirements addressed (vertical traceability).

Which types of tools are you using to implement this traceability?

(a) Configuration management tools.
(b) Test management tools.
(c) Test data management tools.

(d) Defect management tools.
(e) Requirement management tools.

Select TWO answers.

**Question 1.3.7B**

Which of the following is a task of the test analyst concerning the configuration management tool used in their organization?

(a) Ensure that the versions of the test cases used in a test level are consistent with the test basis of the software version under test.
(b) Maintain the traceability link from requirements to test conditions, test cases, and test runs.
(c) Review the configuration of the software under test before starting test execution.
(d) Structure the test case repository by creating separate test sets for each software configuration tested.

Select ONE answer.

# Chapter 2 The Test Analyst's Tasks in Risk-Based Testing

**Keywords** Impact analysis · Product risk · Regression testing · Risk analysis · Risk assessment · Risk control · Risk identification · Risk mitigation · Risk monitoring · Risk-based testing

## Introduction to the Test Analyst's Tasks in Risk-Based Testing

**Definitions**

**Risk-based testing**: A test approach in which the management, selection, prioritization, and use of test activities and resources are based on corresponding risk types and risk levels.

In the unpredictable world of software development, things rarely go as planned. Unforeseen problems, unexpected failures, and undesirable effects—collectively known as risks—can arise at any stage of the Software Development Lifecycle, threatening its success. ISTQB® defines risk as "a factor that could result in future negative consequences." The word "could" means that the consequences are *unpredictable*. The word "negative" implies that risks are unwanted effects of an event or factor that can lead to harm, such as financial loss, damage to reputation, or even harm to individuals or the environment.

One way to reasonably manage risks related to the quality of software is through risk-based testing—a test approach that prioritizes test efforts based on the risk levels of the test items. The test manager determines this approach. The role of a test



A. Roman and M. Hamburg, *Practical Software Test Analysis*,
https://doi.org/10.1007/978-3-032-27986-6_4

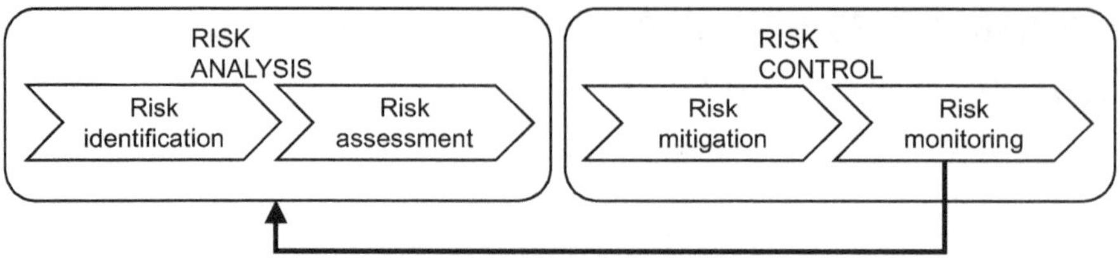


**Fig. 2.1** Risk management process

analyst in this context is to implement it by systematically identifying, assessing, and prioritizing quality risks, focusing test efforts on areas that pose the greatest threat to the objectives of software development. By tailoring test activities to risk levels, the test analyst helps ensure that critical issues are resolved early and effectively, enabling development to stay on course and achieve its objectives despite inherent uncertainty.

In general, the risk management process consists of two main stages: risk analysis and risk control, as shown in Fig. 2.1. These stages, in the context of a test analyst's tasks, are discussed in Sects. 2.1 and 2.2. The figure illustrates that the risk management process is iterative rather than linear. This is because risks are not static and change over time. Risk-based testing involves ongoing risk monitoring, and the results of risk monitoring are used for re-evaluating risks. This may occur due to the emergence of new risks or the need to adjust the prioritization of known risks. In software development, the test manager is responsible for managing the quality risks and typically maintains a risk register that lists the identified risks, risk levels, and mitigation measures. The sections below describe how a test analyst actively contributes to the analysis and control of quality risks.

## 2.1 Risk Analysis

TA-2.1.1 (K2) Summarize the test analyst's contribution to product risk analysis

Risk analysis consists of two phases: risk identification and risk assessment. In each of these phases, the test analyst contributes their unique skills to ensure the correct implementation of a risk-based test approach. As a role closer to business than technology, the test analyst has the knowledge and experience to identify the impact of specific quality risks. They are also able to select mitigation measures for these risks related to particular forms of testing. This makes the test analyst a valuable participant in product risk analysis.

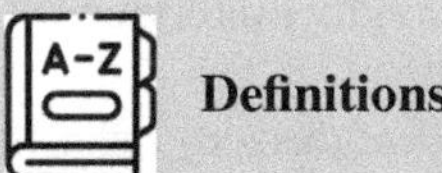

**Definitions**

**Product risk**: A risk that impacts the quality of a product.

**Risk analysis**: The overall process of risk identification and risk assessment.

**Risk identification**: The process of finding, recognizing and describing risks.

**Risk assessment**: The process to examine identified risks and determine the risk level.

**Risk identification** is the phase in which the team attempts to identify as many potential risks as possible in the shortest possible time. The team often categorizes these risks according to the quality characteristic that the risk affects (e.g., according to the ISO 25010 product quality model [6], as described in Chap. 4). This grouping facilitates further risk analysis activities, as similar mitigation strategies can typically be applied to risks of a similar nature.

The most commonly used risk identification techniques are presented in Table 2.1, along with their descriptions and typical situations in which their use is most common or most effective.

The test analyst actively contributes to all these techniques. They participate in brainstorming sessions and risk workshops, adding risks from their own experience.

**Table 2.1** Common risk identification techniques

| Technique | Description | Typical context of use |
|---|---|---|
| Brainstorming | A group of stakeholders generates a list of potential risks through open discussion. Brainstorming encourages creativity and broad input | Early stages of project planning, or when a wide range of perspectives is needed |
| Interviews with stakeholders | One-on-one or group conversations with key stakeholders to elicit potential risks. They give deep insights from experienced individuals | Complex or high-stakes projects where a detailed understanding is needed |
| Checklists | Using a predefined list of known risks (e.g., from previous projects or industry standards) to identify risks in the current context. Simple and quick technique | Common in regulated industries or repetitive project types |
| Risk workshops | A structured, facilitated meeting where stakeholders collaboratively identify, assess, and sometimes prioritize risks. Brings together diverse perspectives for more comprehensive risk identification | The early planning phase of complex projects, especially when collaboration across multiple stakeholders or disciplines is required |

They can create and maintain risk checklists. They can also conduct interviews with stakeholders to identify risks from the stakeholders' perspective.

The outcome of the risk identification phase is a list of (categorized) risks. This list also serves as input for the second phase of risk analysis, namely risk assessment.

**Risk assessment** involves estimating the parameters of a risk: its likelihood and impact. Based on these parameters, the so-called *risk level*, or "risk importance," is calculated. Risk prioritization, based on risk level, ranks risks from most important to least important. The likelihood of product risk occurrence is usually influenced by technical factors, such as the complexity of the source code, which is why this parameter is usually estimated by developers and technical test analysts. Test analysts work with the client and are familiar with the business side of the product being developed, so they are often able to determine the risk impact accurately. Of course, this does not mean that test analysts cannot also estimate the risk likelihood, e.g., based on their experience with defect-prone areas of the software or with typical quality assurance bottlenecks in the process.

During risk assessment, the test analyst, together with other stakeholders, contributes to the determination of the risk level by estimating several factors such as:

- frequency of use and criticality of the affected features,
- criticality of the affected business objectives,
- financial, environmental, and reputational damage,
- quality of the test basis,
- legal or safety needs.

The risk level is often not uniformly distributed across the test object. In such cases, the test analyst should break down the test object into test items (e.g., components, interfaces, and features) and assess a given risk for each test item separately.

**Quantitative, Qualitative, and Hybrid Risk Analysis**

There are three general approaches to risk analysis: quantitative, qualitative, and hybrid. The ISTQB® Advanced Test Management Syllabus [12] points out in Sect. 1.3.3 that a quantitative approach should be based upon extensive and statistically valid risk data, whereas the qualitative approach commonly used in IT is based on the stakeholders' subjective perceptions. In this section, we discuss in detail how the test analyst should apply the different approaches.

**Quantitative risk assessment**. In the quantitative approach, the estimated likelihood and impact are expressed on a *ratio* scale. The risk likelihood is a number greater than zero and less than one (a risk with zero probability could never occur, while a risk with a probability of one would be a specific event and therefore not a risk). The risk impact is a positive number expressing the loss we will incur if the risk occurs. The unit of impact is usually money, because ultimately every loss boils down to a financial loss.

The risk level is calculated by multiplying the risk likelihood and risk impact. Since likelihood is dimensionless and impact is expressed in monetary terms, the product of these two values is described in financial terms. In a quantitative approach, the level of risk is interpreted as the expected loss that will be incurred due to the occurrence of specific risks. From a practical point of view, it does not make much sense to consider the level of a single risk, because a risk will either occur or it will not. For example, if we have estimated the likelihood and impact of a risk to be 10% and $40,000, respectively, then its level is 0.1 * $40,000 = $4000. However, this risk will either occur, in which case, we will incur a loss of $40,000, or it will not occur, in which case, we will incur no loss. Therefore, the average value, $4000, is "virtual" in the sense that it is only a statistical measure that will never actually occur (it is like saying that a dog and its owner have an average of three legs; from a statistical point of view, this is true, even though neither the dog nor its owner has three legs).

The risk level, on the other hand, makes sense when considered as the total risk level, which is the sum of the risk levels for all identified risks. This value is interpreted as the expected total loss that will occur because some risks will materialize and others will not.

The advantage of a quantitative approach to risk assessment is that the result of the evaluation is easy to interpret: it is the expected amount of loss that we will incur as a result of the risks occurring. This value can be reported periodically and tracked over time, which greatly assists decision-makers in making business decisions.

The disadvantage of the quantitative approach is that quantitative estimation is often difficult or subjective. If someone estimates that the risk likelihood is, say, 15%, we can always ask: Where does this specific value come from? Why is it not 14%? or 16%?

**Qualitative risk assessment**. In the qualitative approach, the estimated likelihood and impact are expressed on an *ordinal* scale, e.g., "low/medium/high," or by assigning some points, e.g., from 1 to 10, to these parameters, where 1 is the minimum value, and 10 is the maximum. Since the risk level is the product of likelihood and impact, we need to define a so-called risk matrix, i.e., a kind of "multiplication table," to determine the level of risk, so that we know, for example, what "low likelihood * high impact" means. An example of such a risk matrix is shown in Table 2.2. We assume that both likelihood and impact are expressed on a four-point scale: low, medium, high, and very high.

**Table 2.2** Example of a risk matrix

| Risk level | | Risk likelihood | | | |
|---|---|---|---|---|---|
| | | Low | Medium | High | Very high |
| Risk impact | Low | Very low | Low | Medium | Medium |
| | Medium | Low | Medium | Medium | High |
| | High | Medium | High | High | Very high |
| | Very high | High | Very high | Very high | Very high |

This means that if, for example, the risk likelihood is classified as "high" and its impact as "medium," then the level of that risk is "medium." Note that the risk matrix in Table 2.2 is not symmetrical, which is often the case in practice. For example, low impact * very high likelihood is defined as "medium," but low likelihood * very high impact is defined as "high." The reason for this asymmetry is that the risk impact is usually more important to us than its likelihood. A risk with a negligible likelihood but a huge impact is usually more important to us than a risk with a high likelihood but a negligible impact.

In some risk analysis methods, such as FMEA, the above-mentioned point scale is used, e.g., from 1 to 10 to assess both factors (likelihood and impact), and then they are multiplied to obtain the risk level value. However, great care must be taken here, as the elements of the scale (symbols 1, 2, …, 10) do not represent any physical quantities, but only elements of an ordinal scale. From the perspective of measurement theory, multiplying them does not make sense, but in practice, it is done for convenience. Furthermore, when we treat these elements of the scale as numbers, the multiplication of numbers is commutative, so the symmetry mentioned above will occur here. A risk with a likelihood of 1 and an impact of 10 will have the same risk level as a risk with an impact of 1 and a likelihood of 10, because $1 * 10 = 10 * 1$.

Some teams, especially those working in Agile methodologies, sometimes employ a more straightforward method of risk assessment, comparing identified risks in pairs and defining their likelihood and impact relatively, without referring to any particular measurement scale. This approach is practical when we are not interested in the absolute magnitude of the risk, but only in the order in which we should address the risks.

This idea is illustrated in Fig. 2.2. The team places cards (e.g., sticky notes) on a two-dimensional board, each representing a risk. The X-axis represents risk likelihood, and the Y-axis represents risk impact. Let us assume that the team has already placed cards for risks R1, R2, R3, and R4, and now intends to place a card for risk R5. During the discussion, the team concludes that the impact of risk R5 is comparable to that of risk R1. This means that the R5 card will be at a similar level (on the Y-axis) as the R1 card. The team also determines that the likelihood of R5 will be slightly higher than the likelihood of R3. This means that the R5 card will be moved to the right of the R3 card. This is how the position of the R5 card is determined.

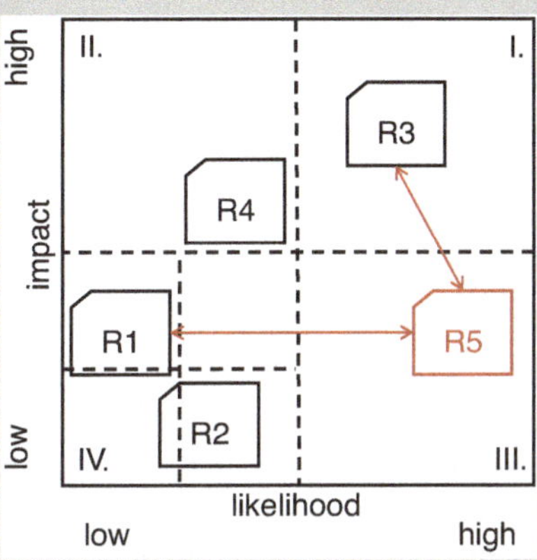


**Fig. 2.2** Risk assessment by pairwise comparison

Once all the cards have been placed on the board, divide it into four quadrants, as shown in Fig. 2.2. Quadrant I represents risks with high impact and high likelihood, so these should be addressed first. R3 is in this quadrant, so it will be the highest level risk (and therefore the highest priority). Next, address the risks in quadrant II (high impact, low likelihood), which in our case is risk R4. The next quadrant is III (low impact, high likelihood), which is risk R5. The last quadrant is IV (low impact and low likelihood). Since there are two risks in this quadrant, R1 and R2, we can recursively divide this quadrant into four quadrants and apply the same method. As a result, we determine that we must first address risk R1 and then R2.

The final prioritization of risks is as follows: R3, R4, R5, R1, R2.

The advantage of a qualitative approach to risk analysis is that it is easier to estimate risk parameters than with a quantitative approach. This is because the scale used in the qualitative approach is more "coarse" than the scale used in the quantitative method (where values are on a continuous scale). This ease is even more apparent in the case of the relative risk comparison method.

The disadvantage of the qualitative approach is that it is less accurate than the quantitative approach. If the measurement scale has only three levels (1 = low, 2 = medium, 3 = high), the number of combinations of these values is six—the possible products are 1, 2, 3, 4, 6, 9. We can therefore only classify the risk level on a six-point scale. It may turn out that there are many risks at the same level, and we then do not know how to prioritize them within such a group.

**Hybrid risk assessment**. This approach combines the advantages of both previous approaches. It involves expressing risk parameters using numbers, but in what is known as *interval arithmetic*. For example, the risk likelihood can be estimated using the interval [10%, 15%]. This means that, in our opinion, the likelihood of this risk lies somewhere between 10 and 15%. To calculate the level of a single risk, multiply the two intervals representing likelihood and impact. This is done according to the formula:

$$[a, b] \cdot [c, d] = [a \cdot c, b \cdot d].$$

For example, if likelihood and impact are estimated as [10%, 15%] and [$2, 000, $4, 000] respectively, the risk level will be

$$\left[0.1 \cdot \$2000, 0.15 \cdot \$4000\right] = \left[\$200, \$600\right].$$

The width of the intervals naturally represents the error (or uncertainty) in our estimation.

In order to calculate the total risk level, the intervals representing the levels of individual risks should be added together, according to the formula:

$$[a, b\} + [c, d] = [a + c, b + d].$$

For example, for three risks with levels of [$200, $600], [$500, $700], and [$1000, $1400] the total risk level is

$$\left[\$200 + \$500 + \$1000, \$600 + \$700 + \$1400\right] = \left[\$1700, \$2700\right].$$

In the hybrid method, all estimates are by definition subject to error, because each estimated parameter is represented as an interval rather than a single-point value. Furthermore, usually, the more operations we perform on intervals, the greater the range of the resulting interval, and thus the greater the error (uncertainty) of the estimate.

**Proposing mitigation measures**. During risk assessment, each risk is assigned a specific mitigation measure. From a test analyst's perspective, various forms of testing are natural risk mitigation measures. These may include, for example:

- test levels that should focus on the risk (e.g., component testing, integration testing, system testing, acceptance testing);
- test types that can mitigate the risk (e.g., functional testing, accessibility testing, compatibility testing, conversion testing, disaster/recovery testing, installability testing, interoperability testing, localization testing, maintainability testing, performance testing, portability testing, reliability testing, security testing, usability testing);
- test approaches that are appropriate for the risk level (e.g., model-based testing, scripted testing, exploratory testing, manual testing, A/B testing, back-to-back testing, mathematical-based testing, fuzz testing, keyword-driven testing, automated testing);

- static testing where applicable (e.g., reviews, static analysis, model verification);
- test techniques that are suitable for mitigating the risk (e.g., equivalence partitioning, domain analysis, boundary value analysis, syntax testing, combinatorial testing, decision table testing, state transition testing, scenario-based testing, random testing, metamorphic testing, error guessing, checklist-based testing, statement testing, branch testing, decision testing, MC/DC testing, data flow testing);
- independence of testing from development (e.g., no independence, independent testers within the team, independent testers outside the team, external test team).

In the spirit of shift left, the test analyst indicates which test activities can mitigate risk earliest to minimize testing effort.

The risk level also usually determines the thoroughness of the proposed approach. For example, if the test analyst decides that the best measure for mitigating risks R1 and R2 is to use the same test technique, the test analyst may propose that stronger coverage criteria be applied to R1 than to R2.

**Risk Mitigation Measures Depending on the Risk Level**

Examples of different approaches for different types of risks, depending on the risk level, are shown in Table 2.3.

**Table 2.3** Examples of risk mitigation measures depending on the risk level

| Risk type | Mitigation measure | Risk level | | |
|---|---|---|---|---|
| | | Low | Medium | High |
| Functionality | Equivalence partitioning/ BVA | Each choice coverage | 2-value BVA | 3-value BVA |
| Functionality | State transition testing | 0-switch coverage | 1-switch coverage | 2-switch coverage + loop coverage |
| Functionality | Combinatorial testing | Base choice | Pair-wise | All combinations |
| Usability | Learnability testing | Technical review | Interviews with users | Experiments in a usability lab |
| Performance | Time behavior testing | Load testing | Scalability testing | Scalability testing + stress testing |

**Case Study**

Based on the description of the FoodApp system, the team conducted a risk analysis. The following risks were identified:

Functionality risks

- F1: incorrect filtering—users may not receive accurate restaurant or food search results due to bugs in filter criteria implementation.
- F2: basket or checkout failure—basket functionality may not accurately reflect the selected items or total costs, resulting in incorrect orders or payment issues.
- F3: incorrect localization—misinterpretation or incomplete translation for users from different countries and languages may lead to wrong usage.

Performance risks

- P1: slow response time under load—high concurrent usage (especially during lunch/dinner peaks) may lead to long loading times or timeouts.
- P2: inefficient route calculation for couriers—route optimization algorithms may not perform efficiently in real-time, delaying deliveries.
- P3: unoptimized image and menu data—large media files from restaurants (e.g., menus, dish images) may increase data usage and slow app performance on mobile networks.

Reliability risks

- R1: service unavailability—microservices could fail or be unavailable, impacting core functionalities like ordering or courier tracking.
- R2: order synchronization failures—orders may get lost or desynchronized between client, Delivery Management, and Courier Components.

Security risks

- S1: payment data breaches—sensitive payment data could be intercepted or stored insecurely if not handled according to industry standards (e.g., PCI-DSS).
- S2: authentication vulnerabilities—insecure login or session management could allow unauthorized access to client, courier, or management interfaces.

Maintainability risks

- M1: inconsistent code quality across microservices—teams working on separate components may introduce divergent coding styles, making integration difficult.

A qualitative approach was used for the risk assessment. Both the likelihood and impact were assessed on a three-point scale (low, medium, high). The risk matrix was defined as in Table 2.4.

**Table 2.4** Risk matrix for the FoodApp project

| Risk level | | Risk likelihood | | |
|---|---|---|---|---|
| | | Low | Medium | High |
| Risk impact | Low | Low | Low | Medium |
| | Medium | Medium | High | High |
| | High | High | Very high | Very high |

The technical team members estimated the likelihood of all risks. The test analyst estimated their impact. For example, in the case of risk F1 (incorrect filtering), the test analyst determined that the frequency of use of the search and filter functions is very high. This is a critical application functionality that will be used by hundreds of thousands of users every day. Its incorrect operation could therefore result in very high losses—the impact of risk F1 was consequently determined to be "high."

As a risk mitigation measure for F1, the test analyst proposed black-box testing using techniques such as domain analysis and decision table testing. Due to the high impact of the risk, the test analyst proposed the use of reliable coverage for domain testing, which is a stronger coverage criterion than simplified coverage (see Sect. 3.1.1). The complete risk analysis is shown in Table 2.5.

**Table 2.5** Product risk analysis for the FoodApp project

| Risk | Likelihood | Impact | Risk level | Risk mitigation actions |
|---|---|---|---|---|
| F1: Incorrect filtering | Medium | High | Very high | Functional correctness testing |
| F2: Basket failure | Medium | High | Very high | Functional correctness testing |
| F3: Incorrect localization | Low | High | High | Functional appropriateness testing, reviews |
| P1: Slow response time | High | Medium | High | Load testing, stress testing |
| P2: Inefficient route calc. | Medium | Low | Low | Scalability testing |
| P3: Unoptimized images | Low | Low | Low | Stress testing |

(continued)

**Table 2.5** (continued)

| Risk | Likelihood | Impact | Risk level | Risk mitigation actions |
|---|---|---|---|---|
| R1: Service unavailability | High | High | Very high | Reliability testing |
| R2: Synchronization failures | Medium | High | Very high | Code reviews, reliability testing |
| S1: Payment data breach | Low | High | High | Security testing |
| S2: Authentication vulnerabilities | Medium | Medium | High | Security testing, penetration testing, security attacks |
| M1: Inconsistent code quality | High | Low | Medium | Code reviews, static analysis |

The four risks with the highest risk level are F1, F2, R1, and R2 (very high). This means that functional and reliability tests will most likely constitute the core of the testing strategy. On the other hand, the two risks with the lowest level are P2 and P3, which means that the scope of performance testing, especially in terms of scalability, is likely to be somewhat limited and indeed prioritized lower than other tests.

## Sample Question

### Question 2.1.1A

Which of the following is an example of the test analyst's contribution to risk analysis?

(a) Selecting regression tests based on an impact analysis.
(b) Applying mitigation actions for each identified product risk.
(c) Performing code reviews to detect security vulnerabilities.
(d) Estimating the frequency of use of the features affected by a risk.

Select ONE answer.

### Question 2.1.1B

The test analyst considers the risk of "slow response time," estimates its likelihood as "low," and its impact as "very high." Then, using the risk matrix, they estimate the risk level as "high."

This is an example of a test analyst's contribution to risk analysis in which phase of risk-based testing?

(a) Risk evaluation.
(b) Risk mitigation.
(c) Risk assessment.
(d) Risk identification.

Select ONE answer.

## 2.2 Risk Control

TA-2.2.1 (K4) Analyze the impact of changes to determine the scope of regression testing

**Definitions**

**Risk control**: The overall process of risk mitigation and risk monitoring.

**Risk mitigation**: The process through which decisions are reached and protective measures are implemented for reducing or maintaining risks to specified levels.

**Risk monitoring**: The activity that checks and reports the status of known risks to stakeholders.

**Impact analysis**: The identification of all work products affected by a change, including an estimate of the resources needed to accomplish the change.

**Regression testing**: A type of change-related testing to detect whether defects have been introduced or uncovered in unchanged areas of the software.

The risk control phase consists of two main activities: risk mitigation and risk monitoring.

**Risk mitigation** proactively reduces the likelihood and impact of potential risks identified during the risk analysis. Test analysts understand both system functionality and the associated product risks. Therefore, test analysts play a central role in risk control. Their tasks include:

- Performing reviews (see Sect. 5.2.2). Reviews of various work products, such as requirements, design documents, or code, enable the early detection of defects,

particularly those that may not be easily identified through testing alone. The test analyst contributes by identifying ambiguous, incomplete, or inconsistent requirements that may result in failures later. Early defect detection reduces the cost of fixing issues and enhances the system's reliability.
- Applying the appropriate test techniques and coverage levels (see Sect. 3.5). Different test techniques (such as domain analysis, combinatorial testing, or state transition testing) are suited to varying types of risk. High-risk areas require higher levels of coverage, whereas low-risk regions may only need basic testing. By aligning test techniques with risk levels, the test analyst ensures that critical risks are mitigated cost-effectively.
- Applying the appropriate test types (see Chap. 4). The choice of test types (e.g., functional, non-functional, black box, white box) is guided by the system's risk profile. For instance, an application dealing with sensitive user data might prioritize security testing. The test analyst selects test types to address specific risk categories, ensuring comprehensive mitigation strategies are in place.
- Performing regression testing (see below). Regression testing ensures that new changes do not negatively affect existing functionality. It is essential in risk mitigation, especially in complex systems where a small change can have unintended side effects.

**Risk monitoring** continually assesses the system for new or changing risks throughout the Software Development Lifecycle. Unlike risk mitigation, which is more proactive and preventive, risk monitoring ensures that identified risks are being controlled effectively and that new risks are detected and addressed promptly as the project evolves. During risk monitoring, the test analyst:

- verifies the status of previously identified risks (has their level increased, decreased, or remained the same?),
- detects new or emerging risks as the system or environment changes, and documents them in a risk register, which is a living document used to log and track risk status,
- performs risk reassessment when new defects occur or risk levels have changed,
- assesses the effectiveness of existing risk mitigation strategies,
- supports decision-making by providing timely and accurate information about the current risk landscape.

The test analyst monitors test execution and analyzes patterns in defects (e.g., frequent failures in a specific component). Consistent issues in a component may indicate increased risk or ineffective mitigation strategies. Metrics such as defect density, failure rates, or number of reopened defects help quantify risk levels over time.

**Selecting appropriate regression tests**. As mentioned above, one of the test analyst's tasks within risk mitigation is to perform regression testing. However, it may be impossible to execute all regression tests during regression testing due to various constraints, such as time, budget, test environment, or test data restrictions. This issue is primarily a concern for manually executed tests, but also affects automated tests, particularly in CI/CD pipelines, where test cycles are short and numerous tests may take a long time to run. Therefore, it is necessary to select appropriate tests for the regression test suites based on specific criteria. It is essential to review the scope of regression testing with every test cycle, as this review may determine that adjustments to the existing regression test suite are needed.

The most reliable technique for selecting automated tests for a regression test suite is impact analysis. When it comes to manual test execution, there has not been conclusive evidence of a technique in regression test selection that is clearly superior, as the results depend on various factors (Engström, 2010). Therefore, the test analyst must decide which technique to use based on the given situation. Examples include:

- risk-based selection,
- history-based testing,
- coverage-based testing,
- requirements traceability matrix,
- testing based on operational profiles.

We will now discuss all the above-mentioned test selection techniques in detail.

**Impact analysis** is a powerful and reliable technique used to identify the consequences of a change within a software system [11]. In the context of regression testing, it helps test analysts determine which test cases should be executed after a change, ensuring testing is focused, efficient, and effective. Impact analysis is usually supported by tools such as configuration management systems (CMSs). CMSs monitor and record dependencies among configuration items, such as code, test cases, scripts, and data files. They also support version control. When a test is executed, the CMS logs which configuration items are exercised or accessed during the test. Suppose a developer modifies a configuration item later (e.g., by committing a new version of a source code file to a repository). In that case, the tool can determine which test cases previously interacted with this item.

When traceability is set up correctly, tools supporting impact analysis can also be used for selecting regression tests using other techniques described below.

**Case Study**

Consider the following scenario for the FoodApp project. A new change request was raised: introduce a new payment option, Apple Pay, in the Client Component. How does it impact regression testing?

Black-box impact analysis that uses the traceability matrix technique allows the test analyst to see the obvious regression scope in the areas of payment workflow, basket functionality interaction with payment screens, error handling when payment is declined, etc.

White-box impact analysis uses a configuration management system (CMS) in combination with runtime tracing. This allows the test analyst to reveal impacts hidden from the black-box tester. For example, suppose that our FoodApp uses a CMS such as Git. When the Apple Pay feature is added, the CMS may show the following modifications in the code:

```
Modified: PaymentService.cs
Modified: OrderController.cs
Modified: OrderEntity.json
Modified: PaymentTypesEnum.cs
Added: ApplePayProvider.cs
Modified: DeliveryManagementAPIContract.yaml
```

A black-box tester sees only "payment option," but CMS reveals a change in OrderController and DeliveryManagementAPIContract, meaning that other components could be affected, and tests must include creation of orders, order lifecycle transitions, and communication with the Delivery Management Component.

Once the Apple Pay feature is exercised in test mode, tracing tools show the actual call flow. Suppose it looks like this:

```
Client → PaymentService(ApplePayProvider)
           → OrderService(updatePaymentMethod = APPLE_PAY)
              → DeliveryManagementAPI (POST /orders)
                 → CompensationFeeCalculator
```

Moreover, tracing shows additional calls to AnalyticsService.logEvent("payment_method = APPLE_PAY").

The trace reveals unexpected paths:

Impact 1: OrderService updates affect Delivery Management. Even though only Apple Pay was added, the order creation flow invoked the DeliveryManagementAPI, which now must accept the new payment method value.

Impact 2: CompensationFeeCalculator touched. Runtime tracing shows that adding Apple Pay triggered code in CompensationFeeCalculator, because internal modules use the payment method to compute risk-based delivery compensation and priority of courier assignment.

Impact 3: AnalyticsService (logEvent) invoked. Calls to AnalyticsService.logEvent ("payment_method = APPLE_PAY"). This indicates regression tests in reporting/analytics must be updated.

Below are two examples of test cases that use the changed configuration items:

**Regression test 1**—PaymentService: existing payment method processing (credit card).

Purpose: verify the correctness of existing credit card payment processing logic in PaymentService.cs.

Preconditions:

- Credit-card payments are already supported and stable.
- User has a valid saved credit card or token.
- User has a basket with valid items.

Steps:

- Proceed to checkout and select "credit card" as the payment method.
- Submit the order.

Expected Results:

- PaymentService routes the request to the correct existing provider (CreditCardProvider).
- The provider receives the correct payload: amount, currency, orderId, and card token.
- Payment succeeds and returns a PaymentSuccess response.

Regression test 1 ensures that after adding the Apple Pay method, there are no regressions such as misrouting to the wrong provider, rejection due to enum mismatch, or null or missing payment method data.

**Regression test 2**—OrderController: order creation with existing payment types.

Purpose: verify that OrderController.cs creates orders correctly and unchanged when an existing payment method (e.g., PayPal) is used.

Preconditions:

- PayPal is an existing, functioning payment method.
- Order creation API was stable before the new feature.

Steps:

Start order creation via checkout, selecting PayPal.

Submit order.

Capture:

- The request that OrderController sends to OrderService.
- The returned order object.

Expected Results:

- Order lifecycle initiated with status = "CREATED."

- All existing fields (orderId, items, amounts, and userId) are populated correctly.
- OrderController receives the request and processes it.
- The outgoing request to OrderService includes "payment_method: PAYPAL."
- Order is created successfully with no schema or mapping errors.

Regression test 2 verifies there are no accidental side effects from the Apple Pay changes (e.g., null enum values, incorrect mapping, additional fields).

**Risk-based test selection**. In this technique, the test analyst maintains the traceability of the regression test suite to a risk register. When a change is made and the risk register is updated accordingly, the test analyst adjusts the regression test suite to cover the highest risk levels.

Consider the example from Sect. 2.1, but suppose that now we performed not qualitative, but quantitative risk analysis. Its results are presented in Table 2.6. The last column presents the traceability from risks to test cases.

**Table 2.6** Risk register before change

| Risk | Likelihood (%) | Impact | Risk level | Risk priority | Test cases |
|---|---|---|---|---|---|
| F1: Incorrect filtering | 20 | $500,000 | $100,000 | 2 | 1, 2 |
| F2: Basket failure | 15 | $500,000 | $75,000 | 3 | 1, 2, 3 |
| F3: Incorrect localization | 5 | $350,000 | $17,500 | 6 | 2 |
| P1: Slow response time | 40 | $150,000 | $60,000 | 4 | 4 |
| P2: Inefficient route calculation | 20 | $20,000 | $4000 | 8 | 5 |
| P3: Unoptimized images | 5 | $10,000 | $500 | 9 | 4, 6 |
| R1: Service unavailability | 35 | $500,000 | $175,000 | 1 | 7 |
| R2: Synchronization failures | 25 | $400,000 | $100,000 | 2 | 7, 8 |
| S1: Payment data breach | 10 | $1000,000 | $100,000 | 2 | 1, 9 |
| S2: Authentication vulnerabilities | 20 | $100,000 | $20,000 | 5 | 1, 10 |
| M1: Inconsistent code quality | 60 | $10,000 | $6000 | 7 | 11 |

Based on this information, the regression test suite should be executed according to risk priorities. First, we should execute TC7 because it is traced back to risk R1, which is the highest risk level. Next, we should execute TC1, TC2, TC8, and TC9 (test cases related to priority 2 risks). These should be followed by TC3 (yet uncovered priority 3 risk), then by TC4, TC10, TC11, TC5, and TC6.

Now, suppose that due to some changes in the project, risk analysis was conducted again, and it turned out that:

- risk F2 seems to occur twice as often as we thought (15% → 30%),
- the impact of risk P2 is estimated to be five times greater than we thought ($20 K → $100 K),
- likelihood of R1 is less than we thought (35% → 10%).

The new situation, compared with the old one, is presented in Table 2.7. The bold values represent the risk parameters that have changed.

Based on the new risk levels, risk priorities were updated accordingly. Now, the test execution order is as follows. First, we should execute TC1, TC2, and TC3, as these are related to the highest priority risk. Next, we should execute TC7, TC8, and TC9, followed by TC4, TC5, TC10, TC11, and TC6.

Let us now compare the two test case execution orders, before and after the change:

Before: TC7, TC1, TC2, TC8, TC9, TC3, TC4, TC10, TC11, TC5, TC6.
After: TC1, TC2, TC3, TC7, TC8, TC9, TC4, TC5, TC10, TC11, TC6.

As we see, the order is different due to changes in risk levels. If we had time for only five test cases, before the change, we would execute TC7, TC1, TC2, TC8, and TC9. After the change, we would execute TC1, TC2, TC3, TC7, and TC8.

**Table 2.7** Risk register before and after the change

| Risk | Before | | | After | | | | Test cases |
|---|---|---|---|---|---|---|---|---|
| | Likelihood (%) | Impact | Risk priority | Likelihood (%) | Impact | Risk level | Risk priority | |
| F1 | 20 | $500 K | 2 | 20 | $500 K | $100 K | 2 | 1, 2 |
| F2 | 15 | $500 K | 3 | **30** | $500 K | **$150 K** | 1 | 1, 2, 3 |
| F3 | 5 | $350 K | 6 | 5 | $350 K | $17.5 K | 6 | 2 |
| P1 | 40 | $150 K | 4 | 40 | $150 K | $60 K | 3 | 4 |
| P2 | 20 | $20 K | 8 | 20 | **$100 K** | **$20 K** | 5 | 5 |
| P3 | 5 | $10 K | 9 | 5 | $10 K | $0.5 K | 8 | 4, 6 |
| R1 | 35 | $500 K | 1 | **10** | $500 K | **$50 K** | 4 | 7 |
| R2 | 25 | $400 K | 2 | 25 | $400 K | $100 K | 2 | 7, 8 |
| S1 | 10 | $1000 K | 2 | 10 | $1000 K | $100 K | 2 | 1, 9 |
| S2 | 20 | $100 K | 5 | 20 | $100 K | $20 K | 5 | 1, 10 |
| M1 | 60 | $10 K | 7 | 60 | $10 K | $6 K | 7 | 11 |

**History-based testing** is an approach where the test analyst evaluates past test executions, code changes, and defect history to determine which test cases have exposed defects or were sensitive to similar modifications made after the last test execution. Executing the corresponding tests again as part of the regression test increases the likelihood of exposing similar defects. The test analyst can also include some tests that have not been executed for a long time to ensure they still pass.

To illustrate this approach, let us consider a simple example. Suppose the test execution history looks as shown in Table 2.8.

From the version management tool, you can see that the code change history is as follows. Between version 1.0 and 1.1, the FilterRestaurants.java file was modified in four separate commits. Between versions 1.1 and 1.2, the same file was modified in two different commits. In one of these commits, two other files, PaymentService.java and Login.java, were also modified.

Using the traceability matrix, you retrieve from the test management tool the following test-to-code mapping:

- TC028 covers PaymentService.java.
- TC029 covers FilterRestaurants.java.
- TC030 and TC036 cover Login.java.

The team is now preparing to release version 1.3. The commit history indicates that after version 1.2, there were two commits, one changed FilterRestaurant.java and another changed Login.java.

You know that FilterRestaurant.java is covered by test case TC028, and Login.java by test cases TC030 and TC036. The defect history indicates that there have been recent issues with FilterRestaurant.java, as TC029 failed in both versions 1.1 and 1.2. On the other hand, neither test case TC030 nor TC036 triggered any failures caused by defects in Login.java.

Suppose we have time to execute only one test case, or we want to prioritize the regression test suite and identify the highest-priority test case. The history-based

**Table 2.8** Test execution history for the last two builds

| Date | Build version | Test case executed | Result | Defect source |
|---|---|---|---|---|
| 10.05, 11:35 | 1.1 | TC028 | Fail | PaymentService.java |
| 10.05, 11:37 | 1.1 | TC029 | Fail | FilterRestaurants.java |
| 10.05, 11:38 | 1.1 | TC030 | Pass | |
| 11.05, 14:03 | 1.1 | TC028 | Pass | |
| 12.05, 10:22 | 1.1 | TC029 | Pass | |
| 15.05, 8:05 | 1.2 | TC028 | Pass | |
| 15.05, 8:08 | 1.2 | TC029 | Fail | FilterRestaurants.java |
| 15.05, 8:11 | 1.2 | TC030 | Pass | |
| 15.05, 8:12 | 1.2 | TC036 | Pass | |
| 17.05, 17:33 | 1.2 | TC029 | Pass | |

approach suggests that TC029 should be prioritized highest for test execution due to a significant likelihood that changes in FilterRestaurants.java could introduce defects, which TC029 may be able to detect.

Test cases TC030 and TC036 should be prioritized just after TC029. Although they did not detect any defects previously, they are related to code that has changed in version 1.3. On the other hand, TC028 should be given the lowest priority. In version 1.1, it triggered a failure caused by a defect in PaymentService.java, but it passed in version 1.2. Since PaymentService remained unchanged after version 1.2, the test analyst can reasonably conclude that the likelihood of TC028 detecting any defects during regression testing for version 1.3 is low.

EXTRA **Bayesian Probability**

Bayesian probability can be applied in regression testing as a rigorous type of history-based technique that builds on statistics. It allows us to calculate the probability with which a regression test case should be executed in the next test run, based on previous execution history and on how often a given test has been failed. Let $p(T)$ be such a probability for a given test case $T$. The value $p(T)$ can be interpreted as the probability that $T$ will fail in the next test run. At the beginning, we set $p(T)$ to an arbitrary value and we set $\alpha(T) = p(T)$, $\beta(T) = 1 - p(T)$. Suppose we set $p(T) = 0.5$. This means that $\alpha(T) = \beta(T) = 0.5$. Notice that the values of $\alpha$ and $\beta$ may be different for different test cases.

In the forthcoming test run, we decide whether $T$ is executed or not. It will be executed with probability

$$p(T) = \frac{\alpha(T)}{\alpha(T) + \beta(T)}.$$

Suppose that $T$ has been executed. If it passed, we leave the value $\alpha$ unchanged, and we increase $\beta$ by one: $\beta(T) := \beta(T) + 1$. If it failed, we increase $\alpha(T)$ by one: $\alpha(T) := \alpha(T) + 1$. Table 2.9 shows a sample realization of execution of a specific test case $T$.

**Table 2.9** Sample execution history regarding a specific test case T

| Test run | $\alpha(T)$ | $\beta(T)$ | Test execution probability | Result | New $\alpha(T)$ | New $\beta(T)$ |
|---|---|---|---|---|---|---|
| 1 | 0.5 | 0.5 | $0.5/(0.5+0.5)=0.5$ | Failed | 1.5 | 0.5 |
| 2 | 1.5 | 0.5 | $1.5/(1.5+0.5)=0.75$ | Failed | 2.5 | 0.5 |
| 3 | 2.5 | 0.5 | $2.5/(2.5+0.5)=0.83$ | Passed | 2.5 | 1.5 |
| 4 | 2.5 | 1.5 | $2.5/(2.5+1.5)=0.625$ | Failed | 3.5 | 1.5 |
| 5 | 3.5 | 1.5 | $3.5/(3.5+1.5)=0.7$ | Passed | 3.5 | 2.5 |
| 6 | 3.5 | 2.5 | $3.5/(3.5+2.5)=0.58$ | Passed | 3.5 | 3.5 |
| 7 | 3.5 | 3.5 | $3.5/(3.5+3.5)=0.5$ | Passed | 3.5 | 4.5 |
| 8 | 3.5 | 4.5 | $3.5/(3.5+4.5)=0.44$ | Passed | 3.5 | 5.5 |
| 9 | 3.5 | 5.5 | $3.5/(3.5+5.5)=0.39$ | Failed | 4.5 | 5.5 |
| 10 | 4.5 | 5.5 | $4.5/(4.5+5.5)=0.45$ | Passed | 4.5 | 6.5 |

The table contains only the test runs in which $T$ was executed (if a test case is not executed in some test run, the values $\alpha(T)$ and $\beta(T)$ are not modified, and the probability for the next test run remains unchanged). Observe that each time a test case fails, the likelihood of its execution in the next test run increases. And each time a test case passes, the probability of its execution in the next test run decreases. Therefore, if a test case fails frequently, the likelihood of its execution increases, as it is more likely to detect a defect.

This example illustrates the use of Bayesian probability, in which the probability distribution of a particular action is continually modified based on the observed events. In our case, the action is the execution of a test case, and the observed event is the test case result (pass or fail).

**Coverage-based testing**. In coverage-based testing, the test analyst selects a small number of tests that achieve maximum coverage possible, based on the chosen test technique(s). In this approach, the changes in the system under test are not as significant as the coverage that we want to achieve. There are two common variants of this technique.

In the first approach, test prioritization (and the order of test execution) is based solely on coverage (e.g., code coverage, requirements coverage, etc.). However, this technique may be inefficient. If the test cases with the highest coverage (i.e., exercising the highest number of coverage items) focus on the same group of coverage items, test cases exercising the remaining coverage items may be given a low priority. Therefore, if we do not have enough time to execute all test cases, these remaining coverage items may never be executed.

Consider a simple example. Suppose we have 5 test cases, TC1-TC5, and five requirements, A-E. We follow the requirements coverage. TC1 covers A, B, C, D; TC2 covers A, B, C; TC3 covers A, B; TC4 covers A; TC5 covers E. The approach above yields the following test execution order: TC1 → TC2 → TC3 → TC4 → TC5.

Notice that requirement E will be covered only at the end, when TC5 is executed. However, if we have time to execute only four test cases, requirement E will never be covered.

The second, more reasonable approach, is called the additional coverage-based prioritization. In this approach, the number of tests is carefully balanced with the coverage increase per test. First, the test case achieving the highest coverage is executed. Then, each subsequent test case is selected in a way that achieves the highest coverage among the *remaining* (i.e., not yet covered) coverage items of the test object.

Let us consider the previous example once again. First, we need to execute TC1, as it achieves 4/5 = 80% of the requirements coverage. Now, only requirement E remains uncovered. Therefore, the second test case will be TC5, as it covers 1/1 = 100% of the remaining requirements, whereas any of TC2, TC3, and TC4 covers 0% of the remaining requirements. Notice that after executing TC1 and TC5, all five requirements are covered. The remaining test cases can be prioritized using the first approach. So, the final order is: TC1 → TC5 → TC2 → TC3 → TC4.

**Requirements traceability matrix**. The requirements traceability matrix is used to assess the impact of requirement changes on the associated tests. It can be particularly valuable when new or changed requirements indirectly impact existing features. The test analyst selects regression tests for the directly affected and for related features to cover possible unintended side effects. In Agile software development, this can be done similarly by selecting tests that cover the acceptance criteria impacted by new or changed user stories.

Figure 2.3 illustrates a sample traceability matrix that demonstrates how test cases are linked to requirements.

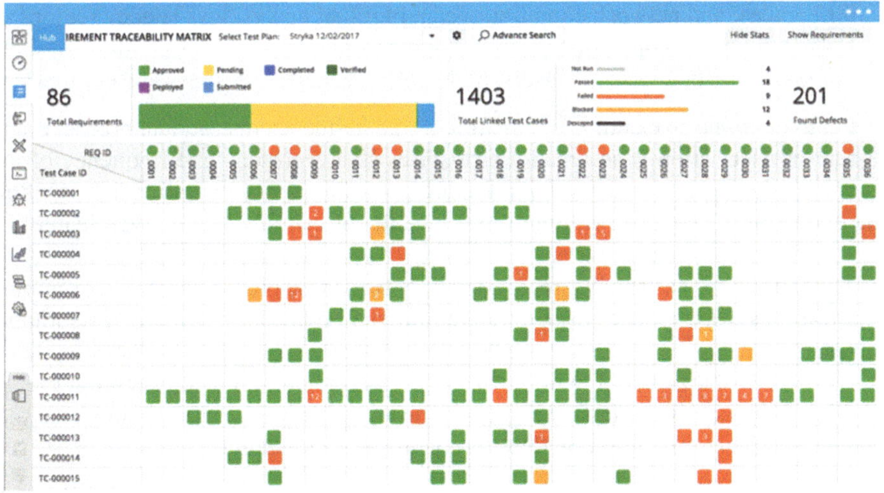


**Fig. 2.3** Traceability matrix (*source* github.com/reportportal/reportportal/issues/507)

For example, if we know that a client decided to modify requirement no. 0015, the traceability matrix indicates that this requirement is exercised by test cases TC-000002, TC-000005, TC-000014, and TC-000015. Hence, we know which test cases are impacted by a given change.

**Testing based on operational profiles**. In this technique, the test analyst selects the regression test cases to be executed based on the usage patterns of the test object. For example, when testing an online store, one such test can include the user logging in, searching for products, adding them to the cart, and placing the order. When an application is significantly changed, this technique provides a quick overview of the overall system's functionality. If this results in too many tests, the test analyst prioritizes critical patterns of use that occur often and cover critical features and business processes.

In this technique, regression tests are selected based on the most frequently used or the most typical patterns of use. A test analyst can use one operational profile or combine two or more operational profiles to select regression tests.

There may be different types of operational profiles that can be used for selecting and prioritizing regression test cases, such as:

- User-based operational profile—models different types of users, including registered clients, unregistered users, and administrators.
- Feature usage frequency operational profile—models the frequency at which different features are used in production.
- Environment-based operational profile—models the distribution of target environment parameters, such as operating system types, web browsers, and mobile devices.
- Geographic/regional operational profile—models location-specific behaviors and characteristics, such as date and time formats, number formats, regulatory differences, and network conditions (e.g., high-latency vs. low-latency regions).
- Load/concurrency operational profile—models real-world traffic conditions, such as the number of concurrent users, high-traffic scenarios, or stress and edge cases.

Let us examine an example of a feature usage frequency operational profile. Each feature or user action is assigned a probability that represents the frequency of its use. Table 2.10 presents an example feature usage frequency operational profile for the FoodApp. The second column represents the probability that a given feature is used within a single session.

The test analyst can execute regression tests with these probabilities. For example, suppose a test case T traces back to the requirement related to browsing restaurants, or verifies some test condition in the "Browse restaurants" feature. In that case, there is a 95% probability that T will be run in a given regression test execution cycle. Another approach is to classify regression tests by frequency of use, and base the frequency of their execution on these probabilities, for example:

- Test cases related to features with the frequency of use of 60% or more must be executed in every regression test execution cycle.

**Table 2.10** Feature usage frequency operational profile for the FoodApp

| Feature | Frequency of use (%) |
|---|---|
| Browse restaurants | 95 |
| Add to cart | 78 |
| Place order | 66 |
| Payment | 62 |
| Track delivery | 13 |
| Apply the coupon code | 18 |
| Rate delivery | 10 |
| Reorder from history | 6 |
| Delete account | 1 |
| Contact support | 3 |
| Change payment method | 1 |

- Test cases related to features with the frequency of use between 20 and 60% should be run every second regression test execution cycle.
- Test cases related to features with the frequency of use of 20% or less should be run every fifth regression test execution cycle.

Another form of feature usage frequency operational profile is the profile that models a single user's actions and probabilities for the following action. It uses the formal stochastic model known as a Markov chain. An example of such an operational profile is presented in Sect. 3.1.3 (Fig. 3.8), together with a script that allows the test analyst to execute regression test cases according to this profile.

**Dependencies between Test Cases**

In a regression test suite, some test cases may depend on other test cases. Such dependencies may influence the desired test execution order. For example, it may be necessary to execute a low-priority test case (or even a test case that was not selected for the regression test execution cycle) to "unblock" the execution of another important regression test case. Consider the following test suite for the FoodApp shown in Table 2.11.

**Table 2.11** Regression test suite for the FoodApp

| TC | Description | Priority | Depends on |
|---|---|---|---|
| 1 | User registration | Medium | |
| 2 | User login | High | TC1 |
| 3 | Add delivery address | Medium | TC2 |
| 4 | Add items to the cart | High | TC2 |
| 5 | Place an order | High | TC3, TC4 |
| 6 | Track order | Low | TC5 |
| 7 | Cancel order | High | TC5 |
| 8 | Rate order | Low | TC5 |

The column "priority" results from applying one of the regression test selection techniques described earlier. Looking at priorities only, the ordering should be as follows:

First, TC2, TC4, TC5.
Then, TC1, TC3.
Then, TC6, TC8.

However, we see that, for example, we cannot execute TC2 because it depends on TC1: a user must first be registered to log in. The following algorithm can be used to find the final, optimal test execution order:

**Input**: List of test cases with priorities and dependencies

**Output**: Optimal test execution order

1. Order test cases by priority only.
2. **while** (execution is infeasible due to some dependencies) **do**:
    2.1 Let t be the first test case that cannot be executed.
    2.2 Let X be the set of test cases that t depends on.
    2.3 Move all test cases from X (preserving their order) just before t.

    **end while**
3. **return** the final ordering.

Let us apply this algorithm to our problem. First, we order test cases by priorities only (the ordering within the group of test cases with the same priority is arbitrary):

TC2 → TC4 → TC5 → TC1 → TC3 → TC6 → TC8

TC2 is the first test case that cannot be executed. TC1 blocks it, so we move TC1 just before TC2, and we get the modified ordering:

TC1 → TC2 → TC4 → TC5 → TC3 → TC6 → TC8

Now TC1 and TC2 can be executed. TC4 can also be executed, because it depends on already executed TC2. However, TC5 is blocked by TC3. We move TC3 just before TC5:

TC1 → TC2 → TC4 → TC3 → TC5 → TC6 → TC8

Now, all test cases can be executed because their dependencies are executed earlier. Notice that this final ordering forces us, in some moments, to execute test cases with lower priorities before test cases with higher priorities. For example, TC1 (medium priority) must be executed before all high-priority test cases.

**Combining the techniques**. It is often necessary to use a combination of selection techniques to create a more comprehensive and practical regression test suite. However, the test analyst must carefully balance the need for thorough coverage with the need for a manageable size of the test suite. After each test cycle, the test analyst analyzes the test results to evaluate the effectiveness of the techniques applied (see Sect. 5.3.1). In the next cycle, the test analyst will retain effective techniques and replace ineffective ones, continuously improving regression test selection over time. This process is essential in iterative and incremental development models, where changes occur frequently.

**Case Study**

Assume that FoodApp consists of three components, M1, M2, and M3. They implement five different requirements, Req1–Req5. Your regression test suite contains seven test cases, TC1–TC7. The test analyst is asked to select the regression test cases for the FoodApp. These test cases are to be executed at the end of the present iteration. Figure 2.4 presents the data available to the test analyst regarding traceability and the probability of defect detection for each test case, based on Bayesian probability (see the "Bayesian probability" optional section above).

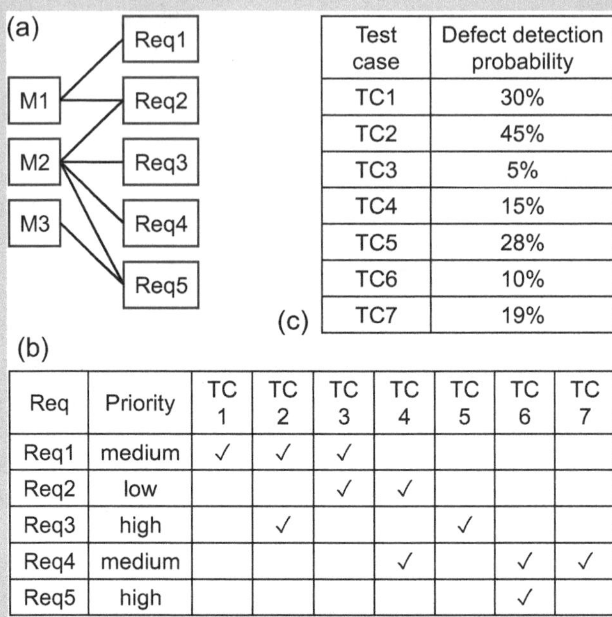


| Test case | Defect detection probability |
|---|---|
| TC1 | 30% |
| TC2 | 45% |
| TC3 | 5% |
| TC4 | 15% |
| TC5 | 28% |
| TC6 | 10% |
| TC7 | 19% |

| Req | Priority | TC 1 | TC 2 | TC 3 | TC 4 | TC 5 | TC 6 | TC 7 |
|---|---|---|---|---|---|---|---|---|
| Req1 | medium | ✓ | ✓ | ✓ | | | | |
| Req2 | low | | | ✓ | ✓ | | | |
| Req3 | high | | ✓ | | | ✓ | | |
| Req4 | medium | | | | ✓ | | ✓ | ✓ |
| Req5 | high | | | | | | ✓ | |

**Fig. 2.4** Traceability and defect detection information for the FoodApp regression test suite

The test analyst checks the version control system to confirm that since the last iteration, changes have only been made to modules M1 and M3. From the components-to-requirements traceability matrix (Fig. 2.4a), the test analyst observes that changes in M1 and M3 may impact requirements Req1, Req2, and Req5. From the requirements-to-test cases traceability matrix (Fig. 2.4b), the test analyst deduces that the following test cases cover the area subject to change:

- TC1, TC2, TC3, which cover Req1,
- TC3, TC4, which cover Req2,
- TC6, which covers Req5.

In total, five test cases should be selected for the forthcoming regression testing: TC1, TC2, TC3, TC4, and TC6.

The test analyst takes into account the fact that, due to time constraints, not all test cases can be executed. They must therefore decide how to prioritize the test cases within the upcoming regression tests so that the most important tests are performed first. The test analyst uses information about the priority of requirements defined by the product owner. Of the three requirements analyzed, Req5 (high) has the highest priority, followed by Req1 (medium) and finally Req2 (low). Therefore, the TC6 regression test will be run first. This will be followed by the TC1, TC2, and TC3 test set. Finally, the TC4 test will be performed, which, together with the previously executed TC3, will cover Req2.

Within the TC1, TC2, and TC3 test set, the test analyst also applies prioritization based on information about the probability of defect detection (Fig. 2.4c). Among these three tests, TC2 detected defects most often (45%), followed by TC1 (30%), and TC3 least frequently (5%). Therefore, the order within this group will be as follows: TC2, TC1, TC3.

Hence, the test analyst finalized the final regression test selection and obtained the final test execution order:

TC6 → TC2 → TC1 → TC3 → TC4

This example illustrates that selecting regression tests can be non-trivial. Test analysts often employ a variety of selection and prioritization techniques, which they combine to ensure that the final selection is as close to optimal as possible (i.e., the selected set of tests is likely to detect any defects introduced during recent code changes as quickly as possible).

## Sample Questions

### Question 2.2.1A

You are preparing to perform regression testing for an aircraft autopilot software. The test strategy requires prioritizing regression tests according to risk level. The table below shows the results of the risk analysis for this software.

| Risk | Risk likelihood (%) | Risk impact | Mitigation actions | Test case covering the risk |
|---|---|---|---|---|
| Sensor data inaccuracy | 20 | $5,000,000 | Fault injection testing | TC1 |
| Algorithmic decision errors | 10 | $12,000,000 | Model-based testing | TC2 |
| Environmental condition mismanagement | 5 | $10,000,000 | Metamorphic testing | TC3 |
| Security vulnerabilities | 1 | $15,000,000 | Penetration testing | TC4 |

All four test cases, TC1 to TC4, must be executed.

Which test case should be executed as the **THIRD** one?

(a) TC1.
(b) TC2.
(c) TC3.
(d) TC4.

Select ONE answer.

**Question 2.2.1B**

The test strategy requires that regression tests be prioritized based on the so-called additional coverage criterion. This means that the test case with the highest coverage is executed first, followed by the remaining test cases, so that each of them exercises as many coverage items as possible that have not been exercised by the test cases already executed.

Your team uses requirement coverage. The traceability matrix below shows which regression test cases cover which requirements (X means that a requirement is covered).

| Regression test case | Requirements | | | | | | |
|---|---|---|---|---|---|---|---|
| | 1 | 2 | 3 | 4 | 5 | 6 | 7 |
| TC1 | | X | | X | X | X | |
| TC2 | X | | | X | X | | |
| TC3 | X | X | X | | | | |
| TC4 | | | | X | X | | X |

You must perform all regression tests in accordance with the accepted additional coverage criterion.

Which test case will be executed **LAST**?

(a) TC1.
(b) TC2.
(c) TC3.
(d) TC4.

Select ONE answer.

## Exercise 2—Determining the Scope of Regression Testing

TA-2.2.1 (K4) Analyze the impact of changes to determine the scope of regression testing

You are part of a team testing the new release of a Banking Web App. The release includes bug fixes and changes in the *Funds Transfer* and *Account Statement* modules, as well as a new feature for *Scheduled Payments.*

Your task is to select and prioritize test cases for execution under a tight schedule. The test execution includes both the regression test suite and test cases for the new features. Test cases for the new features have higher priority than regression tests.

You are given:

- requirements-to-test cases traceability matrix (Table 2.12),
- defect history per test case (Table 2.13),
- dependencies between test cases (see below).

The dependencies between test cases are:

- T2 depends on T1 (Authentication requires a working login).
- T3 depends on T2 (Transfer requires a working authentication).
- T5 depends on T4 (Verifying transfer requires a working balance check).
- T11, T12, T13 depend on T1 (Scheduled payments require a working login).
- T14 depends on T11 (Canceling a scheduled payment requires a working schedule).

**Table 2.12** Requirements-to-test cases traceability matrix

| Requirement | Requirement description | Related test cases |
|---|---|---|
| R1 | User login & authentication | T1, T2 |
| R2 | Funds transfer (domestic) | T3, T4, T5 |
| R3 | Funds transfer (international) | T6, T7 |
| R4 | View account balance | T8 |
| R5 | Generate account statement | T9, T10 |
| R6 | Schedule future payments | T11, T12, T13 |
| R7 | Cancel scheduled payments | T14 |

**Table 2.13** Defect history based on the last three regression test cycles

| Test case ID | Defects found previously | Severity of defects |
|---|---|---|
| T2 | 2 | High, high |
| T3 | 3 | Critical, critical, high |
| T7 | 1 | Low |
| T10 | 1 | Medium |

Select the test cases that should be executed given the new changes, traceability, and past failures. Prioritize the test cases in order of execution, considering:

- requirements impacted by recent changes,
- historical defect detection effectiveness,
- dependencies between test cases,
- execution time constraints,
- criticality of requirements.

Provide a selected subset of test cases (with reasoning) with a prioritized execution order and a short justification for why the chosen order maximizes defect detection and minimizes risk under time constraints.

# Chapter 3 Test Analysis and Design

**Keywords** Checklist-based testing · Behavior-based technique · Combinatorial testing · Crowd testing · CRUD testing · Data-based test technique · Decision table testing · Domain testing · Equivalence partition · Experience-based testing · Metamorphic relation · Metamorphic testing · Random testing · Rule-based test technique · Scenario-based testing · Session-based testing · State-based testing · Test charter

## Introduction to Test Analysis and Design

The Test Analyst syllabus addresses black box and experience-based test techniques. White-box test techniques are typically used by developers and technical test analysts; therefore, they are not discussed in this syllabus. The test techniques discussed deepen the knowledge acquired in the Foundation Level syllabus [1] and supplement that knowledge with a broader set of test techniques. A test analyst should be capable of applying all of them. The syllabus has selected these techniques based on their general applicability and their proven effectiveness and efficiency. In addition, it categorizes the black-box test techniques based on the type of test condition addressed. Let us start with a brief overview of these test techniques.

**Definitions**

**Data-based test technique**: A test technique in which test conditions are model elements of the test object data.

 
A. Roman and M. Hamburg, *Practical Software Test Analysis*,
https://doi.org/10.1007/978-3-032-27986-6_5

**Behavior-based test technique**: A black-box test technique in which test conditions are model elements of the state-dependent behavior of a test object.

**Rule-based test technique**: A black-box test technique in which test conditions are model elements of the state-independent behavior rules of a test object.

**Experience-based testing**: A test approach based on the tester's experience, knowledge, and intuition.

**Data-based test techniques** aim to verify that the implementation handles specific domain areas correctly. The syllabus describes three such techniques:

- domain testing, which extends equivalence partitioning and boundary value analysis (described in the Foundation Level syllabus) to domains with multiple parameters, as well as to complex partitions,
- combinatorial testing, which focuses on interactions of multiple parameters in a multidimensional domain,
- random testing, which selects random inputs from the domain based on a specified probability distribution.

**Behavior-based test techniques** derive test conditions from specifications of the dynamic behavior of the test item to verify that the test item behaves as expected. The syllabus describes three such techniques:

- CRUD testing, which verifies the lifecycle of entities processed by the test item,
- state-based testing, familiar from the Foundation Level syllabus and explored in greater depth here,
- scenario-based testing, which evaluates the test item behavior in realistic scenarios. It generalizes the use case testing from earlier versions of this curriculum.

**Rule-based test techniques** focus on software failures that occur due to the mishandling of some rules in the specification (e.g., business rules). The syllabus describes two such techniques:

- decision table testing, which expands on the Foundation Level syllabus knowledge with advanced techniques for designing and minimizing decision tables,
- metamorphic testing, which generates new test cases from an existing source test case based on consistency rules of the feature being tested.

**Experience-based test techniques** leverage the test analyst's knowledge, intuition, expertise, and past encounters to guide test activities.

# 3.1 Data-Based Test Techniques

## *3.1.1 Domain Testing*

TA-3.1.1 (K3) Apply domain testing

**Definitions**

**Equivalence partition**: A subset of a value domain for which a component or system is expected to treat all values the same based on the specification.

**Domain testing**: A black-box test technique in which test conditions are points on, near to, inside, or outside the boundaries of different equivalence partitions of the input value domain.

**Introduction**. Domain testing is a test technique that generalizes boundary value analysis, discussed in the Foundation Level syllabus [1]. Both techniques require the equivalence partitioning of the value domain. Boundary value analysis applies to the case of a one-dimensional ordered domain determined by the values of a single variable. However, in practice, the tester usually encounters much more complicated, multidimensional domains determined by multiple variables. In addition, these variables may interact with each other, and the relations between variables may be nonlinear.

**Domain Testing for the BMI Calculator**

Let us consider a simple example of a body mass index (BMI) calculator app called BMI-Calc. The application takes two positive numbers as input, height ($h$) and weight ($w$), and then calculates the BMI by dividing weight (in kilograms) by the square of height (in meters):

$$\mathrm{BMI} = \frac{w}{h^2}.$$

A BMI of at least 18.5 and less than 25 is classified as normal weight. For example, if the user enters $w = 70$ kg and $h = 1.75$ m as input, the BMI value is $\mathrm{BMI} = 70/(1.75^2) \approx 22.86$. So, the app should return a message stating that the user's BMI is within the normal range.

In the following, we want to check whether BMI-Calc has correctly implemented the equivalence partition "normal range." The input value domain is two-dimensional, since it is a set of points with coordinates $w$ and $h$. The equivalence partition "normal range" is defined as a subset of this domain determined by the following condition:

$$w > 0 \text{ AND } h > 0 \text{ AND } \frac{w}{h^2} \geq 18.5 \text{ AND } \frac{w}{h^2} < 25$$

Figure 3.1, taken from the World Health Organization (WHO), visualizes the normal range in a relevant section of the $(w, h)$ plane with yellow coloring. It is a set of points lying between the curves represented by the equations $\frac{w}{h^2} = 18.5$ and $\frac{w}{h^2} = 25$, respectively. The points lying on the former belong to the equivalence partition and the points lying on the latter do not belong to it, due to the strong inequality in the boundary condition $\frac{w}{h^2} < 25$ .

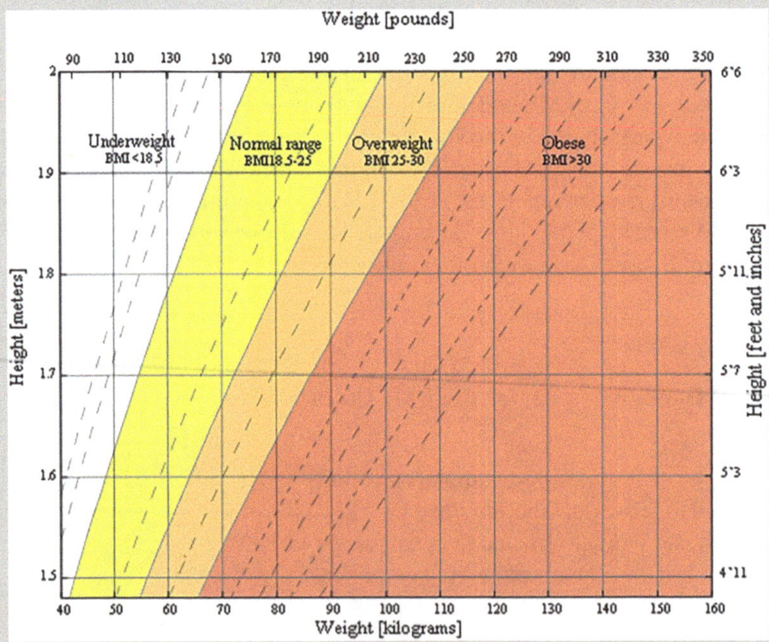


**Fig. 3.1** Graph of BMI categories based on the World Health Organization data (*source* www.calculator.net/bmi-calculator.html)

Suppose that when implementing BMI-Calc, the programmer could have made a mistake and forgotten to implement the conditions $w > 0$ and $h > 0$ for the "normal range" equivalence partition. In such a case, the program could categorize negative inputs for height and weight, which would not make sense.

Or it could run into a division-by-zero exception when entering h = 0. The programmer could also, for example, forget to include the square of the height in the implementation of the formula for BMI and instead of the formula BMI = $w/h^2$ implement the formula BMI = $w/h$. This would shift the normal range equivalence partition. For example, for the input values $w = 70$ and $h = 1.75$, the system would calculate the BMI as 70/1.75 = 40, and thus give an incorrect result stating that the user is obese, although their BMI (whose correct value is 22.86) is within the normal range.

Domain testing is a technique used to verify that specified equivalence partitions are implemented correctly. The coverage criteria for domain testing enable the detection of the vast majority of defects (such as the one described above) using as few inputs as possible.

As you can see from the example above, domain testing can handle much more complex equivalence partitions than boundary value analysis. They may involve several variables in combination, nonlinear functions, and a logical combination of several atomic conditions.

Before discussing the coverage criteria described in the syllabus, let us introduce the key terms for this section.

**Domains**. By the term domain, we mean the set of all possible inputs of a test item. In other words, a domain means in this context the value domain of all possible inputs.

**Equivalence partitions and borders**. The equivalence partitions addressed by domain testing must be defined by expressions that combine atomic conditions by Boolean operators (AND, OR, and NOT) and involve one or more interacting variables. Each atomic condition defines a border of the equivalence partition. A border can be closed or open with respect to the equivalence partition it defines. A closed border is formed by a relational expression with a $\leq$, $\geq$ or $=$ operator. An open border results from a relational expression with a $<$, $>$ or $\neq$ oprator.

**Compound Conditions**

In our example with BMI-Calc, the "normal range" equivalence partition is defined by a compound condition combining the following four atomic conditions with the logical operator AND:

$w > 0$ (open border)
$h > 0$ (open border)
$\frac{w}{h^2} \geq 18.5$ (closed border)
$\frac{w}{h^2} < 25$ (open border)

Any point, i.e., pair of values ($w$, $h$), satisfying all four of the above atomic conditions belongs to the equivalence partition "normal range." Points that do not satisfy them all are outside the equivalence partition.

**ON, OFF, IN, and OUT points**. Coverage criteria for domain testing are defined using special points identified for specific borders. There are four types of such points, which are called ON, OFF, IN, and OUT points.

The intuitive idea behind these types of points is as follows: When crossing a border of the equivalence partition from the outside, membership switches on at an ON point. In the opposite direction, membership switches off at an OFF point. The more precise formal definitions are as follows:

- For a closed border of an equivalence partition, an ON point is located within the equivalence partition on this border, and an OFF point is outside the equivalence partition but is closest to the border according to the given accuracy.
- For an open border of an equivalence partition, an ON point is located within the equivalence partition and is closest to the border according to the given accuracy. An OFF point lies outside the equivalence partition and is situated on the border.
- An IN point related to a border belongs to the equivalence partition and is not an ON point for that border.
- Similarly, an OUT point related to a border lies outside the equivalence partition and is not an OFF point for that border.

Note that in complex partitions, only the portion of the border that is adjacent to the equivalence partition is relevant for these types of points.

Figure 3.2 illustrates this concept. Suppose that in a two-dimensional domain some equivalence partition $P$ is defined by a region bounded by conjunction of four atomic conditions: $x \geq 0$ AND $x \leq 10$ AND $y \geq 0$ AND $y < 10$. Equivalence partition $P$ is marked as a gray square in the figure. Suppose further that points are represented with an accuracy of 0.01. So, for example, point (1, 1) has four immediate neighbors: (1, 1.01), (0.99, 1), (1.01, 1), and (0.99, 1).

Consider the closed border $x \geq 0$. Point $A$ with coordinates (0, 5) is an ON point for this border, and point $B$ with coordinates $(-0.01, 4)$ is an OFF point for this border, because it lies outside the equivalence partition but at the smallest possible distance of 0.01) to the point (0, 4) in the equivalence partition. Point $C$ with coordinates (3, 7) is an IN point, because it is located within the equivalence partition and is not an ON point for this border. Point $D$ with coordinates (−5, 7) is an OUT point for the border because it lies outside the equivalence partition and is not an OFF point for $x \geq 0$.

Now consider the open border $y < 10$ for $P$. Point $F$ is an OFF point for this border, because it lies exactly on the line $y = 10$, but this line does not belong to $P$. On the other hand, point $E$, lying just under the line $y = 10$, belongs to $P$, so it is an ON point for the border $y < 10$.

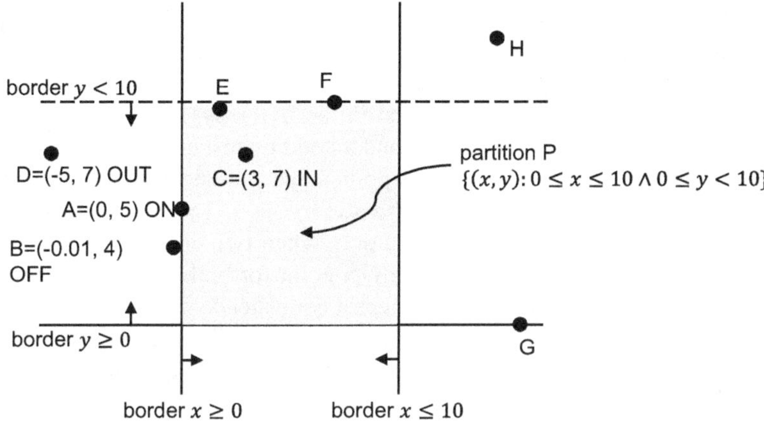


**Fig. 3.2** Four borders delineating a partition

Note that every point for a certain border is also a point of a certain type for every other border. For example, point $A$ is an ON point for border $x \geq 0$, but at the same time is an IN point for borders $y < 10$, $y \geq 0$ and $x \leq 10$. Point $G$ is an ON point for $y \geq 0$, an IN point for both $x \geq 0$ and $y < 10$, and an OUT point for $x \leq 10$. Point $H$ is an OUT point for borders $y < 10$ and $x \leq 10$, and an IN point for borders $x \geq 0$ and $y \geq 0$.

The fact that each point is a point of some type for each border allows the tester to identify a small number of test data, which, taken together, can detect a great number of different types of defects in the implementation of the domain.

The Test Analyst syllabus describes two coverage criteria for testing a specific partition. We will now discuss them in detail.

**Simplified domain coverage** [2]. It requires that for each inequality border using the $\leq$ or $\geq$ operator, one ON point and one OFF point are selected. The OFF point should be as close to the ON point as possible. For each equality border (i.e., defined with the $=$ operator), one ON point and two OFF points lying on different sides of the border are required. Similarly, for an inequality border using the $\neq$ operator, one OFF point and two ON points are required. Simplified domain coverage requires a limited number of coverage items but may not detect some simple defect types, like using '=' instead of '≥.'

**Reliable domain coverage** [3]. For each inequality border using the $\leq$ or $\geq$ operator, one ON, one OFF, one IN, and one OUT point should be selected. For the equality border, one ON and two OUT points should be selected. For an inequality border using the $\neq$ operator, one OFF and two IN data points are required, with the IN data points being on different sides of the border.

The reliable domain coverage requires a slightly larger number of coverage items than the simplified domain coverage, but can detect considerably more domain defects. This is because the required set of coverage items is, in fact, a superset of the set of coverage items required for the simplified domain coverage.

The number of coverage items can be optimized. Systematic optimization in general cases is complex and not covered in the Syllabus. However, some simple cases are straightforward and should be understood by test analysts.

In the example of Fig. 3.2, the same IN point C can be selected for all four borders. Moreover, an ON point for a border might also serve as an IN point for other borders of the same equivalence partition. In addition, when two closed borders intersect, their intersection can serve as a common ON point for both borders. Optimization can also involve coverage items from different equivalence partitions. For example, a pair of ON and OFF points of the equivalence partition, like E and F in the example above, can serve as the OFF and ON points of the adjacent equivalence partition at the common border.[1]

Figure 3.3 illustrates the difference between the two coverage types, regarding the number of coverage items. On the left-hand side, we see the test points required to achieve reliable domain coverage. We need ON, OFF, IN, and OUT points for each of the four borders. Without optimization, that would give us $4 \cdot 4 = 16$ coverage items. However, point M can be an IN point for all four borders. Hence, we need at most $4 \cdot 3 + 1 = 13$ coverage items. Further optimization could completely remove M: The ON point G of border $x \leq 10$ could serve as an IN point for any of the other borders. Moreover, ON points A and J could be merged into one common ON point (0, 0) for the two closed borders $x \geq 0$ and $y \geq 0$. Similarly, ON points D and G could also be merged. This would leave us with an optimized set of 10 coverage items: 4 separate OFF points, 4 separate OUT points, and 2 ON points, which serve two borders each and are also IN points for the other two borders.

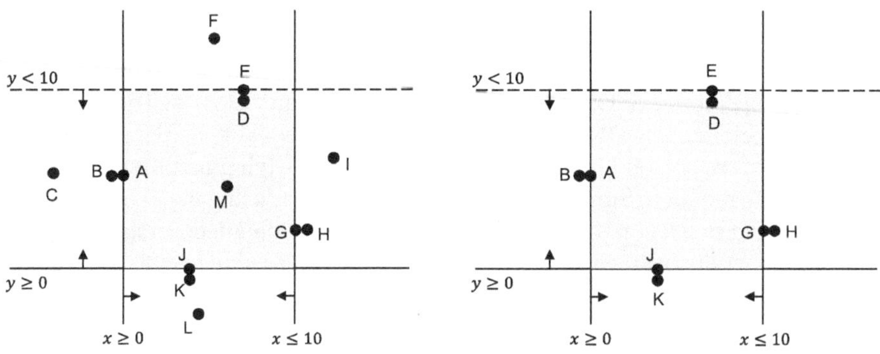


**Fig. 3.3** Coverage items for reliable and simple domain coverage

[1] This is feasible if the partition is convex, but in general case may not be possible. A simple example is when a partition is composed of two disjoint squares: no ON point can be an IN point for all eight borders that define these two squares.

On the right-hand side, we see the test points required to achieve the simplified domain coverage. We need to provide two points for each of the four borders: ON and OFF. Hence, without optimization, we need $4 \cdot 2 = 8$ coverage items. As with the reliable coverage, the ON points A and J, and the on points D and G could be merged. In this case, the OFF points must be moved to be placed next to them. Moreover, each pair of ON and OFF points for a given border can simultaneously serve as a pair of OFF and ON points for the adjacent equivalence partition. So, the minimized set will contain 6 coverage items: two ON points, which serve two borders each, and four separate OFF points.

In Fig. 3.4, we see how the coverage criteria work for the borders defined with the $=$ or $\neq$ operators. Fig. 3.4a shows the coverage items for the simplified domain coverage. For an equality border, one ON and two OFF points are needed. The OFF points must lie on the opposite sides of the border. In the case of inequality, we also need three points: an OFF point lies on the border, and two ON points lie on the opposite sides of this border.

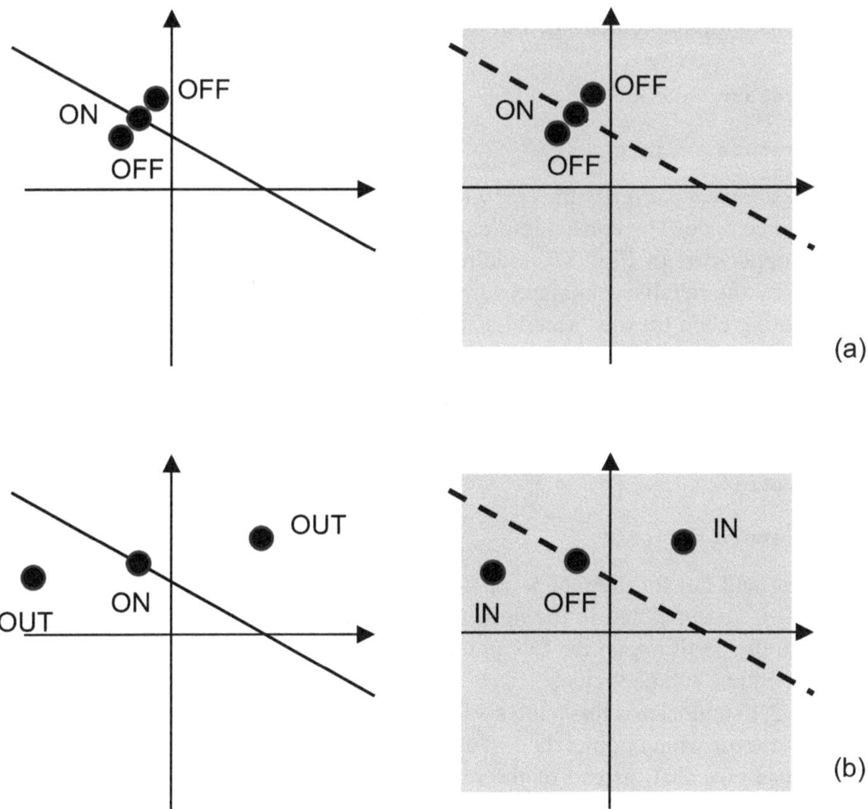


**Fig. 3.4** Coverage items for equality and inequality borders

Figure 3.4b shows the coverage items for reliable domain coverage. The difference is that in the case of an equality border, we do not take two OFF points but two OUT points. In the case of an inequality border, we do not take two ON points but two IN points.

**The number of coverage items**. Let us provide the formulae for the number of required coverage items for both coverage types. We perform this analysis for a single equivalence partition. Suppose an equivalence partition is defined in a $K$-dimensional space (i.e., it is defined with $K$ variables) as a conjunction of $N$ inequality borders using the $\leq$, $<$, $>$, or $\geq$ operators. Then the simplified domain coverage of that equivalence partition requires $2N$ test points, while the reliable domain coverage usually requires $3N + 1$ test points. Notice that for both coverage criteria discussed, the number of coverage items does not depend on the domain dimension $K$. It only depends linearly on the number $N$ of borders, which makes the technique efficient, especially for partitions in high-dimensional domains.

**Types of defects detected by domain testing**. Now, let us analyze what type of defects can be found using the above-mentioned coverage criteria. Suppose the developer should implement the following requirements:

```
if (y <= x)
    return "accept"
else
    return "reject"
```

The tester wants to verify the correctness of this implementation but has no access to the source code. The correct implementation of the "accept" domain is shown in the left upper part of Fig. 3.5, together with ON, OFF, IN, and OUT points, as required by the reliable domain coverage. The developer can make some mistakes when writing code for the "accept" partition. In Fig. 3.5, the effects of seven types of errors are shown. Notice that in each of these cases, there is at least one test point for which the test fails. These points are denoted as white points.

For example, for the defective implementation:

```
if (y < x)
    return "accept"
else
    return "reject"
```

the test will fail for the ON point. This is because the expected response for the ON point is "accept," but in the defective implementation, the line $y = x$ does not belong to the partition, so the ON point will not be a part of the partition, and the system's output will be "reject."

Table 3.1 summarizes this analysis for all seven types of typical defects, showing in each case for which points the test cases fail.

Suppose now that instead of the reliable domain coverage, we used simplified coverage. This approach requires only ON and OFF points. Notice that for all defects except $y = x$, a test case for at least one of these points will fail. But for the defective implementation $y = x$ both ON and OFF points will result in the correct answer. This example shows that reliable domain coverage is stronger than simplified coverage,

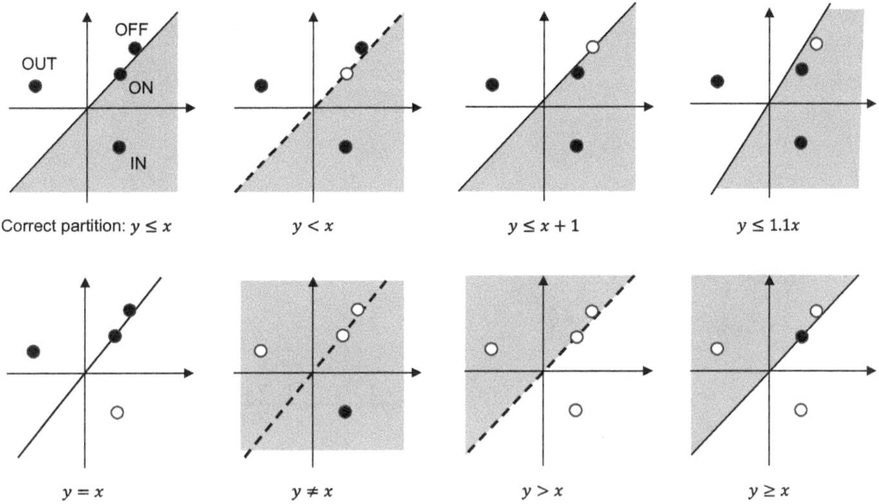


**Fig. 3.5** Correct partition, its possible defective implementations, and test points

**Table 3.1** Analysis of typical defects in implementing the partition y ≤ x

| Defect | Test results for test points | | | |
|---|---|---|---|---|
| | ON | OFF | IN | OUT |
| $y < x$ | **Fail** | Pass | Pass | Pass |
| $y \leq x + 1$ | Pass | **Fail** | Pass | Pass |
| $y \leq 1.1x$ | Pass | **Fail** | Pass | Pass |
| $y = x$ | Pass | Pass | **Fail** | Pass |
| $y \neq x$ | **Fail** | **Fail** | Pass | **Fail** |
| $y > x$ | **Fail** | **Fail** | **Fail** | **Fail** |
| $y \geq x$ | Pass | **Fail** | **Fail** | **Fail** |

i.e., it is able to detect more typical defects by requiring a larger set of coverage items.

**Case Study**

Let us apply domain testing to our FoodApp. Suppose that a client can find restaurants of a certain type in an area where they live (Fig. 3.6). Each restaurant R defines a maximum distance Max(R) to the meal delivery location. If the distance *d* between the customer's location and the location of restaurant R is no greater than Max(R), that restaurant is shown on the map, and the customer can order a meal there. Otherwise, the restaurant is not shown on the map.

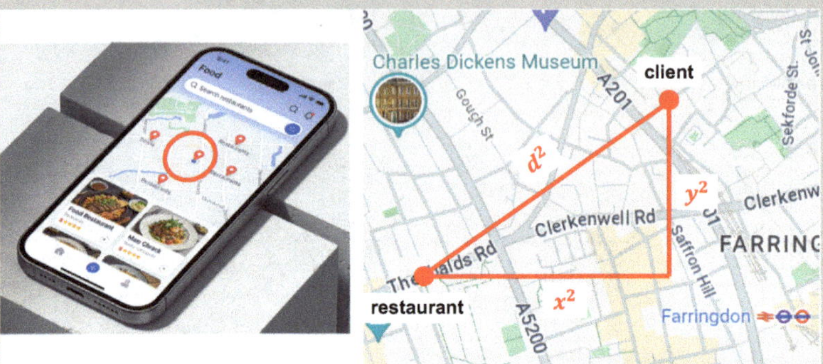


**Fig. 3.6** Food App: finding restaurants near the client's location and verifying the distance

The system calculates the customer's distance as follows: the coordinates of the restaurant are defined as (0, 0), and the coordinates of the customer are defined as (x, y) relative to the restaurant's position. Using Pythagoras' theorem, the system calculates the square of the distance between the customer and the restaurant as follows:

$$d^2 = x^2 + y^2$$

The test analyst may assume that the logic for checking the distance condition is implemented as follows:

```
function CheckDistance(R, x, y)
    x, y as distance components relative to R
    if x*x + y*y <= Max(R)*Max(R)
      Show the restaurant R on the map
    else
    Do not show the restaurant R on the map
end
```

The input parameters *R*, *x*, and *y* denote, respectively, a restaurant and the absolute coordinates of the client's location. First, the function `CheckDistance` calculates the client's distance components x and y relative to the restaurant's R location. Max(*R*) returns the maximal allowed distance for restaurant R. If the distance between R and the client does not exceed the maximal allowed distance for R, the restaurant is shown on the map. Otherwise, it is not shown on the map.

The test analyst decides to use a simplified domain coverage to verify the correctness of the implementation of the partition *P* defined as a set of points (*x*, *y*) fulfilling the relation $x^2 + y^2 \leq$ Max $(R)^2$, where Max(*R*) is a constant.

Before the test analyst designs test cases, some preconditions must be met. First, the test analyst creates a restaurant R and defines its maximal allowed distance as Max($R$) = 20 km.

Now, to achieve the simplified coverage for $P$, two coverage items are needed: an ON point and an OFF point. An ON point must lie on the border of $P$, that is, its coordinates $(x, y)$ must fulfill the relation $x^2 + y^2 = 20^2$. An example of such an ON point can be (12, 16), because $12^2 + 16^2 = 400 = 20^2$. An OFF point must lie outside $P$, but closest to the border according to the given accuracy. Suppose the accuracy is set to 10 meters. Now, the accuracy can be understood in at least two ways.

First, the accuracy may be related to the client's coordinates. This means that, for example, the closest points to (12, 16) are, for example, (12.01, 16), (12, 16.01), (11.99, 16), and (12, 15.99). The test analyst can choose (12, 16.01) as the OFF point, because $12^2 + 16.01^2 = 400.3201 > 20^2$, which means that the calculated distance is $d = \sqrt{400.3201} \approx 20.008$.

However, the accuracy may be also related to the calculated distance. In this case, the test analyst should choose as an OFF point a point $(x, y)$ such that $x^2 + y^2 = 400.01$. It may be difficult to find the exact $x$, $y$ for which this equation is true, so the test analyst may try to find the values that give the reasonable margin. For example, if $x = 10.1$, then $y = \sqrt{400.01 - 102.01} = \sqrt{298} \approx 17.275$. For $(x, y) = (10.1, 17.275)$ we have $d \approx 20.01$.

Now the test analyst is ready to design the test cases. Suppose we relate accuracy to the calculated distance. The test cases are shown in Table 3.2.

**Table 3.2** Test cases achieving simplified domain coverage for the distance calculation

| Test case | Input data | | Expected result | |
|---|---|---|---|---|
| | $x$ | $y$ | $d$ | Decision |
| TC 1 (ON) | 12 | 16 | 20 | Show restaurant R on the map |
| TC 2 (OFF) | 10.1 | 12.27 | ≈20.01 | Do not show restaurant R on the map |

If we want to apply reliable domain coverage, we must provide two more test points: IN and OUT. This task is easier than for the OFF point. For example, for an IN point we can take (10, 15), because $8^2 + 15^2 = 17^2 < 20^2$, and for an OUT point we can take (10, 24), since $10^2 + 24^2 = 26^2 > 20^2$. The full test suite for achieving the reliable domain coverage is shown in Table 3.3.

**Table 3.3** Test cases achieving reliable domain coverage for the distance calculation

| | Input data | | Expected result | |
|---|---|---|---|---|
| Test case | $x$ | $y$ | $d$ | decision |
| TC 1 (ON) | 12 | 16 | 20 | Show restaurant R on the map |
| TC 2 (OFF) | 10.1 | 12.27 | ≈20.01 | Do not show restaurant R on the map |
| TC 3 (IN) | 8 | 15 | 17 | Show restaurant R on the map |
| TC 4 (OUT) | 10 | 24 | 26 | Do not show restaurant R on the map |

## Sample Questions

### Question 3.1.1A

A system accepts age as an input for a form where age is divided into three equivalence partitions:

Child: Ages 0 to 12, defined by the borders age $\geq 0$ and age $\leq 12$
Teen: Ages 13 to 17, defined by the borders age $\geq 13$ and age $\leq 17$
Adult: Ages 18 to 120, defined by the borders age $\geq 18$ and age $\leq 120$

The valid range for age input is 0 to 120. Assume the user can only enter valid age values.

You design test cases using domain testing to verify the correct implementation of the equivalence partitions.

Which of the following input data sets achieves the highest **reliable coverage**?

(a) 18, 120.
(b) 12, 17.
(c) 6, 15.
(d) 0, 5.

Select ONE answer.

### Question 3.1.1B

You are testing a system that gets two integer values, X and Y, representing the values of two variables, as input. On the output, the system determines whether the relationship between the variables is correct. The set of points representing the correct relationship is marked with a gray area in Fig. 3.7 and defined by the following conditions:

$$X \leq 6 \text{ and } Y \leq 6 \text{ and } X + Y \geq 9$$

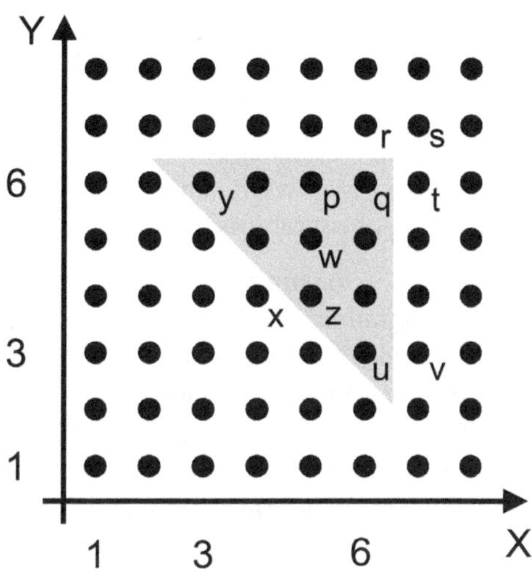


**Fig. 3.7** A domain split into two partitions

You apply domain testing to design test cases.

Which set of test points achieves the **simplified coverage** for this scenario?

(a) y, u, x, s.
(b) x, w, q, r, v.
(c) p, u, v, w.
(d) q, r, t, x, z.

Select ONE answer.

## Exercise 3—Domain Analysis

TA-3.1.1 (K3) Apply domain testing

You are testing a hotel reservation system, and currently you are focusing on the component that verifies the correctness of the length of stay. The business rules are as follows:

- check-in can take place at the earliest on the current day
- the minimum length of stay is 1 night, and the maximum is 30 nights
- checkout must take place no later than 180 days after the day on which the user books the room

The system accepts two inputs: the check-in date and the number of nights (integer), and, based on them, sends two integers to the component that verifies the correctness of the data:

- D—denoting the "delay", i.e., the number of days that elapse from the date of booking to the check-in date (R < 0 means the check-in date is earlier than today, R = 0 means today, R > 0 means the check-in date is later than today)
- N—denoting the number of nights booked.

Based on these two numbers, the system checks if the business rules are met. If so, the component returns TRUE; otherwise, it returns FALSE.

1. Perform a domain analysis for this problem using the variables D and N. To do this, formulate a set of constraints representing the set of values (D, N) in a two-dimensional space for which the system should return TRUE. Its complement will express the set of values (D, N) for which the system should return FALSE.
2. Draw the domain with the constraints defining both equivalence classes.
3. Design a minimal set of test cases (input data is understood as a pair of points (D, N), and the expected output is TRUE or FALSE) that satisfy the simplified coverage criterion for both equivalence classes. First, ignore the rule that each ON and OFF point for a given border should be an IN point for other borders. Show that in such a case, there exist defects that may not be detected by the test points. Then, design another minimal set of test cases, this time following the rule that each ON and off point for a given border should be an IN point for other borders. Show that the above-mentioned defects can now be detected.
4. Design a minimal set of test cases (input data is understood as a pair of points (D, N), and the expected output is TRUE or FALSE) that satisfy the reliable coverage criterion for both equivalence classes.

### *3.1.2 Combinatorial Testing*

TA-3.1.2 (K3) Apply combinatorial testing

**Definitions**

**Combinatorial testing**: A black-box test technique in which test conditions are specific combinations of values of several parameters.

**Introduction**. Testers constantly face complexity issues in their daily work. This complexity can involve many issues, for example:

- a very large number of combinations of values that together constitute the input to the software—many software failures arise from the interaction of two or more such factors

- a very large number of configurations of potential environments in which the developed application may run—a program may run perfectly fine on a browser P under an operating system Q, but incorrectly perform some functionality when run on a browser R under an operating system S.

**A Failure Resulting from the Parameters Interaction**

Consider a typical example of a failure resulting from the interaction of two parameters. Assume that a web server uses a combination of specific PHP and MySQL settings, namely `memory_limit` for PHP, representing the amount of memory a script can consume, and `max_allowed_packet` for MySQL, representing the maximum packet size the server can handle in a single request. Let us assume that PHP's memory limit can be set to 32 MB, 64 MB, or 128 MB, while MySQL's maximum packet size can be set to 32 MB or 64 MB. Since there are three possible values for the PHP memory limit and two possible values for the maximum MySQL packet size, the number of combinations of these two parameters is $3 \cdot 2 = 6$.

If we want to test all of them, we need six test cases. For five of them, everything may work fine. However, for the combination (memory limit = 32 MB, max packet size = 64 MB), we have a situation in which a user tries to perform a large database query, and the PHP script will attempt to handle this large data packet. Since the `max_allowed_packet` is set to 64 MB, the MySQL server will accept large queries up to this size. However, the PHP script will not be able to allocate sufficient memory to process the large data packet. This will result in a failure due to a memory allocation error in PHP.

The situation described in the example above was very simple—we dealt with only six possible combinations of two environmental parameters. In reality, environments are often defined by dozens or even hundreds of parameters with many possible values. It is usually impossible for testers to test all combinations of factors considered in testing. To illustrate this, let us consider a simple example involving the FoodApp. Since it is a commercial-off-the-shelf application, it can be used by any user anywhere in the world. We do not know in advance the configurations of devices on which our app will run.

Suppose we want to test the correctness of the FoodApp due to several factors that define the app's environment. Let us assume that we have a set of functional tests that test basic scenarios of system use. We want to run these tests for as many environment configurations as we can. The first environment parameter is the type of device (D) on which the user runs the application. Assume that it can take one of four values: desktop, laptop, tablet, or cell phone. Users can also use different operating systems (OS). Assume that FoodApp can be run under one of the five most popular operating systems: Win 11, Win 10, Linux, Android 14, iOS. The third parameter is the alphabet type (A) that the user uses. Assume it can be one of the following five options: Latin alphabet, Cyrillic alphabet, Arabic alphabet, Hebrew alphabet, and Japanese simplified alphabet. Consider also: 5 possible types of memory (M), 4 possible types of screen size (S), and 4 possible types of processor (P).

To test the FoodApp regarding only the parameter D, we need 4 test cases. If we add the OS parameter, the number of combinations increases from 4 to $4 \cdot 5 = 20$, because the number of combinations results from multiplying the number of possibilities for each parameter. Adding another parameter (A), we get $4 \cdot 5 \cdot 5 = 100$ combinations. As you can see, the number of combinations grows very quickly. This is shown in Fig. 3.8.

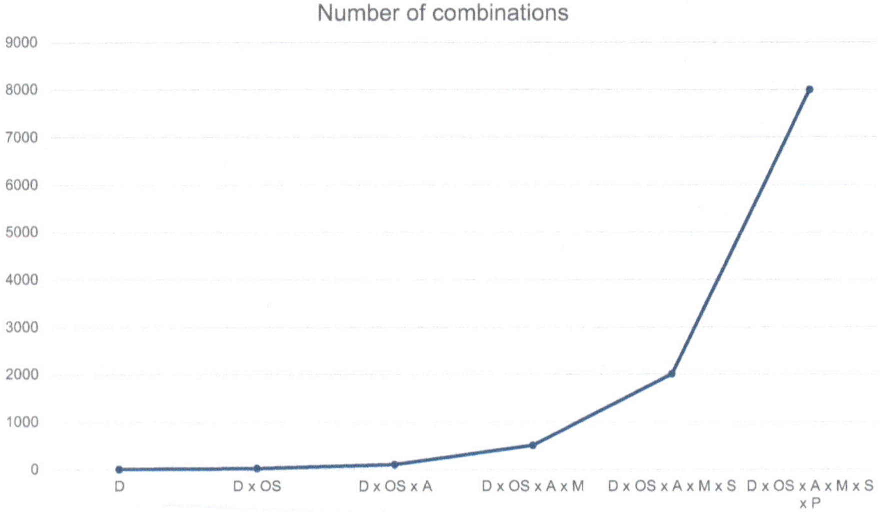


**Fig. 3.8** Combinatorial explosion of configuration parameters for FoodApp

**Combinatorial explosion**. In order to test *all* combinations of *all* identified parameters, we would need $4 \cdot 5 \cdot 5 \cdot 5 \cdot 4 \cdot 4 = 8000$ test cases. This is completely unrealistic. The number of combinations is huge. In testing, such a phenomenon is called a *combinatorial explosion.*

Combinatorial testing is a technique designed to deal with this complexity. The combinatorial coverage criteria that we describe later in this chapter allow us to reduce the number of test cases significantly. However, as the popular proverb says, "There is no such thing as a free lunch." The price we have to pay for test set reduction is that in our tests, we cannot include all possible combinations of all possible values of all parameters. Some combinations will remain untested, but combinatorial techniques allow us to select the set of combinations in such a way that the resulting test set is still capable of detecting many defects.

Another way to deal with the combinatorial explosion is to apply the equivalence partitioning technique beforehand. For example, if a parameter can take a lot of (or even infinitely many) values, we can first use the equivalence partitioning technique [1] to divide the set of possible values into equivalence partitions and then consider representatives of the equivalence partitions as the values of this parameter. For example, if the possible values of the "memory type" parameter are thousands of memory types from different manufacturers, we can divide them into equivalence partitions, for example, by memory capacity, obtaining a small set of values (e.g., 2 GB, 4 GB, 8 GB, 16 GB, 32 GB, 64 GB). Of course, such a decision should be justified by the testing context. If we take care only of the memory size, it may be reasonable. However, if the RAM memory type is also important (e.g., SRAM, DRAM, and ECC), it should not be ignored. In such a case, we can introduce a new parameter, "memory type."

**Configurations representation**. Configurations can be represented in at least two ways. The first one simply involves listing the parameters and their possible values. The second one does the same thing but in the form of a so-called *classification tree*. This is a way to represent the structure of a combinatorial problem graphically. A classification tree consists of:

- a root, representing the entire problem,
- inner vertices, representing the parameters (also called classifiers),
- leaves, representing the possible values of the parameters or equivalence partitions (also called classes).

Notice that classification trees themselves are *not* a test technique. They are merely a form of input representation for a combinatorial testing problem. In order to design test cases, it is still necessary to use the combinatorial test technique associated with a specific coverage criterion (below, we discuss several coverage criteria).

**Classification trees**. Figure 3.9 shows the classification tree for the FoodApp example mentioned earlier. The root represents the entire application. The vertices just below the root represent the individual parameters. The leaves of each of these vertices, in turn, represent all the possible values a parameter can take.

Test cases can be generated based on a given classification tree. Figure 3.10 shows an example of automatic test case generation by the CTE XL tool. The domain consists of three parameters, "Property B," "Property C," and "Property D" with, respectively, 2, 2, and 3 possible values. Vertical lines represent parameter values, and horizontal lines represent individual test cases. A dot at the intersection of lines indicates a concrete parameter value for a test case. For example, the test case called "Partition 1" has the following input data: Property B = "1–4," Property C = "Yes," and Property D = "0."

Classification trees can also be represented in a way that reflects a more precise structure of the problem. In Fig. 3.11, we see a fragment of a tree representing the same configurations as in Fig. 3.9, but with a more detailed division of parameters

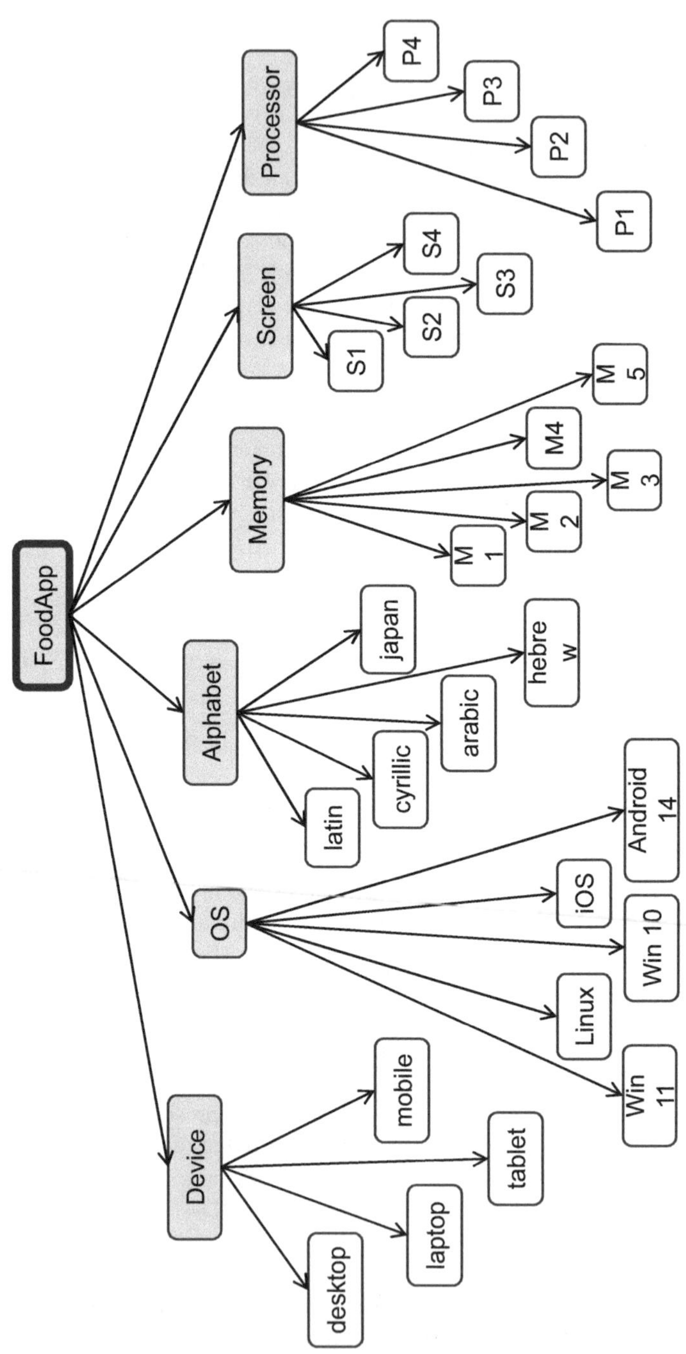


**Fig. 3.9** Classification tree for FoodApp configurations

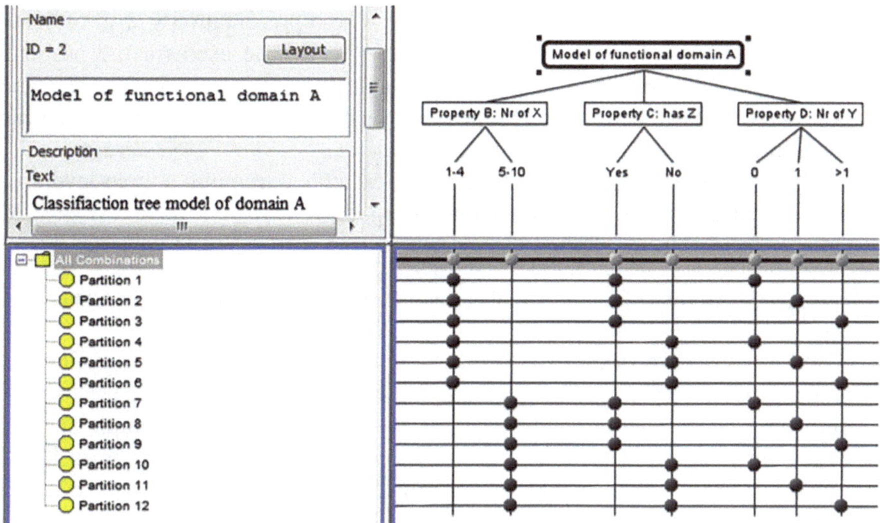


**Fig. 3.10** Test cases generated from a classification tree (from [4])

into "subpartitions." This is analogous to the process of hierarchically dividing equivalence partitions into finer partitions. For example, the parameter "OS" is divided into two types: Windows family and Unix-based. The Windows family is represented with two possible values, Win 11 and Win 10, while Unix-based is represented with three possible values: Linux, iOS, and Android 14. The parameter "Device" is divided into a subcategory "portable" and a single (non-portable) value "desktop." Portable devices can be of three possible types: laptop, mobile, or tablet.

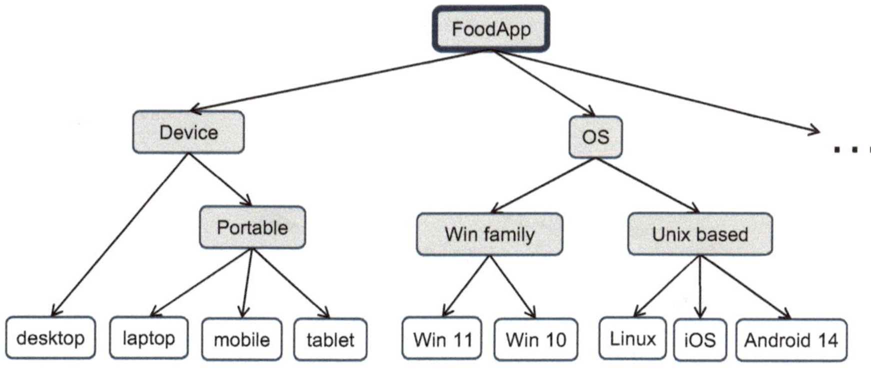


**Fig. 3.11** Fragment of an extensive classification tree for FoodApp configurations

The representation in Fig. 3.11 is equivalent to that in Fig. 3.9. In both cases, each test case will consist of exactly the same set of inputs (a device, an OS, an alphabet, memory type, screen type, and processor type). The representation's level of detail is, therefore, irrelevant to the combinatorial test technique used for the problem represented by the classification tree. It only matters to the tester who creates and analyzes such a classification tree. Sometimes the hierarchical nature of the tree can facilitate the structuring of large, complex problems.

We can always "flatten" the structure of a hierarchical tree into a three-level tree (root, parameters, and values) like the one in Fig. 3.9.

## EXTRA Modeling Constraints Between Parameters: Feature Models

In some cases (like in our FoodApp example), parameters are independent. This means that a test case can contain *any* combination of parameter values. But sometimes, the relations between parameters may be more complicated. For example, some constraints may exist, such as if the "OS" is Android 14, then the "device" must be "mobile" or "tablet." This kind of constraint is often found in so-called software product lines (SPL). A software product line is an engineering approach to create a collection of similar software systems from a shared set of software assets using a common means of production. The concept is analogous to product lines in manufacturing, where a family of related products is produced from a core set of components.

Configurations in SPL can be modeled with a special kind of classification tree called a *feature model*. It is basically a classification tree with some extra notation that allows us to model different dependencies and constraints. Figure 3.12 presents an example of a feature model for online shops based on the example from [5].

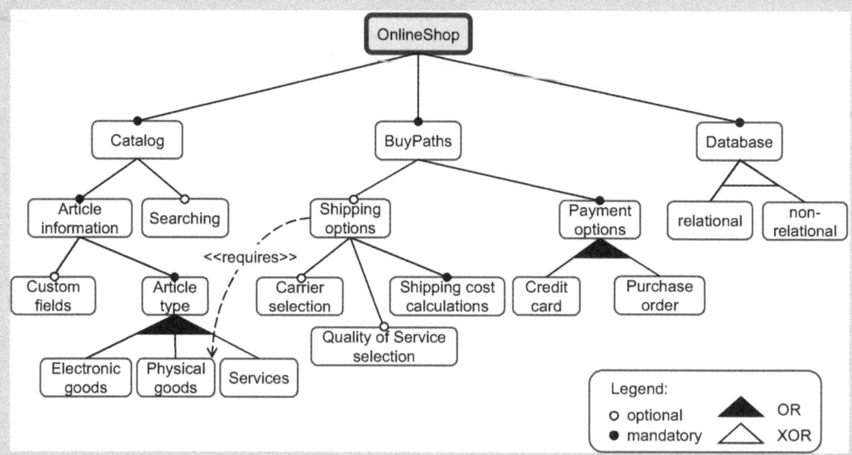


**Fig. 3.12** Feature model for online shops

From the feature model, we see that each online shop must have three features: Catalog, BuyPaths, and Database. The database must be relational or non-relational, and the choice of one of them excludes the other one. The catalog must contain Article information, but the Searching feature is optional. Article information must contain the Article type, which can contain one or more of the three types: electronic goods, physical goods, and services. BuyPaths may contain Shipping options, but if it does, this necessarily requires that physical goods are one of the possible article types.

When the system is modeled with a feature model, the constraints may impact the configurations of parameter values. For example, if we design a test case with Shipping options enabled, we must include both Shipping cost calculations and Physical goods as one of the article types. This impacts the test data, test environment, coverage items, etc.

SPLs can help testers in several ways. It allows the design and implementation of reusable, shared test assets, such as test cases, test scripts, or test data, which can be used across multiple products within the product line. This reduces the time and effort required to create tests for each individual product. Analysis of a feature model can also reduce the redundancy in testing: features that are common across products need to be tested only once (e.g., if all products share the same login module, testing this module once can ensure it works across all products). Common features can also form a base configuration for the base choice coverage (see below).

**PV pairs**. Before we move on to discuss combinatorial coverage criteria, let us introduce the concept of a *parameter-value pair* (or, simply, PV pair). A parameter-value pair is a pair consisting of the name of a parameter and its value. In the example considered above, we considered six different parameters. One of them was the "operating system." Possible values for this parameter are Win 11, Win 10, Linux, Android 14, and iOS. An example of a PV pair could be (operating system, Win 10). PV pair thus represents a specific value of a particular parameter. In combinatorial techniques, the test conditions are specific combinations of PV pairs for different parameters.

The Test Analyst syllabus describes two combinatorial coverage criteria. Let us discuss them in detail.

**Base choice coverage**. This criterion is based on the idea that some parameter-value pairs are more important than others. For each parameter, a base PV pair is selected. First, a base coverage item is designed that combines these base PV pairs. Then, additional coverage items are designed by keeping all but one base PV pair fixed and combining that with each non-base value for the parameter that is varied.

The base choice coverage criterion makes sense when most users use the same or very similar configurations. Let us see how this criterion works in practice. Assume that we are testing a university library system, and we want to perform a test case for lending a book. Let us further assume that each lending is characterized by three parameters in particular:

- reader type (3 possible options): student, Ph.D. student, academic
- limit of borrowed books achieved? (2 possible options): yes, no
- type of loan (3 possible options): ordinary, reading room, reservation

Thus, each test case will be characterized by three parameters: reader type (3 possible options), max limit information (2 possible options), and type of loan (3 possible options). There are $3 \cdot 2 \cdot 3 = 18$ different combinations of these parameters, but the base choice will allow us to reduce the test set size significantly.

Assume that we analyzed the library database and observed that, typically, a student who has not reached the max borrowing limit is borrowing a book to take it home. We therefore create a base test case that represents this configuration:

TC1: reader = student, limit = no, type = ordinary

We create each subsequent test case by replacing the value of one of the parameters in the base case with another value. Since there are two other types of readers besides the student, we add two new test cases, TC2 and TC3, in which we replace the value of the "reader" parameter; the values of the other parameters remain the same (values in bold indicate those that have been changed from the base selection):

TC2: reader = **Ph.D. student**, limit = no, type = ordinary
TC3: reader = **academic**, limit = no, type = ordinary

Next, we modify TC1 regarding the "limit" parameter. Besides the value "no," the only possible value of this parameter is "yes," so we add one test case:

TC4: reader = student, limit = **yes**, type = ordinary

We do the same with the "type" parameter by replacing its value with two others, thus adding thc two new test cases:

TC5: reader = student, limit = no, type = **reservation**
TC6: reader = student, limit = no, type = **reading room**

### Strength of the Base Choice Coverage

Let us analyze the effectiveness of the base choice technique. Assume that 80% of readers are students, 15% are academics, and 5% are Ph.D. students. Only 1% of readers try to borrow a book after reaching the borrowing limit, and in 99% of cases, the limit is not reached. 90% of borrowings are regular, 8% are for the reading room, and 2% are reservations. Let us further assume for the purpose of this analysis that these parameters are independent of each other. Therefore, the probability that a randomly selected borrowing is characterized by specific values of the three parameters (reader = $x$, limit = $y$, type = $z$) is

$p = p(x) \cdot p(y) \cdot p(z)$, where $p(x)$, $p(y)$, $p(z)$ are the probabilities of values $x$, $y$, $z$ occurrence.

Now let us calculate what is the probability $P$ that a randomly selected borrowing is covered by one of the test cases constructed earlier. Let us denote by $P(TC)$ the probability that a borrowing is covered by a test case $TC$. Thus, we have:

$$P = P(TC1) + P(TC2) + P(TC3) + P(TC4) + P(TC5) + P(TC6),$$

where

$P(\text{TC1}) = p(\text{student}) \cdot p(\text{no}) \cdot p(\text{ordinary}) = 0.8 \cdot 0.99 \cdot 0.9 = 0.7128,$
$P(\text{TC2}) = p(\text{PhD student}) \cdot p(\text{no}) \cdot p(\text{ordinary}) = 0.05 \cdot 0.99 \cdot 0.9 = 0.04455,$
$P(\text{TC3}) = p(\text{academic}) \cdot p(\text{no}) \cdot p(\text{ordinary}) = 0.15 \cdot 0.99 \cdot 0.9 = 0.13365,$
$P(\text{TC4}) = p(\text{student}) \cdot p(\text{yes}) \cdot p(\text{ordinary}) = 0.8 \cdot 0.01 \cdot 0.9 = 0.0072,$
$P(\text{TC5}) = p(\text{student}) \cdot p(\text{no}) \cdot p(\text{reading room}) = 0.8 \cdot 0.99 \cdot 0.08 = 0.06336,$
$P(\text{TC6}) = p(\text{student}) \cdot p(\text{no}) \cdot p(\text{reservation}) = 0.8 \cdot 0.99 \cdot 0.02 = 0.01584,$

Hence,

$$P = 0.7128 + 0.04455 + 0.13365 + 0.0072 + 0.06336 + 0.01584 = 0.9774.$$

This means that only six test cases cover almost 98% of combinations of parameter values. Notice that if we want to achieve 100% coverage, we need all $3 \cdot 2 \cdot 3 = 18$ test cases. But only one-third of them cover almost all of the cases. This is due to the fact that there is a high probability that a randomly selected configuration will be the base or "almost" base configuration (i.e., base configuration with only one parameter value replaced with some other value).

In general, when there are $n$ parameters $x_1, \ldots, x_n$, the parameter $x_i$ has $v_i$ possible values, and the parameters are independent (i.e., any combination of their values is feasible), the minimal number of test cases that achieve base choice coverage is equal to

$$1 + \sum_{i=1}^{n} (v_i - 1),$$

because we need one test case for the base configuration, and for each parameter $x_i$ we need to replace the base value with all the remaining $v_i - 1$ values. In the library example we have three parameters with resp. 3, 2, 3 possible values, so, indeed, the number of test cases achieving base choice is $1 + (3 - 1) + (2 - 1) + (3 - 1) = 1 + 2 + 1 + 2 = 6$.

**Pairwise coverage**. In this case, the coverage items are pairs of parameter-value pairs for any two parameters. This criterion assumes that most failures occur due to a specific value of a single parameter or due to the interaction of two parameter values. This result is supported by empirical evidence [6], which shows that about 97% of failures are caused by only one or two interacting parameters. This makes pairwise testing a very effective test technique.

### Pairwise Coverage of Three Parameters with Latin Squares

For the simple case of three parameters, a popular algorithm, inspired by the Latin squares of Swiss mathematician Leonhard Euler (1707–1783), is available that generates a minimal set of PV pairs which achieves pairwise coverage.

First, we sort the parameters in descending order of the number of their possible values, so we assume that for $x_1, x_2, x_3$ we have $v_1 \geq v_2 \geq v_3$. Obviously, the pairwise coverage needs at least $v_1 \times v_2$ PV pairs. Next, we design a table with $v_1$ rows and $v_2$ columns, mark the rows with the values of $x_1$, and the columns with the values of $x_2$.

Then, we fill in the values of $x_3$ into the table row by row. We start with the first value at the beginning of the first row, the second value at the beginning of the second row, and so on. (Note that, in the special case when $v_1 = v_2 = v_3$, this yields a Latin square as studied by Euler, in which every value of $x_3$ occurs exactly once in each row and in each column.) The combinations of row mark, column mark, and cell value then form a minimal set of $v_1 \times v_2$ triples that achieves 100% pairwise coverage of the three parameters.

For example, in a variation of the university library system discussed above, let us assume that each lending is characterized by the following three parameters:

- reader type (4 possible options): student, Ph.D. student, academic, guest
- publication type (3 possible options): book, periodical, audio recording
- loan type (3 possible options): ordinary, reading room, reservation

Since the parameters are in the right order, we can set up the Latin square for reader type and publication type:

| | Book | Periodical | Audio recording |
|---|---|---|---|
| Student | | | |
| PhD student | | | |
| Academic | | | |
| Guest | | | |

Next, we fill in the values of the loan type row by row as indicated:

| | Book | Periodical | Audio recording |
|---|---|---|---|
| Student | Ordinary | Reading room | Reservation |
| PhD student | Reading room | Reservation | Ordinary |
| Academic | Reservation | Ordinary | Reading room |
| Guest | Ordinary | Reading room | Reservation |

This yields a minimal set of 12 combinations (reader type, publication type, loan type) with 100% pairwise coverage:

1. (student, book, ordinary)
2. (student, periodical, reading room)
3. (student, audio recording, reservation)
4. (PhD student, book, reading room)
5. (PhD student, periodical, reservation)
6. (PhD student, audio recording, ordinary)
7. (academic, book, reservation)
8. (academic, periodical, ordinary)
9. (academic, audio recording, reading room)
10. (guest, book, ordinary)
11. (guest, periodical, reading room)
12. (guest, audio recording, reservation)

The problem of finding a *minimal* set of test cases achieving pairwise coverage is, in general, difficult (in terms of theoretical computer science, we say that the decision version of this problem[2] is NP-complete). There are tools available for generating test data. These tools use different heuristics in order to find the best possible solution in a short time. In many cases, they are able to find the optimal solution, but in some cases, they may return a sub-optimal solution (e.g., they may provide the solution with 17 test cases, while the optimal value is 15).

Let us consider an example of a control panel for a smart house, shown in Fig. 3.13. The panel has five switches, and each of them can be either in an ON or OFF state. The panel is used to turn on or off intelligent algorithms that control the operation of five systems: lights in the house, air conditioning, burglar alarm, garden sprinklers, and TV/entertainment.

Suppose we want to test the system's correctness using pairwise testing. Since we have five parameters, each of which can take one of two values, the number of all

[2] A decision version of the problem is as follows: the algorithm takes as an input a configuration data (parameters and their values) and a number N. It should return YES if it is possible to achieve pairwise coverage for the given problem with at most N test cases, and NO otherwise. A problem is NP-complete if a non-deterministic Turing machine could solve it really fast, basically by "guessing" the right solution out of many possibilities and then checking it quickly. However, a real-world computer cannot magically guess, so we do not know whether there is any fast (polynomial-time) algorithm that can solve an NP-complete problem.

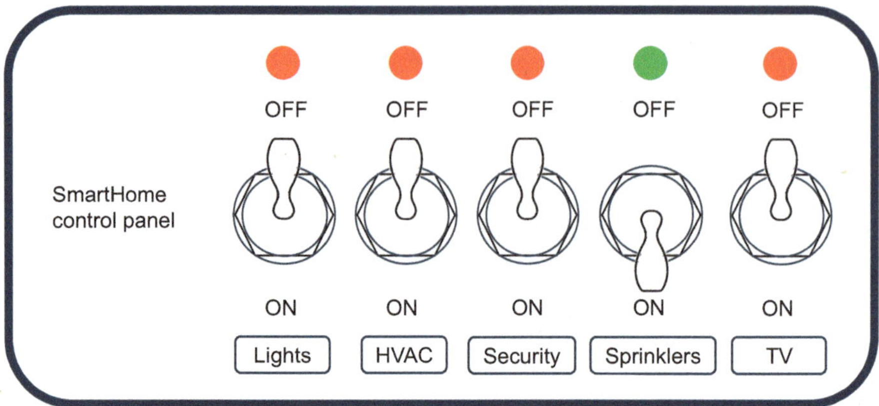


**Fig. 3.13** Control panel for a smart home

combinations of values of these five parameters is $2^5 = 32$. However, the pairwise coverage can be achieved using a much smaller number of test cases.

Consider the test cases shown in Table 3.4. These six test cases achieve pairwise coverage because for each of the two parameters and each combination of their values, there exists at least one test case (a row in the table) covering such a pair. To verify it, let us analyze all 40 coverage items and the corresponding test cases that cover them. The results are shown in Table 3.5. Each entry in the table represents test cases that cover one coverage item.

As we can see, each combination of any two PV pairs for two different parameters is covered by at least one test case. We reduced the number of test cases from 32 to 6. The technique guarantees to achieve pairwise coverage, but it does not guarantee to cover all triplets, quadruplets, etc., of PV pairs. For example, our test set does not cover the combination (Lights = OFF, HVAC = ON, Security = OFF).

As we said before, determining the *minimal* number of test cases that achieve pairwise coverage is, in general, difficult. However, there are simple upper and lower boundaries on the test set size $S$, assuming the parameters are independent. First, notice that since we need to cover all pairs of PV values, we need, in particular, to cover all the combinations for two parameters with the largest number of values.

**Table 3.4** Test cases achieving pairwise coverage for the smart home control panel

| TC | Lights | HVAC | Security | Sprinklers | TV |
|---|---|---|---|---|---|
| TC1 | OFF | OFF | OFF | OFF | OFF |
| TC2 | OFF | ON | ON | ON | ON |
| TC3 | ON | OFF | ON | ON | OFF |
| TC4 | ON | ON | OFF | ON | OFF |
| TC5 | ON | ON | ON | OFF | ON |
| TC6 | OFF | OFF | OFF | ON | ON |

**Table 3.5** Coverage items and corresponding test cases for the smart home control panel

| Parameters pair | Test cases covering the combinations | | | |
|---|---|---|---|---|
| | OFF/OFF | OFF/ON | ON/OFF | ON/ON |
| Lights/HVAC | TC1, TC6 | TC2 | TC3 | TC4, TC5 |
| Lights/security | TC1, TC6 | TC2 | TC4 | TC3, TC5 |
| Lights/sprinklers | TC1 | TC2, TC6 | TC5 | TC3, TC4 |
| Lights/TV | TC1 | TC2, TC6 | TC3, TC4 | TC5 |
| HVAC/security | TC1, TC6 | TC3 | TC4 | TC2, TC4 |
| HVAC/sprinklers | TC1 | TC3, TC6 | TC5 | TC2, TC4 |
| HVAC/TV | TC1, TC3 | TC6 | TC4 | TC2, TC5 |
| Security/sprinklers | TC1 | TC4, TC6 | TC5 | TC2, TC3 |
| Security/TV | TC1, TC4 | TC6 | TC3 | TC2, TC5 |
| Sprinklers/TV | TC1 | TC5 | TC3, TC4 | TC2, TC6 |

Suppose these values are $a$ and $b$. Then, $S \geq a \cdot b$. On the other hand, the number of test cases must be lower than the number of all combinations for all parameters. In case of three or more parameters, it must also be lower than the number of coverage items since each test case covers more than one coverage item.

In our case of a smart house control panel, we have $a = 2$, $b = 2$, so $S \geq 2 \cdot 2 = 4$. We know that we need at least four test cases. On the other hand, $S < 40$, because we have five parameters and there are 40 coverage items. We also have that $S < 2^5 = 32$, because there are 32 combinations of values for all five parameters. This gives us that $4 \leq S \leq 31$. We were able to provide a test set of size 6.

EXTRA

### Other Combinatorial Coverage Criteria

Apart from the two combinatorial coverage criteria described above, many other criteria exist that are not discussed in the Test Analyst syllabus but are used in practice. These are:

**Multiple choice coverage**. This is a generalization of the base choice coverage. Multiple choice coverage assumes there is no one but several base combinations. We need to create test cases for each of them, and then we proceed as in the base choice, i.e., we replace a single parameter value. Consider our university library example and assume we have three base combinations covered by the following test cases:

TC1: reader = student, limit = no, type = ordinary
TC2: reader = academic, limit = no, type = ordinary
TC3: reader = student, limit = no, type = reading room

We now follow the base choice coverage for each of TC1, TC2, and TC3. For TC1, we get the same set of test cases as in the base choice example, that is:

TC4: reader = Ph.D. student, limit = no, type = ordinary
TC5: reader = academic, limit = no, type = ordinary
TC6: reader = student, limit = yes, type = ordinary
TC7: reader = student, limit = no, type = reading room
TC8: reader = student, limit = no, type = reservation
Notice that TC5 is the same as TC2 in the base set, so we do not need to include it in our test set.
For TC2, we obtain the following set of test cases:
TC9: reader = student, limit = no, type = ordinary
TC10: reader = academic, limit = yes, type = ordinary
TC11: reader = academic, limit = no, type = reading room
TC12: reader = academic, limit = no, type = reservation

Again, TC9 is identical to TC1, so we exclude it from our test set to avoid repeating ourselves.

For TC3, we obtain the following set of test cases:

TC13: reader = academic, limit = no, type = reading room
TC14: reader = student, limit = yes, type = reading room
TC15: reader = student, limit = no, type = ordinary
TC16: reader = student, limit = no, type = reservation

Again, TC13 is identical to TC11, TC15 is identical to TC1, and TC16 is identical to TC8.

Hence, we obtain the final set of 11 test cases:

TC1, TC2, TC3, TC4, TC6, TC7, TC8, TC10, TC11, TC12, TC14.

**N-wise coverage** is an extension of pairwise coverage. It requires that every possible N-tuple of values of PV pairs is covered by at least one test case. For instance, in the smart home control panel example, 3-wise coverage would focus on triplets of values for three PV pairs. For the triplet (lights, HVAC, security), the following eight combinations of these values must be covered:

(ON, ON, ON) (ON, ON, OFF) (ON, OFF, ON) (ON, OFF, OFF)
(OFF, ON, ON) (OFF, ON, OFF) (OFF, OFF, ON) (OFF, OFF, OFF)

The greater the *N* is, the more coverage items are required to be covered, and the larger the test set size is. Of this coverage family, the most widely used one is pairwise, that is, 2-wise coverage. Notice that 1-wise coverage is equal to each choice coverage for equivalence partitioning, described in the Foundation Level syllabus [1].

**Case Study**

Sometimes, just applying pairwise testing is not enough. Consider the password validator for the FoodApp system, shown in Fig. 3.14. When users define their passwords, the validation procedure checks whether the password has the correct syntax.

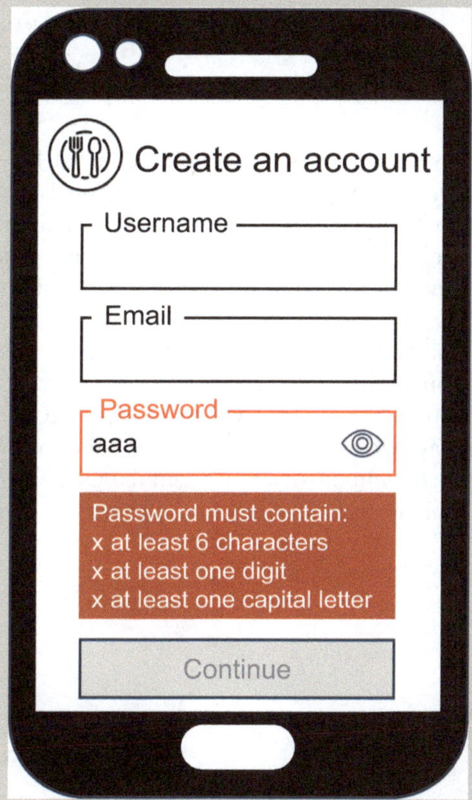


**Fig. 3.14** FoodApp password validator feature

The password has the correct syntax if all of the following conditions are met:

- length condition (L): the password has at least 6 characters,
- digit condition (D): the password has at least one digit,
- capital letter condition (C): the password has at least one capital letter.

Each password is characterized by three parameters: L, D, and C. Each parameter can take one of the two possible values: yes (when the condition is fulfilled) or no (if the condition is not fulfilled). We apply pairwise testing and design the set of test data as shown in Table 3.6.

**Table 3.6** Test data combinations for the password validator, achieving pairwise coverage

| # | L | D | C | Sample password |
|---|---|---|---|---|
| 1 | yes | yes | no | abc123 |
| 2 | yes | no | yes | ABCdef |
| 3 | no | yes | yes | A1 |
| 4 | no | no | no | abc |

It is easy to observe that pairwise coverage is achieved. However, notice that none of these passwords are syntactically correct! This is because, in our test set, we do not have a combination of three "yes." In practice, we would like to test not only the combinations of values for any two properties of a password but also the most natural test condition: check if it is possible to log in with the correct password.

We can fix our test set in at least two ways. The first one is to consider, as one of the test data combinations, the values (L = yes, D = yes, C = yes). This will guarantee that accepting the password will be the expected result for at least one test case. Another way is to add to the existing test suite an additional test case, representing the most common situation when the user enters a syntactically correct password (this is similar to defining a base configuration in the base choice technique).

## Sample Questions

### Question 3.1.2A

You test a computer network characterized by four parameters:

- Protocol—3 possible values: TCP, UDP, ICMP
- Encryption—4 possible values: None, SSL, AES, WPA2
- Authentication—4 possible values: None, Username/Password, Token, Biometric
- Connection speed—3 possible values: Low, Medium, High

You follow the base choice coverage to test the combinations of network configuration parameter values. Historical data suggest that 85% of users use the TCP protocol, SSL encryption, Username/Password authentication, and Medium connection speed.

What is the **MINIMUM** number of configurations that should be tested in order to achieve the required coverage?

(a) 4.
(b) 10.
(c) 11.
(d) 14.

Select ONE answer.

**Question 3.1.2B**

[*Preliminary note on Question 3.1.2B: typical real-exam questions on pairwise testing list an incomplete set of combinations and ask which combinations are required to achieve 100% pairwise coverage. Question 3.1.2B may be more challenging because it requires the reader to design a minimal set of combinations from scratch. However, we have included this question deliberately to demonstrate that it is generally difficult to construct a minimal set of combinations for 100% pairwise coverage.*]

You test a computer network characterized by four parameters:

- Protocol—2 possible values: TCP, UDP
- Encryption—2 possible values: SSL, AES
- Authentication—2 possible values: Token, Biometric
- Connection speed—3 possible values: Low, Medium, High

What is the **MINIMUM** number of configurations that should be tested in order to achieve the full pairwise coverage?

(a) 6.
(b) 7.
(c) 8.
(d) 9.

Select ONE answer.

## Exercise 4—Combinatorial Testing

TA-3.1.2 (K3) Apply combinatorial testing

You are working in a team that develops a web platform with its login system. In the current iteration, your task is to test the login feature. The system's configuration options are as follows:

- 2-factor authentication (Boolean)—enabled/disabled
- allowing "Remember me" function (Boolean)—enabled/disabled
- password expiration policy (Boolean)—active/not active

- account lockout after failed attempts (Boolean)—enabled/disabled
- authentication method (3 values)—password-only, OAuth2, SAML

Each combination of the parameter values is possible. Your team has decided to follow combinatorial testing using the pairwise coverage. Each test case has five values representing the values of the five above-mentioned parameters.

1. What is the total number of all possible combinations of parameter values?
2. What is the total number of pairs that need to be tested to achieve the pairwise coverage?
3. Design the minimal test set that achieves the pairwise coverage.
4. Design the minimal test set that achieves the base choice coverage, assuming the base coverage item is:
   - 2-factor authentication disabled
   - "Remember me" function enabled
   - password expiration policy active
   - account lockout after failed attempts disabled
   - authentication method is password-only

### 3.1.3 *Random Testing*

TA-3.1.3 (K2) Summarize the benefits and limitations of random testing

**Definitions**

**Random testing**: A black-box test technique in which input values are randomly generated.

**Introduction**. Random testing involves selecting test data randomly from the input domain of the test item based on a given probability distribution. The probability distribution can be uniform (i.e., each value is drawn with the same probability) or based on an operational profile, which describes the way users use the system. For validation purposes, a distribution based on operational profiles is recommended. For verification purposes, the distribution should be usage-agnostic to avoid biases.

Random testing comes in several approaches or variations, such as:

- monkey testing—involving the execution of random actions on a test object, usually without reference to specifications, with the intention of causing observable failures

- fuzz testing—delivering high volumes of meaningless data, both correct and incorrect, to the test object; the tool that generates the data (called a fuzzer) may be able to distinguish between correct and incorrect data
- chaos engineering—generating random failures and adverse conditions of the environment at random points in time (e.g., intentionally disabling computers, simulating server outages, etc.)
- generating random test data in other test design techniques—for example, using equivalence partitioning [1], one representative must be selected for testing for each partition, and this representative can be chosen randomly

Some authors equate monkey testing and fuzz testing. Others distinguish between the two by saying that monkey testing refers to random actions when using the test object, while fuzz testing refers to generating random inputs.

**Faker—A Python Library for Random Test Data Generation**

There are many programming libraries that help testers with random test data generation. An example may be the Python library called `Faker`. It is able to generate different random data that looks like the real data, so the generated name will look like "John Smith" and not like "dH&sdh js2*sa". For example, when the test analyst wants to generate five datasets containing name, surname, and US address, they can write a script like the one shown in Fig. 3.15.

genRandomData.py

```python
from faker import Faker
fake = Faker()

for i in range(1, 6):
    print("Test data - set", i)
    print("Name: ", fake.name())
    print("Address: ", fake.address(), "\n")
```

**Fig. 3.15** A script for generating random names and addresses using Python's `Faker` library

This simple script generates five datasets with random names (generated by the `fake.name()` function) and random addresses (generated by the `fake.address()` function). The result of the script execution is shown below.

```
D:\FoodAppTesting>genRandomData.py
Test data - set 1
Name: Keith Bailey
Address: 325 Julia Glen
Kimberlyborough, NH 17807
```

```
Test data - set 2
Name: Lindsay King
Address: 4823 Best Fall
Clayfort, AS 81839
Test data - set 3
Name: Kayla Sanchez
Address: 210 Carolyn Stravenue
East Malloryberg, NC 92219
Test data - set 4
Name: Julie Wong
Address: 95855 Luna Mills Suite 231
Perkinsmouth, WI 50663
Test data - set 5
Name: Mrs. Melissa Neal
Address: 0106 Barbara Skyway
North Sheilatown, SD 84017
```

In random testing, each test run will have different inputs and provide different actual results. However, testers might want to be able to verify if the same inputs produce the same actual results. This requires using the same set of randomly generated input and output data in each test run. Random generators have a feature that allows them to do that. It is called a *seed*. It is an initial value used to initialize a pseudo-random number generator. The seed determines the sequence of numbers that the generator will produce. For example, if we add a line "`Faker.seed(182)`" after line 2 in the script from Fig. 3.15, the generator will always generate exactly the same set of data. This allows reproducibility in test execution.

**Oracle problem**. In general, the process of generating random data is easy. However, each test case should also include the expected results. This necessitates a test oracle. If we do not have an automated test oracle, we must provide (manually or semi-automatically) the expected results for test cases, which may be difficult and time-consuming. Therefore, special attention must be paid to the availability of an automated test oracle when performing random testing. The presence of an oracle problem can make random testing inefficient (see Sect. 1.3.4).

In some cases, it is possible to provide a test oracle easily, for example:

- when the correctness of the program's output can be easily verified (for example, if a string of numbers is given to the input, and on the output, the program is supposed to return the same string sorted in ascending order, the correctness of sorting can be easily verified)
- when the input can be easily generated on the basis of the output (e.g., if we are testing a program that calculates the square root, verification of the correctness of the operation consists of raising the value from the output to the square and assimilating it to the input data).

**Guided and unguided random testing**. Random testing can be guided or unguided. In unguided random testing, the probability distribution remains fixed throughout the process. Guided random testing, exemplified by techniques like Adaptive Random Testing (ART) [7], adjusts the distribution based on previously selected values, evolving over time. Guided testing aims to cover the input domain efficiently, considering that defects often cluster in specific domain regions.

ART is an attempt to improve random testing so as to minimize the risk of generating a bad set of input data (i.e., one that fails to detect an existing problem in the test object). ART is based on the concept of the so-called failure pattern. Empirical data indicate that areas of the input domain corresponding to software malfunctions tend to form dense, uniform regions [8] like the ones presented in Fig. 3.16.

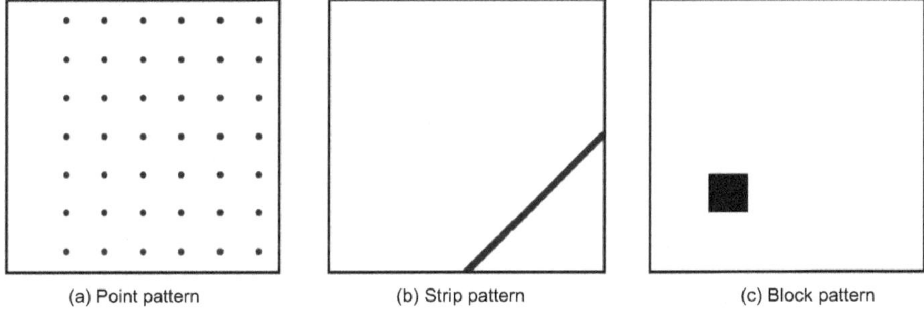


**Fig. 3.16** Examples of patterns of failure-causing inputs

For the ART approach, there are several strategies for generating domain coverage that is "even" and, at the same time, gives a high chance to detect anomalies like the ones from Fig. 3.16:

- Fixed Size Candidate Setthe next input data is generated by generating $k$ random inputs, calculating the closest distance of each input to existing ones, and selecting the one with the greatest distance (see Fig. 3.17a–c),
- Restricted Random Testing—for each drawn input data, an "exclusion region" is created around it; new input data are drawn from areas outside the exclusion regions (see Fig. 3.17d–e),
- Random Partitioning—the drawn point divides the domain into regions, and the next point is drawn from the largest region (see Fig. 3.17f–h).

Notice that the ART approach is an example of guided random testing. In each step, the probability distribution is not uniform for the whole domain. For example, in Fig. 3.17d, initially, the probability is uniform across the whole area. But after drawing the first point, the probability that the next point will be within the dashed circle is set to 0, while for the remaining area, it remains uniform.

**Coverage**. Random testing lacks recognized coverage criteria. Therefore, the exit criteria can only rely on the number of tests executed, testing time, or another measure of completion.

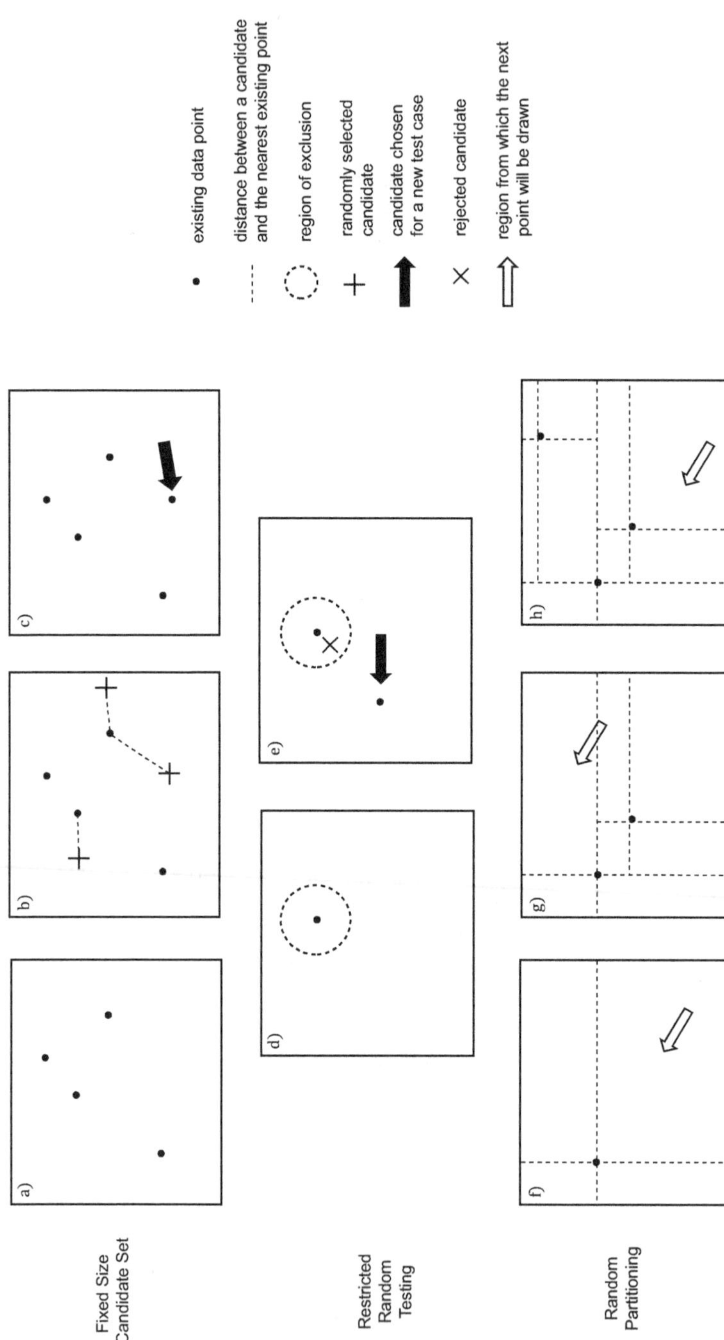


**Fig. 3.17** Three variants of adaptive random testing

**Applications**. Random testing is a valuable technique in various contexts due to its ability to identify unexpected problems. It helps to avoid biases such as overlooking defects in manual testing due to misplaced trust in some code. Below, we present several scenarios where random testing can be particularly beneficial:

- Limited domain knowledge, especially when there is a need for a large volume of test data, such as in performance testing. It is cost-effective and provides, in probabilistic terms, insights into test object reliability.
- Complex systems, where the number of possible states, inputs, or configurations is extremely large, and it is impractical to test all combinations.
- Early development stages, when the code is rapidly changing. At this stage, random testing can identify major issues without the need for comprehensive test cases, which saves time and makes testing more efficient.
- Testing non-deterministic systems. For systems where behavior might vary with different inputs, such as those involving machine learning or AI, random testing can provide a broad spectrum of scenarios to ensure the system's consistent performance.
- Exploratory testing. When a test analyst wants to explore the behavior of the system in an unscripted manner, random testing can help them generate diverse inputs that might reveal unexpected behaviors.

**Challenges**. Random testing is useful in many situations, but it also has a number of challenges, including neglecting data semantics, potentially missing defects related to data meaning, overlooking certain defects, generating redundant tests, dependency on an automated test oracle, and random inputs leading to test flakiness. Balancing the advantages and limitations of random testing is essential in each testing context.

**Effectiveness**. Traditionally, random testing has been considered less effective than other test techniques. In recent years, this hypothesis has been investigated in numerous empirical studies. The finding is that under the circumstances mentioned above, random testing can be more effective and efficient than other data-based test techniques [9, 10].

**Case Study**

A part of FoodApp's ordering process is presented in Fig. 3.18. After logging in, users can search for restaurants, or they can display their last order. From the historical data, we know that 90% of users will select the first option, and only 10% will go with the second one. We have such data on probabilistic distributions of the next action for all steps of the process, as shown in Fig. 3.18. For example, 95% of payments are successful, but in 5% of cases, the payment cannot be realized, and the process goes back to the "place order" step. Notice that for each state, the probabilities of outgoing transitions sum up to 100%.

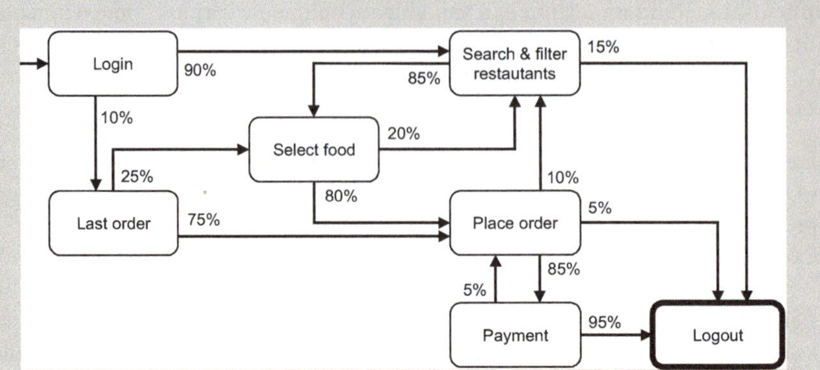


**Fig. 3.18** Operational profile for the food ordering process in FoodApp

The test analyst can write a script that simulates the user's behavior. The script executes an appropriate test case when entering a given step and then randomly chooses the next step, using the appropriate probability distribution as shown in Fig. 3.18.

An example script is presented in Fig. 3.19.

```python
import numpy as np

class WalkthroughModel:
    def __init__(self, transition_matrix, states):
        self.transition_matrix = np.array(transition_matrix)
        self.states = states
        self.state_index = {state: index for index, state in enumerate(states)}
        self.current_state = states[0] # Initial state is Login

    def next_state(self):
        current_index = self.state_index[self.current_state]
        next_state_index = np.random.choice(
            len(self.states), p=self.transition_matrix[current_index]
        )
        self.current_state = self.states[next_state_index]
    # Here execute a test case corresponding to self.current_state
        return self.current_state

    def simulate(self, steps):
        chain = [self.current_state]
        for _ in range(steps - 1):
            chain.append(self.next_state())
        return chain

# Define states and transition matrix
states = ['Login', 'Search', 'LastOrder', 'SelectFood', 'PlaceOrder', 'Pay', 'Logout']
transition_matrix = [
    [0.0, 0.9, 0.1, 0.0, 0.0, 0.0, 0.0],  # Probabilities from state Login
    [0.0, 0.0, 0.0, 0.85, 0.0, 0.0, 0.15],  # Probabilities from state Search
    [0.0, 0.0, 0.0, 0.25, 0.75, 0.0, 0.0],  # Probabilities from state LastOrder
    [0.0, 0.20, 0.0, 0.0, 0.80, 0.0, 0.0],  # Probabilities from state SelectFood
    [0.0, 0.1, 0.0, 0.0, 0.0, 0.85, 0.05],  # Probabilities from state PlaceOrder
    [0.0, 0.0, 0.0, 0.0, 0.05, 0.0, 0.95],  # Probabilities from state Pay
    [1.0, 0.0, 0.0, 0.0, 0.0, 0.0, 0.0]   # Probabilities from state Logout
]

# Initialize the model
wm = WalkthroughModel(transition_matrix, states)

# Simulate for 20 steps
simulation_result = wm.simulate(20)
print("Simulated user's walkthrough:", simulation_result)
```

**Fig. 3.19** A script for generating random users' behavior

The walkthrough model is defined by a set of states and a transition matrix that represents probabilities of transitions between states. The function `next_state` calculates for a given state the next state with the probability distribution defined for the current state. The commented line should be replaced with a code that executes a test case related to a calculated state. The next state is chosen randomly using the function `random.choice` from the `numpy` library. Its parameter is the row of the transition matrix that represents the probability distribution for the current state. The function `simulate` runs the model for a defined number of steps. The transition matrix is defined based on the model from Fig. 3.18. After executing the script, we get the following results:

```
D:\FoodAppTesting>randomWalk.py
Simulated user's walkthrough: ['Login', 'Search', 'Select-
Food', 'PlaceOrder', 'Logout', 'Login', 'Search', 'Select-
Food', 'PlaceOrder', 'Logout', 'Login', 'Search', 'Logout',
'Login', 'Search', 'Logout', 'Login', 'Search', 'SelectFood',
'PlaceOrder']
```

Of course, another execution would result in a different scenario. As we see, the script simulated a random sequence of steps: after logging in, the user searches for food, then selects the food, places the order, and logs out; next, they log in again, search for food, select food, etc. Notice that since the probabilities reflect the real behavior of users, the generated scenarios will “mimic” these behaviors. That is why the most natural sequence of steps (placing an order successfully) will occur most often.

## Sample Questions

### Question 3.1.3A

You use random testing, in which the test data (natural numbers) are generated by the following procedure:

1. Draw a number from the set {1, 2, ..., 10}
2. Draw a number from the set {x + 1, x + 2, ..., x + 10}, where x is the last number drawn
3. Repeat step 2 a hundred times

What kind of random testing is used here and why?

(a) Guided random testing, because the probability of drawing a given number may change.

(b) Guided random testing, because each number is drawn from a specific range of numbers.

(c) Unguided random testing, because we are sure that no number drawn will be repeated.
(d) Unguided random testing, because there is a limited number of iterations.

Select ONE answer.

**Question 3.1.3B**

Which of the following is an advantage of random testing?

(a) It is dependent on an automated test oracle.
(b) It has a well-defined, easy-to-compute coverage criterion.
(c) It does not take into account data semantics.
(d) It can be used when domain knowledge is limited.

Select ONE answer.

## 3.2 Behavior-Based Test Techniques

### *3.2.1 CRUD Testing*

TA-3.2.1 (K2) Explain CRUD testing

**Definitions**

**CRUD testing**: A black-box test technique in which test conditions are operations of the types create, read, update, and delete for an entity.

**Introduction**. CRUD testing verifies the lifecycle of entities processed by the test item. This technique can be applied to a wide range of applications and systems where data management and data manipulation are crucial. Examples of such systems include:

- content management systems (CMS), which process entities such as articles, pages, or files,
- customer relationship management systems (CRM), which process entities such as clients, accounts, and messages,
- e-commerce platforms, which process entities such as users, orders, invoices, or reviews,
- inventory management systems, which process entities such as stock items, suppliers, orders, or shipments.

The vast majority of information systems operate on data, which is processed intensively by the system's functions. These functions perform various types of operations on the data. CRUD testing verifies the correctness of performing these operations in the context of the entity's entire lifecycle.

CRUD is an acronym that stands for Create, Read, Update, and Delete. These are the four basic operations that functions (e.g., features, use cases, user stories, procedures, methods in object-oriented design) can perform on entities.

**CRUD matrix**. The lifecycle of the entities is represented by a CRUD matrix. Its columns represent the entities, and its rows represent functions. If a function executes one or more particular operations on a given entity, this is shown in the matrix by means of the initials of these operations: C, R, U, or D. To create a CRUD matrix, the test analyst determines, for each function:

- which entities are used by this function,
- which operations (C, R, U, D) are carried out on these entities.

Let us consider an example of a system that supports the work of a scientific journal's editorial board. The author, having written an article, sends it to the editor. The editor can send the article to selected reviewers. The reviewers write reviews, and the editor, based on these reviews, makes the final decision to accept or reject the article. If accepted, the editor signs a publishing contract with the author. Once the contract is signed, the website administrator adapts the article to the editorial requirements of the journal and publishes it on the site.

We can distinguish the following functions used to perform the above operations:

- Write—a function used by an author
- Edit—a function used by an editor
- Review—a function used by a reviewer
- Publish—a function used by a web administrator

and entities on which the functions operate:

- Article
- Review
- Contract

The test analyst, together with the architects, can analyze which operations on the entities can be performed by which roles. For example, the author deals with articles, reviews, and contracts. The author should always be able to create, read, and update their article in the system, but if they want to resign from the publication, they can ask the editor to remove their paper from the system. Authors can only read the reviews of their articles. Regarding contracts, they can only read them or sign them (update). The same analysis is carried out for all the other functions and entities. Table 3.7 presents the results of the analysis for our system in the form of a full CRUD matrix. A dash symbol means that a given entity is not used by a given function. For example, a web administrator does not use reviews or contracts.

CRUD matrix is useful for several reasons. CRUD matrix:

**Table 3.7** CRUD matrix for the system supporting the scientific journal's editorial board

| | Article | Review | Contract |
|---|---|---|---|
| Write | C, R, U | R | R, U |
| Edit | R, D | R, D | C, R, U, D |
| Review | R | C, R, U | – |
| Publish | R, U | – | – |

- provides a clear way to visualize which operations are allowed on each entity,
- helps define the responsibilities of different functions regarding data manipulation,
- allows the test analyst to verify that all necessary CRUD operations on entities have been identified and implemented,
- helps in identifying any gaps or missing functionalities or data operations in the requirements,
- aids in setting appropriate access controls by specifying who (or which function) can perform which operation on each entity.

Lifecycles of entities can be CRUD tested at least twofold: by completeness check and by consistency testing.

**Completeness check**. It is a static test that is based on an analysis of the CRUD matrix. It verifies that all four operations are defined for each entity. It is, therefore, a form of verification of lifecycle completeness for each entity. However, the absence of an operation does not necessarily mean that the system is flawed. Consider again the example of a system supporting a scientific journal editorial office. Imagine that the client requires that the submitted articles may be archived, but never deleted. Then, for the entity "article," the CRUD matrix will contain only three types of operations: Create, Read, and Update. Similarly, some static entities, such as a geographic area, might be created, read, and deleted, but never updated. Therefore, a test analyst should investigate deviations from completeness as anomalies and evaluate whether they are actual gaps or intentional.

**Consistency testing**. This dynamic test is focused on verifying the integration of various functions. The consistency test verifies that different functions use an entity in a consistent way. Failures detected in consistency testing can be, for example, that a specific entity was incorrectly processed by a function, causing another function, applying a specific CRUD operation on that entity, to work incorrectly. Test cases are derived by putting together the entire lifecycle of an entity. This is done as follows [11]:

- Every test case starts with a "C," followed by all the possible "U"s, and ends with a "D." If further possibilities exist for creating or removing an entity, additional test cases are designed.
- After every "C," "U," or "D" action, an "R" is carried out once or more. This is to establish that the entity has been correctly processed and is usable for the other functions (i.e., has not been corrupted).
- The test cases should cover all the occurrences of actions (C, R, U, and D) in all the functions of the relevant entity.

Consider again the CRUD matrix for our editorial office supporting system and, for the sake of simplicity, let us restrict ourselves only to testing the "article" entity. It can be created by one role, four roles can read it, it can be updated by two roles, and it can be deleted by one role. All these eight operations need to be tested. We can do it with the following two test cases (for the sake of simplicity, we only present the general description of test steps, ignoring preconditions, expected results, postconditions, etc.):

Test case 1: rejection of an article

- Author uploads the article to the system (Write, C)
- Author reads the article before the final acceptance (Write, R)
- Author updates the article and submits it (Write, U)
- Editor reads the article (Edit, R)
- Editor decides to desk reject the article (Edit, D)
- Editor verifies that the article is deleted (Edit, R)

Test case 2: publication and removal of an article

- Author uploads the article to the system and submits it (Write, C)
- Editor reads the article and sends it to the reviewer (Edit, R)
- Reviewer reads the article and accepts it (Review, R)
- Editor reads the article and sends it to the web administrator (Edit, R)
- Web administrator reads the article (Publish, R)
- Web administrator modifies the text to meet the journal formatting (Publish, U)
- Web administrator publishes the article, and reads it on the webpage (Publish, R)
- Editor removes the article (Edit, D)
- Editor verifies that the article is deleted (Edit, R)

Notice that these two test cases follow the procedure described above. Each operation performed by each role has been tested at least once. Also, after each "C," "U," and "D," an "R" operation is performed. In the last test step in test case 1, the editor performs an "R" after a "D." This action could, for example, confirm that the article we just deleted is no longer in the article database.

**More thorough coverage for consistency testing** can be achieved by requiring that certain combinations of actions also be fully covered. For example, we may require that after each "U," all the functions with an "R" should be carried out. More thorough coverage helps test analysts detect more defects that could be otherwise missed. An example is shown below.

**Case Study**

Consider our FoodApp. Suppose that the entity "order" is processed as follows by the following functions:

- Create order (C)—operation done by a client
- Cancel order (D)—operation performed by a client, delivery person, or restaurant
- Change order status (U)—performed by a delivery person and restaurant between placing and final execution of the order (i.e., between creating the order and its delivery to the customer)
- Overview of orders (R)—performed by a client
- Check status (R)—performed by a delivery person or restaurant

The test analyst prepared the following standard CRUD test:

| | |
|---|---|
| 1. Create order | (C) |
| 2. Check status | (R) |
| 3. Change order status | (U) |
| 4. Overview of orders | (R) |
| 5. Cancel order | (D) |
| 6. Overview of orders | (R) |

Suppose there is a defect in the system: after changing the order status (e.g., from "new" to "being prepared"), the check status function no longer works correctly, because it is (wrongly) treating the whole order as being delivered. This defect would not be found with the above-mentioned test case. However, applying more thorough coverage may do the trick. Suppose we require that *all* "R"s are carried out after each "C," "U," or "D." The modified test case would look like this:

| | | |
|---|---|---|
| 1. Create order | (C) | |
| 2. Overview of orders | (R) | |
| 3. Check status | (R) | |
| 4. **Change order status** | **(U)** | **(causes a failure in "Check status")** |
| 5. Overview of orders | (R) | |
| 6. **Check status** | **(R)** | **(the failure is found)** |
| 7. Cancel order | (D) | |
| 8. Overview of orders | (R) | |
| 9. Check status | (R) | |

## Sample Questions

### Question 3.2.1A

Which of the following correctly describes the purpose of CRUD testing?

(a) Verifying if all possible operations on entities occur with every entity
(b) Verifying the correct behavior of a system when different events occur
(c) Verifying that business rules are implemented correctly
(d) Distributing tests among a group of testers of diverse backgrounds

Select ONE answer.

### Question 3.2.1B

What is the CRUD matrix modeling?

(a) Transitions between different data operations.
(b) Sequences of operations performed by functions on entities.
(c) Equivalence partitioning of a data domain.
(d) Lifecycle of the data entities.

Select ONE answer.

### *3.2.2 State Transition Testing*

TA-3.2.2 (K3) Apply state transition testing

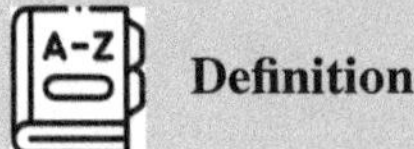

**State transition testing**: A black-box test technique in which test cases are designed to exercise elements of a state transition model.

**Introduction**. Most real-life systems are stateful, i.e., their behavior depends to a certain extent on their state. A state refers to the stored information or data that represents the system's current condition or context at a given time. For example, the state of a web dialog application could be determined by the screen that the user currently encounters. Some key aspects of what a stateful behavior of a system entails are:

- **Data persistence**. The system maintains information about past interactions or transactions. A state represents its memory. Information can be stored in memory, databases, files, or other storage mechanisms. In a state transition model, it is modeled by the fact that the system stays in a certain state for a certain amount of time.
- **Contextual information**. The state contains information that provides context for current operations. For example, the state of a user's session in a web application might include login status, preferences, and shopping cart contents.
- **Influence on behavior**. The current state can affect how the system responds to a new event. For example, a vehicle's response to pressing the start/stop button depends on its operating state (whether the key is present and whether the engine is idle or running).
- **State transitions**. States can change over time due to events or input data. Transitions are governed by defined rules or logic in the system. Transitions are usually assumed to occur instantaneously.

**State transition models**. In software engineering, there are many different types of state transition models. The common examples include finite state machines (FSM) [12], extended finite state machines (EFSM) [13], or Harel statecharts [14]. These models differ in their expressive power. FSM is the simplest model, consisting of states and transitions labeled with input signals called events and (optionally) outputs, called actions. EFSM extends this model to include so-called guard conditions. It also allows the use of variables and operations on them, which increases the possibility of modeling system memory. These additions often make it possible to significantly simplify the system diagram created with FSM. Harel statecharts allow for modeling the hierarchy of states (so-called super-states), the independence of events through parallelized computation (orthogonality), and so-called general transitions, simplifying the diagram. There are many other models, like sequence diagrams, activity diagrams, Petri nets [15], etc. Standards such as UML [16] also include models of state diagrams.

Since the Foundation Level syllabus refers to EFSM, we will discuss this state transition model in detail.

**Extended Finite State Machines**. FSM becomes difficult to use and understand as the number of states and transitions increases. Since the only form of memory in the FSM is the state of the system, it is often necessary to use multiple states to model even simple systems. For example, if we are modeling an elevator and want to remember the floor the elevator is on, we need at least as many states as there are floors. EFSM, through the use of variables and guard conditions, allows a significant reduction in the number of states in the model. EFSM also allows us to label transitions with no events but with guard conditions only, making the model more readable in some situations.

Let us describe the EFSM model using a simple example of a finite buffer. A buffer is a queue of items with two possible operations: *insert*, which inserts an element at the rear of the queue, and remove, which deletes an element from the front of the queue. The only observable states of our interest are those that correspond to empty and non-empty buffers. We also want to model the number of elements in a buffer. This information will be stored in a variable *size*. We assume the buffer is finite, which means that it can store only a certain number of elements. This number will be modeled by a constant *max*. We assume that *max* is a positive integer ($max \geq 1$).

The EFSM model of the buffer is shown in Fig. 3.20. The model consists of two states: *Empty* and *Non-empty*. The initial state is *Empty*. If the system is in this state and an *insert* event occurs, the system goes to the *Non-empty* state and sets the value of the *size* variable to 1, since there is now one element in the buffer. Being in the *Non-empty* state, the system remains in it when more elements are inserted into the buffer. Each time, the *size* variable increases by one (*size*++). However, this transition can only be executed if the guard condition [$size < max$] is true. If it is false, it means that the buffer is full, and the next *insert* event will have no effect on the system.

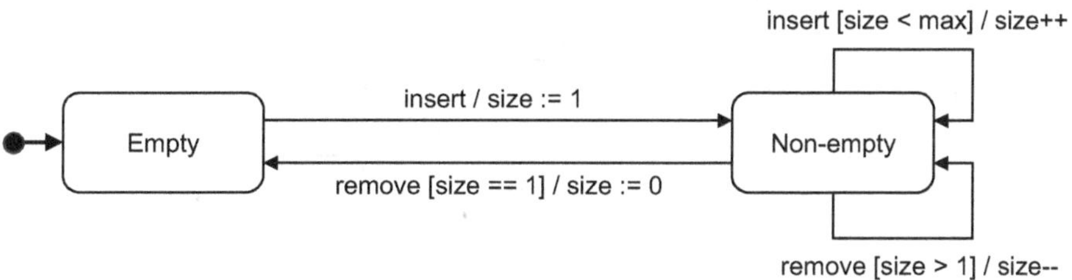


**Fig. 3.20** Extended finite state machine for a finite buffer

When the system is in the *Non-empty* state, and the *remove* event occurs, two possible situations can happen:

1. There is only one element in the buffer. This means the guard condition [*size==1*] is true, so the transition to the *Empty* state will be executed, and the *size* variable will take the value 0.
2. There is more than one element in the buffer. This means the guard condition [*size > 1*] is true, so the system stays in the *Non-empty* state and decreases *size* by 1 (*size--*).

In general, an EFSM model consists of the following elements:

- states, including the initial state and, optionally, one or more final states,
- transitions, labeled by events, guards, and/or actions.

A typical test case exercises a path in the model, consisting of a sequence of states, the transitions between every two consecutive states, and the events that trigger them. A usual precondition is that the system is in the initial state, but in general, the system may start its operation in an arbitrary state before test execution. If a system arrives at a final state, the system ends its execution. This means that a test case must end when its path arrives at a final state. In the case of our finite buffer from Fig. 3.20, there is no final state, so we assume the system runs indefinitely.

All elements of transition labels are optional, but the label must contain at least an event or a guard condition. Otherwise, we could not decide when a transition should be made. All the possible labeling options are shown in Fig. 3.21.

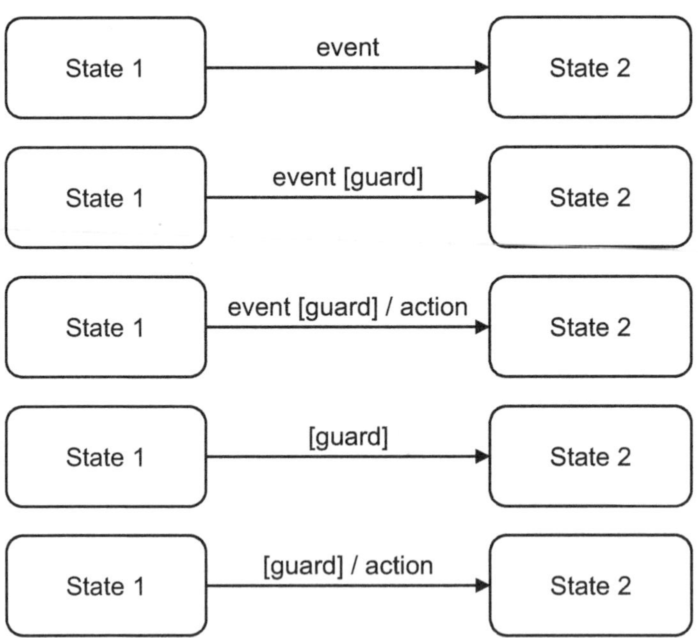


**Fig. 3.21** Possible transition labelings in EFSMs

**State table**. State diagrams are usually represented graphically, as in Fig. 3.20. However, there is an equivalent form of presentation, called a state table. The state table for the EFSM in Fig. 3.20 is shown in Table 3.8. The individual rows of the state table correspond to states, and the columns correspond to transitions. The cell at the intersection of the row corresponding to state S and the column corresponding to event E represents a transition on the state diagram. It contains the target state (after being in S when E occurred) and the action, if defined.

**EFSMs and testing**. EFSM is a very popular model for software systems, so test analysts often use it to design test cases. In test design, the test analyst defines the appropriate coverage criteria based on the risk, test objectives, and the kind of model used.

The idea of testing based on the state transition model is to verify the *behavior* of the system under the influence of various events. Let us consider an example of the FoodApp application model from Fig. 3.26 on page 38. In this system, an event *modify* may occur, but the system's behavior under this event should be different, depending on the state the system was in when this event was triggered. For example, if the system were in the Last order state, the test analyst expects that the system goes to the *Select food* state. However, if the system was in the *Place order* state, the occurrence of the *modify* event should result in a state change to *Search & filter restaurants*.

A variety of coverage criteria have been proposed for the state transition model. The Foundation Level syllabus [1] discusses three relatively simple ones: all states coverage, valid transitions coverage (also called 0-switch coverage), and all transitions coverage. It notes that valid transitions coverage subsumes all states coverage and is the most widely used coverage criterion. The Test Analyst syllabus introduces two additional, more advanced coverage criteria that have been empirically proven to have high defect detection effectiveness: $N$-switch coverage and round-trip coverage. We will now explore these coverage criteria in detail.

**N-switch coverage**. Let N be a positive integer. An N-switch is a path in the state model with $N + 1$ consecutive events. An N-switch can be understood as a sequence of $N + 2$ states, where each successive state results from the previous state via a transition initiated by a corresponding event. The value N is the number of intermediate states on this path, which are also called switches.

Consider a state diagram for the so-called Circuit Breaking Pattern, shown in Fig. 3.22. Figure 3.23 shows examples of 0-switch, 1-switch, and 2-switch.

**Table 3.8** State table for the finite buffer system

| State\event | Insert | Insert [size < max] | Remove [size == 1] | Remove [size >1] |
|---|---|---|---|---|
| Empty | Non-empty/size := 1 | | | |
| Non-empty | | Non-empty/size++ | Empty/size := 0 | Non-empty/size-- |

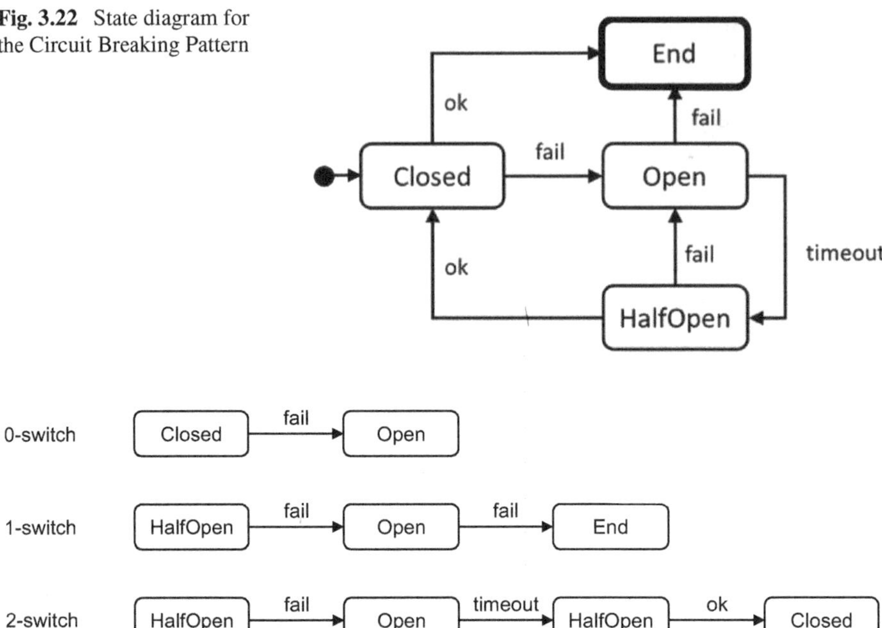


**Fig. 3.22** State diagram for the Circuit Breaking Pattern

**Fig. 3.23** Examples of 0-switch, 1-switch, and 2-switch for the Circuit Breaking Pattern

For example, the sequence *HalfOpen*, *Open*, *HalfOpen*, *Closed*, starting with the state *HalfOpen* and triggered by the events *fail*, *timeout*, and OK, is a 2-switch because there are two intermediate states (*Open* and *HalfOpen*) between the first one (*HalfOpen*) and the last one (*Closed*).

The N-switch coverage measures the percentage of N-switches exercised in a state model. 100% N-switch coverage requires that test cases cover all N-switches. Therefore, the test analyst must be able to determine them. Determining 0-switches is very simple—they are simply the valid transitions in the state diagram. For example, the diagram in Fig. 3.22 has six 0-switches (the notation S (E) T used below means the transition from S to T by event E):

- *Closed (ok) End*
- *Closed (fail) Open*
- *Open (fail) End*
- *Open (timeout) HalfOpen*
- *HalfOpen (ok) Closed*
- *HalfOpen (fail) Open*

Determining 1-switches is also easy. For each state, consider all incoming and all outgoing transitions (Fig. 3.24) and combine them in every possible way. In Fig. 3.24, the 1-switches are all $n \cdot m$ sequences of states of the form $R_i \rightarrow S \rightarrow T_j$) for all $1 \leq i \leq n$ and $1 \leq j \leq m$.

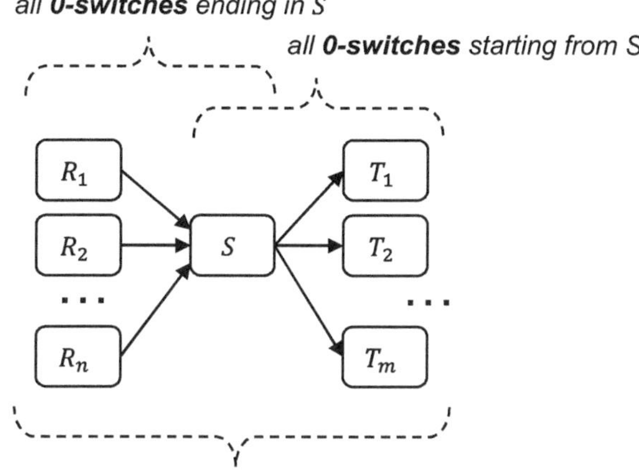


**Fig. 3.24** Determining all 1-switches from 0-switches for a given state

Consider the Circuit Breaking Pattern from Fig. 3.22 again. There are eight 1-switches in total:

- two 1-switches for the state *Closed*, because there is one incoming transition from *HalfOpen* and two outgoing transitions to *End* and to *Open*; the 1-switches are *HalfOpen* (*ok*) *Closed* (*ok*) *End*, *HalfOpen* (*ok*) *Closed* (*fail*) *Open*;
- four 1-switches for the state *Open*, because there are two incoming and two outgoing transitions from it; the 1-switches are: *HalfOpen* (*fail*) *Open* (*fail*) *End*, *HalfOpen* (*fail*) *Open* (*timeout*) *HalfOpen*, *Closed* (*fail*) *Open* (*fail*) *End*, *Closed* (*fail*) *Open* (*timeout*) *HalfOpen*;
- two 1-switches for the state *HalfOpen* because there is one incoming and two outgoing transitions; the 1-switches are: *Open* (*timeout*) *HalfOpen* (*fail*) *Open*, *Open* (*timeout*) *HalfOpen* (*ok*) *Closed*;
- there are no 1-switches with *End* as the middle state because there are no outgoing transitions from End.

There is also a simple method for determining all N-switches inductively for an arbitrary $N > 0$. The idea is shown in Fig. 3.25.

When we determined all the (N-1)-switches, we considered their final state for each and extended it by one more state in all possible ways. In other words, we "glue" together a given (N-1)-switch with all possible 0-switches at its end.

Once the test analyst determines all the N-switches, they can design the test cases. An indelible trade-off occurs here. The larger the N, the stronger the test cases, and the more coverage items (N-switches) to cover. The number of N-switches usually increases very rapidly as N increases. Moreover, if the test analyst wants to derive the *smallest* possible number of test cases achieving N-switch coverage, the problem becomes even more difficult.

As indicated in the Foundation Level syllabus [1], 0-switch coverage is most often used in practice. For higher risk levels related to stateful behavior, 1-switch coverage

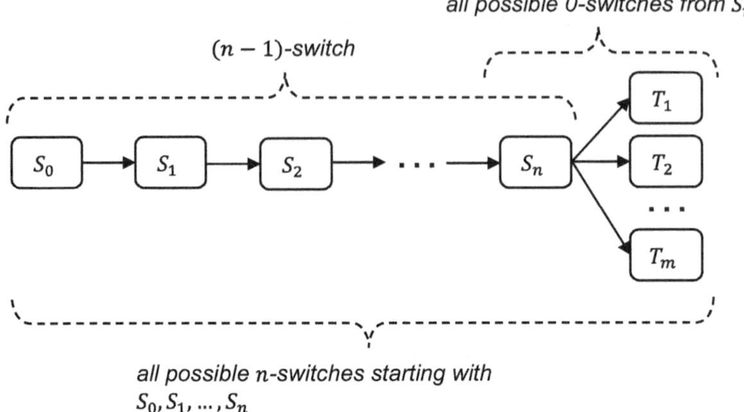


**Fig. 3.25** Determining N-switches from (N-1)-switches

should be used. The use of N-switching for $N > 1$ is very rare and is applied mostly to safety-critical systems.

Consider the state diagram for the FoodApp shown in Fig. 3.26. Suppose we want to achieve 0-switch coverage with a *minimal* number of test cases that exercise paths from the start to the end state.

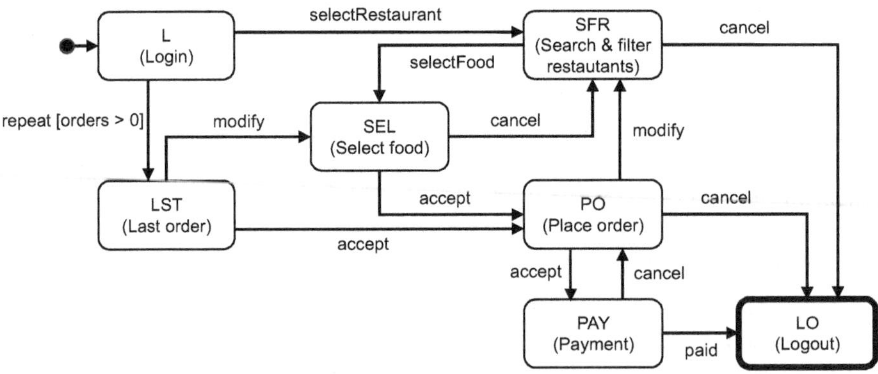


**Fig. 3.26** EFSM model for the client's FoodApp web interface

Notice that there are three incoming transitions to the final state *Logout*. This means that we need at least three test cases since no two of these transitions can occur within the same path: if any of them occurs, the system must end its operation because it reaches the final state. So, we know we need at least three test cases. The question is whether three paths are enough to cover all the 0-switches, or will we need more than three test cases?

It is easy to see that three test cases will be enough. Consider, for example, the following three test cases:

TC1: L (selectRestaurant) SFR (selectFood) SEL (cancel) SFR (selectFood) SEL (accept) PO (accept) PAY (paid) LO.
TC2: Precondition: orders >0. L (repeat) LST (modify) SEL (accept) PO (modify) SFR (cancel) LO.
TC3: Precondition: orders >0. L (repeat) LST (accept) PO (accept) PAY (cancel) PO (cancel) LO.

TC1 (dashed line in Fig. 3.27) covers 6 out of 13 transitions (ca. 46% 0-switch coverage). TC2 (solid line) covers 4 additional transitions (5 in total, so ca. 38% 0-switch coverage). TC3 (dotted line) covers 3 additional transitions (5 in total, so ca. 38% 0-switch coverage). Altogether, TC1, TC2, and TC3 cover 13 out of 13 transitions, so together, they achieve 100% 0-switch coverage.

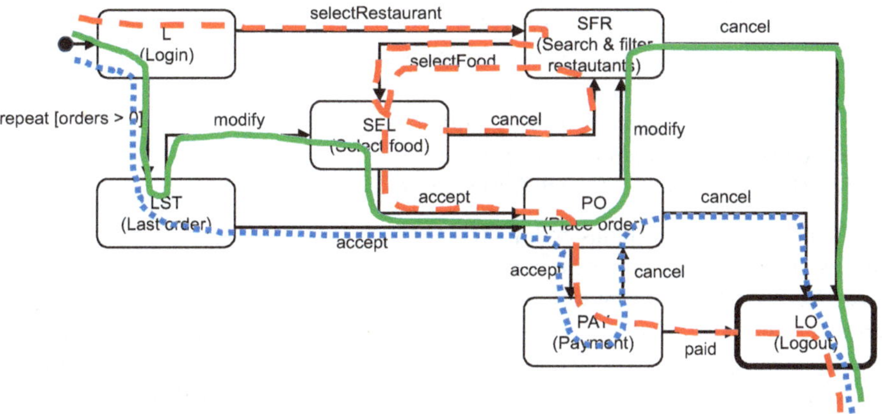


**Fig. 3.27** Three test cases achieving 100% 0-switch coverage for the FoodApp system

Notice a subtle issue with this example. If we start with the empty database, in order to have the guard condition [orders >0] be true to be able to go from L to LST, the first test case must go from L to SFR and must end with the transition PAY (paid) LO. This way, the first test case will result in placing the order. This makes the guard condition true, and only now is it possible to execute TC2 and TC3. This is a classic example of how different logical or technical conditions influence the test execution order. Of course, the test analyst could solve this issue in another way, using the configuration of the test environment. For example, before executing any test case, the test analyst could define a precondition: "There is at least one order in the database." When this precondition is fulfilled, the test execution order does not matter since we can execute the transition L (repeat) LST at any time.

Now, let us consider the state diagram for the Circuit Breaker Pattern again. We provide this diagram again in Fig. 3.28 for convenience.

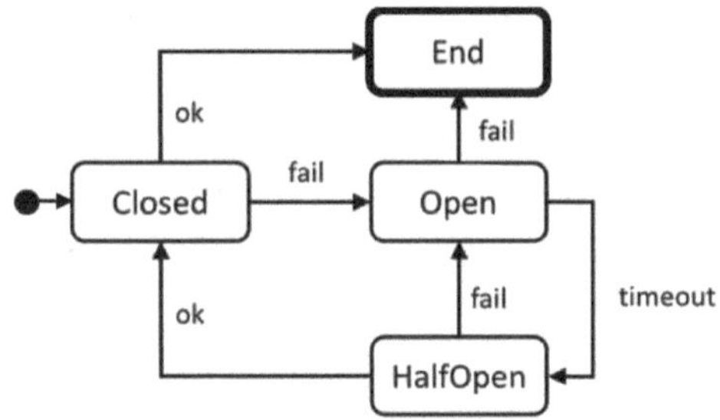


**Fig. 3.28** State diagram for the Circuit Breaking Pattern (repeated)

Suppose we want to achieve 1-switch coverage with the smallest possible number of test cases now. First, we need to identify all 1-switches. We already did it earlier. There are eight 1-switches, labeled S1 to S8:

S1: *HalfOpen* (*ok*) *Closed* (*ok*) *End*,
S2: *HalfOpen* (*ok*) *Closed* (*fail*) *Open*,
S3: *HalfOpen* (*fail*) *Open* (*fail*) *End*,
S4: *HalfOpen* (*fail*) *Open* (*timeout*) *HalfOpen*,
S5: *Closed* (*fail*) *Open* (*fail*) *End*,
S6: *Closed* (*fail*) *Open* (*timeout*) *HalfOpen*,
S7: *Open* (*timeout*) *HalfOpen* (*fail*) *Open*,
S8: *Open* (*timeout*) *HalfOpen* (*ok*) *Closed*.

Three of these 1-switches end in the final state *End*. This means we need to have at least three test cases since no two of these 1-switches can be tested within one test case. Let us define the first test case, TC1, and let's try to design it in a way that it covers as many 1-switches as possible. We start in *Closed* since it is the initial state. We can cover S5, but we must end immediately since S5 ends with the final state. So, let us first cover S6. It ends with the sequence *Open* (*timeout*) *HalfOpen*, so we can extend the test case with *HalfOpen* (*fail*) *Open*, thus covering S7. Extending it with *Open* (*timeout*) *HalfOpen*, we cover S4. Extending it with *HalfOpen* (*ok*) *Closed*, we cover S8. Extending it with *Closed* (*fail*) *Open*, we cover S2. Now we can extend it with *Open* (*failed*) *End*, thus covering S5. Our test case is this:

TC1: *Closed* (*fail*) *Open* (*timeout*) *HalfOpen* (*fail*) *Open* (*timeout*) *HalfOpen* (*ok*) *Closed* (*fail*) *Open* (*failed*) *End*.

Notice that the first test case is quite long but covered 6 out of 8 1-switches: S6, S7, S4, S8, S2, and S5, achieving 6/8 = 75% 1-switch coverage. The two remaining 1-switches to cover are S1 and S3. We need to cover them in separate test cases, for example:

TC2: *Closed* (*fail*) *Open* (*timeout*) *HalfOpen* (*ok*) *Closed* (*ok*) *End*, which covers S1,
TC3: *Closed* (*fail*) *Open* (*timeout*) *HalfOpen* (*fail*) *Open* (*fail*) *End*, which covers S3.

The test set {TC1, TC2, TC3} achieves 100% 1-switch coverage.

Notice another subtlety. Our test set achieved 1-switch coverage but did not cover the 0-switch Closed (ok) End. This is because this 0-switch starts in the initial state and ends in the final state. For practical reasons, we would like to have the subsumption criterion that says that if a test set achieves 100% N-switch coverage, then it achieves 100% M-switch coverage for all $M < N$. This is possible if the criterion is defined in this way: N-switch coverage requires that all M-switches are covered, for all $M = 0, 1, \ldots, N$.

**Round-trip coverage**. The second coverage discussed in the Test Analyst syllabus deals with loops. Loops are problematic because they mean that there can be an infinite number of paths in this system if the loop can execute an arbitrary number of times. The round-trip criterion is limited to testing simple loops called round trips. A round trip is a path in which the first and last states are the same, and no other state within the path can repeat. Especially, a round trip cannot contain another round trip (or "sub-loop.") The idea behind this criterion is to check that if we start in a given state and we execute a sequence of events that form a round trip, the system's state goes back to the state from which we started.

Consider the FoodApp transition diagram from Fig. 3.26 again. It has seven round trips:

- *SEL (cancel) SFR (selectFood) SEL,*
- *SFR (selectFood) SEL (cancel) SFR,*
- *PO (accept) PAY (cancel) PO,*
- *PAY (cancel) PO (accept) PAY,*
- *SFR (selectFood) SEL (accept) PO (modify) SFR,*
- *SEL (accept) PO (modify) SFR (selectFood) SEL,*
- *PO (modify) SFR (selectFood) SEL (accept) PO.*

Notice that, for example, states *SFR* and *SEL* define two different round trips because one of them starts and ends in *SEL*, and the other starts and ends in *SEL*. Round-trip coverage requires covering all the round trips. In our example, we can do it with only one test case, for example:

> *TC1: L (selectRestaurant) SFR (selectFood) SEL (cancel) SFR (selectFood) SEL (accept) PO (modify) SFR (selectFood) SEL (accept) PO (accept) PAY (cancel) PO (accept) Pay (paid) LO.*

Notice, however, that we did not achieve 100% 0-switch coverage. For example, we did not exercise the transition SFR (cancel) LO. This shows that loop coverage does not subsume N-switch coverage. However, the opposite is true: if the longest round trip has N transitions, then (N-1)-switch coverage subsumes round-trip coverage since each round trip of length M forms a (M-1)-switch.

Round-trip coverage is a valuable additional coverage criterion to N-switch coverage. It targets defects that trigger failures only when a test case does not follow a short path through the state model, which is commonly seen in N-switch testing. A case study based on mutation analysis [17] provides evidence for the effectiveness of round-trip coverage in detecting defects. In this study, researchers implemented a specific container class and applied a set of mutation operators designed for object-oriented code, which included defects that went unnoticed during 1-switch testing. Round-trip testing identified 87% of these defects, whereas size-equivalent random tests only detected 69%. Furthermore, the study suggested that domain testing is particularly effective at uncovering the mutations left undetected by state transition testing.

## Case Study

This real-life example shows that even small and simple systems cause big and complicated problems regarding test design. Consider an ATM machine whose state diagram is presented in Fig. 3.29. This diagram has 8 states and 19 transitions, which can be considered a relatively small model.

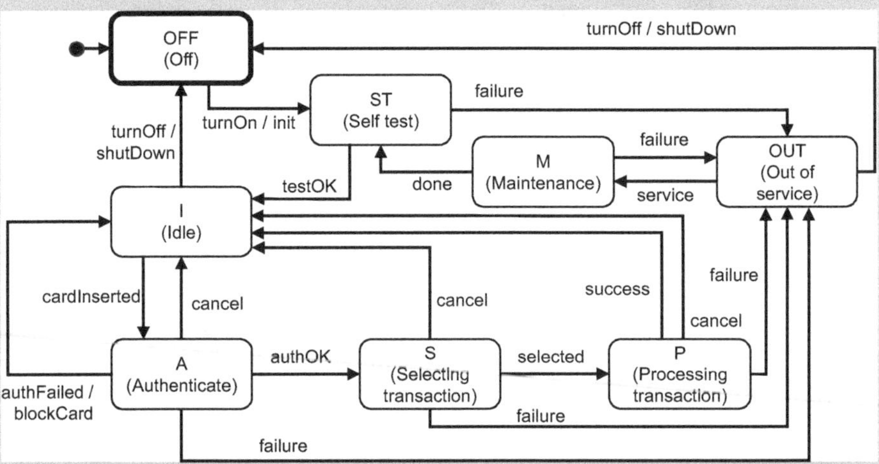


**Fig. 3.29** State diagram for an ATM machine

Initially, the system is in the *OFF* state. At the same time, *OFF* is the final state. This means that whenever the ATM arrives at the *OFF* state, the test case must end since the ATM turns off. After turning the ATM on, it changes its state to *ST* and executes a self-test. If everything goes OK, the ATM goes to the *I* (Idle) state and is ready to be used by a client. However, if there is a failure during the self-test, the ATM goes into the *OUT* (out of service) state. It can then be turned off or put into maintenance mode (the *M* state). Maintenance can be successful (the ATM goes again into the *ST* state) or not (the ATM goes again into the *OUT* state).

Being in the $I$, when a user inserts a card, the system goes into an $A$ (Authenticate) state. If authentication is OK, the ATM goes into the $S$ (Selecting transaction) state; otherwise, it blocks the card and goes back to the $I$ state. After the selection is done, the system goes to the $P$ (Processing transaction state), and once it is done, it goes back to the $I$ state. Whenever a user cancels the operation during this process, the system returns to the $I$ state. If a failure occurs, the system goes to the $OUT$ state.

Suppose we want to achieve the round-trip coverage for the ATM state diagram. Let us count how many round trips we have to cover (remember that whenever we arrive at $OFF$, the test case must end; this property will eliminate many possible round trips that would be there if $OFF$ were not the final state). All the round trips to cover are presented in Table 3.9. For the sake of simplicity, we omit the events when there is only one possible transition between two states. The only two exceptions are for the transitions between $P$ and $I$ (because there are two possible transitions caused by *success* or *cancel* events) and between $A$ and $I$ (*cancel* and *authFailed* events).

**Table 3.9** Round trips to be covered for the ATM state diagram

| Initial state | Round trips |
|---|---|
| OFF | (1) OFF, ST, OUT, OFF<br>(2) OFF, ST, I, OFF<br>(3) OFF, ST, I, A, OUT, OFF<br>(4) OFF, ST, I, A, S, OUT, OFF<br>(5) OFF, ST, I, A, S, P, OUT, OFF |
| ST | (6) ST, OUT, M, ST<br>(7) ST, I, A, OUT, M, ST<br>(8) ST, I, A, S, OUT, M, ST<br>(9) ST, I, A, S, P, OUT, M, ST |
| M | (10) M, OUT, M<br>(11) M, ST, OUT, M<br>(12) M, ST, I, A, OUT, M<br>(13) M, ST, I, A, S, OUT, M<br>(14) M, ST, I, A, S, P, OUT, M |
| OUT | (15) OUT, M, OUT<br>(16) OUT, M, ST, OUT<br>(17) OUT, M, ST, I, A, OUT<br>(18) OUT, M, ST, I, A, S, OUT<br>(19) OUT, M, ST, I, A, S, P, OUT |

(continued)

**Table 3.9** (continued)

| Initial state | Round trips |
|---|---|
| I | (20) I, A (cancel), I<br>(21) I, A (authFailed), I<br>(22) I, A, S, I<br>(23) I, A, S, P (success), I<br>(24) I, A, S, P (cancel), I<br>(25) I, A, S, OUT, M, ST, I<br>(26) I, A, S, P, OUT, M, ST, I<br>(27) I, A, OUT, M, ST, I |
| A | (28) A, I (cancel), A<br>(29) A, I (authFailed), A<br>(30) A, S, I, A<br>(31) A, S, P (success), I, A<br>(32) A, S, P (cancel), I, A<br>(33) A, S, P, OUT, M, ST, I, A<br>(34) A, S, OUT, M, ST, I, A (35) A, OUT, M, ST, I, A |
| S | (36) S, I, A, S<br>(37) S, P (success), I, A, S<br>(38) S, P (cancel), I, A, S<br>(39) S, P, OUT, M, ST, I, A, S<br>(40) S, OUT, M, ST, I, A, S |
| P | (41) P (success), I, A, S, P<br>(42) P (cancel), I, A, S, P<br>(43) P, OUT, M, ST, I, A, S, P |

The number of coverage items is large—we identified 43 round trips. This is a typical problem in software testing: even for small systems that look simple to test, when the test analyst applies some test design technique to achieve a typical coverage (like round-trip coverage in our case), the number of coverage elements can become very large. This is an example of the combinatorial explosion mentioned earlier in Sect. 3.1.2 on combinatorial testing.

Now, the question is how to design test cases to achieve 100% round-trip coverage. First, notice that we need 5 separate test cases TC1-TC6 to cover round trips starting from the OFF state, since OFF is also the final state. The remaining 38 round trips can be covered by a single, but *very* long test case with a total number of 158 transitions:

TC6: *OFF*, *ST*, (6), (7), (8), (9), *OUT*, *M*, (10), (11), (12), (13), (14), *OUT*, (15), (16), (17), (18), (19), *M*, *ST*, *I*, (20), (21), (22), (23), (24), (25), (26), (27), *A*, (28), (29), (30), (31), (32), (33), (34), (35), *S*, (36), (37), (38), (39), (40), *P*, (41), (42), (43),

where numbers in parentheses refer to the round trips from Table 3.9, hence, the minimal number of test cases is 6, but testers would not design test cases like that in practice. The TC6 test case is unnatural. First of all, it is too long, which can cause very long execution times, maintenance problems, and analysis problems if a failure occurs during execution. Second, this test case does not represent any meaningful scenario that we might observe during actual ATM use. Usually, in such cases, testers create a larger number of shorter and simpler test cases. For example, the test analyst might decide that each loop should be tested within a separate test case. Then, the test suite would consist of 43 test cases. This is an example of the other extreme—we have small, simple, fast, and cheap-to-maintain test cases, but there are many of them. Test analysts will always face a trade-off in which they will have to weigh the number of test cases versus their length and complexity.

## Sample Questions

### Question 3.2.2A

You test the system that reads files and prints reports based on their content. The system's state transition model is presented in Fig. 3.30. The initial state is "Init," and the final state is "END". A test case is a sequence of transitions between states, starting from the initial state and ending in the final state.

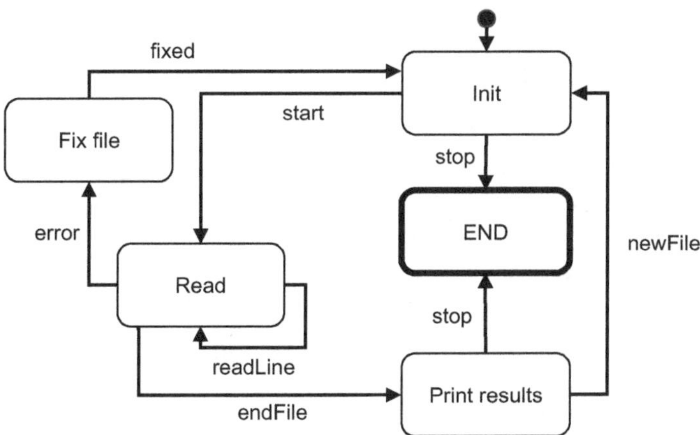


**Fig. 3.30** State transition model for a file-reading system

You have already designed the following test cases:

- TC1: Init, Read, Read, Print results, Init, Read, Print results, END
- TC2: Init, Read, Fix file, Init, Read, Fix file, Init, Read, Print results, END

Which test case, when added to TC1 and TC2, will allow you to achieve 100% round trip coverage?

(a) No test cases are needed—the existing ones already achieve round trip coverage.
(b) Init, Read, Print results, Init, Read, Print results, END.
(c) Init, END.
(d) Init, Read, Read, Print results, END.

Select ONE answer.

**Question 3.2.2B**

You test the system that reads files and prints reports based on their content. The system's state transition model is presented in Fig. 3.30 (see Question 3.2.2A). The initial state is "Init," and the final state is "END." A test case is a sequence of transitions between states, starting from the initial state and ending in the final state.

What is the **MINIMUM** number of test cases needed to achieve 100% 1-switch coverage?

(a) 3.
(b) 8.
(c) 2.
(d) 4.

Select ONE answer.

## Exercise 5—State Transition Testing

TA-3.2.2 (K3) Apply state transition testing

You are testing a login mechanism modeled by a state diagram shown in Fig. 3.31. If the user enters the correct login and password, they are logged in. Otherwise, the system asks the user to enter their credentials again. If the user enters incorrect credentials three times, their account is locked.

Using state transition testing, design a minimal set of test cases that will achieve:

1. Valid transitions coverage (i.e., 0-switch coverage)
2. 1-switch coverage
3. Round-trip coverage

Each test case should be documented in a tabular format as shown in Table 3.10.

### *3.2.3 Scenario-Based Testing*

TA-3.2.3 (K3) Apply scenario-based testing

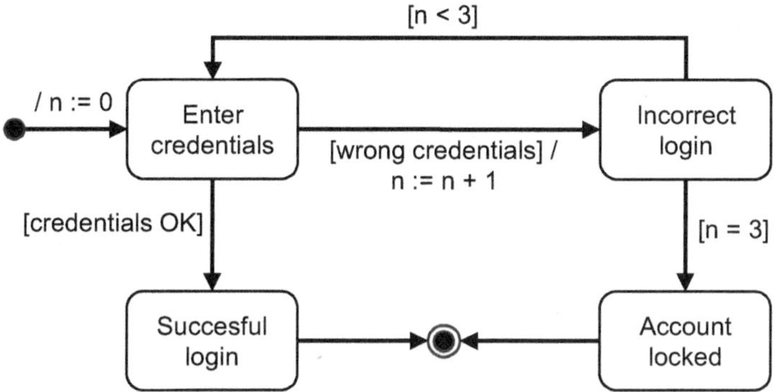


**Fig. 3.31** State diagram for a login feature

**Table 3.10** A format of a test case for a login feature

Test case ID: …
Preconditions: …

| Test step | State | Event [guard condition] | Expected action | Expected next state |
|---|---|---|---|---|
| 1 | | | | |
| 2 | | | | |
| … | | | | |

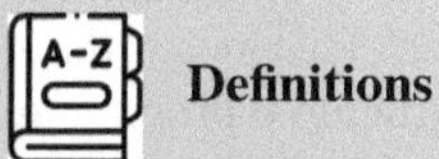

**Definitions**

**Scenario-based testing**: A black-box test technique in which test conditions are sequences of interactions between external actors and the test item.

**Introduction**. Scenario-based testing and state-based testing seem to be similar, but they have important differences. State-based testing involves testing the system's responses to various events or inputs in various states. Scenario-based testing involves testing software by simulating realistic situations or "scenarios" that represent how users will interact with the system. It focuses on ensuring that the software behaves correctly in these practical, real-world conditions.

Scenarios are typically high-level descriptions of user business processes in a system. Scenario-based testing is, therefore, a natural technique for test analysts because they are "closer to the business than to the technology" (as opposed to technical test analysts).

Scenario-based testing is often performed in system testing or acceptance testing. It takes the form of end-to-end testing focused on the functional suitability (see Sect. 4.1) of a system from the user's perspective. However, scenario-based testing can also be used at other test levels (e.g., integration testing with scenarios based on the interaction protocols or component testing of stateful, object-oriented classes with scenarios invoking various methods), as well as in non-functional testing (e.g., scenarios may constitute the elements of the operational profiles used in reliability, portability, or compatibility testing).

**Scenario modeling.** The test analyst designs test cases based on a particular scenario model. The most common types of scenario models used in practice are:

- **Use cases** [18]. They describe the interaction between actors and the test object to achieve a specific goal. The actors can be users, administrators, other systems, or software components. Use cases consist of a sequence of steps containing an individual action by the actor and the respective response from the system. For example, a use case for an ATM might include steps for a user to withdraw cash, including authentication, selecting a withdrawal amount, and receiving cash.
- **User stories** [19]. Short descriptions of a feature from the perspective of a particular end-user, for whom they bring added value. User stories are common in Agile software development. They usually follow the "as a (role)/I want (action)/so that (purpose)" format, followed by a set of acceptance criteria (e.g., "As a customer, I want to be able to track my food order status online so that I can know when it will arrive". They also include acceptance criteria, like "After clicking on the order, a map is shown with the position of a delivery person, together with the estimated time of arrival".
- **Flowcharts** [20]. They are simple diagrams that represent the flow of logic or steps in a process. Flowchart notation supports the three basic constructs of structured programming: sequence, selection, and repetition. This means that any "well-formed" flowchart can be coded in an imperative, structured programming language.
- **Activity diagrams** [16]. They provide a closer look at the implementation of a single use case. From the technical point of view, they extend the basic idea of flowcharts to an object-oriented paradigm. The most interesting parts of an activity diagram are so-called "swim lanes" that show the devices or classes that perform activities.
- **Business process models** [21]. They outline the business processes that the software supports or realizes. The most common notation used is Business Process Model and Notation (BPMN). An example is a business process model for the food ordering process realized by FoodApp, including steps such as searching for a restaurant, order entry, payment processing, order fulfillment, and shipping.
- **Personas** [22]. Personas are fictional characters representing different types of users that might interact with the system. They help test analysts derive different scenarios for different groups of users. Examples of personas for the FoodApp might include a regular customer that orders lunch several times a week, prefers quick reordering of favorites, values loyalty rewards; a first-time user, new to the app, needs easy navigation and clear instructions, values introductory discounts; a family user who orders for family dinners, needs diverse menu options to satisfy

everyone, values bulk order discounts and kid-friendly meals. By using personas to guide scenario-based testing, the test analyst can better ensure that the system under test meets its users' diverse needs and expectations, leading to a more satisfying and user-friendly experience.

- **User journey maps** [23]. They are visual representations that outline a user's steps to achieve a specific goal when interacting with a product or service. They help understand the user's experiences, including their emotions, pain points, and motivations throughout their journey (see Fig. 3.32). A user journey map is usually defined for a given persona with a particular scenario or goal. It breaks the journey into distinct phases, such as awareness, consideration, purchase, and postpurchase.

The Test Analyst syllabus focuses only on two of these models, namely use cases and activity diagrams. We discuss them below in detail.

**Use cases**. A use case describes how users interact with a system to achieve a specific goal. In software engineering, use cases are used to capture the functional requirements of a system. They provide a narrative of how a system should operate, detailing the steps and interactions between users (also called actors) and the system.

Use cases are primarily written in text form but can also be represented with flow charts, sequence charts, Petri nets, or programming languages. They are used to communicate between people, often without special training, so text in natural language usually fits best. Use cases can help a team discuss an upcoming system and document the requirements and final design later. They can be used for both large systems and small software applications. Regardless of the situation, the same basic writing rules apply, though the level of detail and rigor may vary [18].

The main elements of a use case are:

- Title—a brief, descriptive name of the use case (what business process does it describe?).
- Actors—individuals, groups, or external systems that interact with the system to achieve the goal. A primary actor initiates the interaction.
- Preconditions are conditions that must hold before the use case can start. They describe the system's and environment's initial state.
- Triggers—events that initiate the use case. A trigger could be a user action, a system condition, or a scheduled event.
- Main scenario (also called "happy path")—the standard sequence of steps taken by the actors, with no errors or failures along the way. It represents the system's "ideal" use.
- Extensions (also called "alternative scenarios" or "alternative flows")—variations from the main scenario that handle different conditions that may result in taking a path other than the main scenario. Extensions still allow the actor to achieve the goal described in the use case.
- Exceptions (also called "errors")—variations from the main scenario that handle conditions that do not allow the user to achieve the goal.

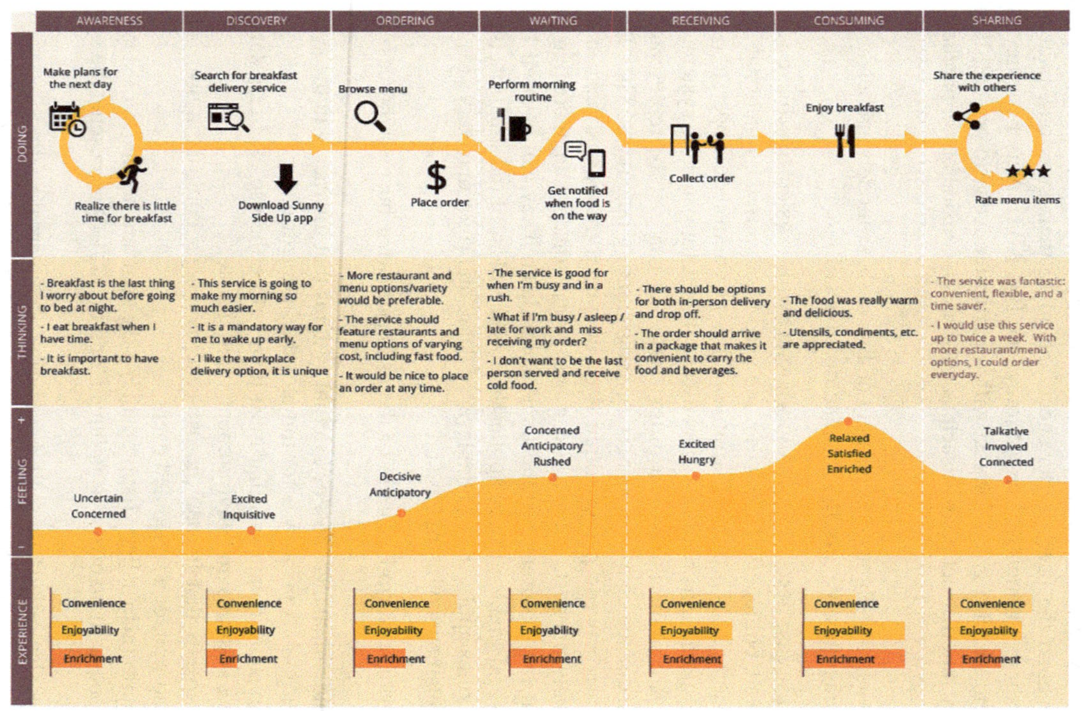


**Fig. 3.32** Example of a user journey map for the food delivery app. Source futuremiraekim.com/sunny-side-up/)

- Postconditions—conditions that must be true after the use case has been successfully completed. They describe the system's final state.

An example of a use case is shown in Table 3.11. It describes a process of cash withdrawal from an ATM.

**Use case-based testing and coverage**. Use cases provide almost a ready-made functional test description for the system. Transforming the main scenario, extensions, and exceptions into test cases is very simple. The scenario steps performed by the primary actor usually correspond to test steps, and the actions taken by the system in response to those steps usually correspond to the system's expected behavior. For example, a high-level test case testing the main use case scenario from Table 3.11 could look like the one shown in Table 3.12.

**Table 3.11** Use case "Withdraw cash from the ATM"

| **Title** | Withdraw cash from the ATM |
|---|---|
| **Actors** | Customer (primary actor), ATM |
| **Main scenario** | 1. Customer inserts a card into the card reader.<br>2. ATM reads the card (bank ID, account number, encrypted PIN from the card) and validates the bank ID and account number with the main banking system.<br>3. ATM asks for PIN.<br>4. Customer enters PIN.<br>5. ATM validates the PIN against the encrypted PIN read from the card, shows the main menu, and asks the customer to choose an operation type.<br>6. Customer selects "Withdraw cash".<br>7. ATM asks about the amount of money.<br>8. Customer enters an amount, a multiple of \$5.<br>9. ATM notifies the main banking system of a customer account, requests the amount to withdraw, and receives back acknowledgment plus the new balance.<br>10. ATM delivers the cash, card, and receipt showing the new balance.<br>11. ATM logs the transaction. |
| **Postcondition** | The customer receives the requested cash, and the account balance is subtracted from this amount. The transaction is logged in the ATM database. |
| **Extensions** | 5A. PIN validation failed (for the first or second time). The system shows the "Invalid PIN" message and asks the customer to enter the PIN again. The use case goes back to step 3.<br>8A. The amount is not a multiple of \$5. The system shows the message "Amount must be a multiple of \$5." The use case goes back to step 7.<br>8B. Customer uses one of the buttons with a predefined amount. |
| **Exceptions** | 2A. Invalid card. The system rejects it. The use case ends.<br>5B. PIN validation failed a third time. The system shows the message "Invalid PIN—third time. The card is blocked! Please contact your bank." The card is blocked, and the bank is informed that the card is blocked. The use case ends.<br>8C. Customer does not select anything for 1 minute. The system cancels the transaction, blocks the card, and shows the message "Waiting time too long. The card is blocked! Please contact your bank". The use case ends. |

**Table 3.12** High-level test case based on the main scenario of the use case "Withdraw cash from the ATM"

**Test case: successful cash withdrawal from an ATM ID: TC-001-01**
**Preconditions**: the customer has a valid card and sufficient funds in their account, and the ATM has enough suitable banknotes to make the withdrawal
Test steps:
**Step 1**. Customer inserts card into the card reader. **Expected behavior**: ATM reads the card (bank ID, account number, encrypted PIN from the card), validates bank ID and account number with the main banking system, and asks for PIN
**Step 2**. Customer enters the correct PIN. **Expected behavior**: ATM validates the PIN against the encrypted PIN read from the card, accepts it, shows the main menu, and asks the customer to choose an operation type.
**Step 3**. Customer selects "Withdraw cash". **Expected behavior**: ATM asks about the amount of money
**Step 4**. Customer enters the correct amount (a multiple of $5). **Expected behavior**: ATM notifies the main banking system of a customer account, requests the amount to withdraw, and receives back acknowledgment plus the new balance. ATM delivers the cash, card, and a receipt showing the new balance. ATM logs the transaction
**Postconditions**: Customer receives requested cash, account balance is subtracted by this amount, and the transaction is logged in the ATM database

As we can see, the test case is almost a copy-paste of the main scenario from the use case. In practice, when designing use case-based test cases, test analysts often combine them with other test techniques to increase coverage. In our example, the test analyst could use boundary value analysis and design a low-level test case based on the high-level test case from Table 3.12, as shown in Table 3.13.

**Table 3.13** Low-level test case based on the main scenario of the use case "Withdraw cash from the ATM"

**Test case: successful cash withdrawal from an ATM ID: TC-001-01-01**
**Preconditions**: the customer has a valid card (no. 1234–5678–9012-3456) with PIN 1234; the customer has a $5 balance on their account; the ATM has one $5 bill
Test steps:
**Step 1**. Customer inserts card into the card reader. **Expected behavior**: ATM reads the card (bank ID, account number, encrypted PIN from the card), validates bank ID and account number with the main banking system, and asks for PIN
**Step 2**. Customer enters '1234'. **Expected behavior**: ATM validates the PIN against the encrypted PIN read from the card, accepts it, shows the main menu, and asks the customer to choose an operation type
**Step 3**. Customer selects "Withdraw cash". **Expected behavior**: ATM asks about the amount of money
**Step 4**. Customer enters '$5'. **Expected behavior**: ATM notifies the main banking system of a customer account, requests the amount to withdraw, and receives back acknowledgment plus the new balance of $0. ATM delivers the cash, card, and a receipt showing the new balance. ATM logs the transaction
**Postconditions**: Customer receives $5, account balance is $0, and the transaction is logged in the ATM database

With this one test case, the test analyst checked several interesting "edge cases." First, the boundary value for the account balance was checked. The customer wants to withdraw $5 from the account with exactly the same balance. Second, the boundary value for the banknote holder was checked: the customer wants to withdraw the same amount of money available at the ATM.

Of course, the test analyst should also design test cases for all the extensions and exceptions. Extensions and exceptions are where the most interesting system requirements reside. Handling them often uses business rules that the developers did not anticipate. Hence, the sole test design, when such a situation occurs, may result in a need to add or modify the system response, introduce a new actor or new extension condition, or even a new use case.

The use case from Table 3.11 has six extensions and exceptions defined, but there may be more. The test analysts, business representatives, and other development team members can use brainstorming during the use case analysis to identify as many unpredictable behaviors as possible that may occur during the main scenario. Some possible examples that go beyond the ones already identified in Table 3.11 are:

- alternate success path (e.g., choosing "fast withdrawal of $50");
- failure of the validation steps (e.g., the bank account associated with the card is terminated);
- integration failure (e.g., no Internet connection between ATM and bank);
- inaction by the primary actor (e.g., timeout waiting for the PIN, the customer does not take the money within a certain amount of time);
- insufficient banknotes at the ATM (less than the requested amount);
- lack of specific denominations of banknotes (e.g., the customer requested $15, but there are only $10 and $20 banknotes);
- internal failure within the system under test (e.g., cash dispenser jams, receipt paper runs out);
- critical non-functional failures (e.g., too long ATM response time);
- critical functional failures (e.g., power down in any step of the main scenario).

Each identified extension or exception should be tested with an appropriate test case.

Although there is no universally accepted precise definition of use case coverage, it is reasonable to adopt the following rules:

- there should be at least one test case that exercises the main scenario;
- there should be enough test cases to cover all extensions and exceptions;
- exceptions should be tested in isolation, i.e., each exception should be exercised in a separate test case.

The test strategy may allow for different approaches to meeting these criteria. For example, if the level of risk associated with the system is high, the test strategy may require each extension and exception to be tested in a separate test case. If the risk is low, the test strategy may allow more than one extension to be tested within a single test case. Sometimes, separate testing of exceptions may not be feasible, for example, if one exception lies on a path that implements another exception ("exception within another exception").

Let's see how applying the above criteria to our ATM example (use case from Table 3.11) will result in the number of test cases. For a strategy that mandates testing extensions and exceptions in separate test cases, the test analyst must prepare at least 7 test cases covering the main scenario, three extensions, and three exceptions. The test cases will implement the following scenarios (the numbers here denote the steps of the use case):

- TC1 (main scenario): 1, 2, 3, 4, 5, 6, 7, 8, 9, 10, 11.
- TC2 (PIN validation failed): 1, 2, 3, 4, 5A, 3, 4, 5, 6, 7, 8, 9, 10, 11.
- TC3 (wrong amount): 1, 2, 3, 4, 5, 6, 7, 8A, 7, 8, 9, 10, 11.
- TC4 (predefined amount): 1, 2, 3, 4, 5, 6, 7, 8B, 9, 10, 11.
- TC5 (invalid card): 1, 2A.
- TC6 (PIN validation failed third time): 1, 2, 3, 4, 5B.
- TC7 (user inaction when selecting an amount): 1, 2, 3, 4, 5, 6, 7, 8C.

If our test strategy allows for combining multiple extensions within one test case, we could reduce our test suite from seven to 5 test cases:

- TC1 (main scenario): 1, 2, 3, 4, 5, 6, 7, 8, 9, 10, 11.
- TC234 (testing extensions 5A, 8A, and 8B): 1, 2, 3, 4, 5A, 3, 4, 5, 6, 7, 8A, 7, 8B, 9, 10, 11.
- TC5 (invalid card): 1, 2A.
- TC6 (PIN validation failed third time): 1, 2, 3, 4, 5B.
- TC7 (user inaction when selecting an amount): 1, 2, 3, 4, 5, 6, 7, 8C.

Test cases 1, 5, 6, and 7 remain the same. Test cases 2, 3, and 4 are combined into one longer test case, TC234, that exercises all three extensions.

If a scenario does not contain loops (i.e., returns to earlier steps), then the number of possible executions of the scenario, understood as the number of possible sequences of steps, is finite. Each of them can be tested with a separate test case. When loops exist, there can be infinite ways to execute a given scenario. To deal with this problem, the test analyst can apply a coverage criterion called "simple loop coverage." This criterion requires that each loop should be executed:

- zero times (i.e., do not enter the loop at all),
- exactly once,
- more than once (a typical number of loop executions),
- the maximum number of times (if possible).

Consider the structure of our use case, presented in Fig. 3.33. The scenario has two possible loops: 3, 4, 5A, 3, and 7, 8A, 7. Each represents a specific scenario workflow, but each may be realized in many ways due to the loops. To achieve the simple loop coverage for the first loop, we need to test the following coverage items, which represent realizations of the scenario with extension 5A (PIN validation failed):

- zero loop executions (this is realized by the test case TC1 for the main scenario);
- one execution (this is realized by the test case TC2 above);
- more than one execution (this can be realized by a test case that exercises the step 5A twice, e.g., PT8: 1, 2, 3, 4, 5A, 3, 4, 5A, 3, 4, 5, 6, 7, 8, 9, 10, 11);
- maximal number of loop executions—notice that 5A can occur no more than two times, since when the PIN is incorrect for the third time, the exception 5B occurs. So, the PT8 covers this coverage item at the same time.

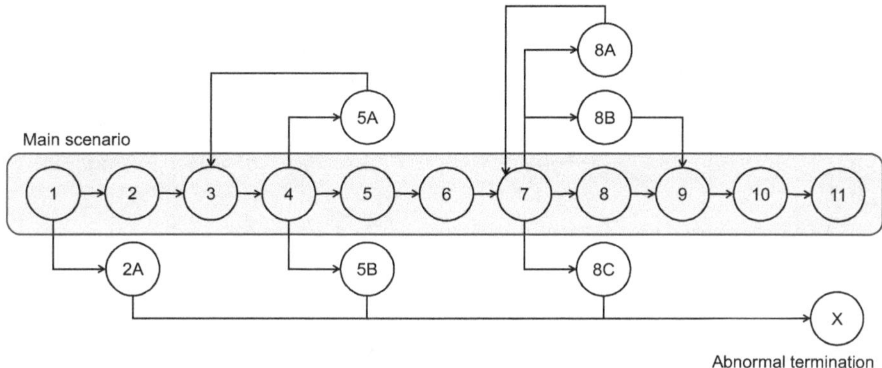


**Fig. 3.33** Workflow structure for the use case "Withdraw cash from the ATM"

To achieve the simple loop coverage for the second loop, we need to test the following realizations of the scenario with extension 8A (wrong amount):

- zero loop executions (this is realized by the test case TC1 for the main scenario);
- one loop execution (this is realized by the test case TC3 above);
- more than one execution (this can be realized by a test case that exercises step 8A three times, e.g., PT9: 1, 2, 3, 4, 5, 6, 7, 8A, 7, 8A, 7, 8A, 7, 8, 9, 10, 11);
- maximal number of loop executions—infeasible.

Note that the requirements say nothing about whether there is any maximal number of possible occurrences of 8A. This means that there is no maximum number of loop calls defined. However, the test analyst can ask the architect or the customer whether this should be the case. Perhaps there should be some sort of upper limit beyond which the system would, for example, return the card and terminate the operation. This observation is a good example of how modeling can help detect problems or anomalies in specification. Based on models, test analysis, and test design can reveal some gaps or misstatements in the specification and suggest changes to the requirements so that the quality of the final product increases. We describe this approach in more detail in Sect. 5.2.1.

**Activity diagrams**. An activity diagram is a graphical representation of the workflow within a system. Activity diagrams are particularly useful for modeling business processes, but they can also model control flow or data flow. They provide a closer look at the implementation of a single use case. From the technical point of view, they are an extension of the basic idea of flowcharts to an object-oriented paradigm, allowing also to model concurrency. One interesting part of an activity diagram is the so-called "swim lanes." Swim lanes show the devices or classes that perform activities within a modeled scenario.

The main elements of the activity diagrams are start and end nodes, swim lanes, actions, transitions, decision nodes, merge nodes, fork nodes, and join nodes (see Fig. 3.34).

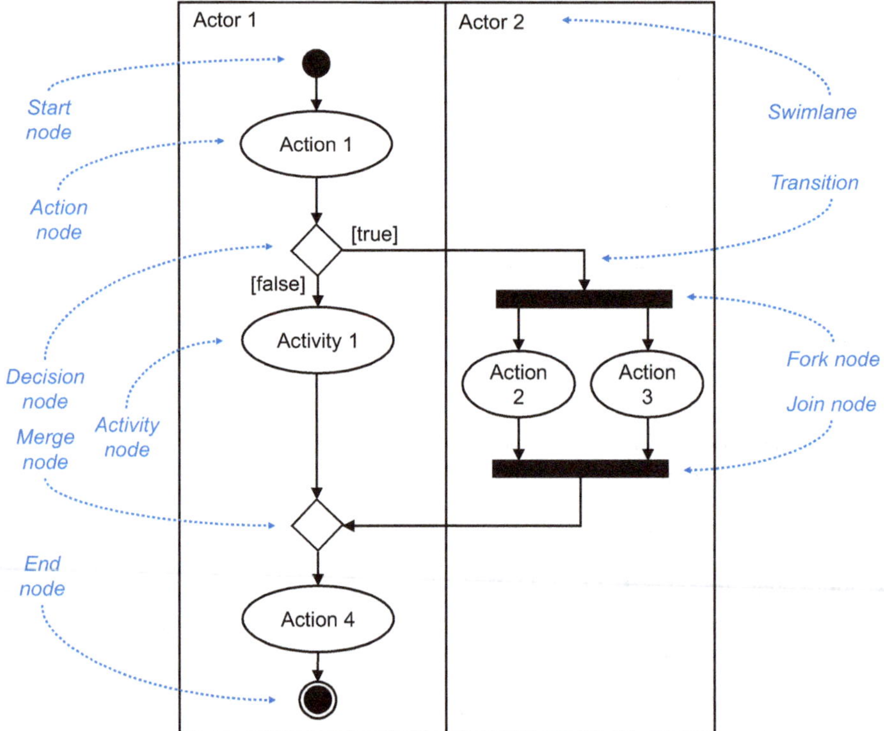


**Fig. 3.34** Structural elements of an activity diagram

The action represents a single operation or behavior of a system (i.e., an atomic step within an activity). A list of actions can be grouped together into one node that looks exactly like the action node but is called an activity node. Decision nodes control the action flow depending on the fulfillment of certain conditions. The decision node in Fig. 3.34 shows that after Action 1 is completed, the workflow can go either to Activity 1 or to the parallel execution of Actions 2 and 3. Parallel execution of activities is modeled with fork nodes. Join nodes represent a "synchronization" point of parallel activities—from a join node, we can move on only when all the activities incoming to this node are completed. In Fig. 3.34, when Action 2 and Action 3 run in parallel, we can go to Action 4 only if both Action 2 and Action 3 are completed. Merge nodes represent possible input points to actions or activities. In Fig. 3.34, we see that Action 4 can be initiated in two possible ways: either by completion of Activity 1 or by completion of Actions 2 and 3.

**Activity diagram-based testing and coverage**. Figure 3.35 shows an example activity diagram. It represents the detailed PIN verification process for our ATM cash withdrawal example.

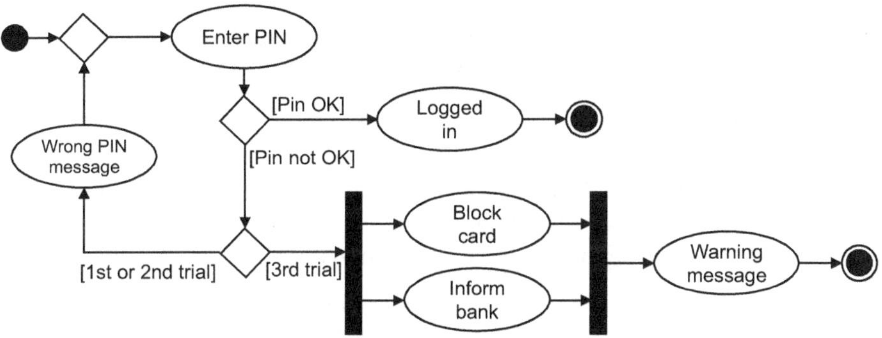


**Fig. 3.35** Activity diagram for the PIN validation process

Since the activity diagram is a kind of state machine, coverage criteria known from the technique of testing transitions between states can be used. For example, one can require coverage of every activity or coverage of every transition (0-switch coverage). One can also adopt coverage criteria analogous to those described earlier for use cases (one test case for the main scenario, enough test cases for all extensions and exceptions, and simple loop coverage). In this case, three test cases should be designed:

- TC1 (main scenario) Enter PIN [Pin OK] Logged in;
- TC2 (extension: wrong PIN) Enter PIN [PIN not OK] [first trial] Enter PIN [PIN OK] Logged in;
- TC3 (exception: block card) Enter PIN [PIN not OK] [first trial] Enter PIN [PIN not OK] [second trial] Enter PIN [PIN not OK] [third trial] {Block card, Inform bank} Warning message.

Events within curly brackets in TC3 can run in parallel. Time-related coverage criteria can also be used for such sets of activities (located between a fork node and a join node). For example, we can require testing every combination of the order in which the parallel activities are completed. For the system depicted in Fig. 3.35, we have one area with two parallel activities: Block card and Inform bank. This coverage criterion requires testing two situations: one in which the card is blocked before the bank is informed, and the other in which the bank is informed before the card is blocked. To achieve this coverage, the test case TC3 has to be replaced by two test cases:

- TC3a Enter PIN [PIN not OK] [first trial] Enter PIN [PIN not OK] [second trial] Enter PIN [PIN not OK] [third trial] Block card, Inform bank, Warning message.
- TC3b Enter PIN [PIN not OK] [first trial] Enter PIN [PIN not OK] [second trial] Enter PIN [PIN not OK] [third trial] Inform bank, Block card, Warning message.

This type of testing can detect time-dependent problems. For example, when an ATM informs the bank that a card has been blocked before actually blocking it, the banking system may expect that the card is already blocked when processing the following business logic:

```
1   IF (card blocking information received) THEN
2   B: = number of a card with the status "blocked"
3   M: = email address of the cardholder of the card B
4   Send an email to the M address about the card being blocked
    END IF
```

However, since the card is not yet blocked when instruction 2 is executed, the B variable has a NULL value. Attempting to retrieve the email address for an invalid client (with a NULL value) may cause the system to crash.

**Case Study**

A test analyst is asked to help design the "Food delivery" use case for the FoodApp's application for delivery persons and create test cases based on this use case. The use case must be written from the perspective of a delivery person, who will be the primary actor. The team proposes the first version of the use case as follows:

**Use case**: Successful food delivery

**Primary actor**: delivery person

**Secondary actors**: customer, restaurant, system

**Preconditions**

- the delivery person is logged into the app and is available for deliveries
- a customer has placed the correct order (within the distance in which the restaurant operates), and the restaurant is preparing the food
- the system assigned this order to a delivery person

**Main scenario**

1. The system sends a notification on the delivery person's app about a new delivery assignment, including order details, pickup location (a restaurant), and distance from the restaurant to the client's location

2. The delivery person accepts the assignment, confirming their availability to pick up and deliver the order
3. The system changes the delivery person's status to "Occupied" and provides the delivery person with GPS directions to the restaurant
4. The delivery person arrives at the restaurant, checks the order details to ensure accuracy, and marks the order as "Picked up" in the app
5. The system provides the delivery person with GPS directions to the customer's delivery address and notifies the customer that their food is on the way
6. The delivery person arrives at the customer's location, confirms the delivery address, hands over the food to the customer, and marks the order as "Delivered" in the app

**Postconditions**

- the customer receives the food
- the restaurant is informed of the successful delivery
- the delivery person is available for the next assignment

The system updates the delivery status, changes the delivery person's status to "Available", and notifies the customer and the restaurant of the successful delivery

Based on this initial version of the use case, the test analyst can design a test case for successful food ordering. Table 3.14 presents an example of such a (low-level) test case.

**Table 3.14** Test case for a successful food ordering

| Test case ID: FA-001-01 | Title: successful food ordering |
|---|---|
| **Preconditions**<br>• John is the only logged-in delivery person with the status "available.<br>• A customer ordered a pizza "quattro formaggi" from the restaurant "President's Pizza" (address: 1789 Union St. NE, Washington, DC 20002) at 1600 Pennsylvania Avenue, N.W. Washington, DC 20500<br>• President's Pizza is notified about the order<br>• The system assigned the order to John | |

(continued)

**Table 3.14** (continued)

| Test case ID: FA-001-01 | Title: successful food ordering |
|---|---|
| **Input** | **Expected result** |
| John opens the app | A “New delivery” notification is shown in the app with:<br>• order details: order = “Pizza quattro formaggi”, pickup location = “President’s Pizza, 1789 Union St. NE, Washington, DC 20002, distance from the restaurant to the client = “5.7 km,”<br>• a button “Accept” |
| John clicks the “Accept” button | The restaurant address, “1789 Union St. NE, Washington, DC 20002,” and the route from the current location to the restaurant are shown on the map.<br>John’s status changed to “occupied” |
| The GPS coordinates of John’s mobile phone match the ones with the restaurant address | The order details (“Pizza quattro formaggi”) are shown together with a button “Food picked up” |
| John clicks the “Food picked up” button | The client’s address (“1600 Pennsylvania Avenue, N.W. Washington, DC 20500”) and the route from the restaurant to the client’s location are shown<br>Client receives a notification, “Your order is on the way!” |
| The GPS coordinates of John’s mobile phone match the ones with the client’s address | A message “You arrived at the client’s location” is shown together with a button “Confirm delivery” |
| John clicks the “Confirm delivery” button | The order is marked as “Delivered” in John’s app |

**Postconditions**:
- John’s status changed to “Available”
- Customer is notified about the successful delivery
- The restaurant is notified about the successful delivery

The test analyst can also analyze the use case to provide the possible extensions and exceptions for the main scenario. For each of them, a separate test case should be designed. Examples of extensions and exceptions (with possible system reactions) are as follows:

- (exception) The delivery person rejects the assignment within 1 minute. The system reassigns the assignment to another delivery person.
- (extension) The delivery person does not accept the assignment within 1 minute. The system notifies the delivery person with a sound.

- (exception) After a sound message, the delivery person does not accept the assignment within 1 min. The system cancels the assignment and reassigns it to another delivery person.
- (extension) When a delivery person arrives at the restaurant, the food may not be ready yet. The delivery person may log this situation by changing their status to "Waiting at restaurant".
- (exception) The client refuses to receive the food. The delivery person changes the status to "Rejected by customer" and enters a short explanation about the reason. This exception could trigger a separate use case, "Customer rejects the food," which would include the process of returning the food to the restaurant.

Note that the system may be unable to assign an order to any delivery person (e.g., if all delivery persons were busy when the order was placed). However, such a situation cannot be considered an extension or exception since assigning an order to a delivery person is a *prerequisite* in our use case. So, we assume it holds. This situation could be considered in a separate use case (e.g., "Placing an order when there are no free delivery persons"), which would describe how the application should behave in such a case. For example, the app could notify the customer that the waiting time for food will be longer than usual due to the lack of delivery persons and ask the client whether they accept this situation or not (which might result in order cancelation).

## Sample Questions

### Question 3.2.3A

You are testing the operation of an automatic scheduling assistant, whose operating model is described by the activity diagram shown in Fig. 3.36. You use scenario-based testing when designing test cases.

What is the **MINIMUM** number of test cases that will test all the scenarios described by the diagram in Fig. 3.36?

(a) 2.
(b) 3.
(c) 4.
(d) 5.

Select ONE answer.

### Question 3.2.3B

You design test cases based on the following online shopping use case.

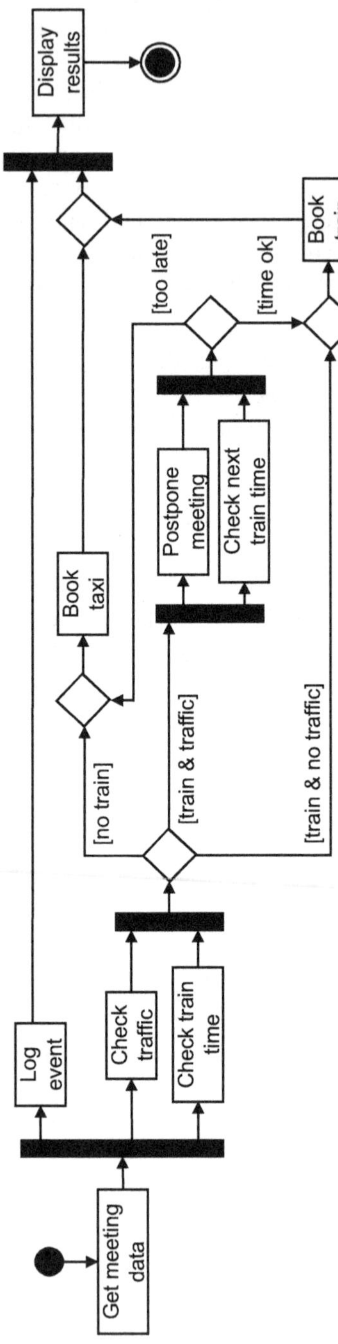


**Fig. 3.36** Activity diagram for an automatic scheduling assistant

Use case: online shopping—purchase products

**Main scenario**

1. Customer logs into their account.
2. The system verifies the login credentials and grants access to the product catalog.
3. Customer browses the catalog and adds a product to the cart.
4. The system updates the cart with the selected product details.
5. Customer proceeds to checkout.
6. The system displays the cart summary.
7. Customer accepts the summary.
8. The system processes the payment with the registered customer's data.
9. The system sends an order confirmation email.
10. Customer receives the email and can view the order details.

**Alternative flows**

1A. Customer enters incorrect login credentials. The system displays the error message "Invalid credentials. Please try again." The use case goes back to step 1.

5A Customer enters a promo code during checkout. The system validates the promo code and updates the total price in step 6.

7A. Customer chooses to pay using a digital wallet. The system redirects to the digital wallet's interface for authentication, and the payment is confirmed. The system goes to step 9.

**Exceptions**

7AA. (within alternative flow 7A) Payment declined by the digital wallet provider. The system displays an error message: "Payment was declined." The use case ends.

8A. Payment declined by the payment provider. The system displays an error message: "Payment was declined." The use case ends.

8B. The system fails to process the payment due to a timeout. It displays an error message: "We are experiencing technical difficulties. Please try again later." The use case ends.

The test strategy requires testing the main scenario and all extensions and exceptions. The strategy allows for the exercise of more than one alternative flow within a test case.

What is the **MINIMUM** number of test cases needed to cover all scenarios?

(a) 3.
(b) 4.

(c) 5.
(d) 6.

Select ONE answer.

## Exercise 6—Scenario-Based Testing

TA-3.2.3 (K3) Apply scenario-based testing

You have been asked to design test cases for a loan application analysis system. The business process implemented by this system is presented in the form of an activity diagram in Fig. 3.37.

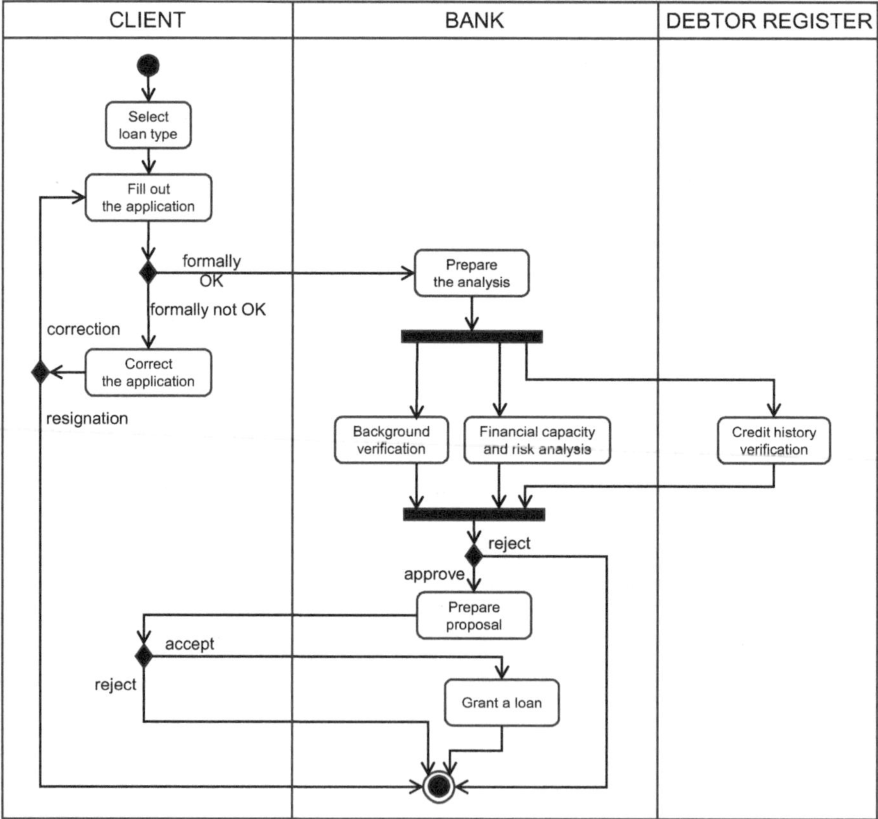


**Fig. 3.37** Loan application process

Using scenario-based testing, design functional test cases for this system.

# 3.3 Rule-Based Test Techniques

## 3.3.1 Decision Table Testing

TA-3.3.1 (K3) Apply decision table testing

**Definitions**

**Decision table testing**: A black-box test technique in which test cases are designed to exercise the combinations of conditions and the resulting actions shown in a decision table.

**Introduction**. Decision tables are used to test the implementation of system requirements that specify how different combinations of conditions result in different outcomes. They are an effective way of recording complex logic, such as business rules.

Decision tables help test analysts ensure that all possible combinations of conditions and their corresponding actions are considered. Test analysts identify any missing conditions or business rules by systematically listing all conditions and actions. This helps create a complete set of test cases and ensures thorough testing by covering all possible scenarios. Each unique combination of conditions in the decision table translates into one or more specific test cases, depending on factors like requirement importance or related risk. In case of lower risk, decision tables can be minimized, which may significantly reduce the decision table size and, hence, the number of test cases.

The structured format of decision tables provides a clear and concise way to represent complex rules. It also makes understanding, analyzing, and communicating the test scenarios easier for other stakeholders. Decision tables help detect errors in the requirements or business logic by providing a clear view of all conditions and their outcomes. This allows for early detection and fixing of defects in requirements.

**Decision table structure and notation**. We recap the basics of decision tables, which were already covered in the ISTQB® Foundation Level [1]. They form the basis for the more in-depth investigations in Advanced Test Analyst.

The main structural elements, as well as the notation used in creating decision tables, are illustrated by the example given in Table 3.15. It shows the business rules of the bank transfer processing system. Only registered users can make bank transfers. Three types of transfers are possible: by credit card, contactless by phone, or by internet wire transfer. The user must enter a valid PIN for card payments and internet wire transfers. If it is incorrect, the system informs the bank about the transfer attempt. Each transfer is subject to a processing fee ($1 for phone payments, $2 for card payments, and $3 for internet wire transfers). The system refuses to process the transaction if the payment amount plus the processing fee is greater than the account balance. The payment is processed only if the amount of funds is sufficient, and in the case of card payments and internet wire transfers, it is also processed if the PIN entered is correct.

The top part of the decision table contains conditions. Based on the combination of their values, appropriate actions will be taken, as described in the lower part of the decision table. The first column gives the names of the conditions and actions. Each of the other columns (headings numbered in Table 3.15 from R1 to R9) contains a rule, consisting of a specific combination of condition values (in the top part) and the corresponding actions (in the bottom part). For example, rule 2 describes the following situation: if a user is registered, withdraws money with the card, has entered the correct PIN, and has enough funds in the account, then the system processes the payment, charges a handling fee of $2, and the bank is not informed that the transaction was processed correctly. In turn, Rule 9 describes the following situation: if a user is registered, wants to make a transfer over the Internet, and has entered an incorrect PIN, then—regardless of whether he has enough funds in his account or not—the system does not execute the transfer, does not charge any processing fee, but informs the bank about the attempted operation.

The symbol "–" ("irrelevant" or "don't care") means any value. It is used in rules where actions depend only on certain conditions. In the case of rule 9, the system's response does not depend on the amount of funds in the account.

The symbol "N/A" ("not applicable") means that the condition cannot be given any value for a given rule. For example, in the case of payment by phone (rules 5 and 6), the payment procedure does not provide for the use of any PIN number.

The symbol "X" means that the action occurs. On the other hand, a blank box at the bottom part of the decision table means that the action should not happen.

**Limited-entry and extended-entry decision tables**. In limited-entry decision tables, all the values of the conditions and actions (except for not applicable or

**Table 3.15** Decision table for payment rules

| | R1 | R2 | R3 | R4 | R5 | R6 | R7 | R8 | R9 |
|---|---|---|---|---|---|---|---|---|---|
| **Conditions** | | | | | | | | | |
| User registered? | NO | YES | YES | YES | YES | YES | YES | YES | YES |
| Transfer type | – | card | card | card | phone | phone | wire | wire | wire |
| PIN correct? | – | YES | YES | NO | n/a | n/a | YES | YES | NO |
| Sufficient funds? | – | YES | NO | – | YES | NO | YES | NO | – |
| **Actions** | | | | | | | | | |
| Realize operation | | X | | | X | | X | | |
| Processing fee | | $2 | | | $1 | | $3 | | |
| Inform bank | | | | X | | | | | X |

infeasible ones; see below) are shown as Boolean values (true or false, or, equivalently, "yes" or "no"). In our example, this is the case for the conditions "User registered?", "PIN correct?" and "Sufficient funds?" and actions "Realize operation" and "Inform bank". In contrast, in extended-entry decision tables, some or all the conditions and actions may also take on multiple values (e.g., ranges of numbers, equivalence partitions, and discrete values). In our example, this is the case for the condition "Transfer type" (which has three possible values) and for the action "Processing fee" (also with three possible values). Because not all conditions and actions are Boolean, the example in Table 3.15 is an extended-entry decision table.

**Full decision table and the number of rules**. A decision table containing all possible condition values in all possible combinations is called a full decision table. A full decision table does not contain any "- "(irrelevant) condition values. The number of columns in the full decision table is the product of the possible values each condition can take and increases exponentially when the number of conditions and their possible values increase. For example, a limited-entry full decision table with 10 conditions has $2^{10} = 1024$ rules. Note that it is not uncommon for a real-life system to have business rules with 10 or more conditions. This is another case for the so-called combinatorial explosion, which we already mentioned in Sect. 2.4.

The full decision table for our bank transfer processing system has four conditions with resp. 2, 3, 2, 2 possible values. This means that the total number of rules equals $2 \cdot 3 \cdot 2 \cdot 2 = 24$. Notice that some of the rules are infeasible (combinations with transfer type = "phone" and PIN = "yes" (or "no")). For some others, some conditions do not impact actions (e.g., when the PIN for the card is not correct, the account balance is irrelevant for the related actions).

In decision table testing, the coverage items are the columns containing feasible combinations of conditions. To achieve 100% coverage with this technique, test cases must exercise all these columns. Coverage is measured as the number of exercised columns divided by the total number of feasible columns and is expressed as a percentage.

The advantage of using decision tables is that test analysts can easily check whether the correct actions occur for each combination of conditions. But to do this, the test analyst (or anyone who creates the decision table) must first determine all possible combinations of conditions. If the number of conditions and their values is low, combinations can be generated manually. Figure 3.38 shows this technique for our bank transfer processing system problem.

First, we calculate the number of columns of the full decision table (a). Then, we divide the array into as many equal parts as the number of values the first condition can take. In the columns in each part, we write the individual values of this condition (b). In our example, the first condition can take two possible values, so we divide the 24 columns into two equal parts of 12 columns each. In the first one, we write the value "NO"; in the second, "YES." Then, for each group of columns, we repeat the above procedure for the next conditions. The second condition (transfer type) can take three different values, so we divide each of the parts containing 12 columns into three equal parts of four columns each (c), entering the corresponding values of the

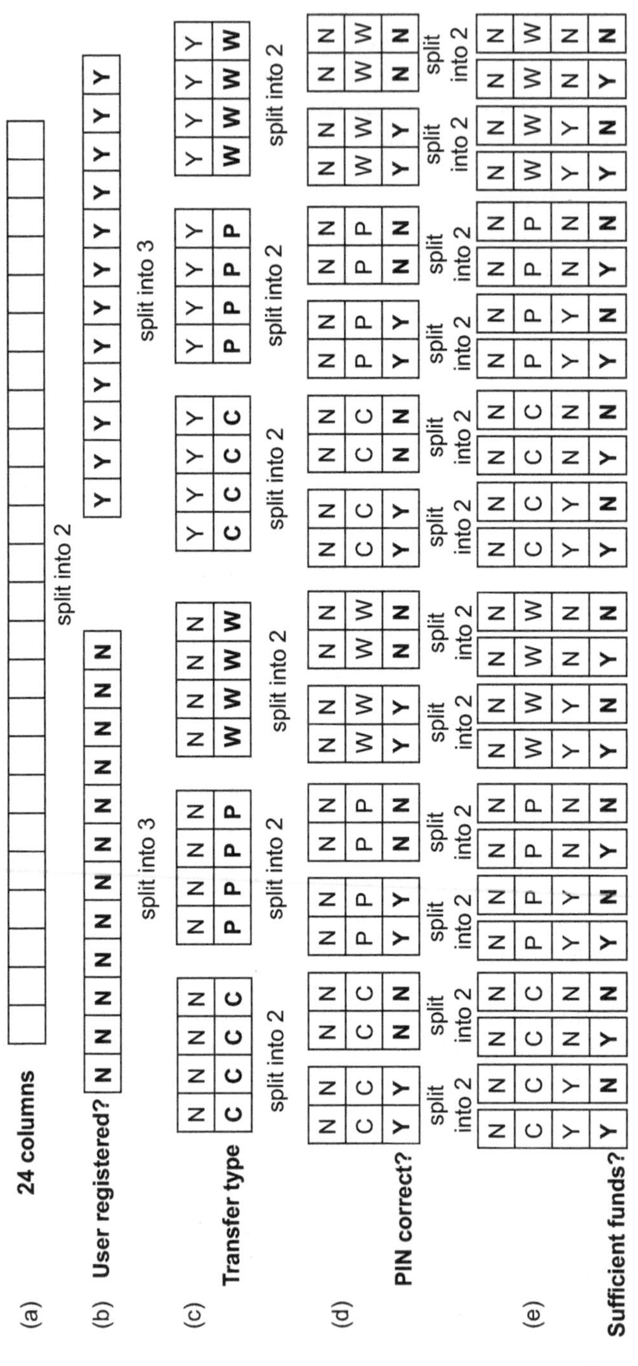


**Fig. 3.38** Deriving all combinations of condition values

second condition into them. Similarly, we divide each of these groups into two parts (d) since the third condition can take two different values. After dividing due to the last condition (e), each group contains one column. After entering the conditions, the set of finally obtained columns includes all possible combinations of condition values.

**Automating the Generation of Combinations of Elements**

If the number of combinations is large, some automation can become handy. A simple script, such as the one in Fig. 3.39, written in Python, can be used for this purpose. This script uses the `itertools` library, which allows us to generate all sorts of combinations of elements. In lines 18–21, the parameters and their possible values are defined for our bank transfer processing system.

```
1  import itertools
2
3  def generate_combinations(param_dict):
4      # Extract the keys and values from the dictionary
5      keys = param_dict.keys()
6      values = param_dict.values()
7
8      # Generate all combinations using itertools.product
9      combinations = list(itertools.product(*values))
10
11     # Convert the combinations into a list of dictionaries
12     combination_dicts = [dict(zip(keys, combination)) for combination in combinations]
13
14     return combination_dicts
15
16     # Define the parameter dictionary
17 params = {
18     "Reg?": ["YES", "NO "],
19     "Tr type": ["CARD ", "PHONE", "WIRE "],
20     "PIN cor?": ["YES", "NO "],
21     "Suff funds?": ["YES", "NO "]
22 }
23
24 # Generate combinations
25 all_combinations = generate_combinations(params)
26
27 # Print the combinations
28 for combination in all_combinations:
29     print(combination)
```

**Fig. 3.39** Script for generating all combinations of condition values

After running the script, we get the following result: all combinations of condition values.

```
D:\BankTransferProcessingSystem>genCombinations.py
{'Reg?': 'YES', 'Tr type': 'CARD ', 'PIN cor?': 'YES', 'Suff
funds?': 'YES'}
{'Reg?': 'YES', 'Tr type': 'CARD ', 'PIN cor?': 'YES', 'Suff
funds?': 'NO '}
{'Reg?': 'YES', 'Tr type': 'CARD ', 'PIN cor?': 'NO ', 'Suff
funds?': 'YES'}
{'Reg?': 'YES', 'Tr type': 'CARD ', 'PIN cor?': 'NO ', 'Suff
funds?': 'NO '}
```

```
{'Reg?': 'YES', 'Tr type': 'PHONE', 'PIN cor?': 'YES', 'Suff
funds?': 'YES'}
{'Reg?': 'YES', 'Tr type': 'PHONE', 'PIN cor?': 'YES', 'Suff
funds?': 'NO '}
{'Reg?': 'YES', 'Tr type': 'PHONE', 'PIN cor?': 'NO ', 'Suff
funds?': 'YES'}
{'Reg?': 'YES', 'Tr type': 'PHONE', 'PIN cor?': 'NO ', 'Suff
funds?': 'NO '}
{'Reg?': 'YES', 'Tr type': 'WIRE ', 'PIN cor?': 'YES', 'Suff
funds?': 'YES'}
{'Reg?': 'YES', 'Tr type': 'WIRE ', 'PIN cor?': 'YES', 'Suff
funds?': 'NO '}
{'Reg?': 'YES', 'Tr type': 'WIRE ', 'PIN cor?': 'NO ', 'Suff
funds?': 'YES'}
{'Reg?': 'YES', 'Tr type': 'WIRE ', 'PIN cor?': 'NO ', 'Suff
funds?': 'NO '}
{'Reg?': 'NO ', 'Tr type': 'CARD ', 'PIN cor?': 'YES', 'Suff
funds?': 'YES'}
{'Reg?': 'NO ', 'Tr type': 'CARD ', 'PIN cor?': 'YES', 'Suff
funds?': 'NO '}
{'Reg?': 'NO ', 'Tr type': 'CARD ', 'PIN cor?': 'NO ', 'Suff
funds?': 'YES'}
{'Reg?': 'NO ', 'Tr type': 'CARD ', 'PIN cor?': 'NO ', 'Suff
funds?': 'NO '}
{'Reg?': 'NO ', 'Tr type': 'PHONE', 'PIN cor?': 'YES', 'Suff
funds?': 'YES'}
{'Reg?': 'NO ', 'Tr type': 'PHONE', 'PIN cor?': 'YES', 'Suff
funds?': 'NO '}
{'Reg?': 'NO ', 'Tr type': 'PHONE', 'PIN cor?': 'NO ', 'Suff
funds?': 'YES'}
{'Reg?': 'NO ', 'Tr type': 'PHONE', 'PIN cor?': 'NO ', 'Suff
funds?': 'NO '}
{'Reg?': 'NO ', 'Tr type': 'WIRE ', 'PIN cor?': 'YES', 'Suff
funds?': 'YES'}
{'Reg?': 'NO ', 'Tr type': 'WIRE ', 'PIN cor?': 'YES', 'Suff
funds?': 'NO '}
{'Reg?': 'NO ', 'Tr type': 'WIRE ', 'PIN cor?': 'NO ', 'Suff
funds?': 'YES'}
{'Reg?': 'NO ', 'Tr type': 'WIRE ', 'PIN cor?': 'NO ', 'Suff
funds?': 'NO '}
```

**Decision table minimization**.

In addition to removing infeasible rules, decision tables can be minimized by merging action-equivalent rules that depend only on a subset of conditions. Two rules are considered action-equivalent if they have the same values for every action in the decision table. As we see in Table 3.15, our minimized decision table has only 9 columns compared to 24. While the ISTQB® Foundation syllabus only mentions that minimization is possible, the Advanced Test Analyst syllabus focuses on the minimization procedure.

In practice, especially in non-critical systems, test analysts do not operate on full decision tables due to the combinatorial explosion regarding the number of columns. In most cases, large decision tables can be minimized.

The procedure for decision table minimization is as follows.

1. Remove infeasible columns (or mark them as "infeasible"; they will be ignored in the minimization process).
2. Group the columns according to action-equivalent rules. Minimization can only be done within a group of columns with the same actions.
3. For each such group, find a set of columns for which some conditions have constant values and all the other conditions have all possible combinations of their values.
4. All columns from each set from Point 3 can be minimized into one column, where the values of the first group of conditions remain as they are, while the values of the second group of conditions get the value of "– "(irrelevant).

The minimization procedure is shown in Fig. 3.40. Full decision table (a) is decomposed into three action-equivalent groups of columns (b). In the first group, columns 1, 2, 3, and 4 can be minimized because Cond1 is constant, and Cond2 and Cond3 are combined in all four possible ways (YES/YES, YES/NO, NO/YES, and NO/NO). Similarly, columns 5 and 7 can be minimized because Cond1 and Cond3 are constant, and Cond2 has all possible values (YES and NO). Values for the irrelevant conditions are replaced with a "–" symbol, and we obtain the minimized table (c).

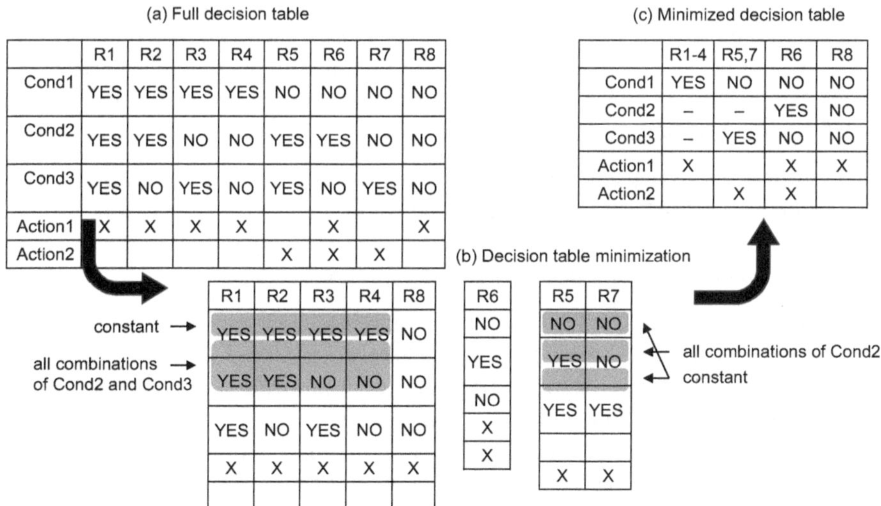


**Fig. 3.40** Decision table minimization procedure

A minimized decision table is simpler and easier to understand. Reducing the number of conditions and actions to only those essential helps avoid unnecessary complexity, making the table more user-friendly. By minimizing the decision table, test analysts can focus on the most critical combinations of conditions and actions, creating efficient and targeted test cases. This helps in avoiding redundant or duplicate test cases. With fewer test cases derived from a minimized decision table, the time required for test execution is reduced. This leads to faster testing cycles and quicker feedback, which is crucial in agile and iterative development environments. Minimized decision tables are also easier to maintain. When business rules change or new requirements are introduced, a minimized table can usually be updated more quickly and with less risk of introducing defects.

While minimizing decision tables has several benefits, there are also potential risks associated with this approach compared to using a full decision table. These risks include:

- **Incomplete coverage**. For a minimized group of columns, the test analyst usually designs one test case, so the concrete values of all the conditions must be given. There is a risk that a certain combination of values that results in a failure will be missed in test cases. This can lead to gaps in coverage, potentially allowing defects to slip through.
- **Oversimplification**. In the minimization process, especially when the minimized table is created directly, not from the full decision table, there is a risk of oversimplifying the decision table and omitting important conditions or actions. This can result in an incomplete representation of the business logic and lead to insufficient testing.
- **Risk of incorrect assumptions.** Minimization can often be processed in many different ways, leading to different minimized tables. In such cases, minimizing a decision table involves making assumptions about which conditions and actions are less critical. This influences the order of column minimization. If the assumptions are incorrect, important scenarios might be overlooked, leading to potential defects in those areas remaining undetected.

To mitigate these risks, it is important to approach the minimization of decision tables with care. This involves thorough analysis, validation of the minimized table against the full set of conditions and actions, and possibly combining minimized tables with other test techniques to ensure comprehensive coverage.

**Checksum procedure**. Decision tables can be minimized using tools or manually. Sometimes, decision tables are created immediately in a minimized form. In any case, the test analyst should be able to verify that the minimization was done correctly. This can be done in various ways. For example, one can verify that each unique combination of conditions matches exactly one column. However, such checking can be lengthy. The syllabus describes another, simpler technique, called the "checksum procedure."

The checksum procedure begins by calculating a score for each rule, representing the number of rules in a full decision table that it reflects. By summing the scores of all rules within the table, we arrive at the decision table checksum. If the minimization has been executed correctly, the checksum of the minimized table will equal the checksum of the original decision table. Typically, the original decision table is either a full decision table or one derived from the full version by omitting infeasible rules.

The score for a specific rule is calculated as follows. If the rule does not contain any "irrelevant" or "not applicable" condition values, its score is set to one. If the rule contains any values represented by a "–" or "n/a" symbol, we assign each of them the number of possible values that the corresponding condition can take. The rule score is then calculated by multiplying these values together. For example, in Table 3.15, the score of column 1 is computed as $3*2*2 = 12$, as it includes "irrelevant" values for three conditions with 3, 2, and 2 possible values, respectively. The score of rule 5 is two, because it contains one condition with "n/a" value, and this condition can take two possible values.

Summing all rule scores provides the checksum. It is straightforward to see that the checksum of the decision table in Fig. 3.41 equals the total number of combinations of condition values.

**Number of possible values for each condition**

| | | R1 | R2 | R3 | R4 | R5 | R6 | R7 | R8 | R9 |
|---|---|---|---|---|---|---|---|---|---|---|
| | Conditions | | | | | | | | | |
| 2 | User registered? | NO | YES | YES | YES | YES | YES | YES | YES | YES |
| 3 | Transfer type | – | card | card | card | phone | phone | wire | wire | wire |
| 2 | PIN correct? | – | YES | YES | NO | n/a | n/a | YES | YES | NO |
| 2 | Sufficient funds? | – | YES | NO | – | YES | NO | YES | NO | – |
| | **Rule sums for each column** | **3*2*2 =12** | **1** | **1** | **2** | **2** | **2** | **1** | **1** | **2** |

Checksum = sum of rule sums

12 + 1 + 1 + 2 + 2 + 2 + 1 + 1 + 2 = **24**

Number of combinations: 2 * 3 * 2 * 2 = **24**

**Fig. 3.41** Illustration of the checksum procedure

Let $S$ denote the checksum of a minimized table, and let $C$ denote the number of all combinations of condition values, i.e., the checksum of the corresponding full decision table. Notice that if the decision table is minimized correctly, then $S = C$. If $S \neq C$, for sure optimization did something wrong: if $S > C$, there must be a combination of conditions that matches more than one column; if $S < C$, some conditions are omitted from the table. However, $S = C$ does not guarantee that the minimization is correct. Figure 3.42 shows such an example.

The original, full decision table has 8 columns. The checksum for the minimized version is also 8, but the minimized decision table is incorrect. It contains two defects. The first one is an inconsistency: the combination (NO, YES, YES) matches both the first and second columns. The second one is a gap: the combination (YES, YES, NO) is missing.

| Condition 1 | NO | NO | NO | NO | YES | YES | YES | YES |
|---|---|---|---|---|---|---|---|---|
| Condition 2 | NO | NO | YES | YES | NO | NO | YES | YES |
| Condition 3 | NO | YES | NO | YES | NO | YES | NO | YES |
| Action | A | A | A | A | C | C | B | B |

$$C = 2 \cdot 2 \cdot 2 = 8$$

| Condition 1 | NO | – | YES |
|---|---|---|---|
| Condition 2 | – | YES | NO |
| Condition 3 | – | YES | – |
| Action | A | B | C |

$$S = 4 + 2 + 2 = 8$$

**Fig. 3.42** Correct checksum for an incorrectly minimized decision table

**Decision table review**. The test analyst should review the decision table, possibly with the other stakeholders, with the following criteria:

- consistency (i.e., if two different rules apply to a combination of condition values, then they are action-equivalent)
- feasibility (i.e., each rule contains a combination of condition values that is achievable in the test item)
- completeness (i.e., no feasible combination of condition values is missing)
- correctness (i.e., the rules model the system's intended behavior)

It is also recommended that the rules be non-overlapping (i.e., for any combination of condition values, there is at most one rule that applies). Overlapping rules may happen when the original decision table is already minimized or if rules are merged incorrectly. If the rules are non-overlapping, they are consistent.

Table 3.16 shows a decision table with several problems:

- Rules 2 and 3 are not consistent. They both match the combination (NO, YES, NO), but they are not action-equivalent: rule 2 admits a 20% discount, while rule 3 admits a 30% discount.
- Rule 1 is infeasible. It is impossible to be more than 18 years old and not more than 14 years old simultaneously. Such mutually exclusive conditions can be merged into one; in this case, we could have only one condition, "age," with three possible values, ">18", "between 15 and 18", and "≤14".
- The table is not complete. The rule for the combination (YES, NO, NO) is missing.
- The table is probably incorrect. An honorary blood donor should receive a non-zero discount (if not a free ride ticket!).

If we change the ticket discount from 30 to 20% in rule 3, the table will still have overlapping rules, but at least these rules will be consistent. However, it is a bad practice to have non-overlapping rules in decision tables. The good practice is

**Table 3.16** Very defective decision table

| | R1 | R2 | R3 | R4 |
|---|---|---|---|---|
| **Conditions** | | | | |
| Age > 18 | YES | NO | – | YES |
| Age $\leq$ 14 | YES | – | YES | NO |
| Honorary blood donor? | – | NO | NO | YES |
| **Action** | | | | |
| Ticket discount | | 20% | 30% | 0% |

that each feasible combination of condition values should match one and only one column in the decision table.

**Decision table coverage**. Once the decision table is checked, minimized (if necessary), and contains only achievable rules, the test analyst can start designing test cases. The decision table coverage criterion requires that each rule in the table be tested with at least one test case.

The test case's defined inputs and expected behavior are often in the form of condition values and actions from the corresponding column of the decision table. However, sometimes, forcing certain conditions to occur may require more complicated inputs and actions. For example, consider the condition "total value of account operations during the month > $10,000" to take the truth value. There may not be a variable in the system that directly expresses this value. To perform the test case, the test analyst must ensure that the condition is met, for example, by creating bank transfers in a given month for an amount exceeding $10,000.

**Decision Tables and Cause-and-Effect Graphs**

Cause-and-effect graphs are an equivalent form of presenting the rules defined in a decision table, but they do it in a more compact way. Cause-and-effect graphs represent the logical relationships between different inputs (causes) and the resultant outputs (effects). The components of the cause-and-effect graphs are:

- Causes—inputs or conditions that influence the system's behavior, usually represented as nodes in the left part of the cause-effect graph
- Effects—outputs or results that occur due to the causes, usually represented as nodes in the right part of the cause-effect graph
- Logical connectors—these include AND, OR, and NOT operators that connect the causes and effects, defining the logical relationship between them
- Edges—lines connecting causes with effects (sometimes via some "internal" nodes that may be defined when the logical relations are complex)

The cause-and-effect graph equivalent to the decision table from Fig. 3.40c is shown in Fig. 3.43.

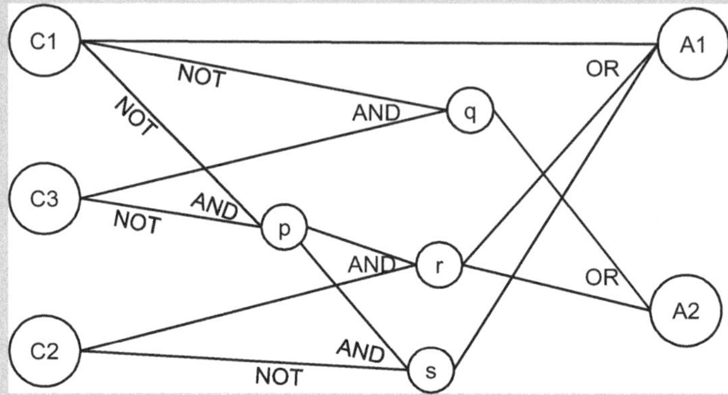


**Fig. 3.43** Cause-effect graph

When we want to see which actions should occur for a given combination of conditions, we set the condition values in cause nodes C1, C2, and C3, and we propagate them along the edges according to the logical operators. Equivalently, we can derive logical formulae for effects A1 and A2 by analyzing the graph backward. For example:

$$\begin{aligned} A1 &= C1 \vee r \vee s \\ &= C1 \vee (p \wedge C2) \vee (p \wedge \neg C2) \\ &= C1 \vee (\neg C1 \wedge \neg C3 \wedge C2) \vee (\neg C1 \wedge \neg C3 \wedge \neg C2) \\ &= C1 \vee (\neg C1 \wedge \neg C3). \end{aligned}$$

Now, if, for example, C1 = FALSE, C2 = TRUE, C3 = FALSE, then

$$A1 = \text{FALSE} \vee (\neg\text{FALSE} \wedge \neg\text{FALSE}) = \text{FALSE} \vee \text{TRUE} = \text{TRUE}.$$

This means that action (effect) A1 holds.

There are tools to create cause-and-effect graphs and convert them into decision tables. There are also algorithms that allow one to derive a small number of test cases from the cause-effect graph, taking into account the logical structure of the expressions corresponding to each effect. An example is the backward propagation algorithm described in [24].

### Case Study

Consider the discount system for the FoodApp. The rules for admitting discounts are presented in Table 3.17.

**Table 3.17** Decision table for the FoodApp discount rules

| | R1 | R2 | R3 | R4 | R5 | R6 | R7 | R8 |
|---|---|---|---|---|---|---|---|---|
| **Conditions** | | | | | | | | |
| Regular customer? | YES | YES | YES | YES | NO | NO | NO | NO |
| Order amount > $50? | YES | YES | NO | NO | YES | YES | NO | NO |
| Promo code applied? | YES | NO | YES | NO | YES | NO | YES | NO |
| **Action** | | | | | | | | |
| Discount | 20% | 10% | 20% | 10% | 20% | 10% | 5% | 0% |

The test analyst was tasked with designing test cases based on this decision table. Due to the small amount of time and relatively low risk related to this feature, management decided to design test cases based on the minimized decision table.

The test analyst first makes sure that the decision board is correct. Each of the three conditions is binary (yes/no), meaning the full decision table should have 2 * 2 * 2 = 8 columns. Each of the eight columns contains a different combination of conditions, so the test analyst concludes that the decision table is full and the rules are non-overlapping, which also means that the rules are consistent.

Next, the test analyst checks whether the rules are achievable. The rules describe the size of the discount depending on three conditions: whether the customer is a regular customer, the size of the order, and whether the customer entered a promotional code. The test analyst may find that these conditions are independent of each other, which would mean that each rule is attainable. However, it is worth making sure that, for example, the ability to enter a promo code is not, for example, limited to regular customers only. If this were the case, rules 5 and 7 would have to be removed as unattainable.

The final step in checking the decision table is to verify that the business rules meet the user's requirements. The test analyst could, for example, raise doubts about whether the assigned discount for rule 5 (non-regular customer) should be the same as for rule 1 (regular customer). Let's assume that after inquiring about this issue, the customer responds that the size of the discount in the case of rule 5 is correct and is the result of the company's marketing policy.

Once the decision table has been validated, the test analyst minimizes it. Within a group of columns 1, 3, and 5, a pair of 1, 3, or a pair of 1, 5 can be minimized, but all three cannot be minimized. Within the group of columns 2, 4, and 6, the pair 2, 4, or the pair 2, 6 can be minimized, but the whole three cannot be minimized. In addition, you can only minimize two columns among columns 1, 3, and 5 or only two columns among columns 2, 4, and 6.

As you can see, there are many possible minimization methods. All eight possibilities are shown in Fig. 3.44. Let us examine them closely to understand the relationship between the minimization method and the risks we want to mitigate during testing.

(a)

| | R1,3 | R2,4 | R5 | R6 | R7 | R8 |
|---|---|---|---|---|---|---|
| **Conditions** | | | | | | |
| Regular customer? | YES | YES | NO | NO | NO | NO |
| Order amount > $50? | – | – | YES | YES | NO | NO |
| Promo code applied? | YES | NO | YES | NO | YES | NO |
| **Action** | | | | | | |
| Discount | 20% | 10% | 20% | 10% | 5% | 0% |

(b)

| | R1,5 | R3 | R2,4 | R6 | R7 | R8 |
|---|---|---|---|---|---|---|
| **Conditions** | | | | | | |
| Regular customer? | – | YES | YES | NO | NO | NO |
| Order amount > $50? | YES | NO | – | YES | NO | NO |
| Promo code applied? | YES | YES | NO | NO | YES | NO |
| **Action** | | | | | | |
| Discount | 20% | 20% | 10% | 10% | 5% | 0% |

(c)

| | R1,3 | R2 | R4 | R5 | R6 | R7 | R8 |
|---|---|---|---|---|---|---|---|
| **Conditions** | | | | | | | |
| Regular customer? | YES | YES | YES | NO | NO | NO | NO |
| Order amount > $50? | – | YES | NO | YES | YES | NO | NO |
| Promo code applied? | YES | NO | NO | YES | NO | YES | NO |
| **Action** | | | | | | | |
| Discount | 20% | 10% | 10% | 20% | 10% | 5% | 0% |

(d)

| | R1 | R2,4 | R3 | R5 | R6 | R7 | R8 |
|---|---|---|---|---|---|---|---|
| **Conditions** | | | | | | | |
| Regular customer? | YES | YES | YES | NO | NO | NO | NO |
| Order amount > $50? | YES | – | NO | YES | YES | NO | NO |
| Promo code applied? | YES | NO | YES | YES | NO | YES | NO |
| **Action** | | | | | | | |
| Discount | 20% | 10% | 20% | 20% | 10% | 5% | 0% |

(e)

| | R1,3 | R2,6 | R4 | R5 | R7 | R8 |
|---|---|---|---|---|---|---|
| **Conditions** | | | | | | |
| Regular customer? | YES | – | YES | NO | NO | NO |
| Order amount > $50? | – | YES | NO | YES | NO | NO |
| Promo code applied? | YES | NO | NO | YES | YES | NO |
| **Action** | | | | | | |
| Discount | 20% | 10% | 10% | 20% | 5% | 0% |

(f)

| | R1,5 | R2,6 | R3 | R4 | R7 | R8 |
|---|---|---|---|---|---|---|
| **Conditions** | | | | | | |
| Regular customer? | – | – | YES | YES | NO | NO |
| Order amount > $50? | YES | YES | NO | NO | NO | NO |
| Promo code applied? | YES | NO | YES | NO | YES | NO |
| **Action** | | | | | | |
| Discount | 20% | 10% | 20% | 10% | 5% | 0% |

(g)

| | R1,5 | R2 | R3 | R4 | R6 | R7 | R8 |
|---|---|---|---|---|---|---|---|
| **Conditions** | | | | | | | |
| Regular customer? | – | YES | YES | YES | NO | NO | NO |
| Order amount > $50? | YES | YES | NO | NO | YES | NO | NO |
| Promo code applied? | YES | NO | YES | NO | NO | YES | NO |
| **Action** | | | | | | | |
| Discount | 20% | 10% | 20% | 10% | 10% | 5% | 0% |

(h)

| | R1 | R2,6 | R3 | R4 | R5 | R7 | R8 |
|---|---|---|---|---|---|---|---|
| **Conditions** | | | | | | | |
| Regular customer? | YES | – | YES | YES | NO | NO | NO |
| Order amount > $50? | YES | YES | NO | NO | YES | NO | NO |
| Promo code applied? | YES | NO | YES | NO | YES | YES | NO |
| **Action** | | | | | | | |
| Discount | 20% | 10% | 20% | 10% | 20% | 5% | 0% |

**Fig. 3.44** All possible ways to minimize the decision table from Table 3.17

Let us first compare tables (c) and (g). The former minimizes columns 1 and 3, while the latter minimizes columns 1 and 5. In the case of (c), the minimized column ignores the order amount, while in the case of (g), it ignores the type of customer. If, in the case of granting a 20% discount, verification of the order amount is for some reason more important to us than the type of customer who will receive this discount, then, deciding to minimize this group of columns, the test analyst should choose option (g). This is because this table forces the test analyst to perform two test cases in the case of a 20% discount, in one of which the order amount exceeds $50, and in the other, it does not (and in the former case, the type of customer is not important). However, if, for some reason, the customer type is more important than the order amount, the test analyst should select option (c). This is because this decision table forces the test analyst to perform two test cases for a 20% discount for two different customer types (with the order amount not being important in one case).

Similarly, the test analyst can decide to minimize the columns corresponding to the 10% discount, that is, minimizing columns 2, 4, or 2, 6, shown in tables (d) and (h). Option (d) should be selected when the type of customer is more relevant to this type of discount than the order amount, and option (h) otherwise.

Finally, the test analyst can decide whether to minimize both groups of columns or only one of them. In the former case, he has four choices: (a)–(d). If the order amount is always more important than the type of customer (regardless of the discount type), it will be logical to choose option (f), which corresponds to the "combined" options (g) and (h), which both prioritize order amount over client type. If the customer's type is more important than the number of purchases, it will be logical to choose option (a), which corresponds to the "combined" options (c) and (d), which both prioritize client type over order amount. In turn, the selection of option (b) or (e) will make sense if the priorities of the conditions "customer type" and "total amount of purchases" are different for the two types of discount (10% and 20%).

Suppose the test analyst chooses option (f). This table has six columns, so in order to achieve the decision table coverage, the test analyst has to design at least six test cases—one for each column. Assuming the test analyst designs low-level test cases, they must define a concrete order amount for each test case. The example set of six test cases may look as follows:

- TC1: regular customer with an order amount $60 and promo code applied (expected result: 20% discount)—covers the rule "1, 5";
- TC2: non-regular customer with an order amount of $71 and promo code not applied (expected result: 10% discount)—covers the rule "2, 6";
- TC3: regular customer with an order amount of $15 and promo code applied (expected result: 20% discount)—covers the rule "3";
- TC4: regular customer with an order amount of $11 and promo code not applied (expected result: 10% discount)—covers the rule "4";
- TC5: non-regular customer with an order amount of $45 and promo code applied (expected result: 5% discount)—covers the rule "7";
- TC6: non-regular customer with an order amount of $20 and promo code not applied (expected result: 0% discount)—covers the rule "8".

Suppose now that the management decides that the condition "order amount" is much more important than they thought earlier. This means there's a high risk related to incorrect discount admissions based on this value. The test analyst may combine decision table testing with the two-value boundary value analysis (see the Foundation Level syllabus). The boundary values for equivalence classes representing the order amount are $0.01, $50, and $50.01. The test analyst can modify TC1 by replacing $60 with $50.01, which is the minimal value for which the condition "Order amount > $50" is fulfilled. TC3 can be modified by replacing $15 with $50, since this is the maximal value for which the condition "Order amount > $50" is not fulfilled. TC4 can be modified by replacing \$11 with \$0.01, which is the smallest possible amount of order (at least, in theory; it could also be the price of the cheapest thing that can be ordered from the restaurant). Such a modified set of test cases still achieves the decision table coverage but also achieves the boundary value coverage for the "order amount" domain.

## Sample Questions

### Question 3.3.1A

The university admission system implements the following rule for deciding if an applicant is eligible for a university program:

An applicant is eligible for a university program if both of the following conditions are fulfilled:

(1) Applicant has a Grade Point Average (GPA) of 3.5 or higher.
**AND**
(2) Applicant scored at least 1200 on the SAT exam **OR** participated in at least two extracurricular activities in high school.

Otherwise, the applicant is not eligible for a university program.

The system uses three variables to model the appropriate conditions:

- GPA—the GPA value
- SAT—the SAT exam result
- EXTRA—number of extracurricular activities in which an applicant participated in high school

You design the minimized decision table with conditions "GPA >= 3.5?", "SAT >= 1200?" and "EXTRA >= 2?" to model the admission rules. The decision table must be complete and have non-overlapping rules.

What is the number of columns representing business rules in the minimized decision table?

(a) 5.
(b) 3.
(c) 2.
(d) 4.

Select ONE answer.

**Table 3.18** Decision table for the customer order acceptance system

| | R1 | R2 | R3 | R4 | R5 | R6 | R7 | R8 |
|---|---|---|---|---|---|---|---|---|
| **Conditions** | | | | | | | | |
| Credit limit exceeded? | Y | Y | Y | Y | N | N | N | N |
| Prompt payer? | Y | Y | N | N | Y | Y | N | N |
| Special clearance? | Y | N | Y | N | Y | N | Y | N |
| **Action** | | | | | | | | |
| Accept order? | Y | N | Y | N | Y | Y | Y | Y |

*Source* youtube.com/watch?v=zHokvz4fRGY

### Question 3.3.1B

You want to design test cases for the system that accepts or rejects a customer order. The business rules are based on the decision table shown in Table 3.18.

You decided to design the test cases for the minimized version of this decision table, with as few columns as possible. You currently have the following test cases:

(i) Credit limit not exceeded, prompt payer, special clearance.
(ii) Credit limit exceeded, prompt payer, no special clearance.
(iii) Credit limit exceeded, prompt payer, special clearance.
(iv) Credit limit not exceeded, prompt payer, no special clearance.
(v) Credit limit not exceeded, no prompt payer, special clearance.

Which subset of these test cases is the **SMALLEST** test set that achieves the coverage for the minimized decision table?

(a) ii, iii, iv.
(b) i, iii, v.
(c) ii, v.
(d) i, iv.

Select ONE answer.

## Exercise 7—Decision Table Testing

TA-3.3.1 (K3) Apply decision table testing

You have been given the decision table shown in Table 3.19. This table presents the business rules of a fraud-prevention/payment authorization system.

**Table 3.19** Business rules of a fraud-prevention/payment authorization system

| | R1 | R2 | R3 | R4 | R5 | R6 | R7 | R8 | R9 | R10 | R11 | R12 |
|---|---|---|---|---|---|---|---|---|---|---|---|---|
| **Conditions** | | | | | | | | | | | | |
| Payment method | C | C | C | C | D | D | D | D | B | B | B | B |
| User verified? | Y | Y | N | N | Y | Y | N | N | Y | Y | N | N |
| High-risk transaction? | Y | N | Y | N | Y | N | Y | N | Y | N | Y | N |
| **Actions** | | | | | | | | | | | | |
| Approve the transaction immediately | | X | | | | X | | | | X | | |
| Request manual review | X | | X | | X | | X | | X | | X | |
| As for additional verification | | | | X | | | | X | | | | |
| Reject transaction | | | | | | | | | | | | X |

*C* Credit card, *D* Digital wallet, *B* Bank transfer

1. Minimize the decision table to obtain the minimum possible number of columns
2. Use the checksum procedure to increase confidence that the minimization was performed correctly
3. Design a test case for one of the columns of the minimized decision table

## 3.3.2 *Metamorphic Testing*

TA-3.3.2 (K3) Apply metamorphic testing

**Definitions**

**Metamorphic relation**: A description of how a change to an input for a test case affects an expected result based on the required behavior of a test item.

**Metamorphic testing**: A test technique in which test conditions are metamorphic relations.

**Introduction**. Metamorphic testing (MT) is a test technique used to address the challenges of testing systems for which it is difficult to derive the correct output for a given input. It is exactly the oracle problem discussed earlier in Sect. 1.3.4. Practical examples in which the oracle problem occurs (and makes MT a useful technique) include:

- **Machine learning algorithms**. Suppose a machine learning algorithm is to return the optimal route for a courier using FoodApp. For a given input (the location of the restaurant and the customer), the algorithm will return some route, but it is very difficult to verify that this route is indeed optimal.

- **Randomized algorithms**. Suppose that when an order arrives, the FoodApp algorithm assigns the task of delivering the meal to a randomly selected delivery person who is available and whose distance from the restaurant does not exceed a certain threshold value. For the same initial data (availability and location of delivery persons), the system may return a different answer each time, selecting a different person. Strictly determining the expected output (i.e., choosing a specific delivery person) is impossible.
- **Simulation software**. Testing complex simulations with multiple variables and uncertain outputs may be challenging since simulation results may differ depending on initial conditions and other factors.
- **Data-related complexity.** Testing the correctness of results of search and retrieval from big data or from legacy systems with several generations of data structures, or testing route optimization in a complex traffic network, are challenging because the accurate expected results are typically hard to determine.

In MT, instead of relying solely on known input-output pairs to verify correctness, new (follow-up) test cases are designed from an existing source test case based on knowledge of the function being tested. The follow-up test cases are generated using a metamorphic relation (MR), which defines a property of the test item and describes how a change in a test case's test inputs should be reflected in the test case's expected results.

Key concepts of metamorphic testing. Three key concepts of MT are:

- metamorphic relations,
- source test cases,
- follow-up test cases.

*Metamorphic relation* is a property that defines how the output should change when the input is modified in specific ways. MRs are derived from the expected behavior of the software and are used to create new test cases from existing ones.

**Examples of Metamorphic Relations**

In a sorting algorithm, an MR might state that if you permute the order of the input list, the output should not change, because it depends on the input elements only, and not their order.

On a hotel reservation website, if a user performs a hotel search and then adds a new filter (e.g., price range or star rating), the resulting set of hotels should be a subset (or equal) of the original result.

A *source test case* is the first test case, which is based on knowledge of the function being tested. It is good if the test analyst is able to verify the expected result, but even if they cannot, they may run the test case and assume temporarily that the result is correct. The test analyst may define one or more source test cases. These form the basis for the follow-up test cases.

A *follow-up test case* is a test case derived from an existing source test case. It is basically the source test case with test input data changed according to a given metamorphic relation. The whole idea of metamorphic testing is that we do not need to know the expected result of a follow-up test case. It is enough to observe the actual result and check if the metamorphic relation holds between the actual results of the source and follow-up test cases.

Let us consider two examples regarding the FoodApp to see how metamorphic testing can be applied.

**Example 1**. A test analyst tests the function of assigning an order to a delivery person. Suppose the algorithm selects a delivery person randomly from the ones that are available and located within a certain distance from the restaurant (let's call this area R).

Consider now the following metamorphic relations:

- M1: if there is only one available delivery person D in R, then moving its position within R does not affect the expected result, i.e., the algorithm still assigns the task to D.
- M2: if there is only one available delivery person D in R, then changing the location of all the other available delivery persons within the complement of R does not affect the expected result, i.e., the algorithm still assigns the task to D.
- M3: if there is only one available delivery person D in R and R is moved or resized so that it still contains D only, then the expected result is not affected, i.e., the algorithm still assigns the task to D.

The test analyst creates a source test case in which there is only one available delivery person, D1, in area R. In addition, there are two other available delivery persons, D2 and D3, outside R. The expected result for this test case is assigning a task to delivery person D1. This situation is depicted in the left part of Fig. 3.45.

The right part of Fig. 3.45 shows how these three metamorphic relations can be used to generate follow-up test cases based on the source test case using the metamorphic relations M1, M2, and M3 (two examples for each relation are shown). Gray elements are the ones that are changed according to the relation between inputs.

Metamorphic relations M1, M2, and M3 may seem to be "trivial" or "simple" because the output relation is simply equality: if input changes in a certain way, then the expected result does not change. However, even this type of simple relationship can reveal many defects during testing. But we may also think about some more complex relations, as in the next example.

**Example 2**. Consider a restaurant search function in the FoodApp. Let us assume that each restaurant determines the distance to which it pays to deliver meals. In addition, each restaurant has its own menu. A FoodApp customer indicates on a form what

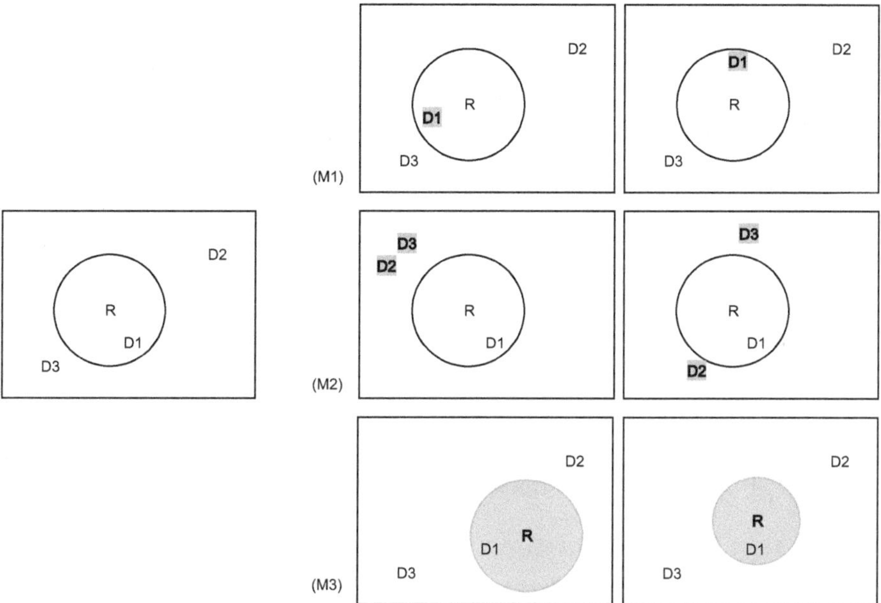


**Fig. 3.45** Three different metamorphic relations for the FoodApp delivery person selection

type of meal they want. The app automatically checks which restaurants prepare the type of meal while being at the right distance from the customer's location. It then filters only those that meet both conditions and marks these restaurants on the map, from which the customer can choose one of them.

The test analyst could define the following metamorphic relations for this function:

- M4: if the distances for some restaurants are decreased, then the search results should be a subset of the set for the original distances;
- M5: if a customer selects some extra options for meal type, then the search results should still contain the original set of restaurants (and possibly some new ones).

An example of source and follow-up test cases for M4 is shown in Fig. 3.46.

The setting for the source test case is presented in the left part of the figure. Client C is in the range of three restaurants, R1, R2, and R3. The expected result should be a list of these three restaurants. The setting for the follow-up test case is presented in the right part of the figure: when we decrease the distances for R2 and R3 (bolded circles), the only restaurant whose range covers the client's position is R1. So, the expected result should be R1, which indeed is a subset of {R1, R2, R3}, the expected result for the source test case. Notice that if the actual result of the follow-up test case contained R4, we would know that something is wrong, even if we may not know what the correct result should be. This is because R4 is not an element of {R1, R2, R3}.

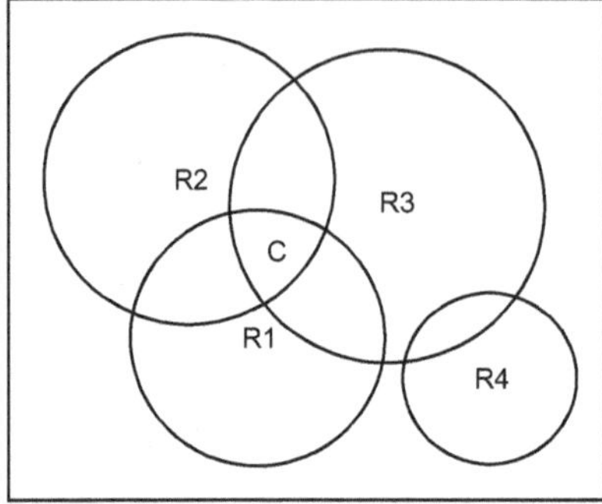


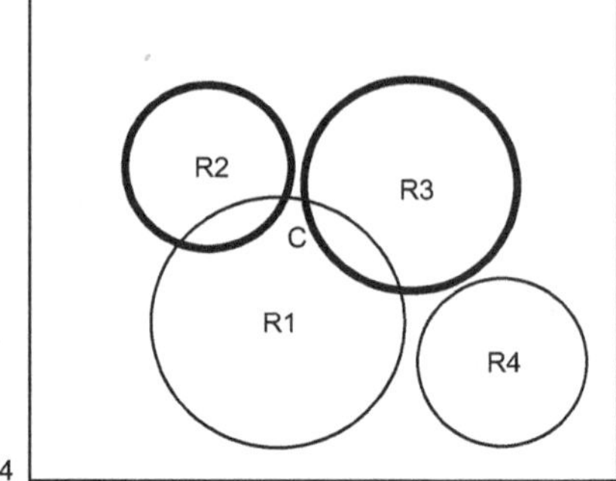


**Fig. 3.46** Example of a non-trivial metamorphic relation M4

EXTRA+

### Metamorphic Testing Formalized

Let $I$, $O$ be resp. input and output domain and let $f : I \rightarrow O$ be a function under test that transforms inputs into outputs. Let $T_f(i)$ denote a test case $T_f$ verifying $f$ with input data $i \in I$ and let $A_{T_f}(i)$ denote the actual result of $T_f(i)$. Let $P \subset I \times I$ and $Q \subset O \times O$ be two predicates representing relations between elements from input (resp. output) domain that should always hold.

We say that $P$ and $Q$ are in a metamorphic relation regarding a function under test $f$ (and we denote it as $P{\sim_f}Q$) if and only if for any test case $T_f$ and any inputs $i, j \in I$ it holds that

$$P(i, j) \Rightarrow Q\left(A_{T_f}(i), A_{T_f}(j)\right).$$

Let $P{\sim_f}Q$ and let $T_f(i)$ be a source test case $T_f$ verifying $f$ with $i \in I$. A follow-up test case for $T_f$ is a test case $T_f(j)$ for any input $j \in I$ such that $(i, j) \in P$. If $Q\left(A_{T_f}(i), A_{T_f}(j)\right)$ does not hold, then $T_f(j)$ fails.

Notice that we do not need to know the *expected* results of $T_f(i)$ and $T_f(j)$, but only the *actual* ones. This addresses the oracle problem. Notice also that, by the Law of Contraposition, if $T_f(j)$ passes, then the relation $Q\left(A_{T_f}(i), A_{T_f}(j)\right)$ holds. But the reverse relation is not true in general: if $Q$ holds, we cannot be sure that the test case should actually pass. We may only increase our confidence about it, based on the *abductive* (so, fallible) reasoning.

**Coverage**. Currently, there are no recognized coverage measures for MT that provide useful exit criteria. Running at least one test (or $n$ tests) for each MR is an insufficient test exit criterion because the actual results have only been partially verified.

This means on the one hand that the test analyst must perform the analysis separately for each problem to find enough metamorphic relations. Metamorphic relations should be defined based on knowledge of how the system works. Relevant features, characteristics, or relationships that may occur in the system itself or in the test data should also be taken into account.

On the other hand, to compensate for the partial verification, test analysts may consider executing metamorphic tests multiple times with varying inputs. For instance, consider the sorting algorithm mentioned above, where the metamorphic relation states that any permutation of the input set should yield the same output. Test analysts can generate numerous input sets for the source test case using a random generator. Additionally, they can create various follow-up test cases using a permutation generator. The verification process, which involves checking that the actual results are the same, can easily be automated, making this approach efficient. This scenario illustrates a common combination of metamorphic testing and random testing. With this approach, test analysts may establish defect-based exit criteria, such as ceasing testing if the last 100 test runs did not reveal any new defects. Alternatively, they may set budget-based exit criteria, stopping the tests when time or resources are exhausted.

The key advantages of MT include:

- addressing the oracle problem, making it a convenient test technique for complex or non-deterministic systems,
- enhancing coverage by generating additional (follow-up) test cases based solely on MRs,
- improving test efficiency because generating the test procedures can be automated (partially or fully),
- ensuring that the system behaves consistently under different conditions by testing the system against invariant properties defined by MRs, thus enhancing the system's robustness and reliability,
- creating practical test cases because MRs often reflect real-world properties, usage scenarios, and transformations, ensuring the system performs well in practical situations,
- no need for knowledge of the system's internal details, making MT suitable for black-box testing, where the focus is on input-output behavior, and for combining MT with random testing,
- versatility since MT is applicable to a wide range of domains.

While MT provides significant advantages, it also has its own set of risks, difficulties, challenges, and limitations. These include:

- challenges with identifying effective and sufficient MRs that actually capture the expected behavior of the system and cover its relevant aspects,
- risk of overlapping or redundant MRs,
- dependency on domain knowledge—effective use of MT requires a deep understanding of the domain to define meaningful and accurate MRs; this can limit the applicability of MT in less familiar domains,
- scalability—applying MRs to generate follow-up test cases can lead to a significant increase in the number of test cases, which might require substantial computational resources and time for execution,

- dependence on initial test case—the effectiveness of MT heavily relies on the quality and comprehensiveness of the initial source test cases. Poor initial test cases can lead to ineffective follow-up test cases,
- limited tooling—there may be limited tool support for automating MT, requiring significant custom development and integration effort,
- difficulty in defining the coverage—it is very difficult (if at all) to define reasonable coverage criteria for MT; currently, no such universally accepted criteria are known,
- failing test does not indicate which test case fails.

**Metamorphic Testing Versus Property-Based Testing**

Metamorphic testing (MT) and property-based testing (PBT) are both advanced test techniques based on certain relations, but they differ in the type of relations they use. MT uses metamorphic relations, which describe how the output should change when the input is changed in a certain way. Metamorphic relations involve two test cases: source and follow-up.

PBT uses the relations between input and output. These relations involve only one test case. In order to define these relations, the test analyst must have access to a test oracle. Suppose the test analyst tests the correctness of the calculations of the square root of a given input number. Let $x$ be the input and $y = \sqrt{x}$ be the output. An example of a PBT relation for this function is as follows: $y^2 = x$. It means that if we square the result, we should get the original input.

**Case Study**

This case study refers not to the FoodApp, but to the actual, existing system—the ISTQB® Glossary App website (www.glossary.istqb.org). We will now describe a real example of how metamorphic testing was used to detect a defect in this system. Figure 3.47 presents the results of the test case TC1: search results for the terms that contain the phrase "test."

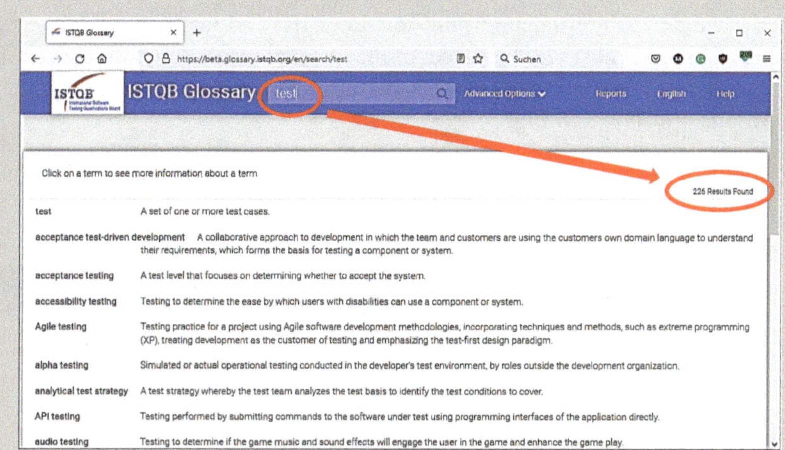


**Fig. 3.47** Search results for the string "test" in the ISTQB® Glossary App

The actual result is 226 terms found (out of 590). We assume that the result is correct. We could also run a direct SQL query on the system's database for that, but since this is an unchanged, proven function, verifying the result this way is not worth the pain. The TC1 will be our source test case.

The Glossary App has a filter option. This option allows the user to restrict the search results only to terms that are keywords in selected syllabi. Figure 3.48 shows such a filter that only restricts the results to keywords in the Foundation Level syllabus v3.1.

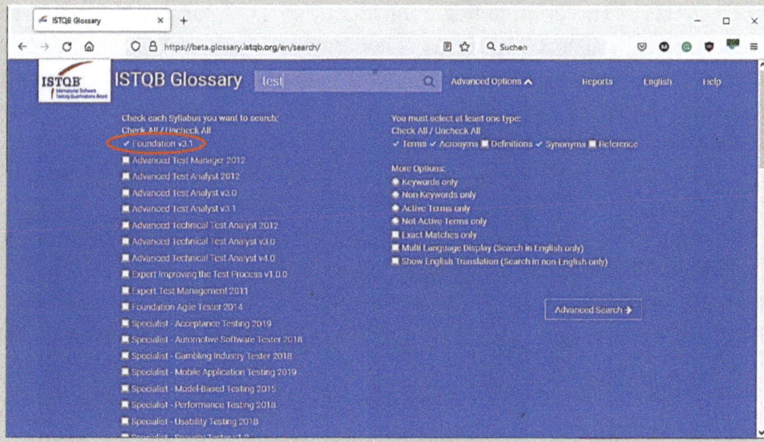


**Fig. 3.48** Filter function in the ISTQB® Glossary App

Now we define the metamorphic relation MR1: adding a filter for terms used in a syllabus must yield a subset of the original results. We run the search again with the "Foundation v3.1" filter on (this is the follow-up test case, TC2). The results are shown in Fig. 3.49.

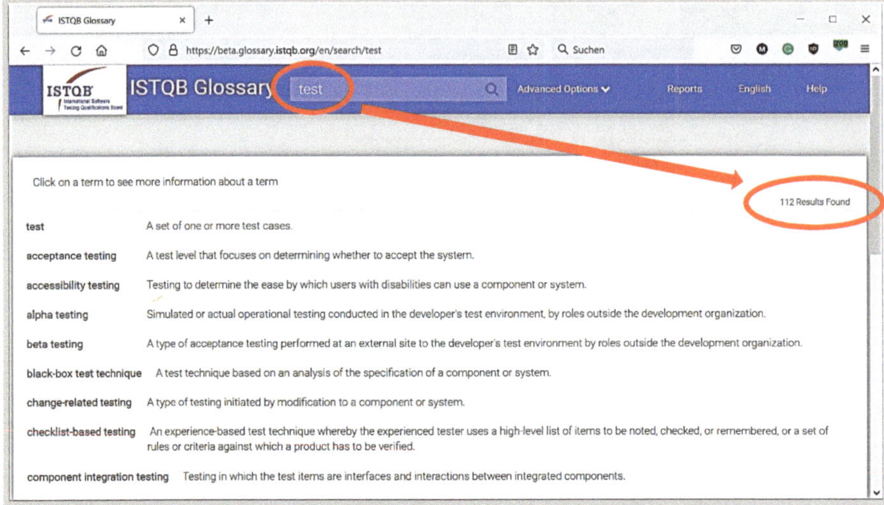


**Fig. 3.49** ISTQB® Glossary App results with a filter used

The Glossary App returned 112 terms. We verify MR1 with a comparator that checks if the returned 112 results are indeed a subset of the 226 results returned in TC1. The comparator confirms it, so TC2 passes. Notice that we do not know if the list of 112 terms is accurate. We just know that it does not contain results that do not match the search string "test". It might have omitted some terms containing "test" that actually are in the Foundation Level syllabus v3.1 (e.g., in plural), or it may contain some terms that are actually not used in this syllabus. We only know that MR1 is fulfilled for the pair of test cases TC1 and TC2.

Let us now make TC2 a source test case for a new metamorphic relation, MR2. Adding the filters for Keywords only/Non-keywords only (see Fig. 3.50) must partition the output of the source test case. MR2 is true because each glossary term that occurs in a given syllabus is either a keyword or a non-keyword.

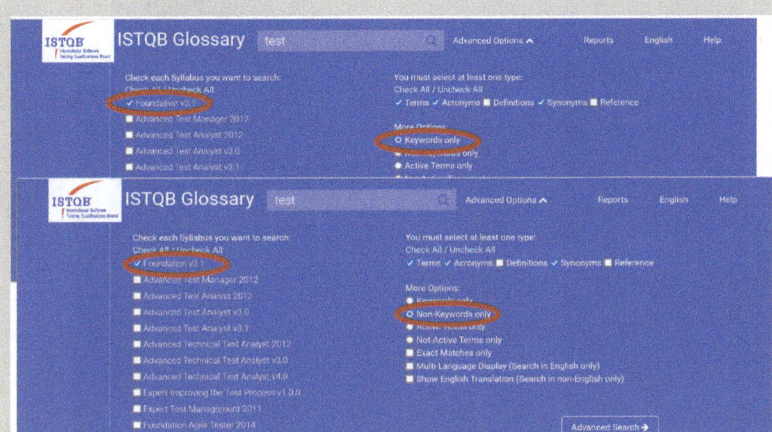


**Fig. 3.50** Using additional filters in the ISTQB® Glossary App

Now the plot thickens. The follow-up test case TC3 checks two searches for the string "term" in Foundation Level syllabus v3.1: one with the "keywords only" filter, and the other with the "non-keywords only" filter. The search results are shown in Fig. 3.51.

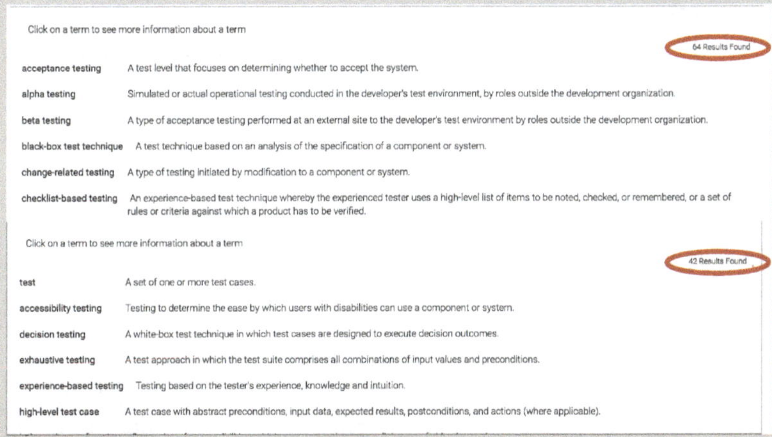


**Fig. 3.51** Search results for "keywords only" and "non-keywords only" filters

The actual result for the "keywords only" filter is 64 terms found, while for the "non-keywords only"—42 terms. But $64 + 42 = 106$, and according to MR2 this sum should be 112. Six terms are missing—we detected a defect. Notice that we *know* there is a defect, even if we *do not know* if these 64 (resp. 42) results are correct!

The test analyst raises a defect report and the developer starts a debugging process. The developer knows that the relevant data is stored in a table called "SyllabusIn". Moreover, the developer knows that the ID for the Foundation Level syllabus v3.1 is 18 and that the attribute relevant to the "keywords only/ non-keywords only" attribute is an integer called "Keyword" (last column in the table in Fig. 3.52). This value is 0 for a non-keyword and 1 for a keyword, because this number encodes the number of times the term occurs in a syllabus as a keyword. Since the MR2 was not fulfilled, it means that there may be some keywords with other codes than 0 and 1. The developer runs the SQL query:

```
SELECT *
FROM 'SyllabusIn'
WHERE 'SyllabusID' = 18 AND Keyword NOT IN (0, 1)
```

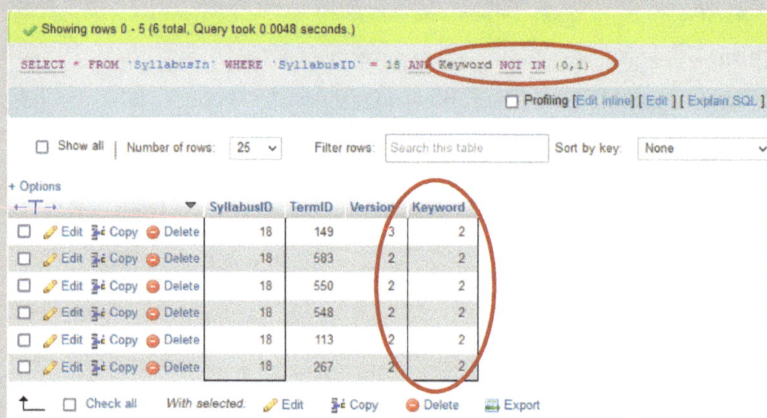


| | SyllabusID | TermID | Version | Keyword |
|---|---|---|---|---|
| Edit Copy Delete | 18 | 149 | 3 | 2 |
| Edit Copy Delete | 18 | 583 | 2 | 2 |
| Edit Copy Delete | 18 | 550 | 2 | 2 |
| Edit Copy Delete | 18 | 548 | 2 | 2 |
| Edit Copy Delete | 18 | 113 | 2 | 2 |
| Edit Copy Delete | 18 | 267 | 2 | 2 |

**Fig. 3.52** Results of an SQL query in the ISTQB® Glossary App database

The search results are shown in Fig. 3.52.

The query returned 6 results (the terms with IDs 149, 583, 550, 548, 113, and 267)—exactly the number of the missing terms. These six terms are marked as keywords in two different chapters of the syllabus, which is legitimate. The defect is that the Glossary App stores the *number of occurrences* of terms (in our case, two for each of the six terms) rather than a *Boolean value* for denoting if a term is a keyword (0 = false, 1 = true).

The developer changes the "Keyword" type to a Boolean one. All entries that had the "Keyword" value greater than zero previously get the value of "TRUE." Similarly, all entries that had the "Keyword" value equal to zero previously get the value of "FALSE." Now, when we retest the corrected version of the system with TC3, the results are OK: there are 70 terms for the "keyword only" filter and 42 for the "non-keywords only" filter. 70 + 42 = 112, so we assume TC3 passes, since its result, compared to the result of TC2, fulfills MR2.

## Sample Questions

### Question 3.3.2A

You are testing a credit risk assessment system based on advanced artificial intelligence algorithms. The system assesses credit risk (on a scale of 0 to 100%) based on three variables: age (in years), annual income (in USD), and seniority (in full years).

You apply metamorphic testing using the following metamorphic relationships:

- MR1: if annual income increases and the other variables do not change, the credit risk remains the same or decreases.
- MR2: if seniority decreases and other variables do not change, credit risk will remain at the same level or increase.

The source test case has the form:

Input: age 45, annual income USD 62,000, seniority 19 years. Output: risk score = 32%

Which follow-up test case reveals a failure?

(a) Input: age 45, annual income USD 62,000, seniority 19 years. Output: risk score = 35%.
(b) Input: age 35, annual income USD 62,000, seniority 19 years. Output: risk score = 35%.
(c) Input: age 45, annual income USD 70,000, seniority 18 years. Output: risk score = 32%.
(d) Input: age 45, annual income USD 70,000, seniority 19 years. Output: risk score = 35%.

Select ONE answer.

### Question 3.3.2B

You are testing a function F that calculates the square root $\sqrt{x}$ of a number $x$ given as input: $F(x) = \sqrt{x}$. The square root is defined only for non-negative numbers, as follows: $\sqrt{x} = y$ if and only if $y^2 = x$. The F function is more efficient than other existing functions because it uses novel, complex quantum algorithms.

Which of the following is an example of a valid metamorphic relation that can be used in testing the F function?

(a) If the output $F(x)$ is squared, we get the number given in the input: $[F(x)]^2 = x$.
(b) If the input is increased, the output $F(x)$ must also increase.
(c) If the input is a negative number, $F$ should return an error message.
(d) If the output $F(x)$ is given as input, the result is smaller that $F(x)$: $F(F(x)) < F(x)$.

Select ONE answer.

## Exercise 8—Metamorphic Testing

TA-3.3.2 (K3) Apply metamorphic testing

You are testing a search engine's ranking algorithm for an e-commerce application selling electronic items. Users can enter keywords (e.g., "laptop," "iPhone 15," "Bluetooth headphones") into the search bar. The system retrieves relevant electronic items from the catalog and presents them to the user as a list. The users can refine search results by applying filters such as category, price, brand, and specifications. They can also sort the results by price (low → high and high → low).

The challenge is that search engines often work as "non-test oracles," which means we cannot always know what the correct ranking should be. Therefore, you decide to use metamorphic testing that helps validate consistency and expected properties of the system by defining metamorphic relations (MRs).

Give examples of five metamorphic relations for this system, and for each of them, give examples of source and follow-up test cases, explaining what the expected relation should be between the results of these two test cases.

## 3.4 Experience-Based Test Techniques

### *3.4.1 Test Charters Supporting Session-Based Testing*

TA-3.4.1 (K3) Prepare test charters for session-based testing

**Definitions**

**Test charter**: The definition has changed. The current definition is: A mission statement that guides an exploratory test session.

**Session-based testing**: A test approach in which test activities are planned as test sessions.

**Introduction**. The Foundation Level syllabus [1] describes exploratory testing, indicating the relevance of session-based testing. Testers at the foundation level should understand the fundamental concepts and main benefits of session-based testing. In contrast, a test analyst at an advanced level must demonstrate greater competence, specifically in preparing high-quality test charters for session-based testing. Therefore, we will first explain session-based testing, detailing its benefits and challenges. Following that, we will focus on the form and content of test charters used in session-based testing.

Session-based test management is an enhancement of exploratory testing that allows one to control, manage, and structure exploratory testing better. Three key elements of session-based test management are explicitly stated test mission, test charter, and time-boxed test sessions. A test charter is a concise document that outlines the scope, objectives, and constraints of a test session within exploratory testing. It serves as a roadmap or a mission statement for testing, providing structure to the test sessions. Test charters are a key element in session-based testing because they help testers stay focused on specific areas or features to be tested while allowing them the flexibility to explore the system when necessary. The test charter does not pre-specify the test cases to be executed in each session, but it may include ideas that guide testers during testing.

The benefits of using test charters in testing include:

- providing clear objectives for each session, ensuring that testers understand what they need to accomplish,
- helping testers to concentrate on relevant parts of the application, ensuring appropriate coverage,
- balancing flexibility with specificity by offering a structured guide to testing and, at the same time, allowing testers to utilize their intuition, creativity, knowledge, and experience,
- providing a baseline against which the reports from session findings can be compared, helping to assess whether the session's objectives were met.

However, there are also some risks and challenges related to using checklists, for example:

- narrow focus—if a test charter is too specific or restrictive, it can limit the tester's ability to explore beyond the defined scope, so critical defects outside of this scope can be missed,
- insufficient coverage—some important areas of a system under test may be overlooked if a test charter does not cover all necessary aspects of the system,
- inconsistent quality—test charters written by different team members may vary significantly in detail and quality, leading to inconsistencies in thoroughness and effectiveness of testing,
- required skills and experience—designing effective test charters requires an excellent understanding of both the test object and the test process; otherwise, the balance between freedom and focus may be disturbed, making testing ineffective.

**Factors influencing a test charter design**. From the test analyst's point of view, one of the most important tasks related to session-based testing is to design test charters for exploratory testing sessions. When preparing the test charter for session-based testing, the test analyst must consider certain factors that influence test charter design, in particular:

- risks and their priorities,

- customer and requirement factors (e.g., requirements elicited from clients, business use case for the system, quality requirements, user journey maps, i.e., user interaction with the product over time, questions raised by stakeholders),
- product factors (e.g., product analysis including functional flows, principal goals of the product, product features, software design, interfaces),
- project management factors (e.g., time constraints, project purpose, estimated effort, business value).

**Test charter format**. The charter test should describe three main issues: what to explore, what resources are available, and what information we want to discover during an exploratory testing session. Therefore, the simplest charter test can be structured as shown in Fig. 3.53.

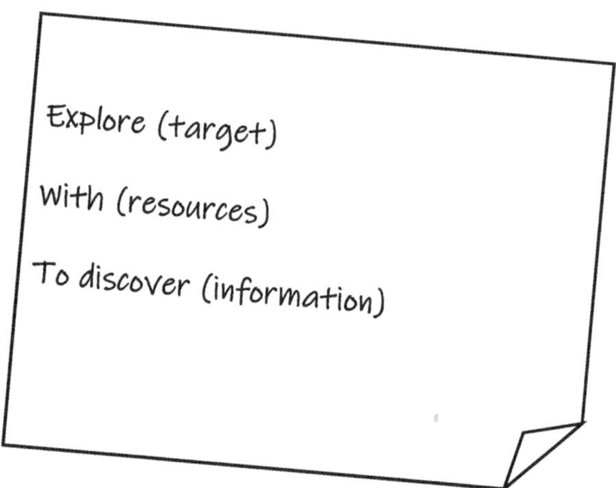


**Fig. 3.53** Example of a simple test charter format

An *object of exploration* can be a requirement, a software feature, a business process, a specific software module, etc. The choice of this object should never be arbitrary or random but should always be based on rational reasons, such as the purpose of testing, prioritization of requirements, risk analysis, or discussions with the customer. Test conditions, if the test analyst has defined them earlier in the test analysis phase, can be a guideline for determining the object of exploration.

*Resources* are anything that the tester will have at their disposal when conducting an exploratory testing session.

Examples of resources are:

- tools and libraries—including general-purpose testing tools (e.g., bug trackers, test management tools), development tools (e.g., IDEs or version control systems), and specialized tools for concrete purposes (e.g., performance testing tools, security testing tools, data generation tools),

- test data—including pre-prepared data sets tailored for different scenarios (e.g., user credentials, product listings) and connections to production or test databases with necessary permissions,
- permissions—including access to user accounts for different roles (e.g., admin, user, guest) to test various access levels, API keys and tokens to interact with APIs securely, and network access (e.g., VPN credentials or other network access requirements for remote testing),
- environments and configurations—including target test environment (e.g., development, staging, or production), configuration details (e.g., specific versions of operating systems, browsers, devices, installed libraries, and network settings), virtual machines and containers (e.g., Docker), that replicate the production environment,
- documentation—including a detailed description of features, design documents (e.g., architectural diagrams, flowcharts, design specifications), user manuals, Service Level Agreements (SLA), API documentation, industry standards that the application should adhere to (e.g., GDPR guidelines), previous test results (to identify patterns and areas needed re-testing or more thorough testing) and known issues (e.g., list of existing bugs or known limitations to avoid redundant reporting),
- stakeholders—including contact information to team members or subject matter experts available during the exploratory session for quick consultation, communication channels, and support resources (e.g., access to IT technical support or third-party vendors if specialized help is needed),
- test scripts and automation—including pre-written scripts for repetitive tests,
- techniques (e.g., specific test design techniques that may be useful during exploration),
- standalone features or applications (e.g., third-party services like payment gateways or cloud services).

The above list of sample resources is quite comprehensive. In practice, the test analyst does not describe the resources in such an extensive way when designing a test charter but focuses on a few of the most important ones from the point of view of a particular exploratory testing session.

Including relevant resources in a test charter enables testers to perform their tasks efficiently and effectively. By detailing these resources, the test analyst ensures that all of them are readily available, minimizing disruptions and enhancing the overall quality of the testing process.

By describing the *information to discover*, the test analyst provides clear objectives for the testing session. It helps testers know what specific information or insights they should be looking for during the session. This can prevent aimless exploration and ensure that the testing efforts are directed toward meaningful goals.

Apart from the three sections described above, test charters usually also contain some other important information, including:

- organizational information (duration of the test session, start date and time, tester's name),

- product-related information (system definition, data and workflow among components, system architecture),
- limitations (what the product must never do),
- current open questions that refer to the "known unknowns."

**Designing the test charter**. Let's assume that a test analyst has been tasked with designing a test charter for exploratory testing of the user registration function. The goal defined in this way is quite general, so the test analyst may decide that the test session will not be limited, for example, to validating the registration form fields, but will cover the entire registration process. The first step in defining the test charter is shown in Fig. 3.54.

**Fig. 3.54** Describing the goal of the test session

Next, the test analyst must decide what resources the tester will need during the session. The registration process does not require any specialized tools, but sample test data, including login, email address, or password, can be useful. The test analyst also knows that the system allows logging in via social media as well. This means that in order to test this way of logging in, the tester must have, for example, a Facebook account or a Google account before starting the session. The test analyst may also recall that in the past, there were problems rendering some pages of the application under test in certain types of browsers. Therefore, he may decide to have the session run on a few basic browser types. The second step in defining the test charter is shown in Fig. 3.55.

The final step is to define the purpose of the session. The test analyst may decide that, due to the high risk associated with the login functionality, the session will have a number of goals related to form validation, UX, performance, security, and integration with other systems. The last step in defining the test charter is shown in Fig. 3.56. Notice that the test analyst also updated the "With" part of the charter with points 4) and 5). This is due to the last two goals defined in the "To discover" section.

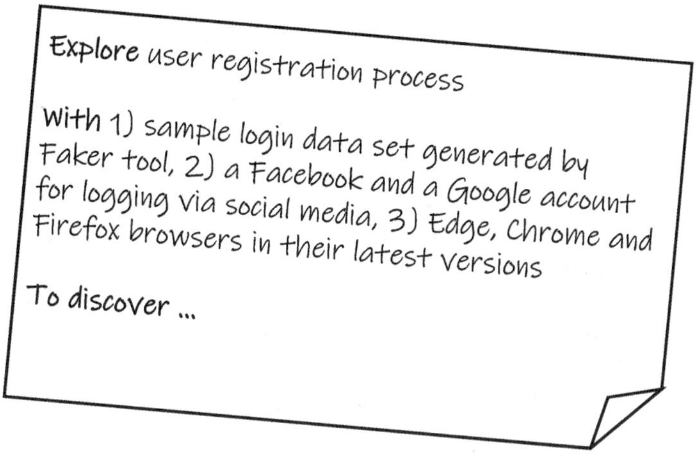

Explore user registration process

With 1) sample login data set generated by Faker tool, 2) a Facebook and a Google account for logging via social media, 3) Edge, Chrome and Firefox browsers in their latest versions

To discover ...

Fig. 3.55 Describing the resources for the test session

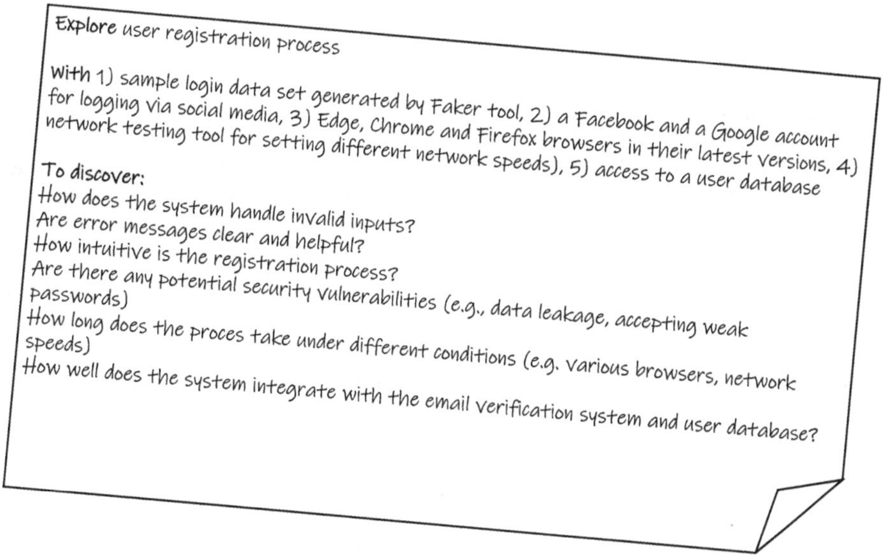

Explore user registration process

With 1) sample login data set generated by Faker tool, 2) a Facebook and a Google account for logging via social media, 3) Edge, Chrome and Firefox browsers in their latest versions, 4) network testing tool for setting different network speeds), 5) access to a user database

To discover:
How does the system handle invalid inputs?
Are error messages clear and helpful?
How intuitive is the registration process?
Are there any potential security vulnerabilities (e.g., data leakage, accepting weak passwords)
How long does the proces take under different conditions (e.g. various browsers, network speeds)
How well does the system integrate with the email verification system and user database?

Fig. 3.56 Final test charter

**Case Study**

The FoodApp has recently undergone significant updates, including a new user interface, enhanced filtering options, additional payment methods, and improved error-handling mechanisms. The development team has completed initial testing, but before releasing the new version 2.0 to the public, an in-depth exploratory testing session is needed to ensure the updates work seamlessly and provide a positive user experience.

Given the extensive nature of the updates, the development team aims to uncover any unexpected issues or user experience problems that might not have been identified during traditional testing. The goal is to validate that all new functionalities work as intended and that the overall user experience has been improved without introducing new bugs. As a test analyst, you have been tasked with preparing a test charter for exploratory testers.

The result could look as follows. Notice that "Focus areas" reflect the main changes in version 2.0 of the application.

**Test charter: exploring the FoodApp 2.0 ordering process**

**Mission**. To explore and validate the entire food ordering process, from selecting a restaurant to placing an order and receiving a confirmation.

**Time box.** 2 hours.

**Focus areas**

Restaurant selection

- Verify that the list of available restaurants is displayed correctly.
- Check that filtering options (e.g., cuisine type, ratings, delivery time) work as expected.
- Ensure that selecting a restaurant takes the user to the restaurant's menu.

Menu navigation

- Confirm that the menu items are categorized correctly.
- Validate that item details (name, description, price, image) are displayed accurately.
- Test the add-to-cart functionality for different menu items.

Cart and checkout

- Verify that items added to the cart are displayed correctly with the correct quantities and prices.
- Check the update and remove item functionalities within the cart.
- Explore the checkout process, including entering a delivery address, selecting the payment method, and applying discount codes.
- Ensure the order summary and total amount calculations are accurate.

Order confirmation

- Validate that an order confirmation screen is displayed after placing an order.

- Check that the order confirmation details (items, prices, delivery address, estimated delivery time) are correct.
- Ensure that an order confirmation email/SMS is received.

Error handling

- Test the application's behavior under different error conditions (e.g., no internet connection, invalid payment details, item out of stock).
- Verify that appropriate error messages are displayed and that the user can recover gracefully.

Usability

- Evaluate the overall user experience and ease of use, including learnability, user error protection, user engagement, inclusivity, and user assistance.
- Verify the correct display of the interface on different types of devices.
- Identify any usability issues or potential improvements.

**Proposed test approaches and techniques**

- Scenario-based testing—use real-world scenarios (e.g., ordering during peak hours, using different payment methods) to simulate typical user actions and ensure coverage of common user journeys.
- Boundary Value Analysis—test boundary values for input fields (e.g., minimum and maximum character limits for input fields, minimum amount eligible for discount).
- Equivalence Partitioning—e.g., valid and invalid discount codes, restaurant types.
- Heuristic evaluation—to identify usability issues based on established usability principles (e.g., Nielsen's heuristics).

**Data and tools required**

- Test account(s) with necessary permissions.
- Access to a variety of restaurants and menu items within the application.
- Test credit cards and other payment methods for placing orders.
- Device with different internet connectivity conditions (Wi-Fi, mobile data, offline).

## Sample Questions

### Question 3.4.1A

You prepare a test charter for an exploratory testing session for an online retail e-commerce platform enabling users to browse products, manage the shopping cart, and make purchases. The system is designed for desktop and mobile devices, emphasizing personalized recommendations, real-time order tracking, and secure payments. Two quality characteristics are especially important: scalability (to handle traffic surges, especially during peak seasons like holidays) and security (to protect the system from security attacks).

Which of the following elements of the charter test **LEAST** fits the above scenario?

(a) Entry criteria: Tools, namely browser emulators and payment gateway simulators, are configured and accessible.
(b) Test ideas: Test adding, updating, and removing items in the shopping cart; assess compatibility on different browsers and devices.
(c) Limitation: The platform must never allow unauthorized users to access internal company financial reports.
(d) Historical information: Previously found defects: slow response times during catalog browsing; payment gateway timeout under high load.

Select ONE answer.

### Question 3.4.1B

A financial institution has developed a mobile banking application with a new feature allowing users to view and search their transaction history. This feature will be used by thousands of customers every day. The feature has been recently integrated, and time constraints have made it difficult to finalize a complete set of predefined test cases. The development team suspects potential functional issues with search functionality and edge-case handling for transaction records.

You are asked to prepare a test charter for an exploratory testing session.

Which test charter fits this scenario **BEST**?

(a) Explore the transaction history search feature.
With a set of randomly generated test data.
To discover inconsistencies in search results.
(b) Explore the mobile banking application.
With different test data.
To discover potential issues in the application.
(c) Explore the transaction view feature.
With a set of existing functional test cases.
To discover performance issues.
(d) Explore the edge cases in the transaction history search feature.
With a set of boundary values.
To discover potential issues with search functionality.

Select ONE answer.

## Exercise 9—Preparing Test Charters for Session-Based Testing

TA-3.4.1 (K3) Prepare test charters for session-based testing

A new version of the FoodApp is being prepared for release. In this new version, the following new features and changes are introduced:

- loyalty points system—users earn points on every purchase, which can be redeemed for discounts,
- split payment—customers can split payments between two payment methods (e.g., part wallet, part credit card),
- real-time order tracking—improved live tracking with map integration to show the rider's movement,
- new notification system—push notifications for order updates and promotional offers.
- support for multiple currencies—supporting transactions in USD, EUR, and GBP.

The development team requests an exploratory testing session to evaluate these new features before formal test cases are finalized, focusing on usability, system integration, and potential edge cases.

Prepare a test charter for an exploratory testing session outlining:

- mission (what to explore),
- areas of focus (key features at risk),
- risks/concerns,
- test ideas (possible paths to investigate).

### *3.4.2 Checklists Supporting Experience-Based Test Techniques*

TA-3.4.2 (K3) Prepare checklists supporting experience-based testing

**Definitions**

**Checklist-based testing**: An experience-based test technique in which test cases are designed to exercise the items of a checklist.

**Introduction**. The Foundation Level syllabus [1] summarizes what checklist-based testing is, what it typically looks like, how it is managed, and what its main benefit is. Testers at the foundation level should understand these fundamental aspects of checklist-based testing. In contrast, a test analyst at an advanced level must demonstrate greater competence, specifically in preparing and maintaining high-quality checklists for testing. Therefore, we will first explain checklist-based testing, detailing its benefits and challenges. Following that, we will describe in detail a structured process of preparing and maintaining checklists and the criteria for high-quality checkpoints for testing.

A checklist is a systematically arranged list of items, actions, or criteria designed to ensure that all necessary steps or elements are considered and completed. It serves as a tool to guide individuals through a process, ensuring thoroughness, consistency, and accuracy in the execution of tasks.

Checklists are typically organized in a logical sequence that aligns with the process or task they are meant to facilitate, allowing users to follow them step-by-step. They aim to encompass all critical components or steps required for the task, ensuring no significant detail is overlooked. By providing a standardized set of criteria or actions, checklists help maintain uniformity in task execution across different instances and among various individuals. Checklists are designed to be user-friendly, often featuring simple, clear language and a straightforward format that is easy to follow. They serve as a record-keeping tool, allowing users to track completed items and identify outstanding tasks. This can be particularly useful for documentation and auditing purposes.

In various fields, including aviation, healthcare, and construction, checklists enhance performance, safety, and quality by ensuring that all necessary actions are taken and all essential criteria are met.

Checklists support experience-based test techniques. Checklist-based testing is a test technique where a predefined list of items, actions, or criteria (a checklist) guides the testing process. This technique ensures that critical aspects of the software are evaluated, leveraging the structure and thoroughness provided by the checklist to enhance the overall testing effectiveness.

The benefits of using checklist-based testing include:

- Ensuring thoroughness—checklists provide a clear and organized list of tasks or criteria that must be addressed, helping testers ensure that no critical aspects are overlooked.
- Enhancing consistency in coverage—by following a standardized list, testers can achieve a uniform level of coverage across different testing phases and projects.
- Leveraging experience—checklists often incorporate lessons learned and best practices from previous projects, allowing testers to benefit from accumulated knowledge and experience. The high-level nature of the checklist items also allows testers to use their own experience during testing.
- Supporting documentation and reporting—checklists clearly record what has been tested and what remains to be done. This documentation is essential for reporting purposes and for meeting regulatory or compliance requirements.

- Facilitating adaptability and flexibility—checklists can be easily modified and tailored to suit the specific needs of different projects or testing scenarios. This adaptability makes them suitable for various testing contexts and methodologies.

Using checklists, while beneficial, comes with its own set of difficulties, risks, and limitations, such as:

- Developing comprehensive and effective checklists requires significant time and expertise. Incomplete or poorly constructed checklists can lead to inadequate testing.
- Checklists need to be regularly updated to reflect software changes, new requirements, and lessons learned from previous projects. This ongoing maintenance can be resource-intensive.
- Testers might become overly dependent on checklists, using them as a crutch rather than a guide, inhibiting their ability to think critically and creatively during testing. Checklists are a powerful and effective tool, but only in the hands of experienced testers.
- The structured nature of checklists can limit the scope for exploratory testing, where testers deviate from predefined paths to uncover unexpected issues.
- Checklists are often high-level and may not provide the detailed guidance needed for complex testing scenarios. This can limit their effectiveness in thoroughly evaluating intricate software features.
- The effectiveness of checklist-based testing is highly dependent on the testers' skills and judgment. Poor interpretation or application of the checklist can lead to ineffective testing.

**Preparing checklists**. Setting up a proper checklist for experience-based testing involves a systematic approach to ensure that all critical aspects of the software are covered. The general checklist creation process is shown in Fig. 3.57. Let us discuss it in detail.

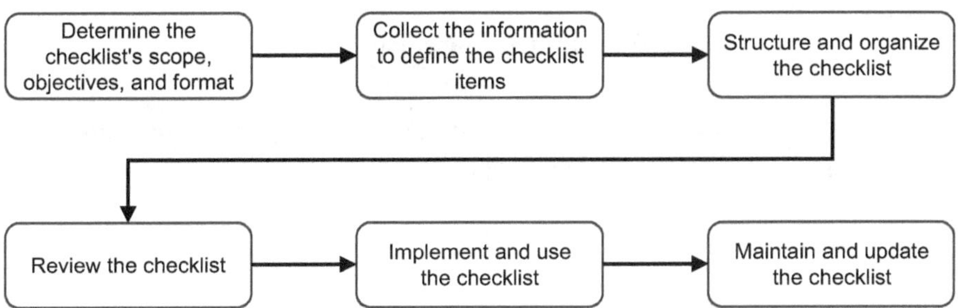


**Fig. 3.57** The checklist creation process

**Determine the checklist's scope, objectives, and format**. The test analyst determines the checklist's scope, objectives, and format because they influence the testing depth and required level of detail. The test analyst must clearly define what aim is to be achieved with the checklist. This could include ensuring coverage of all critical functionalities, improving test efficiency, or maintaining consistency across testing cycles. If the objective is to mitigate risks, the checklist will focus on areas that historically have higher defect rates or are critical to business operations.

The test analyst outlines the scope, i.e., boundaries of the checklist, specifying which parts of the software or which types of tests will be included. The test analyst decides which functions and features of the software will be covered by the checklist. This ensures that critical and high-risk areas receive adequate attention while less critical areas may be covered less extensively. The test analyst also decides on the non-functional scope. This includes aspects like performance, security, usability, and compliance. The analyst determines which non-functional requirements are critical for the project and must be included in the checklist. The scope may also define which phases of testing (unit, integration, system, and acceptance testing) the checklist will cover. This ensures that the checklist is relevant to the specific stage of the testing process.

The format can vary from simple itemized lists to more descriptive narrative formats. Itemized lists are useful for quick reference and ticking off completed tasks, while narrative formats provide more context and details for each check. The syllabus distinguishes between two types of itemized lists: read-do and do-confirm. In a "read-do" checklist, the tester reads each item and then performs the task immediately before moving on to the next item. This type of checklist is often used when tasks must be carried out sequentially and in a specific order. In a "do-confirm" checklist, the user performs the tasks and then checks each item to confirm it has been completed. This type of checklist is often used in scenarios where tasks can be performed out of sequence or where verification after completion is crucial.

**Read-Do and Do-Confirm Checklists**

The checklists shown in Figs. 3.58 and 3.59 are examples of read-do and do-confirm checklists for the FoodApp.

A read-do checklist for the food ordering process

**Select Food Category**: Read the list of available categories and choose one.
**Browse Menu**: Scroll through the items in the chosen category and select the desired dish.
**Customize Order**: Add any special instructions or customization options.
**Add to Cart**: Confirm the selection and add the item to the cart.
**Review Cart**: Read through the items in the cart to ensure all selections are correct.
**Proceed to Checkout**: Initiate the checkout process.
**Enter Delivery Details**: Provide the delivery address and contact information.
**Select Payment Method**: Choose a payment method (e.g., credit card, PayPal).
**Confirm Order**: Review the entire order summary and confirm the order.

**Fig. 3.58** Example of a read-do checklist

A do-confirm checklist for the food ordering process

□ Each selected item is correct and includes all customizations.
□ The cart accurately reflects all selections and quantities.
□ No items in the cart are missing or incorrectly listed.
□ The checkout process has been initiated without errors.
□ The entered delivery details are correctly processed.
□ The payment method has been correctly selected and processed.
□ All order details are correct before final submission

**Fig. 3.59** An example of a do-confirm checklist

The checklist shown in Fig. 3.58 guides the tester through a sequence of precisely defined steps. Its purpose is to validate the food ordering process.

The checklist shown in Fig. 3.59 forces the tester to check the system's behavior *after* the actions are done.

Read-do checklists are more rigid and sequential, suitable for processes that must follow a strict order. Do-confirm checklists allow for more flexibility and are useful for verifying tasks after they have been performed.

**Collect the information to define the checklist items**. This can include gathering insights from experienced professionals, browsing defect libraries and defect taxonomies (e.g., [25, 26]), reviewing relevant documentation (e.g., software requirements, design documents, user manuals), and analyzing risks, test cases, and potential test scenarios. The test analyst can use insights and lessons learned from previous projects and testing efforts to identify common pitfalls and critical areas needing attention. Checklist items should refer to the core features and functions of the software that are essential for its operation. They may include checks for performance, security, usability, and other non-functional aspects. Checklist items can also be related to the areas that have historically been prone to bugs and issues. Developers, product managers, and other stakeholders can also be engaged to gather diverse perspectives on what should be tested.

Checklist items should be clear, specific, unambiguous, consistent, relevant, maintainable, actionable, and measurable. They should be formulated as questions that can be answered with "yes," "no," or "not applicable." They require assigned priorities based on their importance, potential impact, and risk level. The test analyst should consider typical and edge-case user interactions with the software to ensure real-world usage is covered.

**Structure and organize the checklist.** When the checklist items are defined, the test analyst groups related items into categories or sections, such as functional tests, user interface checks, performance tests, etc., to make the checklist easy to navigate. The items are ranked based on their importance and potential impact on the software's quality to focus efforts where they are most needed. This will ensure that the most important defects are detected early.

The test analyst provides a clear and concise description of each task or check, specifying what needs to be done and what criteria need to be met. The language used should be straightforward and unambiguous to avoid misunderstandings.

**Review the checklist.** Once the checklist is ready, the test analyst may ask other testers and stakeholders to review it to catch any missing items and ensure its comprehensiveness and clarity. The checklist can be tested on a small scale to see how well it works in practice and to identify any adjustments that might be needed.

**Implement and use the checklist.** The test analyst ensures that all testers understand how to use the checklist effectively and are aware of its importance in the testing process. Once the checklist is in use, the test analyst observes how it is used during testing to ensure it is being followed correctly and to identify any areas for improvement.

**Maintain and update the checklist.** A checklist is never finalized. The test analyst should continuously review and refine it and adapt it to reflect new findings, changed priorities, feedback from testers, or lessons learned from previous test cycles. By sharing the checklist with other testers, the test analyst promotes consistency and collaboration and helps them better understand the test items and the critical areas to focus on during testing.

**Case Study**

Below, we present a well-known example of ten usability heuristics by Jakob Nielsen [27]. The following list is a modified original version from Nielsen's other paper [28].

1. **Simple and natural dialogue**. Dialogues should not contain irrelevant or rarely needed information. Every extra unit of information in a dialogue competes with the relevant information units and diminishes their relative visibility. All information should appear in a natural and logical order.
2. **Speak the user's language**. The dialogue should be expressed clearly in words, phrases, and concepts familiar to the user, rather than in system-oriented terms.
3. **Minimize the user's memory load**. The user should not have to remember information from one part of the dialogue to another. Instructions for the use of the system should be visible or easily retrievable whenever appropriate.
4. **Consistency**. Users should not have to wonder whether different words, situations, or actions mean the same thing.
5. **Feedback**. The system should always keep users informed about what is going on by providing appropriate feedback within a reasonable time.
6. **Clearly marked exits**. Users often choose system functions by mistake and will need a clearly marked "emergency exit" to leave the unwanted state without going through an extended dialogue.
7. **Shortcuts**. Accelerators—unseen by the novice user—may often speed up the interaction for the expert user so that the system can cater to inexperienced and experienced users.
8. **Good error messages**. They should be expressed in plain language (no codes) and precisely indicate the problem. and constructively suggest a solution.
9. **Prevent errors**. Even better than good error messages is a careful design that prevents problems from occurring.
10. **Help and documentation**. Although it is better if the system can be used without documentation, it may be necessary to provide it. Any such information should be easy to search, focused on the user's task, list concrete steps to be carried out, and not be too large.

Figure 3.60 shows an example of a violation of Rule 1. The interface consists of more than a dozen areas, each containing several fields. A user using such an interface will be overwhelmed by its complexity. This is a common case in ERP (Enterprise Resource Planning) applications such as SAP, Microsoft Dynamics 365, or Oracle ERP.

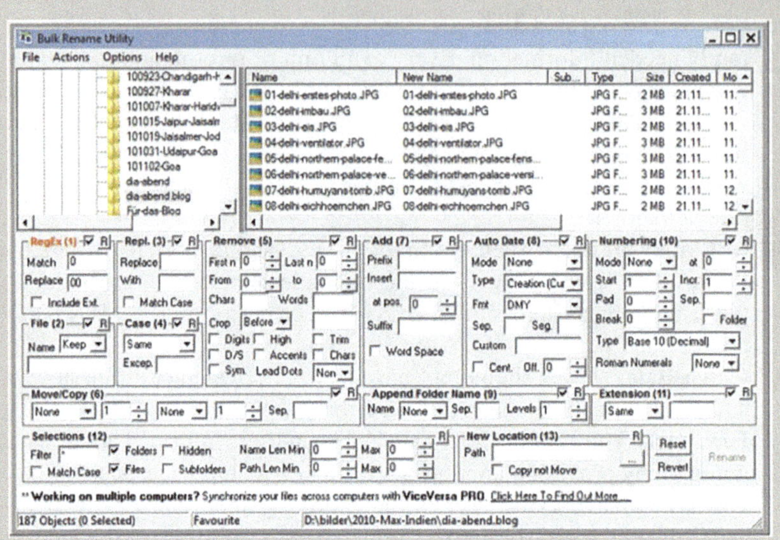


**Fig. 3.60** Example of an overcomplicated interface (source: smarties2013.wordpress.com/2013/04/27/the-importance-of-a-well-designed-user-interface-figure/)

A good example of following Rule 4 is the menus in Microsoft Office applications (see Fig. 3.61). Beyond maintaining uniformity in application icons, home windows, and main menus, Microsoft Office employs a ribbon interface across its products to facilitate task execution. Although the ribbon adapts contextually depending on the active product, tasks can be performed consistently across different applications. For instance, customizing text, copy/paste, and text alignment are accomplished in the same manner in Word (top), Excel (middle), and PowerPoint (bottom).

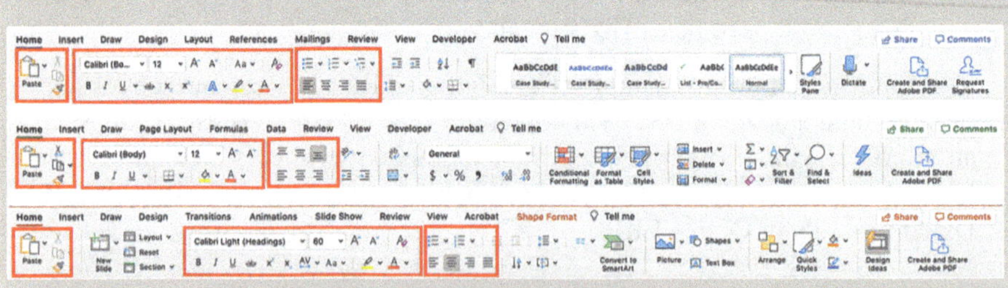


**Fig. 3.61** Consistency in Microsoft Office applications' menus

## Sample Questions

### Question 3.4.2A

A company is developing a facial recognition system for secure access to restricted areas in a corporate office. The system must accurately identify employees, differentiate authorized personnel from unauthorized individuals, and handle various conditions like lighting changes, facial accessories, and different poses. The requirements and expected system behaviors are clearly defined, making a checklist approach practical.

Which checklist will be **MOST** useful for testing this system?

(a) Ensure the camera captures a clear and well-lit image of the user.
Verify that the system normalizes facial data for consistency across different cameras.
Confirm that the system stores encrypted facial data securely in the database.
(b) Test recognition under varying lighting conditions (bright light, shadows, etc.).
Check the system's performance in different backgrounds (plain vs. cluttered).
Test recognition with changes in user appearance (hats, masks, makeup, etc.).
(c) Validate that the system collects explicit user consent before storing facial data.
Ensure compliance with regional privacy regulations (e.g., GDPR, CCPA).
Verify that users can delete their stored facial data on request.
(d) Confirm the system can process live video streams and detect faces in real-time.
Ensure system performance is stable when handling multiple streams simultaneously.
Verify that recognized faces are logged accurately with timestamps in the database.

Select ONE answer.

### Question 3.4.2B

Your company works on a password validator—a system designed to evaluate the strength and validity of a password based on a set of predefined rules. It helps ensure that passwords meet certain security standards and are difficult for attackers to guess or crack. The system's requirement specification contains both functional and non-functional requirements.

You are asked to prepare a **READ-DO** checklist for a password validator.

Which of the following is the best example of such a checklist?

(a) The system responds correctly to passwords with varying complexity.
The error messages are correct for the incorrect passwords.
The system gracefully rejects inputs used to perform SQL injection attacks.
(b) Enter a password that is too short and verify that it is rejected.
Enter a password missing the required uppercase letter, and verify that it is rejected.

Enter a password containing all required types of characters and verify that it is accepted.

(c) Confirm performance under different loads.
Confirm security with different security attacks (SQL injection, XSS, brute force attacks).
Confirm compatibility across various browsers and devices.

(d) Error messages are user-friendly.
The password strength indicator works properly.
"Show password" toggle works properly.

Select ONE answer.

## Exercise 10—Preparing Checklists for Experience-Based Testing

TA-3.4.2 (K3) Prepare checklists that support experience-based testing

A retail company develops customized software for online sales and implements it for many customers. The generic features for such a web-based e-commerce application are as follows:

- search for products,
- add them to a shopping cart,
- proceed to checkout,
- enter payment and shipping details,
- place an order.

You are tasked with creating a checklist for exploratory testing of these applications. The goal is to ensure usability, data integrity, and proper error handling. The checklist should focus on:

- shopping cart functionality,
- checkout process—user information,
- payment details,
- order review and confirmation.

Prepare a checklist.

### *3.4.3 Crowd Testing*

TA-3.4.3 (K2) Give examples of benefits and limitations of crowd testing

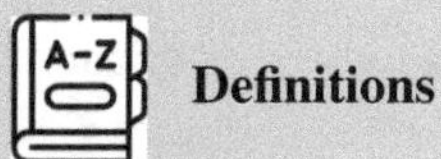

**Definitions**

**Crowd testing**: A test approach in which testing is distributed to a large group of testers.

**Introduction**. Crowd testing, also known as crowdsourced testing, is a test approach that leverages a large and diverse group of people (often from various geographical locations) to test software applications in real-world conditions. Unlike traditional in-house testing, where testing is conducted by a dedicated team within an organization, crowd testing utilizes the collective efforts of external testers, who are often part-time or freelance workers. This approach enables software to be tested across multiple devices, operating systems, and environments that closely mimic actual user conditions.

**Difference Between Crowd Testing and Beta Testing**

For the above-mentioned reason, crowd testing may seem to be a form of beta testing of COTS (commercial off-the-shelf) products. Recall that beta testing is a type of acceptance testing performed at an external site to the developer's test environment by roles outside the development organization. However, crowd testing and beta testing are two different things for many reasons. One of crowd testing's strengths is that it may be applied early during development. With crowd testing, you can acquire testers without addressing the general public. You can, for instance, evaluate software mock-ups or designs, and conduct early verification and validation tests. In contrast, beta testing functions as the final quality gate before software release. Whereas beta testing usually has a strong explorative focus ("Use the software and report bugs"), crowd testing tasks can be much more specific. Testers may be asked to go on a user journey and test certain use cases or even conduct traditional test-case-based testing. This leads to feedback having less noise—that is, ill-advised or irrelevant feedback. In beta testing, testers usually do not receive a concrete reward. In crowd testing, testers frequently receive a monetary reward, often based on the number of defects (bugs) they catch. Sometimes, the payment is on a first-come, first-served basis, such that testers have a strong incentive to be the first to report a defect. So, the individual tester is motivated to learn and improve their testing skills, which will also lead to faster and better feedback. In beta testing, the call for participation is rather open. With crowd testing, companies can select testers from a large pool of users on the basis of a variety of factors and characteristics (for example, testing experience, language, and devices, but also age, gender, and so on). So, the selection provides an efficient way to match tasks to testers (who aren't necessarily customers or clients), ensuring that only suitable people test the software [29].

**Benefits and limitations of crowd testing.** Some of the benefits of crowd testing include:

- **Diverse test environments.** Testers come from various geographical locations, using multiple environment configurations with various devices, browsers, and network conditions. This helps test the application under diverse real-world conditions. For example, if a global e-commerce site is crowd-tested by users in India, Brazil, and Germany using different phones, browsers, and 3G/4G/Wi-Fi connections, testers in rural areas can discover that product images load extremely slowly on older Android devices. This issue may not have appeared in the company's internal test lab.
- **More flexibility.** Crowd testing is easily scalable to handle a large number of tests in a short period of time. The organization can select from a large number of popular crowd testing platforms and tester profiles. For example, a streaming service preparing for a major movie premiere may recruit 500 crowd testers overnight on a popular testing platform. Within hours, they are able to gather performance and usability results from testers with varied profiles, something their small internal test team couldn't scale to handle in time.
- **Cost-effectiveness.** Crowd testing is typically less expensive than maintaining a large and diverse in-house test team or supplementing with external testing services. For example, suppose a small healthcare startup needs to validate its appointment-booking app across many device types but cannot afford a large in-house test team. Using crowd testing, they pay only for completed test cycles, keeping costs low while still getting broad coverage.
- **Rapid feedback.** Testers can provide quick feedback, helping to find failures and fix the underlying defects early. For example, if a mobile banking app releases a beta version to a crowd-testing group, within the first hour, multiple testers may report that fingerprint login fails on certain types of devices, allowing developers to fix it before the official launch the next day.
- **Real user perspective.** Testers can be real users of the application, able to better provide insights into the user experience and usability of the application. This can be especially valuable when using crowd testing to perform user acceptance testing with a group of actual application users. For example, suppose that a city's public transport authority crowd-tests its journey-planning app with real passengers. Users provide insights such as confusing route suggestions and unclear icons for bus transfers—feedback that internal testers might miss because they do not use the system daily.
- **Variability.** Since a wide variety of testers execute tests, this leads to broader coverage and a higher chance of identifying defects. However, this approach may limit the repeatability of tests compared to when they are conducted by a dedicated

team. For example, suppose that a gaming company crowd-tests a new multiplayer feature. Because testers play with different strategies, skill levels, and play styles, they uncover edge cases (e.g., an exploit triggered only when rapidly switching weapons), which could be difficult to encounter by the internal test team.

Some of the limitations of crowd testing include:

- **Unreliable quality of testing**. The quality of testing can vary significantly based on the skills and expertise of individual testers, although this may not be relevant, for example, when the goal is feedback on user experience.
- **Communication challenges**. Coordinating with a large number of testers from various locations with varying time zones, cultural differences, and language barriers can be challenging.
- **Security risks**. Sharing software with external testers in crowd testing poses data security and confidentiality risks. Proper measures can mitigate these risks, allowing for the responsible use of crowd testing without disclosing sensitive details or facilitating plagiarism.
- **Documentation and reporting**. Ensuring comprehensive test documentation and managing a large number of findings can be challenging when dealing with a large and diverse group of testers.

(optional box)

**Crowd Testing Process**

The typical workflow of a crowd testing project involves several key stages.

1. **Defining objectives and scope**. The test analyst must determine their goal with the crowd testing project. The goal may be general (e.g., validate if the product meets users' needs) or specific (e.g., identify functional bugs, performance, or usability problems). The project's boundaries must also be defined, including which features, platforms, devices, and operating systems will be tested.
2. **Selecting the crowd testing approach**. Three main types of crowd testing can be distinguished, as shown in Table 3.20 (after [29]). The classification is based on the type of testers involved.

**Table 3.20** Three approaches to crowd testing

| Approach | Main characteristics |
|---|---|
| Engaging an external crowd of Internet users | • Especially suited for functional testing.<br>• Can be set up quickly and is useful under high time pressure.<br>• Helps overcome testing departments' capacity limits. |
| Engaging the company's own employees | • Promotes high motivation and interest among employees.<br>• Fosters acceptance of new applications as part of IT change management.<br>• Enables easy identification of training needs. |
| Engaging the customers | • Obtains feedback from real customers without exposing the software to the general public.<br>• Offers a new channel for interaction with customers.<br>• Is especially suited for usability testing or user experience feedback combined with functional testing. |

3. **Selecting a crowd testing platform**. Many crowd testing platforms and companies offer crowd testing services, such as uTest, Crowd4Test, Test IO, BetaTesting, UXTweak, MyCrowd QA, Global App Testing, and many others. They differ in the features they offer, the quality of support they offer, and the pricing. Therefore, it is important to establish the budget for the project and set clear timelines for each test activity.
4. **Testers recruitment and onboarding**. The test analyst must specify the demographic and geographic criteria for selecting testers (e.g., age, location, language). This may not be so important in some cases, but in others, it may be crucial, e.g., when localizing a computer game for a given market. The required devices, operating systems, and testers' technical expertise should also be specified. After recruiting testers, they must receive detailed instructions and training materials to help them understand their tasks and the project's goals. They must also be trained in how to report defects.
5. **Test planning**. Depending on the approach, the test analyst may prepare.
   - detailed, low-level test cases outlining specific tasks for the testers to perform,
   - general, high-level test cases to give testers a general idea of what should be tested,
   - acceptance criteria for specific scenarios to be tested.

   The test analyst must also ensure that the necessary test environments, including servers and user accounts, are set up and accessible to testers.

6. **Test execution**. Test cases or test scenarios are assigned to testers based on their devices, expertise, knowledge, and availability. Testers document and report any issues they encounter. They may also classify defects based on severity and priority to facilitate defect management, triage, and resolution.

During test execution, defect reports are collected and analyzed. Defects are reviewed by the persons responsible for this (e.g., test analyst) to validate their authenticity and relevance. The test analyst should also check for duplicate reports to ensure each issue is counted and addressed only once. Defects are prioritized and assigned to the appropriate development teams for fixing. Once they are fixed, the crowd testers may be assigned re-testing tasks to verify that the issues they raised have been resolved.

Feedback and communication with testers should be maintained throughout the process. The test analyst should use the platform's communication tools to interact with testers, answer their questions, and provide necessary clarifications. Testers should be encouraged to provide feedback based on their experience and any difficulties they encounter during testing.

**Case Study**

Suppose you want to perform crowd testing for a new version of the FoodApp.

The primary goals are to ensure the app's functionality across different devices, assess its usability, and identify critical bugs. The app should be tested on iOS and Android platforms, focusing on key features such as user registration, menu browsing, order placement, payment processing, and order tracking. Since testing will be focused mostly on functional testing, and it is important to set it up quickly, you decide to engage an external crowd of Internet users.

You selected the MyCrowd platform (https://mycrowd.com/). Your market researchers informed you that 28% of mobile phone users use iOS, while 72% use Android (see Fig. 3.62). You decide that both these operating systems should be taken into account, as well as the most popular operating systems for desktop applications. You also decide that the FoodApp should be tested on all the most popular browsers. Testers should be recruited from all over the world, but since the app's language is English only, you decided to restrict testing to English-speaking users. The considerations mentioned above are translated to the configuration of the crowd testing process shown in Fig. 3.63. The platform calculates the cost of the crowd testing, which is $4000. This matches your planned budget for crowd testing.

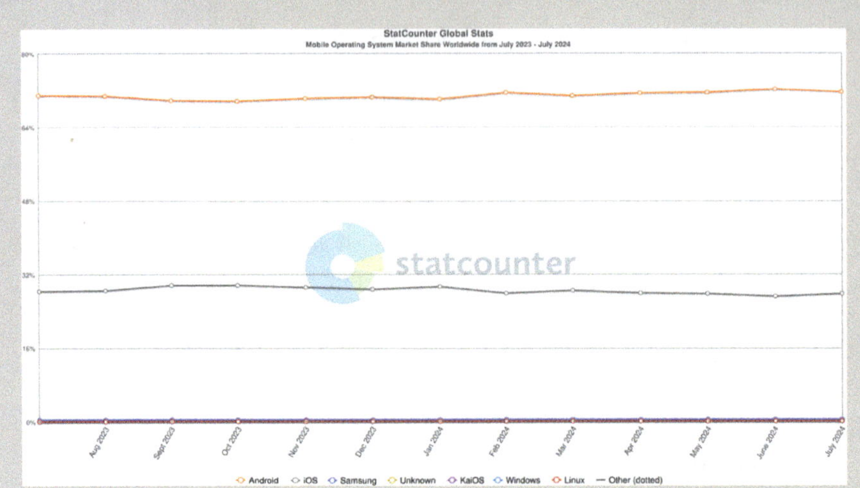


**Fig. 3.62** Mobile operating system market share worldwide 2023–2024, source: gs.statcounter.com/os-market-share/mobile/worldwide

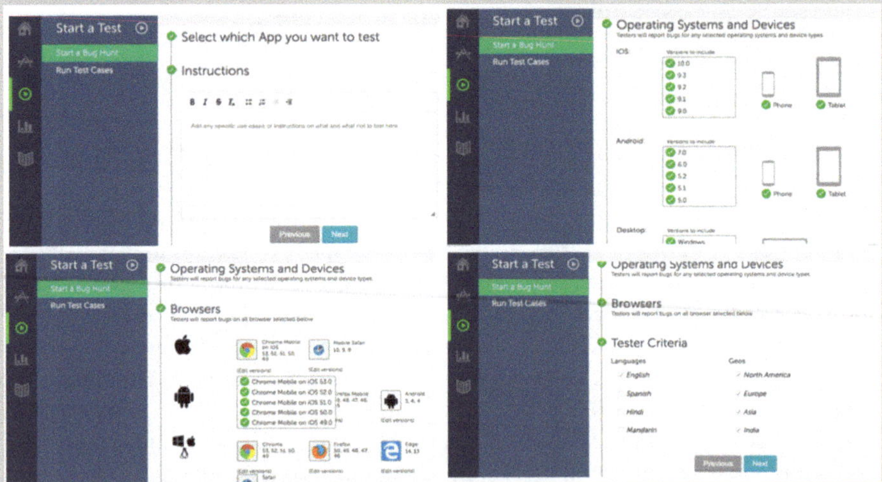


**Fig. 3.63** Configuring the crowd testing process using the MyCrowd platform

The recruitment process is on the platform side, so you do not need to do anything more. You only decide that there should be 200 testers. This group should be representative regarding device type, operating system, and geolocation. As for the onboarding, you fill in the "Instructions" section during the configuration process (top left part of Fig. 3.63). You write all the necessary instructions for the testers, including how to download the app, what specific features to test, and how to report defects. You decide not to provide detailed test cases to the crowd testers. You only inform them about several use cases that should be taken into consideration, namely:

- user registration and login,
- browsing menus and searching for dishes,
- adding items to the cart,
- placing an order,
- payment process (including different payment methods),
- order tracking and delivery notifications,
- user feedback and rating system.

Since crowd testers should not pay real money for the orders, you instrument the FoodApp for the testing process. You use sandbox environments offered by most payment gateways so that transactions can be simulated without involving real money. Crowd testers will use the test card numbers provided by the payment gateways to simulate various transaction outcomes (e.g., successful payments, declined payments, errors). Also, the order tracking and delivery notification features will be mocked, so no real delivery persons are involved in the ordering process.

Once everything is set up, the testers start crowd testing. 55 of them reported that the payment processing fails for Visa credit cards. 10 of them reported difficulty navigating the menu on small screens. 4 crowd testers reported delays in push notifications for order updates on iOS phones. After removing the duplicates, you fill out three bug reports regarding the issues mentioned above.

## Sample Questions

### Question 3.4.3A

Which of the following is a benefit of crowd testing?

(a) It allows the repetition of performed tests in a consistent manner.
(b) It allows for quick achievement of wide coverage.
(c) It allows the use of historical knowledge about failures.
(d) It allows good control of environment configurations.

Select ONE answer.

### Question 3.4.3B

Which of the following is a limitation of crowd testing?

(a) Low flexibility.
(b) Poor cost-effectiveness.

(c) Communication challenges.
(d) No real user perspective.

Select ONE answer.

## 3.5 Applying the Most Appropriate Test Techniques

Testing should be as effective and efficient as possible in the given context. During test planning, the test manager is responsible for selecting the most appropriate test technique(s) and the tooling to be used, considering the context of testing. Thereby, the test analyst supports the test manager with their expertise. In addition, the test analyst can recommend automation measures to optimize the efficiency of dynamic testing activities. This includes automating the test design, described in this section, and supporting test execution automation, described in Sect. 1.3.6 above.

### *3.5.1 Selecting Test Techniques to Mitigate Product Risks*

TA-3.5.1 (K4) Select appropriate test techniques to mitigate product risks for a given situation

The main area in which the test analyst works is test analysis and design. The tests designed by the test analyst should be effective. That is, they should reach the test objectives as far as possible. However, the test analyst must consider a broad context when selecting test techniques. This context includes product and project risks, but in this section, we focus only on mitigating product risks. Project risk mitigation is usually the responsibility of a test manager.

A well-designed test covers a specific risk in risk-based testing. Therefore, one of the key skills of a test analyst is to select the right test techniques for effective and efficient product risk mitigation. Many factors, including the following, influence this selection.

**Test objectives**. They define which aspects of the test object need to be evaluated. Test objectives impact the general approach to risks. Hence, different test objectives may require different test techniques to mitigate risks effectively in accordance with these objectives. Test objectives may be defined based on discussions with the customer, may be directly derived from the adopted test policy and test strategy, but may also be derived from the type of system under test. For example, a program for engineering calculations will require intensive testing of the numerical correctness using domain-based testing. In contrast, a decision-oriented system like credit risk management software will require applying rule-based test techniques.

Table 3.21 shows how a given test objective may affect the choice of test techniques from the risk mitigation perspective.

**Table 3.21** Typical test objectives and their impact on test techniques selection

| Test objective | Impact on test techniques selection |
|---|---|
| Evaluating work products | This is a general and high-level test objective, so the choice of test techniques depends on the type of work product and the type of identified risks. For documentation, it will usually be some static test technique, e.g., applying a review type such as a walkthrough, technical review, or inspection. Executable software usually needs some form of dynamic testing, such as black-box or experience-based test techniques |
| Triggering failures and finding defects | If the test analyst has some particular failures or defects in mind, they can use error guessing or checklist-based testing. If the test analyst focuses on certain defect types or failures, they may choose specific black-box techniques designed to detect this type of defect |
| Ensuring the required coverage of a test object | The coverage type may directly determine the test technique (e.g., boundary value coverage requires applying the boundary value analysis). The coverage strength may depend on the risk level. For example, a standard approach may be to use a 2-value boundary value analysis. However, if the risk related to a test item is high, the test analyst may decide to use a 3-value boundary analysis |
| Reducing the level of risk | The choice of the test technique depends on a particular risk category and its parameters, such as probability, impact, and risk level |
| Verifying fulfillment of requirements | The choice of the test technique depends on the type of requirements (e.g., use cases, user stories, or acceptance criteria), their criticality, and related risks (e.g., according to the Product Owner or the client) |
| Verifying compliance with contractual, legal, and regulatory requirements | This may require a formal review, such as an inspection. Other legal or regulatory requirements, especially in safety-critical industries and system-relevant businesses, require rigorous test techniques to be used for high-risk levels |
| Providing information to stakeholders to allow them to make informed decisions | This goal does not directly influence the choice of a test technique. It rather requires traceability. The results of applying a certain test technique must be reflected in the coverage level achieved and the residual risk level, in terms of the stakeholders' requirements |
| Building confidence in the test object quality | This is a general and high-level test objective, so the choice of test techniques depends on how confidence is understood. Applying techniques that can be easily understood by the stakeholders, like scenario-based testing, might be an option. Demonstrating a steady, successive reduction in the level of residual risk may also increase confidence |
| Validating whether the test object is complete and works as expected | Usually requires some form of acceptance testing. Since this test level should be (at least in theory) performed by end-users, operations, or other stakeholders, they may not follow any particular black-box test technique but use less formal techniques, like error guessing, exploratory testing, or checklist-based testing |

**Product risks**. Product risks are associated with potential defects. These defects, in turn, can best be detected using specific test techniques, as most techniques focus on detecting specific types of defects. Knowing what kind of defects are detected by specific test techniques is therefore crucial for the test analyst. This is because it allows the selection of a test technique to effectively mitigate a specific risk. Below, for each test technique described in the syllabus, we provide examples of generic risks that can be mitigated by using that technique.

- **Domain testing** is a data-based test technique, so it focuses on domain errors. Generic risks that can be mitigated by domain testing include border shifts of the equivalence partitions, data type mismatches, and invalid input handling. For example, a system might fail when trying to handle a negative age, an age over 100 years, could fail to handle users as adults on their 18th birthday, or fail to display points of interest close to the boundary of the map section displayed.
- **Combinatorial testing** focuses on interactions between inputs or, in general, parameters. Generic risks that can be mitigated by combinatorial testing include interaction faults, configuration issues, or complex logic flaws. For example, the system fails to process a tax calculation correctly for a shipment when the input contains a specific combination of source country, destination country, and merchandise type, or when a mobile client is used on a specific combination of mobile devices, browsers, and operating systems.
- **Random testing** is a data-based test technique, so it focuses on domain errors, similar to domain testing. However, the test data are drawn from a given probability distribution, and usually this can be automated, so it is possible to execute test cases with many different test data. Therefore, random testing can mitigate risks related to reliability and robustness issues or detect problems with edge cases overlooked by other techniques.
- **CRUD testing** focuses on the lifecycle of entities processed by the test item. It was originally introduced for database management systems but quickly proved its worth for all types of entities. Typical risks that this technique can mitigate include data integrity failures, data loss, or transaction errors. For example, the system may be unable to read and display a flight booking after upgrading it, or a system action of deleting an open shopping cart after a timeout may result in losing the customer's addresses. Transaction errors often occur in multi-step data transactions, so CRUD testing can be used to verify if the transactions are atomic and consistent.
- **State-based testing** focuses on the system's state-dependent behavior modeled by the state machine model. Generic risks that can be mitigated by this technique include incorrect state handling, incorrect responses to an action in a specific state, unexpected behaviors, or deadlocks. For example, an overheating warning signal may incorrectly turn off when the sensor fails while the engine is overheating, or a car-sharing vehicle may not enter the "key recognized" state and enable starting the engine when the renter gets in.
- **Scenario-based** testing focuses on a system's behavior in real-world scenarios and use cases. Generic risks that can be mitigated by this technique include missing scenarios or their parts, end-to-end flow issues, or usability problems.

For example, the scenario of paying for a shopping cart in online shopping could omit the entry of discount codes and credit notes, or the scenario of a registered customer making a booking could unnecessarily require them to re-enter their address details that are already stored in the system.

- **Decision table testing** focuses on verifying the correctness of rule handling. Generic risks that this technique can mitigate include improper handling of rules, omissions of cases, or contradictions. For example, in a complex tax calculation system, for a given set of conditions, the system calculates an incorrect tax rate, or the system does nothing because this rule is not implemented.
- **Metamorphic testing** verifies if the expected output of a test case changes appropriately when the input test data changes in a certain way. Generic risks that this technique can mitigate include inconsistencies in the system's behavior that occur due to violations of some invariants formally described by the metamorphic relations. For example, an autonomous driving system that correctly steers the vehicle through a left-hand bend on a country road with oncoming traffic in good visibility conditions might fail to do so in rain, fog, backlighting, or through a right-hand bend.
- **Session-based testing** is an experience-based test technique, so the risks it can mitigate vary and depend on many factors, such as the session's goal or the tester's intuition, knowledge, and experience. Like other experience-based test techniques, it is particularly effective for validation, thereby reducing the risk that the software will fail to adequately meet the stakeholders' needs. Such risks are difficult to identify using formal, verification-oriented black-box test techniques. In addition, due to its informal approach, session-based testing is particularly useful when the risk level is low or when the schedule is tight. Some examples of risks that session-based testing can address include usability issues, unanticipated user behaviors, complex interaction problems, missed requirements, regression defects, performance bottlenecks, and security vulnerabilities.
- **Checklist-based testing** relies on a checklist, so the risks it can mitigate depend on the items within that checklist. Common risks this technique can mitigate include overlooking test conditions, inconsistent coverage, and deviations from best practices.
- **Crowd testing** is an experience-based test technique. One of the primary benefits of this technique is the ability to test software in various environments and on a wide range of devices, platforms, and configurations. Therefore, the generic risks that crowd testing can mitigate include usability and localization issues, and risks related to various runtime environments.

**Differentiated use of the same test technique**. Most test techniques can be used with different coverage levels assumed. For example, in domain testing, the test analyst can choose between simplified or reliable domain coverage. The choice of coverage strength is part of risk analysis and is closely tied to project risks. Stronger coverage demands more testing, which in turn requires more time, effort, and resources. For low risk levels, less stringent coverage criteria are usually appropriate. Conversely, when the risk level is high, the coverage strength must be correspondingly higher. It is also important to recognize that the test object usually consists of multiple test items, each with its own risk level. Therefore, the test techniques and coverage criteria might differ for each test item. For example, in our case study, the test items in the Client Component generally carry a higher risk level than those in the delivery component. This is because clients are more likely to input incorrect data and are less tolerant of errors in the software.

**Coverage Requirements in the IEC 61508 Standard**

Some standards impose a given coverage level regarding the risk likelihood. For example, IEC 61508 standard [30] recommends certain risk mitigation measures according to the so-called SIL (Safety Integrity Level) assigned to a test item, as shown in Table 3.22. The higher the SIL level is, the more thorough methods are required or recommended.

**Table 3.22** Example relations between Safety Integration Level and risk mitigation measures as defined in IEC 61508–3 standard

| Measure | SIL1 | SIL 2 | SIL 3 | SIL 4 |
|---|---|---|---|---|
| **Component and component integration testing** | | | | |
| Random testing | – | R | R | R |
| Functional testing and black-box testing | HR | HR | HR | HR |
| **Static analysis** | | | | |
| Boundary value analysis | R | R | HR | HR |
| Checklists | R | R | R | R |
| Error guessing | R | R | R | R |
| Formal inspections | R | R | HR | HR |
| Walkthroughs | R | R | R | R |
| **Dynamic analysis and dynamic testing** | | | | |
| Test case execution from boundary value analysis | R | HR | HR | HR |
| Test case execution from error guessing | R | R | R | R |
| Equivalence classes and input partitioning testing | R | R | R | HR |
| 100% statement coverage | R | HR | HR | HR |
| 100% branch coverage | R | R | HR | HR |
| 100% MC/DC coverage | R | R | R | HR |
| **Modeling** | | | | |
| Data flow diagrams | R | R | R | R |
| Finite state machines (state-based models) | – | R | HR | HR |

HR = highly recommended, R = recommended, – = no recommendation

The **test basis** includes various sources of information, such as requirements, user stories, or design specifications. This information significantly influences the choice of test techniques because it determines the type and depth of information available to the test analyst regarding the system under test. This, in turn, shapes how the test analyst can effectively mitigate product risks. For example, suppose the specification of the test object includes a requirement modeled with a decision table. In such a case, it is natural for the test analyst to choose the decision table testing because this is the most straightforward way to test this requirement. The test analyst, however, must also decide whether to use a full or a minimized decision table. This requires some further risk analysis.

When the test basis includes detailed functional specifications or requirements documents, test analysts clearly understand the system's expected behavior and can verify it by selecting the appropriate test techniques. For example, if the test basis for a room reservation system includes a requirement that describes the reservation process, the first natural choice would be to apply scenario-based testing. Further, detailed analysis may reveal that it would also be beneficial to use some other test techniques. For example, there may be some business rules for the reservation best addressed by decision table testing; time/date issues may suggest the use of some data-based techniques, such as boundary value analysis or combinatorial testing.

If, in contrast, the test basis does not specify the features in sufficient detail to derive a test oracle, then metamorphic testing and experience-based test techniques may be more suitable.

**Knowledge of recurring defect types** may indicate selecting the test technique(s) that focus on detecting such types of defects. This approach assumes that similar risks as in previous projects or iterations will most likely occur again. For example, suppose that in previous iterations no major defects were found regarding the functional correctness, but functional appropriateness was a recurring issue. Therefore, it may be reasonable to focus on scenario-based testing, which has successfully detected in the past if users could not appropriately accomplish specified tasks and objectives. In contrast, equivalence partitioning may suffice for testing functional correctness.

**Tester's knowledge and experience**. If the test analyst is not familiar with a given test technique, it is not a good idea to use it in critical test assignments. Incompetent use of a technique with which the tester is unfamiliar can cause a number of problems, such as wasting time designing ineffective tests or the occurrence of false positives or false negatives. However, a test analyst should strive to constantly gain knowledge of new testing methods and techniques. In this way, they broaden the scope of their skills and are better able to select appropriate measures to mitigate the risks under analysis.

Domain knowledge may also influence the selection of test techniques. For example, little or no domain knowledge indicates that techniques like exploratory testing will be ineffective.

**Software development lifecycle model used**. The adopted lifecycle model significantly influences the choice of techniques to mitigate risk, as the role and responsibilities of the test analyst may vary across lifecycles (see Sect. 1.1.1). A sequential development model typically requires that the test analyst focuses on static test techniques in the initial phases of the project, since no executable code is ready at that time. When dynamic testing can be applied, the test analyst may use more formal techniques since there is usually a well-defined test basis, and the requirements are stable. An iterative development model might be more appropriate for adopting more lightweight test techniques (e.g., experience-based test techniques) or test techniques for which the test design can be automated. This is due to the fact that iterative models assume the requirements may change from iteration to iteration.

**Customer and contract requirements**. Contracts can explicitly require performing certain testing, which influences the selection of test techniques (e.g., acceptance criteria with a set of scenarios provided by the client suggest the use of a scenario-based test technique).

**Regulatory requirements**. When a project follows a standard that imposes specific coverage criteria, it may require the use of specific test techniques that can provide this coverage.

**Coverage Requirements in the DO-178C Standard**

The standard DO-178C [31], Software Considerations in Airborne Systems and Equipment Certification, is the regulatory document by which certification authorities such as the FAA in the US, EASA in the EU, and Transport Canada approve all commercial software-based aerospace systems. It requires achieving different coverage levels for components with different criticality levels, as shown in Table 3.23.

**Table 3.23** The relation between the risk level and the structural coverage objective as defined by DO-178C

| Level | Failure definition | Associated white-box coverage required |
|---|---|---|
| A | Software resulting in a catastrophic failure condition for the system | Modified Condition/ Decision coverage |
| B | Software resulting in a hazardous or severe/major failure condition for the system | Decision coverage |
| C | Software resulting in a major failure condition for the system | Statement coverage |
| D | Software resulting in a minor failure condition for the system | (None required) |
| E | Software resulting in no effect on the system | (None required) |

**Project constraints**, such as time and budget, may prevent the use of time-consuming techniques or those that require expensive resources. For example, a proper review of the extensive decision tables testing the business rules could exceed the availability of the business experts. In such a case, the test analyst could recommend equivalence partitioning with classification trees as an alternative, which is easier to review.

**Combining test techniques.** Test techniques are often combined to increase the efficiency and effectiveness of testing. For example:

- Equivalence partitioning can be used together with boundary value analysis to test both typical and extreme values of partitions.
- Boundary value analysis can be used in state-based testing when evaluating the value of guard conditions.
- Domain analysis can be used to determine the value of a condition from a decision table or a variable occurring in a scenario under test in scenario-based testing.

**Case Study**

You are a test analyst working on the FoodApp application. The app integrates with third-party APIs for payment processing, restaurant data, and delivery tracking. The app is expected to support high traffic during peak times like weekends and holidays.

[Project constraints] The project has a tight deadline due to a planned launch three months before a major holiday season. Limited resources are allocated for testing, so manual and automated testing must be balanced efficiently. The app has multiple integrations (e.g., payment gateway, restaurant data, and delivery services) and requires performance, security, and functional testing.

[Test basis] Functional and non-functional requirements are only partially documented, with some areas (like performance under heavy load) lacking detail. Clear use cases are provided for basic functionalities like user registration, ordering food, and making payments. The app has a very rich set of rules for promotional programs, discounts, etc. Initial prototypes have been tested with early users, and some common issues have been reported, such as crashes during payment processing and slow performance during order tracking.

[Tester's knowledge and experience] Testers in your team have good knowledge of e-commerce and are experts in the food ordering domain. They are skilled in black-box test techniques. They have experience using tools for automated UI testing and test case management.

[Software development lifecycle] The project follows a fast-paced Agile methodology with two-week sprints. Testers work closely with developers but often receive late-stage changes, leading to rework and increased risk. Automated tests are integrated into the CI pipeline, but manual testing is required for specific edge cases and exploratory tests due to unpredictable behavior with third-party services.

[Recurring defect types] Frequent issues occur with third-party payment and restaurant APIs, leading to failed transactions or missing data. User interface bugs, such as buttons not responding or text not displaying correctly, have been observed during prototype testing. The app struggles under heavy load, especially during peak ordering times, leading to slow response times and timeouts. Early penetration tests revealed security risks, especially in handling payment data and user sessions.

Based on the analysis of the above-mentioned context, you may come to the following conclusions about the choice of test techniques to minimize risks.

1. Apply domain analysis. Rationale: Since testers have limited knowledge of the internal workings of the code, black-box test techniques like domain analysis are useful. By breaking down the user inputs into valid and invalid domains (e.g., valid restaurant IDs, correct payment details, coupon codes), testers can explore edge cases and error-handling scenarios, thus mitigating risks such as incorrect handling of payment data, missing data, or failed transactions.
2. Apply decision table testing. Rationale: decision table testing is valuable for testing the different combinations of rules in the app, such as applying coupons, handling payment options (credit card, wallet, etc.), and order

cancelation policies. This type of testing will mitigate risks related to a complex system of discount rules in promotional programs.

3. Apply combinatorial testing. Rationale: given the app's complex interactions (e.g., restaurants, payment methods, and delivery options), combinatorial testing helps identify defects in various combinations of inputs and conditions. This is especially important for testing interactions across restaurant selections, menu items, delivery options, and user locations. This testing will mitigate risks such as failure to correctly handle input combinations, which can cause inconsistent behavior, incorrect orders, or failed transactions. Since risks related to these complex iterations are high (they involve payment methods and delivery options, which are a core part of the business), you decide to apply pairwise coverage rather than base choice coverage.
4. Apply CRUD testing. Rationale: CRUD testing is a good option to ensure data consistency, especially in user management, order history, and payment details. Applying this technique will mitigate risks such as failures in order processing and management.
5. Apply session-based exploratory testing. Rationale: exploratory testing is critical for uncovering unexpected issues, especially in areas with limited documentation or where integrations with third-party services occur. Testers can adapt as they find defects, using their knowledge of typical issues like usability and API integration problems. This technique fits well into the project context: the testers are experienced and have domain knowledge. Moreover, the project is being conducted in an agile methodology, which may mean that there will be little time for lengthy test planning, and the client may change its mind frequently on some requirements.

## Sample Questions

### Question 3.5.1A

An online shopping platform allows users to browse products, add them to their shopping cart, and proceed to checkout. It includes various product categories (electronics, clothing, etc.), filtering options (e.g., price range, ratings, brand), and payment methods (credit card, PayPal, etc.). The application supports both web and mobile platforms and offers features like saving preferences, viewing recommendations, and applying discounts or promotional codes.

The goal is to test the platform's core functionality, ensuring that it correctly handles different combinations of actions, inputs, and states that users might encounter. The application must function correctly across different user profiles, device types, and product selections. The correctness of the filtering mechanism is also important, but you do not have clear requirements about how it should work.

Which **TWO** test techniques will be most useful to apply in this scenario?

(a) CRUD testing.
(b) Pairwise testing.
(c) Random testing.
(d) Metamorphic testing.
(e) Equivalence partitioning.

Select TWO answers.

**Question 3.5.1B**

You are asked to design test cases for the university course enrollment system, based on the specification shown in Fig. 3.64. GPA stands for Grade Point Average, and year stands for year of study.

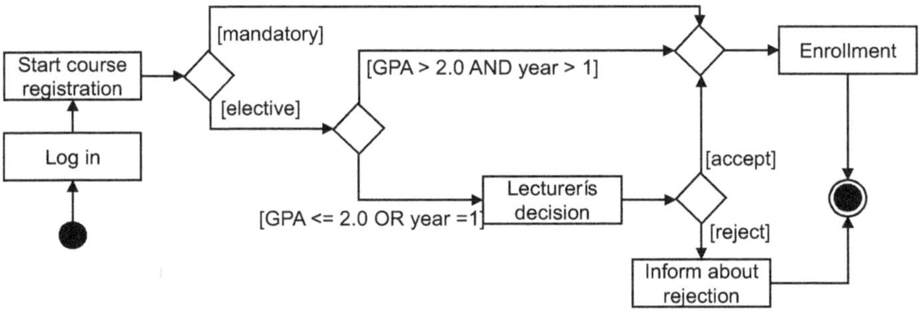


**Fig. 3.64** University course enrollment process

Which **TWO** test techniques will be **MOST** useful for test case design?

(a) Combinatorial testing.
(b) CRUD testing.
(c) Scenario-based testing.
(d) State transition testing.
(e) Domain testing.

Select TWO answers.

## Exercise 11—Test Technique Selection

TA-3.5.1 (K4) Select appropriate test techniques to mitigate product risks for a given situation

A software development team is building a web-based inventory management system for a retail chain. The system allows warehouse staff to add, update, delete, and search inventory items, and it includes complex business rules for stock level thresholds, reorder notifications, and discounts applied based on combinations of product type and quantity. You have been tasked with designing a test plan to mitigate the risks associated with the system's core functionalities before the first release.

The following risks were identified:

- Risk 1: input fields may accept invalid or unexpected data (e.g., negative stock, invalid product codes).
- Risk 2: certain combinations of product attributes may trigger incorrect discount or reorder logic.
- Risk 3: users might perform unexpected sequences of operations on data items that could corrupt the inventory database.
- Risk 4: certain workflows, such as placing a reorder, applying a discount, and generating reports, have complex state-dependent behaviors (e.g., low stock triggers reorder, but only if discount rules are not violated).
- Risk 5: end-to-end-user scenarios might reveal issues missed in isolated testing (e.g., adding items, applying discounts, and generating a report may cause inconsistent outputs).

Based on the provided information, propose a set of black-box test techniques that would be the best choice for mitigating the identified risks. Justify the choice.

### *3.5.2 Benefits of Automating the Test Design*

TA-3.5.2 (K2) Explain the benefits of automating the test design

Typically, when people talk about "test automation," they mean automating test execution. However, automation can also be applied to other test activities, including test design. The test analyst may use tools to automate test design activities, especially for the black-box test techniques discussed earlier. When automating the test design, the test analyst creates a test model and uses appropriate tools to generate testware from that model. Typically, the testware generated in test design consists of test cases, but may also include test data requirements and test environment requirements (see sect. 1.2.2 above).

Automating the test design has several benefits, such as:

**Defect prevention**. Early modeling from the testing perspective is an effective quality control of the test basis. (See Sect. 5.2.1). Automated test design tools can generate a wide range of test cases, covering, for example, all possible combinations of inputs, boundary values, or edge cases. This comprehensive approach ensures that the software is thoroughly tested for potential issues that might otherwise be missed in manual testing.

**Extended capability**. Automated test design can handle complex systems more efficiently than manual testing. It can automatically generate tests for specific workflows or interactions involving many variables or dependencies. This helps to identify defects that might arise from complex integrations or concurrency issues, which would be difficult to anticipate manually. Some test techniques can only be realistically carried out with the help of automation, e.g., combinatorial testing, random testing, or N-switch coverage in state-based testing.

**Improved comprehensibility**. The specification of the test selection criteria in the tool makes the coverage more coherent and intelligible. Automated test design can be configured to focus on high-risk areas of the application, where defects are more likely to occur. By concentrating testing efforts on these areas, it becomes easier to identify potential problems and address them proactively before they lead to larger issues.

**Less repetitive work**. Relevant testware is derived from the test model automatically. This relieves the test analyst from carrying out repetitive work such as manually specifying tests with redundant parts.

**Less maintenance efforts**. In many approaches to automated test design, the test model is the single source of truth used to derive the testware. As a result, only the test model needs to be maintained. Automated test designs can adapt to changes in the system more easily than manual test cases. If the software requirements or system architecture change, automated tools can quickly regenerate or update test cases, preventing defects that could arise from outdated or insufficient tests.

**Less defective testware**. Manual work is prone to errors. Tools may visualize gaps in the test model and perform static analysis on the test model during its creation. Automated test design tools can ensure that the test design is aligned with the system requirements and specifications, reducing the chances of errors that can occur if a tester misinterprets a requirement. This precision provided by tools reduces human error in test design and helps catch defects related to incorrect or incomplete testing early on.

**Enhanced team collaboration**. Automated test design tools usually rely on specifications, models, or requirements to generate test cases. This ensures that everyone—developers, testers, and other stakeholders—has a consistent understanding of the project's goals and quality criteria. With clear, automated tests derived from these requirements, teams can ensure that all members align on the system's expected behavior, minimizing misunderstandings. Stakeholders may review the test model to find defects or to get a better understanding of the test conditions.

**Enhanced traceability**. It is easier to link the elements of a test model to the test conditions or specification items than the test cases themselves. If supported by the utilized tool, the generated test cases will inherit those links, providing overall traceability in testing.

**Compatibility with other test tools.** Most test automation tools are compatible with other tools, such as test management or test execution tools.

As with automated solutions in general, automating the test design leads to a more efficient test process. It is possible to produce higher-quality testware in less time in a more systematic, yet comprehensible way.

**Case Study**

Let us see the example of applying test design automation to our FoodApp. Suppose we want to design a minimum set of test cases achieving 100% of the correct edge coverage criterion for the diagram of state transitions from Sect. 3.2.2. For the convenience of the reader, this diagram is repeated in Fig. 3.65.

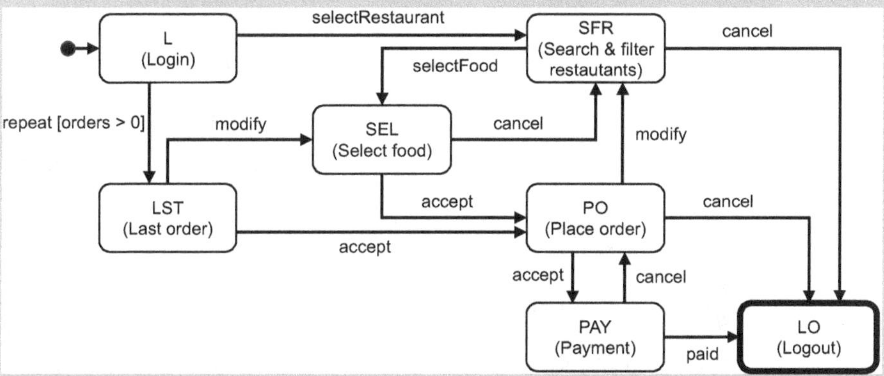


**Fig. 3.65** State diagram for the ordering process in the FoodApp

The following source code automatically generates the minimum set of test cases for this criterion.

```
from collections import defaultdict, deque
import itertools
import networkx as nx

class FiniteStateMachine:
   def __init__(self):
      self.graph = defaultdict(list)
      self.states = set()
      self.final = "LO" # set the final state
      self.added = []
      self.OrigG = None
```

```
    def add_transition(self, from_state, to_state, input_
symbol=None):
        # Add a transition between two states
        self.graph[from_state].append((to_state, input_symbol))
        self.states.add(from_state)
        self.states.add(to_state)

    def _build_nx_graph(self):
        # Helper function to build a NetworkX graph from the FSM tran-
sitions
        G = nx.MultiDiGraph()
        for from_state, transitions in self.graph.items():
            for to_state, input_symbol in transitions:
                G.add_edge(from_state, to_state, label=input_symbol)
        return G

    def _make_graph_eulerian(self, G):
        # Balance the in-degrees and out-degrees
        in_degrees = {v: G.in_degree(v) for v in G.nodes()}
        out_degrees = {v: G.out_degree(v) for v in G.nodes()}

        # Create lists to track vertices with imbalance
        excess_out = []  # vertices where out-degree > in-degree
        excess_in = []   # vertices where in-degree > out-degree

        for v in G.nodes():
            if out_degrees[v] > in_degrees[v]:
                    excess_out.append((v, out_degrees[v] - in_
degrees[v]))
            elif in_degrees[v] > out_degrees[v]:
                excess_in.append((v, in_degrees[v] - out_degrees[v]))

        # Match vertices from excess_in to excess_out
        for u, in_deficit in excess_in:
            for _ in range(in_deficit):
                v, out_deficit = excess_out.pop(0)
                G.add_edge(u, v)
                self.added.append([u, v])
                if out_deficit > 1:
                    excess_out.insert(0, (v, out_deficit - 1))
        return G

    def _find_eulerian_circuit(self, G):
        #Find an Eulerian circuit (or path) in the graph
        eulerian_circuit = list(nx.eulerian_circuit(G))
        return eulerian_circuit

    def generate_test_cases(self):
            #Generate minimal test cases that achieve transi-
tion coverage
```

```
        G = self._build_nx_graph()

        # Ensure the graph is Eulerian
        if not nx.is_eulerian(G):
            G = self._make_graph_eulerian(G)
        # Find an Eulerian circuit
        eulerian_circuit = self._find_eulerian_circuit(G)
        final_circuit = []
        # Replace added edges with shortest path consisting of
        # original edges
        for u, v in eulerian_circuit:
            if [u, v] in self.added:
                path = nx.shortest_path(self.OrigG, u, v)[:-1]
            else:
                path = [u]
            final_circuit.extend(path)
        #final_circuit.append(eulerian_circuit[-1])

        # Generate the test cases from the Eulerian circuit
        test_cases = []
        current_path = []
        for u in final_circuit:
            if (u != self.final):
                current_path.append(u)
            if (u == self.final):
                current_path.append(u)
                test_cases.append(current_path)
                current_path = []
        return test_cases

fsm = FiniteStateMachine()
# Create the state transition model
fsm.add_transition('L', 'SFR', 'selectRestaurant')
fsm.add_transition('L', 'LST', 'repeat')
fsm.add_transition('SFR', 'SEL', 'selectFood')
fsm.add_transition('SFR', 'LO', 'cancel')
fsm.add_transition('SEL', 'SFR', 'cancel')
fsm.add_transition('SEL', 'PO', 'accept')
fsm.add_transition('LST', 'SEL', 'modify')
fsm.add_transition('LST', 'PO', 'accept')
fsm.add_transition('PO', 'SFR', 'modify')
fsm.add_transition('PO', 'LO', 'cancel')
fsm.add_transition('PO', 'PAY', 'accept')
fsm.add_transition('PAY', 'PO', 'cancel')
fsm.add_transition('PAY', 'LO', 'paid')
fsm.OrigG = fsm._build_nx_graph() # remember original graph
# Add three artificial transitions so that in-degree = out-
degree
# for the final state, and make the diagram strongly connnected
fsm.add_transition('LO', 'L', ")
fsm.add_transition('LO', 'L', ")
```

```
fsm.add_transition('LO', 'L', '')

test_cases = fsm.generate_test_cases()
print("\nMinimal Test Suite Achieving 100% Transition Coverage:")
for idx, test_case in enumerate(test_cases):
    print(f"Test Case {idx + 1}: {' -> '.join(test_case)}")
```

When run, the script will generate a minimum set of test cases achieving the set coverage.

```
D:\FoodApp>python mbt3.py
Minimal Test Suite Achieving 100% Transition Coverage:
Test Case 1: L -> LST -> SEL -> PO -> PAY -> PO -> SFR -> SEL ->
SFR -> SEL -> PO -> PAY -> LO.
Test Case 2: L -> LST -> PO -> LO
Test Case 3: L -> SFR -> LO
```

### EXTRA Why Does the Script Work?

The script works as follows. The state diagram is enriched with "artificial" additional transitions (in the _make_graph_eulerian() function) so that for each state, the number of incoming transitions equals the number of outgoing transitions. In particular, as many transitions are added from the final state to the initial state as there are transitions entering the final state (the last three calls to the fsm.add_transition() function). The idea is that when the final state is reached, the only possible transition is to the initial state. Such a transition will represent the beginning of a new test case.

A diagram modified in this way is a so-called Eulerian graph. This means that there is a cycle in it that passes through each transition exactly once. This cycle is split into chunks: each chunk ending in the final state constitutes a separate test case. However, if a test case contains an artificially added transition between states x and y, we need to replace it with the feasible path in the original diagram. Such an edge is, therefore, converted into the shortest path from x to y composed only of the transitions from the original diagram.

Notice that the above-mentioned procedure guarantees that the resulting number of test cases will be minimal.

## Sample Questions

### Question 3.5.2A

Which of the following is a benefit of automating the test design that results in fewer maintenance efforts?

(a) Automated tests can run much faster than manual testing.
(b) Test scripts can be reused across multiple test execution cycles.
(c) Early modeling effectively evaluates test basis quality.
(d) The test model is the single source of truth.

Select ONE answer.

### Question 3.5.2B

Which of the following is an example of a test design automation risk?

(a) Limited flexibility of automated tests.
(b) False positives or false negative results.
(c) Overlooking test conditions.
(d) Automated test scripts' fragility.

Select ONE answer.

# Chapter 4 Testing Software Quality Characteristics

**Keywords** Adaptability · Compatibility · Flexibility · Functional appropriateness · Functional completeness · Functional correctness · Functional suitability · Functional testing · Installability · Interaction capability · Interoperability · Usability · User experience

## Note on the Relation Between the Syllabus and the ISO 25010 Standard

The Test Analyst syllabus utilizes the software product quality model outlined in the ISO 25010 standard [6] as a guide and discusses the quality characteristics that are in focus for a test analyst. This international standard defines product quality as the capability of a system or its components to satisfy stated and implied quality needs when used under specific conditions. Therefore, product quality focuses on the known needs of the users.

The terminology used in the Test Analyst syllabus for quality characteristics basically follows that of the international standard ISO 25010. However, some terminology used in the syllabus differs from that provided in ISO 25010. This is because the previous syllabi were based on the former version of this standard, which used a slightly different terminology for interaction capability and flexibility. To remain consistent with existing ISTQB® syllabi, the Test Analyst syllabus uses the term "usability" for the characteristic that is now called "interaction capability" in the international standard [6] and mentions that the term "flexibility" is also known as "portability."

Figure 4.1 provides an overview of the product quality model of the current ISO 25010 standard. Terms in parentheses refer to the old names used in previous ISTQB®



A. Roman and M. Hamburg, *Practical Software Test Analysis*,
https://doi.org/10.1007/978-3-032-27986-6_6

syllabi. The characteristics and subcharacteristics highlighted in red bold type are within the scope of a test analyst's responsibilities.

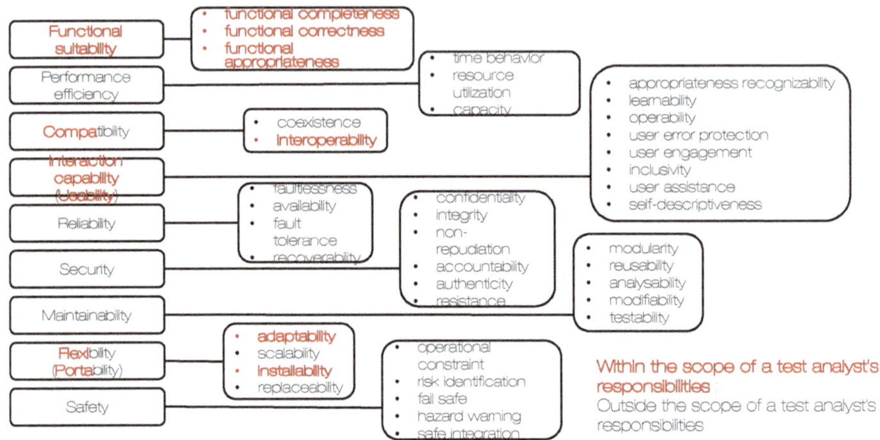


**Fig. 4.1** ISO 25010:2023—software quality model

The standard subdivides product quality into several quality characteristics and subcharacteristics, which play an essential role in software testing because different quality characteristics need different test approaches and techniques. For example, functional testing, performance testing, usability testing, or security testing are different disciplines of software testing needing different qualifications. Therefore, it is important for a test analyst to understand the product quality model and know which quality characteristics they are responsible for, which they can support, and which should be evaluated under the responsibility of a different specialist. Note that ISTQB® offers specialist qualifications for several quality characteristics.

The test analyst is the primary person responsible for testing the following quality characteristics:

- Functional suitability—with all its subcharacteristics.
- Interoperability within the compatibility.

In addition, the test analyst supports testing the following quality characteristics:

- Usability (interaction capability)—with all its subcharacteristics.
- Adaptability and installability within the flexibility (portability).

## 4.1 Functional Testing

TA-4.1.1 (K2) Differentiate between functional correctness, functional appropriateness, and functional completeness testing

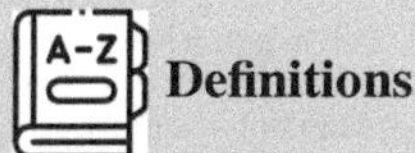

**Functional testing**: Testing performed to evaluate if a component or system satisfies functional requirements.

**Functional suitability**: The degree to which a component or system provides functions that meet stated and implied needs when used under specified conditions.

**Functional correctness**: The degree to which a component or system provides the correct results with the needed degree of precision.

**Functional appropriateness**: The degree to which the functions facilitate the accomplishment of specified tasks and objectives.

**Functional completeness**: The degree to which the set of functions covers all the specified tasks and user objectives.

The Foundation Level syllabus describes functional testing as a test type focusing on functional suitability without going into more details of this quality characteristic. Due to their role, assessing functional suitability is one of the most important tasks of a test analyst. Therefore, the Test Analyst syllabus describes this quality characteristic in detail, discussing how and when to test each of its three subcharacteristics: functional correctness, functional appropriateness, and functional completeness.

The formal basis for functional testing is descriptions of functionality defined by functional requirements. Figure 4.2 shows where the functional requirements come from and how functional tests are derived from them.

Let us assume that a client has ordered an online bookstore application from a software developer. During the discussions, the team asks the client how they imagine the product and what it should do. The client informs the team that the users of the application (readers) will particularly want to buy subsequent volumes of their favorite book series. This is a so-called business need. Note that this has nothing to do with technology, software development, or software requirements yet. This need directly concerns business issues.

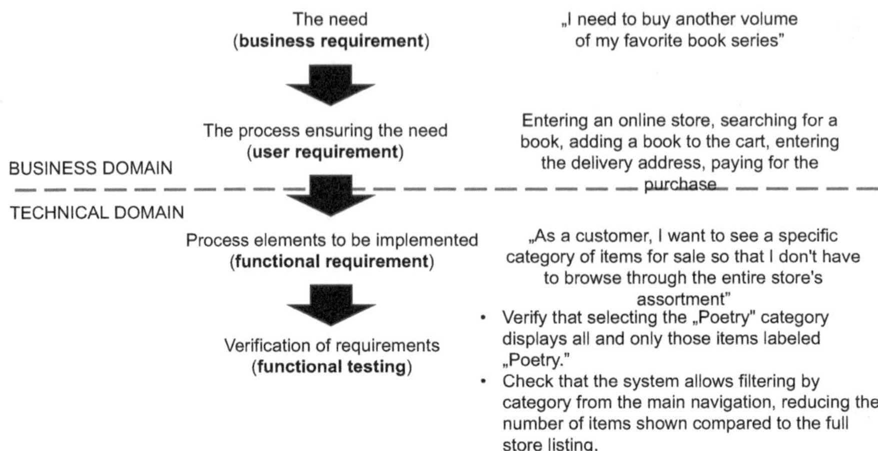


**Fig. 4.2** Translating business needs into functional requirements

The team maps this need into a process, i.e., they consider what actions the reader will have to take to fulfill their business needs. The tasks in this process (e.g., logging into the store, searching for a book, adding it to the cart, etc.) are referred to as user requirements. These are more detailed descriptions of the tasks that must be performed to fulfill the business need. Still, they remain independent of any implementation and are situated on the "business" side, not the "technology" side.

In particular, one of these steps describes the action of "searching for a book." The business analyst translates this step from business language into technical language that programmers can understand, creating a so-called functional requirement, e.g., in the form of a user story:

**As a** customer.

**I want to** see a specific category of items for sale.

**So that** I do not have to browse through the entire store's assortment.

This user story may have various acceptance criteria added, which may describe the details of the search function in particular.

The above user story represents a specific functional requirement for which a test analyst can design various types of test cases. We will discuss them in detail below when discussing individual subcharacteristics of functionality according to the ISO 25010 model.

**Functional completeness testing** assesses the extent to which the specified tasks required by stakeholders are implemented, and the user needs can be fulfilled.

Gaps in functionality often arise as early as requirements analysis. In consequence, functional completeness should be addressed as early as possible by reviewing the requirements specification in sequential development models and by discussing user stories, including acceptance criteria, during collaborative user story writing in Agile software development.

Gaps can also arise as a result of later development activities, like technical design and implementation. However, the test analyst can contribute little to testing the intermediate products that arise because these are usually technical in nature. The test analyst should therefore also dynamically test functional completeness in system testing, system integration testing, and acceptance testing, using the functional requirements as a test basis.

In dynamic testing, traceability between test basis, test conditions, and test cases plays a crucial role in determining the achieved level of functional completeness. The requirements traceability matrix is particularly suitable for evaluating functional completeness, as it provides a systematic, measurable, and transparent method to ensure that all functional requirements are implemented and tested.

An example of a requirements traceability matrix is shown in Fig. 4.3. It presents seven requirements for the online bookstore application (rows) and six test cases designed for this product. If the intersection of a row and column is not empty, it means that the test case is tracked to a specific requirement. The "no run" mark indicates that the requirement is covered by a test case that has not yet been run. The words "pass" and "fail" indicate that the requirement is covered by a test case that has been executed and that the latest execution ended in success or failure, respectively. Another example of such a matrix was shown earlier in Fig. 2.3.

| Req ID | Requirement | TC-001 Login | TC-002 Search | TC-003 Add to basket | TC-004 Remove from basket | TC-005 Process the order | TC-006 Log out inactive user |
|---|---|---|---|---|---|---|---|
| REQ-001 | User can log in with valid credentials | pass | | | | | |
| REQ-002 | User can search for a book | | fail | | | | |
| REQ-003 | User can use cart functionalities | | | pass | pass | | |
| REQ-004 | User can enter delivery address | | | | | pass | |
| REQ-005 | User can pay for the transaction | | | | | pass | |
| REQ-006 | User can view the transactions history | | | | | | |
| REQ-007 | System can log out an inactive user | | | | | | no run |

**Fig. 4.3** Requirements traceability matrix for functional completeness testing

The requirements traceability matrix in Fig. 4.3 enables the test analyst to easily identify two problems related to REQ-002 and REQ-006. In case of REQ-006, we observe that there are no test cases traced back to this requirement, indicating that REQ-006 is not covered. The test analyst should investigate the reason for this. If it turns out that REQ-006 is not implemented, we have identified a functional incompleteness. Conversely, if REQ-006 is implemented, there is no functional incompleteness; however, we have identified a gap in our test set.

In case of REQ-002, the corresponding test case TC-002 failed. Depending on the reason for this failure, functional incompleteness regarding this requirement may hold or not. If the test case fails because the functionality is not completely implemented, this is clear proof of functional incompleteness. However, if the test case fails due to, for example, an inaccurate search result list, the failure is rather impactful on functional correctness.

In case of REQ-007, we know there is a test case, TC-006, that covers this requirement. However, since this test case has not yet been executed, we cannot determine whether the test object implemented REQ-007 completely. We will only be able to do so after TC-006 has been executed.

Behavior-based test techniques (see Sect. 3.2 above) are best suited for dynamic testing of functional completeness. Such techniques are effective for evaluating functional completeness because they validate the software from the user's perspective, ensuring that all required behaviors and use-case flows are covered, not just the presence of individual functions. Test cases from Fig. 4.3 can be designed based on use cases. For example, TC-005 can follow the "Ordering process" use case, which assumes that the order items are already in the cart (hence, there is no traceability to REQ-001, REQ-002, and REQ-003) and includes steps such as entering the delivery address and paying for the transaction (hence, there is a traceability to REQ-004 and REQ-005).

In addition to behavior-based test techniques, other black-box and experience-based test techniques can also address functional completeness, even if they do not focus on it. For example, data-based test techniques like domain testing or random testing can detect if functionality does not cover the entire input domain. Rule-based test techniques can detect if specific rules are not implemented. And checklist-based testing may include items asking for specific functions to be available.

**Functional correctness testing** addresses the question of whether the actual results are correct (i.e., exact, accurate, and precise) for both valid and invalid inputs. Functional correctness can be defined via several attributes, such as:

- exactness—the degree to which a function provides a reasonable and acceptable outcome to achieve the specific intended objective,
- accuracy—the degree to which a function's results meet the specified threshold,
- precision—the degree to which a function consistently produces results that fall within the acceptable range of error.

**Functional Correctness of an Online Bookstore Application**

Consider the online bookstore application. Here are some examples of the functional correctness of some of its features:

- a "shipping country" form is exact if it allows the user to select from a drop-down list all possible countries to which the order can be shipped,
- a "recommendations" function is accurate if the recommendations based on the user's browsing and purchase history are appropriate and relevant,
- a "tax calculation" component is precise if it applies the correct tax rate and returns the correctly calculated tax amount of the payment, rounded to the nearest amount with the number of decimal places of the currency (e.g., if the currency is in Euros, the amount shall be rounded to the nearest 0.01 EUR = 1 Euro-Cent; if the currency is Japanese Yen, the tax amount shall be rounded to the nearest integer JPY; if the currency is Chinese Yuan, the tax amount may be rounded to 0.1 Yuan = 1 Jiao).

Due to the nature of functional correctness, it is crucial to find an effective test oracle that provides the expected results in detail. For example, a set of rules and formulas for applying discounts, taxes, etc., can serve as a test oracle for test cases that verify if the "price calculation" component is precise. However, sometimes it may be difficult to find such a test oracle. For example, for AI-based components such as the "recommendation" function mentioned above, this may be challenging. In such cases, techniques such as metamorphic testing can be helpful (see Sect. 3.3.2).

Functional correctness can be tested dynamically at any test level. According to the shift-left approach, most functional correctness testing should take place during component testing and component integration testing. Even if the test analyst is not responsible for these test levels, they should provide input and advice to help best achieve the test objectives.

All black-box test techniques, experience-based test techniques, and collaboration-based testing are suitable. For example, techniques such as boundary value analysis, decision table testing (see Sect. 3.3.1), or domain testing (see Sect. 3.1.1) are a good choice for testing precision, and checklist-based testing (see Sect. 3.4.2) is well-suited for exactness.

**Functional appropriateness testing** assesses the capability of a product to provide functions that facilitate the accomplishment of specified tasks and objectives. The focus is on whether everything implemented fulfills the users' needs. Unlike functional correctness testing, functional appropriateness testing does not focus on the operation of individual system functions, but on real-world tasks that will be performed by future users of the system. It therefore focuses more on the "business" side of the system.

An early test activity that can evaluate functional appropriateness is reviewing user interfaces. Such a review can already use the dialog design to evaluate whether the dialog windows offer the inputs and outputs relevant to the user, are clear and understandable, and whether the dialog steps follow a logical sequence for the user.

Dynamic testing of functional appropriateness starts with system testing and acceptance testing in sequential development models, as well as demo sessions in Agile software development, because testing real-world tasks typically requires the implementation of corresponding business processes.

The most useful test techniques in this case are those that focus on the business needs of the users. Experience-based techniques such as exploratory testing or error guessing are most appropriate. In Agile software development, collaboration-based techniques are also a good choice. Behavior-based black-box techniques are also suitable, like scenario-based testing (e.g., use case-based testing or activity diagram-based testing), state transition testing (in which states represent dialog screens or high-level steps in a business process), or CRUD-testing.

Consider the online bookstore application mentioned above. Examples of functional appropriateness include:

- finding books using a search/filter option,
- adding books to the cart,
- performing the checkout process.

If the application offers these functionalities, the client is able to fulfill their business need, i.e., buying books and filtering the catalogue. Examples of corresponding high-level test cases are as follows.

Test case 1: finding a book in the catalogue. Enter full or partial book title, author name, or ISBN, and verify that matching results appear. Enter gibberish to verify that the system returns a "no results" message.

Test case 2: adding books to the cart. Add an individual book or multiple books to the cart and verify that the cart content is correct. Add the same book multiple times and check if the quantity updates correctly. Try adding more copies of the book than are available in the warehouse. Check that the system is communicating the lack of the requested number of copies correctly.

Test case 3: verifying the checkout process. Complete checkout with all required fields filled and verify that the payment gateway is triggered and the order is logged. Try to complete checkout with one or more mandatory fields missing or incorrect, and verify that the system displays an appropriate error message.

These test cases ensure the *appropriateness* of functionality for real user tasks like searching, buying, and managing books, rather than just verifying individual functions in isolation.

## Functional Suitability Metrics

The ISO 25023 standard [1] provides a set of quality measures for the characteristics of software products that can be used for specifying requirements, measuring, and evaluating the product quality. Functional suitability measures are used to assess the capability of a product to provide functions that meet the stated and implied needs of intended users when it is used under specified conditions. In Table 4.1, we present the example measures for functional suitability.

**Table 4.1** Example measures for functional suitability

| Subcharacteristic | Measure name | Formula | Description |
|---|---|---|---|
| Functional completeness | Functional coverage | FCov = $1 - A/B$<br>$A$ = number of functions missing, $B$ = number of functions specified | What proportion of the specified product functions are implemented? |
| | Functional requirement coverage | FRC = $A/B$<br>$A$ = number of functional requirements implemented, $B$ = total number of specified functional requirements | What proportion of the specified functional requirements have been implemented? |
| Functional correctness | Functional correctness | FCor = $1 - A/B$<br>$A$ = number of incorrect functions, $B$ = number of functions considered | What proportion of functions provides the correct results? |
| | Functional accuracy | FAcc = $1 - A/B$<br>$A$ = number of test cases with inaccurate results, $B$ = number of test cases | How accurate are the results provided by a specific function? |
| | Functional precision | FPr = $1 - A/B$<br>$A$ = number of test cases with imprecise results, $B$ = number of test cases | How precise are the results provided by a specific function? |

(continued)

**Table 4.1** (continued)

| Subcharacteristic | Measure name | Formula | Description |
|---|---|---|---|
| Functional appropriateness | Functional inappropriateness | FI = 1 − *A*/*B* *A* = number of functions which are not traceable to the specified requirements, *B* = number of functions considered | What number of functions are not traceable to the specified requirements? |

**Coverage metrics for functional suitability**. Functional suitability coverage can be defined on a high level, by metrics such as functional completeness coverage, which can be defined as FCC = *A*/*B*, where *A* = number of functions tested, *B* = total number of functions. But what does it mean that a function was *tested*? Is one test case per one function enough? What if a function is more complex and contains a complicated control or data flow?

More precise coverage metrics are the ones based on test conditions. They are suitable for particular test techniques that can be used for functional suitability testing. For example, if we use scenario-based testing to test functional completeness (see Sect. 3.2.3), and we model the system under test with use cases, we can utilize use-case coverage metrics, such as the number of scenarios tested divided by the total number of scenarios. Such metrics can be more accurate and better reflect the actual coverage of functionality by tests than requirements-based metrics.

**Case Study**

Consider the following functional requirements for the FoodApp.

Functional correctness

- R1: Clients can place a food order from a selected restaurant.
- R2: Orders are correctly routed to the appropriate restaurant dashboard.
- R3: Couriers can accept an order only if it is marked as "ready for delivery."
- R4: Payment must only be processed when the order is confirmed.
- R5: The calculated delivery routes are time optimal.

Functional appropriateness

- R6: Clients can filter restaurants based on food type, rating, and distance.
- R7: Delivery managers can assign couriers based on real-time availability.

- R8: Couriers can view the most optimal delivery route.
- R9: Clients can track their order status in real time.

The test analyst designed the following high-level test cases:

- HLTC1: Place an order for a selected menu item.
- HLTC2: Process payment before order confirmation.
- HLTC3: Filter restaurants by food type, rating, or distance.
- HLTC4: Assign a courier with real-time availability.

For each high-level test case, the test analyst designed several low-level test cases. Table 4.2 shows detailed information on how many low-level test cases were designed, implemented, and executed with pass and fail status.

**Table 4.2** Statistics on low-level test cases for the FoodApp functional requirements

| High-level TC | Number of low-level test cases | | | | |
|---|---|---|---|---|---|
| | Designed | Implemented | Executed | Passed | Failed |
| HLTC1 | 5 | 5 | 4 | 4 | 0 |
| HLTC2 | 3 | 3 | 3 | 1 | 2 |
| HLTC3 | 10 | 8 | 8 | 6 | 2 |
| HLTC4 | 4 | 4 | 4 | 4 | 0 |

Assume that all nine requirements were implemented. This means that functional completeness is 100%, but the test analyst is interested in coverage metrics, not in implementation. Four high-level test cases, HLTC1, 2, 3, and 4, are traced back to requirements 1, 4, 6, and 7, respectively. Functional completeness coverage is therefore 4/9 = ca. 45%. However, if we delve into the details, we can obtain some more precise functional coverage information. For example, requirement R1 is covered, but only four out of five test cases were executed, and all of them passed. Therefore, we may assume that tests for R1 achieve 4/5 = 80% coverage after the last test run. Similarly, the achieved coverage for R4, R6, and R7 is, respectively, 33%, 60%, and 100%. The overall functional completeness coverage is (4 + 1 + 6 + 4)/(5 + 3 + 10 + 4) = 15/22 = ca. 68%.

## Sample Questions

### Question 4.1.1A

Which of the following test cases verifies the functional appropriateness of a route-finding app?

(a) Verify that the app provides route suggestions for walking, driving, and cycling.
(b) Verify that the app displays the shortest distance with an accuracy of 10 meters.
(c) Verify that the app correctly avoids closed roads when the "avoid road closures" option is enabled.
(d) Verify that the app displays an error message when the destination address does not exist.

Select ONE answer.

**Question 4.1.1B**

Which test technique is suitable for testing all three subcharacteristics of functional suitability?

(a) Domain testing.
(b) Use case-based testing.
(c) Random testing.
(d) Pairwise testing.

Select ONE answer.

## 4.2 Usability Testing

TA-4.2.1 (K2) Explain how the test analyst contributes to usability testing

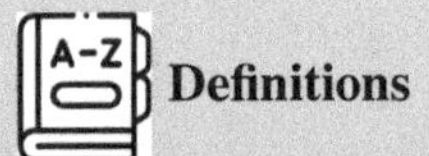


**Definitions**

**Interaction capability**: The degree to which a component or system can exchange information via the user interface with its specified users to complete an intended task.

**Usability**: The degree to which a component or system can be used by specified users to achieve specified goals in a specified context of use.

**User experience**: A person's perceptions and responses resulting from the use or anticipated use of a software product.

Usability is a broad concept. It encompasses both the "interaction capability" from the product's perspective used in the product quality model [2] and the "beneficialness" from the user's perspective used in the quality-in-use model [3]. Usability in a product quality model focuses more on a "technical" aspect of usability, that is, on interactions between product and users, while usability in a quality-in-use model focuses more on a "business" aspect of usability, that is, on benefits resulting from the use of a product, system, or service.

The test analyst is responsible for testing usability in both of these areas. The syllabus specifies that usability testing usually focuses on evaluating the following aspects:

- interaction capability—enabling users to complete tasks in specific contexts of use effectively, efficiently, and satisfactorily,
- user experience—addressing the users' perceptions before, during, and after interacting with the test object,
- accessibility—ensuring that users with disabilities, diverse cultural backgrounds, or language barriers can use the system both effectively and efficiently.

**Interaction capability** is one of the product quality characteristics defined in the ISO 25010 standard [2]. It is comprised of the following eight subcharacteristics:

*Appropriateness recognizability*—the degree to which users can recognize whether a software product or system is suitable for their needs. This refers to the clarity of the system's purpose and relevance from the user's first interaction. It involves things like clear branding, proper categorization, intuitive language, and visual cues that match user expectations. Example test task related to appropriateness recognizability for the FoodApp could be: "Open the app and tell us what kind of service this app provides, without using any help or tutorials." The user should be able to infer that the app is for ordering food based on icons, screen text/images, or layout.

*Learnability*—the degree to which the software can be used by specified users to achieve specified goals of learning how to use it. Learnability is critical for new users. It focuses on how easily users can understand and remember how to perform tasks. A highly learnable system minimizes onboarding time. Example test task related to learnability for the FoodApp could be: "Find and place an order for a vegetarian pizza without any guidance," assuming that the user has never used this app before. The user should be able to figure out how to search, apply filters, and complete checkout.

*Operability*—the degree to which a system has attributes that make it easy to operate and control. Operability includes responsiveness, clarity of commands, consistent interactions, and efficient navigation. It is about how smooth and intuitive the system feels to operate on a daily basis. An example test task related to operability for the FoodApp could be: "Change the delivery address and update the payment method before completing your order." The user should be able to do so easily without unnecessary steps or confusion.

*User error protection*—the degree to which the system protects users against making operational errors. This includes preventing errors before they happen (e.g., disabling unavailable actions) and helping recover from them easily (e.g., undo, warnings, confirmations). An example test task related to operability for the FoodApp could be: "Try placing an order without selecting a delivery address. What happens?"

The app should prevent this action and display a helpful message indicating that an address is required.

*User engagement*—the degree to which the product is perceived to be satisfying and emotionally engaging to use by presenting functions and information in an inviting and motivating manner, supporting continued interaction. This refers to properties of the product that increase the pleasure and satisfaction of the user, such as harmonious colors, an intuitive user interface, and friendly voice guidance. An example test task related to user engagement could be: "Use the app for 5 min. Rate how enjoyable and satisfying it felt to use." User feedback should indicate how much the interface feels modern, fun, or pleasing to interact with.

*Inclusivity*—the degree to which a product or system can be used by people of various backgrounds (such as people of various ages, abilities, cultures, ethnicities, languages, genders, economic situations, etc.). Inclusivity goes beyond accessibility (which typically focuses on disabilities) to ensure that the system respects and accommodates a broad spectrum of human diversity. This includes:

- cultural sensitivity (e.g., not using regionally inappropriate colors or images),
- language diversity (support for multiple languages, avoiding idioms or slang),
- gender-neutral design (e.g., not assuming binary gender identity),
- age inclusiveness (e.g., readable font sizes for older users),
- socioeconomic awareness (e.g., minimizing data usage, offline options),
- digital literacy variance (e.g., avoiding jargon, offering simple modes).

The goal is to make the system welcoming and usable by all, reducing exclusion. An example test task related to inclusivity for the FoodApp could be: "Imagine a user who is a 65-year-old non-native speaker with limited technical experience. Ask them to use the app to find a local restaurant and place an order in their preferred language. Observe and evaluate whether they encounter any cultural, linguistic, or usability barriers."

*User assistance*—the degree to which a product can be used by people with the widest range of characteristics and capabilities to achieve specified goals in a specified context of use. This is also known as accessibility (the term "user assistance" replaced the term "accessibility" used in the older version of the ISO 25010 standard from 2011). Accessibility is described in detail below.

*Self-descriptiveness*—the degree to which a product presents appropriate information where needed by the user and makes its capabilities and use immediately obvious to the user without excessive interactions with a product or other resources. Self-descriptiveness focuses on clarity of labels, icons, menu items, and workflows. An example test task related to self-descriptiveness for the FoodApp could be: "Look at the homepage. Without tapping anything, tell us what actions are available to you." The user should be able to describe core functions like "Search for a restaurant," "View previous orders," "Track orders," etc., based on the layout and labels.

**User experience (UX)** is defined in the ISO 9241-210 standard as "user's perceptions and responses that result from the use and/or anticipated use of a system, product or service." UX includes emotional responses (frustration, satisfaction, enjoyment), ease of use and efficiency, accessibility and inclusivity, context of use (mobile, desktop, noisy environments, etc.), trust, and credibility. It entails social and cultural value-sensitive design and emotional impact. UX is holistic—it includes interaction capability, but also usefulness, desirability, and emotional impact. UX is broader than interaction capability, because it covers all aspects of user interaction, while interaction capability focuses mostly on task performance.

As shown in Fig. 4.4, user experience is a combination that includes four factors: usability, usefulness, emotional impact, and meaningfulness.

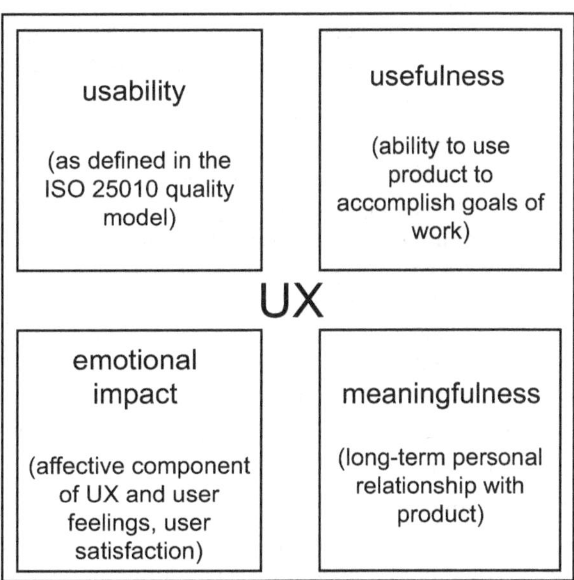


**Fig. 4.4** Components of UX (after [4])

Usability is a very important part of UX. Without good usability, there is little chance that the other components of UX will be satisfactory. Usefulness is about utility. It is the real underlying reason for a product or system. From the ISO 25000 point of view, usefulness is part of the quality-in-use model described in ISO 25019 standard [3]. Emotional impact embraces how users feel emotionally about an interaction. Emotional impact can be experienced in many ways, including joy of usage, pleasure, excitement, fun, curiosity, aesthetics, novelty, surprise, delight, play, exploration, coolness, appeal, happiness, engagement, pride of ownership, "wow" factor, etc. Meaningfulness comes out of a personal relationship of the product with its human user that endures over time [4].

**Accessibility** refers to the design and development of systems, applications, and environments in a way that ensures people of all abilities, particularly those with disabilities, can perceive, understand, navigate, and interact with them effectively. In the context of software and digital systems, accessibility ensures that people with visual, auditory, motor, cognitive, or neurological impairments can use digital products with equal ease. Accessible systems often support alternative input and output methods (e.g., screen readers, keyboard navigation, captions, voice input).

The importance of accessibility in software development is increasing for several reasons. It ensures that all users, regardless of ability, can access and benefit from digital services. Failure to meet accessibility standards can result in lawsuits, fines, and reputational damage. Accessible systems broaden the potential user base, including the elderly and those with temporary impairments. Many accessibility improvements (like clear navigation or captions) benefit all users, not just those with disabilities. Last but not least, accessible systems show a commitment to diversity, equity, and inclusion.

There are many accessibility standards and regulations that the test analyst should be aware of when designing and performing accessibility testing. Most well-known examples include:

- WCAG (Web Content Accessibility Guidelines [5]—developed by the W3C organization, defines three levels of conformance: A (basic accessibility features), AA (addresses the biggest and most common barriers for disabled users and is often the minimum legal requirement for an accessible software), and AAA (highest level of accessibility, difficult to achieve across all content).
- European Accessibility Act—an EU directive [6], designed to create equal access for Europeans with disabilities by defining a single set of accessibility standards for all member states of the European Union.
- Section 508 of the Rehabilitation Act [7]—a national regulation in the United States, requires federal agencies to make their electronic and information technology accessible.

Although accessibility testing is mainly a type of compliance testing, accessibility is not just a legal requirement—it is a fundamental aspect of good design that ensures digital equality. By integrating accessibility into the software development lifecycle and employing both manual and automated testing approaches, the test analyst plays a vital role in building inclusive, user-friendly systems.

**Test techniques for usability testing**. As mentioned earlier, usability is a very broad topic, and so is usability testing. This type of testing involves specific techniques and approaches, the description of which is well beyond the scope of this publication. They are usually the task of a specialist role in usability testing. Therefore, below we only briefly discuss how a test analyst can contribute to the most important techniques used in usability testing. Three such techniques are mentioned in the Test Analyst syllabus, namely:

- usability reviews,
- usability test sessions,
- user questionnaires and surveys.

**Usability reviews** involve experts (such as usability specialists or trained testers) evaluating an application against usability heuristics or standards (e.g., Nielsen's 10 Heuristics [8] or ISO 9241 [9]). This is sometimes called a *heuristic evaluation*. Usability reviews may vary from informal reviews to inspections. The test analyst can adapt the review criteria to the specific needs of the user groups, the particular business objectives and priorities, and the context of use (e.g., tailoring a generic usability checklist).

Usability reviews are typically performed by the development team (including test analysts) and evaluate the product from the "interaction capability" point of view. During a usability review, experts systematically go through the user interface (UI), and they assess the design, layout, interactions, and error messages. Each issue is noted and mapped against predefined usability principles. The test analyst designs test cases by translating heuristic violations into concrete scenarios. For example, a heuristic "Users should not have to remember information across pages" can be translated by the test analyst into a test case "Verify that a multi-step form preserves input when navigating back and forth." The test analyst also prioritizes usability issues based on severity, frequency, and user impact, and identifies key user tasks to evaluate further in test sessions.

**Usability test sessions** are a direct observation of real users (or representative users) as they interact with the system while performing specific tasks. Users are given tasks (e.g., "Book a train ticket"), and observers (including test analysts and UX experts) note where users struggle, need much time, get confused, or fail. The experience gained is then used to improve the system's usability. Usability test sessions are often conducted in a lab setting (i.e., in so-called usability labs, see Fig. 4.5), but can also be remote. Think-aloud protocols, where users verbalize thoughts as they navigate, may be used during the sessions.

The role of the test analyst in usability test sessions also includes test design. The test analyst defines realistic scenarios that reflect actual user goals. For example, instead of "Order a meal," the test analyst can define the task "A client has ordered pizza from restaurant X 30 minutes ago, and it has not been delivered yet. When will it arrive?" The task of the call center agent could be: identify the order and customer; find out where the courier is and what their planned route to the customer is; identify any obstacles; reply to the customer indicating details of the expected delivery time.

The test analyst uses findings to create test cases based on observed pain points: if several users fail to find a feature, the test analyst designs a test case to verify its discoverability and visibility. If users misinterpret UI elements that help solve the problem, test cases should assess clarity and alignment with user expectations.

The test analyst can also measure usability metrics to quantify the results of usability testing. The usability metrics include:

- Task success rate—percentage of users who can complete a given task correctly. A low task success rate implies that the user interface confuses users when performing the task. This may require redesigning the flow, simplifying the dialog screens, or improving guidance.

**Fig. 4.5** Usability lab (from: www.zhaw.ch/en/linguistics/research/human-machine-communication/usability-lab)

- Time spent on task—the average time users take to complete a task. High time spent on a task indicates navigation inefficiency or difficulty in understanding or learning the system. This may require improving layout, reducing steps, or clarifying instructions.
- Number of errors or help requests—the number or frequency of user errors (e.g., incorrect inputs, misclicks) or help requests per task. High values of this metric indicate poor design or feedback. This may require adding validation, improving labels, or revising controls.
- Click path length—number of clicks or screens needed to complete a task. High click path length indicates an overcomplicated structure. This may require redesigning the information hierarchy (e.g., flattening or balancing the web page structure).
- Abandonment rate—percentage of users who start a task but do not complete it. A high abandonment rate indicates frustration among the users or excessive complexity of the product. This may require reducing friction and optimizing process steps.

Usability metrics are quantitative indicators that help measure how effectively users interact with a system. They provide objective data to assess usability and identify areas for improvement. These metrics enable teams to track usability issues, compare design alternatives, and justify design decisions based on real user data.

Moreover, the test analyst creates negative test cases to simulate common user errors, verifying system guidance and error handling.

**User questionnaires,** or **surveys,** are structured or semi-structured tools used to gather subjective feedback from users after interacting with the system. These tools can be quantitative (e.g., using a Likert scale) or qualitative (open-ended). User questionnaires, or surveys, are distributed postsession or remotely. Standard tools include SUS (System Usability Scale) standard questionnaire [10], and the commercial questionnaire-based services SUMI (Software Usability Measurement Inventory) [11] and WAMMI (Website Analysis and Measurement Inventory) [12].

These tools play a significant role in evaluating, quantifying, and benchmarking usability. They are standardized, research-based instruments that collect user feedback to assess a product's usability from the user's perspective. One of the key advantages of tools like SUMI and WAMMI is that they are norm-referenced, meaning they come with benchmark datasets collected from hundreds of other products and websites. This allows our product's usability scores to be compared to industry standards or competitor averages. For example, if our WAMMI score for a certain area is 35, and the industry average is 50, we know we are below par, and our software needs improvement in this area.

### EXTRA System Usability Scale

System Usability Scale (SUS) is a widely used, reliable tool for measuring the usability of a system, product, or service. It provides a quick and dirty, yet effective, way to assess user satisfaction and identify usability issues. SUS was created by John Brooke at Digital Equipment Corporation in the UK in 1986 as a tool to be used in usability engineering of electronic office systems.

SUS is a 10-item questionnaire, where items are assessed on a five-level Likert scale (see Fig. 4.6). The purpose is to assess the overall usability of a system from the user's perspective.

The formula for computing the final SUS score for one person is:

$$\text{SUS} = 2.5 \cdot (20 + s_1 + s_3 + s_5 + s_7 + s_9 - s_2 - s_4 - s_6 - s_8 - s_{10}),$$

where $s_i$ is the answer to the $i$th question on the Likert scale (from 1 to 5). The final score is scaled to be within 0 (minimum) and 100 (maximum) points. Because it yields a single score on a scale of 0–100, it can be used to compare even systems that are outwardly dissimilar. This one-dimensional aspect of the SUS is both a benefit and a drawback because the questionnaire is necessarily quite general.

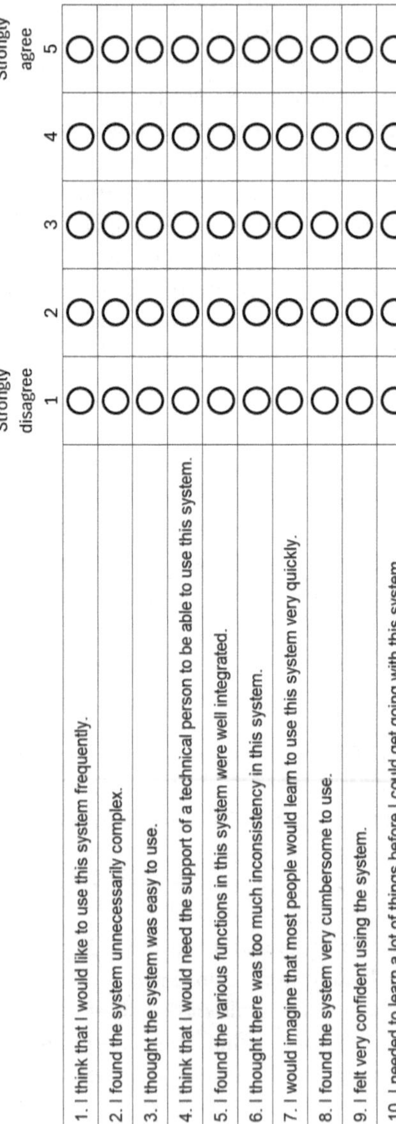

| | Strongly disagree 1 | 2 | 3 | 4 | Strongly agree 5 |
|---|---|---|---|---|---|
| 1. I think that I would like to use this system frequently. | O | O | O | O | O |
| 2. I found the system unnecessarily complex. | O | O | O | O | O |
| 3. I thought the system was easy to use. | O | O | O | O | O |
| 4. I think that I would need the support of a technical person to be able to use this system. | O | O | O | O | O |
| 5. I found the various functions in this system were well integrated. | O | O | O | O | O |
| 6. I thought there was too much inconsistency in this system. | O | O | O | O | O |
| 7. I would imagine that most people would learn to use this system very quickly. | O | O | O | O | O |
| 8. I found the system very cumbersome to use. | O | O | O | O | O |
| 9. I felt very confident using the system. | O | O | O | O | O |
| 10. I needed to learn a lot of things before I could get going with this system. | O | O | O | O | O |

**Fig. 4.6** System usability scale questionnaire

The test analyst can help design a questionnaire, or use an existing one, and analyze responses to identify usability themes. For example, low SUS scores may indicate usability issues that need deeper testing, while recurring user complaints can become the basis for new test cases. The test analyst uses feedback to enhance scenario coverage. If users say, "I couldn't find the settings menu," a test case might be "Verify that the settings menu is visible and accessible from the homepage." The test analyst also captures expectations vs. experience by using surveys to understand what users expect to happen during a process, and tests for mismatches.

### EXTRA Questionnaires Versus Surveys

The terms "questionnaire" and "survey" are often used interchangeably, but they refer to different things. A questionnaire is used to describe the set of questions we are asking an individual user. A survey is the process of collecting, analyzing, and interpreting data from many individuals. It aims to determine insights about a group of users. A survey goes much deeper than a questionnaire and often involves more than one form of data collection. A questionnaire may be part of a wider survey.

### EXTRA Usability Testing Tools

Usability testing uses a wide range of tools to observe, measure, and analyze how real users interact with a system. These tools help identify pain points, track user behavior, and collect qualitative and quantitative data to improve the user experience. Examples of popular usability tools include:

- Eye-tracking tools—they track where users look on the screen and transform it to so-called heatmaps (see), helping to understand attention, focus, and visual hierarchy. They identify elements that draw (or fail to draw) attention, evaluate ad placements and form visibility, and help in refining visual hierarchy and layout.
- Screen recording and session replay tools—they capture user sessions, e.g., mouse movements, clicks, scrolls, and sometimes voice or face video. They help discover where users get stuck or drop off, identify confusing UI elements or hidden features, and replay issues reported by users.
- Survey and feedback tools—used to gather qualitative feedback before, during, or after usability testing. They assess subjective satisfaction, measure usability perception with standardized scores, and gather open-ended feedback for deeper insights.
- Prototyping and task simulation tools—help simulate user tasks and gather early feedback even before the product is fully developed. They are used to

test navigation and structure early in development, validate task flows before coding, and reduce development rework by identifying usability issues early (Fig. 4.7).

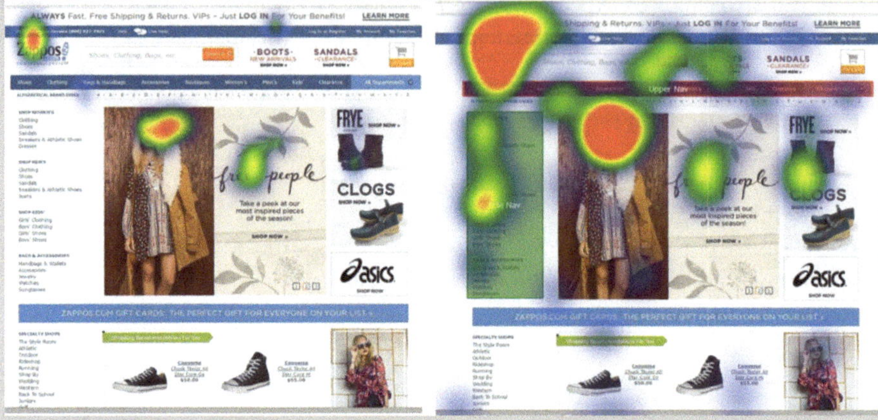


**Fig. 4.7** Heatmap of one user (left) and 13 users (right) on e-commerce website. *Source* measuringu.com/eye-tracking

### Case Study

Usability testing for FoodApp requires a structured approach to ensure the application is intuitive, accessible, and meets the needs of a diverse user base. Below, we present an example of how to conduct usability testing, focusing on usability subcharacteristics and types of usability testing.

**Learnability**. How easy is it for users to accomplish basic tasks the first time they interact with the system? The test approach involves first-time user testing. Testing users are recruited from people who have never used FoodApp. They are split into three groups: customers, couriers, and restaurant owners. Each group is asked to perform key tasks; for example, clients are asked to register, search for a restaurant, add items to a basket, and place an order.

Metrics: time taken to complete tasks, number of errors or help requests, and user feedback on task difficulty.

**Operability**. How easy and comfortable is the system to operate? The test approach involves task-based scenario testing. Test scenarios include filtering restaurants by dietary preferences, managing active orders, and route optimization. Testers observe if users can smoothly perform tasks without confusion or frustration.

Metrics: click counts, error rate, satisfaction rating.

**User error protection**. Does the system help prevent errors or make it easy to recover from them? The test approach involves error simulation testing. Users are intentionally prompted to make mistakes (e.g., incomplete form submission, selecting unavailable items). The test analyst evaluates the clarity and helpfulness of error messages and the ability to recover from the error.

**User interface aesthetics**. Is the interface visually pleasing and well-organized? The test approach involves aesthetic appraisal sessions. The test analyst shows participants different UI versions (A/B testing) and gathers preferences. Likert scale questionnaires are used for design aspects like color, spacing, font, and layout.

**Accessibility**. Can users with disabilities or limitations use the system effectively? The test approach involves accessibility compliance testing against WCAG 2.1. The test analyst performs screen reader testing, analyzes color contrast, tests for keyboard navigation, and considers localization and cultural nuances (e.g., right-to-left languages, color symbolism).

## Sample Questions

### Question 4.2.1A

Which of the following is an example of how a test analyst contributes to usability testing?

(a) Verifying that the test object works properly after installation or update.
(b) Verifying that the test object can be adapted to the intended target environment.
(c) Verifying that the test object complies with the WCAG standard.
(d) Verifying that the test object correctly interacts with other systems or components.

Select ONE answer.

**Question 4.2.1B**

A test analyst performs the usability test of a financial system with the following objective: evaluate how easily a user can perform a funds transfer (a routine but critical operation) using the system, focusing on clarity of the interface, responsiveness, logical flow, and error handling.

What subcharacteristic of usability does this test check?

(a) Learnability.
(b) Operability.
(c) User assistance.
(d) Self-descriptiveness.

Select ONE answer.

## 4.3 Flexibility Testing

TA-4.3.1 (K2) Explain how the test analyst contributes to adaptability and installability testing

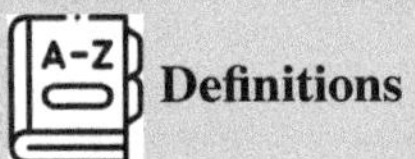

**Definitions**

**Flexibility**: The degree to which a component or system can be adapted to changes in its requirements, contexts of use, or system environment.

**Adaptability**: The degree to which a component or system can be adapted to various or evolving hardware, software, or other operational or usage environments.

**Installability**: The degree to which a component or system can be successfully installed and/or uninstalled in a specified environment.

Flexibility testing (or portability testing) ensures that a system can perform effectively in different environments or under changing conditions. According to ISO/IEC 25010 standard, the subcharacteristics of flexibility are:

- Adaptability,
- scalability,
- installability,
- replaceability.

Adaptability refers to the system's ability to be used in various environments without requiring changes in code. Examples include changing languages, currencies, date format, or adjusting to user interface themes or layouts. These aspects are user-centric and context-of-use dependent, and do not typically require deep knowledge of the system's internal architecture or code. That is why adaptability testing falls within the responsibility of test analysts.

Scalability measures how well the system performs as load or volume increases. This requires deep technical knowledge of system architecture, performance metrics, resource management, and the use of specialized performance testing tools. Such tasks go beyond the scope of a test analyst.

Installability measures the degree to which the software can be installed or uninstalled in the targeted environments. Installability tests are procedural and user-focused, involving installation workflows and user experience, which typically do not require advanced programming or system integration knowledge. Therefore, test analysts are well-equipped to perform them.

Replaceability assesses the degree to which a component can be substituted by another with the same functionality. Replaceability testing includes component-based testing, interface compatibility, or dependency isolation. Evaluating replaceability requires a thorough understanding of system interfaces, architecture, dependencies, and integration points. These, in turn, require programming knowledge, system design insight, and often involve collaboration with developers, making it suitable for technical test analysts. Therefore, replaceability testing is out of scope of the Test Analyst syllabus.

**Adaptability testing** is important for several reasons. Many systems are designed to be usable on different operating systems, devices (mobile, desktop, tablet), browsers, screen resolutions, or languages. Adaptability ensures consistent behavior and usability in all these contexts. Software that adapts to different locales, languages, and settings becomes accessible to a broader audience, improving customer satisfaction and increasing market share. In some cases, local language support, date/time formats, and accessibility settings are mandatory for legal or compliance reasons.

By designing for adaptability early and testing it properly, maintenance costs decrease since fewer environment-specific bugs arise during deployment. Adaptability testing helps catch issues that only occur under specific configurations (e.g., translated labels are cut off or overlap, GUI layout breaks on small screens).

Adaptability testing should be conducted throughout the whole software development lifecycle, but particularly during:

- system testing and acceptance testing—when the system is mostly complete and can be evaluated in different environments or configurations,
- regression testing—after environment-related changes (e.g., new browser version support, new operating system) to ensure previous adaptability still holds,
- release to new markets—when localizing the product for new regions or user groups (language, regional settings, culture-based workflows),
- cross-browser or cross-platform testing—whenever multi-platform/multi-device compatibility is a requirement.

Since adaptability focuses on external behavior and user-facing functionality, it is typically handled by test analysts using black-box test techniques. Adaptability testing often deals with combinations of environmental/contextual factors such as operating system, browser, device type, language, screen resolution, time zone, or region settings. Testing all combinations exhaustively would be too time-consuming and costly. Combinatorial test techniques (such as pairwise testing) and models (such as classification trees) are a great choice for adaptability testing because they allow test analysts to systematically and efficiently test many combinations of environment factors, which is exactly what adaptability testing requires. In some cases, test analysts can use less rigorous techniques, such as equivalence partitioning (for example, when only one parameter is taken into account, or when the number of combinations of parameters is small).

Domain analysis (or its simpler variant, boundary value analysis, discussed in the Foundation Level syllabus) can be used for locale-sensitive inputs such as data ranges, currency formats, postal codes, and number formats. Test analysts can also follow exploratory testing (e.g., resizing the browser window to simulate different screen widths) or checklist-based testing, using adaptability testing checklists. An example of such a checklist is shown in Table 4.3.

Configuration matrices help test analysts track which combinations of key environmental factors have been tested and whether they passed or failed. An example of a configuration matrix is shown in the example below.

**Table 4.3** Adaptability testing checklist

| Category | Checklist item |
|---|---|
| Language and locale | 1. Can the application be launched in each supported language?<br>2. Are all labels, messages, and UI elements properly translated?<br>3. Is the text fully visible and not truncated in different languages?<br>4. Are date, time, and number formats correct for each locale?<br>5. Are decimal separators, currency symbols, and measurement units appropriate per region?<br>6. Does the system handle right-to-left (RTL) languages like Arabic or Hebrew correctly? |
| Regional and cultural settings | 1. Does the application correctly detect and apply user region settings?<br>2. Are culturally sensitive icons, images, or colors appropriate for each target market?<br>3. Are sorting and collation rules adjusted for language/locale (e.g., accented letters)? |
| Operating system and platform | 1. Does the system run without issues on all supported operating systems (e.g., Windows, macOS, Linux)?<br>2. Are system-specific behaviors (file paths, fonts, shortcuts) handled properly?<br>3. Is the UI consistent across OS platforms? |
| Device and screen resolution | 1. Is the UI responsive and usable on various screen sizes (mobile, tablet, desktop)?<br>2. Do layout elements adjust correctly on low or high resolutions?<br>3. Is font readability preserved across screen types? |
| Time zones and clocks | 1. Does the system display the correct local time for different time zones?<br>2. Are time-based operations (e.g., scheduled tasks, logs) adjusted for local time zones?<br>3. Is daylight saving time handled correctly? |
| Browser and rendering | 1. Is the application compatible with all supported browsers (e.g., Chrome, Firefox, Edge, Safari)?<br>2. Are JavaScript/CSS features rendered consistently across browsers?<br>3. Is layout and interactivity preserved in each browser version? |
| Configuration and user settings | 1. Does the application adapt to user-specific system settings (e.g., dark mode, accessibility preferences)?<br>2. Are changes in settings (language, region) applied dynamically or after a restart?<br>3. Does the application restore properly after being resumed from sleep/lock mode? |

(continued)

**Table 4.3** (continued)

| Category | Checklist item |
|---|---|
| Error handling and fallbacks | 1. Is there a fallback mechanism if a language pack or locale file is missing?<br>2. Are error messages shown in the correct language/context?<br>3. Do broken translations or unsupported settings fail gracefully? |
| Documentation and support | 1. Is user documentation localized and consistent with the UI?<br>2. Are installation/uninstallation instructions adapted to the platform and language?<br>3. Are help links and contact info relevant to the user's region? |
| Test process | 1. Have test cases been executed across the defined matrix of supported environments (see the example below)?<br>2. Were combinatorial techniques used to reduce test effort while maximizing coverage?<br>3. Are any adaptability-related bugs logged, categorized, and prioritized? |

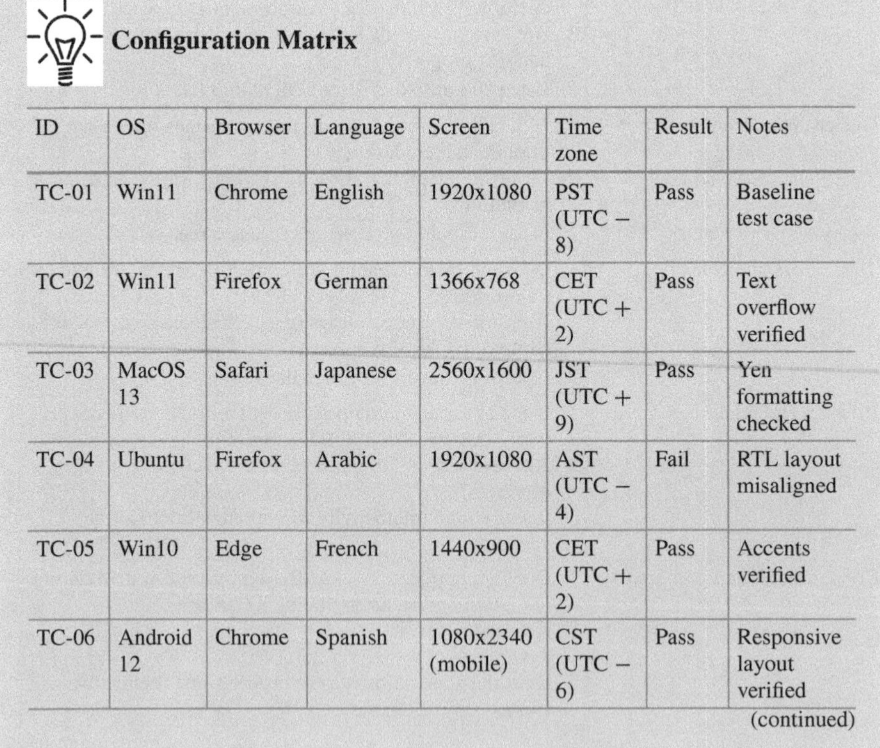

**Configuration Matrix**

| ID | OS | Browser | Language | Screen | Time zone | Result | Notes |
|---|---|---|---|---|---|---|---|
| TC-01 | Win11 | Chrome | English | 1920x1080 | PST (UTC – 8) | Pass | Baseline test case |
| TC-02 | Win11 | Firefox | German | 1366x768 | CET (UTC + 2) | Pass | Text overflow verified |
| TC-03 | MacOS 13 | Safari | Japanese | 2560x1600 | JST (UTC + 9) | Pass | Yen formatting checked |
| TC-04 | Ubuntu | Firefox | Arabic | 1920x1080 | AST (UTC – 4) | Fail | RTL layout misaligned |
| TC-05 | Win10 | Edge | French | 1440x900 | CET (UTC + 2) | Pass | Accents verified |
| TC-06 | Android 12 | Chrome | Spanish | 1080x2340 (mobile) | CST (UTC – 6) | Pass | Responsive layout verified |

(continued)

(continued)

| ID | OS | Browser | Language | Screen | Time zone | Result | Notes |
|---|---|---|---|---|---|---|---|
| TC-07 | iOS 17 | Safari | Hebrew | 1170x2532 (iPhone) | IST (UTC + 2) | Fail | RTL and font clipping on button |

In order to perform adaptability testing that helps ensure thorough, efficient, and reliable validation of a system's ability to operate correctly across different environments, configurations, and user contexts, the test analyst should follow some good practices. These include:

- Defining a clear configuration matrix that identifies all supported combinations of operating systems, browsers, devices (e.g., desktop, tablet, mobile), languages and locales, time zones, and screen resolutions.
- Prioritizing the combinations based on usage statistics, market targets, or risk. This helps prevent testing unnecessary combinations and ensures critical configurations are tested.
- Using combinatorial test techniques and combinatorial coverage types such as Each Choice, pairwise, or N-wise coverage to reduce the number of test cases while ensuring good coverage of possible environment interactions.
- Reusing functional test cases when possible. Adapting existing functional tests for different configurations by varying inputs and system settings (e.g., language, region, browser) saves time and effort and ensures consistent validation across environments.
- Automating (where feasible) repetitive adaptability checks such as launching the app in different languages, checking layout responsiveness on multiple screen sizes, and verifying time/date formatting. This increases test efficiency and assures consistency across many environments.
- Testing with both real and emulated devices. Emulators are efficient, but using a mix of real and virtual devices (emulators/simulators) to test adaptability, especially for mobile apps and screen responsiveness, allows for efficient catching of issues with rendering, hardware, or touch interaction.
- Including "edge case locales," such as right-to-left (RTL) languages (e.g., Arabic, Hebrew), languages with long words (e.g., German), or locales with unique date/currency formats (e.g., Japanese yen, Swiss franc). This helps uncover layout issues, formatting bugs, or UI defects.
- Checking dynamic context switching. Changing language, region, or device orientation at runtime (if supported) and observing behavior ensures that UI and data adapt correctly and gracefully. This validates the robustness of live adaptability features (like changing locale without restarting the app).

- Verifying fallbacks and defaults by simulating missing translations or unsupported locales. This confirms the system falls back to a default (e.g., English) and doesn't crash, ensures graceful degradation, and prevents user-facing failures.
- Reviewing localization files for consistency. Test analysts should work with translators to maintain tone and clarity, ensure terms are consistently translated, and overflows in buttons or menus are avoided. Localization affects adaptability, and UI can break if text lengths vary wildly.
- Documenting and tracing environment coverage. Maintaining a testing log or matrix to track which combinations were tested and which defects were found in which contexts provides traceability, simplifies defect reproduction, and supports impact analysis.
- Testing under various network and system conditions. Simulating slow networks, low memory, or low battery allows us to observe whether the application adapts or degrades gracefully.

**EXTRA Responsive Design**

Below is a simple, real-world example of HTML and CSS that demonstrates responsive design principles using flexible layout, media queries, and relative units. This example includes a responsive header, navigation menu, and content cards that adapt to different screen sizes.

File index.html:

```
<!DOCTYPE html>
<html lang="en">
<head>
  <meta charset="UTF-8">
      <meta  name="viewport"  content="width=device-width,
initial-scale=1">
  <title>Responsive Design Example</title>
  <link rel="stylesheet" href="styles.css">
</head>
<body>
  <header>
   <h1>My Responsive Site</h1>
   <nav>
    <ul class="nav-links">
     <li><a href="#">Home</a></li>
     <li><a href="#">About</a></li>
     <li><a href="#">Services</a></li>
     <li><a href="#">Contact</a></li>
   </ul>
   </nav>
</header>
```

```
    <main class="card-container">
       <article class="card">
        <h2>Card 1</h2>
          <p>This is a responsive card.</p>
        </article>
        <article class="card">
          <h2>Card 2</h2>
         <p>This card adjusts to screen size.</p>
        </article>
        <article class="card">
          <h2>Card 3</h2>
          <p>Resize to see layout changes.</p>
        </article>
    </main>
  </body>
  </html>
```

File styles.css:

```
/* Base Reset and Styling */
* {
  box-sizing: border-box;
  margin: 0;
  padding: 0;
}



body {
  font-family: Arial, sans-serif;
  padding: 1rem;
  background-color: #f8f8f8;
}



/* Header */
header {
  background-color: #333;
  color: white;
  padding: 1rem;
text-align: center;
}



.nav-links {
  list-style: none;
  display: flex;
  justify-content: center;
  flex-wrap: wrap;
  gap: 1rem;
```

```
    margin-top: 1rem;
  }


  .nav-links a {
    color: white;
    text-decoration: none;
    font-weight: bold;
  }


  /* Cards */
  .card-container {
    display: flex;
    flex-wrap: wrap;
    gap: 1rem;
    justify-content: center;
    margin-top: 2rem;
  }


  .card {
    background-color: white;
    padding: 1rem;
    border-radius: 8px;
    flex: 1 1 300px;
    max-width: 400px;
    box-shadow: 0 0 8px rgba(0, 0, 0, 0.1);
  }


  /* Responsive Design: Small Screens */
  @media (max-width: 600px) {
    .nav-links {
      flex-direction: column;
      align-items: center;
    }


    .card {
      flex-basis: 90%;
    }
  }
```

The tag "<meta name = "viewport">" ensures proper scaling on mobile devices. Relative units (%, rem) adapt to screen size and user settings. Media query in the styles.css file adjusts the layout for smaller screens.

Flexboxes enable flexible layout for nav and cards. The `flex-wrap` allows elements to wrap on smaller screens. The `max-width` and `flex-basis` prevent elements from being too wide.

**Installability testing** verifies that a software can be successfully installed, uninstalled, updated, and reconfigured correctly across supported environments with minimal effort and without causing issues. Testing this subcharacteristic of flexibility is important for several reasons. Installation is the first interaction users have with the product, so a smooth and successful installation builds trust, while a failed installation leads to frustration and abandonment. Good installability ensures the product installs properly across OS versions, hardware configurations, and permission settings. Identifying install/uninstall issues early avoids a flood of technical support requests and negative user feedback. It also prevents leftover files, registry entries, or corrupted system settings after deinstallation that may cause future problems. Installability testing ensures installers follow security policies, like running with the correct permissions or using signed packages. Finally, since installation is the process of making the software system ready for execution, installability testing ensures that the test object works properly after installation. Therefore, it goes beyond just running the installation procedure to completion.

Below, we describe the typical installability test objectives in focus for the test analyst, as described by the syllabus. For each of them, we also indicate test techniques and activities that can be useful in designing test cases related to these test objectives:

- **Verifying that the installation procedures are executed correctly under various environment parameter configurations**. Since installation should be tested across different configuration parameters, combinatorial test techniques such as pairwise testing or base choice testing are useful in this context. Test analysts can also use negative testing to verify how the installation process behaves in case of invalid paths (e.g., network drivers or read-only directories), removed or restricted system resources (e.g., disk space), or interruptions (e.g., power failure, cancelation). Installability checklists may cover required preconditions (e.g., hardware, OS, permissions), installation steps and validation points, and cleanup and rollback procedures.
- **Designing and executing tests to determine whether the test object works properly after installation or update**. This can be verified by performing a smoke test. Also, regression tests, as well as scenario-based testing (end-to-end scenarios used in system and acceptance testing), can be utilized.
- **Checking how easy it is for users to install, uninstall, or update the software**. This includes reviewing the installation documentation. This can be verified by applying usability testing and scenario-based testing with usability scenarios. Test scenarios may cover first-time install on a clean system, reinstall over an existing installation, install with default and custom options, install in restricted

user mode, full uninstall, partial uninstall (canceled in the middle of the process). State transition testing can also be applied to model installation states and test different transitions between them (see the optional box).

- **Testing permissions-related behavior, particularly for mobile applications.** The test analyst can apply black-box test techniques, such as boundary value analysis (for defining minimal and maximal required permissions), state transition testing (for modeling transitions between permission-related states, e.g., modifying permissions from system settings after installation), or decision table testing (to model interaction of multiple permissions, such as location + Bluetooth + notifications). Scenario-based testing and checklist-based testing can also be used, where scenarios or checklists may describe situations such as installation on devices with different OS security configurations.

### EXTRA Using State Transition Testing to Model Sequences of Installation States

The state model can represent the installation state. The test analyst can then test transitions between these states, such as not installed → installed → uninstalled, etc. An example of such a state model is shown in Fig. 4.8.

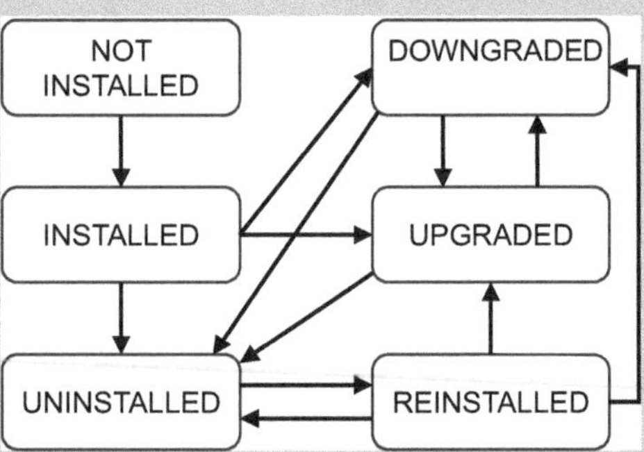


**Fig. 4.8** State transitions between different software installation states

During installability testing, the test analyst should verify:

- Preconditions—to check that the installer validates system requirements, permissions, and dependencies.
- Installation—to check that the installation process completes without errors, displays success messages, and installs all necessary files and components.
- Post-install—to check that the software runs correctly (this can be done with smoke testing or using existing functional test cases).
- Upgrade/patch—to check that the software preserves user data and settings, and avoids file duplication.

- Uninstallation— to check that the installer removes the files, registry entries, shortcuts, and services.
- Rollback—to check that partial installs clean up after failures or interruptions.

**Case Study**

The test team designs the installability tests for the FoodApp. They prepared different test cases categorized by installability testing objectives, as shown below:

1. **Verifying that the installation procedures are executed correctly under various environment parameter configurations**

TC-1.1—Install FoodApp under different OS versions and device types

- Purpose: Validate installation works across supported environments.
- Preconditions: devices with Android 13/14, iOS 16/17; phones/tablets.
- Steps: (1) Attempt installation from Play Store/App Store on each device × OS combination; (2) Launch the app after installation.
- Expected Results: App installs successfully, App opens without crashes. Components initialize (Client/Delivery Management/Courier) based on the chosen mode.

TC-1.2—Install with differing system locale and region settings

- Purpose: Verify app installs under various language and region configurations.
- Steps: (1) Change device locale to English, German, Turkish, Spanish, etc.; (2) Install the app.
- Expected Results: Installation succeeds in all locales. Initial screens display correct localized content.

2. **Designing and executing tests to determine whether the test object works properly after installation or update**

TC-2.1—Postinstallation smoke test for Client Component

- Purpose: Ensure the client app works properly after a fresh install.
- Steps: (1) Install FoodApp; (2) Launch the app; (3) Create a customer account; (4) Browse restaurants, filter by distance or cuisine.
- Expected Results: No crashes.

TC-2.2—Verify the Delivery Management Component after the update

- Purpose: Ensure the Delivery Management Component works properly after the update.

- Steps: (1) Log in as a restaurant owner after updating the app; (2) View the existing restaurant portfolio; (3) Accept a new order and assign a courier.
- Expected Results: No data loss. Order management functions operate correctly. Restaurants load as expected, and filters work.

3. **Checking how easy it is for users to install, uninstall, or update the software**

TC-3.1—Validate clarity and completeness of installation documentation

- Purpose: Ensure user documentation is clear and supports installation.
- Steps: (1) Review installation instructions in help pages and online store; (2) Verify steps match actual installation process.
- Expected Results: Documentation accurately describes installation steps. Screenshots match the app.

TC-3.2—User-friendly installation flow on first install

- Purpose: Ensure the installation process is user-friendly for inexperienced users.
- Steps: (1) Ask a first-time user to install the app using only the instructions available on the app store page; (2) Observe time taken and confusion points.
- Expected Results: User successfully installs without external help. Steps are intuitive.

4. **Testing permissions-related behavior, particularly for mobile applications**

TC-4.1—Install and launch the app with all permissions granted

- Purpose: Validate correct behavior when the user accepts all requested permissions.
- Steps: (1) Install app; (2) Grant all permissions when prompted; (3) Attempt features: GPS delivery location, camera, notifications.
- Expected Results: All functions operate normally.

TC-4.2—Install app and deny all permissions on first launch

- Purpose: Verify graceful degradation.
- Steps: (1) Install FoodApp; (2) Deny location, camera, and notification permissions; (3) Open restaurant search and checkout.
- Expected Results: App shows "location required" message but allows browsing. Camera-based features disabled until permission granted.

## Sample Questions

### Question 4.3.1A

Which of the following is an example of how a test analyst contributes to the adaptability testing of a route-finding application?

(a) Verifying that the app installs successfully on Android devices with limited storage space and older OS versions.
(b) Checking whether the app can share live location data with external navigation systems like Google Maps.
(c) Ensuring that the app works fine when other applications simultaneously use the same GPS-based app.
(d) Executing tests across different screen sizes to ensure the map rendering works OK across target environments.

Select ONE answer.

### Question 4.3.1B

Which of the following is an example of an installability testing objective for the tax calculation application?

(a) Verify that the tax calculation application installs, uninstalls, and updates correctly on Windows 10 and macOS, and that it launches successfully after installation.
(b) Verify that the tax calculation app correctly adjusts its layout and UI components on different screen resolutions (e.g., 1280x720, 1920x1080, 4 K monitors).
(c) Verify that the application accurately computes tax returns based on various income types and regional tax rules after installation.
(d) Evaluate how intuitive the installation process is for users with low technical skills, including clarity of prompts and instructions.

Select ONE answer.

## 4.4 Compatibility Testing

TA-4.4.1 (K2) Explain how the test analyst contributes to interoperability testing

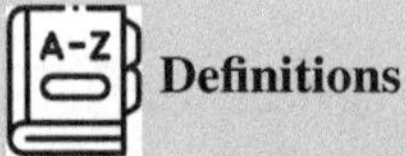
**Definitions**

**Compatibility**: The degree to which a component or system can exchange information with other components or systems, and/or perform its required functions while sharing the same hardware or software environment.

**Interoperability**: The degree to which two or more components or systems can exchange information and use the information that has been exchanged.

Compatibility testing verifies whether a test object is compatible with other components or systems when it is used. The ISO 25010 product quality model (ISO/IEC 25010, 2023) differentiates between two subcharacteristics of compatibility: interoperability and coexistence. Therefore, compatibility testing can be subdivided into the following test types:

- **Interoperability testing**, which verifies compatibility with components or systems with which the test object is intended to interact. These tests are typically black-box functional tests, so the test analyst is usually responsible for them.
- **Coexistence testing**, which verifies that the test object can share its target environment with other components or systems without interference. This technical test type is not a responsibility of the test analyst; it is discussed in the Technical Test Analyst syllabus [13].

The goal of interoperability testing is to ensure that different systems, components, applications, or products can work together seamlessly and exchange information correctly and reliably, even if they were developed by different organizations or use different technologies.

Key objectives of interoperability testing include:

- Verifying that the system under test can communicate and function together with other systems as expected.
- Validating that data is transmitted, received, and interpreted accurately across systems.
- Detecting and resolving mismatches in protocols, formats, or interfaces.
- Ensuring adherence to industry or communication standards (e.g., HTTP, REST, HL7 used in medical applications, etc.).
- Providing users with a smooth, consistent, and functional interaction between integrated systems.

Test analysts should remember that negative testing is crucial in interoperability testing to ensure the system gracefully handles unexpected or incorrect behavior when interacting with other systems. These tests help ensure robust error handling, user-friendly feedback on failure, security and compliance (e.g., no leaking sensitive info in errors), and system resilience during third-party failures or miscommunications.

Interoperability testing has become critically important in modern software architecture due to the rise of distributed, modular, and dynamic systems like cloud computing, web services, microservices, containerization, and the Internet of Things (IoT). These architectures emphasize connectivity, scalability, and independent development, all of which increase the need for reliable integration between components. This is summarized in Table 4.4.

Interoperability usually happens on various architectural levels. The test analyst must understand the possible interactions to define proper test conditions to cover them. Not all interactions may be documented. The test analyst may indirectly retrieve information about the interactions from architecture and design documentation. Hence, it is crucial to understand this documentation to ensure that all important aspects of the interactions will be tested. The examples of interoperability testing at different test levels are discussed below.

**Table 4.4** Modern architectures and their impact on interoperability testing

| Architecture | Why is it important? | Interoperability challenges |
|---|---|---|
| Cloud computing | Applications are no longer monolithic or on-premise. Cloud-based solutions often integrate services from multiple vendors (e.g., AWS, Azure, Google Cloud) | Ensuring systems from different cloud providers or hybrid setups (on-prem + cloud) work seamlessly together |
| Web services | Systems expose services to other systems via APIs. Clients and servers can be built by different teams, organizations, or using different tech stacks | Ensuring that data formats, protocols, and endpoints are interpreted correctly across systems |
| Microservices | Applications are decomposed into small, loosely coupled services that communicate over the network | Each service might be developed in a different language, use different data schemas, or rely on different protocols. Proper coordination is essential |
| Containerization | Applications and services are packaged and deployed independently, often across different environments or clusters | Ensuring containers communicate reliably via network interfaces, shared volumes, or APIs, regardless of where or how they are deployed |
| Internet of Things (IoT) | IoT applications involve numerous devices from diverse vendors using various protocols and data formats | Ensuring integration of many different protocols, closed ecosystems, data schemas, units, and encodings |

- At the component testing level, the goal is to ensure that individual components (functions, methods, classes) can handle data or calls from other components correctly, especially when interfacing with external libraries or APIs. This is usually the task of developers and technical test analysts. For example, a function that parses JSON responses from an external REST API is tested to ensure it can handle varying data structures returned by different versions of the API.
- At the component integration testing level, the goal is to verify that small groups of interacting components can interoperate correctly when integrated together. This is usually the task of developers and technical test analysts. For example, a payment module integrates with a currency conversion module. Tests verify that currency values passed between them maintain precision and expected format (e.g., rounding behavior, decimal separators).
- At the system testing level, the goal is to ensure that the entire system can operate correctly as a whole, including internal subsystems that must work together. This is typically the task of the test analyst. For example, a web application sends order data from the frontend to the backend for processing. System tests confirm that data formats (e.g., date formats, item codes) are consistent and accepted by both layers.
- At the system integration testing level, the goal is to verify that the system can interoperate with external systems, services, or applications in a real or simulated environment. This is typically the task of the test analyst. For example, a hospital information system integrates with a national health database using the HL7 standard. Tests check that both systems interpret and process patient records correctly.
- At the acceptance testing level, the goal is to validate by demonstrating to stakeholders that the entire system interoperates correctly in the intended real-world environment, often with third-party systems. In theory, these tests should be performed by the clients/end users, but in practice, they are performed by the test analysts within the test team. For example, a client-facing e-commerce platform is tested to ensure it integrates smoothly with external logistics providers (e.g., FedEx API) for order tracking and shipping label generation.

Interoperability testing helps uncover defects that arise when systems, components, or services from different sources attempt to work together. These defects usually would not appear in isolated testing of the individual systems but become visible only when systems interact. Interoperability testing can detect defects in:

- data transformations for the exchange of data (e.g., a sending system formats order_total as a decimal (12.50), but the receiving system interprets it as an integer (1250), because the decimal separator is not correctly transformed),
- interpretation or use of exchanged data (e.g., a courier system sends distance in meters, but the delivery dashboard interprets them as kilometers, showing routes that seem 1000 times shorter than they are),
- communication flows and protocols (e.g., the courier location update arrives before the courier assignment message due to incorrect message sequence enforcement, causing tracking errors),

- compliance with standards (e.g., the receiving system requires RFC 8259-compliant JSON, but the sender transmits unquoted property names, making the payload invalid),
- end-to-end functionality (e.g., customer receives order confirmation, courier receives order details, but restaurant inventory is not updated because one downstream API call silently fails),
- design documentation (e.g., API specification states that "delivery_fee" is optional, but the implementation makes it mandatory, causing integration failures for partners relying on the spec).

Examples of general standards in interoperability are ISO 15745:2003 and ISO 16100:2009. The ETSI EG 202237 guide provides an example of a concrete interoperability testing methodology in the telecommunications domain.

**Case Study**

Let us consider interoperability in our FoodApp. Interoperability testing is about checking that different systems, devices, or components can correctly exchange and use information. In the case of the FoodApp, the ecosystem might include:

- multiple platforms (Android, iOS, web browsers),
- multiple backend systems (order management, payment gateways, delivery tracking),
- multiple external services (Google Maps API, payment providers, push notification services, restaurant POS systems).

The test analyst analyzes this ecosystem in order to find possible interoperability issues, which would then be a base for interoperability test cases. The results of this analysis are shown in Table 4.5.

**Table 4.5** Examples of interoperability issues in the FoodApp

| Risk area | Example scenario | Example problem |
|---|---|---|
| Platform/device compatibility problems | A client places an order using the Android app, but the restaurant owner uses an older iOS tablet to receive orders | The order confirmation message uses a newer API format not supported by the older iOS version, so the restaurant app fails to show order details (missing menu items or delivery notes) |

(continued)

**Table 4.5** (continued)

| Risk area | Example scenario | Example problem |
|---|---|---|
| Integration with payment gateways | Client pays via Apple Pay, but the courier's app is supposed to see "Payment Received" in real time | The payment gateway returns status in a format the courier app's backend does not interpret correctly: The courier sees "Payment Pending" and refuses to start delivery |
| External mapping and location tracking | The courier's location is tracked using Google Maps API, but a restaurant uses a different mapping provider in their POS system | Location coordinates use different precision formats or reference systems → restaurant dashboard shows courier far from the actual location |
| Data format mismatches between systems | Restaurant's internal POS expects menu item codes in uppercase (PIZZA_MARGHERITA), but the ordering app sends them lowercase (pizza_margherita) | Orders appear with "Unknown Item" in the restaurant system |
| Version mismatch between components | Client's app is updated to support new discount coupons, but the courier's app doesn't recognize the "discounted total" field in the API | The courier app calculates the wrong total to collect for "cash on delivery" orders |
| Notification delivery across platforms | Courier uses an Android device without Google Play Services (Huawei device), while the restaurant uses a web dashboard | Push notifications fail on the courier's device, resulting in delays of delivery assignments |

Having identified the possible interoperability issues, the test analyst selects a proper set of test techniques that allows them to cover the risk areas appropriately. The test analyst decides to:

- perform compatibility testing across platforms; configuration combinations include different OS versions, payment gateways, and maps APIs,
- perform API testing using tools such as Postman or SoapUI to simulate API calls between systems; the tests cover validation of both data formats (JSON/XML schema validation) and field presence, as well as checking backward compatibility with older API versions,
- performing end-to-end testing to simulate real multi-party transactions (such as: client places order → restaurant confirms → courier accepts → courier delivers → payment processed) by running the same workflow across combinations (e.g., iOS client + web restaurant + Android courier),

- perform protocol testing to ensure that HTTPS, WebSocket, and other protocol implementations are consistent and to test for correct error handling when a protocol is partially supported or unsupported,
- use external service mocking and switching by replacing real APIs (maps, payments) with mock servers to simulate failure cases and test fallback logic (e.g., switching from Google Maps to OpenStreetMap),
- perform data synchronization and format validation to check that timestamps, currency formats, and measurement units are consistent between systems; the test analyst decides also to perform test scenarios with time zone differences (e.g., restaurant in GMT + 1, courier in GMT + 2).

Since the number of possible configurations to test is huge, the test analyst designs an interoperability test matrix to test the most popular versions of the configuration elements. The matrix is shown in Table 4.6.

**Table 4.6** Interoperability test matrix for the FoodApp

| Client app | Restaurant app | Courier app | Payment gateway | Maps API |
|---|---|---|---|---|
| Android 11 | Web POS (Chrome) | Android 9 | Stripe | Google Maps |
| Web (Safari) | Desktop POS | iOS 14 | PayPal | Apple Maps |
| iOS 16 | iPad (iOS 18) | Android v12 | Apple Pay | OpenStreetMap |

Each combination is tested for order creation and confirmation, payment status sync, location tracking accuracy, and notification delivery.

## Sample Questions

### Question 4.4.1A

Which of the following is an example of how a test analyst contributes to compatibility testing when testing the Advanced Driver Assistance System?

(a) Verifying that the decision-making module can accurately detect and classify objects when integrating radar and camera inputs from different sensor vendors.
(b) Verifying that Lane Keeping Assist and Adaptive Cruise Control components can operate simultaneously without degrading each other's performance.
(c) Verifying that the Blind Spot Monitoring radar sensors can be correctly installed on various vehicle body styles without mechanical, electrical, or calibration issues.
(d) Verifying that the system correctly detects a pedestrian in the vehicle's path and automatically applies the brakes to avoid or mitigate a collision.

Select ONE answer.

**Question 4.4.1B**

Which of the following is an example of a compatibility failure of a social media application?

(a) The app download from the App Store fails midway due to an incorrectly packaged build, showing an "Invalid App Bundle" error.
(b) The "Create Post" button is placed in a corner with very small text and a faint color, making it hard for users to find and tap, especially for those with visual impairments.
(c) The app crashes when opened on certain Android devices running an older OS version because it requires a system library that is not present.
(d) When a user tries to upload a photo, the app shows "Upload successful," but the image never appears in their profile or feed.

Select ONE answer.

# Chapter 5 Software Defect Prevention

**Keywords** Ad hoc reviewing · Checklist-based reviewing · Defect prevention · Model-based testing · Perspective-based reading · Review technique · Role-based reviewing · Root cause analysis · Scenario-based reviewing · Test result

## Introduction to the Software Defect Prevention

Defects in software work products can lead to software failures and are the primary factors that compromise the quality of a software product. In the field of software development, defects are typically introduced during the constructive activities by developers, designers, or other roles who make mistakes.[1] Testers, on the other hand, have the task of detecting such defects through analytical activities. Hence, they may feel that they cannot contribute to preventing defects since they do not directly influence those who make the mistakes.

However, this feeling is misleading. The right mindset should be that defect prevention is the responsibility of the whole team. Test analysts have unique knowledge and experience about defects, and they should utilize it to contribute to defect prevention. This chapter explains how test analysts can contribute to software defect prevention.

The goal of defect prevention is to implement actions that reduce the likelihood of (re)occurrence of defects in work products and mitigate the propagation of defects to subsequent phases of the SDLC. These efforts yield a range of significant benefits, including lower costs and labor, increased productivity, and enhanced product quality.

[1] An exceptional case of software failures that do not result from defects and ultimately human mistakes is concept drift in systems based on artificial intelligence, which is discussed in the ISTQB® specialist syllabus for testing artificial intelligence [90].



A. Roman and M. Hamburg, *Practical Software Test Analysis*,
https://doi.org/10.1007/978-3-032-27986-6_7

Defect prevention practices include:

- Preventing defect introduction, which is a part of quality assurance activities, and can be supported by test analysts with practices discussed in Sect. 5.1.
- Preventing defects from escaping to subsequent phases of the SDLC, discussed in Sect. 5.2.
- Preventing defects from recurring, discussed in Sect. 5.3.

## 5.1 Defect Prevention Practices

TA-5.1.1 (K2) Explain how the test analyst can contribute to defect prevention

**Definitions**

**Defect prevention**: The measures that reduce the likelihood of recurrence of defects in work products and limit the propagation of defects in subsequent work products.

Software defect prevention is a proactive approach to reducing or eliminating software defects during the development process. It focuses on identifying potential issues before they manifest as defects in the system or failures. Defect prevention helps to improve software quality by reducing the likelihood of failures. Investing in defect prevention can help reduce the total cost of quality, by reducing appraisal costs (e.g., costs of confirmation testing after defect fixing), internal failure costs (e.g., fixing defects found during testing, or providing workarounds), and external failure costs (e.g., loss of revenue, legal costs, liability for loss of assets, human health, or the environment, postrelease deployment costs, support costs) as discussed in the Advanced Level—Test Manager Syllabus [12], Sect. 3.2.1. It is well known that internal failure costs increase by factors with each subsequent test level [62]. Therefore, early testing is also a measure of defect prevention and lowering the total cost of quality.

Defect prevention activities mainly focus on process improvement, appropriate use of tools, and training [63]. These activities are usually not specific to a single project or product but span the larger organization. The test analyst can support a wide range of defect prevention activities, thereby improving the quality of the software development process and thus contributing to the quality of the final product. The following describes examples of what a test analyst can do in this area.

**Participating in risk analysis**. Risk analysis involves identifying potential risks that could affect the quality of a software product and proposing measures to mitigate the identified risks (e.g., by selecting the most adequate test techniques). Test analysts contribute valuable insights into this process by using their expertise to anticipate defects, focus testing efforts, and improve overall quality. Test analysts are trained to think critically about software behavior and functionality. They can spot potential failure modes or areas where defects are more likely to occur. By identifying risks early, software architects and developers can address potential issues proactively, adjusting designs or coding practices to avoid future defects.

Test analysts can select the most adequate test techniques to mitigate the risks identified as early as possible. They can also prioritize testing based on the risk level of different features or test items (see Chap. 2). This ensures that high-risk areas get the most attention during testing and development, leading to earlier detection of potential defects and reducing the chance of critical defects escaping to production.

**Reviewing requirements, system models, and specifications**. These early-stage documents form the basis of software development, and any anomalies found at this stage can be addressed before they translate into actual code, where defects become more expensive and difficult to fix. Test analysts, with their detailed understanding of how the system should behave, can spot ambiguities, inconsistencies, omissions, or unreliable assumptions early in the lifecycle. By ensuring clear and testable requirements, test analysts help prevent situations where developers implement features that cannot be easily verified, which often leads to undetected defects. The review process prevents introducing defects in the implementation due to misunderstandings, and at the same time reduces the risk of uncertain or incomplete testing that could allow defects to escape into the final product (see Sects. 5.2.1 and 5.2.2).

Reviews foster better communication and collaboration between the testing and development teams. Test analysts' early involvement in this process ensures that all team members have a shared understanding of what needs to be built, how it will be tested, and the system's critical success factors. This improved collaboration leads to fewer misunderstandings and discrepancies, which are common sources of defects. It also reduces the likelihood of rework caused by unclear or miscommunicated requirements.

**Participating in retrospectives**. Retrospectives are conducted to identify improvements in the software development process, including testing. Involving test analysts in these discussions offers several benefits for identifying and addressing the root causes of defects, improving the test process, and enhancing overall software quality.

Retrospectives allow test analysts to assess the effectiveness of the adopted test approach. This can be done by analyzing test results (see Sect. 5.3.1) or the achieved coverage. This feedback allows the team to optimize the test process, making it more robust for future phases or iterations. The test approach can be refined to cover areas that were previously overlooked, thus preventing defects from escaping to the next phases. Retrospectives also offer test analysts a chance to reflect on the quality of test cases. Enhancing test case design based on retrospective discussions ensures more thorough testing in the future, catching defects early and preventing defect escapes.

In retrospectives, test analysts should also evaluate the effectiveness and efficiency of the test techniques used, whether risk areas were appropriately identified and their risk levels appropriately assessed, and whether the test data and test environment appropriately supported test execution and avoided false-positive or false-negative results. In case of shortcomings, they can suggest measures to better prevent defects from escaping with the least effort possible.

Test analysts work closely with developers, architects, product owners, and other stakeholders. In retrospectives, they can discuss any communication breakdowns or collaboration issues that may have contributed to defects. For example, they might highlight areas where clearer communication of requirements, design changes, or user stories could have prevented misunderstandings. Addressing these issues leads to better alignment between testers and other team members, reducing the risk of defects caused by miscommunication or a lack of shared understanding. This encourages a culture of open communication, which is key to preventing issues early.

**Defect data collection and evaluation**. Many teams use defect management tools solely for communicating the status of individual defects. However, it is important to understand that relevant additional pieces of information about defects may be recorded. When the defect is reported by the test analyst, such information includes the test level, severity, or defect trigger (e.g., a link to the test case or test condition that triggered the failure). Other relevant information will only be uncovered in the later stages of the defect lifecycle. This includes the defect type, defect location, insertion phase, resolution efforts, time required to fix the defect, or the root cause. Once defect management tools systematically record and report this information, they become valuable assets for conducting various analyses on the test process quality and product quality. These analyses can, in turn, provide insights that benefit defect prevention (see Sect. 5.3).

Late-stage information, such as the number of defects, their severity, and their distribution across different features or components, allows teams to perform a defect trend analysis. This analysis highlights problematic areas in the codebase or specific features prone to frequent defects. By identifying components or features with a higher-than-expected defect rate, teams can take preventive actions such as allocating more resources to these areas for additional code review, improving coverage in these areas, or providing developer training on specific technologies or coding practices.

As defects go through the lifecycle, their severity and priority are better understood. Recording this information is essential for conducting a thorough analysis and making improvements to the development process. If a significant portion of defects have a high severity, it suggests that critical failures are occurring, likely due to problems such as poor design, incomplete requirements, or ineffective test strategies. This may result in decisions regarding the strengthening of design validation (e.g., through technical reviews), the enhancement of test planning, or the implementation of risk-based testing.

**Participating in root cause analysis**. By participating in root cause analysis, test analysts bring their expertise in understanding testing gaps, system behavior, and test case design, which can directly contribute to identifying the true origins of defects and implementing measures to prevent similar defects from occurring in the future (see Sect. 5.3.2).

When the root causes are identified, test analysts can propose appropriate corrective actions to address them. For example, if the root cause of typical defects in the system behavior is that the stateful behavior is only described informally and typically contains inconsistencies, ambiguities, and gaps, the test analyst may propose collaborating with the system architect and designing state models, from which developers can implement the components and testers can derive tests.

**Case Study**

Let us explore how a test analyst could contribute to defect prevention activities for the FoodApp, applying the above-mentioned techniques and strategies.

- Participating in risk analysis. The test analyst participates in a risk analysis meeting to assess which areas of the app are most likely to introduce defects. Given the complex logic involved in payment processing (e.g., integrating multiple payment gateways like credit cards, digital wallets, and discount codes), they identify this as a high-risk area. An example of defect prevention activity may be a test analyst's recommendation to focus on risk-based testing for the payment feature. By prioritizing high-risk areas such as payment handling, the test analyst ensures that critical defects (e.g., incorrect payments, failed transactions) are caught early. Focusing on payment processes can prevent financial losses, user frustration, and potential security vulnerabilities that could arise from defects in payment handling.
- Reviewing requirements, system models, and specifications. During the requirements review, the test analyst notices that the requirements for order customization (e.g., choosing ingredients for a pizza) are vague. It is unclear whether users can add custom ingredients or only choose from preset options. The requirement also lacks detail about how different customization options affect pricing. An example of a defect prevention activity is a situation where the test analyst raises a concern during the requirement review, pointing out the ambiguity in the order customization rules. Clarifying the requirements helps prevent requirement-related defects, such as users not being able to fully customize their orders or being charged incorrectly.
- Participating in retrospectives. During the sprint retrospective, the team discussed several defects that were found late in the development cycle. Many were related to edge cases that weren't caught in the initial test cases, such as rare scenarios where users attempt to order from a restaurant that's temporarily closed. An example of defect prevention activity is the test analyst's suggestion that the team should implement more exploratory testing to cover these edge cases. The test analyst may propose adding a stage to the sprint where testers focus on unscripted testing of less common scenarios. This activity leads to test process improvement by incorporating

testing, which helps to catch potential defects that are difficult to detect in the current test process.

- Defect reporting and root cause analysis. An example of defect prevention activity is a test analyst's suggestion that defects should be classified according to the functionality affected. During testing, several defects were reported that were related to users facing difficulties when updating their delivery address. The issues range from problems when selecting new addresses to app crashes. Analysis of defect reports indicates that a lot of defects are related to the functionality of modifying user data. Upon investigation, it was revealed that the root cause was a combination of interoperability issues with the third-party address validation system and poor user interface design. Understanding the root cause allows the team to address both the UI design and the interactions with the address validation system comprehensively. The test analyst also suggests improving test scenarios that involve address updates to cover both front-end and back-end processes.

In addition to engaging in defect prevention, the test analyst should evaluate whether the proposed corrective measures have resulted in the desired effect. This evaluation is typically carried out in consultation with the test manager. Examples of metrics that can be used to evaluate the effectiveness of prevention measures include:

- defect removal efficiency,
- phase containment effectiveness,
- cost of quality.

Let us explore these metrics in more detail.

**Defect Removal Efficiency** (DRE) is the percentage of defects eliminated before the release. Hence, one can say that DRE measures the "quality of the test process." This simple metric can lead to some very sophisticated analyses and change "quality" from an ambiguous, amorphous term to a tangible factor [64]. The exact value of DRE is impossible to calculate because it is the ratio of the defects detected and fixed before release and the *total* number of defects in the software product, which is unknown. However, a "practical" version of DRE is very easy to calculate. During software development, the team records all defects it finds. When the product is released to a client, recording the defects continues for a certain period of time (e.g., for six months after the release). Once this is done, the DRE is calculated as follows:

$$DRE = \frac{FB}{FB + FA + R} \times 100\%,$$

where

- $FB$ is the number of defects found and fixed before release,

- *FA* is the number of defects found and fixed after release, during a fixed time period,
- *R* is the number of residual defects, that were found but not fixed.

Notice that, formally, this is an upper bound for the DRE metric. When we collect data on defects found during a longer period of time of system use, the denominator of the metric will increase, lowering the value of the DRE. For example, let us assume that there are no residual defects, i.e., all defects found are fixed quickly. Consider the data on defects found in different project phases presented in Table 5.1.

Six months after the release, DRE = 200/230 = 87%. But in months 7–12, 20 new field defects were found by the client. So now, the total number of defects found after the release increased from 30 to 50, and DRE = 200/250 = 80%. After the next six months, the DRE decreased to 77%, and two years after the release, it is only 75%.

At its most basic level, the DRE metric is simply an informative indicator of the effectiveness of defect prevention practices. However, when applied to specific types of defects and throughout various stages, such as design reviews, code inspections, and testing, it transforms into a powerful tool for analyzing quality. Used thoughtfully, this metric can guide the selection of defect removal processes that optimize efficiency while reducing costs and timelines [64].

The analysis of the DRE metric helps in understanding how effective the defect prevention process is. High DRE values indicate that the test processes are effective and that a majority of defects are caught before release. Consistently high DRE rates reflect a test analyst's capability in thorough test case design, test execution, and defect detection, reducing the likelihood of postrelease issues. However, if the DRE is lower than expected, it indicates that defects are escaping the testing process. This can help test analysts focus on areas that may need more in-depth testing, such

**Table 5.1** Defects found in different phases of the system's lifecycle

| | Development | | | After the release (months) | | | |
|---|---|---|---|---|---|---|---|
| Phase | Design | Code | Test | 1–6 | 7–12 | 13–18 | 19–24 |
| Defects found | 20 | 40 | 140 | 30 | 20 | 10 | 5 |
| Cumulative number of defects found before the release | 20 | 60 | 200 | 200 | 200 | 200 | 200 |
| Cumulative number of defects found after the release | – | – | – | 30 | 50 | 60 | 65 |
| Cumulative number of defects found | 20 | 60 | 200 | 230 | 250 | 260 | 265 |
| DRE | | | | 87% | 80% | 77% | 75% |

as specific functionality, integration points, or performance concerns. For instance, if too many critical issues are found postrelease, defect prevention or testing (or both) may need improvements.

It should be noted that the name of this metric is not entirely accurate. It does not measure the cost/benefit ratio of defect removal, as the name would suggest, but rather its effectiveness, i.e., the degree to which it achieves its objective. However, since the name "defect removal efficiency" has become established in the testing community, it has been retained in the Test Analyst syllabus. An alternative with an accurate name is the metric "defect detection percentage" (DDP), which is just slightly different in that it only measures defect detection and not defect fixing.

**Phase Containment Effectiveness** (PCE) measures the percentage of defects introduced and removed in the same phase in relation to the total number of defects introduced in that phase. This metric is an essential indicator of how effective each development phase is in capturing and resolving defects before they progress to the next stage, where they can become more costly and challenging to fix.

The PCE for a phase P is calculated as follows:

$$PCE(P) = \frac{D(P)}{T(P)} \times 100\%,$$

where

- $D(P)$ is the number of defects introduced and detected in phase $P$,
- $T(P)$ is the total number of defects introduced in phase $P$.

As with the DRE metric, it is not possible to determine the exact value of the PCE metric's denominator $T(P)$. However, it can be approximated by the number of defects introduced in phase $P$ that were detected in a given period of time, or in some given subsequent phases. Also, as with the DRE metric, the calculated PCE value is actually an upper bound for the exact (unknown) PCE value. If any defects introduced in phase $P$ are detected after the PCE($P$) has been calculated, the PCE($P$) will decrease.

By tracking PCE across phases, test analysts can identify which phases are most effective at detecting and resolving defects early on. A high PCE in a phase indicates strong quality practices in that phase, helping prevent defects from escaping into later stages. A low PCE in a specific phase signals areas that require additional focus, such as better review processes or more thorough testing, to improve early defect detection.

Consider the data in Table 5.2, which shows how many defects introduced in particular phases were detected in these and subsequent phases, and how the PCE metric can be calculated from this data. We assume that defect data from the Oper (operations) phase was collected for a period of six months after the software was released to the customer, so it is a good approximation of the total number of defects that remained in the product after its release. We also assume here that the project follows a sequential lifecycle. However, the PCE metric can be calculated for any kind of phase or group of phases. For example, in agile projects, PCE can be calculated for "sprint zero" and for all the other sprints or for each iteration separately.

The last column in Table 5.2 shows the values of the PCE metric for all development phases: requirements elicitation (Req), high-level design (HLD), low-level design (LLD), implementation (Code), and testing (Test). For example, $PCE(Req) = \frac{60}{200} = 30\%$, because 200 defects in total were introduced in the requirements elicitation phase, but only 60 of them were detected in the same phase. Similarly, $PCE(HLD) = \frac{50}{80} = 62.5\%$, $PCE(LLD) = \frac{140}{250} = 56\%$, $PCE(Code) = \frac{40}{190} = 21\%$, and $PCE(Test) = \frac{10}{15} = 66.6\%$.

**Cost of quality** (CoQ) is a metric that measures the total cost incurred to ensure software quality (see [12], Sect. 3.2.1). The CoQ metric is divided into four primary categories:

1. Prevention costs—costs incurred to prevent defects from occurring in the first place, such as training, process improvement, and quality planning. These costs are incurred regardless of what the future quality of the product will be, but we have full control over them because it is up to us to decide how much money we will spend on training, process improvement, etc.
2. Appraisal costs—costs associated with evaluating the product for quality, including testing, reviews, and quality audits. As with prevention costs, we have full control over appraisal costs.
3. Internal failure costs—costs due to defects found before release, such as debugging, fixing, and confirmation testing. These costs depend on how many defects are found before the software is released and how expensive it is to fix them.
4. External failure costs—costs related to defects discovered after release, including customer support, patching, workarounds, data cleanups, warranty claims, reputation damage, and liability for human health, life, and environmental damages. These costs depend on how many defects escape into production, the damage they cause, and the costs of fixing them in production.

CoQ helps organizations evaluate the effectiveness of their quality assurance and defect prevention practices by providing a financial perspective on the investment in quality activities versus the costs resulting from poor quality. The idea behind the CoQ model is that external failure costs are typically much higher than internal removal

**Table 5.2** Defects by phase of introduction and detection

| Number of detected defects | | Phase of defect detection | | | | | | Total defects introduced in the phase | PCE (%) |
|---|---|---|---|---|---|---|---|---|---|
| | | Req | HLD | LLD | Code | Test | Oper | | |
| Phase of defect introduction | Req | 60 | 20 | 50 | 10 | 40 | 20 | 200 | 30 |
| | HLD | | 50 | 20 | 0 | 10 | 0 | 80 | 62.5 |
| | LLD | | | 140 | 20 | 80 | 10 | 250 | 56 |
| | Code | | | | 40 | 85 | 65 | 190 | 21 |
| | Test | | | | | 10 | 5 | 15 | 66.6 |

costs. Internal and external failure costs depend on the number of defects found, which depends on the prevention and appraisal costs. Therefore, it pays to invest in prevention and appraisal, as this will result in lower detection costs, ultimately reducing the total cost of quality.

Let us consider a simple simulation of two strategies regarding the cost of quality, shown in Fig. 5.1.

Assume that there are 100 potential defects at the beginning of the project. This means that if we do not apply any quality-related activities, 100 defects will be released with the product. Assume that in testing, 33% of defects are detected, and the average cost per defect is $800. Finally, assume that the average cost per defect found by the client after release is $2000.

In Scenario A, prevention and appraisal costs are low, which results in the removal of 15 defects and 10 subsequent defects in the review phase. This means that 75 defects escaped to the implementation phase. 33% of them (25) were detected, which cost 25 * $800 = $20,000. The remaining defects (50) were detected by the client, so the cost of their removal was 50 * $2000 = $100,000. The total cost of quality in Scenario A is, therefore,

$$\$15{,}000 + \$2500 + \$20{,}000 + \$100{,}000 = \$137{,}500.$$

In Scenario B, the team invested more in prevention and appraisal ($50,000 in total), which resulted in eliminating 30 potential defects and a further 28 defects in the review phase. This means that 42 defects escaped to the implementation phase. 33% of them (14) were detected, which cost 14 * $800 = $11,200. The remaining defects (28) were detected by the client, so the cost of their removal was 28 * $2,000 = $56,000. The total cost of quality in Scenario B is, therefore,

$$\$40{,}000 + \$10{,}000 + \$11{,}200 + \$56{,}000 = \$117{,}200.$$

This is $20,300 less than in Scenario A. We were able to reduce the total cost of quality by almost 15%.

This simulation shows that defect prevention is cost-effective and worth investing in detecting defects in the early phases. In practice, there is a certain optimal cost of early defect prevention activities since the law of diminishing returns is at work here. For example, the cost of eliminating defect potentials (defect prevention costs) can grow exponentially with the increase in defect potentials eliminated. In our example, this could mean that, for example, the cost of removing 70 defect potentials could exceed the total cost of quality in Scenario B.

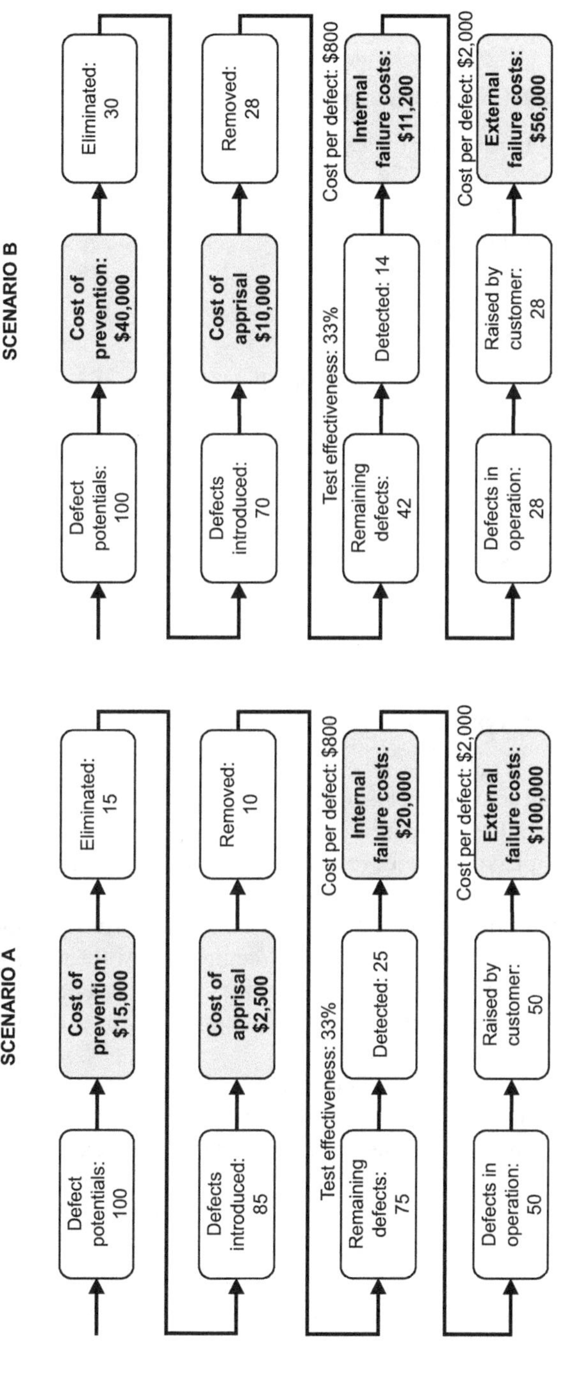


**Fig. 5.1** Two quality strategies and their cost of quality

## Sample Questions

### Question 5.1.1A

How can the test analyst **BEST** contribute to defect prevention?

(a) By participating in retrospectives.
(b) By automating test execution.
(c) By performing exploratory testing.
(d) By determining test oracles.

Select ONE answer.

### Question 5.1.1B

Participating in which of the following is **NOT** an example of how the test analyst contributes to defect prevention?

(a) Risk analysis.
(b) Retrospectives.
(c) Audits.
(d) Root cause analysis.

Select ONE answer.

## 5.2 Supporting Phase Containment

The objective of phase containment is to detect and remove defects in the same phase of the SDLC in which they were introduced. This policy is designed to reduce the cost of quality. In Agile software development, the shift left approach can be used similarly.

One measure supporting phase containment is to perform dynamic testing on differentiated test levels as soon as the intermediate software work products are testable. In addition, the appropriate test techniques should be applied, with a focus on defects introduced at that level of software integration. This is described in detail in Chap. 3.

However, it should be noted that defects can also occur in other work products, not just code. Requirements, specifications, and architecture plans may contain defects that, if not detected in the same phase as they were introduced, can propagate to code. As the test basis is both such a work product in software development and a crucial element in test analysis and test design, the test analyst can most effectively contribute to phase containment by evaluating the quality of the test basis. It is vital to pay close attention to the quality of the test basis at the outset in order to minimize subsequent effort and prevent defects from spreading to later phases of software development. The Test Analyst syllabus outlines two common options for test analysts to identify defects in the test basis: modeling for testing purposes and reviewing the test basis using various review techniques.

### *5.2.1 Using Models to Detect Anomalies in Specifications*

TA-5.2.1 (K3) Use a model of the test object to detect anomalies in a specification.

**Definitions**

**Model-based testing**: Testing based on or involving models.

Modeling is a powerful tool in software engineering because it enables teams to capture, analyze, and communicate the essence of complex systems at different levels of detail. In the context of phase containment, which aims to detect and address defects early in the development lifecycle, modeling can provide critical advantages in terms of cost savings, time efficiency, and overall system reliability. Modeling can support phase containment in at least three ways:

- detecting defects in specifications,
- detecting defects in models,
- detecting defects by using model-based testing.

A prerequisite for the effective use of modeling by a test analyst is, of course, a good working knowledge of it. The test analyst should have at least passive knowledge of the models, i.e., they should be able to read, analyze, and interpret the most commonly used models. In contrast, active knowledge of the models is the ability to create correct models from other formats, like natural-language specifications and informal knowledge. Such knowledge can result from academic education or from practical experience, for example, in system design. It makes the test analyst even more capable of using the models for defect detection and defect prevention.

**More on Software Models**

The software can be modeled in many different ways. There is a plethora of software models that describe different aspects of software. Examples include:

- Models representing static structure and constraints of the system, its parameters, system's architecture or its code, e.g., control flow graph, data flow graph, call graph, domain model, CRUD matrix, formal grammar (BNF),

classification tree, feature model, ERD (entity-relationship) diagram, class diagram, object diagram, component diagram, deployment diagram, database relational model, package diagram, abstract syntax tree, parse tree.
- Models defining static rules and conditions that govern the system's behavior, e.g., decision table, cause and effect graph, decision tree, truth table, predicate logic, constraint satisfaction model, inference rules, fault tree, EAC (Event-Action-Condition model).
- Models representing software workflows or dynamic behavior or interaction between the system's architectural components, e.g., sequence diagram, interaction diagram, collaboration diagram, MSC (Message Sequence Chart), data flow diagram, use case model, activity diagram, business process model, and many versions of a state transition model, such as FSM (finite state machines), EFSM (extended finite states machines), Harel state charts, and Petri nets.

**Detecting defects in specifications by modeling**. Detecting defects in specifications involves identifying issues in the initial requirements and descriptions before any coding or detailed design is underway. Since specifications form the foundation for all subsequent activities, specification defects can propagate throughout the project, becoming increasingly costly to fix as they go unnoticed.

Specifications are often provided in the form of informal text, whether written or verbal. Test analysts can formally represent these specifications using models. The benefits of modeling the specifications include:

- Improved traceability—when creating a model, the test analyst can more easily map test conditions (e.g., requirements, acceptance criteria) to model elements and link them to test cases for traceability. For example, if the test conditions include the state-dependent behavior of the test item, the state transitions in the state model will be the coverage items that can be linked to the test cases on one side and to the specification elements on the other side.
- Early defect detection—models formalize and visualize the test basis. They focus on its relevant aspects and eliminate irrelevant information. This makes complex relationships easier to understand and anomalies easier to identify. Therefore, modeling efficiently reveals defects such as incompleteness, inconsistencies, or ambiguities. For example, it is easier to see in a state model than in a text that an event can lead to different subsequent states, but the guard conditions are missing.
- Improved communication—the strength of modeling is that the specification is transformed while reviews check it in its original form. As a result, the test analyst also contributes to finding appropriate solutions for the defects detected. Models (such as state diagrams or use case diagrams) formalize and visualize abstract requirements, helping stakeholders align on their understanding of system functionality. This alignment reduces the risk of defects arising from misinterpretations. In the example of missing guard conditions mentioned above, the test

analyst can not only point out the anomaly, but also propose guard conditions and discuss them with the stakeholders.
- Reduced quality costs—the earlier a defect is detected, the less expensive it is to fix it. The cost of fixing defects in a model is low, since it usually comes down to modifying the model and the underlying specification documentation, which can be done very quickly. Addressing issues in the specification phase saves resources by avoiding rework in later, more expensive stages like implementation or dynamic testing. For example, if a missing guard condition, as mentioned above, escapes to development and dynamic testing, the test analyst will try to cover it with a test case that will fail. That will cause efforts in debugging, code fixing, and confirmation testing, in addition to updating the specification.

In Tables 5.3, 5.4, and 5.5, we give examples of defects that can be found in requirements by modeling them using three kinds of models described in Chap. 3: data-based, behavior-based, and rule-based.

**Table 5.3** Examples of defects found by modeling the requirements with data-based models

| Requirement | Derived model | Anomaly revealed by the model |
|---|---|---|
| The thermostat shall activate the heater when the room temperature falls below 18 °C and deactivate it when the temperature reaches 22 °C | Domain model | Undefined behavior for temperature between 18 and 21 °C |
| The system shall allow users to remotely schedule smart lights to turn on or off based on daily routines. The system shall also adjust intelligent lighting levels automatically in response to ambient light conditions | Classification tree model | Inconsistent feature names—“smart lights” and “intelligent lightning” are two features, but in fact they are the same feature |
| A student must enroll in exactly one major. Each major belongs to exactly one department | Class diagram | The model implies that a university cannot have any students until at least one department and one major already exist |

**Detecting defects in models**. If the test basis contains models, the test analyst can review these models to detect defects. Detecting defects in models means identifying anomalies within the abstractions made. The benefits of detecting defects in models are as follows:

- Making the test basis more consistent—validate that the model in the test basis aligns with specifications and requirements. Models such as UML (Unified Modeling Language) [37] or BPMN (Business Process Model and Notation) [42] enable teams to visually verify relationships, dependencies, and flows.
- Improved quality of design—any model can contain defects such as syntax errors, typos, duplicates, and inconsistent naming of model elements. Finding

**Table 5.4** Examples of defects found by modeling the requirements with behavior-based models

| Requirement | Derived model | Anomaly revealed by the model |
|---|---|---|
| The system shall allow a manager to update employee records. A manager can always read employee records | CRUD matrix | The matrix reveals that managers can read and update employee records, but does not specify who can create an employee record, or whether employee creation is even allowed |
| The subscription can be deactivated (initial state), activated, or suspended. Subscription can be activated when a payment is made. An activated subscription can be suspended when the subscription time ends or deactivated on demand | State model | Dead-end state: when in "suspended" mode, the subscription cannot be activated or deactivated |
| The online ordering system shall allow a customer to cancel an order at any time before the order is shipped. When an order is canceled, the system shall immediately refund the customer and update inventory. If payment has not yet been processed, the system shall still issue a refund | Activity diagram | Order cancelation occurs while payment is still processing, so there is nothing to refund yet. There is no defined behavior for canceling the pending payment transaction. The system might refund zero or a double refund, depending on timing. The model exposes that refunding and canceling the payment pipeline conflict |

**Table 5.5** Examples of defects found by modeling the requirements with rule-based models

| Requirement | Derived model | Anomaly revealed by the model |
|---|---|---|
| A customer's loan interest rate is determined as follows: if the customer has good credit or high income, apply the low rate. If the customer has poor credit and low income, apply the high rate. If the customer has good credit and low income, apply the medium rate | Decision table | The requirement contains overlapping and conflicting conditions: a customer with good credit and low income fits both the medium rate and the low rate |
| A parking garage charges fees based on vehicle type and time of day. Cars pay $5 per hour during the day, $3 per hour at night. Motorcycles pay $2 per hour at any time. Trucks are not allowed during the night | Decision table | Missing rule: It is not known what the price should be for trucks during the day |

and resolving such defects in the model increases not only the correctness and consistency but also the maintainability of the models in the test basis.

- Easier change management—detecting defects in the model helps manage changes and refinements before the system is fully developed, making it more cost-effective to accommodate evolving requirements without significantly impacting the project timeline or budget.

Examples of defects in models include:

- state models—missing/wrong states, improper transitions, incorrect guard conditions or actions, redundant or unreachable states, and nondeterministic behavior,
- scenario-based models such as activity diagrams—missing, unreachable, or dead-end actions, incorrect order of actions, wrong, non-exclusive, or incomplete guard conditions in decision nodes, missing synchronization points, or improperly synchronized parallel flows that can lead to unintended behavior,
- decision tables—overlapping, inconsistent, or infeasible rules, incompleteness (e.g., missing combinations of conditions or missing actions for a given combination of conditions).

**Detecting defects by using model-based testing**. Model-based testing (MBT) is a test approach that derives test cases and other testware from models of the test item. It relies on the concept that if the model correctly represents system behavior, including the test conditions. Based on the model, it can reveal discrepancies between expected and actual outcomes early in the lifecycle. Typically, MBT involves using an MBT tool that automatically generates the testware from the model. The test analyst can define test selection criteria to set the desired test coverage by the generated test cases. Benefits of using MBT include:

- Effective detection of anomalies—MBT is effective in finding anomalies in the specification because it allows for comprehensive coverage and systematic exploration of the expected behavior of the test object according to the MBT model.
- Automated test case generation—model-based testing facilitates the automated generation of test cases from models, improving coverage and reducing the time and cost associated with manual test case development (see the real-life example in Sect. 3.1.3).
- Flexible coverage—the test selection criteria enable the test analyst to reach a wide range of coverage. High coverage ensures rigorous testing, increasing the likelihood of identifying defects before they reach production (see the real-life example in Sect. 3.5.2).
- Reduction of maintenance effort—since model-based tests are generated from abstract models, they are more resilient to code changes, reducing the maintenance workload for testing teams. Changes to the system only require updates to the model (being the "single source of truth"), from which new test cases can be automatically generated.

### Case Study

Consider a simple example of using modeling to detect defects in a business process, as well as detecting defects in models. Suppose we are designing a system to support the editorial team of a magazine. The publishing process to be supported by the system looks as follows:

(1) The author of the article sends it to the editor, who performs a preliminary review.
(2) The editor decides whether to desk reject the article (if, for example, it doesn't fit the journal's profile) or submit it for review.
(3) The reviewer reads the article and can make one of three decisions: accept the article, reject it, or forward it to the author for improvement.
(4) In the first two cases, the article is forwarded to the editor, who decides whether to publish or reject the article.
(5) In the third case, the article is sent to the author requesting improvements.
(6) After corrections, the author sends the article to the editor, who sends it again to the reviewer. The cycle of article improvement can occur any number of times.

Suppose we modeled the requirements (1)–(6) with a state diagram shown in Fig. 5.2. The test analyst can detect defects in the requirements by performing various types of actions. For example, an analysis of workflows allowed by the transition diagram might reveal that an author always sends an article to an editor but receives requests for improvement from a reviewer. Perhaps more appropriate, from an editorial workflow point of view, would be a situation in which the editor is the single contact point for the author and the reviewer. This can be reflected in the requirements by changing the sentences (3) and (5) to the following ones:

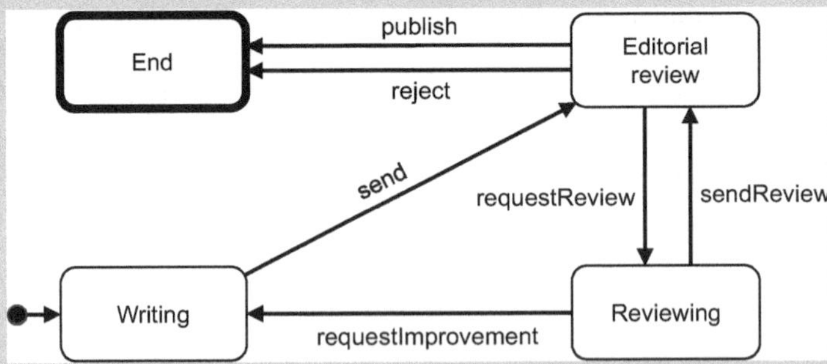


**Fig. 2** First version of the model for the system supporting editorial boards

(3) The reviewer reads the article and can make one of three decisions: accept the article, reject it, or request improvements.
(5) In the third case, the article is sent to the editor, who then requests improvements from the author.

In addition, it is useful to distinguish the type of message the reviewer sends to the editor. Figure 5.3 shows a modified model, taking into account the corrected requirements.

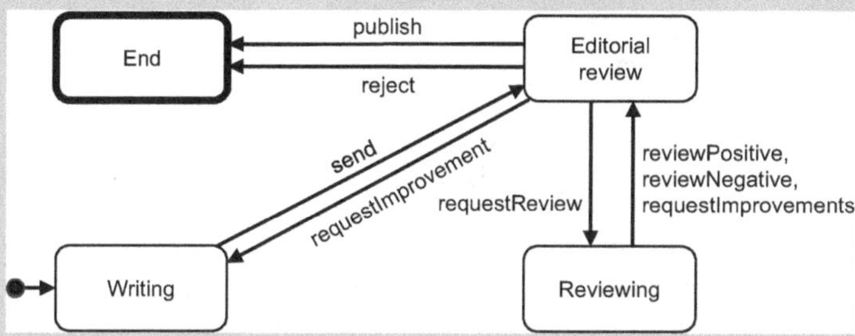


**Fig. 5.3** Improved version of the model

Defects in requirements can also be detected by designing tests based on the model. Suppose we follow the state transition test technique, and we want to design tests that achieve 1-switch coverage. That is, we want to cover all possible sequences of two consecutive transitions in the state diagram. In particular, this requires designing test cases that cover the sequences:

- Writing (send) Editorial review (publish) End.
- Reviewing (reviewPositive) Editorial review (reject) End.
- Reviewing (reviewNegative) Editorial review (publish) End.
- Reviewing (requestImprovements) EditorialReview (publish) End.

The first sequence suggests that the model allows for a situation in which an article is accepted by an editor for publication without performing peer review. Arguably, such a situation should not be allowed. The test analyst may note that the problem stems from the fact that the model does not distinguish between the situations of sending an article to the editor described in sentences (1) and (4) of the specification. This is because these sentences refer to two different situations: sentence (1) refers to an article that has not yet been reviewed, and sentence (4) refers to an article that has already gone through the review process and the editor has just received a revised version. We detected a defect in the model, which does not accurately reflect the process described in the requirements. Note that we detected this problem by almost mechanically applying a coverage criterion for the state transition model. This example shows the power of test design techniques—they can serve as useful tools for static requirements analysis!

The last three sequences from the bullet point list above present a similar problem. The model is not able to "remember" the review status when the editor receives the reviewer's decision.

The test analyst may decide to refine the model and use guard conditions to eliminate the detected issues. The third, final version of the model is presented in Fig. 5.4.

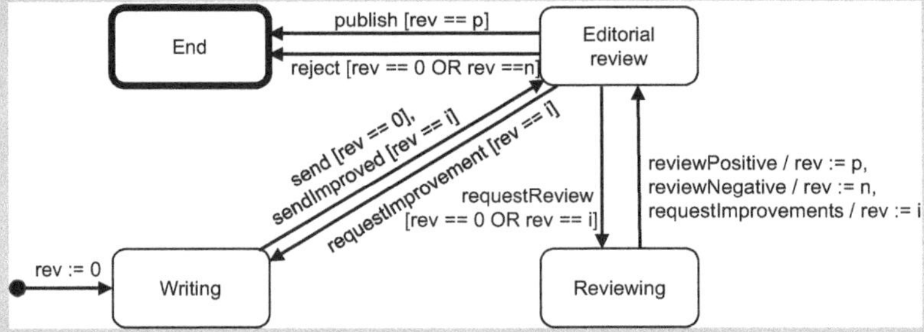


**Fig. 5.4** Final model

The introduction of guard conditions has solved the problems described above. When an article is sent by an author for the first time, the *rev* variable has a value of 0, which means that the article has not yet been reviewed. Sending an article can, therefore, only be accomplished using the *send* event. At this point, the editor can desk reject the article or send it for review. Depending on the outcome of the review, the *rev* variable will take the value *p* (positive review), n (negative review), or *i* (request for improvements). If the review was positive (resp. negative), the only action the editor can take is to publish (resp. reject) the article. If the reviewer requests improvements, the editor can only send this request to the author. At this point, the author, having made the improvements, can only send the corrected article using the *sendImproved* event, since only for this event the guard condition (*rev* = = i) is true.

The above analysis led the test analyst to a number of important insights into the requirements. In particular, they detected an inaccurate description of the document workflow. This made it possible to make the rules of this workflow more precise, thus most likely avoiding the introduction of defects into the code, which could have been detected only at the system testing stage, making them very expensive to fix.

## Sample Questions

### Question 5.2.1A

You want to use a domain model to detect potential defects in the following specification of the language competence evaluation system.

The system assigns a competence level based on two exam results: the reading exam (R) and the writing exam (W). Both R and W are integers between 0 and 100:

- if R >= 50 or W >= 50, the competence level is HIGH,
- if R <= 30 and W < 50, the competence level is LOW,
- if R > 30 and R < 50 and W > 30 and W < 50, the competence level is MEDIUM.

What conclusion can a test analyst draw from analyzing a domain model built from these requirements?

(a) There are no defects. The model represents the domain correctly.
(b) There are overlapping equivalence classes.
(c) Some input elements are not covered by equivalence classes.
(d) Not all competence levels are included in the model.

Select ONE answer.

### Question 5.2.1B

You analyze the state transition model for the online shopping website, shown in Fig. 5.5. The shop offers only one product type. The model was derived precisely from the requirement specification. The action Add adds a single item to a cart, and the action Remove removes a single item from a cart.

What conclusion can a test analyst draw from analyzing this model?

(a) There exists a sequence of events that results in paying for an empty cart.
(b) When a cart is full, it is impossible to remove more than one item from it.

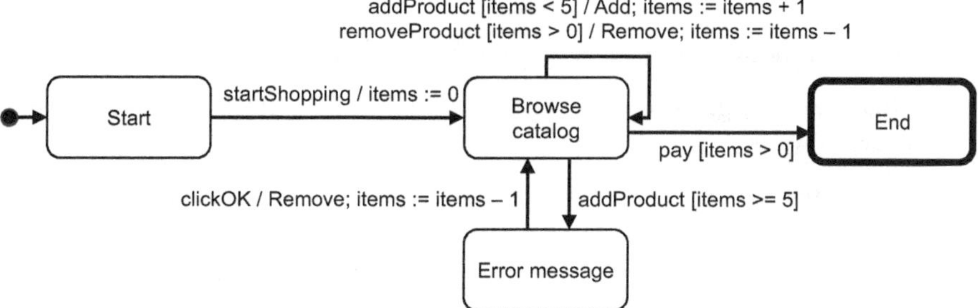


**Fig. 5.5** State transition model for an online shopping website

(c) An attempt to add a product to a full cart results in removing an item from it.
(d) It is possible to pay for a cart containing an arbitrarily large number of items.

Select ONE answer.

## Exercise 12—Using Test Models to Detect Defects in a Specification

TA-5.2.1 (K3) Use a model of the test object to detect defects in a specification

You are analyzing the requirements for the online shopping app. The requirements are as follows.

Shipping cost depends on membership status and shipping speed. Membership status can be regular or premium. Shipping speed can be standard, express, or overnight. Premium members with standard shipping speed pay no shipping costs (0$). For all the other shipping speeds, they pay $5. Regular members placing orders with the standard shipping speed pay $5, and with the express speed pay $10. Overnight shipping speed costs $15, regardless of the membership status.

1. Model the requirements as a decision table.
2. Analyze the decision table for potential defects in the requirements. Have you noticed any defects? If so, suggest corrections to the specification to remove these defects and design a decision table for the corrected specification.

### *5.2.2 Applying Review Techniques*

TA-5.2.2 (K3) Apply a review technique to a test basis to find defects

**Definitions**

**Review technique**: A procedure used to perform a review.

**Ad hoc reviewing**: A review technique performed informally without a structured process.

**Checklist-based reviewing**: A review technique guided by a list of questions or required attributes.

**Perspective-based reading**: A type of role-based reviewing that uses checklists and involves the creation of prototype deliverables.

**Role-based reviewing**: A review technique in which a work product is evaluated from the perspective of different stakeholder roles.

**Scenario-based reviewing**: A review technique in which a work product is evaluated to determine its ability to address specific scenarios.

Reviews are a very powerful form of static testing. They help ensure that both the testware (e.g., test plans, test cases, scripts) and the software work products (e.g., requirements, architectural design) are correct, complete, and aligned with project goals. Some research estimates that reviews such as walkthroughs [65] and software inspections [66, 67] are able to detect 50 to 90% of a software product's defects [68, 69]. Even so, reviews still haven't become common practice in today's software development projects [70]. Probably one of the most popular reviews used nowadays is the so-called Modern Code Review [71] due to its lightweight nature and the popularity of the DevOps-related approach to development. However, Modern Code Review is used mainly for code reviews, and the participants are often restricted to developers.

One of the most important characteristics that make reviews a powerful tool is that they help in identifying defects *early in the lifecycle*. Therefore, the internal failure costs are significantly lower than if they are detected during dynamic testing. In addition, the risk of budget and time overruns is significantly lower than if the same defect is found in a late dynamic test level, possibly shortly before the release date.

During requirements reviews, test analysts often discover missing requirements, conflicting requirements, or requirements that are difficult to test, which can lead to improved requirement documentation and testability. Reviews provide an opportunity for test analysts to clarify requirements with business analysts, developers, and stakeholders, helping them better understand the project goals and what needs to be tested. Test analysts can also review other specifications and design work products, as well as test cases, to improve the effectiveness, efficiency, and maintainability of testing.

An important added value for a test analyst is the opportunity to participate in reviews, which allows them to continually learn and improve their skills. Reviews enable test analysts to benefit from the insights and expertise of other team members. This improves their knowledge of the product as well as their skills in defect detection, critical thinking, and requirements analysis.

While reviews are highly beneficial for improving quality and reducing defects, they do come with certain challenges and risks. Understanding these can help test analysts mitigate potential issues and make the review process more effective. Below we give some examples of challenges and risks. We will refer to them later while describing different review types.

- Reviews, especially formal ones, can be time-consuming, which can lead to project delays if not properly managed.

- Team members with relevant expertise may not always be available to participate in reviews, especially if they are involved in other critical tasks. This can lead to delays or less effective reviews if only limited participants can be involved.
- Not all team members are open to receiving feedback, especially if they perceive it as criticism. This can create tension or conflict during reviews, making the process uncomfortable and less constructive. If individuals become defensive about their work, they may resist changes, leading to a less effective review process and potentially lower-quality output.
- Without clear review standards and procedures, different reviewers may have varying criteria, which can result in inconsistent feedback and missed issues. This inconsistency can lower the quality and thoroughness of the reviews.
- If reviewers are assigned to review large volumes of documentation or code, they can experience fatigue and lose focus, increasing the chances of overlooking defects.
- In group reviews, especially in walkthroughs or inspections, there is a risk that participants may agree with more vocal or senior members, even if they notice issues. This can prevent genuine problems from being raised and addressed.
- If reviewers come from similar backgrounds or roles, they might overlook issues that someone with a different perspective (e.g., a customer representative) might catch.
- Reviews that lack a clearly defined objective (e.g., to identify specific types of defects, or to ensure requirement clarity) can be unfocused and inefficient, as participants may not know what to prioritize.
- Review effectiveness depends heavily on the knowledge and expertise of the reviewers. If the team lacks members with an in-depth understanding of the requirements or code, the review might miss critical issues.
- Measuring the effectiveness of reviews can be challenging. Without metrics, it is hard to determine whether the review process is truly adding value or needs improvement.

The Foundation Level syllabus [11] discusses four different review types: informal review, walkthrough, technical review, and inspection. Table 5.6 briefly summarizes the comparison of these review types in terms of their goals, processes, roles, and levels of formalism.

The Foundation Level syllabus also describes typical steps of a review process:

- Planning. The review leader organizes the review, defining the purpose, scope, participants, materials, and schedule. Objectives and entry criteria are established to ensure the review is focused and effective.
- Review Initiation (kick-off). The review leader briefs participants on the review's goals, process, and expectations. This ensures everyone is aligned and understands the work product being reviewed, setting the stage for a productive review.
- Individual Review. Each reviewer examines the material independently, identifying potential defects, issues, and improvements.

**Table 5.6** Main characteristics of the most common review types

| | Informal review | Walkthrough | Technical review | Inspection |
|---|---|---|---|---|
| Main goals | Detecting defects | Detecting defects, quality improvement | Reaching a consensus, detecting defects | Detecting defects, quality evaluation, and defect prevention |
| Process | No formal process | Optional prior preparation for review | Mandatory prior preparation for review | Formal process based on rules and checklists; mandatory prior preparation |
| Roles | Can be conducted by the author or a group of people | Meeting conducted by a moderator, a scribe is mandatory | Meeting conducted by a moderator, a scribe is mandatory | Strictly defined roles, moderator and scribe are mandatory, reader is optional |
| Documenting the results | Optional, usually no documentation is created | Optional defect logs and review report | Typically, defect logs and review reports are created | Documentation (such as a review report) is mandatory |
| Level of formalism | Informal by definition | Varies from informal to formal | Varies from informal to formal | Formal by definition |

- Communication and analysis. The team discusses the findings collectively, analyzing each issue's significance and prioritizing fixes. This phase promotes consensus and a shared understanding of the review's outcomes.
- Fixing and reporting. The author addresses the identified issues, and the review leader compiles a report documenting the findings, actions taken, and any remaining concerns. This phase ensures that the review's objectives are met and provides a record for future reference.

The main part of this process is called "individual review". The individual review is critical in the review process because it allows each reviewer to examine the material independently, without influence from other participants. Reviewers can concentrate on specific details and go through the document or code at their own pace, leading to a deeper understanding and more comprehensive identification of issues. Without the influence of group discussions, each reviewer can provide an objective assessment. This independent perspective often uncovers unique issues that might be missed in a group setting. Individual review ensures that reviewers are already familiar with the material before group discussions, making meetings more productive and focused on resolving identified issues rather than discovering them. Each reviewer brings their own expertise and approach, which broadens the scope of feedback. This diversity enriches the review process and improves the quality of the final product.

To be as effective as possible during the individual review, the reviewers should apply the appropriate review technique. The test analyst syllabus, which follows the ISO 20246 standard on work product reviews [9], discusses five such review techniques. All of these techniques are commonly used by test analysts. These are:

- ad hoc reviewing,
- checklist-based reviewing,
- scenario-based reviewing,
- role-based reviewing,
- perspective-based reading.

**Ad hoc reviewing** is an informal, unstructured type of review where reviewers evaluate artifacts without a predefined process, structure, or documentation. Unlike formal review methods, ad hoc reviewing doesn't follow a systematic approach like checklists, scripts, document templates, formal procedures, or entry and exit criteria. Instead, it relies on the knowledge, experience, and intuition of the reviewers to identify issues. This review technique is often quicker and less resource-intensive than other techniques, making it suitable for situations where speed and flexibility are prioritized. Ad hoc reviews can be performed almost immediately, providing fast feedback on artifacts. This is particularly useful in Agile or iterative development environments where continuous and rapid assessment is needed.

Without the need for extensive preparation, documentation, or formal meetings, ad hoc reviews are less resource-intensive, making them feasible even with limited time and budget. The unstructured nature of ad hoc reviewing allows it to be applied to a wide range of artifacts, even if they vary in type or complexity. This flexibility allows teams to adapt reviews to specific situations and needs. When done by experienced reviewers, ad hoc reviews can quickly uncover high-level issues, allowing organizations to identify potential defects without formal processes.

However, the success of the ad hoc technique depends heavily on the reviewer's experience and familiarity with the subject. If reviewers lack knowledge or relevant experience, critical issues may go unnoticed. Due to the absence of structure, there is a risk of overlooking certain areas or requirements, leading to gaps in the review process. Different reviewers might focus on different aspects, which can result in inconsistent feedback. Since ad hoc reviews often lack formal documentation, it may be difficult to track which issues were identified and whether they were addressed. This lack of a documented trail is a problem in audits or quality assessments. Without structured checklists or criteria, ad hoc reviews are more likely to miss defects, especially subtle problems that might be identified with a more methodical approach.

**Checklist-based reviewing** is a systematic review technique, where reviewers use a predefined checklist to guide their evaluation of a work product (such as requirements, design, or code). Each item on the checklist represents a specific aspect or quality criterion that the reviewer should verify, helping ensure thorough and consistent coverage of all critical areas. The use of a checklist makes this process a structured approach. This structure helps to avoid oversight and focus on specific criteria. Each item on the checklist represents a question, condition, or guideline that helps reviewers evaluate particular aspects of the artifact. For example, a requirements document might have checklist items like "Is each requirement unambiguous?" or "Are all business rules clearly defined?".

By using the same checklist across similar work products, organizations promote consistency in reviews. This allows for a standardized assessment and ensures that all essential aspects are covered across different work products. Checklist-based reviews often involve documenting observations and issues for each checklist item. This structured documentation provides traceability and can be useful for follow-up actions and audits.

However, the effectiveness of a checklist-based review is highly dependent on the quality and completeness of the checklist itself. If the checklist is outdated, incomplete, or poorly designed, important issues may still be missed. Reviewers may focus too narrowly on the checklist items and overlook issues not explicitly listed. This can lead to "tunnel vision," where reviewers miss defects outside the checklist's scope. Checklist-based reviews may be less adaptable to unique situations or work products that do not fully fit the checklist criteria. This rigidity can make the checklist-based reviewing technique less effective for complex or highly specialized work products. Developing a comprehensive and effective checklist can be time-consuming. Additionally, checklists must be regularly updated to stay relevant, reflecting changes in standards, technologies, or project needs. Reviewers may treat the checklist as a "tick-the-box" exercise, focusing on marking items off without fully engaging with the content. This mechanical approach reduces the depth and effectiveness of the review.

Even with a checklist, the quality of the review still depends on the reviewers' expertise and understanding, as in the case of the ad hoc reviewing technique. Less experienced reviewers may not fully grasp the checklist items, leading to inconsistent or incomplete evaluations.

The process of creating a checklist, as well as a distinction between "read-do" and "do-confirm" checklists, is described in detail in Sect. 3.4.2, where we discussed checklists in the context of dynamic testing.

The test analyst can use a checklist-based reviewing technique not only for requirements and code but also for testware in order to improve the test process quality, which should result in a better quality of the final product. Table 5.7 shows a sample checklist for test plan review. The test analyst can use it to ensure that the test plan covers all the necessary elements. If deficiencies are observed, they can be filled in, which will increase the quality of the document. This, in turn, will have a positive impact on the quality of the test process. Notice that for each element of the checklist, the test analyst should be able to answer "yes, it holds" or "no, it does not hold."

Another example is a checklist for a test case, shown in Fig. 5.6. Its use allows the test analyst to ensure that the test cases are of high quality, allowing for comprehensive testing, better test efficiency, and defect identification. This checklist allows the test analyst to answer not only "yes" or "no," but also "partially." On the one hand, this allows for a more precise evaluation in some cases (e.g., if only part of the preconditions under "all preconditions are explicitly stated" is correctly described). On the other hand, it can be unclear what to do in a situation of partial fulfillment of

**Table 5.7** Checklist for test plan documentation

| | |
|---|---|
| 1. Objectives | ☐ Clearly stated objectives of the test plan<br>☐ Alignment of test objectives with overall project goals |
| 2. Scope | ☐ Defined scope of testing, including in-scope and out-of-scope items<br>☐ Identification of all features, functions, and components to be tested |
| 3. Strategy | ☐ Description of the overall approach to testing<br>☐ Selection of appropriate testing types (e.g., functional, non-functional)<br>☐ Rationale for chosen test strategy and methods |
| 4. Resource planning | ☐ Identification of necessary resources (e.g., people, tools, environments)<br>☐ The roles and responsibilities of team members are clearly defined<br>☐ Adequate resource allocation for all test activities |
| 5. Test environment | ☐ Detailed description of the required test environment<br>☐ Plan for test environment setup, maintenance, and teardown |
| 6. Testware | ☐ List of all test deliverables (e.g., test cases, test scripts, test data)<br>☐ Defined format and content for each deliverable<br>☐ Schedule for deliverable completion and review |
| 7. Schedule | ☐ Comprehensive test schedule with milestones and deadlines<br>☐ Alignment of the test schedule with the overall project timeline<br>☐ Identification of dependencies and critical path |
| 8. Risk management | ☐ Identification of potential project and product risks<br>☐ Risk analysis, risk mitigation, and contingency plans are in place |
| 9. Test case design | ☐ Defined criteria for test case design and selection<br>☐ Test cases cover all functional and non-functional requirements<br>☐ Traceability between requirements and test cases |
| 10. Test data | ☐ Plan for test data creation, management, and maintenance<br>☐ Ensuring test data is representative of production data<br>☐ Protection of sensitive data during testing |
| 11. Defect management | ☐ The process for defect reporting, tracking, and resolution is defined<br>☐ Defined criteria for defect severity and priority |
| 12. Communication | ☐ Defined communication channels and frequency of updates<br>☐ Identification of stakeholders and their information needs<br>☐ The process for escalating issues and risks is defined |
| 13. Metrics | ☐ Metrics and KPIs to measure testing effectiveness and efficiency |

(continued)

**Table 5.7** (continued)

| | |
|---|---|
| 14. Compliance | ☐ Adherence to relevant industry standards and regulations<br>☐ Compliance with organizational policies and procedures<br>☐ Documentation of any deviations from standards and justification |
| 15. Continuous improvement | ☐ Mechanism for capturing lessons learned and feedback<br>☐ Process for incorporating improvements into future test plans |

a criterion (e.g., what does it mean that a test case title is only partially descriptive?). If this means that it is imperative to improve the work product so that the criterion is fully met, then the "partially" option is unnecessary. In the situation of partial fulfillment of the criterion, the test analyst recognizes that the criterion is not fully met and selects the "no" option. However, if there is a legitimate reason for the distinction between full and partial fulfillment of the criterion, both the reviewer and the work product author should know very well what this means in order to avoid problems in the future, such as those related to the inaccurate improvement of the work product.

**Scenario-based reviewing** is a structured review technique that involves evaluating a work product by applying specific scenarios that represent real-world use cases. Reviewers examine the work product to determine if it meets expected outcomes and handles scenarios appropriately, especially those relevant to end-user behavior, common workflows, and potential edge cases.

Scenarios are crafted to reflect realistic usage patterns and interactions with the system, focusing on how end-users will use the product in practice. Instead of focusing solely on isolated elements, scenario-based reviews examine the end-to-end workflow, ensuring all parts of the process work cohesively from a user's perspective. By focusing on realistic user scenarios, this technique helps reviewers evaluate how

| **Test case checklist** | |
|---|---|
| The test case has a descriptive and meaningful title | YES / NO / PARTIALLY |
| The test case has a clear and concise description of the objective | YES / NO / PARTIALLY |
| The test case is aligned with specific requirements or user stories | YES / NO / PARTIALLY |
| All preconditions are explicitly stated | YES / NO / PARTIALLY |
| Dependencies on other test cases or test data are clearly identified | YES / NO / PARTIALLY |
| Environment setup requirements are documented | YES / NO / PARTIALLY |
| The test case has a detailed description of the required test data | YES / NO / PARTIALLY |
| Test data covers all necessary edge cases and scenarios | YES / NO / PARTIALLY |
| Test data is accessible and manageable | YES / NO / PARTIALLY |
| Step-by-step instructions are clear and concise | YES / NO / PARTIALLY |
| Each test step includes specific actions to be performed | YES / NO / PARTIALLY |
| Expected results are clearly defined for each step | YES / NO / PARTIALLY |
| Postconditions are clearly stated and relevant to the test case | YES / NO / PARTIALLY |
| The test case covers the intended functionality comprehensively | YES / NO / PARTIALLY |
| The test case covers both positive and negative scenarios | YES / NO / PARTIALLY |
| The test case is designed for reusability in future testing cycles | YES / NO / PARTIALLY |
| The test case is modular and well-structured, allowing for reuse with different data sets | YES / NO / PARTIALLY |
| The test case is written in clear and simple language | YES / NO / PARTIALLY |
| The test case has been reviewed by peers or stakeholders | YES / NO / PARTIALLY |
| The test case is designed with automation in mind (if applicable) | YES / NO / PARTIALLY |

**Fig. 5.6** Checklist for test case quality

intuitive, efficient, and satisfying the user experience will likely be. It allows teams to identify usability issues that may not be apparent in technical specifications alone. By validating requirements against practical use cases, reviewers can confirm that requirements are aligned with real-world needs and expectations. Scenario-based reviews follow end-to-end flows, often involving multiple components or modules. This makes it easier to spot integration issues or inconsistencies that may arise when different system parts interact. Scenario-based reviews encourage participants to think from the user's perspective, promoting an empathetic approach that can bring insights into how different user roles and skill levels might approach the system.

However, designing comprehensive, realistic scenarios can be time-consuming and requires a thorough understanding of user behavior, system requirements, and use cases. If scenarios are not well-defined, the review may miss critical issues or fail to provide relevant insights. Scenario-based reviews focus on specific use cases and user flows. While this provides deep insights, it may also result in partial coverage, as the review may miss issues outside the defined scenarios. Reviewers may unconsciously focus on "ideal" user flows or scenarios that align with expected behavior, overlooking less common or unexpected user interactions that might expose defects or usability issues. Scenario-based reviewing often requires more time and resources than simpler review techniques, especially if scenarios are complex or need multiple reviewers to cover all relevant aspects. While scenario-based reviews are excellent for detecting functional and usability issues, they may not be as effective in identifying non-functional issues, such as flexibility and compatibility, unless explicitly designed to do so.

An example of a scenario for a scenario-based reviewing technique for our FoodApp would be as follows. The requirements specification document is being reviewed to ensure it effectively supports realistic user scenarios related to the ordering process. The review is intended to catch any gaps, ambiguities, or missing functionalities that could affect the user experience. The team designed four scenarios that will be used during the review:

Scenario 1: The user places an order. The goal is to ensure the requirements support a smooth ordering and delivery process. Using this scenario, the review will focus on:

- checking if the requirements include selecting delivery options, such as standard or express delivery,
- verifying whether there are requirements for capturing and validating delivery addresses, including support for complex or non-standard addresses,
- confirming that the requirements outline a process for tracking the order status in real-time (e.g., "order received," "in preparation," "out for delivery"),
- ensuring there are requirements for notifying the user about the estimated delivery time and providing updates in case of delays.

Scenario 2: The user applies a promotional code. The goal is to assess if FoodApp's requirements allow for applying discounts or promo codes seamlessly. Using this scenario, the review will focus on:

- checking if there are requirements for validating promo codes at checkout (e.g., ensuring they haven't expired or have usage limits),
- verifying whether the requirements specify where and how the user should enter a promo code and see the discount applied in real time,
- ensuring the requirements include handling error messages for invalid or expired codes and providing clear feedback to the user,
- confirming there is a requirement to track promo code usage to prevent unauthorized reuse (if there are limitations).

Scenario 3: The user modifies the order before checkout. The goal is to ensure users can make adjustments to their orders easily before finalizing the purchase. Using this scenario, the review will focus on:

- verifying that the requirements specify the ability to add, remove, or modify items (e.g., change portion sizes or add special instructions) in the cart,
- checking if there are requirements for updating the total cost and estimated delivery time dynamically as items are added or removed,
- ensuring the requirements cover special requests (e.g., extra sauce, no onions) and include a field for additional instructions,
- confirming that the requirements mention error handling for cases where certain items go out of stock while the order is still in the cart.

Scenario 4: The user wants to cancel an order. The goal is to assess if users can easily cancel their orders under specific conditions. Using this scenario, the review will focus on:

- verifying that the requirements specify conditions under which the order can be canceled (e.g., before it is "out for delivery"),
- ensuring there are requirements for refund handling if the user cancels the order, and how the refund process should be initiated and completed,
- checking if the requirements outline how the FoodApp will notify the restaurant of the cancelation, and if there is a confirmation notification to the user,
- confirming that the requirements address any potential fees associated with last-minute cancelations.

**Role-based reviewing** is a review technique that leverages the different types of stakeholders by assigning specific roles to reviewers. Typically, in role-based reviewing, the reviewers take the same perspective on the product (e.g., end-user), but each reviewer evaluates the work product through the lens of a particular role, often defined by so-called personas.

Personas are fictional characters created based on user research, embodying the characteristics of actual users. Personas allow reviewers to consider the diverse needs and motivations of different user segments. By representing specific types of users (e.g., busy professionals, tech-savvy millennials, or parents with young children), personas ensure that the review reflects real-world scenarios and user experiences. Reviewers can empathize with personas during the review process, understanding the challenges and expectations of different user types. This empathy fosters a more user-centered approach to evaluating the work product. Personas can help in determining which roles should be included in the review process. For example, if our FoodApp has personas for "frequent diners," "families ordering for kids," and "health-conscious consumers," these personas can guide the assignment of specific roles (e.g., end-user, parent, nutritionist) to ensure comprehensive coverage.

Personas help in developing realistic scenarios for the review process. By thinking through the scenarios different personas might encounter while using the product, reviewers can assess whether the requirements and design meet the specific needs of those users. Example personas for the FoodApp are shown in Fig. 5.7. Michael represents a technology-averse, occasional app user who is a health-conscious consumer expecting the FoodApp's interface to be simple and user-friendly and show nutritional information about the dish being ordered or to allow for order customization. Reviews would assess nutritional information, customization features for meals, and family meal deals. Reviews would also need to focus on usability aspects, easy navigation, clear instructions, and support features for users unfamiliar with technology. In the case of Anh, reviews should focus on quick ordering, menu recommendations based on previous orders, and efficient payment options. Finally, in the case of Sophia, reviews would focus on ensuring that the app offers robust customization options. This includes adding or removing ingredients and selecting dietary preferences (e.g., vegetarian). Since Sophia is probably a typical representative of "Gen Z," influenced by social media trends, and she probably shares her food experiences, the

**Michael**
Age: 72, retired

A grandparent looking for healthy meal options for his grandchildren.

He is not familiar with technology. Usually cooks at home and orders food rarely.

**Anh**
Age: 26, lawyer in a big international company

A young professional who frequently orders lunch at work.

He doesn't like to experiment with food. He has a few favorite meal sets that he usually orders.

**Sophia**
Age: 19, student, part-time barista in a local coffee shop

She often eats on the go, ordering food delivery to her apartment, library, or even the park when studying with friends. She uses social media every day.

She's mindful of environmental impact and favors restaurants that use recyclable or biodegradable packaging. Sophia often looks for healthy or vegetarian options

**Fig. 5.7** Example personas for the FoodApp

reviews should assess the app's integration with social media platforms like Instagram or TikTok. Features enabling users to share orders, view popular dishes, or see restaurant reviews could increase engagement, especially in this group of users.

Reviewers who analyze requirements and designs with personas in mind can better assess whether the proposed features will meet real-world needs. This can lead to more robust validation and refinement of requirements.

**Perspective-based reading** (PBR) is a structured review technique that involves multiple reviewers evaluating a work product from different stakeholders' *perspectives,* such as end-users, testers, developers, business analysts, or managers. PBR operates under the premise that different information in the requirements is more or less important for the different uses of the document. Many different people use a requirements document to support tasks throughout the development life cycle. Conceivably, each person finds different aspects of the requirements important for accomplishing a particular task. Therefore, PBR provides a set of individual reviews, each from a particular requirements user's point of view, that collectively cover the document's relevant aspects [72].

By examining the work product from distinct perspectives, PBR aims to uncover a wide range of defects that may otherwise go unnoticed if reviewed from a single viewpoint. In PBR, each reviewer is assigned a specific perspective, often representing a stakeholder group or a particular role involved in the product lifecycle. Examples include:

- end-user perspective, focusing on usability, functionality, and user experience,
- developer perspective, focusing on technical and non-functional requirements, feasibility, and code structure,
- tester perspective, focusing on testability, completeness, and adherence to quality standards,
- business analyst perspective, focusing on the alignment of requirements with business needs and goals,
- marketing/sales perspective, focusing on how well the work product aligns with the needs and expectations of potential customers, its market positioning, and its appeal to target audiences.

Each reviewer checks the product against criteria tailored to their assigned perspective. This ensures that reviewers can focus on details critical to their perspective. For example, an end-user might look for user-friendly language and intuitive navigation, while a tester would focus on clarity and completeness of requirements for easy test case creation. By examining the work product from different angles, PBR enables the detection of issues that impact multiple stakeholders. For instance, issues affecting both the user experience and technical implementation are more likely to be identified early, reducing costly changes later in development.

PBR also requires that reviewers, based on the product under review (usually a requirement), develop a prototype or a high-level representation of the work products that a user would typically create. From the perspectives of designers, testers, and customers, these work products may include a high-level system design, a system test plan, and a detailed list of the specified functionalities, respectively. Reviewers can leverage these representations to create more detailed work products later on. Using these representations, they can also analyze how effectively the requirements can support the necessary tasks [72].

PBR is considered one of the most effective review techniques [73], although some research suggests that for PBR to be more effective, the individual perspectives must effectively target different classes of defects [74]. However, there are also some challenges when using this technique. PBR requires each reviewer to prepare thoroughly, focusing on specific stakeholder viewpoints, which can extend the review timeline. Preparing checklists or guidelines for each perspective is time-intensive, and the review process can become resource-heavy if multiple perspectives are covered. Although perspectives are distinct, there may be some overlap in the issues identified. For example, both testers and developers might identify issues related to ambiguous requirements. Managing this overlap and consolidating feedback to avoid redundancy can be challenging and time-consuming. It can sometimes be challenging to clearly define the boundaries of each perspective. If perspectives are too similar or not well differentiated, reviewers may overlook certain aspects or duplicate their efforts, reducing the technique's effectiveness. Ensuring reviewers have the necessary background and knowledge is essential but can be difficult in practice.

**Case Study**

Suppose we have to test some requirements for the FoodApp following the PBR technique. Suppose we have to follow the PBR procedure from the tester's perspective, described in [72] and shown below.

For each requirement, generate a test or set of test cases that let you ensure that a system implementation satisfies the requirement. Follow the procedure below to generate the test cases, using the questions provided to identify faults in the requirements.

**General questions**

Read each requirement once and record the number and page along with the required inputs.

- Q1. Does the requirement make sense based on what you know about the application or from what is specified in the general description?
- Q2. Do you have all the information necessary to identify the inputs to the requirement? Based on the general requirements and your domain knowledge, are these inputs correct for this requirement?
- Q3. Have any of the necessary inputs been omitted?
- Q4. Are any inputs specified that are not needed for this requirement?

- Q5. Is this requirement in the appropriate section of the document?

**Part a: Building equivalence partitions**

For each input, divide the input domain into equivalence partitions; all values in each set will cause the system to behave similarly. Determine the equivalence partitions for a particular input by understanding the conditions that affect the requirement's behavior. You may find it helpful to keep the following guidelines in mind when creating equivalence partitions:

- If an input condition specifies a range, at least one valid (the set of values in the range) and two invalid equivalence sets (the set of values less than the lowest extreme of the range and the set of values greater than the largest extreme) are defined.
- If an input condition specifies a set's member, at least one valid (the set itself) and one invalid equivalence set (the valid set's complement) are defined.
- If an input condition requires a specific value, then one valid (the set containing the value itself) and two invalid equivalence sets (the set of values less than and the set greater than the value) are defined.

Each equivalence partition should be recorded with the appropriate input.

- Qa1. Do you have enough information to construct the equivalence partitions for each input? Can you specify the boundaries of the equivalence partitions at an appropriate level of detail?
- Qa2. According to the information in the requirements, are the equivalence partitions constructed so that no value appears in more than one equivalence partition?
- Qa3. Do the requirements state that a particular value should appear in more than one equivalence partition? (Do they specify more than one type of response for the same value?) Do the requirements specify that a value should appear in the wrong equivalence partition?

**Part b: Testing equivalence partitions.**

For each equivalence partition, write test cases and record them with the associated equivalence partition. Select typical test cases and values at and near the boundaries of the partitions. For example, if the requirement expects input values in the 0–100 range, the test cases selected might be 0, 1, 56, 99, and 100. Finally, for each equivalence partition, record the expected resulting behavior (i.e., how do you expect the system to respond to the test cases you just made up?).

- Qb1. Do you have enough information to create test cases for each equivalence partition?

- Qb2. Are there other interpretations of this requirement that the implementer might make based on the description given? Will this affect the tests you generate?
- Qb3. Is there another requirement for which you would generate a similar test case but would get a contradictory result?
- Qb4. Can you be sure that the tests generated will yield the correct values in the correct units? Is the resulting behavior specified appropriately?

The requirements are as follows:

- **Requirement 1 (user registration)**. The user must provide their email address and password to create an account. The password must be at least 8 characters long and contain at least one number.
- **Requirement 2 (food selection)**. Users can select food items from a predefined list and add them to their cart. Each food item must have a name, description, and price.
- **Requirement 3 (checkout process)**. Users can proceed to checkout after selecting food items. They must enter their delivery address and payment information. The system will accept credit cards and PayPal as payment methods.
- **Requirement 4 (order confirmation)**. Once the payment is processed, the user will receive an order confirmation via email containing the order details.
- **Requirement 5 (order history)**. Users can view their order history. Each order must include the date, items ordered, and total cost.

Using the provided requirements, the test analyst applies the PBR technique by addressing the questions Q1-Q5, Qa1-Qa3, and Qb1-Qb4 to identify potential defects.

**Q1. Does the requirement make sense based on what you know about the application or from what is specified in the general description?** Analysis: Requirement 1 makes sense; however, the specification of a password without indicating whether it needs special characters may be insufficient. The food selection (Requirement 2) assumes a list exists, but does not describe how this list is populated or updated. The order history (Requirement 5) assumes a list of orders, but does not say anything about how many orders can be shown on a screen, or what particular order information should be shown.

**Q2. Do you have all the information necessary to identify the inputs to the requirement? Based on the general requirements and your domain knowledge, are these inputs correct for this requirement?** Analysis: Requirement 1 specifies the email and password as inputs, but it lacks detail on the email format validation. Requirement 2 does not specify how food items are categorized (e.g., by type or dietary restrictions).

**Q3. Have any of the necessary inputs been omitted?** Analysis: yes, Requirement 1 omits a requirement for email format validation. Requirement 3 does not specify that users must confirm their payment before processing.

**Q4. Are any inputs specified that are not needed for this requirement?** Analysis: no unnecessary inputs are specified. All inputs listed in the requirements seem relevant.

**Q5. Is this requirement in the appropriate section of the document?** Analysis: all requirements are in the appropriate sections related to user functionalities and processes. However, clarity could be improved by consolidating related requirements (e.g., user registration and checkout) under a common "User Account Management" section.

**Qa1. Do you have enough information to construct the equivalence partitions for each input? Can you specify the boundaries of the equivalence partitions at an appropriate level of detail?** Analysis: yes, for Requirement 1, equivalence partitions can be created based on valid and invalid password length (e.g., too short (1 to 7 characters) and valid length (8 or more characters)) and valid and invalid number of digits in the password (e.g., invalid (0 digits) and valid (1 or more digits)). However, Requirement 3 could create confusion because it combines different actions (entering address and payment info), which should probably be treated separately. Also, there are no clear partition boundaries for the address (e.g., is there a boundary on the street name length?).

**Qa2. According to the information in the requirements, are the equivalence partitions constructed so that no value appears in more than one equivalence partition?** Analysis: the equivalence partitions for Requirement 1 (valid/invalid password length, valid/invalid number of digits in the password) and Requirement 2 (available/unavailable food items) are disjoint. However, Requirement 3 lacks clarity on how payment information is validated, which may lead to overlapping partitions.

**Qa3. Do the requirements state that a particular value should appear in more than one equivalence partition? (Do they specify more than one type of response for the same value?) Do the requirements specify that a value should appear in the wrong equivalence partition?** Analysis: Requirement 3 is ambiguous. If a user enters payment information without confirmation, the requirement doesn't specify how this affects the equivalence partitions for the checkout process.

**Qb1. Do you have enough information to create test cases for each equivalence partition?** Analysis: for Requirements 1 and 2, sufficient information exists to create test cases. For Requirement 3, the ambiguity in confirming payment affects the test case clarity, making it difficult to generate comprehensive tests.

**Qb2. Are there other interpretations of this requirement that the implementer might make based on the description given? Will this affect the tests you generate?** Analysis: yes, an implementer might interpret Requirement 3 as allowing payment processing without confirming the address. This could affect test cases, particularly around payment authorization and error handling.

**Qb3. Is there another requirement for which you would generate a similar test case but would get a contradictory result?** Analysis: no, all five requirements seem independent (i.e., they describe different aspects of the system) and not contradictory.

**Qb4. Can you be sure that the tests generated will yield the correct values in the correct units? Is the resulting behavior specified appropriately?** Analysis: for Requirements 2 and 5, the specifications of food items and order history are clear. However, for Requirement 3, the expected behavior during the checkout process lacks clarity, leading to uncertainty in test outcomes.

## Sample Questions

### Question 5.2.2A

Below is shown an excerpt of a test basis for the food ordering app. All the requirements have high priority and are related to promo codes and applicable taxes.

1. The system shall calculate the total cost of the order, including promo code, item prices, customizations, delivery fees, and applicable taxes.
2. The promo code can be 5% or 10%. Only one promo code can be used per order.
3. The promo code shall be applied to each item after customization, and before delivery fees and applicable taxes.
4. Taxes shall be calculated for individual items based on their category and aggregated at the order level.
5. The system shall apply a promo code entered by the user to the total order amount after calculating taxes and delivery fees.

You perform a checklist-based review for these requirements, using a general checklist for the requirement quality.

Which item from the checklist is **NOT** fulfilled?

(a) Requirements do not contradict each other.
(b) Requirements are ranked based on their importance.
(c) Each requirement is feasible.
(d) Each requirement can be tested.

Select ONE answer.

**Question 5.2.2B**

A financial software company is preparing to release a new feature in its online banking application that enables customers to schedule recurring bill payments. Before deployment, the development team wants to ensure the feature meets the expectations and needs of various types of end-users, including individual customers, small business owners, and enterprise clients.

The company decides to evaluate the feature by having representatives act as specific user types: one team member simulates a busy individual user trying to manage personal bills, another assumes the role of a small business owner managing multiple accounts, and a third evaluates the feature from the perspective of an enterprise finance manager requiring detailed reporting and authorization workflows.

Each representative focuses on the functionality, usability, and relevance of the feature based on the needs and concerns of their assigned user type. This approach ensures that the review captures insights and potential usability issues unique to each user group.

Which review type is used in this scenario?

(a) Perspective-based reviewing.
(b) Checklist-based reviewing.
(c) Scenario-based reviewing.
(d) Role-based reviewing.

Select ONE answer.

## Exercise 13—Review Techniques

TA-5.2.2 (K3) Apply a review technique to a test basis to find defects

A bank has launched a new online banking system that allows customers to:

- log in securely,
- view account balances and transactions,
- transfer money between accounts,
- pay bills,
- apply for loans.

The system must be reviewed to ensure it meets usability, functionality, and security needs for different types of users. A role-based review will be conducted, with reviewers adopting the perspective of varying end-user personas.

Define 5 example roles that will be most useful when performing this review. For each of them, construct an appropriate persona (defining its background, goals, and concerns) and describe why this persona is important from the testing point of view.

## 5.3 Mitigating the Recurrence of Defects

### *5.3.1 Analyzing Test Results to Improve Defect Detection*

TA-5.3.1 (K4) Analyze test results to identify potential improvements to defect detection.

**Definitions**

**Test result**: The consequence/outcome of the execution of a test.

The primary responsibilities of a test analyst are to analyze the test basis, contribute to risk analysis, and design test cases. However, test analysts should have a much broader view of the test process. Since the quality of the process translates into the quality of the final product ([75, 76]), the test analyst should support the achievement of the highest possible quality in the test process.

One of the most obvious indicators of this quality is the DRE metric, i.e., defect removal efficiency (see Sect. 5.1.1), since it is directly related to the ability of preventing defects from escaping into production. In Chaps. 2, 3, and 4, the syllabus describes how defect detection effectiveness can be increased through risk analysis, execution of tests designed with appropriate test techniques, and performing non-functional testing. However, the ability to detect defects is not only about identifying what is failing but also about recognizing patterns in failures, spotting recurring issues, and pinpointing the areas in the software most vulnerable to defects. In this section, we will see how the test analyst can analyze the *test results* and *statistics on detected defects* to further improve the defect detection. The syllabus discusses five common approaches:

- predicted versus actual defect cluster analysis,
- defect detection percentage analysis,
- structural coverage analysis,
- test gap analysis,
- defect arrival pattern analysis.

**Predicted versus actual defect cluster analysis** helps test analysts refine their defect detection strategies by comparing expected defect distributions with observed outcomes. In the context of software testing, a defect cluster is a concentration of defects in certain areas of the application, typically due to the complexity, high change frequency, or particular risk factors associated with a certain part of the code. One of the test principles discussed by the Foundation Level syllabus ([11], Sect. 1.3) is called "Defects cluster together." The principle says that a small number of system components usually contain most of the defects discovered or are responsible for most of the operational failures [77]. This phenomenon is an illustration of the Pareto principle. Predicted defect clusters and actual defect clusters observed during testing or in operation are important inputs for risk-based testing.

By performing a defect cluster analysis, test analysts can validate assumptions, refine testing focus areas, and improve future predictions to detect defects more effectively. Predicted defect clusters are identified based on historical data, domain knowledge, and risk assessment. Test analysts often predict that certain modules or components will have a higher likelihood of defects based on:

- historical defect data—past projects, releases, and test runs reveal components that have traditionally shown a higher defect density,
- complexity analysis—components with high complexity (e.g., a large number of lines of code, high cyclomatic complexity, high values of information flow metrics) are more prone to defects due to the difficulty in understanding, testing, and maintaining them,
- change frequency and code authorship—areas of code that undergo frequent changes or are being implemented by many developers are more likely to have defects, especially if the changes are significant or introduce new functionality,
- business criticality and risk assessments—features that are critical to business operations may be flagged as high-risk areas where defects are costly, warranting more intensive testing.

Predicted defect clusters guide the test analyst in prioritizing high-risk areas for focused testing efforts, optimizing resources, and ensuring key areas are adequately covered. Actual defect clusters are determined after testing is completed by analyzing the distribution of defects found. By reviewing actual defect clusters, test analysts gain insights into which areas exhibited the most defects and whether these clusters align with initial predictions. In general, there are three possible outcomes of such an analysis, providing three types of information:

- Areas where predicted clusters matched actual clusters validate the test approach and reinforce confidence in predictive models.
- Areas that show unexpectedly high defect rates ("unexpected hotspots"), which were not anticipated as high-risk, suggest that the prediction models may need refinement and possibly indicate missed requirements or unanticipated complexity; according to the "defects cluster together" principle, these areas probably require even more thorough testing, because there are probably many more hidden defects.
- Predicted clusters that did not materialize as actual clusters ("misaligned predictions"), suggest that the prediction models may need refinement.

Let us assume that it is known from historical data that modules classified as high complexity had an average of 15 defects per 1000 lines of code, medium complexity modules had 11 defects per 1000 lines of code, and low complexity modules had 4 defects per 1000 lines of code. In the new FoodApp project, the team will implement six new modules for the application, which are:

- MenuServiceAPI—centralized service that exposes endpoints for accessing and managing menu data, including item descriptions, pricing, and availability status; classified as a medium complexity module.
- OrderEngine—the core component responsible for the end-to-end processing of orders, handling tasks like order validation, state management, and lifecycle events from creation to completion; classified as a high complexity module.
- UserManager—handles user profiles, preferences, and order history, enabling tailored recommendations and personalized menu configurations based on user-specific data; classified as a medium complexity module.
- CartController—manages the shopping cart operations, such as item additions, modifications, and pre-checkout validations; integrates with pricing and discount modules for accurate cart totals; classified as a low complexity module.
- RestaurantIntegrationHub—middleware layer that facilitates seamless communication between the application and the restaurant's kitchen or POS system, ensuring real-time updates and order confirmations; classified as a low complexity module.
- LogisticsDispatcher—oversees delivery logistics, including task assignment for delivery drivers, route optimization, and ETA (Estimated Time of Arrival) calculations, ensuring efficient and timely order fulfillment; classified as a high complexity module.

The test analyst may perform the analysis shown in Table 5.8 (except the last column). Based on complexity classification and historical data, the test analyst estimates the number of defects for each module. For example, MenuServiceAPI complexity is classified as medium. From historical data, we know that medium complexity modules have, on average, 11 defects per KLOC (i.e., 1000 lines of code). The developers estimated that this module will have ca. 10 KLOC. This means that the estimated number of defects for MenuServiceAPI is $11 * 10 = 110$. Instead of LOC estimation, the team may use the so-called Function Points metric, which is also a size complexity measure, but it is independent of the programming language and can be estimated based on architectural design.

The analysis reveals that LogisticsDispatcher and OrderEngine are the most error-prone components, so they should be tested more thoroughly. Suppose now that the actual number of defects for the new six modules is presented in the last column of Table CCC. These two modules were indeed the most error-prone, but when we compare the actual number of defects with estimates, we may observe some discrepancies. For example, for OrderEngine the actual number of defects was much higher, and for LogisticsDispatcher—much lower than estimated. Actual numbers seem to align with estimates in the case of RestaurantIntegrationHub, and probably also for CartController and MenuServiceAPI. For UserManager, it seems we overestimated

**Table 5.8** Predicting defect clusters based on historical data and actual defect clusters

| Module | Complexity | Estimated defects/ KLOC | Estimated KLOC | Estimated number of defects | Actual number of defects |
|---|---|---|---|---|---|
| MenuServiceAPI | Medium | 11 | 10 | 110 | 99 |
| OrderEngine | High | 15 | 18 | 270 | 318 |
| UserManager | Medium | 11 | 12 | 132 | 108 |
| CartController | Low | 4 | 4, 5 | 18 | 27 |
| RestaurantIntegrationHub | Low | 4 | 6 | 24 | 26 |
| LogisticsDispatcher | High | 15 | 40 | 600 | 463 |

the number of defects. The test analyst may update their models to be more accurate with predictions in the next project or iteration.

### Measuring the Significance of the Difference Between the Predicted and Actual Number of Defects

In the above example, the analyzed differences between the actual and predicted number of defects were interpreted at a guess. However, there are more formal, statistical methods to determine whether the observed differences are actually significant or due to some random factors. In our case, the appropriate statistical test would be the Poisson test since the Poisson distribution usually models well the "rare events," such as defects in code. We assume that defects appear in a code with a Poisson distribution $P(X = k; \lambda) = \frac{\lambda^k e^{-\lambda}}{k!}$. This distribution is parameterized by a single parameter, λ, representing the average number of observed events (in our case, an event is a defect in a component), and X is a random variable representing the number of defects in a component. The value $P(X = k; \lambda)$ is the probability that there will be exactly $k$ defects in a component. The test analyst estimates λ (in our case, λ represents the estimated number of defects in a component). From the actual data (i.e., test results), we read $\lambda_1$, the actual, empirical value of λ (i.e., the actual number of defects in this module). The Poisson statistical test verifies, at a given significance level α (which is usually set to 0.05), whether the null hypothesis can be rejected. In our case, the null hypothesis says that $\lambda = \lambda_1$, i.e., the actual number of defects is aligned with the estimated value. Figure 5.8 shows a simple spreadsheet that allows the test analyst to perform such a test. The orange fields are the input fields: estimated number of defects λ, actual number of defects $\lambda_1$, and significance level $\alpha$.

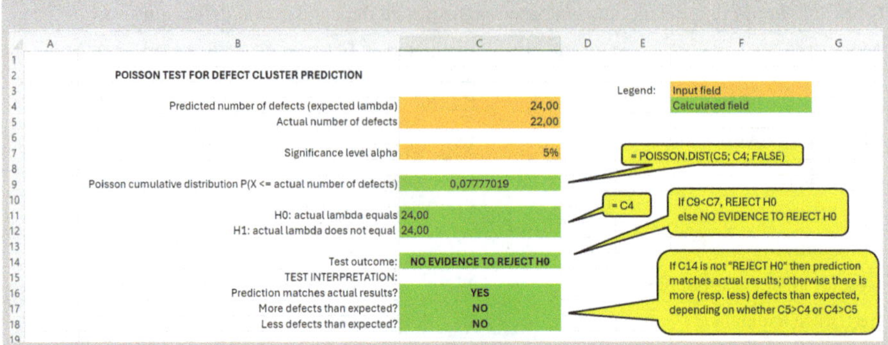


**Fig. 5.8** Excel sheet for Poisson statistical test for defect cluster prediction

The spreadsheet uses the POISSON.DIST($\lambda_1$; $\lambda$; FALSE) Excel function, which calculates the probability $p$ that exactly $\lambda_1$ events (i.e., defects) will occur, when their occurrence is governed by the Poisson distribution parameterized by $\lambda$. This value is compared with the significance level $\alpha$. If $p < \alpha$, the null hypothesis is rejected because it is very unlikely that the observed difference is due to random factors only. If $p \geq \alpha$, there is no evidence for rejecting the null hypothesis—this can be interpreted as our prediction matched the actual observed results. Suppose we estimate that there will be 24 defects.

Figures 5.8 and 5.9 show three different outcomes of the analysis—when the actual number of observed defects equals 22, 18, and 29. In the first case (Fig. 5.8), we have no evidence to reject the null hypothesis. In the second and third (Fig. 5.9), we reject the null hypothesis. In the second case, we can say that we observed significantly fewer defects than we expected. In the third case, we observed significantly more defects than we expected.

**POISSON TEST FOR DEFECT CLUSTER PREDICTION**

| | | |
|---|---|---|
| Predicted number of defects (expected lambda) | 24,00 | 24,00 |
| Actual number of defects | 18,00 | 29,00 |
| Significance level alpha | 5% | 5% |
| Poisson cumulative distribution P(X <= actual number of defects) | 0,041152267 | 0,045343979 |
| H0: actual lambda equals | 24,00 | 24,00 |
| H1: actual lambda does not equal | 24,00 | 24,00 |
| Test outcome: | REJECT H0 | REJECT H0 |
| TEST INTERPRETATION: | | |
| Prediction matches actual results? | NO | NO |
| More defects than expected? | NO | YES |
| Less defects than expected? | YES | NO |

**Fig. 5.9** Two other possible results for the Poisson test

**Defect detection percentage (DDP) analysis** allows test analysts to evaluate how effectively defects are identified in the various phases of the test process. The analysis is based on the defect detection percentage metric. The DDP is the number of defects found by a test level, divided by the number of defects found by that test level and any other means afterward. Of course, the denominator of this metric includes only those defects that were detectable during the phase for which the DDP is calculated.

In the context of analyzing test results to improve defect detection, DDP provides insight into the efficiency of test levels or test phases in detecting defects. Improving DDP is central to strengthening software quality, as it highlights the capability of the test process to catch defects before they escape to subsequent phases. Thus, the DDP gives insight into the "strength" of each test level or test phase in terms of the number of defects it detects relative to the number of total defects it could detect.

Figure 5.10 presents schematically the defect flow model, which will be the basis for the precise definition of the DDP metric. Let us assume that testing is done in phases (iterations, test runs, test levels, etc.) and consider the $N$-th phase in order. In this phase, two types of detectable defects can be distinguished. The first type is defects that escaped into phase $N$ from the previous phase, $N-1$. Let us denote their number by $E(N-1)$. The second type is defects that were introduced only in the $N$th phase. Let us denote their number by $I(N)$. We can also classify all these defects according to whether they were detected in the $N$th phase. Here, too, we have two categories: defects that were detected in phase $N$ (let us denote them by $D(N)$), and those that escaped to the next phase $(N+1)$—let's denote them by $E(N)$.

Since both of these classifications apply to the same defects, a kind of "Kirchhoff's law" occurs here that preserves the amount of defect "flow" through the $N$th phase. This law states that the sum $E(N-1)+I(N)$ of defects entering the $N$th phase must equal the sum $E(N)+D(N)$ of defects leaving the phase. Assume there are $K$ phases in total. Hence, the following equation holds:

$$E(N-1)+I(N)=D(N)+E(N), N=1,\ldots,K,$$

where $E(0)=0$. The value $E(K)$ can be interpreted as defects that escaped to operation phase (after the release). The equation allows us to define the DDP:

**Fig. 5.10** Defect flow model

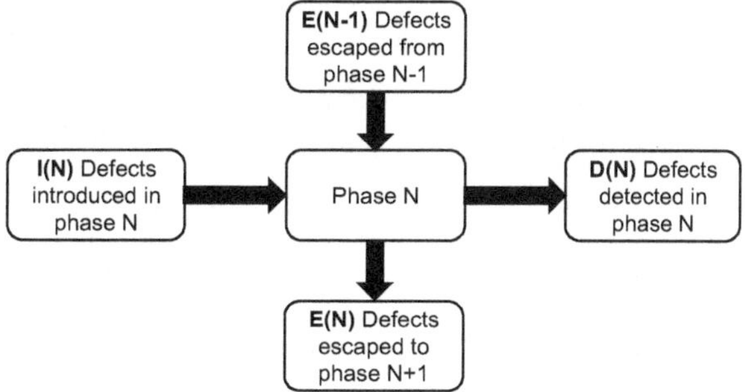

**Table 5.9** Data on defect detection at different test levels

| | The number of defects that... | | | |
|---|---|---|---|---|
| Phase | Escaped from the previous phase $E(N-1)$ | Were introduced in this phase $I(N)$ | Were detected in this phase $D(N)$ | Escaped to the next phase $E(N)$ |
| CT | – | 20 | 10 | 10 |
| CIT | 10 | 45 | 15 | 40 |
| ST | 40 | 70 | 30 | 80 |
| SIT | 80 | 20 | 50 | 50 |
| AT | 50 | 0 | 30 | 20 |

*CT* component testing, *CIT* component integration testing, *ST* system testing, *SIT* system integration testing, *AT* acceptance testing

$$DDP(N) = D(N)/(D(N) + E(N)) = D(N)/(E(N-1) + I(N)).$$

Notice that the model assumes that in the $N$th phase we cannot detect defects introduced after this phase (i.e., it does not take into account the values $I(x)$ for $x > N$).[2]

To be able to count the DDP for each phase, the test analyst must have information on the introduced phase for each detected defect. In general, the problem of determining when a defect was introduced is a non-trivial issue. If the project uses tools such as a code versioning system, and defects—along with information about their repair—are properly logged in defect management systems, determining when a defect was introduced is easier. There are algorithms that do it. For example, the SZZ algorithm [78] detects a bug-introducing change by identifying which code changes (commits) introduced defects that were later fixed. The SZZ algorithm is also widely used in research and industry for defect prediction and software maintenance analysis.

Now, let us see how the test analyst can improve defect detection by using the DDP metric. Suppose the test analyst gathered data on defect detection at several test levels in their organization. The results are presented in Table 5.9.

Let us calculate the DDP for each phase.

$DDP(CT) = \frac{10}{20} = 50\%$, because out of 20 defects that could be detected in CT, only 10 were actually detected, and 10 other defects escaped to CIT.

$DDP(CIT) = \frac{15}{55} \approx 27\%$, because out of $10 + 45 = 55$ defects that could be detected in CIT, only 15 were detected, and 40 other defects escaped to ST.

$DDP(ST) = \frac{30}{110} \approx 27\%$, because out of $40 + 70 = 110$ defects that could be detected in ST, only 30 were detected, and 80 other defects escaped to SIT.

$DDP(SIT) = \frac{50}{100} = 50\%$, because out of $80 + 20 = 100$ defects that could be detected in SIT, only 50 were detected, and 50 other defects escaped to AT.

[2] An example of a metric that takes this into account is Dunn metric [86].

$DDP(AT) = \frac{30}{50} = 60\%$, because out of 50 defects that could be detected in AT, only 30 were detected, and 20 remaining defects escaped to production.

Notice that the defect removal efficiency (DRE) is $\frac{135}{155} \approx 87\%$, so it seems the overall test process effectively detects defects before they escape to production. However, the analysis of the DDP metric gives us a more detailed insight into the process, allowing the test analyst to assess the efficiency of each test level. The analysis shows that the efficiency of component integration testing and system testing is low (ca. 27%).

The test analyst, perhaps in consultation with the technical test analyst, may suggest that some changes be made to these two test levels so as to increase their defect detection ability. For example, in the course of analysis, it may become apparent that developers are not using any structured strategies for component integration testing. The test analyst may suggest using a systematic top-down or bottom-up strategy. They may also review the architecture to check the quality of documentation describing API functions and suggest the use of best practices when documenting API functions, as well as suggest specific API testing strategies. For the system test level, the test analyst may suggest the use of specific black box techniques to increase coverage and test efficiency in a meaningful way.

Let us assume that the changes proposed by the test analyst will increase the DDP of the CIT and ST phases from 27 to 50%, with the effectiveness of the other test levels unchanged. The test analyst (or management) can simulate how such a change will affect the DRE value. This simulation is presented in Table 5.10. Improved phases are denoted in bold.

Assuming that we are able to increase DDP for CIT and ST from 27 to 50%, the simulation shows that the number of field defects will decrease from 20 to 14, which means that DRE will increase from 87% to $\frac{141}{155} \approx 91\%$. This increases the defect detection by 4%. The analysis could also be enriched with economic data. Knowing the cost of fixing a field defect and the cost of making the changes proposed by the test analyst, one can estimate whether the changes are worth it at all.

As defects go through the lifecycle, their severity (impact on the system) and priority (how soon they need to be fixed) are better understood. Using this information allows for a more accurate analysis of the DDP metric. For example, if a significant

**Table 5.10** Simulation of the test process efficiency after the changes proposed by the test analysts

| | The number of defects that... | | | |
|---|---|---|---|---|
| Phase (DDP) | Escaped from the previous phase $E(N-1)$ | Were introduced in this phase $I(N)$ | Were detected in this phase $D(N)$ | Escaped to the next phase $E(N)$ |
| CT (50%) | – | 20 | 10 | 10 |
| **CIT (50%)** | 10 | 45 | 28 | 27 |
| **ST (50%)** | 27 | 70 | 48 | 49 |
| SIT (50%) | 49 | 20 | 34 | 35 |
| AT (60%) | 35 | 0 | 21 | 14 |

```
function FinalPrice(price, adThreshold, adRate, pcRate)
    if (pcRate >= adRate)
        return price * pcRate
    else
        if (price >= adThreshold)
            return price * adRate
        else
            return price
```

**Fig. 5.11** Code for discount calculation

portion of defects are high severity, even for the phase for which the value of DDP is high, it may suggest that not all critical failures are detected in this phase. This can prompt teams to strengthen design validation efforts (e.g., through architectural reviews or prototyping), enhance test planning, ensure critical system functionality is prioritized and thoroughly tested early in the development process, and implement risk-based testing to focus on the most critical and vulnerable areas of the system, preventing high-impact defects from reaching production.

**Structural coverage analysis** helps test analysts improve defect detection by assessing the degree to which the code is executed during testing. By measuring how thoroughly the code structure has been tested, structural coverage analysis provides insight into untested areas, allowing test analysts to design test cases covering these areas.

Structural coverage analysis, often called code coverage analysis, focuses on evaluating how much of the software's internal structure is exercised by the tests. Unlike functional testing, which assesses if the software meets specified requirements, structural coverage analysis evaluates the completeness of testing from a code execution perspective. This is particularly useful in white-box testing, where the internal code structure is known, and allows testers to identify parts of the code that have not been adequately tested.

Structural coverage analysis can use different types of coverage metrics, reflecting different types of coverage measured. The two most popular and used in practice coverage types include statement coverage and branch coverage. Statement coverage measures the proportion of executable lines of code that were actually exercised by tests. Branch coverage measures the proportion of control flow transitions between code instructions.

Let us consider an example of a function that calculates the final price for an order in the FoodApp. There are two sources of price discount: automatic discount (`adRate`), which is applied when the total amount (`price`) exceeds a given threshold (adThreshold), and a promo code discount (pcRate), which is applied when a user enters a valid promo code that gives this discount. Promotions cannot be combined. The final price is one of the two discounted values that is more favorable to the customer. The code for calculating the final price is implemented as shown in Fig. 5.11.

The source code has 5 executable lines numbered as 1–5. Suppose the testers executed the following test cases:

TC1:

- Input: price = 100 EUR, adThreshold = 80 EUR, adRate = 0.15, pcRate = 0.20
- Expected behavior: 15% automatic discount (20 EUR) applicable, but 20% promo code discount (20 EUR) is more favorable
- Expected output: 80 EUR

TC2:

- Input: price = 150 EUR, adThreshold = 100 EUR, adRate = 0.10, pcRate = 0.02
- Expected behavior: 10% automatic discount (15 EUR) applicable, and better than 2% promo code discount (3 EUR)
- Expected output: 135 EUR.

For both TC1 and TC2, the actual results match the expected results. After test execution, the component testing framework can return the coverage results. Structural coverage tools provide real-time feedback on coverage levels, which can be invaluable in an agile or continuous integration environment. This enables test analysts to monitor coverage continuously and quickly address gaps as they develop, rather than waiting until the end of a testing cycle to perform coverage analysis. This real-time feedback loop significantly enhances defect detection efficiency.

The results for statement coverage are shown in Fig. 5.12. The left part is the result of executing TC1, the right part is the result of executing TC2. The highlighted lines are the ones that were exercised during the test execution.

TC1 achieved 2/5 = 40% statement coverage, because it covered two out of five executable statements (1 and 2). TC2 achieved 3/5 = 60% statement coverage, because it covered three out of five executable statements (1, 3, and 4). Both test cases executed four out of five executable statements (1, 2, 3, and 4), so the test suite composed of TC1 and TC2 achieved 4/5 = 80% statement coverage. The test analyst may now notice that line 5 was not covered. This part of the code handles a situation in which an automatic discount is not applied, and the promo code should be applied. The test analyst may design a new test case, TC3, that covers this scenario:

TC3:

```
1.  if (pcRate >= adRate)
2.      return price * pcRate
    else
3.      if (price >= adThreshold)
4.          return price * adRate
        else
5.          return price
```

```
1.  if (pcRate >= adRate)
2.      return price * pcRate
    else
3.      if (price >= adThreshold)
4.          return price * adRate
        else
5.          return price
```

**Fig. 5.12** Coverage analysis after test execution

- Input: price = 100 EUR, adThreshold = 150 EUR, adRate = 0.15, pcRate = 0.10
- Expected behavior: 15% automatic discount (15 EUR) not applicable, but 10% promo code applicable (10 EUR)
- Expected output: 90 EUR.

This test case covers statements 1, 3, and 5, so TC1, TC2, and TC3 together achieve full, 100% statement coverage. After executing the TC3, the actual result is 100 EUR, which is a failure. The test analyst may raise this issue, and in the course of the debugging process, a defect is found in the calculations in line 5. Line 5 should be:

```
return price * pcRate
```

because the promo code discount should be applicable even if the automated discount is not applicable. The defect is probably an effect of the developer's assumption that in line 5 no discount should be applied, since the price does not exceed the automated discount threshold.

Systematic analysis of coverage helps test analysts identify and eliminate gaps in testing. This leads to improved defect detection in the following ways:

- identifying untested code, which is often a hidden source of defects, as shown in the example above; structural coverage analysis highlights these code sections, enabling test analysts to create additional tests that target the untested statements, logic, or paths in code, increasing the likelihood of finding defects that may not be triggered by existing tests,
- ensuring complex code is tested thoroughly enough, since certain code sections, especially those with complex logic, control flow, or algorithmic structure, are more prone to defects,
- detecting unreachable code, i.e., code that is never executed under any tested conditions, which might be a defect itself or suggest logical errors in the code.

While functional testing focuses on validating expected behavior based on requirements, structural coverage adds depth by ensuring that the underlying code is exhaustively tested. This combination allows test analysts to catch defects that may not be apparent from the user-facing functionality alone but could still affect the software quality.

While structural coverage analysis offers many benefits for defect detection, it is not without challenges. First, high coverage does not guarantee high test effectiveness. Achieving 100% coverage does not guarantee a defect-free product. It only guarantees that the tester has used the coverage technique completely, and the technique is no longer able to suggest new structural elements of the code to cover. Some defects might only be detectable under specific data conditions that are not captured by coverage metrics alone. It is also important to remember that neither developers nor testers should be judged by the code coverage achieved. This is because it is very easy for programmers to tamper with the results, artificially inflating the coverage by, for example, adding many instructions in the code that have no meaning, but will always be covered by the tests. For example, suppose the developers run only TC1

```
function FinalPrice(price, adThreshold, adRate, pcRate)
1.    price = price
2.    price = price
3.    price = price
4.    price = price
5.    price = price
...
95.   price = price
96.   if (pcRate >= adRate)
97.       return price * pcRate
      else
98.       if (price >= adThreshold)
99.           return price * adRate
          else
100.          return price
```

**Fig. 5.13** Tampering with the statement coverage

for the code from Fig. 5.11. TC1 achieves only 40% statement coverage. However, when the developer modifies the code as in Fig. 5.13, adding 95 nonsense instructions at the beginning, the coverage will increase from 40 to 97%, since TC1 will exercise 97 out of 100 executable statements.

The second challenge with structural code coverage is that achieving higher levels of structural coverage can be resource-intensive, requiring more tests and computational resources. Test analysts must balance coverage goals with the project's practical constraints. This is also closely related to the risk-based approach, since not all code requires the same level of coverage. Test analysts should prioritize high-risk, complex, or critical areas for coverage and use a risk-based approach to focus efforts on critical or more error-prone code.

The test analyst should also remember that structural coverage metrics should always be used as a guide, not an absolute. They should aim to use coverage as a directional guide for improving tests rather than a strict metric that guarantees quality.

**Test gap analysis** assesses the extent to which tests have exercised recent code changes. This allows the test analyst to focus additional test effort in areas that are especially error-prone (i.e., new changes that have not been tested at all) instead of targeting all areas that have low coverage (e.g., code that has not changed in a long time and has been tested for previous releases).

Non-tested, modified code is much more fault-prone than code that was executed by tests. Test gap analysis identifies such test gaps (i.e., added or modified, but in untested methods) by combining information from static and dynamic analysis [79]. A static analysis uses the data from the version control system to compare the current state of the source code to that of the previous release in order to determine new and changed code areas. The analysis can also differentiate between varying kinds of changes. For example, refactoring, which does not lead to a modification of the behavior of the source code, cannot cause errors and can thus be filtered out. This brings the test analyst's attention to those changes that lead to a change in the behavior of the system. In addition, coverage is determined with the help of dynamic analysis. Both automated and manually executed test cases should be taken into account [80].

Figure 5.14 shows how the test gap analysis is conducted. The rectangles (a), (b), and (c) represent the so-called component treemap. Each box represents one component (e.g., a method). The box size is proportional to the component size (e.g., represented by the number of lines of code). Figure 5.14a shows changes within the system under test since the previous release. This data comes from the version control system. Gray boxes represent unchanged components (or components with changes that should not introduce defects, e.g., due to refactoring). Dashed boxes represent components that were changed and are potentially error-prone. Dotted boxes represent new components, which are error-prone by definition. Figure 5.14b overlays the test data on the component treemap. Dark boxes represent components that are tested, white boxes—components that are untested. This data comes from the test management system.

Finally, Fig. 5.14c represents the "gaps" in testing by combining data from Fig. 5.14a, b. Gray boxes represent unchanged components. They are ruled out from the analysis, since nothing has changed in them, so they do not require additional testing. Light-colored, dashed rectangles represent components that are changed, but also tested. Since they are already tested, they do not require further testing.

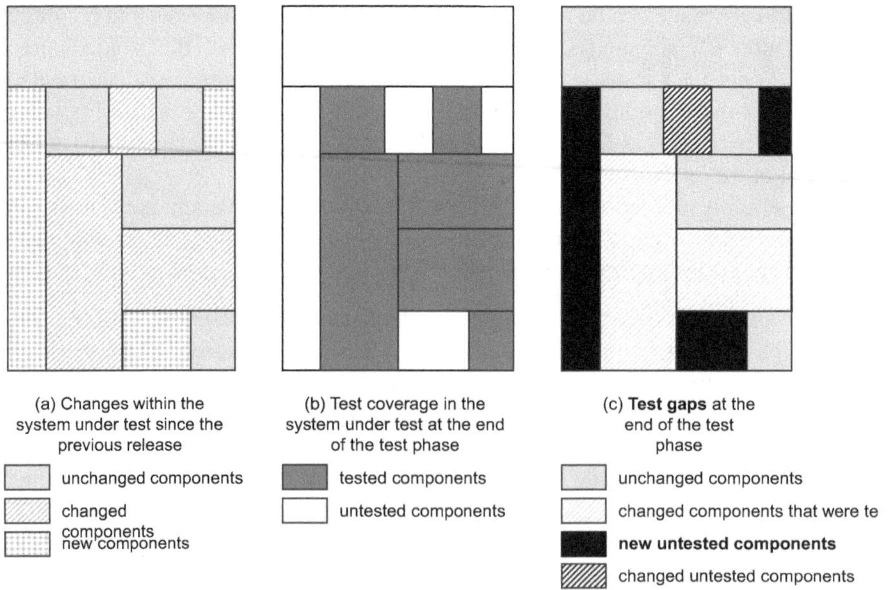


**Fig. 5.14** Test gap analysis

However, the analysis may require that, if, for example, the changes are significant, additional testing is needed. The change significance can be measured using the coverage metrics and churn metrics (e.g., number of lines added, removed, and modified). The most important components are represented by black and dark-colored dashed boxes. These are new and changed components that were not tested. These components represent gaps in testing. These components require testing, since they are error-prone and were not previously tested.

Test gap analysis is supported by tools, such as Teamscale, which can differentiate between different coverage sources, e.g., unit test coverage from a continuous integration pipeline and coverage from manual tests. Test gaps can be identified on a ticket basis [79], as well, using defect tracking tools such as Jira, Mantis, or Bugzilla. Issues with code changes can be linked to test execution information. This helps test analysts to see whether the code changes for a specific ticket (i.e., defect report) have been tested.

Test gap analysis supported by tools allows test analysts to get quick feedback on untested areas after each change in the code repository. This allows test analysts to react quickly and detect defects early, contributing to the increase of Phase Containment Effectiveness.

**Defect arrival pattern analysis** allows test analysts to gain insights into the timing, frequency, and severity of defects. This analysis supports defect detection in several ways:

- Identifying high-risk periods. Defect arrival patterns often show spikes during specific stages, such as during integration testing, when new features are merged, or as release deadlines approach. These spikes can indicate high-risk periods when defects are more likely to appear. Test analysts can allocate additional resources or focus test efforts during these high-risk periods to increase defect detection and mitigate risks better.
- Identifying trends in defect clustering. Analyzing where and how fast defects tend to cluster helps to identify which modules or features are most defect-prone. This analysis can be an input to the "predicted versus actual defect cluster analysis" described above. By focusing more testing on defect-prone areas, test analysts can increase the likelihood of uncovering critical defects, particularly in complex or unstable components of the system under test.
- Identifying test case weaknesses. Certain defect patterns may reveal weaknesses in test case coverage, indicating that some scenarios are consistently missing or under-tested. An example could be a pattern that shows a constant, low number of defect arrivals, while the test analyst expects this trend to be increasing. With this insight, test analysts can try to improve the existing test cases or add new ones, so that the actual pattern matches the expected one.
- Predicting future defect patterns. Historical defect arrival data allows test analysts to make educated predictions about defect patterns in future iterations, test levels, or releases. This allows test teams to proactively prepare, targeting high-risk areas early on and potentially identifying defects before they become critical issues.

One of the most well-known defect arrival patterns is described by the Rayleigh model. This model is based on the Rayleigh probability distribution. It has a single peak and is skewed to the right, showing that the expected number of defects found first increases in time, and after reaching its maximum value, drops slowly toward zero. Formally, the probability density function of the Rayleigh distribution is

$$f(x;\sigma) = \frac{x}{\sigma^2} e^{-x^2/(2\sigma^2)}, x \geq 0$$

where σ is the scale parameter of the distribution.

**Rayleigh Distribution for Different Parameters**

Five examples of the Rayleigh distribution for different parameters $\sigma$ are shown in Fig. 5.15.

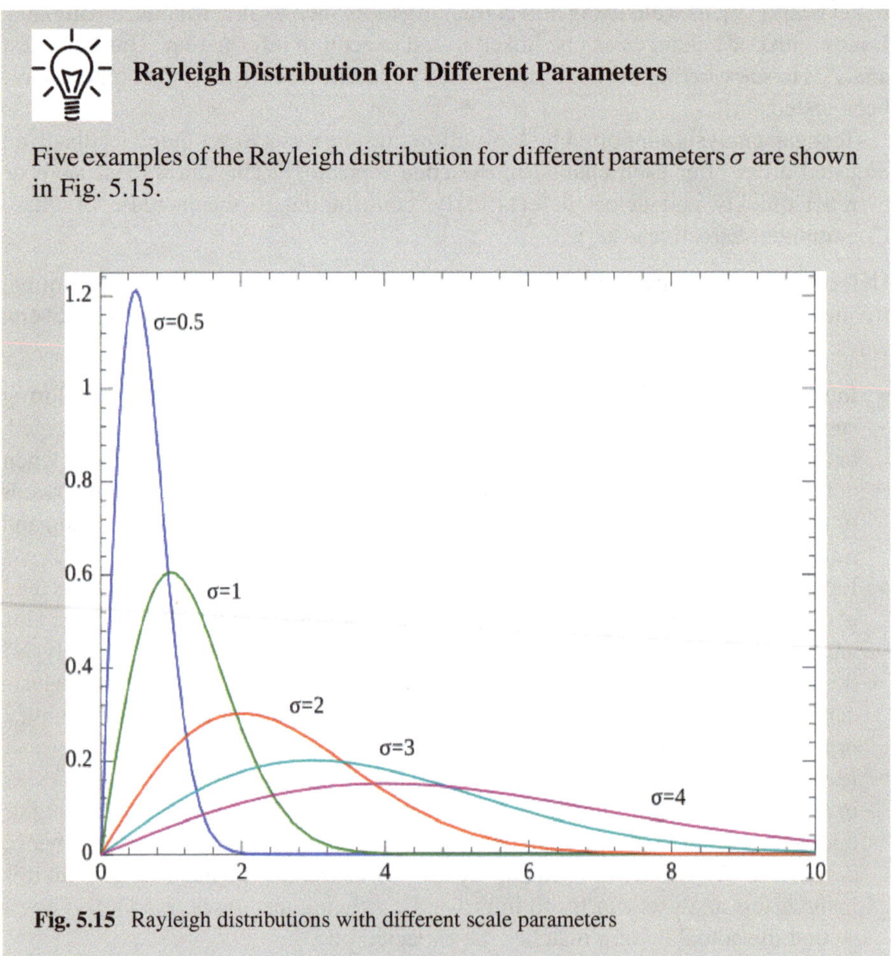


**Fig. 5.15** Rayleigh distributions with different scale parameters

The Rayleigh model has been used for many years in various branches of engineering. In software quality engineering, the Rayleigh distribution represents the number (or frequency) of defects over time. In real-world applications, the right side

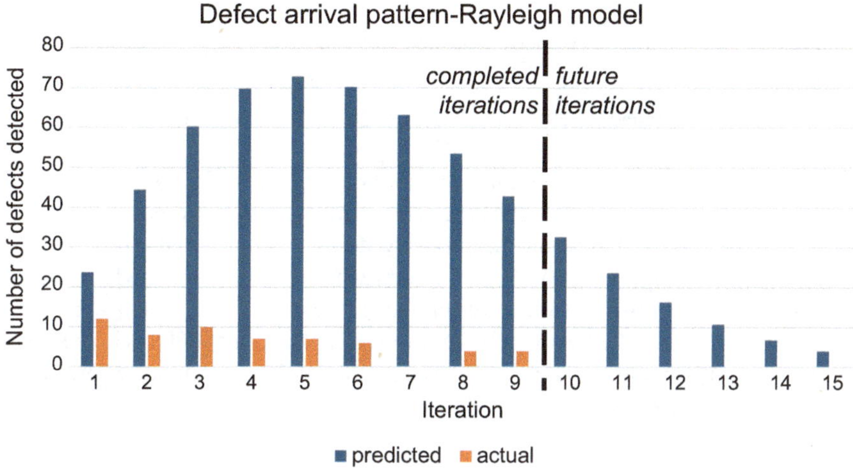


**Fig. 5.16** Comparing the expected and actual defect arrival patterns

of the equation is multiplied by $K$, a number representing the total number of defects (or total defect frequency). This allows us to model the number of defects occurring in consecutive project phases. It has been experimentally proven many times that the pattern of defect appearance in IT projects follows the pattern described by the Rayleigh curve [81].

The Rayleigh distribution has a property that allows for the quick prediction of the total number of defects. If the Rayleigh curve fitted to the existing data reaches a maximum for any of the data points, the total number of defects detected up to that point is approximately 40% of the total number of defects. Knowing this value, you can calculate the total number of defects in the product.

Suppose the test analyst assumes (e.g., by analyzing historical data) that the defect arrival pattern follows a Rayleigh distribution and that the test analyst has estimated the total number of defects. Based on this data, the test analyst can build the model, as shown in Fig. 5.16. Then, the test analyst observes in the first nine iterations, the actual number of defects found. It is clear from the figure that the defect arrival pattern is "flat" and the number of defects found is much smaller than the expected values from the model. This may suggest that the tests are weak and unable to detect most of the defects.

**EXTRA** **Software Defect Prediction with the Rayleigh Model**

Defect arrival patterns can be used to predict the total number of defects, as well as the defect arrival pattern in the future. Assume that the test analyst collected the data on the number of defects found in the first nine iterations of the project, shown in Table 5.11.

**Table 5.11** Number of defects found in the first nine iterations

| Iteration | 1 | 2 | 3 | 4 | 5 | 6 | 7 | 8 | 9 |
|---|---|---|---|---|---|---|---|---|---|
| Number of defects found | 20 | 41 | 48 | 52 | 62 | 59 | 52 | 44 | 33 |

The test analyst wants to estimate the number of defects found in the subsequent iterations 10–15, as well as the total number of defects in the product. The first method is based on the property described earlier: the number of defects detected up to the point when the maximum value is reached accounts for approximately 40% of the total number of defects. Since in our example the maximum is reached in the fifth iteration (62), the sum of defects in the first five iterations is approximately 40% of the total number of defects. Therefore, the total number $K$ of defects equals

$$K = \frac{1}{0.4} \cdot (20 + 41 + 48 + 52 + 62) = \frac{223}{0.4} \approx 558.$$

The second method is more accurate and is based on mathematical modeling. The test analyst can use a simple script written in the R Statistical Package. The script will fit nonlinear functions to data by using the R function called `nls`. Two parameters will be fit: $K$, the total number of defects, and $\sigma$, the scale parameter. The script looks as follows.

```
1> obs <- data.frame(t=c(1:9), d=c(20,41,48,52,62,59,52,44,33))
2> pred <- data.frame(t=c(10:15), d=NA)
3> points <- rbind(obs, pred)
4> model <- nls(d ~ K*2*(t/sigma^2)*exp(-(t/sigma)^2),
data=points[1:9,], start=list(K=450, sigma=8))
5> summary(model)

Formula: d ~ K * 2 * (t/sigma^2) * exp(-(t/sigma)^2)

Parameters:
      Estimate   Std. Error   t value Pr(>|t|)
K   489.7381    13.2938     36.84 2.82e-09 ***
sigma 7.0245      0.1687    41.65 1.20e-09 ***
---
Signif. codes: 0 '***' 0.001 '**' 0.01 '*' 0.05 '.' 0.1 ' ' 1

Residual standard error: 2.977 on 7 degrees of freedom

Number of iterations to convergence: 4
Achieved convergence tolerance: 3.137e-06
```

In line 1, we define the data frame obs consisting of two columns named t and d, denoting the consecutive iterations and the number of defects found in each iteration. In line 2 we define an analogous dataframe `pred` for weeks 10–15, for which we want to make a prediction of the number of defects detected. For now, we do not know these values, so we fill the data frame with the NA (not available) values. In line 3 we define a data frame `points`, which glues `obs` and `pred` into one dataset.

Line 4 is crucial for the whole analysis. It uses the `nls` function to fit the Rayleigh model parameters to the observed data. Its first parameter:

```
d ~ K*2*(t/sigma^2)*exp(-(t/sigma)^2)
```

is the formula we want to fit to the data. This is the Rayleigh model multiplied by the constant $K$. There are two parameters that will be fit to the data, $K$ and $\sigma$. The second parameter is the observed data, which will be used by the `nls` function. The third parameter gives the starting values for $K$ and $\sigma$. The test analyst can make an educated guess to provide these parameters. These are only approximations, but the closer they are to the true values, the faster the method will converge and complete the calculations.

In line 5 we print out the information about the built model. We see that the estimated values of the parameters are $K \approx 490$ and $\sigma \approx 7$. This means that the predicted total number of defects in the product is ca. 490. If we want to have a prediction divided into iterations of 10–15, we simply calculate the values of the Rayleigh function parameterized with the fit parameters $K$ and $\sigma$, using the `predict` function.

```
6> points$predVal <- predict(model, newdata=points)
7> points
    t  d  predVal
1   1 20 19.451786
2   2 41 36.608784
3   3 48 49.621468
4   4 52 57.411464
5   5 62 59.799303
6   6 59 57.419853
7   7 52 51.474341
8   8 44 43.407212
9   9 33 34.601170
10 10 NA 26.159044
11 11 NA 18.801191
12 12 NA 12.868915
13 13 NA  8.399807
14 14 NA  5.233792
15 15 NA  3.115583
```

We added a new column, `predVal`, to our data frame. Its values represent the number of defects predicted by the model. We see that for iterations 1–9, the predicted values fit well with the observed data. For iterations 10–15, the values are the predictions. We can also plot the data using the following R commands:

```
8> points$predVal <- predict(model, newdata=points)
9> lines(points$t, points$predVal, type="o", pch=1)
```

which results in the graph shown in Fig. 5.17. Black points represent the observed data, white circles—the values predicted by the model.

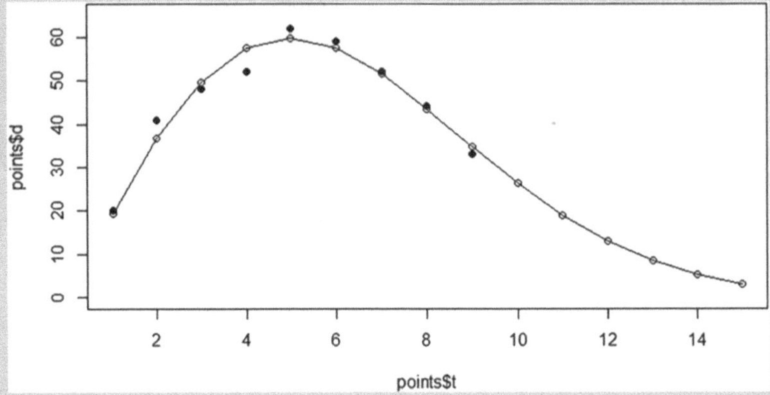


**Fig. 5.17** Graphical representation of predictions by the Rayleigh model

Such defect prediction gives the test analyst several important information, for example:

- We know what to expect in the near future (whether many or few defects will be detected in a given week) and how the number of defects detected will change. If the actual values deviate significantly from the estimates (e.g., they will be much smaller), it is possible that the testing process has become ineffective, and remedial action should be considered.
- We know the estimated total number of defects in the program (490).
- We can fairly accurately determine the dependence of the quality level (in the sense of the number of defects remaining in the program) on the time spent on testing. Already after week 9 of the project, we are able to tell the project manager that if, for example, the test process lasts 12 iterations, we will detect about 467 defects (the sum of the predictions for iterations 1–12), so there will be $490 - 467 = 23$ defects left in the program after release. The defect removal efficiency of the test process will be $\frac{467}{490} \approx 95.3\%$. However, if we extend the testing process by 3 more iterations, we will find about 484 defects in 15 iterations. The efficiency of the process will therefore be about $\frac{484}{490} \approx 98.7\%$, so it is expected to increase by 3.4%.

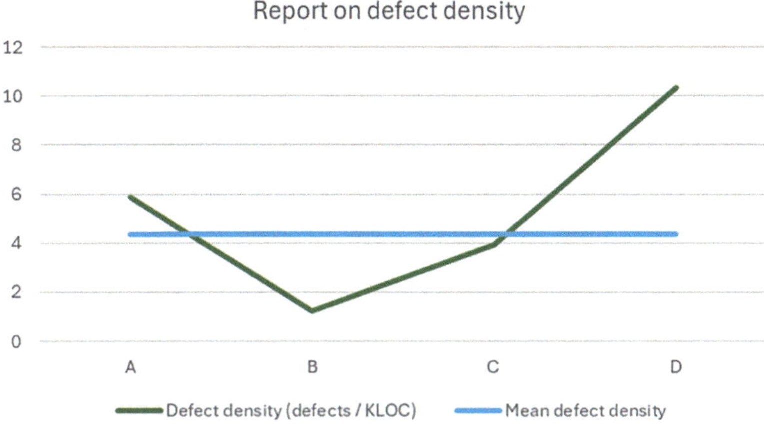


**Fig. 5.18** Report on defect density by components

## Sample Questions

### Question 5.3.1A

Your testing team has completed testing on a project and collected data on defect locations for four software components: A, B, C, and D. The team compares the predicted defect clusters (based on historical data and risk assessment) with the actual defect clusters found during testing using the defect density metric. The results are shown in Fig. 5.18.

Based on the predicted versus actual defect cluster analysis, which of the following actions would **BEST** improve defect detection in future testing cycles?

(a) Compare the defect density report with the previous one and focus future testing exclusively on components with consistently low defect density.
(b) Maintain the same testing approach but increase the frequency of test execution for the components proportionally to defect density in these components.
(c) Expand coverage in Component D and update the risk assessment process to include factors related to Component D that might have been overlooked.
(d) Reduce test effort for Component D, since most defects in D are probably found, and increase test effort for Component B, since defect density for B is below average.

Select ONE answer.

### Question 5.3.1B

You analyze the report on the number of defects found in the first 7 iterations of the project. The report is shown in Fig. 5.19.

You assume the Rayleigh distribution of the number of defects found. The theory says that the cumulative number of defects found counted from the beginning until

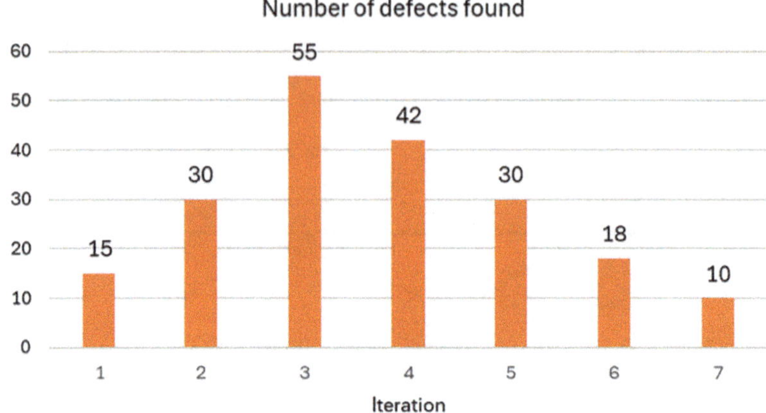


**Fig. 5.19** Statistics on defects found

the Rayleigh distribution reaches its maximum accounts for ca. 40% of the total number of defects.

What is the estimate of the number of defects that go undetected and still remain in the product?

(a) 150.
(b) 50.
(c) 10.
(d) 5.

Select ONE answer.

## Exercise 14—Improving Defect Detection

TA-5.3.1 (K4) Analyze test results to identify potential improvements to defect detection.

An online banking application has been tested in two consecutive test cycles, cycle 1 and cycle 2. The previous test cycle (1) data was used to predict defect-prone areas for the current test cycle (2). The results of the previous test cycle are shown in Table 5.12.

The components have been assigned risk levels based on the critical defect density. The Login and FundsTransfer components were marked high risk, BillPayments—medium risk, and AccountSummary and ProfileManager—low risk.

The results for the current test cycle are shown in Table 5.13.

1. Using the predicted vs actual defect cluster analysis, identify the most important, actual defect-prone areas, i.e., the areas related to critical and major defects.

**Table 5.12** Defect report for the previous test cycle (cycle 1)

| Component | Total defects found | | | Defect density (defects/KLOC) | | |
|---|---|---|---|---|---|---|
| | Critical | Major | Minor | Critical | Major | Minor |
| Login | 10 | 20 | 40 | 4.0 | 8.0 | 16.0 |
| FundsTransfer | 15 | 15 | 25 | 2.5 | 2.5 | 4.2 |
| AccountSummary | 5 | 20 | 20 | 0.4 | 1.6 | 1.6 |
| BillPayments | 2 | 6 | 20 | 1.6 | 4.8 | 16 |
| ProfileManager | 3 | 12 | 24 | 1.2 | 4.8 | 9.6 |

**Table 5.13** Defect report for the current test cycle (cycle 2)

| Component | Total defects found | | | Defect density (defects/KLOC) | | |
|---|---|---|---|---|---|---|
| | Critical | Major | Minor | Critical | Major | Minor |
| Login | 4 | 10 | 10 | 1.6 | 4.0 | 4.0 |
| FundsTransfer | 15 | 10 | 50 | 2.5 | 1.6 | 8.6 |
| AccountSummary | 5 | 10 | 30 | 0.4 | 0.8 | 2.4 |
| BillPayments | 6 | 8 | 10 | 4.8 | 6.4 | 8 |
| ProfileManager | 4 | 6 | 12 | 1.6 | 2.4 | 4.8 |

2. Modify the component risk levels according to the changes in defect density.
3. How should the test effort shift after the test cycle 2 to improve the defect detection?

### *5.3.2 Supporting Root Cause Analysis with Defect Classification*

TA-5.3.2 (K2) Explain how defect classification supports root cause analysis.

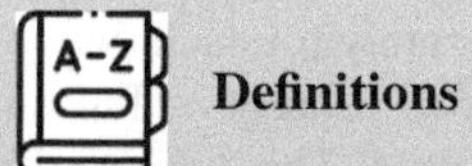


**Definitions**

**Root cause analysis**: A process used to identify the root cause of a defect.

Root Cause Analysis (RCA) is a systematic approach to identifying root causes of defects or failures in software. It focuses on pinpointing the root cause rather than just fixing the symptoms. The root cause is a factor that causes a problem and should be permanently eliminated through process improvement. The root cause is the core issue—the highest-level cause—that sets in motion the entire cause-and-effect reaction that ultimately leads to the problem(s) [21].

By identifying the source of defects, the test analyst can help implement preventive measures, reducing the likelihood of similar issues arising in the future. This makes the RCA an excellent tool for defect prevention improvement. Focusing on root causes helps prioritize critical issues over superficial or less impactful problems, allowing the test analyst to allocate resources effectively. Understanding the root causes of defects can also reveal gaps in test cases or test processes, allowing test analysts to improve test design and increase coverage.

The typical RCA process looks as follows:

1. **Problem identification**. By clearly defining the problem, the symptoms, the context, and the specific conditions under which the problem occurred, the test analyst will be able to determine the direction in which further analysis should go.
2. **Data gathering**. The test analyst collects all relevant and available information about the problem. This includes documentation, reports, measurements, screenshots, error messages, user feedback, and other key information that the test analyst thinks would be beneficial to identify the root cause.
3. **Determining possible causes**. A possible cause is any condition, action, or circumstance that contributes to an outcome or problem but may not be the primary (root) cause of it. Using RCA techniques such as 5 whys, Ishikawa fishbone diagram, or fault tree analysis can help organize potential causes and determine relationships between them.
4. **Root cause identification**. Based on the data and analysis from the previous step, the most likely root causes of the issue are identified.
5. **Recommendations and solution implementation**. Once the root cause is identified, the test analyst (and possibly other relevant stakeholders) develops a solution that is to be implemented. The solution includes preventive measures to ensure that the problem will not happen again.

In the context of software testing, the "problem" described above is usually a failure or a defect. Usually, the number of reported defects is very large. This makes it virtually impossible to perform the RCA, as analyzing each defect individually would take too much time. Instead of conducting RCA separately for each defect, it can be conducted for "categories" of defects. Since there will usually be few such categories, the RCA can be conducted in a short period of time. The way in which defects are classified should make it possible to carry out RCA efficiently, i.e., to propose effective methods for removing root causes. If the classification takes into account factors such as defect priority or impact, defect categories can be prioritized, and RCA can begin with the categories describing the most serious problems.

There are many ways to perform defect classification. Below, we describe some of the well-known approaches, namely:

- orthogonal defect classification,
- IEEE 1044 standard classification for software anomalies,
- severity-based classification,
- defect taxonomy models.

**Orthogonal Defect Classification** (ODC) [82] is a method of categorizing defects in a way that highlights areas of the development process needing attention, similar to how coordinates define a point in a value domain. Software development involves different phases that can vary across organizations, overlap, and involve different teams or even separate organizations. For ODC to be effective and applicable across different projects, the classification scheme must be consistent across phases and not tied to specific products. This consistency and independence create a robust system that can reveal useful patterns and insights over time. Classifying defects can be challenging due to human error, confusion, and reluctance if the purpose of the data isn't clear. These issues can be minimized by keeping the classification process simple, easy to interpret, and using a small number of clear categories. With fewer, distinct options, classification becomes easier, less prone to errors, and more reliable.

ODC classifies defects by assigning values to eight defect attributes:

- activity—the actual activity that was being performed at the time the defect was discovered,
- trigger—represents the environment or condition that had to exist for the defect to surface,
- impact—for in-process defects, the impact that the test analyst judges the defect would have had upon the customer if it had escaped to the field; for field-reported defects, the impact the failure had on the customer,
- target—the high-level identity of the entity that was fixed,
- defect type—the actual reason for the problem,
- qualifier (applies to defect type)—captures the element of a nonexistent, wrong, or irrelevant implementation,
- source—defines the defect in terms of its developmental history.

The attributes are grouped into two sections. The opener section contains attributes that are usually available when the defect is opened. The closer section contains attributes that are usually available when the defect is fixed. The example categories of these eight attributes are shown in Fig. 5.20. They represent a slightly modified approach to ODC that was developed by IBM [83].

**IEEE 1044 standard classification for software anomalies** [8]. IEEE 1044 provides a uniform approach to the classification of software anomalies, regardless of when they originate or when they are encountered within the project, product, or system life cycle. Classification data can be used for a variety of purposes, including defect causal analysis, project management, and software process improvement (e.g., to reduce the likelihood of defect insertion and/or to increase the likelihood of early defect detection). The goal of IEEE 1044 is to provide a shared vocabulary that enables effective

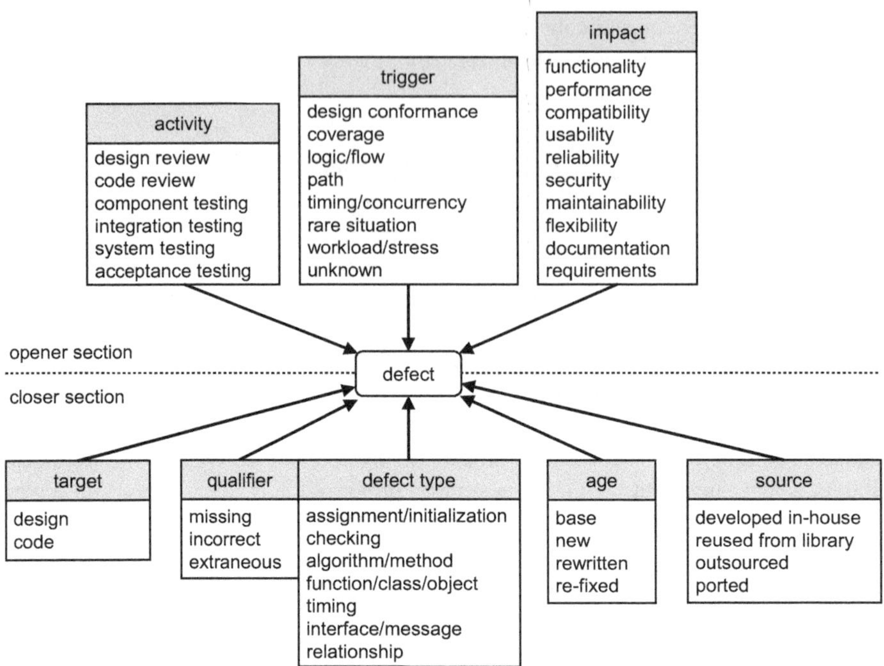


**Fig. 5.20** Example of the ODC schema for analyzing defects related to design and code

communication about software anomalies across individuals and organizations and to define a consistent set of attributes that facilitate industry methods for analyzing software defect and failure data.

IEEE 1044 provides the following defect attributes that can be used for defect classification:

- asset—the software asset (product, component, etc.) containing the defect,
- artifact—the specific software work product containing the defect,
- version detected—identification of the software version in which the defect was detected,
- version corrected—identification of the software version in which the defect was corrected,
- priority—ranking for processing assigned by the organization responsible for the evaluation, resolution, and closure of the defect relative to other reported defects,
- severity—the highest failure impact that the defect could (or did) cause, as determined by (from the perspective of) the organization responsible for software engineering,
- probability—probability of recurring failure caused by this defect,
- effect—the class of requirement that is impacted by a failure caused by a defect,
- type—a categorization based on the class of code within which the defect is found or the work product within which the defect is found,

- mode—a categorization based on whether the defect is due to incorrect implementation or representation, the addition of something that is not needed, or an omission,
- insertion activity—the activity during which the defect was injected/inserted (i.e., during which the artifact containing the defect originated),
- disposition—final disposition of defect report upon closure.

**Severity-based classification** is a simple method of categorizing software defects based on the degree of impact they have on the system, users, or business processes. This is the only parameter used in the classification. This classification method, due to its simplicity, does not allow grouping defects in terms of "substantive" characteristics, which is typically done to simplify the RCA later. However, this method can be used to prioritize defects and perform a kind of "defect triage" before the RCA is used. This will allow only the most serious defects to be identified, and leave the less important ones for later, or even leave them out of the analysis.

Typical severity levels include:

- critical/showstopper—a defect that prevents the system or its major features from functioning; often causes system crashes or data loss; immediate attention and resolution are required,
- major—a defect that causes significant disruption to functionality, but workarounds exist; high-priority resolution is required,
- minor/moderate—a defect that causes inconvenience but does not significantly impair functionality; requires scheduled fixes based on available bandwidth,
- trivial/cosmetic—a defect with negligible impact on system or user experience; fixes have low priority, and such defects are often deferred.

**Defect taxonomies** organize defects into structured, hierarchical categories that share similar characteristics. Taxonomies are based on the nature, source, or impact of defects and provide a systematic way to identify patterns, analyze trends, and prioritize improvements. Examples of defect taxonomies include Beizer's taxonomy [46, 84]. For example, the original Beizer's taxonomy is quite rich and looks as follows:

1xxx REQUIREMENTS

11xx Requirements Incorrect
12xx Requirements Logic
13xx Requirements, Completeness
15xx Presentation, Documentation
16xx Requirements Changes

2xxx FEATURES AND FUNCTIONALITY

21xx Feature/Function Correctness
22xx Feature Completeness
23xx Functional Case Completeness
24xx Domain Bugs
25xx User Messages and Diagnostics

26xx Exception Condition Mishandled
29xx Other Functional Bugs

3xxx STRUCTURAL BUGS

31xx Control Flow and Sequencing
32xx Processing

4xxx DATA

41xx Data Definition and Structure
42xx Data Access and Handling
49xx Other Data Problems

5xxx IMPLEMENTATION AND CODING

51xx Coding and Typographical
52xx Style and Standards Violations
53xx Documentation
59xx Other Implementation

6xxx INTEGRATION

61xx Internal Interfaces
62xx External Interfaces, Timing, Throughput
69xx Other Integration

7xxx SYSTEM, SOFTWARE ARCHITECTURE

71xx O/S Call and Use
72xx Software Architecture
73xx Recovery and Accountability
74xx Performance
75xx Incorrect Diagnostics, Exceptions
76xx Partitions, Overlays
77xx Sysgen, Environment

8xxx TEST DEFINITION AND EXECUTION

81xx Test Design Bugs
82xx Test Execution Bugs
83xx Test Documentation
84xx Test Case Completeness
89xx Other Testing Bugs

9xxx OTHER, UNSPECIFIED

The "xx" notation suggests that subcategories can be further categorized into their own subtypes.

Software quality models, such as ISO/IEC 25010 [6], can also be used as a defect taxonomy (see Fig. 5.21). This approach provides a structured framework to identify,

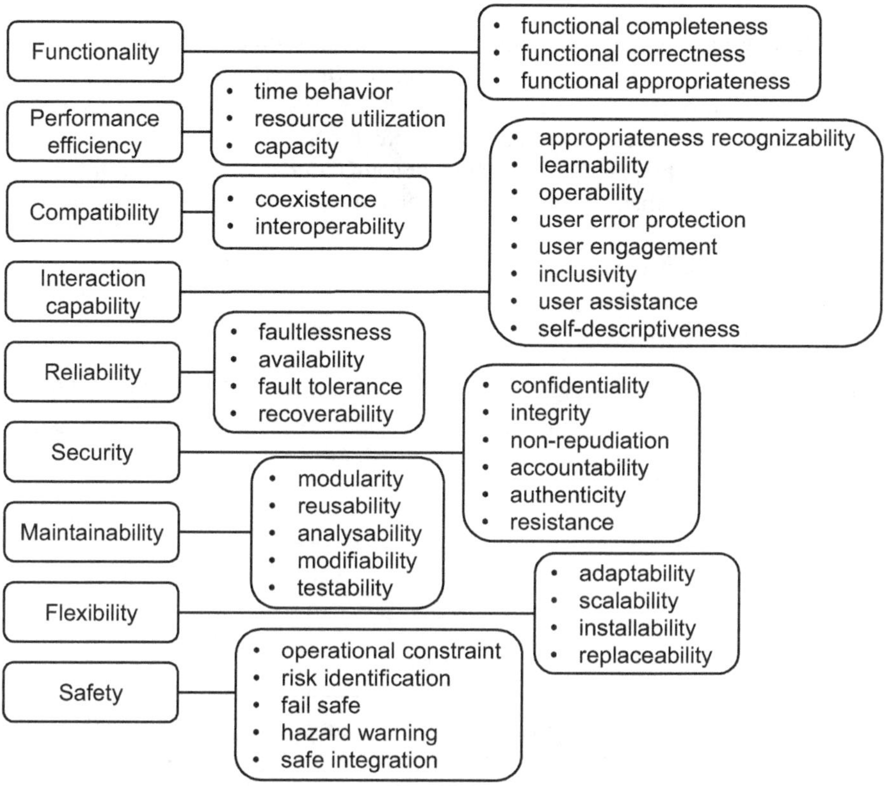

- Functionality
  - functional completeness
  - functional correctness
  - functional appropriateness
- Performance efficiency
  - time behavior
  - resource utilization
  - capacity
- Compatibility
  - coexistence
  - interoperability
- Interaction capability
  - appropriateness recognizability
  - learnability
  - operability
  - user error protection
  - user engagement
  - inclusivity
  - user assistance
  - self-descriptiveness
- Reliability
  - faultlessness
  - availability
  - fault tolerance
  - recoverability
- Security
  - confidentiality
  - integrity
  - non-repudiation
  - accountability
  - authenticity
  - resistance
- Maintainability
  - modularity
  - reusability
  - analysability
  - modifiability
  - testability
- Flexibility
  - adaptability
  - scalability
  - installability
  - replaceability
- Safety
  - operational constraint
  - risk identification
  - fail safe
  - hazard warning
  - safe integration

**Fig. 5.21** ISO/IEC 25010:2023 software quality model

classify, and analyze defects while aligning them with specific quality objectives impacted by these defects.

**Case Study**

The FoodApp project's defect management process requires that throughout the defect lifecycle, information characterizing the defect according to the ODC classification be added to the defect report. An ODC-compliant description of a sample failure found during testing is as follows.

Failure: FoodApp crashes when placing an order for multiple items. The failure was raised by a client during beta testing (activity: acceptance testing). The client tried to achieve boundary value analysis coverage for the "maximum number of items in the cart" (trigger: coverage). This failure prevented the customer from ordering (impact: functionality). After the defect analysis and debugging, it turned out that the defect was in the source code (target: code). The failure occurred because of the incorrect predicate `numberOfItems < maxItems` instead of `numberOfItems <= maxItems` (qualifier and defect type: incorrect checking). The defect was introduced in the new component (age: new) by the development team (source: developed in-house).

Now, suppose that the defect management system contains 850 defects raised and fixed for the latest version of the FoodApp. Performing the RCA for each of these defects is impossible. However, the test analyst can use defect classification in order to "cluster" defects into a smaller number of items, which then will be analyzed within the RCA process. After analyzing the defect attributes stored in the defect management system, the test analyst created a tree-like structure that groups defects according to these categories. Such a tree may be created using the statistical machine learning method, such as a classification tree. A fragment of this tree is shown in Fig. 5.22.

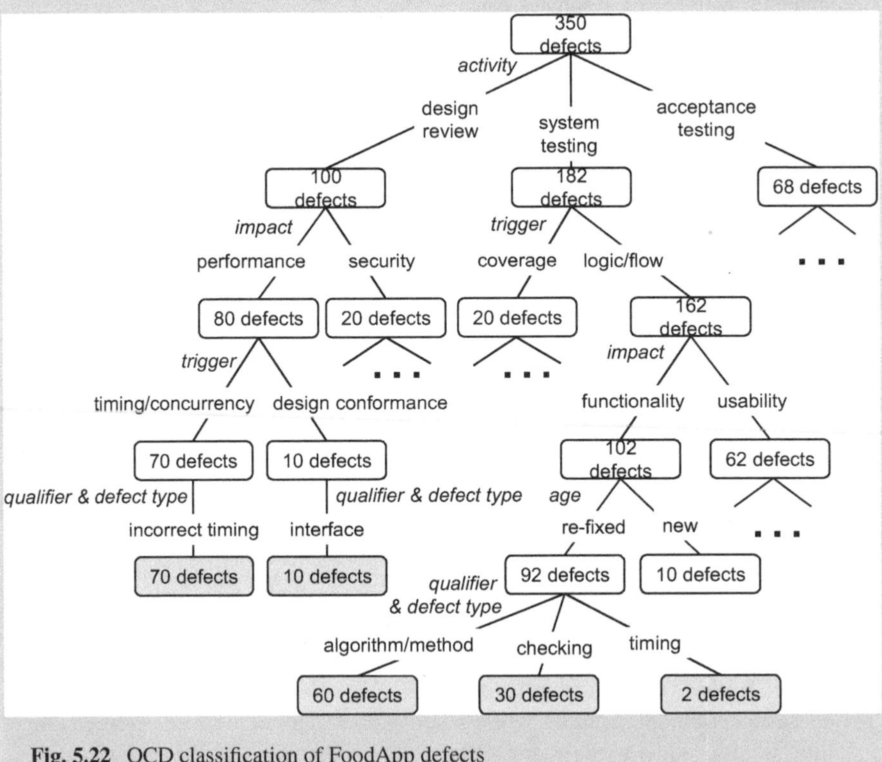


Fig. 5.22 OCD classification of FoodApp defects

Having such a classification, the test analyst can perform the RCA not for single defects, but for groups of defects, denoted by the gray rectangles in Fig. 5.22. First, the test analyst notices the two biggest groups of defects:

- 70 defects were detected during the design review, related to performance, triggered by timing/concurrency activities, whose occurrence was due to an incorrect timing.
- 60 defects detected during system testing, triggered by examining the logic/ flow of data, having an impact on functionality, all of them introduced by the solution provided to fix a previous defect, whose occurrence was due to correctness problems in algorithm implementations.

These two groups of defects are the first candidates for RCA. For the first of these groups, RCA revealed that the defects occurred because the requirements specification omitted requirements for serialization of shared resources, resulting in the introduction of solutions into the design that can result in poor performance. In order to remove the root cause, the test analyst decided to add the item "Does the requirement specification describe timing issues, such as necessary serialization of shared resources?" to the checklist used during the requirements review. This should prevent the recurrence of the defects of the first type.

For the second group of defects, RCA revealed that the defects occurred because of a poor description of complex algorithms related to price calculation, discount assignment, and loyalty programs. All these defects were introduced when trying to fix another defect, which revealed that the source code was also written poorly. The code lacked any comments, was not formatted properly, and used non-informative variable names. The test analyst suggested:

- to introduce the training for developers on how to write clean code and use good practices and design patterns,
- to perform obligatory code reviews focusing on code quality,
- to require that requirements related to complex rules are specified using formal models, such as decision tables, block diagrams, and mathematical formalism.

These improvements should prevent the recurrence of the defects of the second type.

Note that the use of defect classification before performing RCA enabled a significant reduction in the work required to perform RCA. For example, almost half of all defects (172 of 350) are grouped into five categories (gray rectangles in Fig. 5.22). This means that root cause analysis for 172 defects will require only five analyses, for five groups of defects.

## Sample Questions

### Question 5.3.2A

How does defect classification support root cause analysis?

(a) It allows for identifying the causes of a defect rather than its symptoms.
(b) It facilitates choosing an appropriate test technique for each possible defect.
(c) It ensures that risks related to identified defects are properly mitigated.
(d) It enables analysis of defect types rather than individual defects.

Select ONE answer.

### Question 5.3.2B

Which framework is used for defect classification in order to support root cause analysis?

(a) Defect prevention.
(b) Defect taxonomy.
(c) Defect density analysis.
(d) Defect life cycle.

Select ONE answer.

# Part III
# Answers to Questions and Exercises

# Answers to Sample Questions

## Chapter 1

### Question 1.1.1A

Correct answer: (b)

(a) Incorrect answer. The test effort estimation is part of test planning, which is done in an early planning phase of the SDLC.
(b) Correct answer. Test analysis should begin when the test basis is produced. The requirements are the test basis for acceptance testing, and reviewing the test basis is one of the first steps in test analysis.
(c) Incorrect answer. Designing test cases is a test design activity. In a sequential SDLC, the test basis (requirements) must be done before test design can start. Test design should follow at a later phase, in parallel with software design and implementation.
(d) Incorrect answer. Prioritizing test procedures is a test-implementation activity that should be done in parallel with software design and implementation.

### Question 1.1.1B

Correct answer: (c)

This is an incremental development lifecycle. Hence, testing must focus on the new or changed features and include a regression suite that is carefully maintained.

(a) Incorrect answer. The main focus should be on the new or modified features. Testing their happy paths is usually insufficient, unless the risk is low (which is not indicated here).
(b) Incorrect answer. Focusing on the new or modified features is correct, but always running the standard regression test suite is not. The test analyst must pay particular attention to the refactoring and the assembly of regression test suites.

 
A. Roman and M. Hamburg, *Practical Software Test Analysis*,
https://doi.org/10.1007/978-3-032-27986-6_8

(c) Correct answer. The test analyst must pay particular attention to the refactoring and the assembly of regression test suites.
(d) Incorrect answer. In incremental SDLCs, the test analyst performs the same activities for each increment (i.e., test analysis, test design, test implementation, test execution, and test management support).

**Question 1.2.1A**

Correct answer: (a)

(a) Correct answer. According to the syllabus, "During test analysis, the test analyst checks the completeness of the test basis and collects any additional information relevant for testing."
(b) Incorrect answer. Defining the test basis is a test planning activity that must happen before test analysis. "The test basis is defined" is an entry criterion for test analysis.
(c) Incorrect answer. Capturing the traceability between the test basis, test conditions, and test cases is a task in test design. Test cases are only created after test analysis, in the test design activity.
(d) Incorrect answer. The input to keyword-driven testing is test cases, not test conditions. Test conditions using keywords are not helpful.

**Question 1.2.1B**

Correct answer: (d)

(a) Incorrect answer. Prioritizing test conditions is part of the test analysis.
(b) Incorrect answer. Reviewing the test basis is part of the test analysis.
(c) Incorrect answer. Documenting defects in the test basis is part of the test analysis.
(d) Correct answer. Designing test cases is part of the test design, not test analysis.

**Question 1.2.2A**

Correct answer: (c)

The test environment must ensure that a test case that passes or fails in the test environment will have the same test result when executed in production (see [85], Sect. 1.3.3). Hence, the requirements for the test environment can only be completed when the test cases are known.

(a) Incorrect answer. Test scope and objectives are usually insufficient for completing the requirements for the test environment.
(b) Incorrect answer. Test conditions are usually insufficient for completing the requirements for the test environment.
(c) Correct answer. Defining the test environment requirements is a task in the test design activity, see [85], Sect. 1.2.2.
(d) Incorrect answer. During test implementation, the test environment must be provided, and its readiness for test execution must be verified. It is usually too

late to specify the requirements at this stage, because implementing them might take time.

### Question 1.2.2B

Correct answer: (c)

(a) Incorrect answer. This is part of the test analysis.
(b) Incorrect answer. This is part of the test implementation.
(c) Correct answer. This is part of the test design.
(d) Incorrect answer. This is part of the test execution.

### Question 1.2.3A

Correct answer: (c)

The following matches are correct:

1-C: A small test suite that invokes all interfaces is a smoke test (see Glossary). The smoke test is the best means to verify the test environment setup (see syllabus).
2-D: Dependencies, priorities, and skills play a role in the test execution schedule. Even though the first two also play a role in creating test suites, the skills needed for execution do not.
3-A: Grouping test scripts and test procedures for execution creates test suites. A test suite is defined as a set of test scripts or test procedures to be executed in a specific test run (see Glossary).
4-B: Migrating test data to the new structure is creating the test data for execution.

So,

(a) Incorrect answer. It swaps A and B for 3 and 4.
(b) Incorrect answer. It swaps C and D for 1 and 2.
(c) Correct answer.
(d) Incorrect answer. Entirely mismatched, e.g., 2 (dependencies, priorities, and skills for test procedures) does not match B (create test data).

### Question 1.2.3B

Correct answer: (d)

(a) Incorrect answer. This takes place during the test execution.
(b) Incorrect answer. This takes place during the test design.
(c) Incorrect answer. This takes place during the test analysis.
(d) Correct answer. This takes place during the test implementation. The test analyst can assist the test manager in defining a test execution schedule, including resource allocation, to enable efficient test execution by defining the test execution order.

### Question 1.2.4A

Correct answer: (a)

(a) Correct answer. Updating the traceability between the test basis and the latest test results enables the stakeholders to take informed decisions, see syllabus, Sect. 1.2.4.
(b) Incorrect answer. Analyzing the anomalies that have led to the defects must be performed before reporting a defect, not after fixing it.
(c) Incorrect answer. Performing a root cause analysis to support defect prevention does not have to immediately follow confirmation testing, because it is a long-term measure. It may be done before or after that.
(d) Incorrect answer. Running the regression test suite must be performed as foreseen in the test execution schedule. It may, but does not have to, immediately follow confirmation testing.

### Question 1.2.4B

Correct answer: (a)

(a) Correct answer. It sounds reasonable because it relates to documentation and system behavior, but it is not correct—a test analyst can document defects or ambiguities in the requirements, but they do not directly change the official business requirements.
(b) Incorrect answer. This is done during the test execution.
(c) Incorrect answer. This is done during the test execution.
(d) Incorrect answer. This is done during the test execution.

### Question 1.3.1A

Correct answer: (d)

(a) Incorrect answer. The test case is not high-level because it contains the concrete age limit of 12 years for fingerprinting.
(b) Incorrect answer. The test case is not low-level because it contains the abstract data elements birthdate and current_date.
(c) Incorrect answer. A test case does not have to be purely high-level or low-level.
(d) Correct answer. According to the Syllabus, "In practice, many test cases are hybrid, being concrete in some aspects and abstract in others." In our case, the threshold for the age is concrete (12 years), but the age of the traveler is abstract (could be any age from exactly 12 years on).

### Question 1.3.1B

Correct answer: (b)

(a) Incorrect answer. Low-level test cases contain concrete information for input data.

(b) Correct answer. These two sentences correctly characterize both high-level and low-level test cases.
(c) Incorrect answer. Anyone can design both high-level and low-level test cases.
(d) Incorrect answer. There is no rule about which techniques can be used for which type of test case. In fact, black-box test techniques are very useful for defining low-level test cases, because they can identify test data to achieve a required coverage.

### Question 1.3.2A

Correct answer: (d)

Precision means that there is only one interpretation of the test case, and test execution will not result in false positives or false negatives.

(a) Incorrect answer. Lack of information in the test case is a shortcoming of completeness and not of precision.
(b) Incorrect answer. This is a case of a lack of traceability from the test case back to the test condition.
(c) Incorrect answer. There is no reason why a lack of precision would impact maintainability.
(d) Correct answer. This is a false positive, which is a typical consequence of a lack of precision.

### Question 1.3.2B

Correct answer: (a)

(a) Correct answer. The word "suitable" is ambiguous and could mean location, price, accessibility, etc., leading to different interpretations. Therefore, the test case is not precise.
(b) Incorrect answer. The test case can actually be executed, so it is feasible.
(c) Incorrect answer. Although we do not know if the test case is traceable to some requirement, for sure, using the ambiguous word "suitable" does not make this test case untraceable.
(d) Incorrect answer. The test case accurately verifies the intended test condition, so it is correct.

### Question 1.3.3A

Correct answer: (b)

(a) Incorrect answer. Test environment requirements can be defined during test design as well, if they depend on test conditions or test cases. See also Sect. 1.2.2 above.
(b) Correct answer. The requirements should also address the test environment's overarching needs, including administration and maintenance.
(c) Incorrect answer. Test levels and test types influence the trade-off between test environment flexibility and similarity to the production environment.

(d) Incorrect answer. Test environment requirements may include diagrams and tables.

### Question 1.3.3B

Correct answer: (a)

According to the Syllabus:

- unique identifier—used for traceability purposes
- description—in sufficient detail to implement it as required
- period needed—identifies when and for how long the item is needed
- fidelity—the degree to which this item represents or deviates from the production environment.

Therefore:

(a) Correct answer. Matches the syllabus.
(b) Incorrect answer. Does not match the syllabus. For example, 3D is incorrect: the period needed does not indicate the flexibility and similarity with production.
(c) Incorrect answer. Does not match the syllabus. For example, 4B is incorrect: the fidelity does not support traceability.
(d) Incorrect answer. Does not match the syllabus. For example, 4A is incorrect: the fidelity does not ensure the availability of the test environment during test execution.

### Question 1.3.4A

Correct answer: (b)

(a) Incorrect answer. Detailed requirements indicate a complete test basis that can serve as a test oracle.
(b) Correct answer. The factor described indicates that the testers will struggle with missing requirements, which is a typical factor contributing to a test oracle problem.
(c) Incorrect answer. This factor describes deterministic behavior that facilitates test oracles. Only non-deterministic or probabilistic behavior causes an oracle problem.
(d) Incorrect answer. A small amount of test data is not causing an oracle problem by itself; it rather facilitates the test oracle. Oracle problems are rather caused by data-related complexity, e.g., big data or a complex database structure, which are not indicated here.

### Question 1.3.4B

Correct answer: (d)

(a) Incorrect answer. The solution of the test team does not include a test model from which the expected results will be generated, so this is not model-based testing.

(b) Incorrect answer. In this solution, the expected results are not predicted by a human but by the implemented software.
(c) Incorrect answer. The solution does not involve metamorphic relations between source and follow-up test cases, which would be needed for metamorphic testing.
(d) Correct answer. The solution describes an independently derived variant of the test item used to generate expected results, which is, by the Glossary definition, a pseudo-oracle.

**Question 1.3.5A**

Correct answer: (a)

(a) Correct answer. Linking test data requirements with the test cases ensures traceability, a key aspect that ensures test data maintainability.
(b) Incorrect answer. The data format should be indicated in the requirements as well, because it is a key aspect according to the syllabus.
(c) Incorrect answer. Test data may be needed for the coverage criteria of any test technique, according to the key aspect "Purpose."
(d) Incorrect answer. Test data required may contain time-sensitive attributes, which will need data aging before the tests can be executed; see the key aspect "Time sensitivity and data aging."

**Question 1.3.5B**

Correct answer: (d)

According to the Syllabus:

- Supporting every rule in the decision table to be tested (1)—is an aspect of coverage criteria (C).
- Separating high-level test cases, which contain the test logic, from test data (2)—is an aspect of maintainability (A).
- Referential integrity (3)—is an aspect of dependencies (D).
- Synthetic data supporting realistic business scenarios (4)—is an aspect of similarity with production data (B).

Therefore,

(a) Incorrect answer. Does not match the syllabus. For example, 1B is incorrect: supporting every coverage item is not a question of maintainability.
(b) Incorrect answer. Does not match the syllabus. For example, 1D is incorrect: supporting every coverage item is not a question of dependencies.
(c) Incorrect answer. Does not match the syllabus. For example, 2D is incorrect: separating test logic from test data does not support dependencies between test data.
(d) Correct answer. Matches the syllabus.

### Question 1.3.6A

Correct answer: (c)

(a) Incorrect answer. This action keyword is not specific to the new user story USt1. It might be a precondition for a test case addressing USt1, but it should be covered in previous increments.
(b) Incorrect answer. The name of the keyword does not contain a verb. The correct keyword should contain a verb like "verify," "check," or "validate."
(c) Correct answer. This is a valid domain-layer action keyword fulfilling all criteria listed in the syllabus: the name contains a verb in imperative, it has a unique meaning, the description documents it adequately, uses the vocabulary of the user story, and is reusable for any test case involving this action (e.g., for various ways to quit the data entry).
(d) Incorrect answer. This keyword resides on the test interface layer rather than on the domain layer. It assumes that proceeding with the action after a data loss warning is implemented as a button with the label "Confirm."

### Question 1.3.6B

Correct answer: (d)

The scripts cover the hyphen rule as follows:

(i) Yes, a space in the vocabulary is compared with a hyphen in the search text.
(ii) No, this script only covers the equality of upper- and lower-case characters.
(iii) Yes, this script covers the equality of spaces with hyphens (test-f with test f) and the equality of upper- and lower-case characters in combination.
(iv) Yes, a hyphen in the vocabulary is compared with a space in the search list.
(v) No, this script checks that hyphens are not treated the same as slashes. But this is not part of the acceptance criteria about hyphens.

Hence,

(a) Incorrect answer. Script iv) is missing, and script v) does not cover the acceptance criteria.
(b) Incorrect answer. Script iii) is missing, and script v) does not cover the acceptance criteria.
(c) Incorrect answer. Script i) is missing, and script ii) does not cover the acceptance criteria.
(d) Correct answer. These three scripts cover the hyphen rule; the other two do not.

### Question 1.3.7A

Correct answer: (b) and (e)

The traceability involves test results, test cases, specification items, and requirements. Test cases and their latest results are managed by test management tools. This typically also involves the horizontal traceability of test cases to test conditions and test basis elements (in this case: the system specification items). Requirements, specification items, and their vertical traceability are managed in requirement management tools. Therefore,

(a) Incorrect answer. Configuration management tools cannot support the traceability of test results to requirements. They only register information about consistent versions of the testware.
(b) Correct answer. Test management tools register the test results and test cases, so they must be involved in establishing the traceability.
(c) Incorrect answer. Test data management tools do not provide any information about test cases, their execution status, or defect reports.
(d) Incorrect answer. Defect management tools do not manage any of the work products involved (requirements, specification items, test cases, test results). They only register the defect reports and their workflow status.
(e) Correct answer. Requirement management tools typically manage various requirement types, including system requirements and system specification items. They also support establishing vertical traceability between them, which is a system engineering good practice.

### Question 1.3.7B

Correct answer: (a)

(a) Correct answer. The tasks of the test analyst include the configuration management of the test cases.
(b) Incorrect answer. Maintaining the traceability is done in a test management tool and not in a configuration management tool.
(c) Incorrect answer. The test analyst is not responsible for reviewing the software configuration. This is a development or architecture task.
(d) Incorrect answer. Structuring the test case repository is done in a test management tool and not in a configuration management tool. Moreover, grouping tests by software configuration is not recommended by the syllabus.

## Chapter 2

### Question 2.1.1A

Correct answer: (d)

(a) Incorrect answer. Regression test selection is an activity that the test analyst performs during risk control, not risk analysis.
(b) Incorrect answer. Mitigation actions are applied during risk control, not risk analysis.
(c) Incorrect answer. Performing code reviews is an example of a mitigating action, which is performed during risk control, not risk analysis.

(d) Correct answer. Risk analysis consists of risk identification and risk assessment. During the risk assessment, the test analyst evaluates risk level (including risk impact) based on the knowledge of the business domain, such as the frequency of use or criticality of the affected feature.

### Question 2.1.1B

Correct answer: (c)

The scenario describes a qualitative risk assessment. Therefore:

(a) Incorrect answer. There is no such phase as "risk evaluation."
(b) Incorrect answer.
(c) Correct answer.
(d) Incorrect answer.

### Question 2.2.1A

Correct answer: (c)

Risk level is calculated as the multiplication of risk likelihood and risk impact. Therefore, risk levels for the risks covered by resp. TC1, TC2, TC3, and TC4, are:

- 20% * $5,000,000 = $1,000,000
- 10% * $12,00,000 = $1,200,000
- 5% * $10,000,000 = $500,000
- 1% * $15,000,000 = $150,000

This means that the test case prioritization, which follows risk prioritization, is TC2 → TC1 → TC3 → TC4. Hence, the third test case executed is TC3. So:

(a) Incorrect answer.
(b) Incorrect answer.
(c) Correct answer.
(d) Incorrect answer.

### Question 2.2.1B

Correct answer: (b)

TC1 achieves the highest coverage among all test cases (4/7), so it will be executed first. After its execution, requirements 1, 3, and 7 remain uncovered. Among the remaining test cases, TC3 covers the most uncovered requirements (2/3), so it will be executed second. The only requirement not covered so far is 7. It is covered by TC4, so this test case will be executed third. Therefore, TC2 must be executed last. Hence:

(a) Incorrect answer.
(b) Correct answer.
(c) Incorrect answer.
(d) Incorrect answer.

# Chapter 3

## Question 3.1.1A

Correct answer: (b)

There are six borders in the scenario:

- (A1) age >= 0
- (A2) age <= 12
- (B1) age >= 13
- (B2) age <= 17
- (C1) age >= 18
- (C2) age <= 120

A1 and A2 determine the "child" equivalence class. B1 and B2 determine the "teen" equivalence class. C1 and C2 determine the "adult" equivalence class. Reliable coverage requires one of the ON, OFF, IN, and OUT points for each border. This means there are 6 * 4 = 24 coverage items. However, we cannot have OFF and OUT points for A1 and C2 since the only valid input is integers from 0 to 120. This leaves us with 24 – 4 = 20 coverage items.

Table 1 shows which coverage items are covered by the data points from the answers regarding these borders.

Test data 18, 120 cover 9 out of 20 coverage items: IN for A1 and B1, OUT for A2, OFF and OUT for B2, and ON and IN for C1 and C2. This gives 9/20 = 45% reliable coverage.

Test data 12, 17 cover 10 out of 20 coverage items, which gives 50% reliable coverage.

Test data 6, 15 cover 8 out of 20 coverage items, which gives 40% reliable coverage.

Test data 0, 5 cover 7 out of 20 coverage items, which gives 35% reliable coverage.

The test data 12 and 17 achieve the highest coverage, so the correct answer is (b).

**Table 1** Coverage items for all six borders

| Test set | Point | Coverage items covered for the borders | | | | | |
|---|---|---|---|---|---|---|---|
| | | A1 | A2 | B1 | B2 | C1 | C2 |
| (a) | 18 | IN | OUT | IN | OFF | ON | IN |
| | 120 | IN | OUT | IN | OUT | IN | ON |
| (b) | 12 | IN | ON | OFF | IN | OUT | IN |
| | 17 | IN | OUT | IN | ON | OFF | IN |
| (c) | 6 | IN | IN | OUT | IN | OUT | IN |
| | 15 | IN | OUT | IN | IN | OUT | IN |
| (d) | 0 | ON | IN | OUT | IN | OUT | IN |
| | 5 | IN | IN | OUT | IN | OUT | IN |

### Question 3.1.1B

Correct answer: (d)

Simplified coverage requires one ON and one OFF point for each border. The OFF points must be as close as possible to the corresponding ON points.

(a) Incorrect answer. Point y is ON for $Y \leq 6$, but the OFF point for this border is missing.
(b) Incorrect answer. First, point w is unnecessary. Second, the ON and OFF points for $X \leq 6$ are not close to each other.
(c) Incorrect answer. The OFF point for $Y \leq 6$ is missing.
(d) Correct answer. Points q and r are ON and OFF for $Y \leq 6$ and r is closest to q. Points q and t are the similar pair for $X \leq 6$. Points x and z are the similar pair for $X + Y \geq 9$. Due to the symmetry of ON and OFF points for adjacent borders, the same set of points cover all the required ON and OFF points for the borders of the complement partition $X > 6$ *or* $Y > 6$ *or* $X + Y < 9$.

### Question 3.1.2A

Correct answer: (c)

Each choice coverage requires testing the base configuration and all its modifications created from replacing one parameter value with every possible other value. Hence, we need to test the 11 configurations shown in Table 2 (base configuration values are shown in bold).

### Question 3.1.2B

Correct answer: (a)

Pairwise coverage requires covering all possible pairs of parameter values. Table 3 shows 30 such pairs.

**Table 2** Configurations that achieve each choice coverage

| # | Protocol | Encryption | Authentication | Connection |
|---|---|---|---|---|
| 1 | **TCP** | **SSL** | **Username/password** | **Medium** |
| 2 | UDP | **SSL** | **Username/password** | **Medium** |
| 3 | ICMP | **SSL** | **Username/password** | **Medium** |
| 4 | **TCP** | None | **Username/password** | **Medium** |
| 5 | **TCP** | AES | **Username/password** | **Medium** |
| 6 | **TCP** | WPA2 | **Username/password** | **Medium** |
| 7 | **TCP** | **SSL** | None | **Medium** |
| 8 | **TCP** | **SSL** | Token | **Medium** |
| 9 | **TCP** | **SSL** | Biometric | **Medium** |
| 10 | **TCP** | **SSL** | **Username/password** | Low |
| 11 | **TCP** | **SSL** | **Username/password** | High |

**Table 3** All coverage items for pairwise testing of a network configuration

| Pair of parameters | Combinations to cover | Number of combinations |
|---|---|---|
| Protocol x Encryption | (TCP, SSL), (TCP, AES) (UDP, SSL), (UDP, AES) | $2 \times 2 = 4$ |
| Protocol x Authentication | (TCP, Token), (TCP, Biometric) (UDP, Token), (UDP, Biometric) | $2 \times 2 = 4$ |
| Protocol x Connection speed | (TCP, Low), (TCP, Medium), (TCP, High) (UDP, Low), (UDP, Medium), (UDP, High) | $2 \times 3 = 6$ |
| Encryption x Authentication | (SSL, Token), (SSL, Biometric) (AES, Token), (AES, Biometric) | $2 \times 2 = 4$ |
| Encryption x Connection speed | (SSL, Low), (SSL, Medium), (SSL, High) (AES, Low), (AES, Medium), (AES, High) | $2 \times 3 = 6$ |
| Authentication x Connection speed | (Token, Low), (Token, Medium), (Token, High) (Biometric, Low), (Biometric, Medium), (Biometric, High) | $2 \times 3 = 6$ |
| Total number of combinations to cover | | 30 |

Since the greatest number of combinations for two given parameters is 6, we need at least 6 configurations to test. Indeed, 6 configurations are enough, as shown in Table 4.

Notice that each of the 30 pairs of parameter values is covered in this table. For example, the pair (SSL, Medium) is covered in row 4, the pair (TCP, High) is covered in row 6, etc.

**Table 4** Configurations to test to achieve pairwise coverage

| # | Protocol | Encryption | Authentication | Connection speed |
|---|---|---|---|---|
| 1 | TCP | SSL | Token | Low |
| 2 | UDP | AES | Biometric | Low |
| 3 | TCP | AES | Token | Medium |
| 4 | UDP | SSL | Biometric | Medium |
| 5 | UDP | AES | Token | High |
| 6 | TCP | SSL | Biometric | High |

### Question 3.1.3A

Correct answer: (a)

(a) Correct answer. Each time the numbers are drawn from a different set, which means that the probability distribution changes depending on the last number drawn. It is, therefore, an example of guided random testing.
(b) Incorrect answer. While this is indeed an example of guided random testing, the explanation is incorrect. Any random testing, whether guided or unguided, involves drawing values from a well-defined set of values.
(c) Incorrect answer. This is an example of guided random testing—see the rationale for the correct answer.
(d) Incorrect answer. This is an example of guided random testing—see the rationale for the correct answer. Also, the form of the exit criterion is not the reason that random testing is guided or not.

### Question 3.1.3B

Correct answer: (d)

(a) Incorrect answer. This is a limitation, not an advantage, of random testing.
(b) Incorrect answer. Random testing lacks recognized coverage criteria.
(c) Incorrect answer. Neglecting data semantics is a limitation, not an advantage, of random testing.
(d) Correct answer. When domain knowledge is limited, random testing, including unguided random testing, can be used.

### Question 3.2.1A

Correct answer: (a)

(a) Correct answer. This is a description of one type of CRUD testing, which is completeness testing.
(b) Incorrect answer. This is a description of state transition testing.
(c) Incorrect answer. This is a description of decision table testing.
(d) Incorrect answer. This is a description of crowd testing.

### Question 3.2.1B

Correct answer: (d)

(a) Incorrect answer. CRUD matrix is not a state transition model.
(b) Incorrect answer. CRUD matrix is not a scenario model.
(c) Incorrect answer. CRUD matrix is not a domain-based technique.
(d) Correct answer. The CRUD matrix gives an overview of the lifecycle of the data entities. Its columns represent the entities, and its rows represent functions.

**Question 3.2.2A**

Correct answer: (b)

There are seven round trips in the state diagram:

(1) Read, Read
(2) Init, Read, Fix file, Init
(3) Read, Fix file, Init, Read
(4) Fix file, Init, Read, Fix file
(5) Init, Read, Print results, Init
(6) Read, Print results, Init, Read
(7) Print results, Init, Read, Print results

There are two already designed test cases:

TC1: Init, Read, Read, Print results, Init, Read, Print results, END

TC2: Init, Read, Fix file, Init, Read, Fix file, Init, Read, Print results, END

TC1 covers round trips (1), (6), and (7). TC2 covers round trips (2), (3), and (4). The only uncovered round trip is (5). Hence:

(a) Incorrect answer. The round trip (5) is not covered.
(b) Correct answer. The test case "Init, Read, Print, Init, Read, Print results, END" covers the round trip "Init, Read, Print, Init." Together with TC1 and TC2, these three test cases cover all round trips, so they achieve 100% round trip coverage.
(c) Incorrect answer. After adding this test case, the round trip (5) is not covered.
(d) Incorrect answer. After adding this test case, the round trip (5) is not covered.

**Question 3.2.2B**

Correct answer: (a)

There are 13 1-switches:

- Starting from "Init": (1) start, readLine; (2) start, error; (3) start, endFile
- Starting from "Fix file": (4) fixed, stop; (5) fixed, start
- Starting from "Read": (6) readLine, readLine; (7) readLine, error; (8) readLine, endFile; (9) error, fixed; (10) endFile, stop; (11) endFile, newFile
- Starting from "Print results": (12) newFile, stop; (13) newFile, start

Notice that no two out of 1-switches (4), (10), and (12) can occur within one test case because each of these 1-switches ends in a final state. So, we need at least three test cases. Three test cases are indeed enough to cover all the 13 1-switches, for example:

TC1: start, readLine, readLine, error, fixed, start, endFile, stop—covers (1), (6), (7), (9), (5), (3), (10)
TC2: start, error, fixed, stop—additionally covers (2), (9), (4)

TC3: start, readLine, endFile, newFile, start, endFile, newFile, stop—additionally covers (8), (11), (12), and (13).

**Question 3.2.3A**

Correct answer: (c)

The activity diagram shows four scenarios (the parallel actions are shown in curly brackets):

(1) No train: Get meeting data, {Log event, {Check traffic, Check train time}, Book taxi}, Display results
(2) Train & traffic, too late: Get meeting data, {Log event, {Check traffic, Check train time}, {Postpone meeting, Check next train time}, Book taxi}, Display results
(3) Train & traffic, time ok: Get meeting data, {Log event, {Check traffic, Check train time}, {Postpone meeting, Check next train time}, Book train}, Display results
(4) Train & no traffic: Get meeting data, {Log event, {Check traffic, Check train time}, Book train}, Display results

These four scenarios are shown in Fig. 1.
Hence, four test cases are needed to cover all four scenarios.

**Question 3.2.3B**

Correct answer: (c)

We need:

- One test case to cover the main scenario 1, 2, 3, 4, 5, 6, 7, 8, 9, 10
- One test case to cover all the extensions: 1A, 1, 2, 3, 4, 5A, 6, 7A, 9, 10
- Three test cases to cover three exceptions:

  1, 2, 3, 4, 5, 6, 7A, 7AA
  1, 2, 3, 4, 5, 6, 7, 8A
  1, 2, 3, 4, 5, 6, 7, 8B

Notice that we cannot combine exception 7AA with the test case that covers all the extensions (e.g., 1A, 1, 2, 3, 4, 5A, 6, 7A, 7AA) because this way, we would not test the extensions properly. The extension is an alternative scenario that still allows the user to achieve the use case goal (which, in our case, is a successful purchase), and in this case, after step 7AA, the test case would have ended.

**Question 3.3.1A**

Correct answer: (d)

If GPA = FALSE, SAT, and EXTRA do not matter, then the first column can be: GPA = FALSE, SAT = (don't care), EXTRA = (don't care).

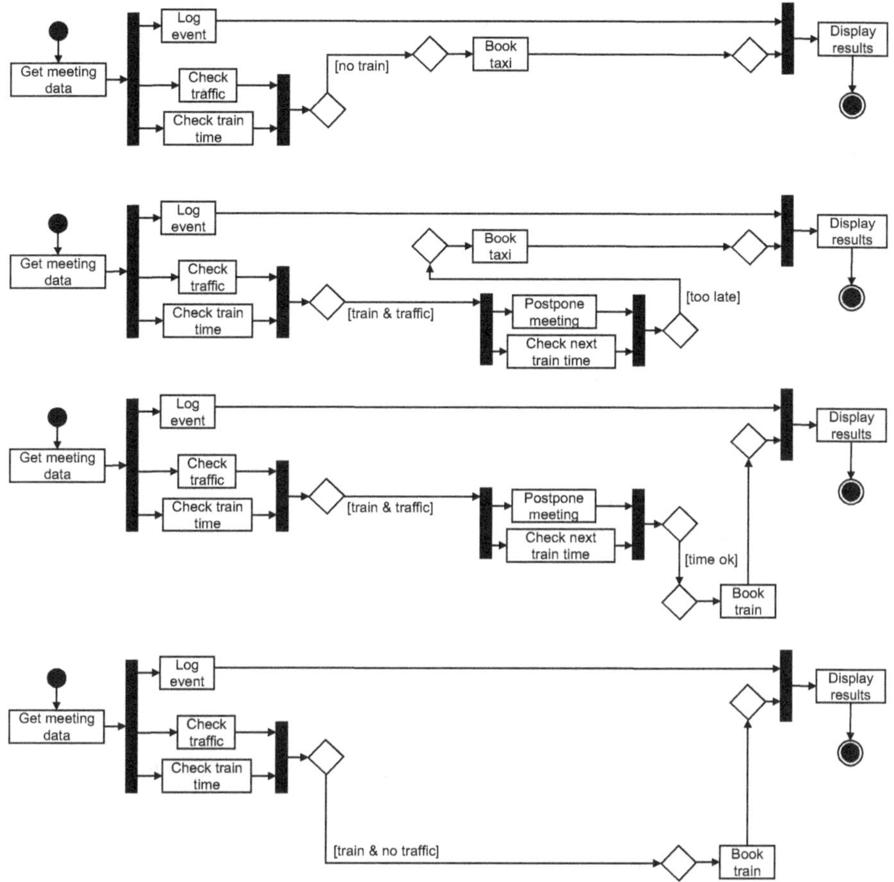


**Fig. 1** Four possible scenarios for the automatic scheduling assistant

If GPA = TRUE, the applicant is not eligible only if SAT = FALSE and EXTRA = FALSE, so we need the second column for this rule: GPA = TRUE, SAT = FALSE, EXTRA = FALSE.

The only remaining combinations to model are GPA = TRUE and (SAT = TRUE or EXTRA = TRUE). Since the rules must be non-overlapping, we can model these combinations with two rules, for example, GPA = TRUE, SAT = TRUE, EXTRA = (don't care), and GPA = TRUE, SAT = FALSE, EXTRA = TRUE.

Hence, the minimized table with complete and non-overlapping rules needs four columns. The minimized table is shown in Table 5. Another possible solution is to construct and minimize the full decision table shown in Table 6 (NE = non-eligible, E = eligible).

The minimized columns must be action equivalent. This means we can minimize the columns from the set {1, 2, 3, 4, 5} and the set {6, 7, 8}. We can minimize the first four columns in the first group since the action does not depend on SAT and

**Table 5** Minimized, complete decision table with non-overlapping rules for the university admission system

| | R1 | R2 | R3 | R4 |
|---|---|---|---|---|
| *Conditions* | | | | |
| GPA >= 3.5? | FALSE | TRUE | TRUE | TRUE |
| SAT >= 1200? | – | FALSE | TRUE | FALSE |
| EXTRA >= 2? | – | FALSE | – | TRUE |
| *Action* | | | | |
| Decision | Non-eligible | Non-eligible | Eligible | Eligible |

**Table 6** Full decision table for the university admission system

| | R1 | R2 | R3 | R4 | R5 | R6 | R7 | R8 |
|---|---|---|---|---|---|---|---|---|
| *Conditions* | | | | | | | | |
| GPA >= 3.5? | FALSE | FALSE | FALSE | FALSE | TRUE | TRUE | TRUE | TRUE |
| SAT >= 1200? | FALSE | FALSE | TRUE | TRUE | FALSE | FALSE | TRUE | TRUE |
| EXTRA >= 2? | FALSE | TRUE | FALSE | TRUE | FALSE | TRUE | FALSE | TRUE |
| *Action* | | | | | | | | |
| Decision | NE | NE | NE | NE | NE | E | E | E |

EXTRA. In the second group, we can minimize columns 7 and 8 because the actions on 7 and 8 do not depend on EXTRA. No more columns can be minimized. The resulting table is exactly the one shown in Table 5.

Instead of 7 and 8, we could minimize columns 6 and 7, but the resulting table will still have four columns. It is impossible to minimize it further, so the smallest possible decision table has four columns.

## Question 3.3.1B

Correct answer: (a)

The minimized decision table is shown in Table 7.

R1 minimizes columns 1 and 3, R2 columns 2 and 4, and R3 columns 5, 6, 7, and 8.

**Table 7** Minimized decision table for the customer order acceptance system

| | R1 | R2 | R3 |
|---|---|---|---|
| *Conditions* | | | |
| Credit limit exceeded? | Y | Y | N |
| Prompt payer? | – | – | – |
| Special clearance? | Y | N | – |
| *Action* | | | |
| Accept order? | Y | N | Y |

Notice that since the minimized decision table has three columns, we need at least three test cases to cover them.

(a) Correct answer. Test case ii matches the combination (Y, Y, N), so it covers R2. Test case iii matches the combination (Y, Y, Y), so it covers R1. Test case iv matches the combination (N, Y, N), so it covers R3. The set of test cases ii, iii, and iv covers all the rules R1, R2, and R3, thus achieving the full coverage for the minimized decision table.
(b) Incorrect answer. Both test cases i and v match R3, and test case iii matches R1. A test case that matches R2 is missing.
(c) Incorrect answer. We need at least three test cases. Two is not enough.
(d) Incorrect answer. We need at least three test cases. Two is not enough.

### Question 3.3.2A

Correct answer: (d)

(a) Incorrect answer. This follow-up test case has the same input data as the source test case but a different output. Although such behavior is unexpected and may be considered a failure, it does not violate either MR1 or MR2.
(b) Incorrect answer. This follow-up test case does not fulfill the assumptions of either MR1 or MR2, so no metamorphic relation is violated.
(c) Incorrect answer. This follow-up test case fulfills MR2 and does not violate MR1 since it does not fulfill MR1's assumptions.
(d) Correct answer. This follow-up test case fulfills MR1's assumptions but fails to fulfill the result: the risk score should remain the same or decrease, but it increased. Therefore, the follow-up test case violates MR1, so we detected a failure.

### Question 3.3.2B

Correct answer: (b)

(a) Incorrect answer. This is a relation between a single input and corresponding output, not between two inputs and two outputs, so it is a relation that could be used in property-based testing, not in metamorphic testing.
(b) Correct answer. This relation shows how the output should change if the input changes in a certain way. This is a valid metamorphic relation.
(c) Incorrect answer. This is not a relation between inputs and outputs but a requirement related to data format.
(d) Incorrect answer. This relation for is not true for $x = 1$, because $\sqrt{\sqrt{1}} = \sqrt{1} = 1$.

### Question 3.4.1A

Correct answer: (c)

(a) Incorrect answer. The system is designed for different devices and requires secure payments. Browser emulators and payment gateway simulators may be helpful during exploratory testing sessions.
(b) Incorrect answer. These test ideas come directly from the requirements: the system shall enable users to browse products, manage a shopping cart, and make purchases.
(c) Correct answer. Limitations may be part of test charters, but this limitation does not fit the scenario. It refers to securing access to internal company financial data, which is typically a concern for enterprise resource planning (ERP) systems or internal financial systems—not an e-commerce platform. An e-commerce platform focuses on securing user data, transactions, and inventory management rather than internal corporate financial data.
(d) Incorrect answer. These defects are related to the functions under test, so it is a good idea to write this historical information in the test charts so that the exploratory tester is aware of past problems.

### Question 3.4.1B

Correct answer: (a)

(a) Correct answer. This test charter ensures that the testing effort is focused on detecting potential issues with search functionality in the transaction history search feature.
(b) Incorrect answer. This test charter is too general.
(c) Incorrect answer. This test charter focuses on performance issues, not on functional issues with search functionality or edge-case handling for transaction records.
(d) Incorrect answer. The "explore" part makes no sense since edge cases are not a feature under test but a technique that can be used to derive tests.

### Question 3.4.2A

Correct answer: (b)

(a) Incorrect answer. This checklist focuses on technical issues, not the system's facial recognition performance.
(b) Correct answer. This checklist focuses on facial recognition.
(c) Incorrect answer. This checklist focuses on data privacy compliance, not facial recognition.
(d) Incorrect answer. This checklist focuses on real-time video streaming issues, not facial recognition.

### Question 3.4.2B

Correct answer: (b)

(a) Incorrect answer. This checklist is a do-confirm checklist because it serves as an aid to guide the thought process, providing experience-based testing ideas to explore the critical elements like usability, security, and robustness.
(b) Correct answer. This checklist ensures systematic testing of the password validator's input handling against specific, well-defined criteria. It is a read-do checklist because it forces the tester to perform specific actions one by one and immediately verify the obtained results.
(c) Incorrect answer. This checklist ensures systematic testing of non-functional characteristics, but the checklist items are rather general—they serve as ideas for non-functional testing, making the checklist a do-confirm, not a read-do one.
(d) Incorrect answer. This checklist focuses on usability aspects but serves as an aid to guide the tester's thought process, providing ideas about what should be checked regarding usability. It is, therefore, a do-confirm checklist, not a read-do one.

### Question 3.4.3A

Correct answer: (b)

(a) Incorrect answer. Crowd tests are difficult to repeat.
(b) Correct answer. Tests are executed by a wide variety of testers every time, which results in wider coverage.
(c) Incorrect answer. Crowd testers are typically randomly sampled, and they may even test the product for the first time, so usually they have no knowledge about previous failures.
(d) Incorrect answer. Crowd testers are typically randomly sampled, so usually we have no control over their environment configurations.

### Question 3.4.3B

Correct answer: (c)

(a) Incorrect answer. Crowd testing is usually flexible because it is easily scalable to handle many tests in a short time.
(b) Incorrect answer. Crowd testing is typically less expensive than maintaining a large and diverse in-house test team or supplementing with external testing services, so it is cost-effective.
(c) Correct answer. Coordinating with many testers from various locations with varying time zones, cultural differences, and language barriers can be challenging.
(d) Incorrect answer. Crowd testing usually gives a real user perspective. Testers can be actual users of the application and can better provide insights into its user experience and usability.

### Question 3.5.1A

Correct answer: (b), (d)

(a) Incorrect answer. CRUD testing ensures the application can correctly create, read, update, and delete data. However, the scenario suggests testing complex workflows and functionalities, such as filtering mechanisms, not just basic data operations.
(b) Correct answer. The need to test different combinations of actions, inputs, and states suggests applying combinatorial testing, such as pairwise testing.
(c) Incorrect answer. Random testing will not be effective in testing different combinations of actions, inputs, and states. It will also not help in thoroughly testing the filtering feature.
(d) Correct answer. Testing the filtering mechanism may have an oracle problem, so metamorphic testing is a very good choice.
(e) Incorrect answer. The scenario does not suggest testing domain-related issues.

### Question 3.5.1B

Correct answer: (c), (e)

The specification is the activity diagram, which suggests using scenario-based testing. Four scenarios can be identified:

1. Mandatory course (enroll)
2. Elective course, GPA > 2.0, year > 1 (enroll)
3. Elective course, GPA <= 2.0 or year = 1, lecturer accepts (enroll)
4. Elective course, GPA <= 2.0 or year = 1, lecturer reject (do not enroll)

Also, one decision involves a two-dimensional domain (GPA and year) and complex conditions, which suggests using domain testing. For example, assuming that the GPA is calculated to 1 decimal place, the boundary for "GPA > 2.0 and year > 1" can be tested with three test data:

A. GPA = 2.1, year = 2 (true, ON point for both borders GPA > 2.0 and year > 1)
B. GPA = 2.0, year = 2 (false, OFF point for GPA > 2.0)
C. GPA = 2.1, year = 1 (false, OFF point for year > 1)

which achieves simplified coverage. By combining both test techniques, the test analyst can provide four test cases: scenario 1, scenario 2 + A, scenario 3 + B, and scenario 4 + C.

The scenario does not suggest that CRUD operations, parameter combinations, or state transitions are important. Thus, combinatorial testing, CRUD testing, and state transition testing are eliminated.

Hence:

(a) Incorrect answer.
(b) Incorrect answer.
(c) Correct answer.

(d) Incorrect answer.
(e) Correct answer.

### Question 3.5.2A

Correct answer: (d)

(a) Incorrect answer. This is a benefit of automating the test execution, not the test design.
(b) Incorrect answer. While this benefit may be related to maintainability, it is a benefit of automating the test execution, not the test design.
(c) Incorrect answer. While automating the test design is a benefit, it results in better defect prevention and not lower efforts to maintain the test design.
(d) Correct answer. Since the test model is the single source of truth, only the test model needs to be maintained, lowering the cost of maintaining the test design.

### Question 3.5.2B

Correct answer: (c)

(a) Incorrect answer. This is a risk of automating the test execution, not the test design.
(b) Incorrect answer. This is a risk of automating the test execution, not the test design.
(c) Correct answer. Test conditions that are not shown in a model may be overlooked.
(d) Incorrect answer. This is a risk of automating the test execution, not the test design.

## Chapter 4

### Question 4.1.1A

Correct answer: (a)

(a) Correct answer. The goal of the route-finding app is to help users find routes for various means of transport. This test case verifies that the system is *appropriate* for this business need.
(b) Incorrect answer. This test case verifies functional accuracy, which is a type of functional correctness, not functional appropriateness.
(c) Incorrect answer. This test case verifies the *correctness* of the mechanism that enables or disables one of the application's features.
(d) Incorrect answer. This test case checks whether the system responds correctly to user errors, so it does not directly relate to the user's business needs, but verifies the mechanisms that protect the user from errors.

### Question 4.1.1B

Correct answer: (b)

(a) Incorrect answer. Domain testing is a domain-based test technique that focuses on the technical aspects of domain implementation. Therefore, it may be useful for functional correctness testing, but not for functional completeness testing, which tests if the set of functions covers all the specified tasks and user objectives.
(b) Correct answer. Use-case testing is a scenario-based test technique. Use cases model business processes that the system should implement. Therefore, they are suitable for testing functional completeness and functional appropriateness. Use cases may also describe more "technical" issues, such as calculations, so this technique is also useful in functional correctness testing.
(c) Incorrect answer. Random testing is a domain-based technique, so, similar to domain testing, it is not suitable for functional completeness testing.
(d) Incorrect answer. Pairwise testing is a domain-based technique, so, similar to domain testing, it is not suitable for functional completeness testing.

### Question 4.2.1A

Correct answer: (c)

(a) Incorrect answer. This is an example of installability testing, which is a subcharacteristic of flexibility testing, not usability testing.
(b) Incorrect answer. This is an example of adaptability testing, which is a subcharacteristic of flexibility testing, not usability testing.
(c) Correct answer. This is a part of accessibility testing, which in turn is a part of usability testing.
(d) Incorrect answer. This is a part of interoperability testing, which is a subcharacteristic of compatibility testing, not usability testing.

### Question 4.2.1B

Correct answer: (b)

(a) Incorrect answer. Learnability is about how easy it is for first-time users to learn to use the system. This test assumes users already understand basic banking operations and interface structure. This test does not evaluate how quickly a new user understands the task flow or interface layout. It does not involve training or observation of new users trying to discover functionality.
(b) Correct answer. Operability is about how effectively and efficiently a user can control and use the system once they already know how it works. It focuses on ease of use, clarity of controls, and user comfort while performing tasks.
(c) Incorrect answer. User assistance refers to help systems, tooltips, documentation, or guided tutorials that support users when they get stuck. This test does not involve evaluating help buttons, FAQs, or chat support. No assessment of the availability or quality of on-screen help is included.

(d) Incorrect answer. Self-descriptiveness assesses whether the interface clearly communicates what actions are possible at any moment, without external help. While some minor overlap exists (e.g., clear labeling of fields), this test does not focus on evaluating whether UI elements make their purpose immediately obvious to first-time users. The goal is not to check whether users understand what to do without prior knowledge, but whether users can easily operate the system based on existing familiarity.

**Question 4.3.1A**

Correct answer: (d)

(a) Incorrect answer. This is an example of installability testing, not adaptability testing.
(b) Incorrect answer. This is an example of interoperability testing, not adaptability testing.
(c) Incorrect answer. This is an example of coexistence testing, not adaptability testing.
(d) Correct answer. This is an example of adaptability testing. It specifically involves testing the app on different screen sizes, which are part of the target environments. The purpose is to verify whether the app adapts correctly to a variety of configurations, ensuring that features (like map rendering and GPS) work properly across those different environments.

**Question 4.3.1B**

Correct answer: (a)

(a) Correct answer. This focuses on the installation lifecycle across target environments, and ensures the app is functional immediately after install/update.
(b) Incorrect answer. It checks if the app adapts to different display environments—not how it installs.
(c) Incorrect answer. This focuses on tax logic accuracy, which is part of functional testing, not the installation process.
(d) Incorrect answer. While related to installation, this focuses on the user experience and intuitiveness, making it usability testing, not verifying the install procedure correctness.

**Question 4.4.1A**

Correct answer: (a)

(a) Correct answer. This is an example of interoperability testing. Interoperability is a subcharacteristic of compatibility.
(b) Incorrect answer. This is an example of coexistence testing. Although coexistence is a subcharacteristic of compatibility, coexistence testing is not the responsibility of a test analyst.
(c) Incorrect answer. This is an example of installability testing.

(d) Incorrect answer. This is an example of functional testing.

### Question 4.4.1B

Correct answer: (c)

(a) Incorrect answer. This is an example of an installability failure.
(b) Incorrect answer. This is an example of a usability failure.
(c) Correct answer. This is an example of a compatibility failure because compatibility in software quality terms means the ability of the application to work correctly across different environments, such as various operating systems, device models, browsers, or hardware configurations. In this answer, the app depends on a specific system library that exists on newer versions of Android, but not on older ones. As a result, the app fails to run on certain devices even though it is supposed to support them. This is a failure to interoperate or run correctly in the intended range of platforms—a core aspect of compatibility testing.
(d) Incorrect answer. This is an example of a functional failure.

## Chapter 5

### Question 5.1.1A

Correct answer: (a)

(a) Correct answer. Retrospectives identify potential improvements in test analysis, test design, test implementation, and test execution that will lead to better defect detection
(b) Incorrect answer. First, automating test execution is not the responsibility of the TA; second, automating test execution does not help in defect prevention.
(c) Incorrect answer. Dynamic testing detects defects rather than preventing them from escaping or recurring.
(d) Incorrect answer. Determining test oracles is the responsibility of the TA, but it has nothing to do with defect prevention.

### Question 5.1.1B

Correct answer: (c)

(a) Incorrect answer. Participating in risk analysis ensures that identified risks are properly mitigated, contributing to defect prevention.
(b) Incorrect answer. Retrospectives allow us to identify potential improvements in test analysis, design, implementation, and execution, leading to better defect prevention.
(c) Correct answer. Audits are not the best method for defect prevention because they are typically reactive rather than proactive in addressing issues. They are

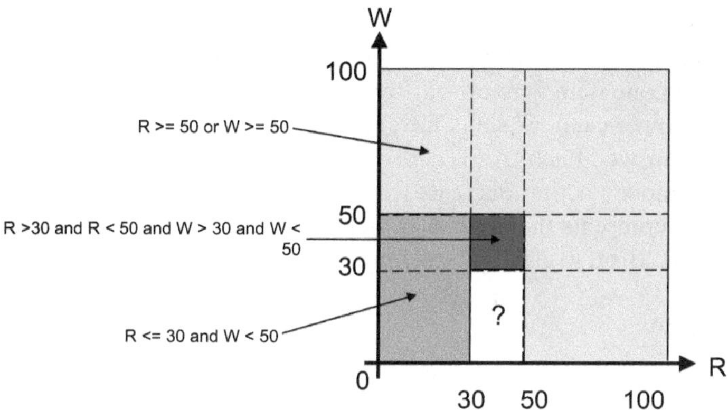


**Fig. 2** Domain model for the language competence evaluation system

conducted periodically, not continuously, and they are typically performed late in the lifecycle. They focus not on prevention but on detection.

(d) Incorrect answer. Root cause analysis prevents defects from recurring by proposing corrective actions to address the identified root causes.

### Question 5.2.1A

Correct answer: (c)

The domain model built based on the requirements is shown in Fig. 2.

Three equivalence partitions, corresponding to HIGH, LOW, and MEDIUM competence levels, are denoted by three different gray areas. As can be seen, the white area designated by the borders R > 30 and R < 50 and W <= 30 does not belong to any equivalence partition. This means that some input elements are not covered by equivalence partitions.

Hence, the correct answer is (c).

### Question 5.2.1B

Correct answer: (c)

(a) Incorrect answer. Paying is possible only when a guard condition [items > 0] is true. Since the variable items always correctly represent the number of items in the cart, it is impossible to pay for a cart with zero items.

(b) Incorrect answer. When a cart reaches its capacity, the system must be in the "Browse catalog" state since the last action must have been "Add," which is possible only in this state. But then it is possible to invoke more than one "removeProduct" event, which may result in removing an arbitrary number of items from the cart.

(c) Correct answer. When the system is in the "Browse catalog" state, the cart is full, and the "addProduct" event occurs, the guard condition [items >= 5] is true. This means that the system goes to the "Error message" state, but does not add the sixth product to a cart. However, after the "clickOK" event, the system goes back to the "Browse catalog" state, but the "Remove" action occurs, which means that one item is removed from the cart. This means that after returning to the "Browse catalog" state, the cart has four, not five, items.

(d) Incorrect answer. Each "Add" action increases the variable "items" by one, and each "Remove" action decreases it by one. So, the variable "items" always correctly represents the number of items in a cart. The guard condition [items < 5] in the "Browse catalog" state prohibits adding an item when a cart is full.

### Question 5.2.2A

Correct answer: (a)

(a) Correct answer. Requirements 3 and 5 contradict each other. Requirement 3 says that the promo code shall be calculated before applicable taxes, while requirement 5 says that it shall be calculated after calculating taxes.
(b) Incorrect answer. All requirements have high priority.
(c) Incorrect answer. Although some requirements contradict each other, each individual requirement is feasible.
(d) Incorrect answer. Each individual requirement can be tested with one or more functional test cases.

### Question 5.2.2B

Correct answer: (d)

(a) Incorrect answer. Perspective-based reviewing involves reviewing the test basis from various perspectives or viewpoints (e.g., designer, tester, marketer, administrator, and end-user). In this scenario, all the reviewers take the same perspective: an end-user.
(b) Incorrect answer. The scenario does not say anything about using checklists.
(c) Incorrect answer. Scenario-based reviewing involves simulating a process or activity to identify anomalies and refine the test basis. This review technique is most effective when the test basis has a scenario-based format, such as a use case or activity diagram. This is not the case.
(d) Correct answer. Role-based reviewing involves assigning specific roles or responsibilities to reviewers. Typical roles are based on specific end-user types and can be described by personas. This is the case, since there are three roles described in the scenario, all taking the same perspective—an end-user.

### Question 5.3.1A

Correct answer: (c)

(a) Incorrect answer. Such a comparison could be a good way to measure the effectiveness of test process improvements, but is not very helpful in the improvement itself.

(b) Incorrect answer. Modifying the frequency of test execution will not help if the test approach is the same.
(c) Correct answer. According to the "Defects cluster together" principle, it is very likely that there are even more defects in Component D. Therefore, expanding coverage for D is a good option, because it allows for the detection of more defects in the forthcoming test cycle.
(d) Incorrect answer. Reducing test effort for Component D and increasing it for Component B is contrary to the "Defects cluster together" principle because there are probably more uncovered defects in D and not so many remaining defects left in B.

## Question 5.3.1B

Correct answer: (b)

The distribution reaches its maximum in iteration 3, so the cumulative number of defects in the first three iterations is 15 + 30 + 55 = 100, which constitutes ca. 40% of the estimated total number of defects. This means that the estimated total number of defects in the product is 100/40% = 250. Since in the first seven iterations, a total of 15 + 30 + 55 + 42 + 30 + 18 + 10 = 200 defects were found, the estimated number of undetected defects is 250 – 200 = 50.

Hence, the correct answer is (b).

# Solutions to Exercises

## Solution to Exercise 1

Table 1. presents a sample set of keywords, organized into three groups as requested.

**Table 1** Sample set of keywords for the login feature

| # | Keyword | Parameters | Description |
|---|---|---|---|
| *"Technical" action keywords for setting up preconditions* | | | |
| 1 | CreateUser | Login<br>Password<br>AccountNumber | Creates a user in the database with the credentials and account number given as parameters |
| 2 | SetBalance | Login<br>Amount | Set the balance *amount* for the user *login* |
| *Action keywords* | | | |
| 3 | Login | Login<br>Password | Attempts to log in a user *login* with a password |
| 4 | Logout | | Logs out the current user |
| 5 | CheckBalance | | Checks the account balance |
| 6 | Transfer | SourceAccount<br>TargetAccount<br>Amount | Attempts to transfer *amount* from *sourceAccount* to *targetAccount* |

(continued)



A. Roman and M. Hamburg, *Practical Software Test Analysis*,
https://doi.org/10.1007/978-3-032-27986-6_9

**Table 1** (continued)

| # | Keyword | Parameters | Description |
|---|---|---|---|
| *Verification keywords* | | | |
| 7 | VerifyUserLoggedIn | Login | Throws an exception if the user *login* is not logged in |
| 8 | VerifyUserLoggedOut | Login | Throws an exception if the user *login* is logged in (i.e., not logged out) |
| 9 | VerifyBalanceShown | | Throws an exception if the balance is not shown on the screen |
| 10 | VerifyBalance | AccountNumber Amount | Verifies that the balance for the account *accountNumber* equals *amount* and throws an exception if this is not the case |
| 10 | VerifyTransferErrorMsg | TRUE/FALSE | Verifies if the error message is shown (TRUE) or not (FALSE) after trying to make a transfer, and throws an exception if the message is displayed for a FALSE parameter value, or not shown with a TRUE parameter value |

Test conditions:

- TCond1: Verify valid login
- TCond2: Verify invalid login (wrong password)
- TCond3: Verify invalid login (wrong username)
- TCond4: Verify logout
- TCond5: Verify balance check
- TCond6: Verify valid transfer fund
- TCond7: Verify invalid fund transfer (insufficient funds)
- TCond8: Verify invalid transfer fund (to the same account)
- TCond9: Verify invalid transfer fund (wrong target account)

Let us define a test procedure that covers all the test conditions:

TProc1: invalid login (TConds 2, 3), login (TCond1), check balance (TCond5), invalid transfer fund (TConds 7, 8, 9), valid transfer fund (TCond6), logout (TCond4).

This test procedure can be conducted using the following test script, written with the help of the keywords defined above.

1. CreateUser(John, JohnPass, 100001)
2. SetBalance(John, 5000)
3. CreateUser(Mary, MaryPass, 100002)
4. SetBalance(Mary, 7000)
5. Login(John, PassJohn)
6. VerifyUserLoggedOut(John) // steps 5 and 6 cover TCond2
7. Login(Anne, MaryPass)
8. VerifyUserLoggedOut(Mary) // steps 7 and 8 cover TCond3
9. Login(John, JohnPass)
10. VerifyUserLoggedIn(John) // steps 9 and 10 cover TCond1

11. CheckBalance()
12. VerifyBalanceShown() // steps 11 and 12 cover TCond5
13. Transfer(100001, 100002, 5000.01)
14. VerifyTransferErrMsg(TRUE)
15. VerifyBalance(100001, 5000)
16. VerifyBalance(100002, 7000) // steps 13–16 cover TCond7
17. Transfer(100001, 100001, 630)
18. VerifyTransferErrMsg(TRUE)
19. VerifyBalance(100001, 5000) // steps 17–19 cover TCond8
20. Transfer(100001, 100003, 420)
21. VerifyTransferErrMsg(TRUE)
22. VerifyBalance(100001, 5000) // steps 20–22 cover TCond9
23. Transfer(100001, 100002, 5000)
24. VerifyTransferErrMsg(FALSE)
25. VerifyBalance(100001, 0)
26. VerifyBalance(100002, 12000) // steps 23–26 cover TCond6
27. Logout()
28. VerifyUserLoggedOut(John) // steps 27 and 28 cover TCond4

Notice that in step 13, we additionally covered a boundary value (the amount being just above the account balance).

## Solution to Exercise 2

First, let us identify the impacted areas. These are:

- New features: *Scheduled Payments* (R6, R7 → T11–T14). These are high priority because they've never been tested before.
- Bug fixes and changes: *Funds Transfer* (R2, R3 → T3–T7) and *Account Statement* (R5 → T9–T10). Must be re-tested.
- Core functionality: *Login* (R1 → T1–T2). It is always critical since everything else depends on it.

*Scheduled Payments* is related to R6 and R7. The traceability matrix tells us that T11, T12, T13, and T14 cover these requirements. These test cases must be run first, since testing the new features has the highest priority. We know that T11, T12, and T13 depend on T1, and T14 depends on T11. Hence, the order of the first group of test cases is:

T1 → T11 → T12 → T13 → T14

The order of T12, T13, and T14 is arbitrary, as we run them for the first time.

Next, we should perform regression testing related to bug fixes and changes of two features: *Funds Transfer* and *Account Statement*, related to requirements R2, R3 (*Funds Transfer*), and R5 (*Account Statement*). The traceability matrix tells us that

R2 and R3 are covered by T3, T4, T5, T6, and T7, while R5 is covered by T9 and T10. T3 detected critical defects in the last run, T10 detected one medium priority defect, T7 detected one low priority defect, and T4, T5, T6, and T9 did not detect any defects. Hence, in this group of test cases, T3 has the highest priority, followed by T10 and T7. T4, T5, T6, and T9 have the lowest priority and can be executed in any order. The desired order is shown below, where the test cases in curly brackets can be executed in any order:

T3 → T10 → T7 → {T4, T5, T6, T9}

However, T3 depends on T2, and T5 depends on T4. This means that we have to execute T2 before T3, and T4 before T5. So, we define the final execution order as follows:

T2 → T3 → T10 → T7 → T4 → T5 → T6 → T9

The only test that we did not consider is T8, which is related to a feature that was neither fixed nor changed, and the impact analysis shows that no actual change impacts this feature. This means we can skip this test case or, if time allows, execute it as the last one. The final test execution order is hence as follows:

T1 → T11 → T12 → T13 → T14 → T2 → T3 → T10 → T7 → T4 → T5 → T6 → T9 → T8

## Solution to Exercise 3

The business rules of the hotel reservation system are as follows:

- check-in can take place at the earliest on the current day,
- the minimum length of stay is 1 night, and the maximum is 30 nights,
- checkout must take place no later than 180 days after the day on which the user books the room.

The component that verifies the correctness of input data gets two integers:

- *D*—denoting the "delay," i.e., the number of days that elapse from the date of booking to the check-in date ($D < 0$ means the check-in date is earlier than today, $D = 0$ means today, $D > 0$ means the check-in date is later than today).
- *N*—denoting the number of nights booked.

Based on these two numbers, the system checks if the business rules are met. If so, the component returns TRUE; otherwise, it returns FALSE.

The domain is a two-dimensional grid of integers. Its elements, pairs of numbers $(d, n)$ represent the delay and the number of nights. Since the component returns only TRUE or FALSE, we have two equivalence partitions, corresponding to these two outputs. Let us model the equivalence partition representing the valid combinations of $d$ and $n$:

- The minimum length of stay is 1 night and the maximum is 30 nights, so $1 \leq N \leq 30$.
- At earliest, check-in can take place at the day of the reservation, so $D \geq 0$.
- Checkout must take place no later than 180 days after the day on which the user books the room. This means that the delay plus number of nights cannot exceed 180, so $N + D \leq 180$

Therefore, we obtained a set of four constraints that define the "TRUE" equivalence partition:

$$N \geq 1 \wedge N \leq 30 \wedge D \geq 0 \wedge N + D \leq 180.$$

The area designated by these restrictions is shown in gray in Fig. 1. Its complement corresponds to the "FALSE" equivalence partition.

Simplified coverage requires having a pair of ON and OFF points for each border. We have four borders for the „TRUE" equivalence partition and the corresponding four borders for the "FALSE" equivalence partition. A pair of ON and OFF points for a given border is also a pair of OFF and ON points for the complementary border. So this suggests we need eight points, two for each of the four borders of the "TRUE" (or "FALSE") equivalence partitions. However, when we ignore the rule that each ON and OFF point for a given border should be an IN point for other borders, we can achieve the simplified coverage with fewer test points, since some points can be ON (or OFF) points for more than one border. We can use only six test points, shown as black points in Fig. 2.

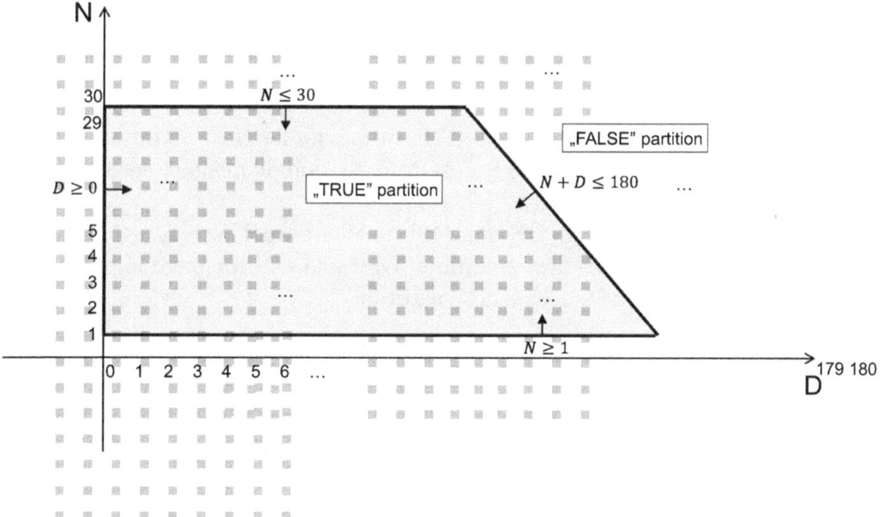


**Fig. 1** Domain and its two equivalence partitions for the hotel reservation system

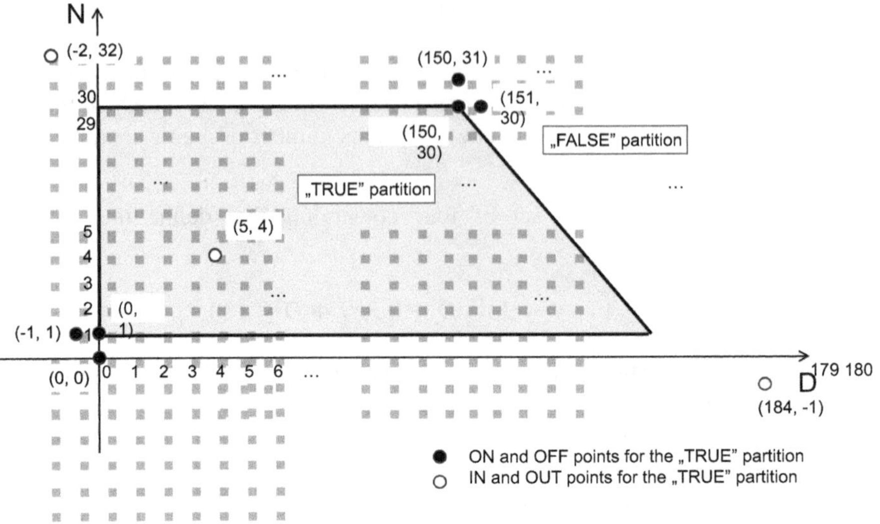


**Fig. 2** ON, OFF, IN, and OUT points for the hotel reservation system

Let us check that these six points fulfill the requirements of the simplified coverage:

- (0, 1) and $(-1, 1)$ are ON and OFF for the border $D \geq 0$ of the "TRUE" partition, and at the same time, OFF and ON for the complementary border $D < 0$ of the "FALSE" partition
- (0, 1) and (0, 0) are ON and OFF for the border $N \geq 1$ of the "TRUE" partition, and at the same time, OFF and ON for the complementary border $N < 1$ of the "FALSE" partition
- (150, 30) and (150, 31) are ON and OFF for the border $N \leq 30$ of the "TRUE" partition, and at the same time, OFF and ON for the complementary border $N > 30$ of the "FALSE" partition
- (150, 30) and (151, 30) are ON and OFF for the border $N + D \leq 180$ of the "TRUE" partition, and at the same time, OFF and ON for the complementary border $N + D < 180$ of the "FALSE" partition

We found the test set that achieves the simplified coverage. It is optimal in terms of the number of test points. Notice we cannot replace two OFF points $(-1, 1)$ and (0, 0) with only one point $(-1, 0)$, because the simplified coverage requires that OFF must be as close to ON as possible. The distance between the ON point (0, 1) and each of the OFF points $(-1, 1)$ and (0, 0) is 1, while the distance between (0, 1) and $(-1, 0)$ is $\sqrt{2}$, which is greater than 1. For the same reason, we cannot replace two OFF points (150, 31) and (151, 30) with only one test point.

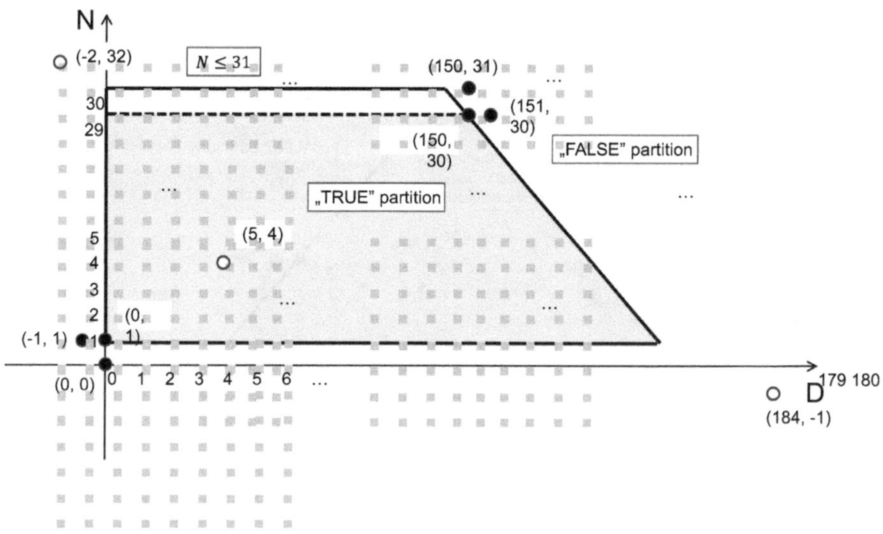


**Fig. 3** Incorrect implementation of one of the borders

Notice, however, that this solution—optimal in the sense of the number of test points—is not able to catch all the possible defects in the equivalence partitions implementation. For example, suppose the border $N \leq 30$ was incorrectly implemented as $N \leq 31$ (see Fig. 3).

None of the six test points would detect this defect. All ON (resp. OFF) points according to the specification are still ON (resp. OFF) in the defective implementation. This means that for each of them, the system's actual result will be the same as the expected one.

In practice, it is better to design a larger amount of test data, but in such a way as to guarantee the detection of a larger number of potential errors in the implementation. In the case of the simplified coverage criterion, ON and OFF points can be selected separately for each border in a way that each of them is an IN point for other borders. This way, the ON points are not located in the "corners" of the area representing the equivalence partition under test, but somewhere in the middle. In our case, this would therefore be a set of not six but eight points—two (ON and OFF) for each constraint of the "TRUE" equivalence partition. By symmetry, each such pair would also be a pair of OFF and ON points for the corresponding constraint defining the "FALSE" partition. Figure 4 presents a sample solution.

Notice that in this case, if the border $N \leq 30$ is incorrectly implemented as $N \leq 31$, the point (6, 31), which is an OFF point for the "TRUE" equivalence partition, would become the ON point for this partition. Hence, the expected result for this point would be "FALSE," but the actual result would be "TRUE," and we would observe the failure.

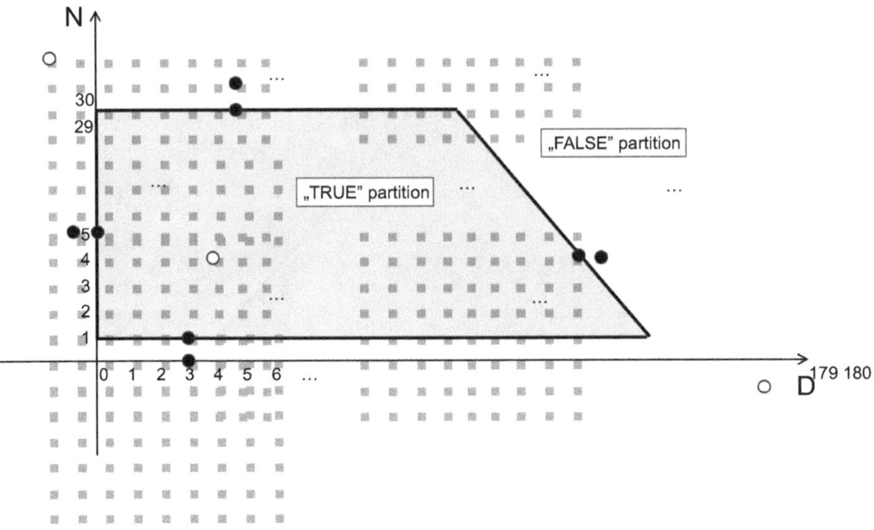


**Fig. 4** Simplified coverage achieved with a larger number of test points

In order to achieve reliable coverage, we need to add some IN and OUT points for each border. Adding three white points, as shown in Fig. 4, will be enough. The (5, 4) point is an IN point for all four borders of the "TRUE" equivalence partition and, at the same time, an OUT point for all four complementary borders of the "FALSE" partition. The (−2, 32) point is OUT for the borders $N \leq 30$ and $D \geq 0$, and (184, −1) is an OUT point for the borders $N \geq 1$ and $N + D \leq 180$. The minimal set of test points fulfilling the reliable coverage has nine points (six ON and OFF points designed for the simplified coverage, plus three points described above. Of course, we could also replace six ON and OFF points with the set of eight points, as discussed before.

## Solution to Exercise 4

In the following, 2FA means 2-factor authentication, RM means allowing the "Remember me" function, PEP means password expiration policy, AL means account lockout after failed attempts, and AM means authentication method. E (resp. D) means "enabled" (resp. disabled), A (resp. NA) means "active" (resp. "not active"), and PO means "password only."

There are four Boolean parameters (2FA, RM, PEP, AL) and one parameter (AM) with three possible values. The total number of parameter values combinations is therefore $2 \times 2 \times 2 \times 2 \times 3 = 48$.

Pairwise testing requires covering each pair of values of each pair of parameters. The pairs of parameters can be derived systematically. First, we write down the parameters in a defined order, numbering them with the numbers 1–5, for example:

(1) AM, (2) 2FA, (3) RM, (4) PEP, (5) AL

Next, we pair parameter 1 with all the parameters that have a larger number, that is:

- (1, 2)—which gives AM paired with 2FA
- (1, 3)—which gives AM paired with RM
- (1, 4)—which gives AM paired with PEP
- (1, 5)—which gives AM paired with AL

Next, we repeat the same with parameter 2:

- (2, 3)—which gives 2FA paired with RM
- (2, 4)—which gives 2FA paired with PEP
- (2, 5)—which gives 2FA paired with AL

Next, we repeat the same with parameter 3:

- (3, 4)—which gives RM paired with PEP
- (3, 5)—which gives RM paired with AL

Finally, we repeat the procedure with parameter 4:

- (4, 5)—which gives PEP paired with AL

This way, we obtained all ten pairs of parameters. For each such pair, we need to derive all possible combinations of their values. They are shown in Table 2.

All the coverage items are presented in Table 2 in the second column. We have six combinations for four parameter pairs and four combinations for six parameter pairs. This gives a total of $4 \times 3 \times 2 \times 6 \times 2 \times 2 = 24 + 24 = 48$ coverage items to test.

**Table 2** Coverage items for pairwise testing of the login feature

| Parameters pair | Pairs of parameters' values to test |
|---|---|
| AM, 2FA | (PO, E), (PO, D), (OAuth2, E), (OAuth2, D), (SAML, E), (SAML, D) |
| AM, RM | (PO, E), (PO, D), (OAuth2, E), (OAuth2, D), (SAML, E), (SAML, D) |
| AM, PEP | (PO, A), (PO, NA), (OAuth2, A), (OAuth2, NA), (SAML, A), (SAML, NA) |
| AM, AL | (PO, E), (PO, D), (OAuth2, E), (OAuth2, D), (SAML, E), (SAML, D) |
| 2FA, RM | (E, E), (E, D), (D, E), (D, D) |
| 2FA, PEP | (E, A), (E, NA), (D, A), (D, NA) |
| 2FA, AL | (E, E), (E, D), (D, E), (D, D) |
| RM, PEP | (E, A), (E, NA), (D, A), (D, NA) |
| RM, AL | (E, E), (E, D), (D, E), (D, D) |
| PEP, AL | (A, E), (A, D), (NA, E), (NA, D) |

Pairwise testing requires covering all pairs of parameter-value pairs for any two parameters, which in our case are the 48 pairs mentioned above. Notice that the two parameters with the largest number of possible values are 3 and 2. Since, in particular, we need to cover their combinations, we see that we need at least $3 \times 2 = 6$ test cases. Let us begin with combinations that cover the pair (AM, 2FA). This is shown in Table 3.

Next, we will fill in the RM column, aiming to cover all possible combinations of both (AM, RM) and (2FA, RM). This is shown in Table 4.

Notice that we changed the order of "D" and "E" values in rows 3 and 4, compared to the 2FA column. Otherwise, we would cover only two out of four possible combinations for the pair (2FA, RM), namely (E, E) and (D, D). Changing this order also allowed us to cover combinations (E, D) and (D, E). We follow the same procedure, filling in the PEP column now, and try to cover all possible combinations of (AM, PEP), (2FA, PEP), and (RM, PEP) simultaneously. This is shown in Table 5.

Notice that, again, we manipulated the order of "NA" and "A" values so that we were able to cover all possible combinations for all three pairs of parameters: (AM, PEP), (2FA, PEP), and (RM, PEP). Finally, we fill the last column, trying to provide the values in a way that allows us to cover all the combinations for the parameter pairs (AM, AL), (2FA, AL), (RM, AL), and (PEP, AL). This is shown in Table 6.

A closer examination of Table 6 shows us that indeed we covered all the required coverage items using only six test cases. For example, a parameter-value pair (2FA, E) and (AL, D) is covered in row 3; a parameter-value pair (RM, E) and (PEP, NA)

**Table 3** First iteration of the pairwise testing

| Test case | AM | 2FA | RM | PEP | AL |
|---|---|---|---|---|---|
| 1 | PO | E | | | |
| 2 | PO | D | | | |
| 3 | OAuth2 | E | | | |
| 4 | OAuth | D | | | |
| 5 | SAML | E | | | |
| 6 | SAML | D | | | |

**Table 4** Second iteration of the pairwise testing

| Test case | AM | 2FA | RM | PEP | AL |
|---|---|---|---|---|---|
| 1 | PO | E | E | | |
| 2 | PO | D | D | | |
| 3 | OAuth2 | E | D | | |
| 4 | OAuth | D | E | | |
| 5 | SAML | E | D | | |
| 6 | SAML | D | E | | |

**Table 5** Third iteration of the pairwise testing

| Test case | AM | 2FA | RM | PEP | AL |
|---|---|---|---|---|---|
| 1 | PO | E | E | NA | |
| 2 | PO | D | D | A | |
| 3 | OAuth2 | E | D | NA | |
| 4 | OAuth | D | E | A | |
| 5 | SAML | E | D | A | |
| 6 | SAML | D | E | NA | |

**Table 6** Fourth iteration of the pairwise testing

| Test case | AM | 2FA | RM | PEP | AL |
|---|---|---|---|---|---|
| 1 | PO | E | E | NA | E |
| 2 | PO | D | D | A | D |
| 3 | OAuth2 | E | D | NA | D |
| 4 | OAuth | D | E | A | E |
| 5 | SAML | E | D | A | E |
| 6 | SAML | D | E | NA | D |

is covered in row 1; and so on. All 48 coverage items defined in Table 2 are covered, so we achieved the pairwise coverage.

To achieve the base choice coverage, we need to design one test case for the base coverage item, and then a separate test case for each configuration in which only one value is changed to another value.

The test cases that achieve each choice coverage are shown in Table 7. The bolded elements are the ones that come from the base coverage item (i.e., from the base configuration).

**Table 7** Test set achieving base choice coverage for the login feature

| Test case | AM | 2FA | RM | PEP | AL | Comment |
|---|---|---|---|---|---|---|
| 1 | **PO** | **D** | **E** | **A** | **D** | **Base configuration** |
| 2 | OAuth2 | **D** | **E** | **A** | **D** | AM value replaced |
| 3 | SAML | **D** | **E** | **A** | **D** | AM value replaced |
| 4 | **PO** | E | **E** | **A** | **D** | 2FA value replaced |
| 5 | **PO** | **D** | D | **A** | **D** | RM value replaced |
| 6 | **PO** | **D** | **E** | NA | **D** | PEP value replaced |
| 7 | **PO** | **D** | **E** | **A** | E | AL value replaced |

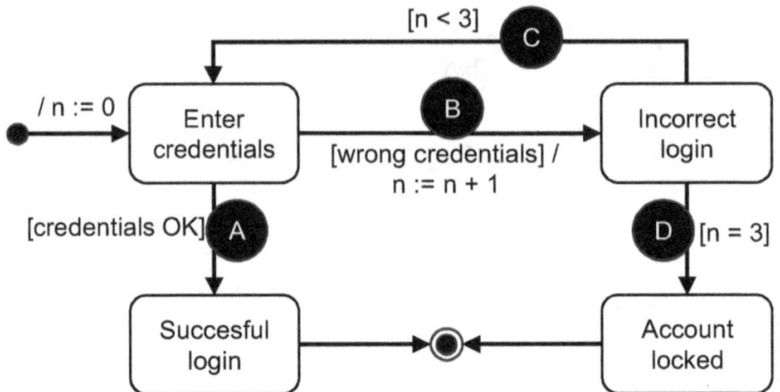


**Fig. 5** State diagram with labeled transitions

## Solution to Exercise 5

For convenience, let us label the four transitions in our system with A, B, C, and D, as shown in Fig. 5.

To achieve 0-switch coverage, we have to exercise each transition at least once. Notice that we are not able to cover both A and D within one test case, so we need at least two test cases, and two is indeed enough, for example:

TC1: A
TC2: B, C, B, C, B, D

Notice that we are not able to achieve D just after the first occurrence of B, because of the guard condition [n = 3]. To exercise D, we must enter incorrect credentials three times.

To achieve 1-switch coverage, we need to cover all 1-switches. These are: B → C, B → D, C → A, and C → B. 1-switches B → D and C → A cannot be covered within one test case, so we need at least two test cases. Again, two test cases are indeed enough, for example, TC2 mentioned above, and

TC3: B, C, A

Notice that TC2 covers three 1-switches: B → C, B → D, and C → B. TC3, in turn, covers the fourth 1-switch, C → A.

To achieve round-trip coverage, we need to cover all round trips. There are two round trips in our system, namely B → C → B, and C → B → C. TC2 covers both of them, so one test case is enough.

The test cases TC1, TC2, and TC3 are shown in the required format in Tables 8, 9, and 10.

TC1 is a simple test case with only one test step, covering the event A. It tests the "happy path", that is, a successful login with no problems.

**Table 8** TC1 for the login system

Test case ID: TC1 (successful login in the first attempt)
Preconditions: registered user with login "John" and password "JohnPass123"

| Test step | State | Event [guard condition] | Expected action | Expected next state |
|---|---|---|---|---|
| 1 | Enter credentials | Enter login "John" and password "JohnPass123" [credentials OK] | | Successful login |

**Table 9** TC2 for the login system

Test case ID: TC2 (account locked because of entering invalid credentials three times)
Preconditions: only one registered user, with login "John" and password "JohnPass123"

| Test step | State | Event [guard condition] | Expected action | Expected next state |
|---|---|---|---|---|
| 1 | Enter credentials | Enter login "John" and password "JohnPass321" [wrong credentials] | n = 1 | Incorrect login |
| 2 | Incorrect login | [n < 3] | | Enter credentials |
| 3 | Enter credentials | Enter login "Mary" and password "JohnPass123" [wrong credentials] | n = 2 | Incorrect login |
| 4 | Incorrect login | [n < 3] | | Enter credentials |
| 5 | Enter credentials | Enter login "John" and an empty password [wrong credentials] | n = 3 | Incorrect login |
| 6 | Incorrect login | [n = 3] | | Account locked |

**Table 10** TC3 for the login system

Test case ID: TC3 (entering invalid credentials followed by a successful login)
Preconditions: only one registered user, with login "John" and password "JohnPass123"

| Test step | State | Event [guard condition] | Expected action | Expected next state |
|---|---|---|---|---|
| 1 | Enter credentials | Enter login "John" and password "JohnPass321" [wrong credentials] | n = 1 | Incorrect login |
| 2 | Incorrect login | [n < 3] | | Enter credentials |
| 3 | Enter credentials | Enter login "John" and password "JohnPass123" [credentials OK] | | Successful login |

TC2 covers the sequence of events B, C, B, C, B, D. Notice that in TC2, we triggered the [wrong credentials] guard condition in three different ways: once with a correct login, but a wrong password, once with a wrong (non-existent) login, and once with a correct login, but with an empty password. We did not need to do this to achieve the required coverage, but this is an example of combining different coverage items within one test case to test as many different situations as possible within a small number of test cases.

TC3 covers the sequence of events B, C, and A.

Notice that the test set that covers both 0-switch coverage and 1-switch coverage allowed us to test three important and distinct scenarios:

- Successful login on the first attempt.
- Successful login after entering invalid credentials first.
- Account locked because of entering invalid credentials three times.

## Solution to Exercise 6

Let us first identify the possible scenarios. The most obvious one is the "happy path" scenario, that is, a scenario in which the client fills out the application correctly, receives a proposal, and accepts it. Notice that "Background verification," "Financial capacity and risk analysis," and "Credit history verification" are executed in parallel, so we do not need three separate test cases, each for one of these activities.

The second scenario is similar to the first one, but in the end, the client rejects the bank's proposal. In the third one, the bank rejects the client's request.

The fourth scenario represents a situation in which a filled form is formally not OK and needs to be corrected, after which it is accepted. The fifth scenario represents a similar situation, but after correcting the application, the client resigns from the loan request.

Notice that these five scenarios cover all the edges in the activity diagram. However, we could apply some more coverage criteria. For example, suppose we want to use the simple loop coverage. In that case, we have to test the loop "Fill out the application" $\rightarrow$ "Correct the application" zero times (skipped, but this is already covered with our first scenario), exactly once (this is already covered with the fourth scenario), and more than one iteration. For this one, we need to prepare a sixth scenario, in which a client corrects the form multiple times, but ultimately, the form is correct and can be processed by the bank.

Below, we present two example high-level test cases that cover the first and third scenarios. Test cases for other scenarios can be created in a similar way.

| Test case ID: LA-001-01 | Title: successful loan application |
|---|---|
| **Preconditions**:<br>• The loan history of the client is not negative | |
| **Input** | **Expected result** |
| Select a loan type | The banking system displays the loan application with the appropriate fields |

(continued)

(continued)

| Test case ID: LA-001-01 | Title: successful loan application |
|---|---|
| Fill in the loan application with the correct values that the loan system should accept | • The banking system prepares the analysis<br>• The banking system verifies the customer's authenticity<br>• The banking system rates the customer's financial capacity and risk<br>• The banking system evaluates the customer's credit history<br>• The banking system approves the loan application<br>• The banking system displays a proposal |
| Read the proposal and accept it | The banking system grants the loan |
| **Postconditions**:<br>• The loan is granted | |

| Test case ID: LA-001-03 | Title: loan application rejected by a bank |
|---|---|
| **Preconditions**:<br>• The loan history of the client is negative | |
| **Input** | **Expected result** |
| Select a loan type | The banking system displays the loan application with the appropriate fields |
| Fill in the loan application with the correct values that the loan system should accept | • The banking system prepares the analysis<br>• The banking system verifies the customer's authenticity<br>• The banking system rates the customer's financial capacity and risk<br>• The banking system evaluates the customer's credit history<br>• The banking system rejects the loan application |
| **Postconditions**:<br>• The loan is rejected | |

## Solution to Exercise 7

Only action-equivalent columns can be minimized. This means that we can try to reduce columns within the sets of columns: {2, 6, 10}, {1, 3, 5, 7, 9, 11}, {4, 8}, and {12}.

Consider the group {2, 6, 10}. These three rules do not depend on the payment method, and have identical second and third condition values (resp. Y and N). This means we can minimize these three columns into one, with conditions (*, Y, N), where * denotes the arbitrary value of a corresponding condition.

**Table 11** Minimized decision table for the fraud-prevention/payment authorization system

| | R1 | R2 | R3 | R4 | R5 |
|---|---|---|---|---|---|
| *Conditions* | | | | | |
| Payment method | * | * | C | D | B |
| User verified? | Y | * | N | N | N |
| High-risk transaction? | N | Y | N | N | N |
| *Actions* | | | | | |
| Approve the transaction immediately | X | | | | |
| Request manual review | | X | | | |
| Ask for additional verification | | | X | X | |
| Reject transaction | | | | | X |

Now let us consider the group {1, 3, 5, 7, 8, 11}. These six rules do not depend on the payment method and on the condition "User verified," and have an identical third condition (Y). This means we can minimize these six columns into one, with conditions (*, *, Y).

Columns {4, 8} cannot be minimized, because we cannot identify a group of constant conditions and a complement set of conditions that vary in all possible ways.

The last column, 12, cannot be minimized, because it is a single column.

The minimized decision table has five columns and is shown in Table 11.

Let us use the checksum procedure. Since one condition has three possible values, and two conditions are binary, there are $3 \times 2 \times 2 = 12$ possible combinations of condition values. The checksums for the columns 1–5 are resp.: 3, $3 \times 2 = 6$, 1, 1, 1. Their sum (i.e., the decision table checksum) is $3 + 6 + 1 + 1 + 1 = 12$ which equals the number of all possible combinations of condition values.

An example test case that covers column 2 would be:

Input: payment method = credit card, user is not verified, transaction is high risk

Expected output: Transaction should not be approved immediately, a manual review should be requested, no additional verification should be performed, and the transaction should not be rejected.

## Solution to Exercise 8

The examples of the metamorphic relations (MRs) for an e-commerce application selling electronic items are:

1. Query augmentation MR
   - Source test case example: query = "wireless headphones."

- Follow-up test case example: query = "wireless Bluetooth headphones."
- Expected relation: the results for "wireless Bluetooth headphones" should be a refinement: all top results from the shorter query that are highly relevant should also appear (possibly ranked lower) in the augmented query's result list.

2. Synonym expansion MR

   - Source test case example: query = "couch covers."
   - Follow-up test case example: query = "sofa covers."
   - Expected relation: Since "couch" and "sofa" are synonyms, the results should be largely overlapping, with at least a significant portion of the top results being consistent.

3. Result set enlargement MR

   - Source test case example: query "laptop" with filter "*price* $\leq$ \$1000."
   - Follow-up test case example: query "laptop" with looser filter "*laptop* $\leq$ \$2000."
   - Expected relation: all laptops shown in the "\$1000" query should also appear somewhere in the "\$2000" results.

4. Permutation invariance MR

   - Source test case example: query = "best budget smartphone."
   - Follow-up test case example: query = "smartphone budget best."
   - Expected relation: since word order in bag-of-words style queries should not change semantics (unless explicitly quoted), the ranking results should be the same or very similar.

5. Sorting invariance MR

   - Source test case example: query = "laptop" + sort prices in ascending order.
   - Follow-up test case example: the same query + sort prices in descending order.
   - Expected relation: the items' order should be reversed.

## Solution to Exercise 9

Test charter for exploratory testing session

Title: Exploratory testing of new features in FoodApp v2.0

Mission: Explore and evaluate the newly implemented features in the food delivery app, with a focus on:

- correctness and reliability of loyalty points system,
- functionality and system integration of the split payment option,
- accuracy and responsiveness of real-time order tracking,

- correctness of the new notification system,
- handling of multiple currencies during transactions.

The aim is to identify functional gaps, usability issues, integration defects, and edge cases that might not be covered in scripted tests.

Scope/areas of focus:

- loyalty points system

  earning and redeeming points
  validating point balance updates after multiple transactions
  points behavior with canceled/refunded orders

- split payment option

  combining wallet + credit card
  combining two cards
  handling an insufficient balance in one method
  applying discounts or promo codes along with split payments

- real-time order tracking

  accuracy of the courier's live location on the map
  behavior with poor or intermittent internet connectivity
  synchronization of ETA with actual progress

- notification system

  receiving push notifications for order confirmation, preparation, pickup, and delivery
  promotional notifications (check timing and duplication)
  notifications on different platforms (iOS vs Android)

- multiple currencies

  correct currency selection based on user location
  consistency of prices across checkout, payment, and receipt
  handling refunds in multiple currencies

Risks and concerns:

- incorrect loyalty point calculation leading to customer dissatisfaction
- payment failures or inconsistencies with split payments
- inaccurate or delayed order tracking, especially under weak network conditions
- missed or duplicated push notifications
- currency conversion errors affecting billing

Test ideas/exploration paths:

- Place multiple orders with different payment combinations and verify loyalty point updates.
- Attempt to redeem more loyalty points than available.

- Apply expired promo codes during split payments.
- Cancel an order after redeeming points—check refund behavior.
- Switch network from Wi-Fi to mobile data during real-time tracking.
- Simulate app backgrounding—confirm notifications still arrive.
- Place an order in EUR, then request a refund in USD—verify conversion accuracy.
- Test notification timing when multiple promotions are active.

Session setup:

- Test data: multiple test accounts with varying loyalty balances and currencies
- Environment: staging environment with live payment sandbox enabled
- Devices: Android (latest OS), iOS (latest OS), Web client (Chrome, Safari)
- Network conditions: stable Wi-Fi, 3G, network interruptions

## Solution to Exercise 10

An example checklist is given below.

1. Shopping cart functionality

| | |
|---|---|
| ☐ Yes ☐ No ☐ Partially | Can multiple items be added to the cart successfully? |
| ☐ Yes ☐ No ☐ Partially | Does the cart update quantities correctly (increase/decrease)? |
| ☐ Yes ☐ No ☐ Partially | Does the cart prevent negative or zero quantities? |
| ☐ Yes ☐ No ☐ Partially | Are prices updated correctly when quantities change? |
| ☐ Yes ☐ No ☐ Partially | Does removing an item update the total cost correctly? |
| ☐ Yes ☐ No ☐ Partially | Is the cart preserved when navigating back to product pages or after a refresh? |

2. Checkout process—user information

| | |
|---|---|
| ☐ Yes ☐ No ☐ Partially | Does the system validate mandatory fields (e.g., name, address, email, phone)? |
| ☐ Yes ☐ No ☐ Partially | Does it prevent invalid inputs (e.g., alphabetic characters in phone number, malformed email)? |
| ☐ Yes ☐ No ☐ Partially | Are optional fields clearly marked and working as expected? |
| ☐ Yes ☐ No ☐ Partially | Can the user enter special characters in name/address fields (and is it handled safely)? |

3. Payment Details

| | |
|---|---|
| ☐ Yes ☐ No ☐ Partially | Is the credit card number validated (length, format, Luhn check[1])? |
| ☐ Yes ☐ No ☐ Partially | Does the system handle expired card dates correctly? |
| ☐ Yes ☐ No ☐ Partially | Does it reject invalid CVV codes? |
| ☐ Yes ☐ No ☐ Partially | Are error messages clear and specific when payment fails? |
| ☐ Yes ☐ No ☐ Partially | Are sensitive details masked (e.g., showing only last four digits of the card)? |

4. Order review and confirmation

| | |
|---|---|
| ☐ Yes ☐ No ☐ Partially | Does the order summary display correct product names, quantities, and prices? |
| ☐ Yes ☐ No ☐ Partially | Are shipping costs, discounts, and taxes calculated correctly? |
| ☐ Yes ☐ No ☐ Partially | Is the final total accurate? |
| ☐ Yes ☐ No ☐ Partially | Can the user go back to edit items before confirming? |
| ☐ Yes ☐ No ☐ Partially | Does the confirmation screen provide an order ID? |

## Solution to Exercise 11

**Risk 1**: input fields may accept invalid or unexpected data (e.g., negative stock, invalid product codes). We want to ensure the system behaves correctly with valid and invalid inputs across all relevant ranges. A good choice is **domain testing**. This technique will allow the tester to cover boundary values, equivalence classes, and edge cases for numerical fields (stock quantities, price, etc.) and categorical fields (product categories).

**Risk 2**: certain combinations of product attributes may trigger incorrect discount or reorder logic. The system applies rules based on multiple attributes (type, quantity, supplier, season). Testing all combinations manually is impractical. A good choice is **combinatorial testing**. This technique helps efficiently test interactions between multiple input parameters, identifying defects that only occur in specific combinations.

**Risk 3**: users might perform unexpected sequences of operations on data items that could corrupt the inventory database. We want to ensure that the system maintains data integrity across all CRUD operations, which is critical. A good choice is **CRUD**

[1] The Luhn check (after IBM scientist Hans Peter Luhn) is a simple check digit formula used to validate a variety of identification numbers.

**testing**. This technique will systematically verify that creating, reading, updating, and deleting items behave correctly under different sequences.

**Risk 4**: certain workflows, such as placing a reorder, applying a discount, and generating reports, have complex state-dependent behaviors (e.g., low stock triggers a reorder, but only if discount rules are not violated). These state-dependent operations may fail if transitions between states are not handled correctly. A good choice is **state transition testing**. This technique will test the system's behavior when moving between states such as stock normal → stock low → reorder triggered → reorder completed.

**Risk 5**: end-to-end user scenarios might reveal issues missed in isolated testing (e.g., adding items, applying discounts, and generating a report may cause inconsistent outputs). Realistic workflows are essential to validate system usability and correctness under typical usage. A good choice is **scenario-based testing**. This technique simulates real-world use cases to verify the system's behavior across multiple modules and workflows.

## Solution to Exercise 12

Let us number the sentences in the requirement specification, to make it easier later, when we refer to the specification:

1. Shipping cost depends on membership status and shipping speed.
2. Membership status can be regular or premium.
3. Shipping speed can be standard, express, or overnight.
4. Premium members with standard shipping speed pay no shipping costs ($0).
5. For all the other shipping speeds, they pay $5.
6. Regular members placing orders with the standard shipping speed pay $5, and with the express speed pay $10.
7. Overnight shipping speed costs $15, regardless of the membership status.

To model the requirements as a decision table, first, we need to identify conditions and actions. There are two conditions (see sentences 1, 2, 3):

- membership status (possible values: regular, premium),
- shipping speed (possible values: standard, express, overnight).

and one action:

- shipping cost (possible values: $0, $5, $10).

There are six possible combinations of condition values, forming Rules 1–6 as shown in Table 12.

Now, let us fill in the actions based on the specification rules. Sentence 4 gives us $0 for Rule 4. Sentence 5 suggests that the shipping cost for Rules 5 and 6 should

**Table 12** Decision table for the shopping app

| | R1 | R2 | R3 | R4 | R5 | R6 |
|---|---|---|---|---|---|---|
| *Conditions* | | | | | | |
| Membership status | Regular | Regular | Regular | Premium | Premium | Premium |
| Shipping speed | Standard | Express | Overnight | Standard | Express | Overnight |
| *Action* | | | | | | |
| Shipping cost | $5 | $10 | | $0 | $5 | $5 |

be $5. Sentence 6 gives us $5 for Rule 1 and $10 for Rule 2. After this part of our analysis, the decision table looks as in Table 12.

Now, when we analyze sentence 7, we see that it imposes the shipping cost $15 for Rules 3 and 6. After taking this rule into account, the decision table looks as shown in Table 13.

We see that there is a contradiction in Rule 6. Sentence 5 of the specification says that for the combination (premium, overnight), the shipping cost is $5, while sentence 7 says that for the same combination, the shipping cost is $15. We detected a defect.

An example of a requirement correction could look like this (changes from the original specification are highlighted in bold):

1. Shipping cost depends on membership status and shipping speed.
2. Membership status can be regular or premium.
3. Shipping speed can be standard, express, or overnight.
4. Premium members with standard shipping speed pay no shipping costs ($0).
5. For **the express shipping speed,** they pay $5.
6. Regular members placing orders with the standard shipping speed pay $5, and with the express speed pay $10.
7. Overnight shipping speed costs $15, regardless of the membership status.

This change would fix the problem. The decision table based on the corrected specification looks as in Table 14.

**Table 13** Decision table for the shopping app—last step

| | R1 | R2 | R3 | R4 | R5 | R6 |
|---|---|---|---|---|---|---|
| *Conditions* | | | | | | |
| Membership status | Regular | Regular | Regular | Premium | Premium | Premium |
| Shipping speed | Standard | Express | Overnight | Standard | Express | Overnight |
| *Action* | | | | | | |
| Shipping cost | $5 | $10 | **$15** | $0 | $5 | $5/**$15** |

**Table 14** Decision table based on the fixed specification for the shopping app

| | R1 | R2 | R3 | R4 | R5 | R6 |
|---|---|---|---|---|---|---|
| *Conditions* | | | | | | |
| Membership status | Regular | Regular | Regular | Premium | Premium | Premium |
| Shipping speed | Standard | Express | Overnight | Standard | Express | Overnight |
| *Action* | | | | | | |
| Shipping cost | \$5 | \$10 | \$15 | \$0 | \$5 | \$15 |

## Solution to Exercise 13

A sample solution is given below.

Role 1. Inexperienced User/Novice Customer

Persona 1: Sarah Green, 22 years old, student

- Background: recently opened her first bank account; limited experience with online banking.
- Goals: check balance and transfer money for rent quickly.
- Concerns: may struggle with technical jargon, complicated navigation, or hidden features.

This persona ensures the review will focus on simplicity and clarity of the system, e.g.:

- ease of navigation (is the dashboard intuitive?),
- simplicity of language (are terms like "IBAN" or "SWIFT" explained?),
- support/help features (is help easily accessible?).

Role 2. Experienced User/Power Customer

Persona 2: Michael Lee, 45 years old, business owner

- Background: runs a small company, uses online banking daily for multiple accounts.
- Goals: manage multiple transactions, pay vendors, download statements for accounting.
- Concerns: efficiency and speed of use; ability to handle bulk payments.

This persona ensures the review will focus on advanced features and efficiency, e.g.:

- advanced functionality (bulk transfers, exporting statements),
- system performance (transaction speed, responsiveness),
- security vs. usability balance (two-factor authentication shouldn't slow him down too much).

Role 3. Elderly User/Technologically Inexperienced

Persona: Margaret Smith, 68 years old, retired teacher

- Background: uses banking mainly for pension withdrawals and bill payments; not tech-savvy.
- Goals: simple, safe, and stress-free access to her money.
- Concerns: small font sizes, complex authentication steps, risk of fraud.

This persona ensures the review will focus on accessibility and safety, e.g.:

- accessibility (font size, contrast, screen reader support),
- clear instructions for login and transactions,
- alerts and confirmations for financial safety.

Role 4. Security-Sensitive User

Persona: David Johnson, 35 years old, IT security analyst

- Background: works in security, distrusts weak systems.
- Goals: ensure his money is secure, and transactions are well-protected.
- Concerns: potential vulnerabilities, phishing risks, weak authentication.

This persona ensures the review will focus on system robustness, e.g.:

- security measures (multi-factor authentication, encryption),
- session timeouts, fraud detection, login attempt limits,
- transparency of the system's security practices.

Role 5. Teenager/Future Customer

Persona: Emily Brown, 12 years old, using a supervised "youth account"

- Background: has a junior savings account, limited access.
- Goals: learn how to save and track allowance.
- Concerns: may not understand financial terminology, could click on things accidentally.

This persona ensures the review will focus on usability for youth accounts and parental oversight, e.g.:

- simplified interface for minors,
- educational aspect (savings goals, gamification),
- strong parental controls.

## Solution to Exercise 14

After cycle 1, we predict that the Login and FundsTransfer modules are expected to remain the most defect-prone clusters regarding critical defects. In contrast, Login, BillPayments, and ProfileManager modules are expected to remain the most defect-prone clusters regarding major defects. This is due to the high density and presence of critical/major defects in these modules.

**Table 15** Comparison of results for two consecutive test cycles

| Component | Total defects found | | | Defect density (defects/KLOC) | | |
|---|---|---|---|---|---|---|
| | Critical | Major | Minor | Critical | Major | Minor |
| Login | 10 → 4 | 20 → 10 | 40 → 10 | **4.0** → 1.6 | **8.0** → **4.0** | 16 → 4 |
| FundsTransfer | 15 → 15 | 15 → 10 | 25 → 50 | **2.5** → **2.5** | 2.5 → 1.6 | 4.2 → 8.6 |
| AccountSummary | 5 → 5 | 20 → 10 | 20 → 30 | 0.4 → 0.4 | 1.6 → 0.8 | 1.6 → 2.4 |
| BillPayments | 2 → 6 | 6 → 8 | 20 → 10 | 1.6 → **4.8** | **4.8** → **6.4** | 16 → 8 |
| ProfileManager | 3 → 4 | 12 → 6 | 24 → 12 | 1.2 → 1.6 | **4.8** → **2.4** | 9.6 → 4.8 |

Table 15 shows the comparison of results from the two consecutive test cycles.

The bolded values show the top defect density values for critical and major defects. After the second test cycle, we see that the two components with the highest defect density for critical defects are FundsTransfer (which we predicted) and BillPayments (which was not expected to have a high critical defect density). This means that BillPayments may be error-prone, and the test effort should focus more on this component, since the results suggest that there are more critical defects in this module than we expected, and there may be even more such defects that are not detected yet. We increase its risk level from medium to high.

The Login module was considered high risk before test cycle 2; however, after this cycle, we could lower its risk from high to medium, as its critical defect density is significantly lower than expected. The critical defect density for the remaining components (AccountSummary and ProfileManager) did not change significantly, so their related risk levels remain low.

Regarding the major defect density, the situation looks exactly as we predicted. After the second test cycle, the top three modules with the highest major defect density are exactly the same modules that we identified after the first cycle, namely: Login, BillPayments, and ProfileManager. We can conclude that, regarding major defects, the situation is as expected, and the test efforts directed at detecting this kind of defect should proceed as we planned.

We do not analyze minor defects, as they have the lowest priority and are less important than critical and major defects.

Testing focus should shift accordingly:

- apply more rigorous testing on AccountSummary and ProfileManager,
- maintain high test effort on FundsTransfer,
- reduce test effort on Login and BillPayments, as their defect trend is declining.

# References

1. ISO/IEC/IEEE, "ISO/IEC/IEEE 29119 Software testing standard - Part 1: General concepts," 2022.
2. ISO/IEC/IEEE, "ISO/IEC/IEEE 29119 Software testing standard - Part 2: Test processes," 2021.
3. ISO/IEC/IEEE, "ISO/IEC/IEEE 29119 Software testing standard - Part 3: Test documentation," 2021.
4. ISO/IEC/IEEE, "ISO/IEC/IEEE 29119 Software testing standard - Part 4: Test techniques," 2021.
5. ISO/IEC/IEEE, "ISO/IEC/IEEE 29119 Software testing standard - Part 5: Keyword-driven testing," 2024.
6. ISO/IEC, "ISO/IEC 25010 Systems and software engineering - Systems and software Quality Requirements and Evaluation (SQuaRE) - Product quality model," 2023.
7. ISO/IEC, "ISO/IEC 25019 Systems and software engineering - Systems and software Quality Requirements and Evaluation (SQuaRE) - Quality-in-use model," 2023.
8. IEEE, "IEEE 1044 - Standard Classification for Software Anomalies," 2009.
9. ISO/IEC, "ISO/IEC 20246 Software and systems engineering — Work product reviews," 2017.
10. L. Anderson and D. Krathwohl, A Taxonomy for Learning, Teaching, and Assessing: A Revision of Bloom's Taxonomy of Educational Objectives, Boston: Allyn & Bacon, 2001.
11. ISTQB, "Certified Tester - Foundation Level Syllabus v4.0," 2023.
12. "Certified Tester - Advanced Level - Test Management Syllabus v4.0," ISTQB, 2024.
13. J. Arthur, M. Groner, K. Hayhurst and C. Holloway, "Computer," vol. 32, no. 10, pp. 79–83, 1999.
14. V. Basili and R. Selby, "Comparing the Effectiveness of Software Testing Strategies," *IEEE Transactions on Software Engineering,* vol. 13, no. 12, pp. 1278–1296, 1987.
15. J. Arthur and R. Nance, "Verification and validation without independence: a recipe for failure," in *Winter Simulation Conference Proceedings*, Orlando, FL, USA, 2000.
16. W. Royce, "Managing the Development of Large Software Systems," in *Technical Papers of Western Electronic Show and Convention*, 1970.
17. G. Myers, Software reliability: principles and practices, John Wiley, 1976.
18. M. v. Genuchten, G. Brethouwer, T. v. d. Boomen and F. Heemstra, "Empirical study of software maintenance," *Information and Software Technology,* vol. 34, no. 8, pp. 507–512, 1992.
19. B. Boehm, "A spiral model of software development and enhancement," *ACM SIGSOFT Software Engineering Notes,* vol. 11, no. 4, pp. 14-24, 1986.
20. RTCA, "DO-178C / EUROCAE ED-12C: Software Considerations in Airborne Systems and Equipment Certification," 2012.



A. Roman and M. Hamburg, *Practical Software Test Analysis*,
https://doi.org/10.1007/978-3-032-27986-6

21. ASQ, "Root cause analysis," 02 01 2025. [Online]. Available: https://asq.org/quality-resources/root-cause-analysis.
22. T. Koomen, L. v. d. Aalst, B. Broekman and M. Vroon, TMap Next for result driven testing, UTN Publishers, 2006.
23. E. Barr, M. Harman, P. McMinn, M. Shahbaz and S. Yoo, "The Oracle Problem in Software Testing: A Survey," *IEEE Transactions on Software Engineering,* vol. 41, no. 5, pp. 507–525, 2015.
24. B. Jeng and E. Weyuker, "A simplified domain-testing strategy," *ACM Transactions on Software Engineering Methodology,* vol. 3, no. 3, pp. 254–270, 1994.
25. I. Forgacs and A. Kovacs, Modern Software Test Techniques, Apress, 2024.
26. E. Rogstad, L. Briand and R. Torkar, "Test case selection for black-box regression testing of database applications," *Information and Software Technology,* vol. 55, no. 10, pp. 1781–1795, 2013.
27. A. Pleuss, B. Hauptmann, D. Dhungana and G. Botterweck, "User interface engineering for software product lines: the dilemma between automation and usability," in *EICS '12: Proceedings of the 4th ACM SIGCHI symposium on Engineering interactive computing systems*, 2012.
28. D. Kuhn, D. Wallace and A. Gallo, "Software Fault Interactions and Implications for Software Testing," *IEEE Transactions on Software Engineering,* vol. 30, pp. 418–421, 2004.
29. R. Huang, W. Sun, Y. Xu, H. Chen, D. Towey and X. Xia, "A Survey on Adaptive Random Testing," *IEEE Transactions on Software Engineering,* vol. 47, no. 10, pp. 2052-2083, 2019.
30. T. Chen, H. Leung and I. Mak, "Adaptive Random Testing," *Lecture Notes in Computer Science,* vol. 3321, p. 320–329, 2004.
31. A. Arcuri, M. Iqbal and L. Briand, "Random Testing: Theoretical Results and Practical Implications," *IEEE Transactions on Software Engineering,* vol. 38, pp. 258–277, 2012.
32. H. Wu, C. Nie, J. Petke, Y. Jia and M. Harman, "An empirical comparison of combinatorial testing, random testing and adaptive random testing," *IEEE Transactions on Software Engineering,* vol. 46, no. 3, pp. 302–320, 2020.
33. J. Hopcroft, R. Motwani and J. Ullman, Introduction to Automata Theory, Languages, and Computation, 3rd ed., Addison-Wesley Longman Publishing Co., Inc., 2006.
34. G. Bochmann and A. Petrenko, "Protocol Testing: Review of Methods and Relevance," in *ISSTA '94: Proceedings of the 1994 ACM SIGSOFT international symposium on,* 1994.
35. D. Harel, "Statecharts: A Visual Formalism For Complex Systems," *Science of Computer Programming,* vol. 8, pp. 231–274, 1987.
36. "ISO/IEC 15909-1 Systems and software engineering - High-level Petri nets - Part 1: Concepts, definitions and graphical notation," ISO/IEC, 2019.
37. "OMG® UML: Unified Modeling Language, version 2.5," Object Management Group, 2017.
38. G. Antoniol, Y. Labiche, L. C. Briand and M. Di Penta, "A Case Study Using the Round-Trip Strategy for State-Based Class Testing," in *Proceedings 13th International Symposium on Software Reliability Engineering,* Annapolis, MD, USA, 2002.
39. A. Cockburn, Writing Effective Use Cases, Addison-Wesley, 2000.
40. M. Cohn, User stories applied: For agile software development, Addison-Wesley Professional, 2004.
41. H. Goldstine and J. von Neumann, "Planning and coding of problems for an electronic computing instrument. Report of US Ord. Dept. (1947)," *Reprinted in: Collected Works of J. von Neumann, ed. A. Taub,* pp. 80–151, 1965.
42. "Business Process Model and Notation Specification v2.0.2," Object Management Group, 2014.
43. A. Cooper, The Inmates Are Running the Asylum: Why High Tech Products Drive Us Crazyand How to Restore the Sanity, Sams - Pearson Education, 1999.
44. L. Carbone and S. Haeckel, "Engineering Customer Experiences," *Marketing Management,* vol. 3, no. 3, pp. 8–19, 1994.
45. G. Myers, T. Badgett and C. Sandler, The Art of Software Testing, 3rd ed., John Wiley & Sons, 2012.
46. B. Beizer, Software Test Techniques, 2nd ed., Itp-Media, 1990.
47. C. Kaner, J. Falk and H. Nguyen, Testing Computer Software, Wiley, 1999.

48. R. Molich and J. Nielsen, "Improving a human-computer dialogue," *Communications of the ACM,* vol. 33, no. 3, pp. 338–348, 1990.
49. J. Nielsen, "Enhancing the explanatory power of usability heuristics," in *Proceedings of the SIGCHI Conference on Human Factors in Computing Systems,* 1994.
50. N. Leicht, I. Blohm and J. Leimeister, "Leveraging the Power of the Crowd for Software Testing," *IEEE Software,* vol. 34, no. 2, pp. 62–69, 2017.
51. IEC, "IEC 61508-3, Functional safety of electrical/electronic/programmable electronic safety-related systems—Part 3: Software requirements," 2010.
52. "ISO/IEC 25023 - Systems and software engineering — Systems and software Quality Requirements and Evaluation (SQuaRE) — Measurement of system and software product quality," ISO/IEC, 2016.
53. R. Harston and P. Pyla, The UX Book: Agile UX Design for a Quality User Experience, Elsevier, 2019.
54. "Web Content Accessibility Guidelines 2.2 (WCAG)," w3.org, 2024.
55. "European Accessibility Act (Directive 2019/882 of the European Parliament and of the Council of 17 April 2019 on the accessibility requirements for products and services)," European Parliament, 2019.
56. "Section 508 of the Rehabilitation Act of 1973," US Government, 1998.
57. ISO, "ISO 9241-210 - Ergonomics of human-system interaction, Part 210: Human-centred design for interactive systems," ISO, 2019.
58. J. Brooke, "SUS-A quick and dirty usability scale," in *Usability Evaluation in Industry,* P. Jordan, B. Thomas, B. Weerdmeester and A. McClelland, Eds., 1996.
59. J. Kirakowski and M. Corbett, "SUMI: the Software Usability Measurement Inventory," *British Journal of Educational Technology,* vol. 24, no. 3, pp. 210–212, 1993.
60. J. Kirakowski and N. Claridge, "WAMMI - Website Analysis and MeasureMent Inventory," 1999. [Online]. Available: https://www.wammi.com/index.html. [Accessed 2025].
61. "Certified Tester - Advanced Level - Technical Test Analyst Syllabus v4.0," ISTQB, 2021.
62. B. Boehm, Software Engineering Economics, Englewood Cliffs, N.J.: Prentice Hall, 1981.
63. SWEBOK, SWEBOK - Guide to the Software Engineering Body of Knowledge v4.0, H. Washizaki, Ed., IEEE Computer Society, 2024.
64. C. Jones, "Software defect-removal efficiency," *Computer,* vol. 29, no. 4, pp. 94-95, 1996.
65. E. Yourdon, Structured Walkthroughs, 4th ed., Prentice Hall, 1989.
66. T. Gilb and D. Graham, Software Inspection, Addison-Wesley, 1993.
67. M. Fagan, "Design and Code Inspections to Reduce Errors in Program Development," *IBM Systems Journal,* vol. 15, no. 3, pp. 182–211, 1976.
68. O. Laitenberger and J. M. DeBaud, "An Encompassing Life-Cycle Centric Survey of Software Review," *Journal of Systems and Software,* vol. 50, no. 1, pp. 5–31, 2000.
69. K. Wiegers, Peer Reviews in Software - A Practical Guide, Addison-Wesley, 2002.
70. M. Ciolkowski, O. Laitenberger and S. Biffl, "Software reviews, the state of the practice," *IEEE Software,* vol. 20, no. 6, pp. 46–51, 2003.
71. D. Badampudi, M. Unterkalmsteiner and R. Britto, "Modern Code Reviews—Survey of Literature and Practice," *ACM Transactions on Software Engineering and Methodology,* vol. 32, no. 4, pp. 1–61, 2023.
72. F. Shull, I. Rus and V. Basili, "How perspective-based reading can improve requirements inspections," *Computer,* vol. 33, no. 7, pp. 73-79, 2000.
73. I. Musleh, N. A. and N. Emran, "An Experimental Study on Checklist-Based and Perspective-Based Requirements Reading Techniques Using E-Review Tool," *Journal of Advanced Research in Applied Sciences and Engineering Technology,* vol. 28, no. 3, pp. 351–367, 2022.
74. J. Maldonado, J. Carver, F. Shull, S. Fabbri, E. Dória, L. Martimiano, M. Mendonça and V. Basili, "Perspective-Based Reading: A Replicated Experiment Focused on Individual Reviewer Effectiveness," *Empirical Software Engineering,* vol. 11, pp. 119–142, 2006.
75. A. N., "The impact of software process improvement on quality: in theory and practice," *Information & Management,* vol. 40, no. 7, pp. 677–690, 2003.

76. J.-C. Liu, V. Chen, C.-L. Chan and T. Lie, “The impact of software process standardization on software flexibility and project management performance: Control theory perspective,” *Information and Software Technology,* vol. 50, no. 9-10, pp. 889–896, 2008.
77. A. Enders, “An Analysis of Errors and Their Causes in System Programs,” *IEEE Transactions on Software Engineering,* vol. 1, no. 2, pp. 140–149, 1975.
78. J. Śliwerski, T. Zimmermann and A. Zeller, “When do changes induce fixes?,” *SIGSOFT Software Engineering Notes,* vol. 30, no. 4, pp. 1–5, 2005.
79. R. Haas, R. Niedermayr and E. Juergens, “Teamscale: Tackle Technical Debt and Control the Quality of Your Software,” in *Proceedings of the Second International Conference on Technical Debt*, Canada, 2019.
80. E. Juergens and D. Pagano, “Did We Test the Right Thing? Experiences with Test Gap Analysis in Practice,” CQSE GmbH, 2016.
81. S. Kan, Metrics and Models in Software Quality Engineering, Addison-Wesley, 2002.
82. R. Chillarege, I. Bhandari, J. Chaar, M. Halliday, D. Moebus, B. Ray and M. Wong, “Orthogonal defect classification - a concept for in-process measurements,” *IEEE Transactions on Software Engineering,* vol. 18, no. 11, pp. 943–956, 1992.
83. IBM, “Orthogonal Defect Classification v5.2 for Software Design and Code,” 2013.
84. G. Catolino, F. Palomba, A. Zaidman and F. Ferrucci, "Not All Bugs Are the Same: Understanding, Characterizing, and Classifying Bug Types," *Journal of Systems and Software,* vol. 152, pp. 165–181, 2019.
85. “Certified Tester - Advanced Level - Test Analyst Syllabus v4.0,” ISTQB, 2025.
86. R. Dunn, "The Quest for Software Reliability," in *Handbook of Software Quality Assurance,* G. Schulmeyer and J. McManus, Eds., Van Nostrand Reinhold, 1987.
87. E. Engström, P. Runeson and M. Skoglund, “A systematic review on regression test selection techniques,” *Information and Software Technology,* vol. 52, pp. 14–30, 2010.
88. J. Rott, R. Niedermayr, E. Juergens and D. Pagano, “Ticket Coverage: Putting Test Coverage into Context,” in *8th Workshop on Emerging Trends in Software Metrics (WETSoM)*, 2018.
89. “General Data Protection Directive (GDPR),” European Commission, 2018.
90. “Certified Tester - AI Testing Syllabus, v1.0,” ISTQB, 2021.

# Index


**A**
Abstract test case, 59
Acceptance criteria, 31, 35
Accessibility, 293
Action, 174
Action (decision table), 206
Activity diagram, 188, 195
Activity diagram-based testing, 197
Activity diagram coverage, 197
Actual result, 51, 53, 73
Adaptability, 302
Adaptability testing, 303
Adaptive random testing, 161
Additional coverage, 115
Ad hoc reviewing, 344, 348
Ad hoc testing, 43
Agile, 98
Agile software development, 35, 115
Alternative flow, 189
Alternative scenario, 189
Anomaly, 51, 53
Appraisal costs, 331
Appropriateness recognizability, 291
Assertion, 73
Automated test, 51, 54
Automated test execution, 32
Automated test oracle, 73
Automated test script, 49, 51

**B**
Base choice coverage, 147
Behavior-based test technique, 75, 126
Beizer's taxonomy, 387
Beneficialness, 290
Beta testing, 253
Boundary value analysis, 127
Business process model, 188
Business Process Model and Notation (BPMN), 337

**C**
Cause-effect graph, 215
Chaos engineering, 159
Checklist, 244, 349
Checklist-based reviewing, 344, 348
Checklist-based testing, 243, 244, 263
Checksum procedure, 212
CI/CD pipeline, 49, 70
Classification tree, 143
Clean code, 32
Closed border, 129
Coexistence testing, 316
Combinatorial explosion, 142, 184, 207
Combinatorial testing, 140, 142, 262
Compatibility, 316
Completeness check (CRUD), 168
Complexity, 32
Compliance, 49
Concrete test case, 60
Condition (decision table), 206
Configuration, 143
Configuration matrix, 304
Confirmation testing, 51
Consistency testing (CRUD), 168
Cost of quality, 331
Coverage, 41, 42, 45, 53, 64
Coverage-based testing, 114
Coverage level, 106



A. Roman and M. Hamburg, *Practical Software Test Analysis*, https://doi.org/10.1007/978-3-032-27986-6

Crowd testing, 253, 263
CRUD matrix, 167
CRUD testing, 166, 262

D
Data-based test technique, 125, 126
Decision table, 205
Decision table coverage, 215
Decision table:minimization, 210
Decision table testing, 205, 263
Defect, 51, 53
Defect arrival pattern analysis, 375
Defect cluster, 54
Defect cluster analysis, 362
Defect clustering, 32
Defect Detection Percentage (DDP), 367
Defect management, 53
Defect prevention, 271, 324
Defect rate, 32
Defect removal efficiency, 328, 362
Defect resolution, 32
Defect taxonomy, 387
Demo session, 35
DevOps, 70
DO-178C, 266
Do-confirm checklist, 246
Domain testing, 127, 262
Driver, 69
Dynamic testing, 64

E
Emotional impact, 293
Equality border, 131
Equivalence partition, 127
Equivalence partitioning, 143, 159
Error (use case), 189
Estimation, 35
European Accessibility Act, 294
Event, 174
Exception, 189
Exit criteria, 45
Expected result, 51, 53, 73
Experience-based testing, 35
Experience-based test technique, 126
Exploratory testing, 51, 235
Extended-entry decision table, 207
Extended finite state machine, 172
Extension, 189
External failure costs, 331

F
Failure, 53
False-negative result, 63
False positive, 54
False-positive result, 64
Feature model, 146
Finite state machine, 172
Flexibility, 302
Flowchart, 188, 189
FMEA, 98
Follow-up test case, 223, 224
Full decision table, 207
Functional appropriateness, 281
Functional appropriateness testing, 285
Functional completeness, 281
Functional completeness testing, 282
Functional correctness, 281
Functional correctness testing, 284
Functional suitability, 281
Functional suitability metrics, 287
Functional testing, 281
Fuzz testing, 159

G
Guard condition, 174
Guided random testing, 160

H
Happy path, 189
Harel statechart, 172
High-level test case, 43, 59, 75
High-level test condition, 41
History-based testing, 112
Human oracle, 74
Hybrid risk assessment, 99

I
IEC 61508, 264
IEEE 1044, 385
Impact analysis, 105, 107
Inclusivity, 292
Increment, 31
Incremental development model, 31
Independence of testing, 101
Individual review, 347
Inequality border, 131
Informal review, 346
IN point, 130
Inspection, 346
Installability, 302
Installability testing, 311

Interaction capability, 290, 291
Internal failure costs, 331
Interoperability, 316
Interoperability testing, 316
ISO 20246, 348
ISO 25010, 279, 282, 292, 388
ISO 25023, 287
ISO 29119-3, 64, 70, 78
ISO 9241-210, 293
Iteration, 34
Iterative development model, 34

**K**
Keyword, 83
Keyword-driven testing, 48, 83

**L**
Learnability, 291
Limited-entry decision table, 206
Log, 52
Logical test case, 59
Low-level test case, 43, 59, 60

**M**
Machine learning algorithm, 222
Main scenario, 189
Maintainability, 32
Meaningfulness, 293
Metamorphic relation, 222, 223
Metamorphic testing, 73, 77, 222, 263
Metamorphic testing coverage, 226
Model, 335
Model-based testing, 72, 75, 335, 339
Monkey testing, 158
Multiple choice coverage, 153

**N**
N-switch coverage, 175
N-wise coverage, 154

**O**
OFF point, 130
1-switch, 176
ON point, 130
Open border, 129
Operability, 291
Operational profile, 116
Oracle problem, 160, 222
Orthogonal Defect Classification (ODC), 385
OUT point, 130

**P**
Pairwise coverage, 150
Parameter-value pair, 147
Partition, 129
Pass/fail criteria, 43
PBR, *see* Perspective-based reading
Persona, 188, 353
Perspective-Based Reading (PBR), 344, 355
Petri net, 189
Phase containment effectiveness, 330
Physical test case, 60
Planning poker, 35
Poisson distribution, 365
Prevention costs, 331
Product risk, 95, 96
Property-based testing, 72, 76, 228
Pseudo-oracle, 72, 75
PV pair, *see* Parameter-value pair

**Q**
Qualitative risk assessment, 97
Quality, 27
Quantitative risk assessment, 96

**R**
Randomized algorithm, 223
Random testing, 158, 262
Rayleigh model, 376
Read-do checklist, 246
Refactoring, 32, 54
Regression risk, 32
Regression testing, 31, 51, 105, 106
Regression tests, 35
Regression test suite, 54
Reliable domain coverage, 131
Replaceability, 303
Requirements review, 31
Requirements traceability matrix, 115, 283
Responsive design, 308
Retrospective, 325
Review, 105, 325
Review technique, 39, 344
Risk, 53, 54, 93
Risk analysis, 31, 32, 94, 95, 324
Risk assessment, 95, 96
Risk-based testing, 93, 260

Risk-based test selection, 110
Risk control, 105
Risk identification, 95
Risk impact, 96, 263
Risk importance, 96
Risk level, 40, 45, 48, 96, 97, 100, 101
Risk likelihood, 96, 263
Risk management, 94
Risk mitigation, 100, 105
Risk monitoring, 105, 106
Risk prioritization, 96
Risk register, 110
Role-based reviewing, 344, 353
Root cause analysis, 326, 383
Round-trip coverage, 181
Rule-based test technique, 126

**S**
Scalability, 303
Scenario, 351
Scenario-based reviewing, 345, 351
Scenario-based testing, 187, 262
Scrum, 35
Section 508, 294
Self-descriptiveness, 292
Sequence chart, 189
Sequential development model, 29
Session-based testing, 51, 60, 234, 263
Session-based test management, 235
Session sheet, 52
Severity-based classification, 387
Simple loop coverage, 194
Simplified domain coverage, 131
Simulation software, 223
Smoke test, 49
Software Development Lifecycle (SDLC), 27, 29, 42, 70, 266
Software model, 335
Source test case, 223, 224
State, 174
State-based testing, 262
Statechart, 172
Statement coverage, 371
State transition model, 172
State transition testing, 172
Static testing, 101, 345
Structural coverage analysis, 370
Stub, 69
System usability scale, 297
SZZ algorithm, 368

**T**
Technical debt, 32
Technical review, 346
Test, 51
Test analysis, 31, 36
Test analyst, 27
Test approach, 42, 100
Test automation, 48, 271
Test automation framework, 69
Test basis, 31, 36, 39, 42, 43, 53, 75, 265
Test case, 31, 35, 42, 43, 46, 49, 51, 53, 63, 64, 69
Test case dependency, 117
Test case quality, 64
Test charter, 51, 60, 234, 235
Test completion, 31
Test condition, 31, 35, 36, 40, 42, 43, 49, 62, 68, 69
Test cycle, 70
Test data, 44, 46, 49, 53, 60, 69, 75, 78
Test data requirements, 31
Test design, 31, 42, 62, 64, 70
Test design automation, 271
Test double, 69
Test effort estimation, 31
Test environment, 44, 46, 49, 60, 68
Test environment specification, 31
Test execution, 31, 50, 51, 54, 60
Test execution schedule, 49, 52
Test gap analysis, 373
Test implementation, 31, 46, 60, 62
Test level, 69, 100
Test log, 51, 52
Test management, 31, 49
Test model, 31
Test object, 40, 42, 46, 53, 54, 60, 73, 75, 76
Test oracle, 39, 72
Test plan, 42, 46, 60
Test planning, 31, 36, 70
Test procedure, 31, 47, 51
Test process, 35
Test result, 51, 68, 362
Test run, 51, 53
Test scope, 38
Test script, 46, 48, 51
Test selection criteria, 75
Test strategy, 31
Test suite, 46, 51
Test technique, 39, 42, 101, 106, 260
Test type, 69, 100, 106
Testware, 53, 89
Traceability, 43, 49, 53, 56, 60, 107, 272
Transition, 174

**U**
Unguided random testing, 160
Unified Modeling Language (UML), 337
Unreachable code, 372
Usability, 290, 293
Usability lab, 295
Usability questionnaire, 297
Usability review, 295
Usability test session, 295
Use case, 188, 189
Use case-based testing, 191
Use case coverage, 191
Usefulness, 293
User assistance, 292
User engagement, 292
User error protection, 291
User experience, 290, 293
User journey map, 189
User story, 35, 188
UX, *see* user experience

**W**
Walkthrough, 346
Web Content Accessibility Guidelines (WCAG), 294

**Z**
0-switch, 176

Zeitfracht Medien GmbH
Ferdinand-Jühlke-Straße 7
99095 Erfurt, Deutschland
produktsicherheit@kolibri360.de